Pearson
Education

We work with leading authors to develop the strongest educational materials in Law, bringing cutting-edge thinking and best learning practise to a global market.

Under a range of well-known imprints, including Longman, we craft high quality print and electronic publications which help readers to understand and apply their content, whether studying or at work.

To find out more about the complete range of our publishing please visit us on the World Wide Web at: www.pearsoneduc.com

A Companion Web Site accompanies *The Internet, Law and Society* edited by Akdeniz, Walker and Wall

Visit the Companion Web Site of *The Internet, Law and Society* at www.booksites.net/akdeniz. There you will find source materials including:

- primary source materials and hyperlinks cited in chapters of the book
- links to other valuable resources on the web
- relevant materials which have become available after the writing of the book

THE INTERNET, LAW AND SOCIETY

YAMAN AKDENIZ, CLIVE WALKER

and

DAVID WALL

Longman

An imprint of **Pearson Education**

Harlow, England · London · New York · Reading, Massachusetts · San Francisco
Toronto · Don Mills, Ontario · Sydney · Tokyo · Singapore · Hong Kong · Seoul
Taipei · Cape Town · Madrid · Mexico City · Amsterdam · Munich · Paris · Milan

Pearson Education Limited

Edinburgh Gate
Harlow
Essex CM20 2JE
United Kingdom

and Associated Companies throughout the world

Visit us on the World Wide Web at
www.pearsoneduc.com

First published in Great Britain in 2000

ISBN 0-582-35656-3

British Library Cataloguing in Publication Data
A CIP catalogue record for this book can be obtained from the British Library.

10 9 8 7 6 5 4 3 2 1
05 04 03 02 01 00

Typeset by 35 in 10/12pt Sabon
Printed in Great Britain by Henry Ling Ltd., at the Dorset Press,
Dorchester, Dorset

CONTENTS

Contents

LIST OF CONTRIBUTORS

Yaman Akdeniz is the founder and has been the director since 1997 of Cyber-Rights & Cyber-Liberties (UK) (http://www.cyber-rights.org), a non-profit civil liberties organisation. He gave written and oral evidence to the Trade and Industry Select Committee inquiry into Electronic Commerce in 1999 and was an NGO representative to the OECD Ministerial Conference, 'A Borderless World: Electronic Commerce', in Ottawa, Canada, 1998. He is currently a member of the Cyberlaw Research Unit within the Department of Law, University of Leeds. He also acts as an Internet consultant and policy advisor for various companies. He has written extensively on Internet-related issues and a full list of publications is at http://www.cyber-rights.org/yamancv.htm.

Andrew Charlesworth is Senior Lecturer in Information Technology Law, and Director of the Information Law and Technology Unit at the University of Hull. He is a member of the Editorial Board of the *Journal of Information Law and Technology*, the International Advisory Panel of the *International Yearbook of Law, Computers & Technology* and the Correspondents Panel of the *Computer Law and Security Report*. In the past, he has been Associate Editor of the *International Yearbook of Law, Computers & Technology*, and a member of both the Executive Committee of the British & Irish Legal Education Technology Association (BILETA) and the General Council of the Society for Computers and Law (SCL). He is a Subject Expert and Project Reviewer for the European Commission under the ESPRIT programme in the areas of Electronic Commerce and Intellectual Property, and provides consultancy services in Information Technology Law to a range of Higher Education organisations, including the Joint Information Systems Committee of the Higher Education Funding Council, and the Arts and Humanities Data Service. He has lectured widely on computer misuse, data protection, intellectual property, social exclusion and the information superhighway, and legal issues of the Internet and World Wide Web.

Paul Eden is presently a lecturer in international commercial law at the School of Legal Studies, University of Sussex. He has previously taught at the Universities of Cape Town and Leeds. He has published in the areas of company law, criminal law and revenue law. In addition to his interests in the field of international commercial law, Paul is well known for his work in relation to international law mooting.

Alan Reed became a Reader in Law at Sunderland University in 2000 after seven years as a law lecturer in the Department of Law at Leeds University. He has written extensively on conflict of laws and criminal law, becoming editor of *The Journal of Criminal Law* in 2000. His books include *European Business Litigation* (Ashgate, Aldershot, 1998), *Criminal Law* (Sweet & Maxwell, London, 1999), and *Readings in Criminal Law* (Anderson Press, Cincinati, 1999). His many published articles on conflict of laws have also concentrated upon multistate defamation jurisdiction and choice of law implications, with consequential effect on the Internet regulation, as well as governance through recognition and enforcement of foreign judgments. He is an academic peer referee in the conflict of laws specialism for *Melbourne University Law Review*.

Horton Rogers was Professor of Law in the University of Leeds from 1977 to 1998. He is now Senior Fellow in the School of Law, University of Nottingham. His main interests are Tort Law and Comparative Tort Law. He is a joint editor of *Gatley on Libel and Slander* (9th ed., Sweet & Maxwell, London, 1998) and has edited several editions of *Winfield and Jolowicz on Tort* (now 15th ed., Sweet & Maxwell, London, 1998). He is a member of the European Group on Tort Law (formerly the 'Tilburg Group') and a member of the Board of the European Centre of Tort and Insurance Law in Vienna.

Stephen Saxby is a Solicitor and Reader in Information Technology Law at Southampton University, teaching IT Law at both undergraduate and postgraduate level. He has written widely on the development of the subject including the history of the technology and more recently public sector policy towards the information and communication technologies. His books have focused on these issues, including *The Age of Information* (Macmillan Press, London, 1990) and *Public Policy and Legal Regulation of the Information Market in the Digital Network Environment* (Tano Press, Oslo, 1996). In 1985 he founded *The Computer Law and Security Report* (Elsevier Advanced Technology) and has edited it ever since. He has also been Editor of *The Encyclopedia of Information Technology Law* (Sweet & Maxwell, London) since its first publication in 1990. He is a member of the Legal Advisory Board of the European Commission and of the Intellectual Property Law Task Force of the British Computer Society.

Barry Steinhardt is Associate Director and chair of the ACLU Cyber-liberties Task Force, which coordinates the ACLU's extensive program on information technology issues. He was a co-founder and served as president of the Global Internet Liberty Campaign (GILC), the world's first international coalition of non-governmental organisations concerned with the rights of Internet users and one of the originators of the Internet Free Expression Alliance (IFEA), which was formed to monitor issues related to Internet content rating and filtering. Barry has spoken and written widely on information technology issues and is a frequent guest on news and talk programs. He is currently at work on the ACLU handbook on *The Rights of Persons Online*, and was co-author of the ACLU public policy paper on Internet filtering and blocking technology – 'Farenheit 451.2 is Cyberspace Burning?' He is a 1978 graduate of the Northeastern University School of Law.

Nadine Strossen, a Professor of Law at New York Law School since 1988, has also been President of the American Civil Liberties Union since 1991. She has published and spoken widely, in both scholarly and general interest forums, on constitutional law and civil liberties issues. She comments frequently on legal issues in the national media and is a monthly columnist for the Webzine, *Intellectual Capital*. Recent recognitions include her listing in *Upside Magazine*'s December 1997 feature on 'The Elite 100: 100 Executives Leading The Digital Revolution' and in *Vanity Fair Magazine*'s November 1998 feature on 'America's 200 Most Influential Women'. In November 1999, *Ladies Home Journal* included Strossen in 'The 100 Most Important Women in America'. Her book, *Defending Pornography: Free Speech, Sex, and the Fight for Women's Rights* (Abacus, London, 1996) was named by the *New York Times* a 'notable book' of 1995. Nadine graduated *Phi Beta Kappa* from Harvard College and *magna cum laude* from Harvard Law School. She is married to Eli M. Noam, Professor at Columbia University's Graduate School of Business and Director of the Columbia Institute for Tele-Information.

Clive Walker is a Professor in the Department of Law and Director of the Centre for Criminal Justice Studies at the University of Leeds. He has written extensively on criminal justice, civil liberties and media issues. His books have focused upon terrorism, including (with Hogan, G.) *Political Violence and the Law in Ireland* (Manchester University Press, Manchester, 1989) and *The Prevention of Terrorism in British Law* (2nd ed., Manchester University Press, Manchester, 1992), and upon miscarriages of justice, including the books (with Starmer, K.), *Justice in Error* (Blackstone Press, London, 1993) and *Miscarriages of Justice* (Blackstone Press, London, 1999). His work in relation to the Internet includes the editorship of *Crime, Criminal Justice and the Internet* (special edition, *Criminal Law Review*, Sweet & Maxwell, London, 1998) and involvement in the project, UK Law Online (http://www.uklaw-online.com).

David Wall is a Senior Lecturer in the Department of Law and Deputy Director of the Criminal Justice Studies at the University of Leeds. He has written and researched the subjects of policing and access to criminal justice and also cybercrimes. He is the convenor of the Cyberlaw Research Unit at Leeds and runs taught undergraduate and postgraduate programmes in cyberlaw. His work on the Internet includes published chapters and journal articles, and he recently edited two special issues of the *International*

Review of Law Computers and Technology (Carfax) on 'E-Commerce' (vol. 13/2) and 'Cybercrimes, Cyberspeech and Cyberliberties' (vol. 14/1). He is currently conducting various funded research projects into a variety of policing cybercrime issues and he is editing a book entitled *Crime and the Internet* for Routledge. He has also written and researched extensively in the fields of policing and criminal justice, including (with Stallion, M.) *The British Police: Forces and Chief Officers 1829–2000* (Police History Society, London, 1999), *The Chief Constables of England and Wales* (Dartmouth, Aldershot, 1998) and (with Young, R.) *Access to Criminal Justice: legal aid, lawyers and the defence of liberty* (Blackstone Press, London, 1996).

Martin Wasik is Professor of Criminal Justice in the Department of Law at the University of Keele. He is the author of much published work, including *Crime and the Computer* (Clarendon Press, Oxford, 1990) and *Emmins on Sentencing* (3rd ed., Blackstone Press, London, 1998). He is co-author of *Blackstone's Criminal Practice* (10th ed., London, 2000) and contributor to *Crime On-Line* (Blackstone and Butterworth). He wrote the UK Report to the COMCRIME study on *Legal Aspects of Computer-Related Crime in the Information Society* (2000), prepared for the European Commission.

TABLE OF CASES

TABLE OF STATUTES

TABLE OF STATUTORY INSTRUMENTS

PART I

THE INTERNET, LAW AND SOCIETY

CHAPTER 1

The Internet, law and society

Clive Walker, David Wall and Yaman Akdeniz

The information society

What started as a prosaic set of wires and switches to enable connectivity between the computers of researchers and technicians[1] has become a fast growing emblem of national economic and social vitality.[2] New telecommunications developments, including the Internet,[3] have created an unlimited virtual market-place for the propagation and sale of ideas, goods and services on a global scale. One can imagine whole new worlds of beings, activities, environments and codes, as encapsulated by the term, 'Cyberspace',[4] which encompasses both the intangible communities and the interactive space made possible by the networks of the Internet. The spread of the Internet is scrutinised closely by national governments, keen to steal a march on rivals in globalised economies.[5] The House of Lords' Select Committee on Science and

---

[1] See Hafner, K. and Lyon, M., *Where Wizards Stay Up Late* (Simon & Schuster, New York, 1996); Reid, R., *Architects of the Web* (John Wiley, London, 1999).

[2] See the international Connectivity Providers Database at http://www.nsrc.org/networkstatus.html and also the statistics relating to .uk domain name registrations at http://www.nic.uk/news/stats/index.html.

[3] The Internet is a network of computers which is able to intercommunicate data split into 'packets' via telephonic connections through the standard of Transmission Control Protocol/ Internet Protocol (TCP/IP). The prototype of the Internet was designed and developed in 1969 by Bolt, Beranek and Newman Inc (see http://www.bbn.com/aboutbbn/history.htm), under contract to the Advanced Research Projects Agency (ARPA) of the US Department of Defense (DoD) (in 1996 ARPA was renamed DARPA – the Defense Advanced Research Projects Agency). (See http://www.arpa.mil). The resulting network became known as the 'ARPANET', and US universities joined ARPANET in the 1970s, and some connections to European universities were made at the end of that decade. Defence applications became partitioned in 1983, forming a distinct MILNNET, and ARPANET ceased to exist in 1990. The World Wide Web was developed by a further governmental agency, CERN, the European Particle Physics Laboratory (http://www.cern.ch/). The Internet began to be opened up to commercial Internet Service Providers after 1992 and, through them, private individuals.

[4] The term was coined in Gibson, W., *Neuromancer* (HarperCollins, London, 1994). 'Cyberspace' means 'The notional environment within which electronic communication occurs, esp. when represented as the inside of a computer system; space perceived as such by an observer but generated by a computer system and having no real existence; the space of virtual reality' (*Oxford English Dictionary*, 2000). See further Jordan, T., *Cyberpower: The Culture and Politics of Cyberspace* (Routledge, London, 1999).

[5] See Department of Trade and Industry, *Moving into the Information Age: An International Benchmarking Study*, 1998, http://www.isi.gov.uk/isi/bench/mitia/.

Technology's paper on the *Information Society*[6] depicts Information Super-highways as being 'one of the most important technological developments of this century' and as taking us into 'the age of the Information Society'.[7] Attention to the Internet is also a staple for international fora. Thus, the *Bangemann Report* to the European Council in 1994 identified information and communications technologies as 'generating a new industrial revolution'[8] which is to be encouraged throughout the European Union by the liberalisation of the telecom sector and the encouragement of legal harmonisation.

The channels of communication and commerce provided by the Internet easily transcend national boundaries (though are not universal),[9] and this transnationality is a noticeable feature which marks out the Internet as different at least in degree, if not in kind, from pre-existing mass media. Another important benefit is instantaneity, which can increase the impact of the message as well as decreasing the opportunity for traditional regulatory intercession. The other accentuated characteristics are multiple linkages, ease of access through low establishment costs (in Western societies) and interactivity.

The potential benefits of the Internet are numerous and range from the simple improvement of communications, to a revolution in commerce and an increased potential for increasing the democratic involvement of citizens whether in the nation state or in some other level of political engagement. Yet, many of these perceived dividends can, unfortunately, be turned against the vulnerable and the unwary. Much of the concern to date on the civil side has revolved around threats to privacy, intellectual property rights, the prospect of universal defamation and the implications for national tax collection.[10] On the criminal side, there are concerns about the security of network systems and unauthorised access and denial of service attacks, concerns about the availability of indecent, obscene and racist content, concerns about the use of computer technologies for traditional property offences such as theft, and fraud, and concerns about threatening hate speech and online stalking.[11] Then there are further fears about the disregard of national legal sensitivities, whether about contempt of court, gambling or otherwise.

Politicians have not been slow to condemn what, to some at least, is both unwanted and unfamiliar territory. Following the crash of the TWA Flight

---

[6] 1995–96 HL 77, London.

[7] Ibid. paras 1.1, 1.6.

[8] Recommendations to the European Council, *Europe and the Global Information Society* (1994), http://www2.echo.lu/eudocs/en/bangemann.html, p.1.

[9] The vast bulk of the traffic is in north America, western Europe and the Far East: http://www.nw.com /. For the UK's standing in the use of information and communications technologies, see: DTI, *Moving into the Information Age: An International Benchmarking Study*, 1998, http://www.isi.gov.uk/isi/bench/mitia.

[10] See House of Commons Select Committee on Trade and Industry, *Electronic Commerce* (1998–9 HC 648, London).

[11] See further Wall, D.S., 'Cybercrimes: New wine, no bottles?' in Davies, P., Francis, P. and Jupp, V. (eds), *Invisible Crimes: Their Victims and their Regulation* (Macmillan, London, 1999).

800 and the pipe bomb that exploded at the Olympics in Atlanta in the summer of 1996, the US took the opportunity to pressure the G-7 meeting in France to address restrictions on the use of cryptography, as cryptographic tools were considered a threat to national security. The G-7 adopted a final statement urging states to 'accelerate consultation on encryption that allows, when necessary, lawful government access to data and communications in order to prevent or investigate acts of terrorism, while protecting the privacy of legitimate communications'.[12] Furthermore, the first-ever G-8 meeting on crime at Washington DC in December 1997 adopted a Ministerial Communiqué relating to high-tech crime which recognised that:[13]

> ... new computer and telecommunications technologies offer unprecedented opportunities for global communication. As nations become increasingly reliant upon these technologies, including wireless communications, their exploitation by high-tech criminals poses an ever-greater threat to public safety.

So, the excesses of cyberspace are viewed as threatening, while the cyberspace attributes of transnationality, instantaneity and accessibility make national regulation or indeed any level of imposed regulation very difficult to accomplish and enforce. Social regulation within modern society has developed within physical bounds of time and space. But the development of cyberspace distances its inhabitants from local controls and the physical confines of nationality, sovereignty and governmentality, leading to regulatory solutions which conduce to a divorce from the old paradigms and the prominence of such features as self-organisation and social interaction rather than institutional authority.[14] The difficulties facing regulators are compounded by the fact there is no overall ownership of the Internet, though that is not to say that no law currently applies to it or that no future laws can be devised to govern it. Life is also made complex by the convergence of media, creating uncertainties as to which authority should act and which sectoral standards should be applied.[15]

The themes of this book

The theme of this book is the Internet within the settings of law and society. It is therefore about the 'law in action' and not just the 'law in books' and covers situations where, firstly, actions take place under the direct spotlight

[12] Schneier, B., and Banisar, D., *The Electronic Privacy Papers: Documents on the Battle for Privacy in the Age of Surveillance*, (John Wiley & Sons, New York, 1997) p.322, GILC Resolution in Support of the Freedom to Use Cryptography, September 1996, http://www.gilc.org/crypto/oecd-resolution.html.
[13] Washington, DC, 9, 10 December 1997, http://www.usdoj.gov/criminal/cybercrime/communique.htm.
[14] See Teubner, G. (ed.), *Global Law without a State* (Dartmouth, Aldershot, 1997) pp.7–8; Castells, M., *The Information Age*, vol. II (Blackwell, Oxford, 1997) p.354.
[15] See House of Commons Select Committee on Culture, Media and Sport, *The Multimedia Revolution* (1997–8 HC 520, London); Gibbons, T., *Regulating the Media* (2nd ed., Sweet & Maxwell, London, 1998) p.299.

of law and, secondly, the occasions where they fall in the shadow of the law. Consequently, it explores areas of behaviour which challenge the rule of law but are met with a wider range of regulatory responses and strategies of governance. In this context, governance is concerned with a complex pattern of interrelationships between social institutions and individuals[16] rather than simply the formal processes of government. According to Rhodes, 'governance . . . is about regulating relationships in complex systems'[17] A further aspect is explained by Hirst and Thompson whereby 'governance . . . is a function that can be performed by a wide variety of public and private, state and non-state, national and international, institutions and practices'.[18] In summary, three themes emerge. One is how the Internet operates. Then there are the implications of its inner workings for those working in the fields of law or political or social policy. Finally, the detailed workings of the law in context must be explored, taking as the context the major policy strands in relation to the Internet.

The organisation and governance of the Internet

What organisation? What governance? Legend has likened the Internet to a wild west frontier, others have seen it as a public space: 'a forum without gatekeepers'.[19] But this is simply not true – if it ever was a wild west frontier, then it has quickly been tamed.[20] As others have observed,[21] there is control and order through the design of the system, through non-legal regulation and through sovereign law. Since Internet law from national and international sovereigns and non-legal regulation (whether quasi-legislative codes or the social norms of the Net) are the prime subjects of most of the chapters of this book, then attention will be given first to the basic architecture of the Internet and the choices it embodies.

The thesis here is that the design of Internet technology and software,[22] whether conscious or not, has consequences in terms of organisation and

---

[16] See generally Osborne, D., and Gaebler, T., *Reinventing Government* (Addison Wesley, Reading, MA, 1992) p.34; Jessop, B., 'The regulation approach, governance and post-Fordism: alternative perspectives on economic and political change ?' (1995) 24 (3) *Economy and Society* 307.

[17] Rhodes, R.A.W., 'The Hollowing Out of the State: The Changing Nature of the Public Services in Britain' (1994) 65 *Political Quarterly* 138 at p.151.

[18] Hirst, P. and Thompson, G., 'Globalization and the Future of the Nation State' (1995) 24 (3) *Economy and Society* 408 at p.422.

[19] Wallace, J. and Mangan, M., *Sex, Laws and Cyberspace* (Henry Holt, New York, 1996) p.xiv.

[20] See Chandler, A. (1996) 'The changing definition and image of hackers in popular discourse', 24 *International Journal of the Sociology of Law*, 229.

[21] Lessig, L., *Code and Other Laws of Cyberspace* (Basic Books, New York, 1999). Also see the respective relevant works of the editors of this collection that are cited elsewhere in this text.

[22] See Wallace, J., *Overdrive* (John Wiley, New York, 1997). The same point can be made about computer technology, an example being the design of the Intel Pentium III processor, which allowed for a unique serial number (PSN) to be accessed by software on the Internet for identification purposes (perhaps to verify the user or to link to the loading of software). See http://www.cyber-rights.org/reports/intel-rep.htm.

governance. In order to work as a network, each user linking to it must have a distinct identifier (an IP address) recognisable by a DNS (Domain Name System) server and must send messages or carry data which are recognisable by the network. Choices are inevitable given the necessary mediation of a common technology which, for most non-computer experts, must be designed by others.[23] But is the architecture of the Internet determinative in any sense of the organisation and governance which will flow from it? This contention was recently proffered by Lessig, who believes that the Internet is not only shaped by the 'code' upon which it is founded, but also that the development of code will allow for 'a perfect tool of control' to be wielded 'by commerce with the backing of government'.[24] Two provisos should be entered to this thesis.

First, looking to the future, this thesis overplays the extent to which a common standard can dominate on the Internet, either as a commercial standard or as a governmental standard, to produce 'the emerging architecture of the panopticon'.[25] The inevitable architecture of the Internet (in essence a technologically based network), which includes competition,[26] ease of access, interlinking, interactivity, spontaneity, transnationality and almost boundless expandability (especially with ever more powerful TCP/IP protocols), conduces against such control. Further, the perceived 'invisible hand' impetus towards control underplays the extent to which the imposition of controls would undermine the essential attractions and efficiencies of the Internet. This is not to say that the culture of Internet of 1995, say, is, or is bound to be, the culture of Internet of 2005. Clearly, commercial influences have grown and will grow further[27] (as will explicit governmental attempts to control and regulate such an increasingly significant part of society). But the dominant culture does not have to be, and has never been, monopolistic. Thus, one should guard against functional determinism within a complex cybersociety that is characterised by reflexivity.[28]

Second, the 'conducive architecture' thesis underplays the extent to which forms of organisation and governance have already become firmly established and which again adhere to such attributes as decentralised operation, openness, freedom of choice and social rather than authoritarian development. Thus, it is true that there is no inevitable architecture of the Internet, as alternative protocols are ever the possibility. But it is also true that the

---

[23] This distinguishes the Internet from other customary modes of communication such as language.

[24] Lessig, L., *Code and Other Laws of Cyberspace* (Basic Books, New York, 1999) pp.x, 6.

[25] Ibid., p.233.

[26] In particular it is not clear why in the light of global economic competition governments would always agree to enforce each other's regulations (compare ibid., p.55), and the treatment of the US government on encryption suggests otherwise (see chapter 14).

[27] See House of Commons Select Committee on Trade and Industry, *Electronic Commerce* (1998–9 HC 648, London) para. 138.

[28] It is admitted that the availability continuance of open code allows the evasion of control: Lessig, L., *Code and Other Laws of Cyberspace* (Basic Books, New York, 1999) p.107.

network is now most unlikely to be wholly reinvented and re-engineered in a way which is wholly distinct from its origins of some three decades ago. This is not to say that the existing architecture is wholly benign, for some of the perceptions formed by many commentators of the pre-commerce Internet may be rather affected by their US-centric vision. In this way, it can be accepted that the coding necessary to transmit data through the Internet inevitably gives rise to regulation and a constitutional structure. But it reflects the philosophy of the academics and researchers who took on Internet development from the US military that this regulation and structure should primarily be related to technical necessity. In the light of this technical imperative, what is remarkable is that the point made earlier, that gatekeepers and regulators have so far remained essentially non-governmental, even if they have an increasingly public function, and their profile much more reflects the technical origins and users of the Internet. Consequently, there exists a multi-tiered structure of governance of which sovereign government is but one tier. It follows that there is a heavy US bias in terms of technology, personnel and libertarian philosophy, all of which is reflected in the constitutional history, structure and spirit of the Internet, which will now be outlined.

The organisation around which much of the constitution has revolved is the Internet Society (ISOC),[29] which is a non-profit, non-governmental, international club of Internet enthusiasts and is located in Virginia, USA. Since its foundation in 1992, ISOC has served as the international organization for standards, education and policy issues. Its guiding principles comprise: open, unencumbered, beneficial use of the Internet; self-regulated content providers operating without prior censorship; online free expression which is not restricted by other indirect means such as excessively restrictive governmental or private controls; an open forum for the development of standards and Internet technology; no discrimination in the use of the Internet; no misuse of personal information; free use of encryption; and encouragement of cooperation between networks.[30] What has followed in terms of the governance of the Internet is a tension between the technologists in ISOC seeking 'to retain control of "their" Internet as it evolved into a commercial medium'[31] (often allied with telecommunications corporate interests who are well represented within ISOC membership) and the public interest agendas of national governments (increasingly non-American) and international organisations.

Perhaps the highest level of governance within the policy network is provided by the Internet Architecture Board (IAB).[32] The IAB was established

[29] See http://www.isoc.org/.
[30] Note that this regulator is a member of the Global Internet Liberty Campaign http://www.gilc.org.
[31] Mueller, M., 'ICANN and Internet governance' (1999) 1 *Journal of Policy Regulation and Strategy for Telecommunications Information and Media* 497 at p.499.
[32] See http://www.iab.org/. See Cerf, V., *The Internet Architecture Board* (RFC 1160, 1990).

in 1983 and was chartered as a component of the Internet Society in 1992. Its responsibilities include: oversight of the architecture for the protocols and procedures used by the Internet; oversight of the process used to create Internet Standards; editorial management and publication of the Request for Comments (RFC) document series, and for administration of the various Internet assigned numbers; and external liaison and advice to ISOC concerning technical, architectural, procedural and policy matters pertaining to the Internet and its enabling technologies. It consists of thirteen voting members, most of whom are members of other governing bodies described below, especially the Internet Engineering Task Force (IETF).[33]

The IETF is a large, open international community of network designers, operators, vendors and researchers concerned with the evolution of Internet architecture and operation. Much of the detailed work about routing, standards and transport is carried out in around two dozen working groups and in conjunction with reviews performed by its top layer Internet Engineering Steering Group (which forwards them to ISOC as Recommended Standards). Each version of an Internet standards-related specification traditionally begins life as part of the 'Request for Comments' (RFC) document series which commenced in 1969.[34]

Research into Internet matters is handled by the Internet Research Task Force (IRTF), the chair of which is appointed by the Internet Architecture Board (IAB).[35] Its Research Groups work on topics related to Internet protocols, applications, architecture and technology. Research collaborations outside the ISOC constellation include the World Wide Web Consortium (W3C), founded in 1994 in collaboration with CERN and so based not wholly in the US but also in Europe and Japan. Its provides a repository of information about the World Wide Web for developers and users, reference code implementations to embody and promote standards, and various prototype and sample applications to demonstrate uses of new technology.[36] Its activities also include the development of much criticized tools such as those for content rating (PICS) and tools in relation to privacy protocols (P3P).

Formed in California in October 1998, the Internet Corporation for Assigned Names and Numbers (ICANN)[37] is the non-profit corporation that was devised from a broad coalition of the Internet's business, technical and academic communities to take over responsibility for the IP address space allocation, protocol parameter assignment, domain name

---

[33] See http://www.ietf.org/.
[34] See http://www.rfc-editor.org/; http://www.cis.ohio-state.edu/hypertext/information/rfc.html.
[35] See http://www.irtf.org/.
[36] See http://www.w3.org.
[37] See http://www.icann.org/. ICANN and the US Department of Commerce entered a Memorandum of Understanding (MoU) on 25 November 1998, which effectively endorsed the *fait accompli* of ISOC.

system management,[38] and specified root server system management functions hitherto performed previously under US government contract by the Internet Assigned Numbers Authority (IANA)[39] and other entities. The transfer of functions should be complete by the end of 2000. The previous technical management system had historically been funded and overseen by the US government, but one of ICANN's tasks is to pave the way for a more broadly based management. The Initial Board members (a chair and nine others drawn from six nations), who were appointed by leading figures within ISOC and IANA, will ultimately be replaced by elected board members chosen by four different Internet constituency groups (three Supporting Organizations and an At-Large Membership[40]), collectively representing a broader and more global range of the Internet's technical and user communities. There are also a Government Advisory Committee[41] and a Country Code (Top Level Domain registries) constituency. The structure is highly elaborate but as yet ineffective if democracy and accountability are important goals. In terms of activities, many of the disputes concerning the Internet have arisen in connection with IANA and ICANN because of the commercial value of domain names as a form of trademark. In addition, there remains much constitutional controversy as ICANN hovers between intergovernmental agency and private club, between global player and US Department of Commerce junior partner.[42] Many of the critics seem to hark back to the days when the Internet could be operated as an American

---

[38] RFC 1591 http://sunsite.auc.dk/RFC/rfc/rfc1591.html describes the top level structure for domain names. RFC 920 http://www.is.co.za/smtprd/docs/rfc.html describes the requirements for domain names themselves. The relationship between country code Top Level Domain (ccTLD) registries (such as the .uk name issued by Nominet), national government agencies and ICANN itself is still the subject of debate, with registries often preferring the dominance of ICANN, but the Government Advisory Committee has proposed that ICANN should delegate the administration of ccTLDs only to organizations that have been designated by the relevant government or public authority. The notion of a 'country' is also contested, with current disputes surrounding the recognition of .eu (European Union – see http://www.ispo.cec.be/eif/InternetPoliciesSite/DotEU/dotEU-en.pdf) and .ps (Palestine).

[39] See http://www.iana.org/. IANA was created at the University of Southern California by John Postel (the first member of ISOC) and transferred to ISOC in 1994. Instead of IANA's model of a single international DNS provider, Network Solutions Inc. (trading as the Internet Network Information Center: http://rs.internic.net/) for global top-level domains (.com, .net, .gov, .edu and .org), ICANN is in the process of additionally accrediting dozens of gTLD registries around the world (http://www.icann.org/registries/accredited-list.html). See further chap.3 for European policy.

[40] The constitution of the At Large Membership has been most problematic. The idea is to have direct membership of ICANN which will eventually elect an At Large Council of 14 members. See http://www.icann.org/minutes/prelim-report-10mar00.htm.

[41] See http://www.noie.gov.au/gac/index.htm. The GAC's role is to 'consider and provide advice on the activities of [ICANN] as they relate to concerns of governments, particularly matters where there may be an interaction between the Corporation's policies and various laws, and international agreements'.

[42] See Orange, A., 'Developments in the domain name system' (1999) 3 *Journal of Information Law & Technology*; Mueller, M., 'ICANN and Internet governance' (1999) 1 *Journal of Policy Regulation and Strategy for Telecommunications Information and Media* 497.

hobby, but this model glosses over the extent to which the US government wielded influence, a position which even the US administrator seems to accept in principle must change, in part under pressure from Europe.[43]

Another important linkage with ICANN concerns the work of Network Solutions Inc. (trading as the Internet Network Information Center)[44] which continues for the present to operate the root server system on behalf of the US Department of Commerce in pursuance of its originally monopolistic registration of top level domains.[45] The result is ultimately that the US Department of Commerce controls entry into the root and the propagation of new forms of recognisable Internet entities (Top Level Domains).

Beneath the overlay of all of these non-governmental bodies are the Internet service providers, who provide the interface to the Internet for the vast majority of users and therefore operate as the gatekeepers of the Net. ISPs are either public or private bodies which offer the facility to their customers to gain access to Internet communications systems. 'Public' ISPs include the Joint Academic Network (JANET), which, since 1984, has served UK universities.[46] There are many more commercial ISPs – for example, America Online and Demon – who mainly market the Internet for commercial purposes with both business and private customers, though there are some private non-profit-making organisations who act as servers for community and political groups. Features of interest at this level include the growing corporatisation of the ISPs – their takeover by large corporate conglomerates,[47] which conduces towards a culture of commerce and entertainment rather than hobby-technology, especially when Internet technology is subsumed within other media technology (such as digital television). In addition, ISPs have always included in their contracts with customers provisions about the terms of use of the Internet. As shall be described in later chapters, these have become more elaborate, as governments have pressured ISPs to exert access and content controls, and ISPs have in turn sought to insert the buffer of trade standards organisations (such as the Internet Watch Foundation).[48]

What is remarkably absent from this list of players in the fields of technical growth and governance is any governmental institution. There are relationships between governmental organisations and, for example, ICANN, but

---

[43] European Union policy is set out in Communication from the European Commission to the European Parliament and to the Council, *Internet Governance* (COM(1998) 476, final). See also http://www.ispo.cec.be/eif/InternetPoliciesSite/InternetGovernance/Main.html.

[44] http://rs.internic.net/.

[45] There are regional routing registries which coordinate local registries and large ISPs – ARIN (the Americas, Caribbean and sub-Saharan Africa), RIPE (Europe, North Africa and the Middle East see http://www.ripe.net) and APNIC (the Pacific Rim and Asia). The backbone of the system runs through several public exchange points (such as the London Internet Exchange). See http://www.nsrc.org/admin-guide/nsrceng.htm.

[46] See http://www.ja.net/.

[47] A prime example in the UK market was the sale of Demon to Scottish Power in 1998.

[48] See http://www.iwf.org.uk/.

both national and international governmental establishments have hesitated to supplant the system of management which has grown up in the private sector. Consequently, a structure of private non-governmental organisations have emerged which, as stated earlier, perform a public function. Aside from the controls exerted by the US Department of Commerce which have already been noted (and the European Commission has also been a strong lobbyist), the closest official body is the World Intellectual Property Organization (WIPO) which is a sub-group of the United Nations. However, its involvement in the design of the Internet has been very limited. For example, following an invitation by the US government, WIPO conducted a study of the relationship between domain names and intellectual property and made recommendations to ICANN in April 1999,[49] the results being subject to revision by ICANN's Board which continues successfully to assert authority over these controversies. One of WIPO's proposals concerns the arbitration system for domain name disputes; ICANN rules allow the complainant to select the dispute resolution provider who will adjudicate the claim from among a list approved by ICANN,[50] thereby reducing the dominance of US law through the choice, for example, of the WIPO Arbitration and Mediation Center.[51]

Overall, we are witnessing an emergent system of Internet constitutional governance, woven primarily by Internet interest groups, ISPs and their associations, ISOC and its related agencies and to a lesser degree than normal by national and international government. The basis for this governance remains technical efficiency and cultures which reflect the essence of the viability of any form of networking, though technical efficiency has never been an exclusive concern even for the founding fathers of the Internet; at very least, political impact has been unavoidable. Accordingly, ISOC has established an Internet Societal Task Force (ISTF) to discuss those aspects of the Internet that deal with policy issues affecting users in the global Internet community from a societal perspective.[52] Another example of political impact was raised by a group of computer security, cryptography, law and policy

---

[49] WIPO, *Internet Domain Name Process Final Report* (http://ecommerce.wipo.int/domains/process/eng/processhome.html, 1999). See Froomkin, M., 'A Commentary on WIPO's *The Management of Internet Names and Addresses: Intellectual Property Issues*', http://www.law.miami.edu/~amf/commentary.htm, 1999.

[50] ICANN Board Resolution 99.83, the Uniform Dispute Resolution Policy (UDRP), http://www.icann.org/udrp/udrp.htm para. 4(d). For a review of ICANN activities see the www site of the group ICANN Watch whose mission statement is 'to serve as a central point of reference about what ICANN is and is not doing', http://www.icannwatch.org/.

[51] See http://arbiter.wipo.int/domains/index.html; Mueller, M., 'ICANN and Internet governance' (1999) 1 *Journal of Policy Regulation and Strategy for Telecommunications Information and Media* 497 at p.505. For case-law, see: Osborne, D., 'The ICANN decisions – what have we learned?' (2000) 11 *Computers & Law* 32. This system of arbitration applies to gTLDs. For ccTLDs, national registries can operate their own process. Thus, Nominet UK has a free Dispute Resolution System (http://www.nic.uk/ref/drs.html).

[52] See also 'Responsible Use of the Network,' (RFC 1855), at http://www.stanton.dtcc.edu/stanton/cs/rfc1855.html.

experts who criticised the IETF's standard setting role and urged the IETF not to adopt new protocols or modify existing protocols to facilitate eaves-dropping by law enforcement bodies.[53] The approaches to questions of technical efficiency are also bounded by US governmental interests, though these intersect with traditional Internet culture to a fair degree. The recent commercial dominance of the Internet brings new ideas and tensions but cannot expect to monopolise Internet use on its own terms.

This history suggests that:[54]

> The origins, development and co-operative ethos of cyberspace are therefore directly related to the real and controlled world of government policy-making and public expenditure.

Furthermore, government policy making has been crucial to control import-ant technologies, such as cryptography, which is fundamental to security over the Internet and is an essential tool for the development of e-commerce. Another form of intervention by some nation-states involves the control of access to the Internet. Such policies and control mechanisms imposed by nation-states have a major impact upon the development of the Internet and one should not forget that different nation-states are at different levels of network development with half of humanity having never made a telephone call.[55]

But at the same time, the very design of Internet technology creates a potentially infinite communications complex which cannot readily be bounded by one government or even several or many acting in concert:[56]

> ... the Internet is too widespread to be easily dominated by any single govern-ment. By creating a seamless global-economic zone, borderless and unregulatable, the Internet calls into question the very idea of a nation-state

In this way, the Internet provides a paradigm of a late modern[57] sub-society, in which the traditional structures of class or other socio-political com-monality are replaced by new élites whose privilege is measured in terms of knowledge and technological access.[58] The Internet is a complex and multi-national environment where traditional concepts of regulation, reliant

---

[53] An Open Letter to the Internet Engineering Task Force, 8 November, 1999, at http://www.cyber-rights.org/interception/ietf-letter.htm.

[54] Loader, B.D. (ed.), *The Governance of Cyberspace* (Routledge, London, 1997) pp.6–7.

[55] Human Rights Watch, 'Silencing The Net: The Threat to Freedom of Expression On-line' (1996) 8 (2) *Monitors: A Journal of Human Rights and Technology* (http://www.cwrl.utexas.edu/~monitors/1.1/hw/index.html). See also Wresch, W., *Haves and Have-Nots in the Information Age* (Rutgers University Press, New Brunswick, NJ, 1996).

[56] Barlow, J.P., 'Thinking Locally, Acting Globally', (1996) *Cyber-Rights Electronic List*, 15 January.

[57] Giddens, A., *The Consequences Of Modernity* (Polity Press, Cambridge, 1990).

[58] See Castells, M., *The Information Age*, Vol. I: *The Rise of Network Society* (Blackwell, Oxford, 1996); O'Malley, P. and Palmer, D., 'Post-Keynesian policing' (1996) 25(2) *Economy and Society* 137.

as they are upon tangibility (rather than distanciation[59]) in time and space, may not be easily applicable or enforceable. The nation state must abjure its traditional monopolisation of the policing and regulatory functions not only on political and philosophical grounds associated with growth of neo-Liberalism or new Conservatism,[60] but also because of the pragmatic difficulties in doing otherwise in a situation of instantaneous, mass participation and global modes of Internet communication.[61] It therefore seeks further sustenance by the activation of more varied levels of power at second hand. In this way, laws, regulations and standards will affect the development of the Internet (and, one might say, self-reflexively, vice versa), and this is also true for self-regulatory solutions introduced for the availability of certain types of content on the Internet. As a result:[62]

> Rules and rule-making do exist. However, the identities of the rule makers and the instruments used to establish rules will not conform to classic patterns of regulation.

Social change and the Internet

Technological change does not occur within a social vacuum. Scientific and technological developments are themselves both driven and shaped by the social milieu from which they emerge and in which they operate,[63] and they certainly impact outwardly on social practices and patterns. The Internet is said to be 'the indispensable tool' in the creation of an Information Society[64] in which status and value is based primarily in informational goods or attributes rather than physical goods or attributes. The capacity of the Internet to store, transfer and add value to information obviously makes it an important factor in this trend. In terms of its impact, it conduces towards networked and horizontal relationships rather than hierarchical relationships. It is global rather than national and so can facilitate new relationships based upon meaningful social interaction on a geographic scale hitherto impractical.

---

[59] See Poster, M. (ed.), *Jean Baudrillard* (Polity Press, Cambridge, 1988). Also see Giddens, A. *The Consequences of Modernity*, (Polity Press, London, 1990).

[60] See Habermas, J., *The New Conservatism* (Polity Press, Cambridge, 1989); Gamble, A., 'The political economy of freedom' in Levitas, R. (ed.), *The Ideology of the New Right* (Polity Press, Cambridge, 1986); Sheptycki, J., 'Policing, Postmodernism and Transnationalism' (1998) 38 *British Journal of Criminology*, 485.

[61] Garland, D., 'The limits of the sovereign state' (1996) 35 *British Journal of Criminology* 445; Walker, C., 'Cyber-Contempt: Fair Trials and the Internet' (1997) 3 *Yearbook of Media and Entertainment Law* 1.

[62] Reidenberg, J.R., 'Governing Networks and Cyberspace Rule-Making' (1996) 45 *Emory Law Journal* 911 at pp.911–12. Also, Karnow, C., *Future Codes* (Artech House, Boston, MA, 1997) pp.5–11, 223.

[63] See Kuhn, T., *The Structure of Scientific Revolutions* (3rd ed., University of Chicago Press, Chicago, IL, 1996); Jasanoff, S., *Science at the Bar* (Harvard University Press, Cambridge, MA, 1995).

[64] Castells, M., *The Information Age*, Vol. III: *End of Millennium* (Blackwell, Oxford, 1998) p.336.

Indeed, one of the more visible impacts of the Internet has been to accelerate some of the qualities which characterise late modernity, particularly the 'discontinuities' highlighted by Giddens[65] as separating the modern and traditional social orders. Social orders bind time and space; however, they have become disembedded and distanciated[66] – 'lifted out' of local contexts of interaction and restructured across indefinite spans of time–space.

Yet one should avoid technological or sociological determinism,[67] including claims about 'bipolar opposition between the Net and the Self' or an inevitable domination of a Network Society.[68] While there exist obvious concerns for the psychological development of individuals from this social de-skilling through the distanciation of traditional social order, it is nevertheless the case that the Internet does not operate in isolation, as new and old technologies and practices have impact side by side.[69] Nor does the Internet offer an autonomous or exclusive state of being,[70] and very few people would view their existence as wholly or even distinctly being based within it. It is therefore useful to employ the term 'Cyberspace' to refer to the cultural and social spaces where being and interaction is grounded within technology,[71] and one can even speak of the 'Netizens' who populate the space. But the space is a virtual adjunct, and so affects just one aspect of personal and social being which allows for enrichment and diversity, including by the adoption of extra identities.[72]

A final concern in relation to social change is the limited and structured access to the Internet that exists even in the rich Western societies[73] and the increasing power to homogenise the web wielded by multinational corporations.[74] Just as radio was turned from a personalised and diffused mode of communication, akin to the telephone, into a mass and passive form of consumption by its capture by corporations such as General Electric and Marconi (in hand with a government fearful of Red revolution), so the controversial and unpopular are increasingly less likely to be noticed on the

---

[65] Giddens, A. *The Consequences of Modernity* (Polity Press, London, 1990) p.6.

[66] Ibid., p.14.

[67] Bellamy, C. and Taylor, J.A., *Governing in the Information Age* (Open University Press, Buckingham, 1998) pp.vii, 19; Hague, B.N. and Loader, B.D., *Digital Democracy* (Routledge, London, 1999) chap.1.

[68] Castells, M., *The Information Age*, Vol. I: *The Rise of the Network Society* (Blackwell, Oxford, 1996) pp.3, 468.

[69] Katsh, M.E., *Law in a Digital World* (Oxford University Press, New York, 1995) p.13; Slevin, J., *The Internet and Society* (Polity Press, Cambridge, 2000) pp.56, 91.

[70] Compare Sadar, Z. and Ravetz, J.R., *Cyberfutures* (Pluto Press, London, 1996) p.1; Volkmar, I., 'Universalism and particularism' in Kahin, B. and Neeson, C., *Borders in Cyberspace* (MIT Press, Cambridge, MA, 1997).

[71] See Wellman, B. *et al.*, 'Computer networks as social networks' (1996) 22 *Annual Review of Sociology* 211.

[72] See Porter, D.A. (ed.), *Internet Culture* (Routledge, London, 1997); Smith, M.A. and Kollock, P., *Communities in Cyberspace* (Routledge, London, 1999) chaps 2, 5.

[73] National Audit Office, *Government on the Web* (1999–2000 HC 87) paras 2.6, 2.7.

[74] Loader, B.D. (ed.), *The Governance of Cyberspace* (Routledge, London, 1997) pp.6, 7; Hague, B.N. and Loader, B.D., *Digital Democracy* (Routledge, London, 1999) p.15.

Internet.[75] It is therefore important to emphasise both diversity and social inclusion in Cyberspace for a truly well founded Information Society. Closing the 'digital divide'[76] mainly remains within the domain of nation-states. Access to the Internet at prices affordable for citizens should be a precondition for an inclusive Information Society, just as efficient access to a communication infrastructure is vital for business participation in the digital economy.[77]

The relationship of law to the Internet

If the 'information society' really does materialise then, as an anti-lawyer joke suggests, 'for every action there is an equal and opposite lawyer'. Accordingly, there will be lawyers (and additionally law-related professionals such as police and judges) in close pursuit, not just to make money out of novel disputes but also to act for the public good – to regularise, protect and enforce.

It has already been asserted that the Internet is not lawless, nor does it operate either as a legal utopia nor dystopia. But special problems are created because of the now-familiar features such as disembedding in time and space of actor and action, the amount of traffic and the instantaneity and universality of the traffic. The consequent legal difficulties are often evidential and procedural.[78] The problems are not insuperable, and there is 'no general normative argument that supports the immunisation of cyberspace activities from territorial regulation'.[79] In substance, there is applicable law, though it was rarely designed with the Internet in mind and so there is a 'hotch-potch' rather than a codified set of rules.[80]

The foregoing describes the situation at present, but what should be the future relationship between the Internet and law? One extreme is to assume that traditional legal approaches alone will cope with the Internet:[81]

> . . . it is not necessary or constructive to treat the Internet as a source of new legal issues that create a new legal discipline called 'internet law'. Instead, we argue the Internet is a new medium in which traditional legal principles are analyzed in novel contexts. There is no 'Internet law' as such, and no such specially designed law is required.

---

[75] See Briggs, A., *The History of Broadcasting in the United Kingdom*, Vol. 1: *The birth of broadcasting* (Oxford University Press, Oxford, 1961); Douglas, S., *Inventing American Broadcasting 1899–1922* (The Johns Hopkins University Press, Baltimore, MD, 1987).

[76] See chap. 6.

[77] For example, the e-Europe initiative of the European Union aims to ensure a socially inclusive Information Society. See 'e-Europe: An Information Society for All initiative' (8 December, 1999), at http://europa.eu.int/comm/information_society/eeurope/index_en.htm.

[78] See Barrett, N., *Digital Crime* (Kogan Page, London, 1997) p.10. See also House of Lords Select Committee on Science and Technology, *Digital Images as Evidence* (1997–8 HL 64, London) and Government Response (1997–8 HL 121, London).

[79] Goldsmith, J.L., 'Against cyberanarchy' (1998) 65 *University of Chicago Law Review* 1199 at p.1250.

[80] Edwards, L. and Waelde, C., *Law and the Internet* (Hart Publishing, Oxford, 1997) p.9.

[81] Delta, G.B. and Matsuura, J.H., *Law of the Internet* (Aspen Law & Business, New York, 1998) p.xix.

But to set one's face entirely against Cyberlaw is to ignore the socially transformative nature of the Internet. New relationships and transactions can be created, and the modalities by which they are secured can also be novel.

Another extreme would be to establish a distinct new international jurisdiction called Cyberspace[82] where 'Cyberlaw' prevails over actions and persons operating within it. The imposition of a centralised, remote and monolithic set of rules on the many communities and relationships within the Internet seems a blunt instrument. The loss of local control would be of increasing concern to governments in economic terms as Internet commerce grows. Even the creation of a wholly distinct body of 'Internet law' at national level seems unwarranted, though it is often favoured by legislators wishing to posture as technically advanced or morally vigilant. By and large, extensive new legislation is not necessary since the Internet creates new contexts for old problems rather than new problems *per se*. One should not confuse technological and substantive innovation. In addition, it is not sensible to proceed with a distinct 'internet law' because of the trend towards convergence which means that fixing special boundaries around the treatment of one medium will tend to break down.[83] Emerging technological developments will continue this trend. At one level, falling prices and more user-friendly technologies will enable a broader section of society to gain access to the computer and to the Internet, thus vastly increasing the number of Internet users. At another level, growing bandwidth on the Net allows more and more complex (especially visually rich) information to be carried, making the Internet able to mimic existing media such as radio, telephones and, most important of all, television. Conversely, digital satellite TV systems allow for an increasing number of Internet related facilities. Likewise, telephones are being adapted to world wide web compatibility, and the trend will be accelerated once current restrictions on BT in relation to broadcast services are lifted by 2002.[84] Convergence undercuts the feasibility and rationale for narrow regulation. The multiplicity of bands makes monitoring very difficult and also answers any arguments about scarcity of spectrum. The House of Commons Select Committee on Culture, Media and Sport has called for a unifying Communications Regulations Commission, but does not accept that the same regulatory approach can apply to all

---

[82] Johnson, D.R. and Post, D., 'The rise of law on the global network' in Kahin, B. and Neeson, C., *Borders in Cyberspace* (MIT Press, Cambridge, MA, 1997),

[83] OFTEL, *Beyond the Telephone, the TV and the PC* (London, 1995) para. 1.1.4. See also European Commission, Green Paper on the Convergence of the Telecommunications, Media and Information Technology Sectors, and the Implications for Regulation: Towards an Information Society Approach (COM(97)623). The licensing of telecommunications systems is dealt with under the Telecommunications Act 1984 s.7. This covers Internet systems providers but not (if different) content providers. Digital broadcasting is within the Broadcasting Act 1996, Pt. I. See Smith, G.J.H., *Internet Law and Regulation* (FT Law and Tax, London, 1996) chap.6.

[84] See House of Commons Select Committee on Trade and Industry, *Telecommunications Regulation* (1997–8 HC 254, HMSO, London).

media.[85] The Government Responses were more cautious, and gradual evolution is to ensue, with public service broadcast standards remaining a benchmark.[86] This avoidance of heavy state regulation is to be welcomed as at least pragmatic:

> Digital space is so vast that every view, no matter how vile, finds a ready outlet. There is room enough for every form of diseased intelligence. No commission can oversee even the tiniest fraction of the telecosm anymore.[87]

The third way, and the approach of most commentators in this book, is to progress through the adaptation of existing law,[88] as augmented by techniques of governance. In this way, it becomes possible to talk of a 'Cyberlaw' – the legal responses to issues that arise within Cyberspace – so long as it is realised that many of the responses are not unique to Cyberspace and may not require the passage of new laws. But there must be innovation since there is looming the 'prospect of a vast array of new services'.[89] Some legal innovations will respond to the features of the Internet outlined above. There is also a need to react in law to the emergent theme of convergence. So, what is advocated in the third way is the adaptation of existing legislation and case law. Examples of the adaptation of both will be given in this book, ranging from changes to the law on obscene publications to the meaning of a signature on a document. Judicial reactions have also occurred, but it may be that there is more room for invention and subtlety in that sphere. For example, it would be useful if the judges were to develop a principle of respect within their national legal system for multi-national communities within the Internet. Use might be made here of the concept of margin of appreciation within European Convention jurisprudence[90] by a recognition that it is often inappropriate (and ineffectual) to impose national, variant standards on materials originating from abroad, provided that there is the real possibility of action abroad. This precept seems very relevant to freedom of expression and may even become a requirement under the Human Rights Act 1998. It also reflects the ability of Internet users to engage in ' "regulatory arbitrage" – to choose to evade disliked

---

[85] House of Commons Select Committee on Culture, Media and Sport, *The Multimedia Revolution* (1997–8 HC 520, HMSO, London), Government Response http://www.culture.gov.uk/medrev.htm.

[86] Department of Trade and Industry, *Regulating Communications* (Cm. 4022, Stationery Office, London, 1998). See also *Converging Technologies* http://www.dti.gov.uk/future-unit, 1998.

[87] Huber, P., *Law and Disorder in Cyberspace* (Oxford University Press, New York, 1997) p.165.

[88] See Goldsmith, J.L., 'Against cyberanarchy' (1998) 65 *University of Chicago Law Review* 1199.

[89] OFTEL, *Beyond the Telephone, the TV and the PC* (London, 1995) para. 1.1.1.

[90] This seems more appropriate than subsidiarity which involves a more hierarchical arrangement. Compare Reidenberg, J.R., 'Governing networks and rule-making in cyberspace' in Kahin, B. and Neeson, C., *Borders in Cyberspace* (MIT Press, Cambridge, MA, 1997) at p.98.

domestic regulations by communicating/transacting under regulatory regimes with different rules'.[91] An international treaty to confirm and encourage such an approach might be helpful (and seems much more attainable than the chimera of universal standards), but is not necessary.

As well as direct legal responses by national or international sovereigns, account should be taken of the new environment of the Internet by an emphasis upon multi-tiered governance by '. . . a complex mix of State, business, technical and citizen forces'.[92] This type of approach has already been encountered in relation to the ISOC-related bodies and the ISP responses to illegal, harmful and offensive content. A mixture of public and private interests is indicative of this form of regulation, with the latter taking a strong role in policing.[93] It has the advantage of diminishing governmental intrusion and the threat of state censorship. But private censorship by an organisation such as the Internet Watch Foundation, can be equally as threatening since it is on the one hand less visible and accountable and on the other hand subject to close government scrutiny.[94] Nevertheless, the strategy of governance entails some advantages. It allows for the commercial development of the Internet as quickly as possible. Regulation on a broadcast model would undoubtedly stifle enterprise. Governance also provides for quick and cheap remedies, especially when dealing with multinational issues. Legal process is expensive, remote and complex, and regulation affords choices often more subtle than the instruments of law.[95] Governance in which the Internet industry and users are involved and committed allows for flexibility in terms of future change of an infrastructure not yet fully developed.[96] It can also encourage the empowerment of the consumer, though much depends on whether filtering rather than blocking is available and whether the filtering system is sensitive to the precise needs of the user.[97] At its best, governance does seek to address issues of public concern in a way which is transparent and ordered, rather than allowing *de facto* control to be placed in the hands of either technocratic or commercial élites who would otherwise dominate Internet decision-making.[98] But governance has

---

[91] Froomkin, A.M., 'The Internet as a source of regulatory arbitrage' in Kahin, B. and Neeson, C., *Borders in Cyberspace* (MIT Press, Cambridge, MA, 1997) at p.142.

[92] See Reidenberg, J.R., 'Governing networks and rule-making in cyberspace' in Kahin, B. and Neeson, C., *Borders in Cyberspace* (MIT Press, Cambridge, Mass., 1997) at p.96.

[93] Rose, N. and Miller, P., 'Political power beyond the state' (1992) 43 *British Journal of Sociology* 173; Jones, T. and Newburn, T., *Private Security and Public Policing* (Clarendon Press, Oxford, 1998).

[94] Department of Trade and Industry, *Review of the Internet Watch Foundation* http://www.dti.gov.uk/iwfreview/, 1999.

[95] See Capitanchik, D. and Whine, M., 'The governance of cyberspace: racism on the internet' in Cooper, J. (ed.), *Liberating Cyberspace* (Pluto Press, London, 1998).

[96] Delta, G.B. and Matsuura, J.H., *Law of the Internet* (Aspen Law & Business, New York, 1998) para.1.21.

[97] See Liberty (ed.), *Liberating Cyberspace* (Pluto Press, London, 1998) chap. 1; Hanley, P., *Internet Regulation: The Way Forward?* (ITC, London, 2000).

[98] See Jordan, T., *Cyberpower* (Routledge, London, 1999).

not always been implemented according to these precepts, and the success of such an appeal to the localised governance of crime or anti-social behaviour will itself raise profound questions as to the constitution of 'community', the choice of moral precepts which are to prevail and democratic account-ability.[99] So, such appeals to a communal spirit should not be allowed to mask the fact that repression will continue, whether through traditional policing institutions or through the tyranny of societal standards.

One further role for law, whether mediated through shadowy 'soft' rules or not, is in standard setting. The enactment of the Human Rights Act 1998, which makes the European Convention on Human Rights a legally relevant consideration in a large proportion of legal discourse, will certainly affect how public authorities treat Internet-related controversies within the UK, arguably requiring a more explicit regard for rights to privacy and free expression and perhaps also a higher priority for them. By way of its 'hor-izontal effect', these rights arguably are equally relevant to the contracts between ISPs and customers.[100] Furthermore, all public policy makers and administrators should take into account the Nolan Committee principles on good standards in public life[101] and the Cabinet Office Regulatory Impact Unit's principles of good regulation.[102]

Frequently answered questions

Reflecting the agendas already described, Part II of his book commences with the theme of the 'Governance of the Internet', including chapter 2 on 'The roles of government and the private sector in national/international Internet administration' by Stephen Saxby and then in chapter 3 an exposition of 'The governance of the Internet in Europe' by Andrew Charlesworth. Others have also noted the significant interest of the European Union in the Internet,[103] which is indicative of the delimitation of the traditional regulatory

---

[99] See Crawford, A., *The Local Governance of Crime* (Clarendon Press, Oxford, 1997); Wall, D., 'Policing and the regulation of the Internet' in Walker, C. (ed.), *Crime, Criminal Justice and the Internet* (special edition, *Criminal Law Review*, Sweet & Maxwell, London, 1998). As Cyber-Rights and Cyber-Liberties (UK) say, 'Who Watches the Watchmen' (see http://www.cyber-rights.org/).

[100] See HL Debs. vol. 583 col. 783 24 November 1997, Lord Irvine; Hunt, M., 'The "horizontal effect" of the Human Rights Act' [1998] *Public Law* 423; Wade, W., 'Opinion: human rights and the judiciary' [1998] *European Human Rights Law Review* 520; Coppel, J., *The Human Rights Act 1998* (John Wiley, Chichester, 1999) p.26.

[101] Nolan Committee, *First Report of the Committee on Standards in Public Life* (Cm. 2850, London, HMSO, 1995). See also the Committee on Standards in Public Life website at http://www.open.gov.uk/cspl/csplhome.htm.

[102] See the Cabinet Office Regulatory Impact Unit's (formerly known as the Better Regulation Unit) Better Regulation Guide, and the Principles of Good Regulation at http://www.cabinet-office.gov.uk/bru/1998/task_force/principles.pdf.

[103] See also Walker, C. and Akdeniz, Y., 'The governance of the Internet in Europe with special reference to illegal and harmful content' in Walker, C. (ed.), *Crime, Criminal Justice and the Internet* (special edition, *Criminal Law Review*, Sweet & Maxwell, London, 1998); Kelleher, D. and Murray, K., *IT Law in the European Union* (Sweet & Maxwell, London, 1999).

powers of national government but, given its 'light-handed' approach,[104] still allows for informal, self-referential and localised normative structures. In chapter 4, 'Jurisdiction and choice of law in a borderless electronic environment', Alan Reed goes on to indicate the further implications of transnationality in relation to specific problems such as Internet defamation and trade marks.

Turning away from legal and political boundaries, the impacts of the Internet upon legal institutions and professions are considered in Part III ('Legal institutions and professions and the Internet'). The cultures and working practices of the legal professions are explained in 'The new electric lawyer and legal practice in the information age' in chapter 5 by David Wall. Having spent an estimated £2 billion on computing equipment during the past 25 years, has the result been good or ill, either for the lawyers or their clients?[105] The take-up in relation to UK political and governmental life is the theme of chapter 6, 'Cyber-constitutionalism and digital democracy' by Clive Walker. Next are examined law-related spheres: the experiences, essentials and opportunities of law enforcement on the Internet, in chapter 7, 'Policing the Internet' by David Wall; and chapter 8, 'Criminal justice processes and the Internet' by Clive Walker.

In the final Part IV ('Legal controversies in cyberspace'), the various authors seek to address specific issues in the light of some of the themes and approaches, such as governance, already described.[106] This point is especially true of the headline-grabbing issue of pornography delivered via the Internet – tackled in chapter 9, 'Sexually orientated expression' by Yaman Akdeniz and Nadine Strossen, and also chapter 10, 'Child pornography' by Yaman Akdeniz. Until the 1990s there were no specific restrictions on Internet content and usage. Governments did not concern themselves, because Internet access was confined to a relatively small community of academics at universities, government research institutions and commercial research institutions. However, once the general public gained admittance in the mid-1990s, the earlier debates over Internet content were fuelled by the 'moral panic' over pornography,[107] and so it seems appropriate to start here. The subject of chapter 11, 'Hate speech' by Barry Steinhardt, has been less prominent in UK Internet debates, so it is very pertinent to see what precedents might flow from the USA. The agenda is certainly developing in the UK. In September 1998, the Home Secretary condemned Holocaust denial and racial abuse on the Internet in a speech also dealing

---

[104] Liberty (ed.), *Liberating Cyberspace* (Pluto Press, London, 1999) p.141. See European Commission, *A European Initiative in Electronic Commerce* (COM(97) 157).

[105] See Christian, C., *Legal Practice in the Digital Age* (Bowerdean, London, 1998) p.6.

[106] See further Akdeniz, Y., 'Governance of Pornography and Child Pornography on the Global Internet: A Multi-Layered Approach,' in Edwards, L. and Waelde, C. (eds), *Law and the Internet: Regulating Cyberspace*, Hart Publishing, Oxford, 1997.

[107] See Elmer-Dewitt, P., 'On a screen near you: Cyberporn' *Time*, 3 July 1995; Wallace, J. & Mangan, M., *Sex, Laws and Cyberspace: Freedom and Censorship on the Frontiers of the Online Revolution*, (Henry Holt, New York, 1996).

with terrorism,[108] and a wide array of political violence (including some forms of racism) can now be labelled as 'terrorism' under the Terrorism Act 2000. There have been calls for a policy response in the form of a code of practice,[109] and the Internet Watch Foundation responded in early 2000 to pressures by the DTI and Home Office to extend their remit to racist materials. As indicated in these chapters the Internet involves risk – being an open environment allows for abuse and some would picture the threat of folk-devils, such as hackers and denial of service attackers, as giving rise to a state of siege or even information warfare.[110] The concerns are unbounded and reflexive in a risk society in that the more society comes to rely on information technology as part of the political economy, the more likely it is that forms of abuse will come to be seen as political as well as criminal.[111] The long-established criminal of the computer world is the hacker – around since the advent of personal computers and therefore pre-dating the Internet by some years. An update and application of the legal position is provided in chapter 12, 'Hacking, viruses and fraud' by Martin Wasik. Turning from criminal to civil anti-social behaviour, chapter 13 by Yaman Akdeniz and Horton Rogers covers 'Defamation on the Internet'.

From this point the book moves more positively towards the implications of e-commerce, though it must be realised that the rapid commercial development of the Internet is also acting as a formidable regulator, and therefore overlaps with issues in the previous parts. For example, it is ironic that many of the e-commerce technologies and practices have been developed in connection with gambling and sexually explicit sites. The irony lies in the fact that, while these activities generated regulatory concerns, they nevertheless contributed to the development of Internet technology, particularly e-commerce. The owners of gambling and sexually explicit sites,[112] particularly the latter, in order to protect their markets, have restricted free supply and eliminated competition, thus greatly reducing the amount of 'first click' materials on display and the more extreme forms of pornography. As indicated earlier, moving away from the libertarian and communitarian philosophy which dominated on the Internet for its early life, a second age is now upon us. That age is the age of business, and it may safely be

---

[108] 'We must defeat racism and terrorism says Home Secretary' (356/9, 14 September 1998, http://www.coi.gov.uk/coi/depts/GHO/coi5696e.ok).

[109] Liberty (ed.), *Liberating Cyberspace* (Pluto Press, London, 1999) chap.13. See further, Brophy, P., Craven, J. and Fisher, S., *Extremism and the Internet* (CERLIM, Manchester, 1998).

[110] See Bainbridge, D., *Introduction to Computer Law* (3rd ed., Pitman, London, 1996) Pt. 3; Denning, D.E. and Denning, P.J. (eds), *Internet Besieged* (ACM Press, New York, 1998); Denning, D.E., *Information Warfare and Security* (ACM Press, New York, 1999).

[111] See further Walker, C. (ed.), *Crime, Criminal Justice and the Internet* (Sweet & Maxwell, London, 1998).

[112] See generally Akdeniz, Y., *Sex on the Net? The Dilemma of Policing Cyberspace* (South Street Press, Reading, 1999).

predicted that commercial pressures will continue to drive the Internet into the hands of 'e-commerce':[113]

> Electronic commerce refers generally to all forms of commercial transactions involving both organisations and individuals, that are based upon the electronic processing and transmission of data, including text, sound and visual images. It also refers to the effects that the electronic exchange of commercial information may have on the institutions and processes that support and govern commercial activities.

A bridge is provided by Yaman Akdeniz and Clive Walker in chapter 14, 'Whisper who dares: encryption, privacy rights and the new world disorder', which emphasises the public interest in private communications as well as examines the policing concerns which are engendered by their use. Finally, the remaining wide-ranging issues surrounding e-commerce are covered by chapter 15, 'Electronic commerce' by Paul Eden. The commercial uses of the Internet have several implications for law[114] and society. Among the legal impacts are those relating to the formation and authentication of contracts,[115] copyright protection, consumer and data protection, and tax implications. The issues have been recognised both at national UK level and also by the European Union.[116]

Altogether, this book reflects the strong academic and professional networks which have been organised in the Department of Law at the University of Leeds around the Centre for Criminal Justice Studies and the CyberLaw Research Unit, together with Cyber-Rights and Cyber-Liberties (UK). Through these sites, we have actioned and discussed Internet-related agendas for nearly ten years, and we have met other academics and professionals involved in Internet governance throughout the world. Our research and that of the authors of this book is ongoing and thus represents a snapshot of work on the subject. One can be sure only that Internet development will be rapid and innovative and that new socio-legal issues will emerge in the wake of that development. Despite the changing environment, we have

---

[113] OECD, *Opportunities and Challenges for Government* (the 'Sacher Report') http://www.oecd.org/dsti/sti/it/ec/prod/sacher_e.pdf, 1997, p.20.

[114] See Bainbridge, D., *Introduction to Computer Law* (3rd ed., Pitman, London, 1996) Pt. 2; Gringras, C. (ed.), *The Laws of the Internet* (Butterworths, London, 1997); Chissick, M. and Kelman, A., *Electronic Commerce* (Sweet & Maxwell, London, 1999); Saxby, S. (ed.), *Encyclopaedia of Information Technology Law* (Sweet & Maxwell, London, 1990–9) chap. 3; Singleton, S., *Business, the Internet and the Law* (Tolley's, Croydon, 1999); Rowe, H. (ed.), *A Practitioner's Guide to the Regulation of the Internet* (City & Financial Publishing, Old Woking, 1999); *New Zealand Law Commission, Report 50: Electronic Commerce Part One: guide for the legal and business community* (NZLC R50, Wellington, 1998).

[115] As to what counted as 'documents', 'signatures' and 'writing' before the Electronic Communications Act 2000, see Reed, C., *Digital Information Law* (Centre for Commercial Law Studies, London, 1996).

[116] See Kelleher, D. and Murray, K., *IT Law in the European Union* (Sweet & Maxwell, London, 1999); Dickie, J., *Internet and Electronic Commerce in the European Union* (Hart Publishing, Oxford, 1999).

attempted to incorporate commentary on events up to 1 January 2000 and in some cases (mindful especially of current legislation) we felt it necessary to go beyond even this deadline and have assumed that pending bills will be passed into law in the near future. We hope that later developments can be highlighted for the benefit of readers through materials and links at the following website:

http://www.booksites.net

At the same time, we acknowledge that web links cited within the book will quickly become dated, though readers are advised that the root address may still contain useful sources.

It remains for us to thank the authors of the chapters for persevering with their subjects as the book took shape and also to thank the publishers (especially Pat Bond) for having faith that a manuscript would indeed materialise one day from Cyberspace.

Clive Walker
David Wall
Yaman Akdeniz

May 2000

PART II

GOVERNANCE OF
THE INTERNET

CHAPTER 2

The roles of government in national/ international Internet administration

Stephen Saxby

Introduction

The title of this chapter invites consideration of the roles of government in national and international Internet administration. Discussion is necessarily confined to the role of the British government both as Internet user and policymaker. The reference in the chapter heading to *Internet administration* will be interpreted so as to permit analysis of three key policy issues that currently dominate the British government's response to the rapid advancement of the Internet. These are the development of policies for Internet usage by government,[1] the modernisation of intellectual property law in the wake of digital technology and the expansion of electronic commerce (e-commerce).[2]

The Internet is a new medium and a resource to be tapped. Its potential is only just being understood. When electricity was first controlled as a means of supply in the nineteenth century, it was initially hailed as a new source of light. Its versatility was only later recognised when it was used as a source of energy for heating and to power the electric motor. Subsequent innovation involved its exploitation as a means of transport and communication, and later in a wide range of services and consumer appliances, including the computer. Relying on this energy source, these later innovations could never have been contemplated when electricity was first brought into supply.

The same is likely to apply to the Internet. What began as a means of data transfer and communication within the US military has extended within thirty years to the coming medium for business and consumer transactions and an interactive channel for information flows and social communication of all kinds. This occurred not by design or deliberate planning, but through evolution within the range of technologies that, combined together, have made it possible. The speed with which the Internet has developed and grown, and the stock market reaction to it, has outpaced the ability of most policy makers to come to terms with it. This has meant that the British

---

[1] See chap. 6 for additional consideration in the context of democracy.
[2] See, further, chap. 15.

government, like others, has first had to come to terms with the implications of what the Internet represents in terms of change. It first had to consider how to prioritise public sector exploitation of the Internet and how it should be promoted both commercially and in education. It has also had to decide upon its initial policy stance towards the Internet in international debate where discussion about commercial regulation, harmful and illegal content and jurisdictional questions is already well underway. The emphasis has been about what needs to be done to take matters forward.

In pursuing this agenda, it is likely that the government will conclude that it needs to respond at several different levels. No single government can or should seek to exercise any direct or systematic control over the Internet because its very existence is multi-national, its infrastructure widely dispersed and its content contributed to, and to some extent determined by, the masses. Indeed, the issue today is not primarily about regulation of the Internet (although this remains important) but how to ensure that 'UK plc' responds fast enough and in the right manner to the opportunities created for it by the global network. While the UK can activate domestic policies to encourage take-up of the commercial opportunities presented, any strategic proposals intended for the Internet as a whole will have to be negotiated and adopted collectively by national administrations. In responding to this challenge, one further consideration will be what sort of public/private sector partnership, if any, might best fulfil these policy goals. To promote the acquisition of IT skills for example, the government has been keen to set out what it thinks should be done while inviting private-sector participation in the supply of the technology.

Until recently the UK had not produced a company of the size and strength of an IBM, Intel, Microsoft or Netscape. It has now generated the world's fourth largest company following the take-over by Vodaphone-Airtouch of the German telecoms giant, Mannesmann.[3] This will give the company global strength to compete in the forthcoming mobile-commerce (m-commerce) market. These exceptions apart, the UK's capacity to draw financial reward from the information economy or to shape the direction of the technology or the market, cannot rely exclusively on the strength of its home-grown businesses which cannot alone compete with the US IT industry giants. However, merger opportunities and strategic sector partnerships give British companies major opportunities to participate in the global Internet economy. Successive UK administrations have also recognised the potential value of inward investment in many industries including high-tech services and manufactures. This is important not only to develop and retain an appropriate skills base in the UK, but also to ensure that the nation has available to it the appropriate technological infrastructure for the modern information economy. Government policy must therefore continue in this direction so as to promote jobs, know-how, innovation and R & D at the required levels.

---

[3] Behind Microsoft, General Motors and Cisco Systems.

This includes an appreciation of the needs of the wider EU economy and the role that the EU can and should play in these matters.[4] Above all else of course it must seek to understand the dynamics of the digital revolution and reassess how, as a government of a nation state, it needs to reposition its policies, alliances and efforts to support the positive changes that are taking place as a consequence of technological change.

Having articulated these basic parameters, it is now possible to focus upon specific policy issues of most immediate concern to the government as it develops its agenda for Internet administration. Some of the issues are apparent now, but others remain on the horizon, not a problem today but a potential one in the future. A government that is prepared to take time to investigate and understand these trends will be better placed to act and to participate in the many fora around the world where these issues are being discussed. In this context the following three topics will be explored, representing the key issues engaging the British government's attention as it formulates its present policy for Internet administration:

- Modernisation of the machinery and process of government; this to include the electronic delivery of services and information.
- Reform of intellectual property law to accommodate access to and exploitation of works via the Internet; this to include administration of Internet domain names on an international basis.
- Facilitation of the development of e-commerce including national and international initiatives and measures to protect both suppliers and consumers operating within this electronic marketplace.

What now follows is an analysis of each of these three topics.

Electronic government

The central issue here is to what extent the government considers that digital technology can improve the quality and efficiency of government and government services. Two particular policy investigations have been initiated that feed this debate. The first is analysis of the scope and prospects for the electronic delivery of government services; the second is a review of Crown copyright regulation of official information in digital form.

Government direct

In November 1996 the then Conservative Administration under John Major published, as part of its Information Society Initiative (ISI), a Green Paper entitled *government.direct*.[5] This came after some internal restructuring and

---

[4] See, further, chap. 3.
[5] Cm. 3438, Stationery Office, London. It was also published on the Internet: http://www.citu.gov.uk/greenpaper/index.htm. It was also the first Green Paper to be published on CD-Rom.

the establishment within government of several new entities with responsibilities for promoting different aspects of the Information Society. In November 1995 for example the Central Information Technology Unit (CITU) was set up within the Office of Public Service (OPS) of the Cabinet Office to devise strategies and policies to help the government exploit what it called the 'Information and Communication Technologies' (ICT), tailored to the efficient delivery of government services to business and the citizen. A Ministerial Group on IT was also created to co-ordinate cross-departmental initiatives designed to exploit IT developments in the national interest.[6] The Green Paper described the government's 'excitement at the prospect of delivering government services electronically to the public', bringing government 'closer to the individual' and giving citizens and businesses 'more control over their dealings with government'.[7] It described how IT advances would enable government to provide better services to individuals and businesses. For business this could be direct to the desktop terminal in the office. For the individual this could be via 'user-friendly' public access terminals with touch-sensitive screens in places such as post offices, libraries and shopping malls. Other services could be available into the home by a network connection via the telephone or via media such as cable or digital television. Among the suggested services that might be delivered in this way would be the provision of access to official information, the collection of taxes and the grant of licences, administration of regulations, the payment of grants and benefits, the collection and analysis of statistics and the procurement of goods and services.[8] Many such services would be available 24 hours per day and seven days per week with immediate or near immediate response times. The former Administration recognised that its proposals would involve fundamental change and a reshaping of service delivery. This in turn would raise individual and business concerns, and a full debate was therefore merited with the Green Paper as the starting point.

The Green Paper proposed seven principles to which a strategy for the electronic delivery of government services might conform. These were *choice* – in the methods of electronic direct delivery of services to maximise access; *confidence* – in the security of information collected from citizens and businesses; *accessibility* – to potential information have-nots; *efficiency* – in streamlining administrative processes; *rationalisation* – sharing resources, reducing costs, simplifying systems; *open information* – to open up electronic access to official information; and *fraud prevention* – protect public funds, protect information and authenticate transactions. The intention

---

[6] Other groups and programmes set up included the Multi Media Industry Advisory Group (MMIAG); the National Information Infrastructure Task Force (NIITF); the IT, Electronics and Communications Technology Foresight (ITEC) Panel, and the DTI's Information Society Initiative.

[7] Foreword by Rt Hon Roger Freeman MP, former Chancellor of the Duchy of Lancaster and Cabinet Minister for Public Service in: *Comments on the Green Paper government.direct* March 1997: http://www.citu.gov.uk/greenpaper/commentresponse.htm.

[8] Ibid., p.2.

was that these guidelines would define a framework for future progress. In addition a series of pilot schemes was initiated involving public access terminals in several locations providing sample information as well as Internet access to government forms and leaflets relevant to business. Comments on the Green Paper were received from nearly 300 individuals and organisations in the public, private and voluntary sectors representing almost all the bodies which might have been expected to take an interest in the proposals. The *Response* document suggested that there was broad general support for the Green Paper's vision and agreement that the correct parameters for the debate had been identified. Nevertheless there was concern for rights of privacy and data protection in that interconnection of government IT systems might 'allow civil servants to browse at random through the private affairs of any citizen' and that the possible use of electronic signature cards, designed to facilitate access to government services, might in fact become an identity card in all but name.[9] There was also concern that the proposals did not 'fully seize the opportunity for a more radical reform or "re-engineering" of government and that being technology-led it might not fully reflect societal needs'.[10] And, further, another view suggested that 'the goal of providing more "open government" did not go far enough'.[11]

Following the change of government in May 1997, policy towards the Internet and the broader exploitation of ICT within the public sector was given further impetus. The Parliamentary Office for Science and Technology (POST) was invited to report on the potential impact of the use of ICT in government as a follow-up to *government.direct*. Its findings confirmed that the new government's agenda for electronic government extended beyond service delivery into a full-scale analysis of how to modernise government and its information flows. This agenda included the introduction of the *Government Secure Intranet* designed to link Departments via the Internet, reform of the procedures of the House of Commons, full-scale reviews of the benefit system, defence and revenue collection, constitutional measures in devolution and a Freedom of Information Act and legislative reform of data protection. The POST Report concluded that 'while countries like the USA, Canada and Australia lead in many areas, the UK Government is certainly among the chasing "pack" and some way ahead of most in the EU and globally'.[12]

A full discussion of this in the context of all that the government is doing in the area of electronic government is beyond the scope of this chapter (but is taken up in chapters 3 and 6). For those keen to see the broader agenda emerge there is, however, no more than cautious optimism to offer. On the one hand, important as they are, the present government seems keen not to

---

[9] *Comments on the Green Paper government.direct*, op. cit., pp.7–8.
[10] Parliamentary Office of Science and Technology, *Electronic Government – Information Technologies and the Citizen*, 1998: http://www.parliament.uk/post/report.htm p.14.
[11] Ibid., p.14.
[12] Ibid., p.17.

limit the *electronic government* initiative to the introduction of improved methods of providing information and transacting services with the public. Its broader interest lies in reducing bureaucracy by developing information systems within government, in using performance measures to check efficiency levels and in providing affordable public access to the technology and the skills to use it widely. The downside of the first 1000 days of the Labour administration is that evidence of policy success in this area is not yet consistently to be found. The *Modernising Government* White Paper[13] of March 1999 was more of an agenda for action than a report on progress. Since then, some nine months on, the National Audit Office has discovered scope for 'enormous' cost savings if government can become more efficient in its exploitation of the Internet.[14] The report criticised the government for its 'patchy and . . . slow' response to the Internet and indicated, in sum, that a new strategy was needed. In addition, the Public Accounts Committee found more than 25 cases in the 1990s 'where the implementation of IT systems [within government] resulted in delay, confusion and inconvenience to the citizen and, in many cases, poor value for money to the taxpayer'.[15]

The review of Crown copyright

Government policy towards the distribution of official information electronically has been subject to considerable scrutiny and debate for some years now. It brings into the open a number of tensions between policies for the efficient operation and funding of public administration, the provision of access to official data and its exploitation by private sector information providers. The substance of this debate has been fully documented elsewhere[16] but, at its heart, is an economic discussion about the best way to manage official information and a constitutional debate about access. The information industry argues that the present policy is inefficient and that a more relaxed Crown copyright regime would open the way for growth in value-added products and services drawn from the wealth of published and unpublished information that the government holds. The government remains cautious, pointing to the £200 million it gains from royalty, licensing and sales income derived from Crown copyright material and the potential loss to the taxpayer if such charges were no longer levied.

Public consultation on these issues took place following publication in January 1998 of a consultation document *Crown Copyright in the Information Age*.[17] This set out the range of options for the future administration of

---

[13] *Modernising Government* (Cm. 4310, Stationery Office, London, 1999).

[14] *Government on the web* (1999–2000 HC 87).

[15] House of Commons Public Accounts Committee, *Improving the delivery of government IT projects* (1999–2000 HC 65, Stationery Office, London) at p.1.

[16] Saxby, S., *Public Policy and Legal Regulation of the Information Market in the Digital Network Environment* (Tano Press, Oslo, 1996).

[17] *Crown Copyright in the Information Age – A Consultation Document on Access to Public Sector Information* (Cm. 3819, Stationery Office, London, 1998).

Crown copyright in respect of official information, in both printed and electronic formats. It is unlikely, however, that the private sector will be fully satisfied with the outcome. For example, unless convinced of the overwhelming strength of the economic arguments, HM Treasury is unlikely to support the abolition of Crown copyright and the revenues that would go with it. As the POST Report has made clear, the access issue brings two policies into conflict: 'open government encourages making access easier and cheaper, while financial pressures on Departments and Agencies to recover costs and maximise returns on their information "assets" lead to controls and charging'.[18] It seems that the British government is not about to follow the United States model whereby public information is available virtually free of charge subject to the marginal cost of distribution.

It is to be hoped, however, that the government will eventually listen to the earlier House of Lords Select Committee on Science and Technology which has said that pricing policies may conflict with the widespread distribution of official information.[19] It would be clearly wrong for potential users of such data to be priced out by access costs, or lost to it because of inconsistencies within departments and agencies about policies and technical standards for making public sector data available.

In the meantime the government is slowly proceeding towards a Freedom of Information Act designed to bring more open government to the UK. As a precursor to the many changes this will bring about, the present and previous administrations have, since November 1994, begun to disseminate official information electronically. It was at that time that the Government Information Service (GIS) was launched providing a single index of all government information on the Internet. The POST Report indicates that, by 1998, more than 400 public sector organisations retained a presence on the GIS with approximately 200,000 'hits' per day on the site – 40 per cent of which emanated from the UK.[20]

In terms of what is available on the site, the government continues to navigate a careful path between what it chooses to provide free of charge and what it thinks should be paid for. This is translated into the type of information available online and the terms of its subsequent use. The latter is defined by Her Majesty's Stationery Office (HMSO) in a statement available from its homepage. The proceedings of Parliament, some case law and all statutes and statutory instruments that subsequently come into force are to be provided free, but other materials must be purchased. The paper and print culture still dominates many of the operations of government. Nevertheless this is a far cry from 1994 when at a symposium on the digital

---

[18] Parliamentary Office of Science and Technology, *Electronic Government – Information Technologies and the Citizen*, op. cit., p.31.

[19] House of Lords, Select Committee on Science and Technology, *Information Society: Agenda for Action in the UK* (1995–6 HL 77, London) para.5.59.

[20] Parliamentary Office of Science and Technology, *Electronic Government – Information Technologies and the Citizen*, op. cit., p.5.

information revolution, in reply to a comment that the UK statute book should be available online, a senior civil servant from the Department of Trade and Industry commented: 'HMSO does tend to charge for its documentation and I was not quite sure when you said could it be made available electronically, *whether you actually really meant could it be made available free?*'[21]

Intellectual property

Reform of IP rights generally

The development of international rules for the protection of intellectual property has been regarded for more than a century now as a necessary safeguard for the protection of authors and as a vital means of stimulating innovation and the application of technology. Today the promotion of adequate and effective intellectual property rights (IPRs) is a *sine qua non* for the Information Society and the convergence of the information and communication technologies. The anticipated expansion of electronic commerce and the broader development of the information market would be undermined unless a regime of IPRs existed that both rewarded creativity while encouraging exploitation and use of the products and services that come about. Striking the balance between the rights of authors, the desire for user access and the interests of educators and researchers to explore the stock of knowledge has long been the objective first articulated in the Berne Convention for the Protection of Literary and Artistic Works of 1886 and in the subsequent treaties across the range of IPRs that have followed since.

Until the passage of the Copyright, Designs and Patents Act 1988 it was fair to say that the development of intellectual property law in the UK was substantially a domestic issue, albeit within the framework of international conventions. Since that time the growth of the single market within the EU, the convergence of the information technologies and the pressure on the industry to compete at a global level has shifted control over IPRs' development to the international arena. Today the European Union, the United States, the World Intellectual Property Organisation (WIPO), the World Trade Organisation (WTO), the International Telecommunication Union (ITU), the Organisation for Economic Co-operation and Development (OECD) and to a lesser extent the countries of the Pacific Rim, are the main locations where the ongoing debate about the intellectual property system and its future is taking place.

---

[21] Exchange reported in: *SuperHighway Symposium*, FEI/EURIM Conference 16/17 November 1994 (Corporate Publishing Services and McCreadie Publishing, London, 1994) p.83. The Statutory Publication Office, an office within the Lord Chancellor's Department, is producing a database of United Kingdom legislation which is due to be completed in 2000. However, the marketing and pricing strategy has not yet been agreed (see http://www.open.gov.uk/lcd/lawdatfr.htm, 2000).

The issue for this discussion is what role the British government should play in relation to IPRs and the Internet. Its most immediate priority in this regard has been to participate in the international debate. Britain was, for example, a participant in the General Agreement on Tariffs and Trade (Uruguay Round) of World Trade talks that led to the formation of the World Trade Organisation and the Agreement on Trade Related Aspects of Intellectual Property Rights (TRIPS). The TRIPS accord has been described as the most comprehensive multilateral agreement ever on intellectual property covering 'copyright and related rights (i.e. the rights of performers, producers of sound recordings and broadcasters); trademarks including service marks; geographical indicators including appellations of origin; industrial designs; patents . . . the layout-designs of integrated circuits; and undisclosed information including trade secrets and test data'.[22]

TRIPS establishes minimum standards of protection requiring first that the rights and obligations laid down by the Berne Convention be respected. It also introduces enforcement and dispute resolution procedures. While it is important for the British government to police the agreement in respect of UK interests, it must also fulfil an educative and informing function to explain the value of the agreement to the business community including those engaged in e-commerce activities.

In December 1996 the British government also took part in the WIPO Diplomatic Conference in Geneva that approved new treaties on intellectual property designed to update the Berne Convention to meet the challenges of the 'digital age' and improve the means to fight piracy worldwide. Berne was last revised in 1971, so the new Copyright Treaty sets out to adapt it for the Internet environment. Accordingly, authors are protected for the distribution, commercial rental, communication and publication of their works online; specific protection is accorded for computer programs and databases, and obligations are established in respect of technological measures (such as fraudulent circumvention of anti-copying devices) and rights management information (the unauthorised deletion or interference with electronic information about a work made available on the digital network). A second Treaty provides related protections for performing artists and phonogram producers.

Work continues, however, since no agreement could be reached on the scope of the right of reproduction of works in a digital environment. This issue has now been taken up within the EU in Commission proposals for an EC Directive 'to harmonise certain aspects of copyright and related rights in the Information Society'.[23] The objective is to achieve further harmonisation

---

[22] An Overview of the Agreement on Trade-Related Aspects of Intellectual Property Rights (TRIPS Agreement): http://www.wto.org/wto/intellec/intell2.htm.

[23] *Proposal for a European Parliament and Council Directive on the harmonization of certain aspects of copyright and related rights in the Information Society* (COM(97) 628 final 10 December 1997) as amended 28 June 1999 [599PC0250] at: http://europa.eu.int/eur-lex/en/com/reg/en_register_1720.html.

of these rights as part of the long-term policy of the EU to eradicate legal impediments to the smooth running of the Internal Market.[24] This is in response to feedback from right-holders and intermediaries who expressed anxieties to the Commission about new potential uses of protected material 'in ways that are not authorised or not foreseen under existing laws in this area'.[25] The whole exercise is 'closely linked to, if not based upon', international developments such as the WIPO Treaties and will implement 'a significant number of these new international obligations'.[26]

The government's role will be to represent Britain's interest in these and other related discussions about the development of the Information Market. Within the EU this will involve a continuing process of harmonisation as the Common and Roman law traditions within the Member States are brought together in the specific areas subject to proposed reforms. This process has been observed in the recent implementation of Directive 96/9 on *Legal Protection of Databases*, where differences in the copyright treatment of databases within the two regimes were harmonised by the new measure.[27]

Much of the work in respect of these initiatives is handled by the Intellectual Property Policy Directorate (IPPD) of the Patent Office. This includes the preparation of responses to international proposals and the handling of consultation among interested parties and groups within the UK. Where amendment to existing domestic law is required to fulfil international and EU obligations, this is also usually led by this unit which is an Executive Agency of the Department of Trade and Industry. One area that could be looked at might be ways of improving the consultation process. This is usually a very important stage designed to help government reach and confirm a view on its response to reform proposals. It is not always clear that all relevant parties have been brought into the review process. One way of improving performance might be through the Internet where documents could be placed alongside guidance notes as to the issues for which public comment is sought. This can then be followed up by meetings of interested parties with the IPPD or the European Commission. This strategy is taking place to a small degree at present both in the UK and at the European Commission where some Green Papers or Consultation Documents are specifically made available online for this purpose. However, the process could be made more systematic to ensure that as many viewpoints as possible are brought into the discussion.

Domain name regulation

Domain names have developed very rapidly into an important form of intellectual property, the subject of some vigorous litigation around the

---

[24] Ibid., p.2.
[25] Ibid., p.2.
[26] Ibid., p.3.
[27] OJ 1996 L77/20.

world. Most actions have involved well-known companies alleging that the use of a particular domain name by an unrelated party has in some way infringed their corporate identity or brand name. Most actions have resulted in the brand-name corporation succeeding on its claims. Litigation of this kind confirms the fact that domain names are now extremely important to those commercial interests that seek to reach their market via the Internet. With the dramatic onset of e-commerce, the domain name is the means by which the company and its products can be located.

Its roots date back to the early days of the Internet when a graduate student of the University of California began to maintain a list of host names and addresses and available research documents for access by other members of the research network.[28] The latter was extended to include technical parameters for use by protocol developers and, after several assignments of the administration of the lists, the responsibility passed, in December 1992, to Network Solutions Inc (NSI). NSI worked in cooperation with the US National Science Foundation (NSF) which has statutory authority for the oversight of scientific research, engineering and educational activities in the US: 'including the maintenance of computer networks to connect research and educational institutions'.[29] In 1992 Congress granted the NSF statutory powers to authorise commercial activity on the largest of the governmental networks – NSFNET – 'a national high speed network based on Internet protocols', and the Internet was launched into the wider world.[30]

Until now the Domain Name System (DNS) has been managed, in the main, by agreement with US government agencies. This has involved the control and distribution arrangements for the assignment of Internet addresses to service providers and end users world-wide, as well as the assignment of Internet protocols necessary to the technical operation of the Internet. These actions have been performed by the Internet Assigned Numbers Authority (IANA) whose head, the late Dr Jon Postel, was the graduate student who first maintained the list when the Internet was still encapsulated within the US Defense Department.[31] The allocation of domain name space must also be distributed and managed. In its policy statement the National Telecommunications and Information Administration (NTIA) described this allocation as a hierarchy of top-level, second-level and further sub-divided domains. It showed how more than 200 top-level domains (TLDs) are 'administered by their corresponding governments or by private entities with the appropriate national government's acquiescence'.[32] Other domain space is not limited by jurisdiction but rather by intended function.

---

[28] A brief summary of the background to DNS development can be found in the NTIA White Paper *Management of Internet Names and Addresses* (1998) p.1:
http://www.ntia.doc.gov/ntiahome/domainname/domainhome.htm.

[29] Ibid., p.3.

[30] Ibid.

[31] This was as part of the ARPANET network established by the Department of Defense's Advanced Research Projects Agency (DARPA). See, further, chap. 1.

[32] NTIA White Paper *Management of Internet Names and Addresses*, op. cit., p.4.

This includes *.com* for commercial users, *.org* for not-for-profit organisations, and *.net* for network service providers. Further proposals have been made for other possible generic categories of domain name. This expansion is inevitable as the commercial and educative role of the Internet expands.[33] In the UK the national registry for domain names ending in *.uk* is Nominet UK. This has been recognised by IANA as the appropriate registration authority for the UK ever since Nominet took over the registration process in Britain in August 1996. Its register exceeded 100,000 domain names for the first time in 1998.

At the end of January 1998 the NTIA published a draft discussion document raising a variety of issues concerning the DNS and its future operation.[34] The main conclusion was that, as the Internet expands from a US-based research vehicle into 'an international medium for commerce, education and communications',[35] a more enduring global system of Internet management would be required. One of the main recommendations was a proposal for the creation of a not-for-profit corporation to take over control of DNS management from IANA. A consultation period followed during which the European Commission expressed concern that, despite words to this effect, the proposals were not paying sufficient attention to the need for an international approach to these management issues. There was a danger that the end product would result in the US consolidating its jurisdiction over the Internet including control over dispute resolution and trademarks used on the Internet. It also called for closer cooperation with WIPO which was itself working to develop a dispute resolution procedure for domain name trademark disputes.

In June 1998 the NTIA published its response to the consultation period in a White Paper. It re-affirmed its commitment to the Internet as a global medium whose management should reflect 'the global diversity of Internet users'.[36] It also indicated its continued desire to consult with the international community as the proposed changes begin to be implemented. The outcome has been the formation of a new administrative framework led by the Internet Corporation for Assigned Names and Numbers (ICANN) set up in October 1998. This non-profit corporation represents a coalition of business, academic and technical groups with responsibilities for domain name system management; the allocation of IP address space; the assignment of protocol parameters; and the management of the root server system.[37] An

---

[33] The White Paper at p.12 discussed proposals for the creation of up to five new registries each of which would be permitted initially to operate one new generic top-level domain (gTLD). In February 1997 an International Ad Hoc Committee (supported by a number of international bodies) produced recommendations for the administration and management of gTLDs which included seven new ones – *.firm, .store, .web, .arts, .rec, .nom* and *.info*.

[34] A *Proposal to Improve the Technical Management of Internet Names and Addresses*: http://www.ntia.doc.gov/ntiahome/domainname/dnsdraft.htm.

[35] Ibid. p.2.

[36] Ibid. p.14.

[37] See, further, the ICANN web page at: www.icann.org.

agreement with the US Department of Commerce and existing operator, Network Solutions Inc., combined with a revised set of bylaws and other actions arising from these, has now successfully established a broader based framework of international regulation of the Internet domain environment. ICANN is now working to establish the new framework.

While the British government and the EU are likely to be reasonably satisfied with the new arrangements, they know that the US has gained a vital head start in the Internet economy with the success of the '.com' domain name. Even now, despite the more democratic environment of domain name regulation, international concerns will remain about the level of US domination. For the British government the task now must be to encourage participation in the new administration and to monitor domestic arrangements for implementation of what has been agreed. This will also involve continued assessment of the effect of existing Intellectual Property rules to ensure that they are up to date and providing regulation consistent with these developments.

One belated proposal designed to wrest back some of the initiative generated by the success of the '.com' US dominated Internet address, is the creation of an 'eu' top-level domain. This would offer an alternative to companies and institutions operating in Europe whose domain names, if not registered as '.com', will vary according to the countries in which their operations are located. The belief is that a European identity will 'strengthen the image and infrastructure of the Internet in Europe, for the European institutions, private users and for commercial purposes including e-commerce'.[38] The plan has some way to go, however, as it will need the support of ICANN as well as the International Standards Organisation in Geneva.

Facilitating the development of e-commerce

International policy development

Whatever views individuals may hold about how the resources of the Internet should be applied, it is becoming clearer by the day that the processing and transmission of digitised data for commercial purposes via the Internet is going to rank very highly indeed on the list of potential uses. One recent study described the Internet as a 'major catalyst in the diffusion of e-commerce into an increasing number of economic spheres' and as 'rapidly harmonising the general environment in which electronic transactions of all kinds take place'.[39] It was inevitable that business would rapidly move in to exploit the Internet as soon as it became clear that there were gains to be made from this new medium, not only in the advertising, sale and distribution of goods

---

[38] *The creation of the .EU Internet Top Level Domain*, 2 February 2000: europa.eu.int/comm/dg13/index.htm.
[39] *Electronic Commerce – Opportunities and Challenges for Government* (the 'Sacher Report', OECD, 1997: http://www.oecd.org/dsti/sti/it/ec /act/sacher.htm p.3.

and services, but in the very methods by which businesses produced their products, conducted their research and development or gathered payment from their customers.[40]

Until now the development of e-commerce has been market driven, and it is clear that, while business is supportive of the need for intergovernmental action to create an environment within which e-commerce can develop, it does, nevertheless, want the private sector to lead by collective action rather than by government regulation.[41] This is likely to pose a significant challenge to the regulators, who may well be tempted to take a more intrusive position than the private sector would prefer. The reason is that governments and the international agencies, being concerned with the world economy, are likely to perceive the development of optimal conditions for the growth of e-commerce as vital to their aims. Governments in particular will be keen to ensure that the conditions which determine how e-commerce is to develop are consistent with domestic needs in terms of job creation, taxation, capital investment and ultimately a stake in, and access to, a share of the information economy. Meanwhile business simply carries on with its e-commerce expansion to the point where established businesses face eclipse by '.com' newcomers unless they adapt to the new environment.

If the Internet is to function as 'a seamless global marketplace with no artificial barriers erected by government',[42] then much work has to be done at international level to agree on the way forward. While many governments have produced their own domestic statements on the issues, with particularly influential contributions from the US and the EU, important work is also underway within the WTO, the OECD and the United Nations (UN). Since international consensus must be achieved before a workable e-commerce regime can be put in place, these fora, among others, including the G8, will provide vital opportunities for governments and market representatives to hammer out agreement on the way forward.

The WTO, for example, has identified a number of policy challenges in e-commerce. It supports a liberal regime within which technical progress and efficient practices can develop but sees market forces as requiring industry self-regulation and/or government intervention in a number of key areas: to secure investment in, and standards for, global telecom infrastructure; the delivery of user-friendly and broad-based access; the creation of a 'predictable legal and regulatory environment which enforces contracts and property rights'; action to ensure the security and privacy of data; the control of illegal and harmful content on the Internet; the development of a suitable tax framework; and education for access by users from all nations.[43] The OECD has been supportive of much of this agenda, undertaking studies into a

---

[40] For a discussion, see US Department of Commerce, *The Emerging Digital Economy* (Washington DC, 1998) chap. 3: http://www.ecommerce.gov/emerging.htm.
[41] Ibid. p.50.
[42] Ibid. p.51.
[43] Ibid. p.35.

number of the policy issues and adopting guidelines to promote technologies for security and privacy and consumer protection in e-commerce transactions.[44] In the UN the United Nations Commission on International Trade Law (UNCITRAL), supported by the US, has completed work on a model law for the commercial use of international contracts in e-commerce.[45]

For the US and the EU the aim is to develop an e-commerce strategy that can bring the greatest benefit to their region. The desire of the US to take a leading role in e-commerce policy development is not surprising for it has been described as 'the country with the highest volumes of data communication, the most network access and service providers, the most Internet hosts, and the highest total number of Internet connections'.[46] Much of its e-commerce policy development has taken place through its National Information Infrastructure (NII) programme which has, throughout the Clinton administration, been the policy incubator for governmental action on the information society. It sees the development of e-commerce as a key element of a Global Information Infrastructure (GII) which is set to transform 'almost every aspect of daily life – education, health care, work and leisure activities'.[47]

The response of the EU has been to build upon policies commenced in the 1980s designed to develop trans-European networking capabilities. Since 1994 the European Commission has supported an 'Electronic Commerce Initiative' to encourage e-commerce development in Europe, provide a coherent policy framework for future action by the EU and a common European position that can feed into the search for global consensus in international negotiations.[48] In December 1997 it published a 'Joint EU–US Statement on Electronic Commerce' which encouraged an open dialogue between governments and the private sector world-wide. The aim was to secure 'a predictable legal and commercial environment for the conduct of business on the Internet'.[49] The statement identified with many of the principles already articulated by the WTO of a market-led expansion of e-commerce supported by 'a clear, consistent and predictable legal framework' in a pro-competitive environment with 'adequate protection of public interest objectives such as privacy, IPRs, prevention of fraud, consumer protection and public safety'.[50] Work therefore continues within the EU on policies to develop the infrastructure, technology and services for accessing the global marketplace, and creating a favourable regulatory framework and business environment. Research and development by European firms in support of e-commerce is being funded within a succession of programmes. These

---

[44] OECD, *Policy Brief No. 1-1997*: www.oecd.org.
[45] See: http://www.transdata.ro/drept/uncitral/index-39.htm.
[46] Sacher Report, op. cit., p.71.
[47] US Dept. of Commerce, *US Framework for Electronic Commerce* (Washington, 1997) p.1.
[48] Sacher Report, op. cit., p.73. See also: *A European Initiative in Electronic Commerce* (COM(97)157): http://www.cordis.lu/esprit/src/ecomcom1.htm.
[49] *Joint EU–US Statement on electronic commerce*, 5 December 1997 p.1: http://www.qlinks.net/comdocs/eu-us.htm.
[50] Ibid. p.1.

involve work on software, multimedia systems, high-performance networking, integrated manufacturing and business process technologies.[51]

Of course at this stage the national policy makers face the dilemma of determining where the priorities lie for regulatory action. Such is the pace of change, accelerating daily, that regulatory proposals face being overtaken by events unless they have strategic significance. In addition, such regulatory steps that are taken must carry support internationally. Otherwise such measures will simply be bypassed by those commercial interests affected exercising the choice to move to other more 'regulatory friendly' territory to pursue their Internet operations. Potential regulators must also take time to assess how e-commerce will develop. E-commerce remains just a generic term to describe business-to-business and business-to-consumer commercial activity on the Internet. The delivery systems of that activity are already spawning fragmentation of the concept with m-commerce beginning to be used to describe interaction with Internet data from the mobile phone. Each development will engender a new set of potential regulatory issues. In the first instance the response will inevitably be market driven in the sense that the UK government will want to act with measures designed to encourage business and consumer participation. In the medium to longer term, however, getting the relationship right between the regulatory push and market pull of e-commerce, in terms of the regulatory response, will be crucial to gaining access to the benefits of this new trading medium.

British government action

Having set out the framework of e-commerce policy development internationally, it is now possible to define the British government's agenda and the priorities it is setting. It is clear of course that a significant proportion of what it does must be in compliance with its international obligations as a Member State of the EU and in fulfilment of a wide range of international commitments.

In April 1998 the government published an e-commerce policy statement which identified the activities it is pursuing with business to develop the e-commerce environment.[52] In its *Statement* the government declared its support for e-commerce development in the UK as 'crucial to the future growth and prosperity of both the national economy and our businesses'.[53] It reaffirmed its commitment to work with the wide range of business sectors with an interest in e-commerce and to support companies in their efforts to 'exploit fully the new opportunities presented by the information age'.[54]

In pursuit of this policy several actions can be identified. First, the DTI has made rapid progress in using the Internet to advise companies on the

---

[51] Sacher Report, op. cit., p.73.
[52] Department of Trade and Industry, *Secure Electronic Commerce Statement* (DTI, London, 1998), http://www.dti.gov.uk/CII/ana27p.html.
[53] Ibid. p.1.
[54] Ibid. p.2.

wide range of help and advice that is now available. In March 1998, in a statement,[55] the Minister for Science, Energy and Industry indicated that, at the DTI, there were now more than 3,000 pages of information, organised into six themed channels and available via its in-house Internet server.[56] This site was continuing to grow at a fast rate 'and a community of regular users that need up to date information from the Department has been established'. The statement indicated that, in February 1998, more than two million hits were recorded at the site.[57] Work would continue to upgrade the content and organisation of the facility.

The government has also established channels through which business can talk directly to it about any concerns relating to domestic e-commerce development.[58] It has also appointed an e-Envoy and e-Minister to drive forward the government's objectives on e-commerce.[59] This will help the government to gain a clearer picture of the agendas of all sectors currently expanding into e-commerce. Among the matters likely to be put to government is the need for measures that secure equality for UK industry as it competes with the rest of the world. The e-content sector, for example, which represents one of the most developed forms of e-commerce (since the entire transaction can be conducted online) is concerned that high data transport costs put the UK e-content sector at a competitive disadvantage with the rest of the world. One company, in evidence to the government, has suggested that its European data transport costs are sixteen times more expensive than those of the United States.[60] In this instance the problem can only be remedied if the European Commission is persuaded that action is needed under its single market policy.

The e-content industry is also concerned about the present legal framework within which the online industry is operating. This applies particularly to what it sees as the lack of a satisfactory product liability regime for illegal and harmful content. The sector feels vulnerable to the range of possible actions that might arise from its online publication of information and seeks similar protections to those already available to the traditional printed media. Apart from long-awaited reforms to domestic defamation[61] and competition law, the government has limited its effort so far to the general policy issue, publishing a Green Paper and conducting a consultation exercise

---

[55] *Strategy for the Internet*, Memorandum from the Hon. John Battle MP, Minister for Science, Energy and Industry, arising from his speech in the House of Commons Private Member's Adjournment Debate on 18 March 1998: http://www.dti.gov.uk/Minspeech/btlspch3.htm.

[56] There are now 9 themed channels. See: http://www.dti.gov.uk/guide/index.htm.

[57] In the final week of January 2000 the top 10 open.gov.uk sites attracted more than 4 million hits.

[58] For example through the Information Age Partnership Taskforce.

[59] The e-Envoy is former High Commissioner to Australia, Alex Allen. The Minister with the overall co-ordination role in e-commerce is Patricia Hewitt.

[60] Industry submission to the Information Age Partnership Taskforce E-Commerce Sub-Committee, 1998.

[61] See, further, chap. 13.

to 'assess the impact of digital convergence on the legal and regulatory framework'.[62] It would like to ensure that, as far as possible, the law is technology-neutral in its application.

One matter that the government will need to engage in is the location of jurisdiction for the e-content industry. The latter, among others, is concerned that in the digital environment it is impossible for a service provider to assess the legal implications of content provision within the multitude of jurisdictions served by the provider. The industry seeks agreement for content to be governed by the country of origin rather than reception. Currently concern on the whole issue of e-commerce jurisdiction has been expressed in the context of proposals under Article 65 of the Amsterdam Treaty to adopt the revised Brussels Convention as an EC Regulation. This would give to a court of a consumer's habitual residence jurisdiction to consider actions against suppliers of goods and services based elsewhere within the EU. It would also mean that domestic law on the issue would likely be applied, potentially complicating the assessment of liability. If the British government supports the industry view, it will need to take the issue direct to the EC. The content industry believes that the EC has not yet understood the 'impracticalities of country of reception jurisdiction over services supplied globally over the Internet'.[63]

Probably of all the policy issues surrounding UK e-commerce development presently under consideration, the one receiving greatest consideration is how to build security and trust into e-commerce activity. An essential component must be the availability of secure communications. Without it business cannot be confident that its online activities are secure or that its assets are not being pirated or interfered with. For the ordinary consumer the issues are about privacy of communication, data protection for the electronic traces left behind and security for the financial transactions that will accompany the purchase of goods or services. In its April 1998 statement,[64] the government indicated that it was planning legislation designed to make e-commerce safe by promoting the legal recognition of electronic signatures and the introduction of a voluntary licensing regime for providers of cryptographic services. Having dropped the idea for mandatory deposit of electronic encryption keys for use by law enforcement agencies ('key escrow'), the voluntary arrangements for cryptography service provision were intended to set minimum technical and competence standards for certification authorities offering electronic signature and other services. This aspect of the policy has been welcomed by the private sector which has

---

[62] *Regulating Communications – approaching convergence in the Information* Age (Cm. 4022, Stationery Office, London, 1998) and *Consultation on the Convergence Green Paper*: http://www.dti.gov.uk/cii/convdoc.pdf. See also UK response to EC Green Paper on Convergence: http://www.culture.gov.uk/CONREP.HTM.
[63] Industry submission to the Information Age Partnership Taskforce E-Commerce Sub-Committee, 1998, p.4.
[64] http://www.dti.gov.uk/CII/ana27p.html. See, further, chap. 14.

always feared that the government would seek to control the use and distribution of cryptography products by industry and commerce or that access to encrypted commercial data by government or its agencies would undermine business confidence in its security.

In November 1999 the government published its long awaited Electronic Communications Bill establishing the legality of electronic signatures and an approvals scheme for cryptography support services. As promised the decision not to proceed with 'key escrow' was confirmed by the Bill. However the law enforcement issue has not gone away with the removal of that part of the original draft Bill dealing with the investigation of protected electronic data. The government instead proposed that the Home Office deal with enforcement issues in relation to encrypted data in its Regulation of Investigatory Powers Bill (now an Act). The government is committed to such a measure as part of proposed reforms to the law on the interception of communications. This is necessary in part to meet the requirements of the European Convention on Human Rights, following the passage of the Human Rights Act in 1998.[65] The government maintains that no 'assault' on individual rights is planned and that full consultation will take place with all interested parties before any intercept requirement is legislated for. However, concern will remain as to the nature of the proposed rule until the exact nature of the proposed arrangements are put into practice. In the meantime discussion continues on the impact of the Electronic Communications Act 2000, which is now confined to the e-commerce issues.

The successful introduction of an e-commerce system is a challenge for the international community as a whole. It cannot be achieved by the actions of any one government or institution. Negotiation is going to be essential, particularly for the cross-border issues that cannot be settled without agreement. Further discussion will include consideration of what to do about taxation and customs duties in respect of electronically transmitted transactions. There are also concerns about the problems associated with data protection policy and the potential distortions to e-commerce transactions and the free flow of information caused by differing approaches to it. This is particularly acute in relation to data transfers between the EU and the US. Further work must also be done to develop data coding and publishing standards for e-commerce which would encourage the growth of services and reduction in costs.

Conclusion

In marking its report card, one can be cautiously optimistic about government responses to the policy development for the Internet. It is clear that, in

---

[65] The Regulation of Investigatory Powers Act 2000, Pt. I, puts into effect proposals found in the consultation paper: *Interception of Communications in the United Kingdom* (Cm. 4368, Stationery Office, London, 1999).

setting the agenda, the government is keen to listen and to learn from all those who wish to contribute. In the past, administrations could be criticised for failing to consult as widely as they should and perhaps for adopting policy positions on the basis that they knew best. How the Internet is to be 'governed' is a complicated issue that raises economic, political, constitutional and human rights issues on a global scale. The government is right, for the time being, to look at what is happening in the development of the global information infrastructure and to define the principles upon which it will negotiate and act. There is evidence that the present government is listening to advice. However, it will need to discern the difference between self-interested lobbying and sound advice. It will be interesting to see where that consultation process leads in the life of this administration.

CHAPTER 3

The governance of the Internet in Europe

Andrew Charlesworth

Introduction

The publication of the Bangemann Report on Europe and the Global Information Society[1] in 1994 demonstrated an early recognition at the highest levels of the European Union (EU) that a clear strategy for dealing with the future development of network-related information technologies would be required. The successful implementation of such a strategy would have the effect of stimulating economic growth, promoting closer integration, and allowing the EU to play a direct role in the setting of international technical, commercial and legal standards.

Prior experience had shown that, without strong intervention from the EU, the Member States of the Union struggled to act in a united fashion when reacting to developments in emerging areas of technological development. There was a chauvinistic tendency to support R&D, standard setting and marketing at a national, rather than EU, level and this tended in the long term to militate against the viability of Union producers in the global marketplace.[2] This was particularly clearly demonstrated by the travails of EU computer hardware producers, such as ICL, Bull and Siemens. These firms, who had initially played an important role in R&D advances in the sector, failed to capitalise on those initial advantages via cooperative intra-European ventures. By the mid-1990s, they found themselves unable to compete with US and Japanese firms, and were either reliant on national subsidies or bought out by successful world producers.[3]

At the same time, despite difficulties in that and other sectors, it was becoming clear from developments in the telecommunications sector that the EU could be capable of effective intervention, even where there remained

---

[1] High-Level Group on the Information Society, *Recommendations to the European Council: Europe and the Global Information Society* (the 'Bangemann Report') (Brussels, 1994), http://www.ispo.cec.be/infosoc/backg/bangeman.html.

[2] See Sharp, M., 'The Community and New Technologies' in Lodge, J. (ed.) *The European Community and the Challenge of the Future* (2nd ed., Pinter Publishers, London, 1993).

[3] For example, ICL, once the UK's largest computer manufacturer, was to become effectively a subsidiary of Fujitsu.

opposition from within the Member States. EU action to increase competition, by breaking up the former national telecommunications monopolies, combined with measures designed to promote technical standardisation, and to harmonise pricing and service levels, has aided in the creation of a telecommunications environment within which European companies, such as British Telecom, have been able to develop the platform for a credible global presence.[4]

The Bangemann Report posited that early action would place the EU in a prime position to take advantage of, and have influence over, the growth of the 'Information Society'. Chapter III of the Report dealt specifically with the need to address divergences between national regulatory regimes that could impact on the successful development of the internal EU market for Information Society services. In addition, it recognised that, in many cases, due to the increasingly global nature of those services, if EU policies were to have any meaningful effect, the EU institutions would have to consider appropriate avenues through which to influence the direction of international policy making. Key policy areas identified as requiring EU action were adequate protection of intellectual property rights (IPRs), a uniform approach to the protection of data privacy, the development of encryption technologies and a legal framework to protect them, and a reassessment of EU competition issues such as market power, joint ventures and alliances, and media ownership, in the light of increasing globalisation. The Report's main recommendation in this area was thus that:[5]

> The information society is global. [. . .] Union action should aim to establish a common and agreed regulatory framework for the protection of intellectual property rights, privacy and security of information, in Europe and, where appropriate, internationally.

EU legislators addressed the issue of personal data privacy, via the means of a directive, relatively rapidly after the publication of the Report,[6] although this was almost entirely due to the fact that a legislative initiative had been somewhat fitfully underway since 1990.[7] Even then, the production of national implementing legislation has been woefully slow, with only three Member States meeting the required implementation date.[8] The areas

---

[4] See Kamall, S., *Spicers European Union Policy Briefings: Telecommunications Policy* (FT Media and Telecoms, London, 1996).

[5] Sharp, M., *op. cit.*, chap. III.

[6] See European Union Council Directive 95/46/EC on the Protection of Individuals with regard to the Processing of Personal Data and on the Free Movement of Such Data OJ 1995 No L. 281 p.31, http://europa.eu.int/eur-lex/en/lif/dat/1995/en_395L0046.html.

[7] See Commission of the European Communities, *Proposal for a Council Directive Concerning the Protection of Individuals in Relation to the Processing of Personal Data* (COM(90) 314 final – SYN 287, Brussels, 1990).

[8] For example, despite passing primary legislation in the form of the Data Protection Act 1998, prior to the implementation date, the UK did not fully implement the Directive until 1 March 2000 when the majority 14 pieces of the secondary legislation required to underpin that Act finally came into force.

of IPRs and communications security, however, were to see relatively little in the way of meaningful action until mid to late 1998, and in both cases resulting legislation was delayed until well into 2000. The reasons behind the delay in addressing these issues, stated in the Bangemann Report to be essential to the successful transition to a European-wide 'information society', are varied, but when viewed in broad terms they can all be seen to be underpinned by one of four key factors:

- spirited resistance from entrenched commercial interest groups to counter perceived threats to their existing rights – for example, the lobbying against the Data Protection Directive carried out by the direct marketing and financial industries;
- a fear among national governments that they were losing the power to effectively control both their citizens' on-line activities, and the activities of non-citizens which had an effect within their respective jurisdictions – a fear exemplified by the initial concentration on aspects of content control at the expense of e-commerce facilitation;
- a clear lack of an understanding of the technical workings of the Internet, and its effect on, and implications for, societal norms, on the part of legislators – such as the apparent abdication of responsibility by the EU for the governance of the Internet infrastructure;
- the rapidly developing nature of the technologies, which both outgrew legislative proposals even as they were being drafted, and threw up new, and ever more complex, problems for which traditional solutions were patently unsuitable. These problems are, of course, not unique to the European Union. In many areas, developments in the EU have clearly mirrored those experienced in the US, although with a time lag of upwards of 18 to 24 months.[9] Given the potential tactical advantages this delay provides, the regularity with which EU legislators, as well as legislators in the respective Member States, have demonstrated their failure to learn from the errors and missteps of their US counterparts is both telling and, at the same time, somewhat disheartening.[10]

Since the publication of the Bangemann Report, two influential developments have played a part in sidetracking the legislators from speedily attaining the aims espoused in it. Both were arguably implicit in any large-scale expansion of the Internet, but their implications seem to have been largely overlooked by the EU institutions and their consultants.

---

[9] Contrast, for instance, the progress of the US Digital Millennium Copyright Act of 1998, and the EU draft Directive on Copyright and Related Rights in the Information Society; or the Communications Decency Act of 1996 and the Decision No. 276/1999/EC of the European Parliament and of the Council of 25 January 1999 adopting a multiannual Community action plan on promoting safer use of the Internet by combating illegal and harmful content on global networks.

[10] Consider, for example, the relationship between the US political debate in the last 5 years over encryption, the Clipper Chip and Trusted Third Parties and the debate in the EU over encryption and electronic signatures. See, further, chap. 14.

The first is the changing nature of the Internet itself. The transfer of the majority of the infrastructure of the Internet from public to private hands was already well underway by the time of the Bangemann Report. This was a natural progression from the US government's decision in the early 1990s to move from a government funded core network (NSFNET)[11] to a more distributed Internet architecture operated by commercial providers such as Sprint, MCI, BBN and others. Additionally, the growth in the number of Internet hosts meant that alterations to the management structure of Internet Domain Name System (DNS)[12] were inevitable, as that management structure was not designed to support a massively expanded, and increasingly commercial, Internet. Given the move towards privatisation, those alterations were likely to occur as part of the process of transferring the publicly funded registry functions carried out by Network Services Inc (NSI)[13] to a private competitive system. The rapid international expansion of the Internet, however, meant that such changes could now have a profound effect on education and e-commerce outside the US, and many countries were beginning to voice concern at the implications of privatisation, not least the potential for US companies to obtain a monopoly position in Internet technologies and access. The key nature of these changes, affecting as they do both the technical and managerial fundamentals of the Internet, means that their outcome will be of vital importance to the political direction of the governance of the Internet.

That having been said, the second development, the increasing perception that there was a need to control the nature of the content carried on the Internet, has received considerably more widespread public attention. This is due largely to the populist nature of the subject matter, it being rather easier for the media to explain, and for legislators to understand, how the Internet could be used for nefarious purposes, than it is to conceptualise the implications of significant changes to the distribution of, and control over, the high level Internet domains. It also reflected the desire amongst lawmakers, both legislative and judicial, to bring the realm of cyberspace clearly within the purview of traditional forms of governance, as for a while the unsettling concept that the Internet was, in some way, a 'governance free zone' seemed to be gaining some popular credence.[14] Such an apparent

---

[11] The NSFNET was the first backbone for the US portion of the Internet. It was originally conceived as a way for researchers to submit jobs to supercomputers located at various universities around the US. See, further, Hafner, K. and Lyon, M., *Where Wizards Stay Up Late* (Simon & Schuster, New York, 1996).

[12] The domain name system (DNS) is the way that Internet domain names (such as www.hull.ac.uk) are located and translated into IP (Internet Protocol) addresses (such as the corresponding 150.237.176.8). A domain name is thus a meaningful and easy-to-remember 'handle' for an Internet address. See
http://www.whatis.com/WhatIs_Definition_Page/0,4152,213908,00.html.

[13] See http://www.networksolutions.com/.

[14] One of the favourite pieces of polemic being some form of the mantra that 'The Internet interprets censorship as damage, and routes around it' See, for example, Greenberg, L.T. and Goodman, S.E., 'Is Big Brother Hanging by His Bootstraps?' (1996) 39(7) *Communications of the ACM* 11, http://som1.csudh.edu/faculty/cis/lpress/devnat/general/bigbro.htm.

control vacuum inevitably led to attempts by legislators and judges to exert some element of governance even where, on any rational analysis, those attempts lacked either legitimacy or enforceability.[15] The EU has not been immune to the effects of such desires, either at the Member State level[16] or centrally.[17] However, in the EU as in the US, the illegal content regulation debate has largely proven to be a costly and time-consuming red herring, arguably distracting legislators from more pressing reforms, such as those required to facilitate the growth of e-commerce.

At least partially as a result of the need to react to these developments, the EU has fallen behind the US in developing a legislative framework for such governance of the Internet as may prove necessary or attainable. In some areas, this has meant that US policy makers have gained a crucial advantage in influencing global technical, commercial and legal standards, to the potential disadvantage of the Union. Even where US legislators have created, or maintained, legislation which would have the effect of restricting the commercial activities of US companies, such as the Communications Decency Act,[18] Child Online Protection Act[19] and the various rules governing the export of encryption technologies,[20] the EU has either failed to take advantage, or has been drawn into rehearsing the same pointless debates. This chapter will examine some of the more important recent issues relating

The original quote is usually attributed to John Gilmore, founder of Cygnus Support and the Electronic Frontier Foundation.

[15] See, further, Johnson, D.R. and Post, D.G., 'Law And Borders – The Rise of Law in Cyberspace' http://www.cli.org/X0025_LBFIN.html.

[16] See, for example, the CompuServe Germany case (Felix Somm decision) http://www.cyber-rights.org/isps/somm-dec.htm.

[17] See the Council Recommendation of 24 September 1998 on the development of the competitiveness of the European audiovisual and information services industry by promoting national frameworks aimed at achieving a comparable and effective level of protection of minors and human dignity, OJ 1998 L270/48. Also Decision No. 276/1999/EC of the European Parliament and of the Council adopting a Multiannual Community Action Plan on promoting safer use of the Internet by combating illegal and harmful content on global networks (OJ 1999 L33/1).

[18] 47 U.S.C. 233. Much of the Act was ruled to be unconstitutional by the US Supreme Court in *Reno v American Civil Liberties Union* 521 US 844 (1997). See further Wallace, J. and Mangan, M., *Sex, Laws and Cyberspace* (Henry Holt, New York, 1996), Cannon, R., 'The Legislative History of Senator Exon's Communications Decency Act: Regulating Barbarians on the Information Superhighway' (1996) 49 *Federal Communications Law Journal*, http://www.law.indiana.edu/fclj/pubs/v49/no1/cannon.html.

[19] 47 U.S.C. 231. A preliminary injunction was granted against the enforcement of the Act in *American Civil Liberties Union v Reno II* No. 98 5591, 1999 US Dist LEXIS 735 (E.D. Pa Feb 1, 1999). The Court of Appeals (3rd Circuit) upheld the injunction on 22 June 2000: 217 F. 3d 162.

[20] The export of encryption technology on the US Department of State's munitions list is subject to the rules and regulations contained in the Arms Export Control Act, 22 USC ss.2751–99 (1994) and the International Traffic in Arms Regulations (ITAR) 22 CFR ss.120–30 (1995). The export of other encryption technologies are dealt with by the US Department of Commerce under the Export Administration Act, 50 USC app. ss.2401–2420 (1988 & Supp. V 1993), and the Export Administration Regulations, 15 CFR ss.768–99 (1995).

to the governance of the Internet in the EU and evaluate the ability of the EU to identify and successfully address those issues likely to have long-term implications for both the Member States and their commercial operators.

Internet structure[21]

Throughout the 1990s, legal academics writing about Internet-related subjects seemed to feel obliged, in their introductory remarks, to provide a potted history of the Internet (and, of course, a citation to William Gibson's *Neuromancer*). A topic that those introductions tended to gloss over was the relatively late international development of the Internet; the UK, for instance, only linked to NSFNET in 1989.[22] Even as late as 1994, somewhere between two-thirds to three-quarters of the hosts on the Internet were still US-based. The increasing sophistication of World Wide Web technology from 1994 onwards was, however, the catalyst for a rapid expansion in the Internet as an international, rather than US, communications medium. This move towards the globalisation of the Internet was aided by the fact that the US government was actively seeking to divest itself of its responsibility for the management of the structure of the Internet. The result of this was that, by April 1995, the US government-funded NSFNET had ceased operation and US Internet traffic had been switched to several privately operated backbones. In keeping with this trend, in July 1997, the Clinton Administration published the document 'A Framework for Global Electronic Commerce' which stated that:[23]

> Though government played a role in financing the initial development of the Internet, its expansion has been driven primarily by the private sector. For electronic commerce to flourish, the private sector must continue to lead. Innovation, expanded services, broader participation, and lower prices will arise in a market-driven arena, not in an environment that operates as a regulated industry.

One of the resulting initiatives was the move to privatise the Internet DNS in order to increase competition and facilitate international participation in DNS management. This began with the publication of an initial consultation document or 'Green Paper' in February 1998.[24]

The EU's response to the US Green Paper was critical of a number of elements, in particular the US-centric nature of the text.[25] It noted that the

---

[21] Refer also to chap. 1.

[22] Zakon, R.H., *Hobbes' Internet Timeline*, http://info.isoc.org/guest/zakon/Internet/History/HIT.html.

[23] White House, *A Framework for Global Electronic Commerce* (Washington DC, July 1997) http://www.ecommerce.gov/framewrk.htm.

[24] National Telecommunications and Information Administration, *Improvement of Technical Management of Internet Names and Addresses* Federal Register (Vol. 63(34) 1998 pp.8825–33). http://www.ntia.doc.gov/ntiahome/domainname/dnsdrft.htm.

[25] Communication to the Council from the Commission: International Policy Issues related to Internet Governance, 1998, http://www.ispo.cec.be/eif/policy/governance.html. Council of the European Union & European Commission, Internet Governance: Reply of the

tone of the document seemed to run counter to the joint position adopted by the EU and US at a contemporaneous summit meeting,[26] and that this was an undesirable development from the point of view of the EU. Particular areas of concern were as follows. First, the proposals failed to recognise the need to implement an international approach. Second, they risked consolidating permanent US jurisdiction over the Internet as a whole, including the areas of dispute resolution and trademark law. Third, despite good intentions, they did not bring about any significant improvements to the application of trademark law to domain names. Fourth, the proposals ignored intensive international efforts to prepare a new dispute resolution procedure for the Internet within the framework of the World Intellectual Property Organisation (WIPO).[27] Fifth, the proposals failed to ensure that the private sector in Europe and the rest of the world, including users and industry, could fully participate at all relevant levels in the process. Sixth, they gave the Internet Assigned Numbers Authority (IANA)[28] a natural monopoly position with respect to Internet numbers and the Internet DNS root server system[29] as well as the exercise of certain regulatory functions, and did not go far enough to ensure a level playing field and fair competition with regard to the possible application of European competition law. Finally, they ignored the new system of Generic Top Level Domains (gTLD)[30] Registries, proposed by the International Ad Hoc Committee (IAHC)[31] and modified on the basis of international consultations.

Following the consultation on the Green Paper, the US Department of Commerce released a statement of policy on the management of Internet DNS in June 1998. This suggested that a new, not-for-profit corporation

---

European Community and its Member States to the US Green Paper, Brussels, 1998, http://www.ispo.cec.be/eif/policy/govreply.html.

[26] Joint EU-US Statement on electronic commerce, Washington DC, 5 December 1997, http://www.eurunion.org/partner/summit/summit9712/electrst.htm.

[27] See http://www.wipo.org/eng/index.htm.

[28] See http://www.whatis.com/WhatIs_Definition_Page/0,4152,214010,00.html and chap. 1. See also http://www.iana.org/.

[29] 'The root server system is the way that an authoritative master list of all top-level domain names (such as .com, .net, .org, and individual country codes) is maintained and made available. The system consists of 13 file servers. The central or "A" server is operated by Network Solutions, Inc., the company that currently manages domain name registration, and the master list of top-level domain (TLD) names is kept on the A server. On a daily basis, this list is replicated to 12 other geographically dispersed file servers that are maintained by an assortment of agencies.' http://www.whatis.com/WhatIs_Definition_Page/0,4152,212922,00.html.

[30] A top-level domain (TLD) is the portion of a Uniform Resource Locator (URL) or Internet address that identifies the general type of Internet domain, such as 'com' for 'commercial'. A Generic Top Level Domain (gTLD) is any TLD not associated with a country, e.g. 'edu', 'org' and 'com'. A Country-Code Top-Level Internet Domain (ccTLD) is a TLD associated with a country, e.g. 'uk', 'de', 'nz'.

[31] IAHC was a coalition to discuss and suggest enhancements to the Internet's global Domain Name System (DNS). Organisations naming members to the committee included the Internet Society (ISOC), the Internet Assigned Numbers Authority (IANA), the Internet Architecture Board (IAB), the Federal Networking Council (FNC), the International Telecommunication Union (ITU), the International Trademark Association (INTA) and the World Intellectual Property Organization (WIPO). It was dissolved on 1 May 1997. See http://www.iahc.org/.

formed by the private sector should assume various responsibilities for DNS administration that were performed by or on behalf of the US Government.[32] This document, or 'White Paper', on Internet Governance was the subject of a Commission Communication to the European Parliament and Council.[33] In its Communication, the Commission noted that it had met several times with US officials prior to the publication of the White Paper and that it was satisfied that its comments and criticisms had been taken seriously, with clear US policy changes as a result. Its assessment of the US White Paper was thus rather more favourable, although it noted that there were subjects that would require further consultation and negotiation. These included, first, the applicability of Community and National law to the Internet generally and to the activities of the new corporation in particular. The effect of incorporating IANA as a not-for-profit US private corporation could potentially lead to difficulties with regard to competition law, trademark law, dispute resolution and other aspects of international trade law. Additionally, the private sector nature of the proposed system meant that a notification to the Commission under competition rules would be needed. Finally, the issue of taxation was not addressed, and the application of current taxation systems would need a sufficient and reliable identification system to be built into the DNS.

The Commission praised the US government for recognising the internationalisation of the Internet, somewhat archly noting that the recognition 'has not come lightly in certain US circles which still identify the Internet with US R&D programmes and US-based organisations'. It emphasised the need for the EU to continue to participate in encouraging an appropriate multilateral environment for the co-ordination of international policies in the area of Internet Governance with the aim of providing an appropriate political and legal framework for the future management of the Internet by the proposed private industry self-regulatory body. Noting that the Internet was currently growing more rapidly in Europe than anywhere else in the world it recommended that the EU obtain and maintain a degree of influence and participation commensurate with its economic and social interests in the area. It proposed that the EU institutions and Member States should: address the question of the membership and structure of the IANA as a matter of urgency; participate in the process of setting up the future organisation, and contribute to defining its basic operating principles to ensure that its eventual legal construction is compatible with EU law; draw the urgent attention of the private sector to this matter via consultation and

---

[32] US Department of Commerce: Management of Internet Names and Addresses (Washington, 1998), http://www.ntia.doc.gov/ntiahome/domainname/6_5_98dns.htm.

[33] Communication from the European Commission to the European Parliament and to the Council: Internet Governance: Management of Internet Names and Addresses: Analysis and Assessment from the European Commission of the United States Department of Commerce White Paper (COM 476, final, Brussels, 1998, http://www.ispo.cec.be/eif/dns/com98476.html).

information; ensure that national ccTLD Registries in the Member States should become active and organised members of the new IANA corporation and ensure appropriate representation in the IANA Names Council and on the IANA Board of Directors; begin discussions about the obligation for registries and registrars to provide necessary information to identify operators of Internet domain names for tax purpose; recognise the growing importance of their roles as major users of the Internet and providers of information and services to the public.

In October 1998, IANA submitted a proposal for a new corporation to be called the Internet Corporation for Assigned Names and Numbers (ICANN),[34] including bylaws for the new organisation, and a list of nominations for an interim board. A month later the US government acknowledged ICANN as the new entity called for in the 'White Paper' in a Memorandum of Understanding between the US Department of Commerce and ICANN. ICANN is incorporated as a non-profit public benefit corporation organised under the California Non-profit Public Benefit Corporation Law for charitable and public purposes.[35] Its functions include co-ordinating the assignment of Internet technical parameters, performing and overseeing functions related to the co-ordination of the Internet Protocol ('IP') address space and the Internet domain name system ('DNS'); and overseeing operation of the authoritative Internet DNS root server system.[36]

The Corporation's structure[37] currently consists of an Interim Board of Directors which will eventually be replaced by a permanent Board, three Supporting Organisations and two Advisory Committees. There is also provision for Committees of the Board. The three Supporting Organisations are the Address Supporting Organization (ASO); the Domain Name Supporting Organization (DNSO); and the Protocol Supporting Organization (PSO). The two Advisory Committees are the Governmental Advisory Committee (GAC) and the DNS Root Server System Advisory Committee.

Space does not permit an in-depth analysis of ICANN, which has inevitably received much critical comment about its structure, operations and future.[38] Suffice it to say that the functions listed above provide ICANN with immense, not to say total, control over the basic infrastructure of the Internet. As Post notes, control of the authoritative Internet DNS root server system is:[39]

---

[34] See http://www.icann.com/.
[35] Article 3, Articles of Incorporation of Internet Corporation for Assigned Names and Numbers. As revised 21 November 1998 http://www.icann.org/articles-pr23nov98.html.
[36] Ibid.
[37] See Bylaws for Internet Corporation for Assigned Names and Numbers. A California Non-profit Public Benefit Corporation, as revised 27 May 1999, http://www.icann.org/bylaws-09apr99.html#I.
[38] Horvath, J., 'Cone of Silence: Internet Democracy is Failing' http://www.heise.de/tp/english/inhalt/te/2837/1.html; Post, D., 'Cyberspace's Constitutional Moment', http://www.temple. edu/lawschool/dpost/DNSGovernance.htm; Post, D., 'Governing Cyberspace: "Where is James Madison when we need him?"' http://www.icannwatch.org/archives/essays/930604982.shtml.
[39] Post, D., 'Governing Cyberspace: "Where is James Madison when we need him?"' ibid.

... quite literally a kind of life-or-death power over the global network itself, because presence in (or absence from) this chain of interlocking servers and databases is a matter of [network] life or death: If your name and address cannot be found on the 'authoritative' server, you simply do not exist – at least, not on the Internet. .... Anyone interested in controlling the rules under which activities on the Internet take place ... is likely to find the existence of a single controlling point awfully tempting ... is likely to view control over the root server as the means to impose [their] particular vision on Internet users worldwide.

If the EU wishes to continue to play a role in determining Internet infrastructure governance, its two main areas of concern would thus appear to be, first, to ensure significant EU-based representation on the ICANN Board, and, second, to maximise the degree of influence to be exerted via the Governmental Advisory Committee.

The EU's initial response to the new Internet governance regime was largely positive. In a letter to the US Secretary of Commerce, William Daley,[40] EU Commissioner Martin Bangemann expressed his satisfaction with the development of ICANN and noted the widespread support it was receiving from the Member States and from the European private sector. He stated that, as the EU had sought to ensure geographically balanced representation in the new Corporation, taking into account global usage of the Internet, the proposal that 'no more than one-half of the total number of members of the Permanent Board serving at any given time shall be citizens of any one geographic region' was pleasing. The EU had lobbied hard for such a restriction to avoid US representation dominating ICANN's managing Board and had supported the proposal that each geographic region should be represented on the Board by at least one member. However, the makeup of the Initial Board is less than geographically diverse. Of the nine members, four are from the US, three from Europe, one from Australia and one from Japan. Large areas of the world therefore currently remain unrepresented. The permanent Board, which may have up to nineteen directors, must have at least one representative from each geographic region and no more than half of the directors elected by the Supporting Organisations may be citizens of any single geographic region. The geographic regions are defined as: Europe; Asia/Australia/Pacific; Latin America/Caribbean Islands; Africa; and North America. This would still appear to place some regions at a significant disadvantage, notably the Asia/Australia/Pacific region. Europe and North America would thus appear to have some advantage but, in the case of Europe, this may depend upon the eventual classification of certain nations, such as those that formerly constituted the Soviet Union.

The Governmental Advisory Committee (GAC) of ICANN is an advisory committee comprising representatives of national governments, multinational government organisations and treaty organisations, and distinct economies as recognised in international fora. Its stated role is to 'consider and

---

[40] See http://www.ispo.cec.be/eif/dns/daley.pdf.

provide advice on the activities of the Corporation as they relate to concerns of governments, particularly matters where there may be an interaction between the Corporation's policies and various laws, and international agreements'.[41] With regard to the actual role of the GAC, observers appear divided upon both the degree of influence that it may exert on the operations of ICANN, and the desirability of that influence. It has been claimed that the GAC is unrepresentative, as some nations are not represented or have had representation refused,[42] and that it is secretive, unaccountable and lacking in due process.[43] However, dissenting voices appear few and far between in the wider media and, while some of ICANN's early actions came under high-profile attack,[44] its structure and operations have generally aroused little widespread concern.[45] What is clear is that the EU has played an important role in the early activities of the GAC, notably in ensuring that key policy initiatives, including the dispute resolution policy for domain names, have been rapidly advanced.[46]

In conclusion, after a slow start, the EU appears to have negotiated a useful role for itself within the new Internet governance regime, ensuring that some European opinions will, at the very least, be noted. Some US commentators see this increased role within the new regime as being a move by the US to placate the EU over the current difficulties in reaching an agreement in the data protection dispute.[47] Others see it as part of a wider attempt by national governments generally to bring the Internet more effectively within their control.[48] However, a further school of thought looks beyond arguments over degrees of government interference and control, fearing instead a global corporatist agenda that sees the Internet simply as a vehicle for e-commerce rather than a valuable medium for online democracy and civic discourse.[49]

Above and beyond the debate over its level of influence within the ICANN organisation, the EU remains faced with two further issues. The first issue relates to the fact that ICANN, regardless of the multinational composition of its Permanent Board and related Committees, remains a private company

---

[41] Article 7, s.3a.
[42] See Cook, G., 'The Cook Report on Internet: At War for the Future of the Internet', Part Three: The GAC. http://www.cookreport.com/icannregulate.shtml
[43] Ibid. See also Macavinta, C., 'Vying for control of country-specific domains' *CNET News.com*, 25 August 1999. http://news.cnet.com/news/0-1005-200-346462.html.
[44] Such as a planned $1 fee on the registration of new Internet addresses, which was withdrawn in the face of stiff US opposition.
[45] But see ICANNWatch http://www.icannwatch.org/.
[46] Macavinta, C., 'Domain name dispute policy approved' *CNET News.com*, 26 August 1999. http://news.cnet.com/news/0-1005-200-346511.html.
[47] Cook, G., The Cook Report on Internet, 27 October 1998 (Extra Edition), Part Three: Electronic Commerce and Privacy on a Global Battlefield. http://www.cookreport.com/whorules.html (no longer available).
[48] Post, D., 'Governing Cyberspace: "Where is James Madison when we need him?"' http://www.icannwatch.org/archives/essays/930604982.shtml.
[49] Sondow, M., 'The Internet and The Public Good', ICIIU Submission to the IANA and the IFWP 1998. http://www.iciiu.org/text.html.

incorporated in the US. This begs the question whether it can thus ever operate in a truly independent manner, representing international rather than purely US interests. The past problems faced by NSI, particularly with regard to domain name litigation, suggests that regardless of the international consensus reached on a legal issue, a company incorporated in the US will not be willing, or indeed able, to ignore the consequences of a ruling of a US court requiring it to engage in a particular course of action.[50] The same would not, of course, necessarily be true of a ruling of the European Court of Justice with regard to the same US company. There is thus an obvious risk that, good intentions aside, litigation against ICANN in the US courts may result, by default, in US law becoming the *de facto* administrative law of Internet governance.[51]

The second issue is how exactly the EU institutions wish to see the Internet develop, whether their vision is of Internet governance that is heavily biased towards the fulfilment of corporate interests or of an Internet that fulfils wider civic interests. The EU institutions have been faced with such issues before, in the form of the 'universal service' debate in the telecommunications sector, and the Commission, in particular, has found itself trying to balance two very different tasks, the active encouragement of competition juxtaposed against the need to ensure that basic telephony services are available to all across the Union, regardless of geographic or economic factors. It has been argued before that if the Internet, or a future 'Information Superhighway', becomes as important as the Bangemann Report would have us believe it will, an important part of the EU's role in the future governance of the Internet would be to ensure that access to both the Internet and to services on it are as equitably available as possible.[52] The temptation may be, however, once the institutions are assured that EU corporate interests are adequately protected, to abdicate responsibility for many aspects of Internet governance and simply to allow those corporate bodies to set and dominate the agenda.[53] If this were the case, the relative paucity of user representation, compared to governmental and commercial representation, on the ICANN Board and its various bodies would appear to bode poorly for the prospects of any significant non-commercial input into future Internet developments, both technical and legal.

---

[50] See, further, Oppedahl, C., 'Recent trademark cases examine reverse domain name hijacking' (1999) 21 *Hastings Comm/Ent L.J.* 535 (draft at http://www.patents.com/pubs/comment.htm); McWilliams, B., 'Court Ruling Could Prohibit Stealth Sites' *Business News* 16 April 1999.
http://www.internetnews.com/bus-news/article/0,1087,3_100051,00.html.

[51] Mendrey, S., 'Internet Corporation for Assigned Names and Numbers (ICANN)', http://cyber.law.harvard.edu/property/domain/icann2.html, 1998.

[52] See Charlesworth, A. and Cullen, H., 'Under my Wheels: Issues of Access and Social Exclusion on the Information Superhighway' (1996) 10 *International Review of Law, Computers and Technology* 27.

[53] See Essick, K., European Commission wants minor role in Internet *The Industry Standard* 23 July 1998. http://www.thestandard.net/articles/news_display/0,1270,1155,00.html (no longer available).

Illegal and harmful content[54]

The debate concerning the need for, and feasibility of, content regulation on the Internet was as inevitable, and often as ill-informed, in the EU as it was in the US. However, the nature of the debate in Europe has differed markedly from that in the US. Key to this difference has been the fragmented nature of the EU on matters of acceptable types of cultural and social discourse when compared to the more homogeneous nature of the US.[55] This is not, of course, to say that different regions of the US do not have different 'community standards',[56] but rather that the influence of the First Amendment to the US Constitution, and its interpretation by successive incarnations of the US Supreme Court, has operated to significantly reduce the margin between them. In the EU, that margin is considerably wider, with some Member States, for example the UK, operating rigorous regimes of censorship over depictions of sexual activity, while others, like the Netherlands, prefer a rather more *laissez-faire* approach to their citizens' proclivities in this area. Even in those areas of moral judgement where some degree of consensus might reasonably be expected, such as the undesirability of child pornography, the extent of that consensus does not appear to extend to the uniform interpretation of subject matter, uniform definition of offences or uniformity of punishment across the EU.

This lack of consensus, combined with the difficulties of imposing national rules on a transnational medium might lead one to assume that, in conformity with the doctrine of subsidiarity, legislative action would be best taken at European Union level. However, when debate on the issue was initiated by the Commission in 1996,[57] it soon became apparent that even a supranational entity like the EU would struggle to provide a workable legislative response to all aspects of the regulation of Internet content. The initial debate did, however, identify several key issues: that self-regulation would play an essential role in content control;[58] that 'illegal content' was going to be easier to categorise for legislative purposes than 'harmful

---

[54] See, further, chaps 9–11.

[55] For a wider discussion of the issues raised here see Walker, C. and Akdeniz, Y., 'The Governance of the Internet in Europe with Special Reference to Illegal and Harmful Content' in Walker, C. (ed.), *Crime, Criminal Justice and the Internet* (special edition, *Criminal Law Review*, Sweet & Maxwell, London, 1998); Akdeniz, Y. and Walker, C., 'The Governance of Internet Content Regulation in Europe' http://www.cfp99.org/program/papers/akdeniz.htm.

[56] See, for example, *US v Thomas* F.3d 701 (6th Cir. 1996).

[57] See European Commission, Communication to the European Parliament, The Council, The Economic and Social Committee and the Committee of the Regions: Illegal and Harmful Content on the Internet (COM (96) 487, Brussels, 1996), http://www.ispo.cec.be/legal/en/internet/communic.html; and European Commission, *Green Paper on the Protection of Minors and Human Dignity in Audiovisual and Information Services*, (COM (96) 483, Brussels, 1996), http://europa.eu.int/en/record/green/gp9610/protec.htm.

[58] See European Commission Working Party Report (1996) 'Illegal and Harmful Content on the Internet' http://www.ispo.cec.be/legal/en/internet/wpen.html.

content';[59] that, to be truly effective, any system of Internet content regulation would have to be global;[60] and that responsibility for content should rest with producers and distributors, and not with intermediaries such as ISPs.[61]

It is clear from the early stages of the debate within the Union that legislative initiatives, of the type seen in the US, to regulate Internet content were never seriously envisaged. Instead, it was recognised that a multi-level approach to content regulation would be a more effective way forward. This was reflected in the Union's decision not to take the legislative approach via a regulation or directive, but rather to adopt, by Council Decision, an Action Plan to promote the safer use of the Internet.[62] The Action Plan, which runs from 1 January 1999 to 31 December 2002, is designed to:

- encourage both industry and users to develop and implement adequate systems of self-regulation by building on existing hotline initiatives, improving liaison with law enforcement, and encouraging further initiatives on self-regulation including the implementation of Codes of Conduct[63] and the promotion of a system of visible quality labels;
- strengthen developments by supporting various means of filtering and rating to provide users with a range of tools to protect themselves and their families against undesirable material. This will include the validation of rating systems for European content providers, the integration of rating into the content creation process, assessing the benefits of these technical solutions and the provision of third-party rating systems;
- prepare the ground for awareness actions to be carried out by the Member States, including alerting and informing parents and teachers, through their relevant associations;
- evaluate the impact of Community measures, to assess legal implications and co-ordinate with similar international initiatives and to foster co-operation and exchange of experiences and best practices;
- promote co-ordination across Europe and between actors concerned;
- ensure compatibility between the approach taken in Europe and elsewhere.

Thus far, within the Member States themselves, there appears to have been a disinclination to engage in any wide-ranging legislative changes with regard to Internet content regulation, and to rely on industry self-regulation. Where there has been legislative activity, it has more often had the aim of limiting

---

[59] See European Parliament, Resolution on the Commission communication on illegal and harmful content on the Internet (COM(96)0487 – C4-0592/96).

[60] Ibid.

[61] See Ministerial Declaration, Global Information Networks, Ministerial Conference, Bonn, 6–8 July 1997 at paras 41–3, http://www.ispo.cec.be/bonn/Min_declaration/i_finalen.html.

[62] Decision No. 276/1999/EC of the European Parliament and of the Council of 25 January 1999 adopting a multiannual Community action plan on promoting safer use of the Internet by combating illegal and harmful content on global networks, OJ 1999 L33/1, http://www.ispo.cec.be/ecommerce/oj/1999/1999L33/276_1999CE_es.pdf.

[63] As suggested in Recommendation 98/560/EC on the protection of minors and human dignity, OJ 1998 L270/1.

the liability, if any, of Internet Service Providers, than of penalising website owners and end users. This is not to say that those providing or obtaining material considered illegal or harmful, via the Internet, may do so with impunity. As the recent UK case, *R v Waddon*, demonstrates, national courts are perfectly capable of using existing laws to cover Internet activities, even if some of the law has to be fairly liberally interpreted in the process.[64]

By way of comment, while the EU has been laudably restrained in the scope of its Action Plan, the devil, as ever, is in the details, or rather in the lack of them. The terminology in the Action Plan is regrettably vague about just what exactly is the nature of the material to be addressed by the various initiatives. It makes a distinction between 'harmful' and 'illegal' content, stating that the two types of material should be treated differently, but then fails to provide a workable definition of either – an issue raised by an Interim report in 1997:[65]

> ... it is crucial to differentiate between content which is illegal and other harmful content .... These different categories of content pose radically different issues of principle, and call for very different legal and technological responses: measures on illegal content should aim to fight the source of content, whereas harmful content calls for measures aimed to raise awareness and to empower users.

While it could be argued that differences in Member State laws and culture justify a certain degree of leeway, it would seem that this approach risks significant disparities between Member States in their regulation of a medium which is uniquely pan-European. The *Waddon* case, mentioned above, demonstrates neatly the type of awkward situation that might result with material considered 'illegal' in one Member State and either 'harmful', or even innocuous, in another.

The heavy reliance upon hotlines and other self-regulatory mechanisms such as Codes of Conduct also seems either naive or disingenuous. Hotlines to report illegal material do appear to play some (if a difficult to quantify) role in regulating the activities of local ISPs, content providers and users. Indeed the Action Plan model resembles in many ways the type of national self-regulatory system in place for premium rate telephone information services, such as the Independent Committee for the Supervision of Standards of Telephone Information Services (ICSTIS) in the UK.[66] However, the resemblance is more limited than it may first appear. ICSTIS is an industry-funded, but independent, regulatory body and all the members of its Committee are independent of the premium rate telephone information service

---

[64] *R v Waddon* (6 April 2000, CA),
http://news2.thls.bbc.co.uk/hi/english/sci/tech/newsid%5F382000/382152.stm. See also
R v Fellows; R v Arnold [1997] 1 Cr.App.R. 244.

[65] Interim report on Initiatives in EU Member States with respect to Combating Illegal and Harmful Content on the Internet, Version 7 (4 June 1997),
http://www.ispo.cec.be/legal/en/internet/wp2en.html.

[66] See http://www.icstis.org.uk/frmain.htm.

industry. Its Code of Practice is approved and revised by the Director General of OFTEL exercising statutory functions under the Telecommunications Act 1984. In addition, by virtue of the expense of international telephone calls, ICSTIS has rather less of an international brief; it has rather more control over the contents of its members' services; and it is able to require prior written permission before certain services are provided.[67]

Walker and Akdeniz state that, despite the availability of an impressive array of statistics from the Internet Watch Foundation, the UK self-regulatory body for ISPs,[68] about its hotline and reporting facility, it remains impossible both to ascertain the amount of 'harmful' and 'illegal' content available on the Internet, or for the IWF to enforce any meaningful measures against many foreign content providers.[69] If anything, reliance on hotlines may lead to the perception that there is less of a problem than actually exists. Self-regulation and Codes of Conduct have proven less than effective in other areas of Internet activity (see the section on privacy below), and it is difficult to see why matters should be significantly different here.

The suggestion that the widespread use of filtering and rating systems should be encouraged is also perhaps more controversial than it might at first appear.[70] Experience in the United States suggests that leaving the definition of 'harmful' and 'illegal' to a private-sector rating or filtering system may have undesirable consequences, for example some filtering software organisations have been accused of effectively marginalising controversial rather than 'harmful' and 'illegal' material, such as information on abortion and homosexuality.[71] This can be seen to be removing choice from the individual rather than increasing choice by empowering the end user. It is also argued that there may be problems with regard to cultural bias, as the majority of currently available rating technology has been developed by US companies. Additionally, filtering technology is not infallible and may be easily circumvented, thus leaving families and other content-using groups with a false sense of the extent to which illegal and harmful materials have been blocked.[72] In short, an uncritical reliance on filtering may reduce desirable cultural differences, remove decision-making from individuals and blur ethical standards between countries. A final point, which has not often been mentioned, perhaps unsurprisingly given the furore that the issue of content

---

[67] KPMG & Denton Hall, Review of the Internet Watch Foundation, http://www.kpmgiwf.org/iwfrevu.pdf.

[68] See http://www.iwf.org.uk/.

[69] Walker, C. and Akdeniz, Y., 'The Governance of the Internet in Europe with Special Reference to Illegal and Harmful Content', op. cit., at p.14.

[70] See, for the industry's stance, Internet Watch Foundation, 'Rating and Filtering Internet Content: A United Kingdom perspective', http://www.iwf.org.uk/label/index.htm, 1998.

[71] See 'The Censorware Project' for a critical evaluation of a range of filtering and rating systems: http://www.censorware.org/.

[72] Walker, C. and Akdeniz, Y., 'The Governance of the Internet in Europe with Special Reference to Illegal and Harmful Content', op. cit., at pp.15–18.

control tends to raise, is that filtering without a focused rationale may in fact critically damage the economic development of Internet.[73]

While it is tempting to assert that the EU, as an important regional supranational organisation, should be engaging in some degree of content regulation, it is debatable how many of the activities outlined in the Action Plan will actually prove effective in the long term. It would seem, in particular, that attempting to deal with both illegal *and* harmful material is over-ambitious, not least because the EU authorities are unlikely to reach any consensus on 'harmful' material that is not already covered by a consensus on 'illegal' material. Indeed, one could plausibly turn the subsidiarity argument for the EU's participation in Internet content regulation on its head. Under the doctrine of subsidiarity, for the EU to act, it requires that the issue be one where the EU and Member States share concurrent powers, and that the action to be taken may be beyond the powers and resources of the individual Member States. At present, there is little compelling evidence that suggests the Internet is so overrun with 'illegal' and 'harmful' content that there is a pressing need for EU action, either to protect its citizens or to ensure economic fair play. Equally, given the global nature of the Internet, it is arguable that the EU is likely to be little more successful than its Member States at achieving significant reductions in the amount of 'illegal' and 'harmful' content available. Under such circumstances, recourse to the principle of subsidiarity would suggest less that the EU should attempt to co-ordinate or harmonise Member States' Internet content regulation activities than that the EU should not be involved in this sphere at all. This analysis might, of course, be altered significantly if the recent developments in Internet governance, outlined in the section above, provide a mechanism through which the EU could in fact have some meaningful input. That is, if ICANN's control of the authoritative Internet DNS root server system is as effective a 'chokepoint' for content regulation as has been suggested, and there is sufficient will among the members of its Permanent Board to use it as a content control mechanism.

Personal data privacy

Personal data privacy has long been a concern of a significant proportion of the Member States, with the German *Land* of Hesse enacting the first data protection legislation in 1970 and Sweden enacting the first European national legislation in 1973. Indeed, by 1980, six of the then nine EEC Member States had adopted, or were committed to adopting, national rules.[74] The process was given further impetus by the production of the Council of the Organization for Economic Co-operation and Development

---

[73] Johnson, D.R., 'Pornography Drives Technology: Why Not to Censor the Internet' (1996) 49(1) *Federal Communications Law Journal*,
http://www.law.indiana.edu/fclj/pubs/v49/no1/johnson.html.
[74] The exceptions being Ireland, Italy and the UK.

(OECD) 'Guidelines on the Protection of Privacy and Transborder Data Flows'[75] in 1980 and the adoption of the 'Convention for the Protection of Individuals with Regard to Automatic Processing of Personal Data', in 1981, under the auspices of the Council of Europe.[76] The Convention required ratifying nations to: protect the privacy rights of individuals in circumstances where information about them was to be processed automatically; and to facilitate a common international standard of protection for individuals, with the aim that the free flow of information across international boundaries could proceed without disruption.

While the EEC had taken notice of these early developments on the part of its Member States,[77] it was not until the late 1980s that it began to show a real interest in the harmonisation of data protection laws. With the completion of the Single Market approaching in the early 1990s, the Commission put forward a proposal for a draft Directive on data protection on the basis that, although all the Member States were signatories to the Council of Europe's Convention, not all had data protection legislation, while, among those that did, the nature and scope of that legislation was extremely varied. The Commission saw these variations as a potential impediment to the objective of the Single Market. The primary aim of the Directive was, thus, to remove the differences in protection afforded to personal data by the different Member States.

The resultant Directive requires Member States to provide a comprehensive data privacy regime, which most Member States have done by means of omnibus legislation.[78] It applies to most situations where personal data are processed wholly or partly by automatic means. 'Personal data' as defined broadly covers a wide range of information, including text, photographs, audio-visual images and sound recordings of identifiable individuals.[79] 'Processing' effectively covers every aspect of personal data use from collection to destruction.[80] Processing of data is legitimate only in certain specified situations, and must comply with data protection principles contained in the Directive. Certain data such as indications as to 'racial or ethnic origin, political opinions, religious or philosophical beliefs, trade union

---

[75] *Guidelines on the Protection of Privacy and Transborder Data Flows of Personal Data* (OECD, Paris, 1980).

[76] *Convention for the Protection of Individuals with Regard to Automatic Processing of Personal Data*, ETS No. 108 (Council of Europe, Strasbourg, 1981),
http://www.coe.fr/eng/legaltxt/108e.htm.

[77] The European Parliament's Legal Affairs Committee discussed the matter in 1979 (PE 56.386/fin Doc 100/79), and in 1981 the Commission adopted a Recommendation to the Member States that they sign and ratify the Council of Europe Convention (OJ 1981 L246/31).

[78] For a detailed history, see Bainbridge, D., *EC Data Protection Directive* (Butterworths, London, 1996); Charlesworth, A., 'Implementing the European Data Protection Directive 1995 in UK Law: The Data Protection Act 1998' (1999) 16 (3) *Government Information Quarterly* 203.

[79] Art. 2 (a), DPD, (1995).

[80] Art. 2 (b), DPD, (1995).

membership and health or sex life' are regarded as particularly sensitive, and may only be processed with the explicit consent of the data subject.[81] The Directive also requires that individuals whose data are processed must be provided with certain information, for example, about the purpose of processing; and that they should have the right of access to their personal data, and the right to have inaccurate data amended, erased or destroyed.[82] Individuals are also provided with rights to object to lawful processing of their data, and to their data being used for direct marketing purposes.[83]

With regard to transfers of data outside the EU and EEA, the Directive sets detailed conditions for transfer of personal data to third-party countries and forbids transfers where, subject to limited exceptions, non-Member States do not provide what the Commission considers to be an 'adequate level of protection'. The key exception is when the transfer of data is 'necessary for the performance of a contract between the data subject and the controller' and the data subject has been informed of both this and the fact that the country receiving the export does not provide 'an adequate level of protection'.[84]

There are two aspects to determining the adequacy of protection of data privacy in non-EEA countries to which personal data are to be transferred. These are the substantive rules that apply to protection of the data; and the methods of enforcement by which compliance with those substantive rules is attained. Thus the transferor must ensure that the substantive rules that apply to the transferee will have the same effect as those contained in the Directive. This can be achieved in several ways: by national legislation in the jurisdiction to which the data are transferred; by codes of conduct at an industry or sectoral level; by specific contractual provisions between the UK-based transferor and the transferee; or by elements of all three.

The second element is potentially rather more problematic, especially if complete concordance with the provisions in the Act must be obtained. It will be difficult, for instance, to provide EU data subjects with the same kind of private rights of action against non-EEA data transferees as they have available against EEA-based transferees under the Act. This aspect of the European Union data protection regime, in particular, has caused a considerable degree of consternation among third-party nations. One of the most vociferous critics of the perceived intrusive extra-territorial nature of the Directive is the United States, which has tended only to regulate the privacy and data practices of government[85] and particular industries[86] while

---

[81] Art. 8, DPD, (1995).
[82] Arts 10–12, DPD, (1995).
[83] Art. 14, DPD, (1995).
[84] Arts 25 & 26, DPD, (1995).
[85] See, for example, the Privacy Act 1974 and subsequent amendments (5 U.S.C. 552(a)).
[86] See, for example, the Right to Financial Privacy Act 1978, Video Privacy Protection Act of 1988, and Telephone Consumer Protection Act 1991. Rotenberg, M., *The Privacy Law Sourcebook 1999* (EPIC, Washington DC, 1999).

relying on market demands, public pressure and industry self-regulation to provide wider privacy protection.

It is clear that there are genuine fundamental differences in the EU and US political and legal approaches to personal data privacy. These differences may potentially make it difficult for the United States to adopt federal laws that could provide a level of personal data protection satisfactory to the EU Commission.[87] The European approach to data protection is mainly concerned with governmental regulation of the private sector. The Directive thus exempts large areas of government activity from regulation, and creates or enhances data protection regulatory and registry bodies which report to, and are funded by, central government. This contrasts sharply with the situation in the United States where Constitutional privacy rights are provided almost solely against the government.[88] The US Constitution, in clearly delimiting the role of federal government, may arguably also prevent it from engaging in European-style regulation of personal data use.[89]

A key difference between the EU position and that of the United States is the extent to which market forces and self-regulatory regimes are viewed as being likely to provide an acceptable level of personal data privacy without some form of underlying legal framework. In the United States, there is little support for either a privacy approach on the European model, or a centralised governmental privacy agency.[90] Indeed, two government reports in the mid-1990s explicitly rejected the adoption of such approaches to data privacy.[91]

The Internet has provided some interesting examples of the effectiveness of US self-regulatory schemes. There are several Internet-related self-regulatory bodies,[92] the best known of which is TRUSTe which provides an 'industry-regulated, cost-effective privacy program' based on a branded online seal, the TRUSTe 'trustmark'. Websites that adhere to established

---

[87] See Swire, P.P. and Litan, R.E., *None of Your Business* (Brookings Institution Press, Washington DC, 1998) at 41; Flaherty, D.H., *Computers and Privacy: How to Regulate the Private Sector* (University of Montreal, Montreal, 1992 at http://www.lexum.umontreal.ca/fr/equipes/technologie/conferences/aqdij/Congres92/FLAHERTY.html).

[88] Cate, F., *Privacy in the Information Age* (Brookings Institution Press, Washington DC, 1997) at 99.

[89] Ibid.

[90] Both Cate, op. cit., and Swire and Litan, op. cit., oppose that approach. Similar sentiments are expressed by Kirsh, E.M., Phillips, D.W. and McIntyre, D.E., 'Recommendations for the Evolution of Netlaw: Protecting Privacy in a Digital Age' (1996) 2(2) *Journal of Computer-Mediated Communication*, http://www.ascusc.org/jcmc/vol2/issue2/kirsh.html. For contrast, see Petersen, S.B. 'Your Life as an Open Book: Has Technology Rendered Personal Privacy Virtually Obsolete?' (1995) 48 *Federal Communications Law Journal*, http://www.law.indiana.edu/fclj/pubs/v48/no1/petersen.html.

[91] The Information Infrastructure Task Force, Privacy Working Group, Privacy and the National Information Infrastructure, *Principles for Providing and Using Personal Information* (Washington DC, June 1995); US Dept. of Commerce, National Telecommunications and Information Industry Administration, *Privacy and the NII, Safeguarding Telecommunications-Related Personal Information* (Washington DC, October 1995).

[92] See also The Online Privacy Alliance http://www.privacyalliance.org/ and BBBonline http://www.BBBonline.org/.

privacy principles and agree to comply with TRUSTe's oversight and consumer resolution process may display this trustmark on their sites. This informs online users about the website's policy on personal data use, and permits them to decide whether to disclose personal data to the website. TRUSTe, which counts among its members America Online, CyberCash, Excite, IBM, MatchLogic, Microsoft, Netcom, Netscape and Compaq, has claimed that it is 'the only organization that provides established, comprehensive oversight and consumer resolution mechanisms to assure that stated privacy policies are being enforced and that users' online privacy is protected'.[93]

However, things have not run entirely to plan. In August 1998, the Federal Trade Commission (FTC) and GeoCities, a provider of free home pages on the Internet with over two million members and a TRUSTe member, agreed on a consent order settling the first FTC case of privacy violation.[94] GeoCities was charged with misrepresenting to users its reasons for collecting the personal information it required to establish a user's home page. Its online form included an option to receive or not 'special offers' from advertisers and individual companies, and a statement that the 'optional' information such as education level and income would not be released to third parties without the member's permission. However, GeoCities disclosed the personal data to third parties who used them to market products and services. GeoCities remained a member of TRUSTe, while publicly maintaining that it did not consider that it had acted deceitfully. More recently, in March 1999 Microsoft admitted collecting hardware serial numbers while registering software. TRUSTe stated that this 'compromise[d] consumer trust and privacy' but, as the violation did not involve the 'trustmarked' Microsoft.com website, TRUSTe said it was outside its jurisdiction.[95] Finally, in June 1999 it was announced that the free email services by Microsoft's Hotmail and Excite contained a software flaw which revealed users' account names to other websites, potentially giving spammers access to personal data. This was again potentially in breach of both organisations' privacy agreements as outlined on their websites.[96]

By way of comment, Internet privacy concerns in the international arena are clearly on the increase, and it is possible that the EU Data Protection Directive may yet provide, or form part of, a viable framework for an international approach to protecting personal data privacy on the Internet. Yet the opposition of the US to omnibus government privacy regulation of this nature has been a formidable obstacle to such an approach. Negotiations

---

[93] See TRUSTe: Frequently Asked Questions at http://www.etrust.com/about/about_faqs.html.
[94] See http://www.ftc.gov/opa/1998/9808/geocitie.htm for details of the consent order. Neither GeoCities nor TRUSTe appear to mention the matter on their respective home pages.
[95] Clark, T., 'TRUSTe clears Microsoft on technicality', *CNET News.com*, 22 March 1999, http://www.news.com/News/Item/0,4,34114,00.html.
[96] Macavinta, C., 'Hotmail, Excite have privacy hole', *CNET News.com*, 29 June 1998, http://technews.netscape.com/computing/technews/newsitem/0,290,23710,00.html. (no longer available).

designed to provide a compromise by way of a proposed 'safe harbor' solution[97] began in mid-1998 and, despite the avowed intent of the negotiators to reach quick settlement, dragged on until March 2000. The 'safe harbor' concept rests on the idea that a set of data privacy principles would be agreed between the US and the EU, and self-certified compliance with these principles would entitle a company to shelter within the 'safe harbor'. A company entitled to 'safe harbor' status would automatically be granted a presumption of adequate compliance with the Directive, and thus data transfers from within the European Union to it would be allowed. The difficulty with this concept was that the US Department of Commerce wanted to devise principles that would provide 'adequate' privacy protection for European citizens but which would in turn 'reflect US views on privacy, allow for relevant US legislation, regulation, and other public interest requirements, and provide a predictable and cost effective framework for the private sector'.[98] In practice, the former aim, and some of the latter aims, were quite simply diametrically opposed. Early negotiations reflected this somewhat schizophrenic approach, with the EU refusing to back down from the position adopted in the Directive, while the US, in offering its 'safe harbor' solution, had serious difficulties in persuading either the Commission[99] or US commercial interests[100] that this would prove a satisfactory way forward.

The announcement in early March 2000 that European and US negotiators had finalised an agreement on the issue of data privacy[101] thus came as something of a surprise, as prior to that point certain issues, notably provision for meaningful enforcement of the safe harbor principles, had seemed almost intractable. However, a closer analysis of the agreement reached suggested that it might not be quite the solution that the negotiators' press releases trumpeted, not least because it did not include the financial services sector. The agreement also set no deadline for compliance, stating instead

---

[97] See http://www.ita.doc.gov/td/ecom/menu.html.

[98] Letter from Ambassador Aaron and Safe Harbor Principles as of November 1998, http://www.ita.doc.gov/ecom/aaron114.html.

[99] WP19 (5047/99) Opinion 2/99 on the adequacy of the 'International safe harbour principles' issued by the Dept of Commerce on 19th April 1999, adopted 3 May 1999, http://europa.eu.int/comm/internal_market/en/media/dataprot/wpdocs/wp19en.htm; WP27 (5146/99) Opinion 7/99 on the Level of Data Protection provided by the 'Safe Harbor' Principles as published together with the Frequently Asked Questions (FAQs) and other related documents on 15 and 16 November 1999 by the US Department of Commerce at http://europa.eu.int/comm/internal_market/en/media/dataprot/wpdocs/wp27en.htm.

[100] See comments on the initial draft at http://www.ita.doc.gov/td/ecom/list1.htm, on the April 1999 revision at http://www.ita.doc.gov/td/ecom/599comments.htm, and on the November 1999 revision at http://www.ita.doc.gov/td/ecom/publiccomments1299.htm.

[101] Draft Safe Harbor Principles – 17 March 2000, http://www.ita.doc.gov/td/ecom/RedlinedPrinciples31600.htm. See also EU press release, Data protection: draft package agreed for protection of data transferred from EU to US, 15 March 2000, http://europa.eu.int/comm/internal_market/en/media/dataprot/news/harbor3.htm; de Bony, E., 'EU and US reach data privacy accord', IDG News Service\Brussels Bureau, 14 March 2000, http://www.idg.net/go.cgi?id=238013.

that US and EU officials would meet in mid-2001 to review the situation. The EU press release stated that a key point that EU negotiators had 'clarified successfully is the way in which the principles of data protection will be enforced in the US, and in particular the accuracy and reliability of the list of companies adhering to the "Safe Harbor" and the possible sanctions for non-compliance.' However, further amplification of how this was to be achieved was not forthcoming.

In any event, if, as that press release suggested, the agreement was to be formalised in late June or July 2000, it appeared that this would be dependant upon the apparently unlikely event of the US Congress, the European Commission, EU Member States[102] and the European Parliament agreeing to its terms. The Parliament had previously expressed a desire for the Working Party set up under the Data Protection Directive to present a final report to it before a decision was made, and it was no secret that the Working Party was largely unimpressed by the previous drafts of the "safe harbor" agreement.[103] However, to the surprise of some, the Article 31 Committee approved the safe harbor proposals, apparently on the grounds that US adequacy status could still be revoked at a later date if significant non-compliance occurred. Then, despite the fact that the European Parliament, in a Resolution dated 5 July 2000, expressed the view that the "safe harbor" arrangement needed to be improved before the Commission found it offered adequate protection, the Commission decided, on 13 July 2000, to push ahead with a Decision determining that the "safe harbor" arrangements provided adequate protection for personal data transferred from the EU to the US. In the US, much will depend upon the acquiescence of the Beltway lobbyists, and the compliance of corporations. The lobbyists, notably the Direct Marketing Association, may yet prove intransigent, and as with so many US data privacy related measures in the past, their supporters in Congress will be in a prime position to kill the agreement. The corporations may be inclined to treat the EU's measures with the cavalier contempt with which they have greeted US legislative measures and self-regulatory bodies.

While much of the early EU/US discussion regarding data privacy was influenced heavily by the posturing surrounding a string of trade-related disputes between the two sides, there is some hope that, when that posturing finally ends, serious thought can be given to finding an appropriate compromise solution either via the use of contractual clauses or by the acceptance of sectoral regulation. This will, however, require the US government to accept that outright denial of the personal data privacy approach taken by the EU Member States cannot be sustained in the long term. It is possible that, as previously occurred in the copyright arena, the US

---

[102] Via the EU Directive's Art. 31 Committee composed of the representatives of the Member States (usually the Data Protection Commissioner of the Member State) and chaired by a representative of the Commission.

[103] See Article 29 of the EU Directive. Note the guarded warning in the Working Party's Opinion 3/2000 on the EU/US dialogue concerning the "Safe harbor" arrangement (WP 31 (5019/00)) at http://europa.eu.int/comm/internal_market/en/media/dataprot/wpdocs/wp31en.html.

may hold out, at least for a while, for an international model of its own devising.[104] On the other hand, a number of high-profile incidents in the US have alerted the public to the potential for the invasion of personal privacy inherent in an unregulated personal data market, resulting in consumer campaigns against both products and developments which are seen as undesirable.[105] Ironically, the Internet has considerably simplified the logistical effect required to create such consumer awareness and mobilisation. Equally, some increased enthusiasm for regulation has occasionally been voiced among key US government agencies.[106] Another source of pressure on the US is the fact that other nations are beginning to adopt data privacy legislation that conforms to the model provided by the EU Directive.[107] The EU, on the other hand, has been at pains to avoid undue conflict with the US. This may be, in part, due to a desire to avoid unnecessary trade disruption, but may also be influenced by the fact that, despite the fact that the General Agreement on Trade in Services recognises the protection of personal data as a legitimate reason for restricting the free movement of services,[108] several of the Member States have themselves thus far failed to implement the Directive.[109] This lack of internal compliance with the

---

[104] The United States was the primary mover behind the creation of the Uniform Copyright Convention in 1952, because US copyright law contained formalities that would have been contrary to the long-established Berne Convention. The US eventually joined the Berne Convention, and abandoned the formalities that were the prime motive for support of the UCC, with the result that the significance of the UCC has significantly waned.

[105] See Gurak, L., *Persuasion and Privacy in Cyberspace: The On-line Protests over Lotus Marketplace and the Clipper Chip* (Yale University Press, New Haven, CT, 1997).

[106] In its the most recent reports, the Federal Trade Commission (FTC) has shown divided opinions. In *Self-Regulation and Privacy Online* (July 1999) the four Commissioners involved split 3-1 in favour of giving self-regulation more time. In *Privacy Online: Fair Information Practices in the Electronic Marketplace* (May 2000) the split was 3-2 that self-regulation alone had not adequately protected consumer online privacy, and as a result, legislation was needed to supplement self-regulatory efforts and guarantee basic consumer protections.

[107] Acting partly in response to the EU Directive, the Canadian government introduced Bill C-54, the *Personal Information Protection and Electronic Documents Act* in October 1998. Opponents of the legislation in the Senate were able to stall its progress with a determined filibuster in June 1999, but the government reintroduced it as Bill C-6 in October 1999, and it became law in April 13, 2000. The basic provisions fall broadly in line with the principles contained in the EU Directive, such that if the EU Commission observes appropriate enforcement, Canada should be able to meet the adequacy requirement.

[108] GATS, Article XIV – General Exceptions:
Subject to the requirement that such measures are not applied in a manner which countries where like conditions prevail, or a disguised restriction on trade in services, nothing in this Agreement shall be construed to prevent the adoption or enforcement by any Member of measures: [...]
(c) necessary to secure compliance with laws or regulations which are not inconsistent with the provisions of this Agreement including those relating to: [...] (ii) the protection of the privacy of individuals in relation to the processing and dissemination of personal data and the protection of confidentiality of individual records and accounts. ...

[109] On 11 January 2000, the Commission announced it was to take legal action against France, Luxembourg, the Netherlands, Germany and Ireland, before the European Court of Justice, for their continuing failure to implement the Directive – the third stage of formal infringement proceedings under Article 226 of the EC Treaty.

Directive would potentially weaken the EU's case should the US choose to bring the matter before the World Trade Organisation's dispute mechanism.[110]

Unlike the issue of content regulation, it is less likely that an international data privacy regime on the lines of the EU Directive will be successfully negotiated via the ICANN structure. The fact that ICANN is incorporated and based in the US leaves it vulnerable to legal challenge in the US courts, should it attempt to enforce such a regime. As far as EU influence at ICANN is concerned, as already noted, the EU has indicated its willingness to leave much of the work of Internet governance up to commercial organisations. While those organisations may have an interest in controlling 'illegal' and 'harmful' material, as removing such material makes the Internet a 'safer' place for e-commerce without impinging unduly on the commercial 'heavy-hitters', a strict privacy regime would have financial and operational implications for commercial organisations across the board. In many cases it would signally interfere with both existing, and planned, online marketing techniques. As such, non-EU commercial organisations, while prepared to pay lip service to the notion of on-line personal data privacy, are generally loathe to support any initiative which would place a legal, as opposed to a moral, obligation on them to affirmatively protect personal data privacy rights. Indeed, the evidence thus far from the US suggests that unless the public are prepared to actively protest and to follow up that protest with economic pressure, commercial self-interest would appear to be sadly lacking when it comes to effective enforcement of personal data privacy rules.

Electronic commerce

While the issues of content regulation and data privacy have been the subject of great debate, from a strictly commercial point of view, both issues are very much secondary to the need to facilitate the growth of electronic commerce within the EU.[111] There have been many estimates as to the potential growth of e-commerce over the next five to ten years but, while the estimates often vary wildly, the consensus is clearly that e-commerce is growing rapidly in economic importance and will continue to do so. The EU institutions have as yet taken little effective action to encourage the development of e-commerce by European companies, and already North American companies fill many of the key e-commerce niches.[112] The size of the US market, combined with its legal, economic and commercial homogeneity, has provided US e-commerce startup companies with ideal conditions for growth. By contrast, despite the development of the Single Market rules and the Single Currency, the EU remains a fragmented market, due

---

[110] See http://www.wto.org/.

[111] See, further, Dickie, J., *Internet and Electronic Commerce Law in the European Union* (Hart Publishing, Oxford, 1999) and chap. 15.

[112] Take, for example, book sales where the Internet market place is dominated by Amazon.com and its subsidiaries (US), with competition from Barnes and Noble (US) and Borders (US).

to differences between Member States' legal and economic systems, notably in the areas of commercial law, contract law, consumer protection law and taxation. This means that, while EU e-commerce companies have often been successful in their particular Member State, they have met with significant legal obstacles to European-wide operation, which hinder their speed of growth and development. This was noted by the Commission in a 1997 Communication entitled 'A European Initiative in Electronic Commerce',[113] which stated that, among other things, a favourable EU regulatory framework would be essential if such companies were to be able to compete in the global arena. It suggested that such a legal framework should take account of the following precepts: no regulation for regulation's sake; any regulation must be based on all Single Market freedoms; any regulation must take account of business realities; any regulation must meet general interest objectives effectively and efficiently.[114] Several key areas were pinpointed as likely to require EU action to ensure uniformity between the Member States, including: differing rules concerning the establishment of service providers across frontiers, including professional requirements, prudential and supervisory systems, and notification or licensing requirements; differing national laws relating to conflicts of law, such as location of establishment, competent jurisdiction and applicable law; divergent national regulations covering promotion and provision of electronic commerce activities including commercial communications such as advertising, direct marketing, self-promotions, sponsorship and public relations; restrictive Member State rules on the marketing of particular financial services, including financial services provided electronically; Member State laws relating to the formation and the performance of contracts inappropriate for an electronic commerce environment; Member State laws relating to book-keeping, accounting and auditing inappropriate for an electronic commerce environment; a lack of compatible, user-friendly, efficient and secure electronic payment systems; divergent national laws restricting the use, exportation, importation and offering of encryption technologies and products; and the need to develop new legal protections for intellectual property rights and conditional access services.

As with the earlier Bangemann Report, the Commission's ability to identify the relevant issues at an early stage has failed to translate into early and effective EU action. Over two years later, concrete legislative action has only just begun to occur, although the EU institutions have succeeded in producing a number of proposed legislative measures designed to smooth

---

[113] Communication to the European Parliament, the Council, the Economic and Social Committee and the Committee of the Regions (COM(97)157), ftp://ftp.cordis.lu/pub/esprit/docs/ecomcom.pdf:

> The Netherlands is now one of the most developed electronic commerce markets in the world, with high PC penetration (38% of households), high use of Internet (22% of PC users have access to Internet, against 16% in the US, and 12% in Germany), and high use of electronic commerce (33% of Internet users use it to buy online, against 22% in the US) [at 6].

[114] Ibid. at 14–15.

the way for the development of e-commerce within Europe, the most recent of which specifically addresses those key legal issues affecting e-commerce in the EU. The proposal for a European Parliament and Council Directive on certain legal aspects of electronic commerce in the internal market aims to deal with the majority of the issues raised by the Communication in one legal instrument.[115] It addresses:

- the establishment of providers of information society services – defining place of establishment, prohibiting special national authorisation rules for information society services, and requiring providers to make available certain information about themselves and their activities;
- commercial communications – defining what a commercial communication is, requiring that commercial communications are recognisable as such, that the parties on whose behalf they are made are clearly identifiable, and that unsolicited commercial communications are clearly labelled;
- contracts – Member States are required to adjust their national laws to ensure that electronic contracting is not hampered, the point at which a contract will be deemed to have been concluded is specified for certain cases;
- liability of intermediaries – online service providers who act as mere conduits are to be exempted from liability, and are granted other exemptions for other intermediary activities;
- implementation – Codes of Conduct are to be developed at a Community level, and administrative cooperation is to be fostered between Member States, provision is made for the facilitation of cross-border alternative dispute resolution systems.

This proposed Directive has not been without its critics. A number of concerns have been raised, including the lack of clarity of a number of the provisions, the scope for ambiguity in its definitions, such as 'commercial communication' and 'offer', and the feeling that the suggested 'opt-out' clause for unsolicited commercial communications should be instead an 'opt-in' clause.[116] The European Parliament was at pains to ensure that cryptographic tools would not be subjected to Member State restriction.[117] However, heavy lobbying has also led the European Parliament to include a number of amendments which do not, on their face, improve the efficacy of the proposed Directive, but do address the concerns of

[115] COM(99) 427 final,
http://www.ispo.cec.be/ecommerce/legal/documents/com1999-427/com427en.pdf.

[116] Opinion of the Economic and Social Committee on the 'Proposal for a European Parliament and Council Directive on certain legal aspects of electronic commerce in the internal market', OJ 1999 C169/36, 1999,
http://www.ispo.cec.be/ecommerce/oj/1999/1999C169/1999C169_14_en.pdf.

[117] Report (A4-0248/99) on the proposal for a European Parliament and Council Directive on certain legal aspects of electronic commerce in the internal market; the European Parliament amended the directive in the first reading on 6 May 1999:
http://www.ispo.cec.be/ecommerce/epreports/EP229_868_en.pdf.

the intellectual property and pro-censorship lobbies.[118] Another potential area of institutional dispute may arise from the European Parliament's proposed amendment to permit Member States to adopt public policy measures designed to 'achieve social, cultural and democratic goals taking into account their linguistic diversity, national and regional specificities as well as their cultural heritage'.[119] It is difficult to see how this increases the effectiveness of the Directive, indeed it could, for example, be construed by some Member States as an invitation to impose certain national linguistic requirements on e-commerce sites based in their jurisdiction. A common position was reached on the Directive in Council on 28 February 2000.[120]

The E-commerce Directive is linked with three other initiatives: a Directive on a common framework for electronic signatures;[121] a Directive on Copyright and Related Rights in the Information Society;[122] a proposal that within the EU no new taxes be imposed on electronic commerce, that 'bit taxes' be avoided, and that e-commerce be kept tariff-free at the international level.[123]

The first proposal is grounded primarily in the pragmatic realisation that without a framework for the European-wide acceptance of electronic signatures, e-commerce would be unduly shackled. The latter two proposals largely mirror legislative moves in the US.[124] For differing reasons, mostly relating to the changes required of Member States' existing laws, all three are controversial within the EU. The Electronic Signatures Directive that was adopted in December 1999[125] provides that electronic signatures cannot be legally discriminated against simply because they are in electronic form. If specific requirements are met electronic signatures will be as legally valid as hand-written signatures. Secondly, the Directive specifies that all products and services related to electronic signatures can circulate freely

---

[118] Ibid. See in particular pp.6–7, 11.

[119] Ibid. at p.13.

[120] See Communication from the Commission to the European Parliament pursuant to the second subparagraph of Article 251 (2) of the EC-Treaty concerning the Council common position on the proposal for a Directive on certain legal aspects of Information Society services, in particular electronic commerce, in the Internal Market (SEC(2000) 386 final 1998/0325 (COD)) at http://www.ispo.cec.be/ecommerce/legal/documents/2000_386/sec_2000_0386_f_en_acte.pdf.

[121] Directive 1999/93/EC of 13 December 1999 on a Community framework for electronic signatures, OJ 2000 L13/12 at http://europa.eu.int/comm/internal_market/en/media/sign/Dir99-93-ecEN.pdf. See, further, Angel, J., 'Why use Digital Signatures for Electronic Commerce?' (1999) (2) *Journal of Information, Law and Technology*, http://www.law.warwick.ac.uk/jilt/99-2/angel.html.

[122] COM(97) 628 final, 10/12/97.

[123] Communication by the Commission to the Council of Ministers, the European Parliament and to the Economic and Social Committee, E-Commerce and Indirect Taxation, COM(98) 374 final; 17/6/98.

[124] The 'No Electronic Theft' Act 1997 (Pub.L. No. 105–147), Digital Millennium Copyright Act 1998 (17 U.S.C. s.1201), and Internet Tax Freedom Act 1998 (Pub.L. No. 105–27).

[125] Op. cit. at n.121.

and will only be subject to the legislation and control by the country of origin. Member States cannot make the provision of services related to electronic signatures subject to mandatory licensing. Next, according to the Directive, there will be minimum liability rules for service providers. There must also be legal recognition of electronic signatures irrespective of the technology used, and there will be mechanisms for co-operation with third countries on the basis of mutual recognition of certificates and on bilateral and multilateral agreements.

The proposed Directive on Copyright and Related Rights in the Information Society addresses the thorny issue of intellectual property in the digital medium. Liability for copyright infringement has been specifically addressed by a number of jurisdictions, not just because of the difficulties that it poses for Internet intermediaries, such as Internet Service Providers (ISPs) but also because of sustained pressure from major rights-holders who are concerned to ensure that their interests are not undermined by digital copying. Much of that legislation reflects the tensions between those two groupings who, while not exactly opposed to each other's point of view, have each been wary to ensure that any concession made to the other does not potentially damage their own interests. The resulting legislation thus tends to display two main threads: ISPs and other Internet intermediaries are granted a carefully crafted limited immunity from liability for copyright infringement; and rights-holders are granted significantly greater powers over digital copying of their works, often at the expense of the traditional economic balance maintained between rights-holders and society. In this respect, the proposed Directive bears a number of striking similarities to the US Digital Millennium Copyright Act 1998 which is already courting controversy in particular with regard to the use of its provisions relating to copyright circumvention mechanisms.

The taxation issue remains a delicate subject. The power of determining the scope and level of taxation is an area over which most Member State governments, not unnaturally, are unwilling to relinquish significant control. The suggestion that the EU might require the restriction, or even the removal, of their ability to tax e-commerce, when it appears that, as the sector develops, it will attract increasing revenues from existing taxed sectors, is unlikely to appeal in the longer term.

Overall, although the EU institutions have been slow to develop a coherent e-commerce legislative framework, so slow, in fact, that some Member States have already begun their own legislative program,[126] it is clear that the process is gathering momentum. The key problem has been resolving conflicts grounded in the significant disparities between the Member States' commercial law, contract law, consumer protection law and taxation policies. However, it is becoming apparent to even the most intransigent Member State that failure to agree at least a basic harmonised e-commerce

---

[126] See the UK's Electronic Communications Act 2000.

agenda in the near future will leave EU businesses unable to compete effectively in the rapidly developing global marketplace for e-commerce services.

Just as the EU has struggled to come to terms with the new e-commerce paradigm, the legal situation in the US, while often appearing to the casual observer relatively settled and uncontroversial, remains equally uncertain in the longer term. The states are increasingly fractious about the extent of their ability to exert control over matters as diverse as sales taxes, liquor laws, gambling laws and junk e-mail in the e-commerce arena. Thus far the federal government's stated aim of ensuring that federal and state legislators refrain from engaging in legislative activity that might harm the development of e-commerce has largely been successful. However, cracks are increasingly beginning to show in the resolve of state legislators, who foresee a potentially precipitous decline in their sales tax revenues, and a loss of control over online activities on which they have maintained tight regulation in the traditional commercial environment. It remains entirely possible that the US e-commerce environment may yet, as a result of unco-ordinated state legislative activity, become a rather less business-friendly place. As such, the delay between policy formulation and legislative activity by the EU institutions may not constitute a fatal hindrance to EU e-commerce operations. If a cohesive and coherent set of e-commerce laws can be adopted and then rapidly implemented by the Member States, then the early advantage enjoyed by US businesses will not necessarily prove decisive.

However, it is equally important that in the haste to provide a legislative framework for e-commerce, to meet the requirements of commercial entities, the wider public interest is not overlooked. If the EU's slow progress towards an e-commerce framework means that such wider public interest issues as the maintenance of adequate consumer protection, and the balance between rights-holders and the public in the intellectual property sphere, are to be given more measured consideration, then again, in the longer term, the delay may in fact prove beneficial for the European public.

Conclusion

Whenever one considers aspects of European Union policy, it is important to remember that, despite the continual widening of the Union's competencies since the Treaty of Rome, its primary purpose has always remained the economic development of its internal market. As such, the governance of the Internet by the EU, as opposed to its constituent Member States, is concerned with social issues only where they have the capacity to distort that internal market or to affect the competitiveness of Union producers on international markets. This is reflected in the concerns over the Internet infrastructure, the facilitation of electronic commerce through the reform of national commercial laws, and the need to ensure the international application of personal data privacy laws. Control of illegal and harmful content is less important, not least because of the difficulty in exercising effective control where no consensus exists between the Member States on content which should be controlled or banned. This policy area can, and should, be safely devolved to the Member States, where there seems to be broad agreement that the imposition of new national laws banning certain types of content would serve little useful purpose.

Given the importance of the remaining three areas, has the EU been successful in establishing a coherent policy and clear objectives for each? With regard to the management of Internet infrastructure, the EU appeared to have wrested some significant concessions from the US during the transfer of the DNS management from public to private control. However, it is questionable whether in the long term the EU has obtained any truly effective degree of control or influence on the new management bodies. These remain heavily influenced by commercial interests outside the EU and are, for the moment at least, effectively governed by US law. It would seem unrealistic to suppose that US policymakers will be able to resist using this domination as leverage in future international negotiations over the application of legal norms to the Internet. With the acceptance of ICANN as the organisation to manage the DNS, the opportunity to obtain truly international governance of the Internet infrastructure may thus have passed for good.

Additionally, the Commission's apparent decision to encourage corporate interests to dictate the Internet governance agenda at ICANN leaves the opinions and needs of the general public woefully underrepresented. Lessig has argued that we have perhaps become too fixated on the notion that traditional governments have no role to play in the Internet and that handing control to the private sector is the only way forward.[127] He queries why we should effectively transfer Internet governance from traditional government, which is at least nominally of the people, to private government which has no constitutional responsibilities and is not bound by checks and balances which are there to protect the individual from the might of government. Traditional government, including that of the EU, may be flawed, but there are principles of governance which still have to be observed, including equality, proportionality and transparency. Governance by private corporation guarantees none of these values. In this respect at least, the EU institutions' attitude towards Internet governance would seem to have failed to strike an equitable balance between the promotion of the commercial aspects of EU policy and the protection of the wider civic interests of EU citizens.

Similarly, the fate of the EU's desired model for the protection of personal data privacy currently hangs in the balance. Failure to reach an acceptable permanent settlement with the US on trans-border data flows could well spell the end for the type of highly structured regulatory system provided for in the Data Protection Directive. While a preliminary agreement has now been reached, it remains doubtful as to whether it will meet the long-term requirements of the EU. The EU's position has not been made any

---

[127] See, further, Lessig, L., *Code and Other Laws of Cyberspace* (Basic Books, New York, 1999).

the easier by the failure of the majority of the Member States to fully implement the Directive within the required timeframe.

It is with the initiatives in the area of electronic commerce that the EU appears to have the greatest chance of achieving a useful and lasting impact upon the governance of the Internet. Despite the current flaws in the draft legislation noted above, the EU has at least formulated a clear policy agenda. If that agenda can be translated to effective legislative action within the Member States, e-commerce operations in the EU will be greatly facilitated. Thus, the fact that the EU has clearly fallen behind the US in terms of legislative activity and e-commerce development need not yet become a cause for concern for, as e-commerce becomes a greater part of national economies, the scope for disagreement on issues such as taxation and content control between the 50 states of the US also grows, without there being a clear mechanism for resolving them. The EU's greatest advantage lies in its potential ability to create a coherent and cohesive internal economic market within which e-commerce enterprises can flourish, via the EU Treaty and its institutions. The success of European telecommunications companies in the international marketplace may well thus be a precursor for a similar success for the European e-businesses of the future.

CHAPTER 4

Jurisdiction and choice of law in a borderless electronic environment

Alan Reed

Introduction

The focus of this chapter will be to evaluate conflict of laws issues in the area of tortious liability that relate to use of the Internet. It is axiomatic that literature, radio and television programmes can now be published, heard and viewed throughout the modern world. These instantaneous and international forms of communication consequentially impart great importance to rules protecting an individual's interest in his or her reputation.[1] This is of particular significance to publications made via the Internet.[2] The Internet comprises a worldwide web, so issues involving multistate defamation will often arise, and it may not be clear which law applies. This chapter analyses when an English court will be able to accept jurisdiction in a case in which an individual's reputation is defamed over the Internet, and also considers what law the English court will apply to determine the action. Similar jurisdiction principles, it will be shown, also apply to other intangible torts facilitated by use of the Internet, encompassing negligent misstatement, passing off, infringement of intellectual property rights, inducement of breach of contract and other economic torts.[3]

The first matter that a conflicts lawyer needs to evaluate when considering the Internet is whether it is a novel form of communication or no more than the natural extension of existing forms of communication. It is suggested that the latter perspective reflects the true position. In terms of relevant

---

[1] See, for example, *Jenner v Sun Oil Co Ltd* [1952] 2 D.L.R. 526 (Ont. HC). This Canadian authority vividly illustrates the significance of international defamation jurisdiction. The plaintiff, who resided and carried on business in Ontario, brought an action against several US defendants for damages for defamatory statements concerning him made during radio broadcasts by the defendants on the National Broadcasting Co. radio network. The network is located in the state of New York, but transmitted the broadcasts into Ontario. It was held that the Ontario Court did have jurisdiction as the publication of the defamatory statement to the third party was the very essence of actionable defamation.

[2] See, generally, Castel, J., 'Multistate Defamation: Should the Place of Publication Rule be Abandoned for Jurisdiction and Choice of Law Purposes' (1990) 28 *Osgoode Hall LJ* 153.

[3] See, generally, Reed, A., 'Multistate Defamation Jurisdiction: A Comparative Analysis of Prevailing Jurisprudence in the United States and the European Union' (1996) 18 *Communications and the Law* 29.

issues that arise, the Internet ought to be considered no differently from extant principles that have developed for newspapers or television; it is essentially old wine in new bottles. Thus, it has been stated that, 'information placed by a website provider for access over the Internet is sent by that person to others (potentially millions of others, simultaneously in many different jurisdictions) just as a fax or letter or TV transmission is sent by its author, albeit that the information passively awaits access being made to it by web users'.[4] However, the Internet does provide unique factual circumstances in which multistate defamation may be committed in that it has the ability of making information available simultaneously in every jurisdiction in the world.

There are two distinct forms of jurisdictional rules that apply in any case to determine whether an English court can hear an action.[5] First, there are rules contained within the Brussels Convention,[6] which apply between Contracting European states, and which were incorporated into English law by the Civil Jurisdiction and Judgments Act 1982.[7] Secondly, there are pre-existing English common law rules that govern defendants domiciled in non-contracting European states. Personal jurisdiction applies with a defendant amenable to our jurisdiction if the person is present here[8] or submits to the jurisdiction,[9] or if the dispute falls under one or more heads of Order 11, rule 1(1) of the Rules of the Supreme Court.[10]

It is the jurisdictional principles laid down by the Brussels Convention that have been of recent concern. The concentration in this chapter will be on the highly significant Court of Justice decision in *Shevill v Press Alliance SA*[11]on multistate defamation and its ramifications for Internet users. Brief comparisons are drawn, where appropriate, with the corresponding jurisprudence of the Supreme Court of the United States. In evaluating the *Shevill* case, it is essential to bear in mind the primary ground of jurisdiction ascription. The basic rule, known as *actor sequitur forum rei* (the law leans in favour of the defendant), is provided by Article 2 of the Convention:

---

[4] Dutson, S., 'The Internet, the conflict of laws, international litigation and intellectual property' [1997] *Journal of Business Law* 495, at p.496.

[5] See, generally, Mayss, A. and Reed, A., *European Business Litigation* (Dartmouth Press, Aldershot, 1998) at pp.7–11.

[6] The Brussels Convention on Jurisdiction and the Enforcement of Judgments in Civil and Commercial Matters entered into force for the six original Member States on 1 February 1973. Subsequently, a Protocol on the interpretation of the Convention by the European Court of Justice was signed at Luxembourg on 3 June 1971. The Luxembourg Protocol is largely based on the provision of art. 177 of the Treaty of Rome. It entered into force for the six original Member States on 1 September 1975. There have been four Accession Conventions concluded on the accession of Denmark, Republic of Ireland, United Kingdom, Greece, Portugal and Spain. The Lugano Convention 1988, containing provisions parallel to those in the Brussels Convention, applies between EC and EFTA Member States.

[7] This entered into force on 1 January 1987.

[8] See, for example, *Maharanee of Baroda v Wildenstein* [1972] 2 QB 283.

[9] RSC Order 10.

[10] Mayss, A. and Reed, A., op. cit., at p.9.

[11] [1995] 2 WLR 499; [1995] ECR 415.

'Subject to the provisions of the Convention, persons domiciled in a Contracting State shall, whatever their nationality, be sued in the courts of that State.' In sporting parlance, the claimant must play away from home.[12] However, Section 2 of the Convention provides for 'special jurisdiction' under which the claimant is given a choice of other fora in the circumstances defined. The relevant provision here for tortious matters is Article 5(3): 'A person domiciled in a Contracting State may, in another Contracting State, be sued ... in matters relating to tort, delict or quasi-delict, in the courts for the place where the harmful event occurred.'[13] The application of these twin central provisions to multistate defamation were exemplified by the court in *Shevill*.[14]

Jurisdiction of the English courts

The facts in *Shevill*

The facts in *Shevill*[15] present an intriguing picture. The first plaintiff, Fiona Shevill, domiciled in England with her main residence in Yorkshire, was employed at a bureau de change operated by the fourth plaintiff, Chequepoint SARL, which was owned by the third plaintiff, Ixora Trading Inc., of which the second plaintiff, Chequepoint International, was the holding company. Chequepoint is a French enterprise operating a number of bureaux de change in France and elsewhere in Europe. The second, third and fourth plaintiffs are French-registered companies. The defendants publish the newspaper, *France Soir*, a daily evening newspaper which has a large circulation in France, in excess of 200,000 copies daily, and a smaller circulation of approximately 15,500 copies outside France. In relation to this latter circulation only 230 copies are said to have been sold in England and Wales, notably only five in Yorkshire where the first plaintiff resided.

---

[12] The basis for this presumption has been asserted by Professor Stone:
  [T]he rationale for this preference for defendants over plaintiffs, a preference which has deep historical roots, goes beyond mere convenience in the conduct of litigation. Rather, it is linked with such general rules as that which places on the plaintiff of proving his claim, and reflects a primordial legal assumption that complaints are presumptively unjustified, and that it is better, where the truth cannot be ascertained with reasonable certainty, that the courts should not intervene, that failure to rectify injustice is more tolerable than positive action imposing it. In the present context, this gives rise to a general rule that the plaintiff must establish his case to the satisfaction of the court in whose goodwill towards him the defendant would presumably have most confidence. (Stone, P., *The Conflict of Laws* (Longman, London, 1995) at p.129)

[13] Essentially the effect of art. 5(3) of the Brussels Convention 1968 is to confer jurisdiction upon the English courts, predicated on a tort or a non-contractual liability, if the defendant is domiciled in another Contracting State, or in another part of the United Kingdom, and the 'harmful event' is determined as transpiring in England; see, for example, *Kalfelis v Schroder, Munchmeyer, Hengst & Co.* [1988] ECR 5565 and *Source Ltd v T.U.V. Rheinland Holding A.G.* [1997] 3 WLR 365.

[14] See, generally, Reed, A. and Kennedy, T.P., 'International Torts and *Shevill*: The Ghost of Forum Shopping Yet To Come' [1996] *Lloyd's Maritime and Commercial Law Quarterly* 108.

[15] [1992] 2 WLR 1 at p.6.

The plaintiffs claimed damages for harm caused by the publication of a defamatory newspaper article. The publication of which complaint was made was published in *France Soir* on 27 September 1989. It referred to an alleged investigation by French police into the laundering of money obtained from the sale of drugs by, in particular, the Paris bureau de change in which the first plaintiff was temporarily employed for three months in the summer of 1989, and to whom reference by name was made in the article. In November 1989 the defendants published a retraction and apology in respect of Fiona Shevill and Chequepoint. The action, subsequent to amendments to the statement of claim, related solely to publication in England and Wales, not France. The defendants sought to strike out the claim as fundamentally there was no jurisdiction since no harmful event had occurred in England.

Before the Court of Appeal it was contended for the defendant that, *inter alia*, none of the plaintiffs had suffered any actual damage so as to constitute a harmful event within the jurisdiction. There was no evidence that there was anyone who could possibly have been affected who knew Fiona Shevill or who had access to any copies of the offending newspaper. These submissions were based upon the necessity of demonstrating for the purpose of Article 5(3) of the Convention that damage had been actually suffered, an approach which was inconsistent with the English law, which assumed that damage had been suffered once the libel had been established. The idiosyncratic nature of current English defamation law demands comment. A libel consists of a defamatory statement or representation in permanent form; defamation consists of the publication of material which reflects on a person's reputation so as to lower the plaintiff in the estimation of right-thinking members of society generally, or which would tend to cause her to be shunned or avoided.[16] A distinction should be drawn between libel which is actionable *per se*, i.e., without proof of special damage (loss of money or of some temporal or material advantage estimable in money) and slander where special damage must be proved except in a limited number of cases.[17] It was the acknowledgement by the Court of Appeal of the peculiar nature of English libel law, contrary to the defendant's submission, which was vital to its actual decision. Purchas LJ, stated:[18]

> The only idiosyncratic aspect arising from the law of England and Wales is the assumption of damage. I do not recognise this as a jurisdictional point. Whether or not there may be detected a publishee in England who both knew the plaintiff and read and understood the French evening newspaper may well arise in the course of the action and be relevant to the assessment of damages. In my judgment, however, to restrict the exercise of jurisdiction to cases where the existence of such a person is established would not be correct.

---

[16] See, for example, *Sim v Stretch* (1936) 52 TLR 669, at 671.
[17] See Rogers, W.V.H., *Winfield and Jolowicz on Tort* (Sweet & Maxwell, London, 1996) at pp.318–20.
[18] [1992] 2 WLR 1, at p.13.

It was held by the Court of Appeal that, since the action was restricted to publication of the defamatory article in England and Wales, the Court could assume jurisdiction under Article 5(3) of the Convention once it was shown that there was an arguable case on which each plaintiff could rely to establish a publication carrying with it the presumption of damage.[19] The defendant appealed to the House of Lords, arguing that the French courts had jurisdiction in the dispute under Article 2, and that the English courts did not have jurisdiction under Article 5(3) as the place where the harmful event occurred was France and no harmful event had taken place in England. The House of Lords, considering that the proceedings raised questions of interpretation of the Convention, decided to stay the proceedings pending a preliminary ruling[20] by the European Court of Justice.

The Court of Justice

In essence, as identified by the Court of Justice, the referral raised two vital matters of interpretation.[21] First, interpretative guidance was needed on 'the place where the harmful event occurred' in Article 5(3), with a view to establishing which court(s) had jurisdiction to hear an action for damages for harm caused to the victim following distribution of a defamatory article in several contracting states. Secondly, it had to be decided whether, in determining if it had jurisdiction as court of the place where the damage occurred pursuant to Article 5(3), the national court was required to follow specific rules different from those laid down by its national law in relation to the criteria for assessing whether the event in question was harmful and whether specific rules were needed in relation to the evidence required of the existence and extent of the harm alleged by the victim of the defamation. This second matter is considered subsequently in this chapter.

The place where the harmful event occurred

The first issue addressed by the court concentrates on the concept of 'the place where the harmful event occurred'. As previously adumbrated, Article 5(3) of the Convention provides special jurisdiction, by way of derogation from the general principle in the first paragraph of Article 2 of the Convention that the courts of the Contracting State of the defendant's domicile have jurisdiction.

The Court of Justice examined in some detail their important earlier decisions of *Bier*[22] and *Dumez*[23] as interpretative aids to establish the place

---

[19] Note that Purchas LJ disposed of the claim of the second plaintiff on the ground that, having regard to its relationship with the third plaintiff, the latter would be accountable to the former for any damages recovered.

[20] Pursuant to art. 3 of the Luxembourg Protocol of 3 June 1971 which empowers the Court of Justice to give preliminary rulings on interpretation at the request of courts of Contracting States.

[21] [1995] ECR 415.

[22] *Handelskwekerij GJ. Bier BV v Mines de Potasse d'Alsace S.A.* [1976] ECR 1735.

[23] *Dumez France and Tracoba v Hessische Landesbank (Helaba) and Others* [1990] ECR 490.

of the harmful event in the international libel context. The *Bier* judgment concerned cross-border pollution, responsibility for which lay with an undertaking established in France, causing harm to a horticultural undertaking domiciled in the Netherlands. The defendant, who was engaged in mining activities in France, allegedly discharged such large quantities of residuary salts into the Rhine that the increased salt content of the water caused damage to the plaintiff's seed-beds. When brought before a Dutch court the French defendant argued that it was not competent to hear the dispute. The Hague Court of Appeal referred the matter to the Court of Justice asking whether 'the place where the harmful event occurred' was to be construed as meaning the place where the damage occurred or where the event which caused the damage took place. The Court held that the special jurisdictional grounds in Article 5 were introduced due to the existence 'in certain clearly defined situations, of a particularly close connecting factor between a dispute and the court which may be called upon to hear it, with a view to the efficacious conduct of the proceedings'.[24] The Court held that there was a significant connection in relation to both the place of the causal event and the place of injury, as each could be helpful in relation to the necessary evidence and the conduct of the proceedings. The Court held, therefore, that the place where the harmful event occurred included 'both the place where the damage occurred and the place of the event giving rise to it'.[25] The plaintiff has the option of suing the defendant in either jurisdiction.

The harm in *Bier* was material property damage, whereas in *Shevill* at issue was non-pecuniary damage to reputation *per se*. Nevertheless, the Court of Justice has now, by parity of reasoning, applied a similar analysis to Article 5(3) irrespective of the type of damage involved. It was expressly stated in *Shevill* that identical principles apply, and the place of the event giving rise to the damage no less than the place where the damage occurred could constitute a significant connecting factor from the point of view of jurisdiction.[26] Each of them, depending on the circumstances, could be particularly helpful in relation to the evidence and the conduct of the proceedings. The observations made in *Bier vis-à-vis* physical or pecuniary loss or damage have now been expressly applied to a case involving injury to reputation and the good name of both natural and legal persons due to a defamatory publication. In a libel scenario where a newspaper article is distributed in several Contracting States, then, according to the Court of

---

[24] [1976] ECR 1735, at p.1746 (para. 11).

[25] Ibid., at p.1748. Note that the rationale of *Bier* is not confined to nuisance claims but will, by parity of reasoning, apply to torts involving physical injury to person or property, incorporating personal injury claims brought against manufacturers of defective goods. In *Hewden Stuart v Gottwald* (unreported, 13 May 1992) the English Court of Appeal applied similar reasoning to uphold jurisdiction of the English courts under art. 5(3) over a German company which had manufactured within Germany a redesigned crane with new parts, and had supplied them ex-works there to an English company for re-assembly. The crane had later collapsed whilst being used in England. See also *Grehan v Medical Inc.* [1988] ECC 6.

[26] Loc. cit. at p.539.

Justice, the place of the event giving rise to the damage (causal event), can only be where the miscreant publisher is established, that is the place where the harmful event originated and from which the libel was used and put into circulation. The court of the place where the publisher is established has jurisdiction to hear the whole action for all damage caused by the unlawful event. That jurisdiction will, as the Court of Justice noted, generally coincide in any events with the Article 2 jurisdiction based on the defendant's domicile.[27] In the context of defamatory material circulated over the Internet, the synergistic effect of the *Shevill* jurisdiction is to ascribe jurisdiction to the territory where the defendant web server is domiciled.[28] This jurisdiction applies to the totality of harmful publications of libellous material that is published in each and every Contracting State.[29]

By identical reasoning to *Bier*, co-existent jurisdiction, at the option of the plaintiff, was also held to exist in *Shevill* in the place where the damage occurred, otherwise Article 5(3) of the Convention would be rendered superfluous. Where does the damage occur in the case of an international libel, published for example, throughout each individual member state and originating from an English website? The Court of Justice has answered this question by stating that the damage caused by a defamatory publication occurs in the places 'in which the publication (via the Internet) was distributed and in which the victim claims to have injury to her reputation'.[30] A multiplicity of different fora will have jurisdiction over the harmful events within their own particular territory. The Contracting States in which the publication was distributed and in which the victim claims to have suffered injury to his reputation have jurisdiction to rule on the injury caused in that state to the victim's reputation. The underlying rationale for such a conclusion was founded by the court on the sound administration of justice in that the state in which the defamatory publication was distributed and in which the victim claims to have suffered injury to his reputation is best suited to assess and determine the corresponding damage.

Similar reasoning was adopted in *Dumez*[31] where the Court again took the opportunity to stress that the jurisdictional rule contained in Article

---

[27] Ibid., at p.540.
[28] This, of course, may also be the jurisdiction where the web provider is domiciled. The question of whether a person is domiciled in the UK, for the purposes of the Brussels Convention, is to be determined in accordance with s.41 of the Civil Jurisdiction and Judgments Act 1982. He is so domiciled if and only if: (a) he is resident in the UK; and (b) the nature and circumstances of his residence indicate that he has a substantial connection with the UK. The domicile of companies in the UK is governed by s.42 of the same Act; see further Mayss, A. and Reed, A., op. cit., at pp.45–51.
[29] This might result in an economic and efficient resolution of a dispute of an international character facilitated by use of the Internet, and may avoid inconsistent results. On the other hand there are undoubtedly anomalies which can result from the court applying its own adjectival rules, especially of procedure and remedy, in relation to a cause of action arising under a different state's law; see below pp.90–91.
[30] [1995] 2 WLR 499, at pp.540–1.
[31] [1990] ECR 49.

5(3) supports the need for a close connecting factor between the dispute and the court hearing the case. In *Dumez*, the Court of Justice had to determine whether the French parent of a German subsidiary company, which had indirectly suffered loss as a result of the alleged harmful act in Germany (cancelling certain bank loans), could bring proceedings in France. It was held that they could not. The general philosophy underlying the Convention denied jurisdiction in the court of the place where the ricochet victim suffers damage.[32] The crucial distinction was between the place where the damage actually occurred (Germany) as opposed to where it was suffered (France). The Court of Justice said that the damage which located jurisdiction for the purposes of Article 5(3):[33]

> [C]an be understood only as indicating the place where the event giving rise to the damage, and entailing tortious, delictual or quasi-delictual liability directly produced its harmful effects upon the person who is the immediate victim of that harmful event.

The underlying thread which runs through the Court of Justice's decisions on Article 5(3) is the establishment of a close connecting factor between a dispute and the court which should hear the matter on the basis of the sound administration of justice. The outcome of the first limb of the decision in *Shevill* is to create a multiplicity of competent fora having jurisdiction over international libels committed via the Internet. By parity of reasoning, it must also ascribe jurisdiction within Member States to other intangible economic torts facilitated by use of the Internet such as negligent misstatement,[34] inducement of breach of contract[35] and passing off, which are discussed further below. The decision in *Shevill* raises a number of interesting issues. The outcome is undeniably correct, but it imposes undesirable consequences on litigants which will now be highlighted.[36]

The impact of the Shevill decision

(i) Article 5(3) and the Internet: the tort of passing off and the issue in Mecklermedia Corporation v D C Congress GmbH

The impact of the *Shevill* decision on multistate jurisdiction ascription has recently been exemplified by the decision in *Mecklermedia Corp. and Another v D C Congress GmbH*.[37] The plaintiffs, a US company, and its

---

[32] Ibid., at p.71.
[33] Ibid. See, generally, Reed, A., 'To Chill a Mocking Word: Applicable Choice of Law and Jurisdiction Principles over Multistate Defamation under English and Australian Jurisprudence' (1997) 5 *Tort Law Review* 33.
[34] See, for example, *Domicrest Ltd v Swiss Bank Corporation* [1998] 3 All ER 577; see below, p.98.
[35] See, for example, *Marinari v Lloyds Bank Plc* [1996] 2 WLR 159; see below, pp.97–98; and in relation to intellectual property rights, see *Peace v Ove Arup Partnership* [1999] 1 All ER 769.
[36] See, generally, Hartley, T., 'Art. 5(3): Place where the "Harmful Event Occurs"' (1996) 21 *European Law Review* 164; Briggs, A., 'The Uncertainty of Special Jurisdiction' (1996) *Lloyd's Maritime and Commercial Law Quarterly* 27.
[37] [1998] 1 All ER 148.

English subsidiary brought proceedings against a German corporation, claiming that it was committing the tort of passing off. In particular, the plaintiffs alleged that they had established goodwill in England in the words 'Internet World' via the business activities of the English subsidiary. They had organised three trade shows in this country under the name of Internet World. Mecklermedia had, since 1993, also published in the United States a magazine called *Internet World*. This was claimed to have some circulation within the United Kingdom, essentially of the 'spill-over' variety. In the autumn of 1996 an English version of the magazine was launched under the same name. It was published by VNU Business Publications but claimed association with the US magazine by saying:

> *Internet World* is already the most popular Internet magazine in the US. Now *Internet World* is to be published in the UK by the people who bring you *Personal Computer World*.

The first edition was given away free with *Personal Computer World*, and there was no dispute that that magazine has a substantial UK circulation. It was claimed that VNU published the English edition under licence from Mecklermedia and that it was specifically agreed by VNU that the goodwill in the name 'Internet World' should belong to Mecklermedia. Finally it was claimed that Mecklermedia owned two websites having the addresses http://www.internet-world.com and http://www.iworld.com. It was asserted that anyone visiting these sites would see prominent use of the name 'Internet World' and promotion of the plaintiffs' trade shows and magazines.[38] The defendants had organised their own trade shows in Germany and Austria using the very same epithet. A writ was served on the defendant corporation in Germany. Thereafter, the defendant applied for an order setting aside the writ on the ground that the English court did not have jurisdiction to hear and determine the claim made against it, relying on Arts 2 and 5(3) of the Convention.

The underlying thread which runs through the Court of Justice's decisions on Article 5(3) is the establishment of a close connecting factor between a dispute and the court which should hear the matter on the basis of sound administration of justice. Did such a close connecting factor exist in *Mecklermedia* given the plaintiffs' establishment of rights to 'Internet World'?

The defendant's application was dismissed. Where Article 5(3) of the Convention applied, the plaintiff was given an option to sue either in the forum of the defendant's domicile, or forum of the place where the harmful event occurred. For the purposes of the English tort of passing off, the harmful event was the harm done to the plaintiffs' goodwill in England and its effect on their reputation in England; that was a direct effect on the plaintiffs' claimed English property. Accordingly, although Article 2 would in theory permit an action in Germany in respect of the passing off in

---

[38] This claim was shadowy and reliance was not placed upon it.

England, it was clear that the place where the harmful event occurred was England and, as such, the case was within Article 5(3). The closest connection test ascribed jurisdiction to the English courts to rule on the harm caused within the territory. This outcome is significant as it will also govern parallel infringement of intellectual rights facilitated by the Internet, and governs the grant of injunctions as well as damages. It means that a plaintiff cannot simply forum shop around Europe for a Europe-wide injunction but can only seek such an injunction in the State of the source of the allegedly infringing goods or piratical activity. In *Mecklermedia* the defendant knew that the plaintiff used the name 'Internet World', and consequentially could not be surprised to be met with actions in places where confusion was considered likely.

(ii) Forum shopping

The decisions in *Shevill* and *Mecklermedia* appear to hold out the prospect of a multiplicity of fora open to the victim of a transnational libel or other intangible economic tort committed via the Internet. The damage to the plaintiff in *Shevill* must have been minimal, given the low number of newspapers circulated in the United Kingdom. It would have been ludicrous if the Court of Justice had allowed any of the national courts where damage occurred to adjudicate on the whole loss. International publication of material by publishers based throughout Western Europe is extremely commonplace. In a similar context widespread dissemination of material by web servers using the Internet is a continuing event. Artists involved in music, sport and acting, such as George Michael, David Beckham or Hugh Grant, have international reputations, and a contrary decision could have given such plaintiffs unduly wide choices of court in which to bring their whole defamation claim. It would have given rise to wholesale celebrity forum shopping and run the risk of irreconcilable judgments in different Contracting States. It must be incorrect that a very insubstantial defamatory publication in, say, Luxembourg would allow a plaintiff to sue there in respect of the whole totality of world Internet publications.[39] The efficacious conduct of proceedings demands simply the ability to sue in Luxembourg for the trifling publication within its territory.

(iii) The correct rejection of alternative jurisdictional approaches

In the course of *Shevill* a number of jurisdictional approaches was examined. The principles which the court laid down in *Bier* were relatively easy to apply in a case involving only two jurisdictions. The judgment, however, did not resolve the difficulty of multi-jurisdictional torts. In the case of a transnational libel a defendant could suffer damage to his reputation in each Contracting State. A strict application of *Bier* could lead to a multiplicity of actions. This spectre of celebrity forum shopping caused many to recoil

---

[39] Of course, if the dissemination arose in Luxembourg then, under *Shevill*, Luxembourg would have jurisdiction over all damage suffered in the European Union.

from a strict application and argue that *Bier* could not be applied to defamation. Some commentators felt that *Bier* did not preclude the eventual adoption of specific rules for particular torts, such as a rule that in defamation the place where the harmful event occurred would be that of publication to a third party.[40] No such rule was ever adopted. Another wrote of a defamatory statement written, broadcast or posted in one state, published in a second and causing damage to reputations in a third. He said that it is the defendant's act in the first state which should be held to be the harmful event.[41]

In *Shevill* the defendant argued that Article 5(3) gives special jurisdiction only to the single court which has the greatest connection with the cross-border tort. This would have been France, owing to the very small circulation of the newspaper in England. This most significant connection test has been subsequently supported by one commentator.[42] However, it was rejected by the Court of Justice which, as we have seen, held that an action could be brought either where the defamatory material was published or where it was distributed. The Court did not entertain the argument that one forum or the other should have exclusive jurisdiction on the basis of a more significant connection.

Another alternative considered was giving the courts of the plaintiff's domicile jurisdiction over the whole loss. It would have been contrary to the whole tenor of the Convention if the plaintiff had been allowed unilaterally always to sue in their peculiar domicile. It was stressed by Warner A.G. in *Ruffer*[43] that:

> It was never suggested . . . much less held by the Court, that the place where the harmful event occurred could be the place where the plaintiff company had its seat or the place where the amount of the damages to its business was quantified . . . to hold that the place where the plaintiff has its seat could be regarded as being 'the place where the harmful event occurred' . . . would be tantamount to holding that, under the Convention, a plaintiff in tort had the option of suing in the courts of his own domicile, which would be quite inconsistent with the scheme of Article 2 et seq. of the Convention.

It was similarly stressed by Darmon A.G. in *Shevill*[44] that to sanction the jurisdictional application of the plaintiff's forum would be equivalent to conferring jurisdiction on the *forum actoris*, an attribution to which, as the Court has pointed out on numerous occasions, the Convention is hostile. It was observed by the Court of Justice in its judgment in *Dumez*[45] that:

---

[40] Lasok, D. and Stone, P.A., *Conflict of Laws in the European Community* (Professional Books, Abingdon, 1987) at p.232.

[41] Kaye, P., *Civil Jurisdiction and Enforcement of Judgments* (Professional Books, Abingdon, 1987) at p.561.

[42] Carter, P., 'Jurisdiction in Defamation Cases' [1992] *British Yearbook of International Law* 519, at p.521.

[43] [1980] ECR 3807, at p.3836 (Opinion).

[44] [1995] 2 WLR 499, at p.519.

[45] [1990] ECR 49, at p.79. See also *Shearson Lehman Hutton v TVB Treuhandgesellschatt für Vermogensverwaltung und Beteiligungen mbH* [1993] ECR 39 at p.187.

. . . the hostility of the Convention towards the attribution of justice to the courts of the plaintiff's domicile was demonstrated by the fact that the second paragraph of Article 3 precluded the application of national provisions attributing jurisdiction to such courts for proceedings against defendants domiciled in the territory of a Contracting State.

In a case involving the dissemination of defamatory material over the Internet, the simple attribution of jurisdiction to the courts of the plaintiff's domicile does not accord with the sound administration of justice or efficacious conduct of proceedings. A hypothetical example presented by the UK Government in *Shevill*[46] is both apposite and pertinent. The scenario was raised of an actor who has chosen to become domiciled in England, where he is generally unknown, but who has a following in Italy. Suppose a scandalous story about him were to be published in an Italian newspaper or alternatively by e-mail correspondence, circulated only in Italy, but that the actor then attempted to bring proceedings for libel in the English courts. Were he to argue that the English courts had jurisdiction because the damage to his reputation had occurred in England, the argument would be incorrect. The damage to his reputation would have occurred in Italy, where the reputation existed and could be damaged, and not in England. No justification whatsoever exists for proceedings before the English courts; the sound administration of justice would be materially prejudiced to allow such jurisdiction.

It should be stressed that the judgment in *Shevill* does not impose an obligation on the plaintiff to sue in each separate Member State where damage occurred through defamatory statements over the Internet. Under Article 2, the plaintiff always retains the right to sue the defendant for the whole loss in the courts of the Member State where the defendant is domiciled. No doubt in the international libel situation there are extreme disadvantages in such an approach, as explained earlier; but, irrespective of the demerits, the primacy of Article 2 within the scheme of the Convention has been maintained in *Shevill*.[47]

(iv) Suitability of forum and plaintiff protection

The potential concurrent state jurisdiction arising from *Shevill* in accordance with Article 5(3) will achieve suitability of forum. The courts of the place where the damage arises over the Internet are best placed to assess the harm done to the victim's reputation and to determine the extent of the damage.[48] It avoids the inherent problems caused by a court in one Member State striving to assess the damage actually caused to the plaintiff by the communication of defamatory material in another Member State. It may otherwise by extremely difficult to ascertain or assess knowledge of the

---

[46] [1995] 2 WLR 499, at pp.519–29 where this hypothetical example was expressly approved by Darmon AG.

[47] See [1995] 2 WLR 499, at p.540 where this point was noted by the Court of Justice in its judgment.

[48] [1995] 2 WLR 499, at p.523. This argument was supported in the opinion of Darmon AG.

social conditions and values in another country. Additionally, it seems self-evident that claims relating to loss of reputation, rather than pecuniary loss, invoke a special requirement, as said in *Bier*, for 'a particularly close connecting factor between a dispute and the court which may be called upon to hear it'.[49] Clearly, if the whole claim is brought in the State of the defendant's domicile, such an evaluation will necessarily occur. It will be time-consuming, though, to obtain accurate knowledge of conditions prevailing in another state. Litigation can proceed expeditiously in the very state where damage occurred, witnesses are present, evidence can be easily assessed, and local knowledge applied forthwith.

If the court in *Shevill* had determined that the only state with competence to determine the issue was where the publisher had a place of business, where the material was edited and printed, then it would have been a catalyst to forum shopping by disreputable publishers. In the context of the Internet identical principles apply to the egregious website provider or web user. The unmeritorious publisher could edit and print material in one state with extremely limited defamation protection for plaintiffs, then distribute widely in other states with tighter plaintiff protection. If by Article 5(3) the plaintiffs could only sue in the first state, then their rights would be inequitably weakened, and the publisher would capriciously circumvent legitimate harmful consequences.

The arguments raised thus far all support the first limb of the decision in *Shevill* concentrating on 'place of the harmful event'. There is further support in that it surely accords with the legitimate expectations of all parties to the dispute that a territory where material is foreseeably disseminated, and the plaintiff has a reputation therein, has corresponding jurisdiction. The benefits of this analysis are predictability of jurisdiction in tandem with a fair insurance position for defendants. If a defendant knowingly distributes material in a number of states or at least consciously takes the risk of such distribution, or makes representations in such states which prove negligent, then it accords with common sense and equity that the defendant should insure against losses where damage foreseeably occurs, that is, within each judicial district. Similar arguments were addressed by Darmon AG when he stated:[50]

> ... the aim of providing legal protection can only be satisfied if the rules governing jurisdiction are foreseeable, a requirement to which the Court referred in its judgments in *Jakob Handte et Cie GmbH v Traitements mecano-chimiques des surfaces SA (TMCS)*[51] and *Custom Made Commercial Ltd v Stawa Metallbau GmbII*.[52] The defendant will be in a position to know precisely, on the basis of the place in which the newspapers are distributed, before which court or courts it

---

[49] [1976] ECR 1735, para. 11.
[50] [1995] 2 WLR 499, at p.524. The web provider or server may take steps to waive their liability in each particular territory.
[51] [1992] ECR 3967.
[52] [1994] ECR 2913.

risks being sued and the pleas on which it may be able to rely in its defence having regard to the applicable law.

(v) Comparison with the US

In general the Court of Justice should be applauded for its rational outcome in *Shevill*. A brief comparison may be drawn with the United States jurisprudence on this issue.

The United States substantive libel rules are conditioned by the need to preserve and protect the freedom of the press.[53] It is difficult for a plaintiff to successfully bring a defamation suit against a media defendant rather than an ordinary individual.[54] Substantive rules, however, are not the basis of this commentary, which concentrates purely on jurisdictional matters and the long-arm process. *In personam* jurisdiction in this regard refers to the court's power over the very person of the defendant. To assert this personal jurisdiction over a defendant who is not a resident of the state in which the suit is brought (the *lex fori*), the court of the forum state first needs to invoke the state's long-arm statute providing for substantial service of process on non-residents.[55] The Court must determine whether the non-resident defendant's contacts with the forum state are sufficient so that the exercise of long-arm jurisdiction over him will not violate the Due Process Clause of the Fourteenth Amendment.[56] In essence, three separate questions need to be addressed as to whether the forum has jurisdiction over a non-resident publisher in the multistate libel context.[57] The US Supreme Court has addressed the forum's jurisdiction over multistate defamation cases in two important cases involving magazine publications.[58] By parity of reasoning, the logic they have applied must also pertain to multistate defamation facilitated by use of the Internet.

---

[53] See, for example, *New York Times Co v Sullivan*, 376 US 254 (1964).

[54] *Gertz v Robert Welch, Inc.* 418 U.S. 323 (1974), limits the *Sullivan* protection to references to public officials and public figures.

[55] See Malloy, T.F., 'Personal jurisdiction over publishers in defamation actions: a current assessment' (1985) 30 *Villanova Law Review* 195, at p.197.

[56] Wright, C.A., *Law of Federal Courts* 64 (4th ed., West Publishing, St Paul, MN, 1983). A state violates the Due Process Clause if it exercises personal jurisdiction over a defendant who does not have adequate contacts with the forum state, because the non-resident must defend suit in a forum with which he has no relationship. See *World-Wide Volkswagen Corp v Woodson*, 444 US 286 (1980).

[57] See Dickerson, S., 'Libel and the long reach of out-of-state courts' (1985) 7 *Communications and the Law*, 27, at p.30. It is stressed that in the typical case challenging a state's reach over a non-resident publisher, due process requires a court to balance the plaintiff's interest in having the suit tried in the forum state against the defendant's right not to be forced to litigate in a foreign court. This balancing typically begins by asking three separate but not mutually exclusive questions: (1) Do the necessary minimal contacts with the forum state exist? (2) Was there notice that the activity would cause the effect? (3) Is it 'fair' to force the defendant to litigate in the foreign court?

[58] See, generally, Reed, A., 'Multistate Defamation Jurisdiction: A Comparative Analysis of Prevailing Jurisprudence in the United States and the European Union' (1996) 18 *Communications and the Law* 29.

In *Keeton v Hustler Magazine Inc*, the plaintiff, a New York resident, brought a libel suit in the US District Court of New Hampshire against *Hustler Magazine*, an Ohio Corporation, having its principal place of business in California.[59] Even though Keeton was a resident of New York and *Hustler* was published by an Ohio Corporation, she sued in New Hampshire because it was the only state where her action was not barred by the statute of limitations. The plaintiff's only connection with New Hampshire was the circulation there of a magazine that she assisted in producing, and the corporation's contacts with New Hampshire consisted of monthly sales of approximately 10,000 to 15,000 copies of its nationally published magazine.[60] These sales amounted to less than 1 per cent of *Hustler*'s total US circulation.

The District Court dismissed the suit, holding that the Due Process Clause of the Fourteenth Amendment forbade application of New Hampshire's long-arm statute to acquire personal jurisdiction over the corporation.[61] This was affirmed by the Court of Appeals for the First Circuit, holding that the plaintiff's lack of contacts with New Hampshire rendered the state's interest in redressing the libel too attenuated for an assertion of personal jurisdiction over the corporation.[62] The Court concluded that it would be unfair to assert jurisdiction over the corporation in view of the single publication rule,[63] which would require an award of damage caused in all states, and in view of New Hampshire's unusually long period of limitations for libel actions.[64] The First Circuit Court concluded that, 'the New Hampshire tail is too small to wag so large an out of state dog'.[65]

In a unanimous result, the Supreme Court reversed the First Circuit.[66] It found *Hustler*'s 'regular circulation of magazines in the forum state . . . sufficient to support an assertion of jurisdiction in a libel action based on the contents of the magazine'.[67] Noting that *Hustler*'s monthly circulation in New Hampshire amounted to 10,000 or 15,000 copies, the Court concluded that *Hustler*'s activity could not be characterised as 'random, isolated

---

[59] 682 F. 2d 33 (lst Cir. 1982); 465 US 770 (1984). Keeton originally brought her libel and invasion of privacy suit in Ohio, but the libel action was barred by Ohio's statute of limitations.

[60] *Keeton*, 682 F. 2d at 33 (1st Cir. 1982). Keeton's only connection with New Hampshire was the circulation there of the rival *Penthouse* magazine, of which she was a corporate officer (and common-law wife of the publisher Bob Guccione who, according to the libel, had infected Keeton with venereal disease).

[61] Ibid., at 33.

[62] 682 F. 2d at 35.

[63] This 'single publication rule' has been summarised as: 'As to any single publication: (a) only one action for damages can be maintained; (b) all damages suffered in all jurisdictions can be recovered in the one action; and (c) a judgment for or against the plaintiff upon the merits of any action for damages bars any other actions for damages between the same parties in all jurisdictions.' Restatement (Second) of Torts s.577 A (4) (1977).

[64] 682 F 2d at 36.

[65] Ibid.

[66] 465 US 770 (1984).

[67] Ibid.

or fortuitous'.[68] Additionally the Court found that it was fair to compel the defendant to defend a multistate libel action in New Hampshire. Justice Rehnquist, writing for the Court, noted that false statements of fact, which are the fundamental basis for a libel action, harm both the subject of the falsehood and those who read them. Thus, New Hampshire was protecting its own citizen-readers from deception and could also legitimately protect the reputation of a non-resident in the state even where the plaintiff was previously unknown there.[69] The libel could create a negative reputation in a jurisdiction where the plaintiff's reputation had been small but unblemished. Similar principles would undoubtedly apply in the US to multistate defamation where the defamatory statement is communicated by means of the Internet rather than a salacious magazine.[70] The Court also noted that New Hampshire had expressed an interest in redressing torts occurring within its borders,[71] especially by deleting from its long-arm statute a restriction that plaintiffs be residents.[72] The reasoning of the First Circuit Court that the plaintiff's contacts with the forum were critical was categorically rejected. The Supreme Court explicitly stated that the plaintiff's residence in the forum was not a separate jurisdictional requirement, although it may play a role in enhancing defendant's forum contacts.[73]

The judgment in *Keeton* concluded with the declaration that by 'continuously and deliberately' marketing its magazine in the forum state, *Hustler* reasonably could anticipate being hauled into court to defend a libel action arising from the content of those magazines.[74] Furthermore, because a defendant can be charged with knowledge of the state's laws, a publisher of a national magazine must reasonably expect that a defamation suit will seek actionwide damages under the single publication rule.

The result in *Keeton* appears somewhat astounding to the author, grounded in applicable English jurisdiction principles. A state where neither the plaintiff nor defendant resided, where neither had any contact whatsoever outside the small circulation of *Hustler* magazine, and where the plaintiff was totally unknown had jurisdiction to rule on the totality of damage to reputation caused by the article in all states. This universal jurisdiction would also apply if the defamatory communication in *Keeton* had been facilitated in New Hampshire via access through the Internet. Indeed, it was controversially stated by Justice Rehnquist in *Keeton* that 'False statements of fact harm both the subject of the falsehood *and* the readers of the statement.

---

[68] Ibid., at 774. The result was also said to satisfy the due process requirement of minimum contacts derived from *International Shoe Co. v Washington*, 326 U.S. 310 (1945) and *World-Wide Volkswagen Corp v Woodson*, 444 U.S. 286 (1980).

[69] Ibid., at 776.

[70] Reed, A., loc. cit., at p.34.

[71] 465 US 770 (1984) (citing *Leeper v Leeper*, 319 A.2d 626, 629 (N.H. 1974), and quoting Restatement (Second) of Conflict of Laws s.36 (1971)).

[72] Ibid., at 779.

[73] Ibid., at 780.

[74] Ibid.

New Hampshire may rightly employ its libel laws to discourage the deception of its citizens.'[75] Yet, it seems inimical to justice to allow such jurisdiction, albeit that the actual applicability of the single publication rule in the peculiar circumstances of the case was a matter of substantive law and not personal jurisdiction. A more blatant example of forum shopping would be harder to conceive, given that the suit was statute-barred in all states except New Hampshire.[76] It is submitted that the approach to international libel over the Internet, recently adopted by the European Court of Justice ensures more satisfactory jurisdictional criteria, as considered further below.

The establishment of minimum jurisdictional contacts was far less controversial in *Calder v Jones*.[77] The actress Shirley Jones and her husband (Marty Ingels) filed suit for libel in California against Ian Calder, who was president and editor of the *National Enquirer*, and also against John South, the writer of the allegedly defamatory article at issue.[78] The plaintiffs were residents of California, and the defendants were residents of Florida.[79] The article was written and edited in Florida but was carried in a national magazine which had its highest circulation in California.[80]

Although the publishing corporation did not contest jurisdiction in California, Calder and South made special appearances and moved to quash service of process on the ground that the court lacked personal jurisdiction over them. Calder claimed that he had not entered California or made any telephone calls to persons there while editing the Jones article.[81] South argued that his only contacts with California while researching the article were one trip to gather information and a few telephone calls to verify it. The trial court granted the motion to quash because the totality of the defendants' conducts were insubstantial and because First Amendment considerations precluded jurisdiction. The California Court of Appeals reversed and held that the First Amendment did not afford publishers' special protection.

The US Supreme Court, in a unanimous opinion by Justice Rehnquist, affirmed the California Court of Appeals, thereby rejecting the view that

---

[75] Ibid., at 776.

[76] Reed, A., loc. cit., at p.35. See also Dickerson, S., 'Libel and the Long Reach of Out-of-State Courts' (1985) 7 *Communications and the Law* 27, at p.33; Marino, J., 'Asserting long-arm in personam jurisdiction over multi-state libel defendants' (1985) 31 *New York Law School Law Review* 311; Levine, D.I., 'Preliminary procedural protection for the press after jurisdiction in distant forums after Calder and Keeton' (1984) 3 *Arizona State Law Journal* 459, at p.463.

[77] 187 Cal. Rptr. 825 (Cal. Ct. App. 1982); *Jones v Calder*, 2 Civ. No. 65403 (Cal. 1983); *Calder v Jones* 465 US 783 (1984).

[78] The article stated that Ingels had 'terrorised his staff, cheated stars, outraged advertisers and scandalised Hollywood', and that Jones had 'been driven to drink' by this bizarre behaviour. Brief for Appellant at 2, *Calder v Jones* 465 US 783 (1984).

[79] Ibid., at p.786.

[80] Ibid. The *Enquirer*'s California circulation of 600,000 was more than 11 per cent of its total circulation and the largest of any single state: ibid., at pp.784–5.

[81] Ibid. He had been in California only twice: once for pleasure and once to testify in an unrelated case.

First Amendment considerations must be weighed in a personal jurisdictional analysis.[82] The Court held that jurisdiction over the reporter and editor in California was proper because of their intentional conduct in Florida calculated to cause injury to the plaintiff in California.[83] It was California that was the focal point of both the story and the harm suffered.[84] The article concerned the Californian activities of a California resident. It impugned the professionalism of an entertainer whose television career was centred on California. The article was drawn from California sources, and the brunt of the harm, in terms of both emotional distress and the injury to Jones's professional reputation was suffered in California. Thus, the Court found jurisdiction over Calder and South proper under the effects test for their intentional acts aimed expressly at California. They must have reasonably anticipated being hauled into court in California to answer for the truth of the article.

It seems eminently logical that California, jurisdiction was established by the Court in *Calder*. By way of contrast to *Keeton*, the plaintiff in *Calder* was a Californian resident bringing suit purely to recover damages for injury to reputation caused within the specific forum. This result replicates the European Court of Justice's approach in *Shevill* on multistate defamation. It is suggested that the European rationale on multistate defamation jurisdiction facilitated by use of the Internet is far more compelling than the position in the United States.[85] If the *Shevill* principles were to be applied in *Keeton*, an action for damages against *Hustler Magazine* could have been brought before the courts of the state of the place where the publisher of the defamatory publication over the Internet was established, and which then have jurisdiction to award damages for all the harm caused by the defamation. Of course, in Ohio such a suit was statute barred by the time the plaintiff commenced her action. Alternatively, *Shevill* prescribes jurisdiction before the courts of each state in which the publication was communicated over the Internet and where the victim claimed to have suffered injury to her reputation, and which then have jurisdiction to rule solely in respect of the harm caused in the state of the court seised. It is axiomatic that this limited *in personam* jurisdiction is directly contrary to the application of the single publication rule in *Keeton*. The approach adopted by the European Court of Justice in *Shevill* appears, as discussed in this chapter, to be the correct path to follow. The single publication rule thus needs to be abolished or severely curtailed to allow a claim for total damage recovery to be determined solely within the forum of the defendant web server. The alternative solution is that the jurisdiction of each state where distribution of defamatory statements facilitated by the

---

[82] Ibid., at pp.789–90 (1984).
[83] Ibid., at p.1487. Soon after the decision was announced, the parties settled out of court for a retraction and an undisclosed sum.
[84] Ibid., at p.788.
[85] Reed, A., loc. cit., at p.63; Reed, A. and Mayss, A., op. cit., at p.138.

Internet occurs is activated, but limited to 'local' harm within that specific territory.

Shevill and other intangible economic torts

(i) Economic loss

By parity of reasoning, similar principles to *Shevill* will apply to other intangible economic torts committed over the Internet. An English court will have jurisdiction where the direct effect of the defendant's actions occur within UK territory, and where a close connecting factor is prevalent with the UK.[86] In *Marinari v Lloyds Bank Plc*,[87] the first major decision to consider Article 5(3) immediately subsequent to *Shevill*, a similar perspective was adopted to economic loss. Although the factual circumstances of the case itself did not involve the Internet, nonetheless an identical outcome will occur where the web system is abused to create economic loss, induce a breach of contract or infringe intellectual property rights.[88] The plaintiff, Mr Marinari, who was domiciled in Italy, had obtained a parcel of promissory notes issued by the Negros Oriental province of the Philippines in favour of Zubaidi Trading Co. of Beirut and having an exchange value of $752 million. After he had deposited them with the Manchester branch of Lloyds, whose registered office was in London, the bank staff, taking the view that the notes were of dubious origin, contacted the police and the plaintiff was arrested and notes sequestrated.[89] Subsequently, Marinari brought proceedings in the Italian courts, claiming as damages the value of the confiscated notes. He attempted to rely on Article 5(3) of the Brussels Convention, arguing that the financial loss of which he complained took place in Italy, as a consequence of conduct which had taken place in England.

The Court of Justice ruled that, in effect, the Italian court did not have jurisdiction. Article 5(3) as a derogation from Article 2 has to be given a narrow interpretation.[90] The *Bier* judgment concerned a complex situation in which the causal event and the harmful consequences occurred from the outset in two different Contracting States. By contrast, in *Marinari*, both the causal event (the conduct imputed to the employees of Lloyds Bank) and the initial damage (the sequestration of the promissory notes and imprisonment) occurred in the UK. Only the alleged consequential damage (financial

---

[86] For matters relating to the choice of law an English court will apply see Reed, A., 'Commercial torts' choice of law provisions' [1994] *Lloyd's Maritime and Commercial Law Quarterly* 248; Reed, A., 'The Private International Law (Miscellaneous Provisions) Act 1995 and the need for escape devices' (1996) 15 *Civil Justice Quarterly* 305.

[87] [1996] 2 WLR 159.

[88] See, generally, Briggs, A., 'The uncertainty of special jurisdiction' [1996] *Lloyd's Maritime and Commercial Law Quarterly* 27; and Hartley, T., 'Art. 5(3): Place where the harmful event occurs' (1996) 21 *European Law Review* 164.

[89] Marinari's criminal prosecution in England resulted in his acquittal but not in the return of the notes.

[90] [1996] 2 WLR 159, at p.170.

losses) could have been suffered in Italy. A distinction, identical to *Dumez*, had to be made between the place where the damage arises and the place where it is suffered. The Court of Justice, again construing the term 'place where the harmful event occurred', determined that it does not include the place where the victim claims to have suffered financial loss consequential on initial damage arising and suffered by him in another Contracting State. The rule of specific jurisdiction in Article 5(3) was based on the existence of a particularly close connecting factor between the dispute and the courts other than those of the state of the defendant's domicile which justified the attribution of jurisdiction to those courts for reasons relating to the sound administration of justice. The result goes a long way to stop a plaintiff from invoking Article 5(3) as a device to sue, as a matter of routine within the *forum actoris*, in its own courts, by arguing that it suffered its damage at its headquarters.[91] It is insufficient that damage is merely suffered there through abuse of the Internet if occurrence of the actual economic harm transpires elsewhere.

(ii) Negligent misrepresentation

In negligent misrepresentation cases the plaintiff is induced to act to his detriment in reliance on what has been carelessly represented; in the case of negligent failure to advise, the plaintiff is induced to act to his detriment in ignorance of a fact which the defendant has carelessly failed to communicate. Defamation and negligent misrepresentation share many features in common in that communications by letter, telephone, telex and, of course, via the Internet, can pass across space or time before completion or operation in a different country. The same jurisdictional arguments must apply equally to both torts, albeit that location of a place proves problematic. Most recently, the English court in *Domicrest Ltd v Swiss Bank Corporation*[92] has applied the *Shevill* principles on defamation to a case involving negligent misstatement. Which court has jurisdiction where a negligent statement is placed on the Internet in state A but accessed and received in state B, causing loss there? It was determined in *Domicrest* that state A has jurisdiction in accordance with Article 5(3) of the Convention. The harmful event occurs where the misstatement was actually made over the Internet rather than where it was received.

Choice of law

The general principles

As previously mentioned, the second limb of the judgment in *Shevill* focused on whether a national court was required to follow specific rules different from those laid down by its national law in relation to the criteria for

---

[91] Briggs, A., loc. cit., at pp.27–9.
[92] [1998] 3 All ER 577.

assessing whether the event in question is harmful and in relation to the evidence required of the existence and extent of the harm alleged by the victim of the defamation. The defendants had argued that the plaintiffs had not suffered any damage so as to constitute a *harmful* event. There was no evidence that the plaintiffs' reputation had actually been harmed or that those who knew the plaintiffs had access to any copies of the newspaper. The defendant argued that the principles in English law which assumed that damage is suffered once a libel is established should be disregarded in favour of a common European interpretation of Article 5(3) and thus proof of actual damage to qualify England as the place where the harmful event occurred. The Court noted that the object of the Convention was not to unify the rules of substantive law and of procedure of the different Contracting States.[93] This approach is undoubtedly correct, given that any requirement by the Court of Justice to define and locate the 'tort' would make litigation slow, expensive and inherently uncertain. It would also substantially impair the efficacious conduct of proceedings. The essence of the Convention was to determine which court has jurisdiction in disputes relating to civil and commercial matters in relations between the Contracting States and to facilitate the enforcement of judgments.[94] A consistent line of court jurisprudence has stressed that, as regards procedural rules, reference must be made to the national rules applicable by the national court, provided that the application of those rules does not impair the effectiveness of the Convention. It was stated quite categorically in *Hagen v Zeehaghe*[95] that:

> ... the object of the Convention is not to unify procedural rules but to determine which court has jurisdiction in disputes relating to civil and commercial matters in intra-Community relations and to facilitate the enforcement of judgments. It is therefore necessary to draw a clear distinction between jurisdiction and the conditions governing the admissibility of an action.[96]

The effect is that it is for the substantive English law of defamation to determine whether the event in question is harmful and the evidence required of the existence and extent of the harm. English law on presumption of damage in libel cases will be applied in tandem, unfortunately, with the manifest vagaries of our current libel law with jury trial, no legal aid, the possibility of exemplary damages, actions barred by victims' death and illogical damage awards.[97]

---

[93] [1995] 2 WLR 499, at p.541.

[94] However, it may be considered that the harmful event has an autonomous meaning which may not be what English law expects. After all, English law also saw the communication of the libel, not the printing, as the harmful act. The conclusion that the act complained of was the printing of the libel, and not its communication, may be viewed as a definition and location of the tort by the Court of Justice itself.

[95] [1990] ECR 1845.

[96] Ibid., at 1865 (para. 17).

[97] See Weir, T., *A Casebook on Tort* (Sweet and Maxwell, London, 1996) at p.511.

A wider issue is at stake here in relation to choice of law in tort: What principles govern this important area of conflict of laws? Suppose a defamatory statement is disseminated from an English website and is accessed in Germany where the victim has a reputation; alternatively a negligent representation is made from a website in Leeds but the statement is accessed, received and acted upon in Paris. In both situations assume that the English court has taken jurisdiction over the litigation (in accordance with the defendant's domicile). Obviously, it becomes important to evaluate which law should be applied by the English court – English, German or French. The process of choice of law in the field of tort has been said to raise, 'one of the most vexed questions in the English conflict of laws'.[98] This is especially true in the commercial field, where the place of a tort may be either hard to locate or a matter of chance. Significantly, it was hoped in the early 1980s that there would be a European Convention dealing with all sorts of obligations generally, in a move towards schematic harmonisation. That Convention came into existence in relation to contracts[99] and legislation was duly enacted, but there is no such Convention in relation to torts.[100] The project for a Convention has been abandoned and no progress at all has been made within the EU on the drafting of a non-contractual obligations Convention, and none seems likely.[101] Against this background, it becomes essential to analyse the independent substantive English conflicts' rules.

A certain symmetry applies in this regard. As for jurisdiction of the English court, where we have seen that two mutually exclusive sets of principles apply to Contracting and non-Contracting States, there is a similar dichotomy for choice of law. However, the distinction here relates to the very nature of the tort. There have been created two entirely separate choice of law rules. The tort of defamation is still governed by the traditional common law rules on double actionability that have existed for over a century. All other courses of action classified as tortious are now governed by the Private International Law (Miscellaneous Provisions) Act 1995 which applies to all torts, with the exception of defamation.

---

[98] *Boys v Chaplin* [1968] 2 QB 1 per Lord Denning. It presupposes that there is a choice of law rule for all torts. See, generally, Reed, A., 'Commercial torts' choice of law provisions' [1994] *Lloyd's Maritime and Commercial Law Quarterly* 248; and Reed, A., 'The Private International Law (Miscellaneous Provisions) Act 1995 and the need for escape devices' (1996) 15 *Civil Justice Quarterly* 305.

[99] Note it was planned that what eventually became the 1980 Convention on the Law Applicable to Contractual Obligations [1980] OJ 286 should also contain provisions on choice of law for torts (see art. 10 of the 1972 Preliminary Draft). However, in 1978 a decision by the Committee of Experts decided to confine the negotiations to contracts.

[100] It was in 1980 that the then Member States of the European Convention concluded in Rome the Convention on the Law Applicable to Contractual Obligations, which was given effect in the UK by the Contracts (Applicable Law) Act 1990.

[101] North, P.M., *Essays in Private International Law* (Oxford University Press, Oxford, 1992) at p.228.

The common law rule of double actionability for defamation

The traditional English common law principles relating to tort choice of law have been based for over a century on the decision in *Phillips v Eyre*.[102] This case marked the formulation of the general rule on the imposition of double actionability under both the *lex fori*[103] and the *lex loci delicti*.[104] The Governor of Jamaica allegedly committed acts of assault and false imprisonment within Jamaican territory. No liability was imposed as an Act of Indemnity retrospectively justified such conduct. It was stated by Willes J that for a plaintiff to successfully bring an action in England for a foreign tort:[105]

> As a general rule, in order to found a suit in England for a wrong alleged to have been committed abroad, two conditions must be fulfilled. First, the wrong must be of such a character that it would have been actionable if committed in England . . . Secondly, the act must not have been justifiable by the law of the place where it was done.

The House of Lords in *Boys v Chaplin*[106] confirmed that the decision in *Phillips v Eyre* laid down a double actionability choice of law rule. This leading authority, derived from a motor accident in Malta, in which the plaintiff, a pillion passenger on a motor scooter, suffered personal injuries as a consequence of the negligent driving of a motor vehicle by the defendant. Both parties were members of the British forces serving in Malta, but normally resident in England, and the defendant had insurance cover through an English company. Proceedings were commenced in England for the injuries caused by the negligent driving, and the central issue for determination was whether the plaintiff could recover general damages for pain and suffering, which were recoverable under only English not Maltese law. Their Lordships, in a judgment lacking in clarity, determined unanimously that damages for pain and suffering should be awarded in accordance with English law. The principles enunciated by Lord Wilberforce have subsequently been adopted by appellate courts, that is to say, that as a general rule the defendant's conduct must be 'actionable as a tort according to English law, subject to the condition that civil liability in respect of the relevant claim exists as between the actual parties under the law of the foreign country where the act was done'.[107] However, this certain general rule is subject to an exception, where clear and satisfactory grounds can be demonstrated, justifying the system of law having the most significant relationship with the issue and the parties being applied instead, i.e. the proper law of the tort. The result in *Boys v Chaplin* of the application of

---

[102] (1870) LR 6 QB 1. For consideration of choice of law rules in other jurisdictions, see Mayss, A. and Reed, A., op. cit., at pp.327–57.
[103] The *lex fori* is always English law as far as English conflicts lawyers are concerned.
[104] The *lex loci delicti* relates to the law of the place where the tort was actually committed.
[105] (1870) LR 6 QB 1, at pp.28–9. Note that the first limb of this test, actionability as a tort under English law, derived from the decision in *The Halley* (1868) LR 2 PC 193.
[106] [1971] AC 356.
[107] Ibid., at p.389.

this exception to the general rule was to apply purely English law, i.e. the *lex fori*. In subsequent English cases the exception was formulated to apply English law to the exclusion of foreign law.[108] What was unclear until the recent Privy Council decision in *Red Sea Insurance v Bouygues SA*,[109] was whether the exception could be applicable to allow the application of the *locus delicti* rules, subverting entirely any application of the *lex fori*. It is now clear, following that case, that such flexibility is permissible at common law.

For ease of exposition let us return to our earlier hypothetical illustration of a defamatory statement disseminated from an English website, that is accessed in Germany where the plaintiff has a significant reputation. In applying the general principles of double actionability enunciated in *Boys v Chaplin*, it would be incumbent on the plaintiff to meet two hurdles to successfully pursue a claim before the English courts. First, it must be shown that civil liability exists in Germany, the *locus delicti* for the defendant's conduct. Secondly, it will be necessary to demonstrate that the statement is defamatory under English law. That means to say that if the publication had occurred in England it would be defamatory, and consequentially actionable as a tort.

Finally, in briefly considering the general rules, it is noteworthy that where a tort is alleged to have transpired in England, for instance a defamatory statement published over the Internet in Leeds, our courts have simply applied English law to the dispute. This rationale has been applied irrespective of the foreign elements involved or the total lack of factual connection with England. A pertinent illustration of this was provided by the decision in *Szalatney-Stacho v Fink*.[110] At issue was a defamatory libel, published in England, where all relevant parties were Czech officials and the published documents alleged misconduct by the plaintiff, the Czech Acting Minister in England. Despite the foreign centre of gravity of this dispute, purely English law was held to be applicable. The *Boys v Chaplin* exception is rendered nugatory under our traditional general rules when the tort occurs in England.

Reform of applicable English choice of law rules: the Private International Law (Miscellaneous Provisions) Act 1995

Following Law Commission recommendations,[111] the old common law position (with the exception of defamation) has now been completely abolished.[112] The Private International Law (Miscellaneous Provisions)

---

[108] See, for example, *Church of Scientology of California v Metropolitan Police Commissioner* (1976) 120 Sol. Jo. 690, CA; and *Johnson v Coventry Churchill* [1992] 3 All ER, 14.

[109] [1995] 1 AC 190.

[110] [1947] KB 1.

[111] Law Com. No. 193 (1990); Scot. Law Com. No. 129 (1990). The new Act came into force on 1 May 1996 (S.I. 1996 No. 995).

[112] Note that a key illustration of this fundamental reform is provided by s.9(6) of Part III of the Private International Law (Miscellaneous Provisions) Act 1995). The old common law rationale was to apply purely English law where the tort occurred in England, irrespective

Act 1995 states quite categorically that the rules of the common law, in so far as they require actionability under the law of the forum and the law of another country for the purpose of determining whether a tort is actionable in the forum are abolished.[113] The new general rule is to apply a modified *lex loci delicti* approach containing certain presumptions on ascertainment.[114] By section 11, the key provision, it is provided that:

(1) The general rule is that the applicable law is the law of the country in which the events constituting the tort or *delict* in question occur.
(2) Where significant elements of those events occur in different countries the applicable law under the general rule is to be taken as being –
   (a) for a cause of action in respect of personal injury caused to an individual or death resulting from personal injury, the law of the country where the individual was when he sustained the injury
   (b) for a course of action in respect of damage to property, the law of the country where the property was when it was damaged; and
   (c) in any other case, the law of the country in which the most significant element or elements of those events occurred
(3) In this section 'personal injury' includes disease or any impairment of physical or mental condition.

The above position can be exemplified by considering the earlier hypothetical postulation of a negligent misrepresentation made from a website in Leeds, but where the statement is accessed, received and acted upon in Paris. The effect of section 11 is to apply the law of the country in which the events constituting the tort of negligent misrepresentation occur. However, in our case the elements are divided between different countries. In such a situation it is incumbent upon the English court to evaluate where the 'most significant element or elements' of the tort occur. Thus it is submitted that as the very essence of negligent misrepresentation is where the statement is received and acted upon, French law would be applicable.

Additionally, the new statutory legislation also allows displacement of the general rule in accordance with the important terms of section 12 which states:

---

of the degree of foreign elements involved, as illustrated by the decision in *Szalatnay Stacho v Fink* [1947] KB 1, considered above. This principle has been totally abrogated by s.9(6) which provides: 'For the avoidance of doubt (and without prejudice to the operation of section 14 below) this Part applies in relation to events occurring in the forum as it applies to events occurring in any other country'.

[113] See Private International Law (Miscellaneous Provisions) Act 1995 s.10.

[114] See, generally, Briggs, A., '*The Halley*: Holed, But Still Afloat?' (1995) 111 *Law Quarterly Review* 18; Rogerson, P., 'Choice of Law in Tort: A Missed Opportunity?' (1995) 44 *International and Comparative Law Quarterly* 650; Morse, C., 'Torts in Private International Law: A New Statutory Framework' (1996) 45 *International and Comparative Law Quarterly* 888; Carter, P., 'The Private International Law (Miscellaneous Provisions) Act 1995' (1996) 112 *Law Quarterly Review* 190; Reed, A., 'The Private International Law (Miscellaneous Provisions) Act 1995 and the Need for Escape Devices' (1996) 15 *Civil Justice Quarterly* 305.

(1) If it appears, in all the circumstances, from a comparison of –
  (a) the significance of the factors which connect a tort or delict with the country whose law would be the applicable law under the general rule
  and
  (b) the significance of any factors connecting the tort or delict with another country
  that it is substantially more appropriate for the applicable law for determining the issues arising in the case, or any of those issues, to be the law of the other country, the general rule is displaced and the applicable law for determining those issues or that issue (as the case may be) is the law of that other country.
(2) The factors that may be taken into account as connecting a tort or delict with a country for the purposes of this section include, in particular, factors relating to the parties, to any of the events which constitute the tort or delict in question or to any of the circumstances or consequences of those events.[115]

Conclusions

This chapter has evaluated the jurisdiction and choice of law principles that apply to torts facilitated by abuse of the Internet. By parity of reasoning, the rules prescribed by the Court of Justice in *Shevill* must also apply to other intangible economic torts facilitated by use of the Internet. Although the Internet provides novel factual circumstances in that it creates the ability for information to be made available simultaneously and instantaneously in every jurisdiction in the world, nonetheless the relevant conflict of laws jurisprudence is of general application. In terms of relevant issues that arise the Internet ought to be considered no differently from extant principles that have developed for newspapers or television. Once an English court has jurisdictions then the conflict of laws rule it applies depends on the nature of the tort; for defamation we apply double actionability, but for other torts the Private International Law (Miscellaneous Provisions) Act 1995 will apply. Two distinct models apply to govern choice of law matters; a corollary exists here with the two models for jurisdiction ascription.

More recently, the *Shevill* principles have been applied by the English Court of Appeal in the context of an international libel where the alternative forum was a US state. In *Berezovsky v Michaels and Others*,[116] the claimant, a Russian national, had commenced libel proceedings, before the High Court in respect of allegedly defamatory articles in one of the defendant's magazines which, although published in the US, had a limited circulation of 2,000 in England (the *lex fori*). The trial court allowed a stay of proceedings on the premise that England was not the most appropriate forum to hear the case; they accepted the defendant's contention that an alleged libel published in more than one jurisdiction gave rise to a single

---

[115] This exception can be criticised on the basis that it is unclear what is meant by 'substantially more appropriate'. No definition is provided in the statute itself.
[116] [2000] 2 All ER 986.

cause of action and that it was for the court to determine the most appropriate forum in terms of where the global cause of action arose. This was rejected by both the Court of Appeal and the House of Lords, following the *Shevill* rationale on cases of international publication of defamatory material, whereby the harm caused to a person's reputation occurs in the places where the publication was distributed and where the victim was known in those places. The significance of the *Shevill* ruling is now deeply entrenched in English law and can be applied with advantage to disputes arising from Internet publication.

PART III

LEGAL INSTITUTIONS AND PROFESSIONS AND THE INTERNET

CHAPTER 5

The new electric lawyer and legal practice in the information age

David Wall

Introduction[1]

As we enter the information age, information technologies are clearly shaping both legal practice and also the legal professions. The Internet and other technologies are providing new vehicles that will allow lawyers to provide legal services instantly and remotely while enabling clients to seek the best advice wherever it is located. Moreover, in the not-so-distant future, it is possible that the Internet may even provide a forum for the determination of some types of justice, say through mediated dispute resolution.[2]

But these are also increasingly difficult times for the legal professions. Not only are they suffering from a highly publicised legitimation crisis,[3] but their traditional concepts of legal professionalism are also undergoing considerable change. While there is a fairly broad consensus that these changes are taking place, there is equally considerable disagreement about their effects. At one extreme is a school of thought which interprets these changes as being symptomatic of the decline of the legal professions.[4] At the other extreme is the more optimistic belief that the reports of the death of the legal professions are grossly exaggerated and that the changes result from the re-negotiation of professionalism.[5] Cutting across both viewpoints is a growing debate over the role played by information technology in changing the nature of both legal practice and also legal professionalism.

---

[1] This chapter is drawn from 'Information technology and the Shaping of Legal Practice', which was delivered at the 1998 BILETA Conference at Trinity College, Dublin. The research was conducted with the very able assistance of Jenny Johnstone, now at the University of Sheffield. The research findings upon which this chapter is based were published in full as Wall, D.S. and Johnstone, J., 'The industrialisation of legal practice and the rise of the new electric lawyer: the impact of information technology upon legal practice' (1997) 25 *International Journal of the Sociology of Law* 95.

[2] See, further, chap. 8.

[3] Sweet, P., 'Survey reveals a demoralised profession' (1996) 10(18) *The Lawyer*, pp.1,12,13; Wachman, R., 'PR guru hired to revive profession' (1996) 10(20) *The Lawyer* 1.

[4] Abel, R., *The Legal Profession in England and Wales* (Blackwell, Oxford, 1988).

[5] Paterson, A., 'Professionalism and the legal services market' (1996) 3(1) *International Journal of the Legal Profession* 137.

This chapter will draw upon contemporary literature and research findings to explore the impact of information technology upon legal practice. The first part will identify the trends in both law and society which have provided the rationale for the introduction of information technology into legal practice. It will also look at those same processes within the context of broader changes in society. The second part draws upon the findings of research into the use of information technology by lawyers. The third part explores the implications of the findings in terms of the impact of new technologies upon the individual practitioner. In part four, some general conclusions will be drawn about the impact of information technology upon legal practice.

Technology and change

A century or so ago, Louis Brandeis perceptively observed that the work of lawyers is 'limited by time and space'[6]. The timing of the legal process was then, and still is, largely dependent upon existing technologies, especially transport and communications, which govern the time taken to give advice, receive instructions, process the case, contact relevant parties and so on. This factor, when combined with the lawyers' exclusive professional knowledge, enables the legal professions to exert considerable control over the legal process. Since Brandeis's time, the pace of the legal process and the world in which it takes place has altered considerably, as the technologies and their delivery have become more sophisticated, thus necessitating the introduction of new organisational cultures and practices. We now live in a world that some contemporary thinkers believe has developed beyond its natural capabilities. In the early 1960s Bourdieu, for example, observed that: '[i]t is useless to pursue the world, no one will ever overtake it'.[7] A decade or so later, Illich warned that:[8]

> . . . once the barrier of bicycle velocity is broken at any point in the system, the total per capita monthly time spent at the service of the travel industry increases . . . Transportation beyond bicycle velocity demands power inputs from the environment. Velocity translates into power and soon power needs rise exponentially.

Illich's point was that the conceptualisation of time in traditional societies was derived from the natural pace of life which was determined by the physical capabilities of humans. However, the technologically driven imperatives of capital have now overtaken the world or at least its natural pace.

---

[6] Address by Louis Brandeis entitled 'The Opportunity in the Law' delivered to Harvard Ethical Culture Society, 4 May 1905, cited in Hazard, G.C. and Rhode, D.L. (eds), *The Legal Profession: Responsibility and Regulation* (Foundation Press, New York, 1985), p.15. Also cited in Katsh, E., *Law in a Digital World* (Oxford University Press, Oxford, 1995) at p.194.
[7] Bourdieu, P., 'The attitude of the Algerian peasant towards time', in Pitt-Rivers, J. (ed.), *Mediterranean Countrymen* (Mouton, Paris, 1963) at p.55, cited in Thompson, E.P., 'Time, Work-Discipline, and Industrial Capitalism' (1967) 38 *Past and Present* 56, at p.96.
[8] Illich, I., *Tools for Conviviality* (Fontana, London, 1973), p.95.

Two decades after Illich, Giddens and other commentators[9] have further informed our understanding of modernity by identifying fundamental changes to our understanding of time and space. Giddens has argued that the rate of change that arises within society's institutions has separated modern and traditional social orders, thus creating 'discontinuities' with the past.[10] These discontinuities have led to the disembedding[11] of the time and space which have traditionally bound social orders. They have also led to the 'lifting out' of social relations from local contexts of interaction and their restructuring or 'distanciation' across infinite spans of time–space.[12] One of the main engines of this change has been the developments of technology, particularly the technologies of transportation and communications. Of special interest here is the way that in recent years the Internet has revolutionised communications technology.

The Internet's key contribution to change is not so much its instantaneity, because this was largely achieved by the fax, telephone and radio before it, but its ability to connect a number of different types of communications technologies together. However, the Internet has had the rather contradictory effect of further accelerating the disembedding and distanciation, while simultaneously enabling communications to take place instantaneously, without the need to respect geophysical or national boundaries, thus redefining our understandings of time and space. Moreover, the Internet has created an infrastructure for the development of *cyberspace*[13], a socially constructed, abstract space, which is not physically bounded[14]. It is within this *virtual community* that we now conduct much of our social[15] and intellectual activity, whether it be in work, leisure or pleasure. So, human social relationships, once separated by time and space could now be united once again as the social relationships of production become restructured. These characteristics will apply just as equally to the following analysis of the legal process and it is perhaps interesting to note that one of the significant growth areas has been the emerging concept of the virtual legal community.[16]

---

[9] Giddens, A., *The Consequences of Modernity* (Polity Press, London, 1990); Cornell, D., 'Time, Deconstruction, and the challenge to Legal Positivism: The Call for Judicial Responsibility' (1990) 2 *Yale Journal of Law and the Humanities* 267.

[10] Giddens, op. cit., at p.6.

[11] Ibid., at p.13.

[12] Ibid.

[13] Gibson, W., *Neuromancer* (HarperCollins, London, 1984); Sterling, B., *The Hacker Crackdown* (Penguin Books, London, 1994).

[14] Wall, D.S., 'Policing the Virtual Community: The Internet, cyber-crimes and the policing of cyberspace', in Francis, P., Davies, P. and Jupp, V., *Policing Futures* (Macmillan, London, 1997).

[15] Whether or not we still have a social is itself the subject of considerable debate; see, further, Rose, N., 'The Death of the Social? Re-figuring the Territory of Government' (1996) 25(3) *Economy and Society* 327.

[16] Not discussed here, but for a very interesting discussion of the future of law, which includes aspects of the virtual legal community, see Susskind, R., *The Future of Law* (2nd ed., Oxford University Press, Oxford, 1998) and also Katsh, M.E., *Law in a Digital World* (Oxford University Press, Oxford, 1995).

But of key importance to the emerging argument is the observation that these technologies do not develop themselves. Driving their development, and adoption, is a set of (managerialist) philosophies[17] which embody the 'logic of industrialism'[18] and which continually seek to rationalise productive activity. These philosophies seek to achieve the holy trinity of economy, effectiveness and efficiency[19] and are largely responsible for driving the introduction of information technology. The technology is merely the means by which such rationalisation can be effected.

Changes in law, legal practice and legal professionalism

Applying the above argument to the legal process, a number of trends can be identified which, during the past thirty years, have been responsible for creating internal pressures within the legal professions to increase operational efficiency, make working practices more economic and make organisational structures more effective.[20] The overall effect, it is argued, is to give considerable impetus to the integration of technology plus its associated philosophies and practices into the legal environment.

The growth of advice culture – Smith has demonstrated the emergence of an 'advice culture' by illustrating the increase in public demands for advice from a wide range of helping organisations over the past two decades.[21] He suggests that the increased use of lawyers follows an upward trend in the numbers of people who are reaching out for help for: 'both the material and psychological aspects of their problems'.[22] When Smith's statistics are aggregated, they show that over the past two decades there has been almost a five-fold increase in the numbers of people seeking legal advice.[23]

An increase in the overall volume and complexity of law – The annual number of Acts of Parliament and statutory instruments has remained fairly constant since 1951 at about 65 and 2,500 respectively, however, the number

---

[17] A useful discussion of these philosophies can be found in Sommerlad, H., 'Managerialism and the Legal Profession: A new professional paradigm' (1995) 2(2) *International Journal of the Legal Profession* 159. For a broader picture see Stewart, G. and Walsh, K., 'Change in the management of public services' (1992) 70 *Public Administration* 499.

[18] Kerr, C., Dunlop, J.T., Harbison, F. and Myers, C.A., *Industrialism and Industrial Man* (Pelican, Harmondsworth, 1971).

[19] See, for general accounts: Osborne, D. and Gaebler, T., *Reinventing Government* (Addison-Wesley, Reading, MA, 1992); Zifcaf, S., *New Managerialism* (Open University Press, Buckingham, 1994); Rhodes, R.A.W., *Understanding Governance: policy networks, governance, reflexivity and accountability* (Open University Press, Buckingham, 1997).

[20] The following section is adapted from Wall, D.S., 'Legal Aid, Social Policy and the Architecture of Criminal Justice: The supplier induced demand thesis and legal aid policy' (1996) 23(4) *Journal of Law and Society* 549.

[21] Smith, R., 'Legal Aid and Justice', in Bean, D. (ed.), *Law Reform for All* (Blackstone Press, London, 1996), p.52.

[22] Ibid.

[23] Wall, D.S. and Johnstone, J., 'The industrialisation of legal practice and the rise of the new electric lawyer: the impact of information technology upon legal practice' (1997) 25 *International Journal of the Sociology of Law* 95.

of pages covered by the Acts has tripled. In 1951 they covered 675 pages, by 1991 they had increased to 2,222, with the number of sections and schedules more than doubling from 803 to 1985.[24] Similarly, the number of pages covered by the statutory instruments almost doubled from 3,500 to over 6,000.[25] So, while the annual number of laws remained the same, their substantive complexity has increased considerably.

The increasing pervasiveness of law – Galanter,[26] and others, have described the legal explosion,[27] excessive litigation and the liability crisis, developments which Galanter argues are the product of 'recondite anxieties' about the 'bureaucratisation of the world',[28] 'the juridification of social spheres'[29] and the 'colonialisation of the life-world'.[30] Galanter compared the legal world of the late 1980s with that of 1960 and concluded that there are now more lawyers, more claims, more strategic players of the law game, and more expenditure, both absolutely and proportionately, on law. In addition to the quantitative expansion of law there have been a number of qualitative changes to the legal environment, such as the increasing concern within legal institutions to operate in a rationalised cost-effective and businesslike manner. Broadly speaking, lawyers, administrators and judges are more entrepreneurial and innovative than they ever were in designing and re-designing institutions and procedures. The law itself is plural, decentralised and now comes from multiple sources with more rules and standards being applied by more participants to more varied situations, which means that legal outcomes are contingent and changing. Galanter also concluded that more outcomes are being negotiated rather than being decreed. Because law is contingent (conditional), flexible and technically sophisticated, he argues that legal work has become increasingly costly, yet desired.

Increase in the size of the legal professions – Not surprisingly, the trends illustrated above contributed to an overall rise in the number of practising lawyers. Skordaki[31] has demonstrated that the number of annual admissions to the roll of solicitors more than doubled from 1,877 in 1970 to 4,265 in 1990, resulting in a rise in the number of practising certificates. Much of this increase occurred between 1983/4 and 1994/5, when the

---

[24] Changes in page dimensions and size of font were taken into account in this calculation.

[25] Hansard Society, *Making the Law; The Report of the Hansard Society Commission on the Legislative Process* (The Hansard Society for Parliamentary Government, London, 1992).

[26] Galanter, M., 'Law Abounding: Legalisation Around the North Atlantic' (1992) 55(1) *Modern Law Review* 1.

[27] Barton, J.H., 'Behind the legal explosion' (1975) 27 *Stanford Law Review* 567

[28] Macneil, I.R., 'Bureaucracy, Liberalism and Community – American Style' (1985) 79 *North Western Law Review* 900.

[29] Teubner, G. (ed.), *Juridification of Social Spheres* (Walter De Gruyter, Berlin, 1987).

[30] Ibid.

[31] Skordaki, E., 'Glass Slippers and Glass Ceilings: Women in the Legal Profession' (1996) 3 *International Journal of the Legal Profession* 7. Also see further, Sommerlad, H. and Sanderson, P., *Gender, Choice and Commitment: Women Solicitors in England and Wales and the Struggle for Equal Rights* (Ashgate, Brookfield, VT, 1998).

overall population of solicitors rose by 50 per cent from 44,387 to 66,123.[32] However, this period was also a time of increasing economic uncertainty. Legal practices, like most businesses, have experienced considerable pressures to adapt to modern market forces in order to survive.

In order to further understand the importance of the foregoing trends, we therefore need to look at the actual use of information technology by lawyers and law firms.

The use of information technology by lawyers in legal practice

This section explores the impact of information technology upon the legal professions and it draws upon the findings of a study of the use of information technology by legal professionals.[33] The main thematic conclusions of this research are outlined below.

The different ways that IT is being used within law firms – Three types of usage of information technology by legal practices emerge from the findings. First, is the usage which supplements the back office function, largely replacing dictated letters and file keeping. Second, is the usage which assists the law firms to improve their administrative efficiency. Again mainly 'back office', this IT tends to combine and assist case handling and billing, readily providing the organisations' managers with performance indicators.[34] Third, is the usage which assists lawyers to engage with the law itself. This IT ranges from Lexis/Nexis, to specialist legal networks, to the use of the many CD-Rom databases that are now becoming available, expert systems and document assembly software.

The legal professions and IT – Although the greater majority of lawyers now use information technology in their work, there is surprisingly little

---

[32] For further discussion of the increase in solicitor numbers see Skordaki, E., 'Glass Slippers and Glass Ceilings: Women in the Legal Profession' (1996) 3 *International Journal of the Legal Profession* 7.; Abel, R., 'The Politics of the Market for Legal Services', in Thomas, P.A. (ed.), *Law in the Balance* (Blackwell, Oxford, 1982) at p.6; Abel, R., *The Legal Profession in England and Wales* (Blackwell, Oxford, 1988); Paterson, A. and Nelken, D., 'The Evolution of Legal Services in Britain: Pragmatic Welfarism or Demand Creation?' (1984) 4 *Windsor Yearbook of Access to Justice* 99.

[33] Questionnaires were sent to the 1273 lawyers practising in Leeds (911 solicitors; 300 barristers). A further 62 were sent to solicitors who worked either in private industry or local government. The overall response rate was 35 per cent. In addition to the postal survey questionnaire, interviews were conducted with solicitors, barristers and practice IT managers to elicit further information about their use of information technology, their firm's strategy and what levels of IT competency they expected of their recruits. Leeds was chosen as the site of the research because it is one of the UK's largest provincial legal centres and contains a broad spectrum of legal specialisations; it was also a convenient location. The questionnaires were administered in the mid-1990s; however, follow-up interviews and focus groups conducted in 1998 and 1999 with some of the law firms who took part in the initial survey confirm the representativeness of the thematic findings.

[34] Sommerlad, H. and Wall, D.S., *Legally Aided Clients and their Solicitors: Qualitative perspectives on quality and legal aid* (Research Study No. 34, Law Society, London, 1999).

difference in the overall level of use of information technology between solicitors and barristers. This finding would appear to contradict Kelly's[35] assertion that solicitors tend to be more involved with the administering of law than barristers, whose role is to deal with 'the law'[36] and therefore will more likely use information technology. However, some significant qualitative differences were found which indicated that both branches of the legal profession clearly make different use of information technology, uses which reflect their respective working practices. Barristers, for example, are more likely to use laptops than desktops and word-processing packages more than any other software application, reflecting a more mobile work life and emphasis on orality in practice. The solicitors, on the other hand, use a much broader range of software applications, mainly on networked desktop machines.

Usage by different areas of law – Broadly speaking, lawyers specialising in the traditional, client-based, areas of law, such as family and criminal law, are least likely to use IT, whereas lawyers working in the more recent, but much smaller areas of law, like environmental law and intellectual property law, are most likely to use IT intensively. In simple numerical terms, however, while the smallest areas of law are in fact the most consistent users of IT, it is the commercial lawyers who are numerically the greatest overall users of IT systems within the legal professions.

Gender and usage of IT – When the types of applications used by lawyers are examined some gendered differences become apparent, such as the women lawyers' overall under-usage of IT and high levels of word-processing where IT is used. These differences tend to arise from the unequal positioning of women within the lower echelons of the legal practice, rather than gendered differences in attitudes towards computers.

Clients' expectations of IT – Not only are legal practices very aware of the expectations that corporate clients have of them in terms of their ability to converse electronically and run IT systems, but their corporate clients also tend to have considerable knowledge about what IT facilities are available for lawyers to use. Clients were found to have quite realistic expectations about what can be achieved by using IT-driven methods, for example the electronic transfer of documents and ability to access their own files. In this way the clients themselves are becoming an important factor in encouraging change and are becoming increasingly responsible for changing attitudes within the legal professions, moulding the development of IT strategies and even encouraging the restructuring of legal business.

Motivations for introducing IT – Most of the larger firms which took part in the survey were planning to, or had introduced, in-house case management databases which allow them to store, process and make available to staff vast amounts of information collected throughout the organisation

---

[35] Kelly, M., 'Hypertext – A Model of Lawyers' Text Handling Methods' (1993) 1(3), *International Journal of Law and Information Technology* 354.

[36] Ibid.

– thus facilitating the development of consistent case management by providing practitioners with information about clients, current cases, cases that have already been dealt with by colleagues and the outcomes of those cases. In addition, these systems seek to eradicate unnecessary duplication of effort, for example by providing up-to-date copies of standard legal forms in electronic format. The growing emphasis on the use of internal know-how databases indicate the extent to which firms were responding to the competitive market for legal services.

Availability versus take-up – Generally speaking, there was quite a considerable gap between the availability and take-up of IT by practitioners. Not only were individual lawyers sometimes unaware as to what IT was available for them for use within their firm, but solicitors also tended to be reliant upon internal know-how databases and rarely used other research databases.

Reasons for non-use of computers – Barristers and solicitors put forward very different reasons to explain why they do not use information technology. The barristers who did not use IT, for example, either tended not to have access to a computer, or did not feel that IT was relevant to their work. The solicitors, on the other hand, tended not to have access to computers and only a few felt that they were not relevant to their work.

Although less than a half of lawyers in the mid-1990s said that they did not use a computer, the number today is far less because the majority of medium and larger sized legal practices have since installed IT-based systems. As indicated earlier, lawyers who do not use computers tend to be located in the more traditional client-based areas of law, such as crime and family.[37] Thus, the architecture of legal practice rather than practitioner attitudes tends to determine usage. In fact even in the mid-1990s comparatively few of those who did not use computers did not know how to use them or were not prepared to learn, a finding which contrasted with Susskind's picture of UK lawyers being up to five years behind US attorneys in terms of their acceptance of IT.[38]

Two further findings explain qualitatively different aspects of computer non-use. On the one hand, many of the lawyers who did not use computers still believed that IT could be important to their work and would like to use it to greater effect. On the other hand, of those who had computers available to them, but did not choose to use them, there was still little dissatisfaction with existing IT capabilities, often this choice was made because they wished to wait for training in IT – a finding which reflects that of a Law Society survey[39].

---

[37] The exception in these fields is likely to erode with the advent of block-contracting and consequent pressures towards economy of scale under the Access to Justice Act 1999.

[38] Susskind, R., 'Electronic Communication for Lawyers – Towards Re-engineering the Legal Process' (1993) 4 *Computers and Law* 3.

[39] Jenkins, J., *Omnibus Survey 1, Report 2, Information Technology* (Law Society, London, 1997); 'Better Training Call' (1996) 93(34) *Law Society's Gazette* 22.

IT training and management of change – During the mid-1990s information technology was very much a symbol of corporate virility amongst the larger law firms. However, many of the larger law firms which implemented IT systems appear to overlook, or simply miscalculate the amount of effort required to introduce IT within their firms. The apparent high level of pro-activity in implementing IT therefore contrasted with the reactive utilisation of information technology, thus indicating the presence of a contradiction between firms' IT strategies and their practice. Firms want to be seen by clients to be up-to-date with technology and yet they clearly under-use the information technology that they have invested in.

Success linked to IT – The above observation is an interesting twist to an argument made by the 1994 Robson and Rhodes IT Survey which predicted that there would develop a polarisation between those firms who invested in IT and those who do not.[40] Clearly, investment is not enough; it has to be accompanied by strategies to facilitate implementation and also integration into legal working practices. This does, nevertheless, highlight the potential problems that areas of legal practice which cannot afford to introduce IT might experience in the future especially as the virtual legal community develops. Small practices or Law Centres, for example, which provide services to inner-city clients are traditionally under-funded and do not usually have sufficient resources available to them to equip with the necessary IT. This imbalance will result in a growing disparity of service between themselves and those practices who can afford to have extensive facilities. Clark and Economides[41] predict that the future development of technology and law will become tailored to those who can afford to fund IT projects. Thus a real danger exists 'that the development of expert systems in law will merely reinforce the already powerful and élitist tendencies operating within the legal profession'. In order to avoid these power imbalances 'a more conscious effort must be made to deploy economic, technological and intellectual resources in ways which are sensitive and responsive to collective legal needs and especially those of the disadvantaged and disempowered sections of society'.[42]

The foregoing findings paint an interesting picture of the legal professions in transition. More importantly, they illustrate that information technology impacts upon legal professionalism in a number of different ways. While it was expected that legal practices would be keen to introduce IT, the overall level of willingness among lawyers to engage with new technology was surprisingly high. And yet, in their haste to introduce IT, legal practices would appear to have underestimated the requirements for the management of change, especially with regard to training programmes. One of the revealing impacts of the above study of information technologies is the degree

---

[40] *The Robson Rhodes Legal IT Survey* (RSM International, London, 1994).
[41] Clark, A and Economides, K., 'Computers, Expert Systems and Legal Processes' in Bennum, M. and Narayanan, A., (eds) *Law, Computers and Artificial Intelligence* (Abex, New Jersey, 1991).
[42] Ibid.

to which it demonstrated how much of a solicitor's job now involves administrative and legal procedures and, by comparison, how little it involves the substance of law – thus indicating the degree to which lawyering has become rationalised and has moved away from the traditional conceptualisation of legal professionalism, towards new types and levels of specialism.[43] In many ways, these observations simply confirm what has been predicted or suspected all along, but in other ways they provide important new information about the impact of IT upon legal practice and practitioners – information which informs the following discussion on the broader impacts of IT.

Information technology and the deskilling of the legal professions

Much of the writing on information technology and the legal professions tends to discuss it in fairly benign terms, as a device by which to increase the efficiency of legal practice. Susskind's popular text *The Future of Law*, for example, paints an inevitablist picture of the future of legal practice which expresses the implicit message that firms must embrace IT in order to survive. While this message is probably true in the long term, it is nevertheless a simplistic assumption to make and does tend to hide the fact that legal practices do still have choices left regarding their futures, particularly with regard to deciding the ways by which they will rationalise their structures and as to what types of IT they will integrate into their work. In a sense, it is probably unfair to single out Susskind's book as it, along with Katsh's *Law in a Digital World*,[44] is one of the more sophisticated analyses of the futures of legal practice. However, it and many others tend to concentrate upon scoping the future in terms of the values of the present. The resulting analyses, therefore, emphasise cost benefits, with the benefits invariably outweighing the costs, and they understate the more subjective, and less measurable, issues like professional ethics. Also, in concentrating upon the organisation, many analyses fail to address the deeper impacts of information technology upon individual legal professionals.

We must therefore shift the focus of analysis from the work place to the workers, and one framework for achieving this is Braverman's deskilling thesis.[45] Braverman argues that the history of capitalism has been marked by the progressive degradation of work which has arisen from the managerial expropriation of control from workers through the deepening division of mental and manual labour. This division is achieved through scientific

---

[43] These new specialisms not only tend to locate the practitioner in a specific area of law, but they also involve practitioners developing new legal business skills. For a fuller discussion of legal professionalism see Paterson, A., 'Professionalism and the legal services market' (1996) 3(1) *International Journal of the Legal Profession* 137. For legal specialism see Susskind, R., *The Future of Law* (2nd ed., Oxford University Press, Oxford, 1998).

[44] Katsh, M.E., *Law in a Digital World* (Oxford University Press, New York, 1995).

[45] Braverman, H., *Labour and Monopoly Capital* (Monthly Review Press, New York, 1976), p.100.

management techniques which seek to subdivide work into core tasks that eventually result in the replacement of workers by machine processes. Braverman illustrates that the outcome of rationalisation is always a more detailed division of labour which degrades or deskills work from high to low levels of generic skill and, of course, from higher to lower rates of pay. Although Braverman was writing primarily about the eclipse of industrial craftwork, Burawoy[46] has argued that his thesis could equally be applied to the intellectual craftwork of the professions.

Frequently contested[47] and very often misunderstood,[48] Braverman's thesis places the individual worker at the centre of the analysis. Moreover, the application of the deskilling thesis to the intellectual craftwork of legal practice enables us to understand further the changes that are being experienced by the legal professions as the continuation of a process that has been common to the production process since the beginning of the industrial revolution. The impact of deskilling is always the reduction of the marketable value of the individual worker's skills; however, a frequent misunderstanding of the deskilling thesis is that it simply polarises the workforce into skilled and unskilled. In fact Braverman himself recognised that the rate of birth of new skilled occupations counteracted, or even overwhelmed, progressive deskilling.[49] So, while the deskilling process has the general impact of deskilling and degrading the quality of the work, it nevertheless requires some individuals to develop new specialised skills, for example to operate the new technologies.

It is important to emphasise further the point that was made earlier, namely that deskilling is not the product of new technologies but the ideas about the organisation of work which are generated by the ideological need to divide labour into its core tasks. Thus, the new ideas behind new technologies serve to accelerate the deskilling process. Sommerlad,[50] for example, has argued that new managerialist practices, such as Total Quality Management are manifestations of the rational scientific management practices pioneered by Taylor and Ford and practised since the early part of the century. These ideas are not restricted to the private sector and can also be found embedded in current public policies. Sommerlad cites as an example the transaction criteria which form the backbone of the legal aid franchising initiative. The transaction criteria seek to gain greater control over the

---

[46] Burawoy, M., 'A classic of its time' (1996) 25 *Contemporary Sociology* 296 at p.299.
[47] Tomich, D., 'Review of Braverman's Labour and Monopoly Capital' (1976) 5 *Contemporary Sociology* 6.
[48] For example in the 'dumbing down' debates.
[49] Burawoy, M., loc. cit., at p.297.
[50] Sommerlad, H., 'Managerialism and the Legal Profession: A new professional paradigm' (1995) 2(2) *International Journal of the Legal Profession* 159; Sommerlad, H., 'Criminal Legal Aid Reforms and the Restructuring of Legal Professionalism', in Young, R. and Wall, D.S. (eds), *Access to Criminal Justice: legal aid, lawyers and the defence of liberty* (Blackstone Press, London, 1996) at p.292. Also see Sommerlad, H. and Wall, D.S., *Legally Aided Clients and their Solicitors: Qualitative perspectives on quality and legal aid* (Research Study No. 34, Law Society, London, 1999).

workers' time.[51] As a rule of thumb, the more differentiated a task becomes, the more vulnerable it is to further differentiation and the easier the task is to mechanise.

The detailed division of labour within the legal professions takes place within an organisational context that has been moulded by the rationalisation of capital. Consequently, a characteristic of legal practices during the past few decades has been the creation of larger firms through the amalgamation of medium and small-sized legal practices.[52] These 'mega-law' firms differ from the old types of legal practice as they are mainly staffed by salaried, rather than self-employed solicitors who are encouraged to specialise. The overall impact of these changes has been to diminish the traditional professional autonomy of lawyers, particularly of solicitors.[53] The decline of professional autonomy has led to the further commodification of labour within the law firm. Firms today quite openly see themselves as selling a product under the guise of a service – which is their fee earners' time. So, information technology can be a double-edged sword as, on the one hand, it enables salaried solicitors to work more efficiently, as the benign interpretations tell us, while, on the other, the same 'enabling' technology also provides management with a tool through which lawyers' work can be monitored and controlled,[54] both in terms of how their time is being spent and also how effective they are in carrying out that work.

A poignant example of new technologies accelerating the detailed specialisation of labour and reducing overall levels of legal skill can be seen in the use of computerised personal injury administration systems that are currently being used in the US and are set to become widely used in the UK. These systems enable personal injury claims to be calculated without recourse to a lawyer, unless of course there are exceptional circumstances. Drawing upon a database which contains all of the statistical data from the Personal Injury Valuation Handbooks, the user (not necessarily a lawyer) can establish whether a claim can be made and, if so, then how much can be claimed. The computerised personal injury system therefore allows a firm to take on many more personal injury cases than before by using cheaper non-lawyers, thus reducing overheads and raising profits. Although it could be argued that the system frees the fully qualified lawyer to deal with the more

---

[51] Sommerlad, H., 'Managerialism and the Legal Profession: A new professional paradigm' (1995) 2(2) *International Journal of the Legal Profession* 159, and Sommerlad, H. and Wall, D.S., loc. cit. (1999).

[52] The findings of a recent survey by FT Professional Publishers Ltd, revealed that 'many of the smaller firms in the top 100 are now considering mergers': 'IT Shortfall' (1995) 92 *Law Society's Gazette* 56; Also see Galanter, M., 'Law Abounding: Legalisation Around the North Atlantic' (1992) 55(1) *Modern Law Review* 1; Flood, J., 'Megalaw in the UK' (1989) 64 *Indiana Law Journal* 569.

[53] Barristers are usually self-employed but work in chambers. This section mainly discusses the solicitors' profession.

[54] For an interesting discussion of employee surveillance in the work place, see Kane, P., *Tinsel Show* (Polygon, Edinburgh, 1992), p.94.

complicated matters, the computerised personal injury system nevertheless serves to degrade and de-professionalise work previously carried out by lawyers, thereby undermining the legal professions' guarded monopoly.

Another side to the mechanisation of legal practice is that it enables legal work to take place outside the traditional legal practice, which for many years contained the critical mass of experience in law. For example, a broad range of professional organisations, such as insurance companies, estate agencies and building societies now carry out legal work under the management of in-house lawyers or suitably qualified individuals. Conveyancing is one area which has been the subject of such change, and a number of insurance companies have recently started to offer conveyancing services. One response to this development by the legal firms has been to adopt similar strategies and rationalise, even semi-automate, their conveyancing process through the use of computerised systems. Consequently, the preparation of the case is now largely performed by clerical staff through the computerised system and is subsequently verified by a licensed conveyancer. In the extreme example, the task is fully automated by software, such as in the case of QuickCourt which is a standalone machine used in, for example, Utah that assists divorce petitioners[55] and enables them to initiate legal proceedings themselves.

The brunt of deskilling is always borne by those whose work has been degraded and deskilled to the point that it ceases to exist. The expansion of unqualified paralegals and the decline in secretarial staff during the past two decades also confirms this trend. The dynamics of this process were expressed during an interview with the head of litigation in a large corporate law firm:

> An experienced but unqualified person doing fairly routine work can cost us about £32,000 including National Insurance and Pension, but I don't need all of these people with such a high level of expertise. I really only need one of them to oversee things. If I lower the skills base by standardising procedures, introducing procedure manuals and by using relevant information technology then I can create savings or employ two people [fee earners] for the cost of the existing personnel and effectively double my team. Either way it becomes more cost-effective.[56]

Solicitors are themselves now performing more basic administrative tasks, especially typing and communications, while their own legal work is becoming more specialised and narrow in focus. Many of their substantive functions have now been reduced to standardised procedures and are now being performed by paralegals with an ever-increasing number of functions now being performed by unqualified, or specifically qualified staff. The

---

[55] http://courtlink.utcourts.gov/howto/qkcrt.htm. See Purcell, T., 'Technology's role in access to legal services and legal information', in Smith, R. (ed.), *Shaping the Future* (Legal Action Group, London, 1995), p.82; McConnell, B., 'Speedy Justice' (1995) 145 *New Law Journal* 126; Smith, R., 'Doing the Future Today' (1995) 145 *New Law Journal* 752. For further interfaces between courts and the Internet, see chap. 8.
[56] Interview 23 November 1996.

research findings that were cited earlier certainly confirm that both solicitors and barristers were initiating some of the basic secretarial work themselves. Word-processing, for example, was by far one of the most frequently used applications, which suggests that lawyers, especially the barristers, are now performing many of the tasks that they previously delegated to secretaries. They no longer have to dictate notes or write them on scraps of paper and can now type them into notebook computers to be communicated directly to the recipient. It is not, therefore, surprising that the use of secretarial staff by lawyers is decreasing. In the US the percentage of secretaries per attorney has decreased from 50 per cent to 33 per cent,[57] a trend that is also found in the UK. All of the legal practice managers who were interviewed in the Leeds research said that they were moving away from the traditional one-to-one ratio of secretary to fee earners, towards two or more.[58] Furthermore, this finding is supported by the 1995 Robson Rhodes Legal IT Survey[59] which found that the ratio of secretaries per fee earner had decreased by five per cent between 1993 and 1995. Interestingly, UK lawyers have a higher percentage of secretaries per fee earner than their US colleagues; in 1995 the UK ratio was the same as that in the US in 1988. The ratio has since decreased but is still higher than the US.

Conclusions: the industrialisation of legal practice

The deskilling thesis provides a framework for a deeper understanding of the impact of information technology upon legal practice. It also enables us to peer behind the benign mask of information technology and develop a more realistic understanding of its origins and implications. Moreover, the preceding analysis suggests that the changes that are currently being experienced by the legal professions bear the hallmarks of a process that has long been going on within legal practice and legal professionalism, but at different rates of change. This observation suggests that the 'golden age' theory of professional stability, which allegedly characterised the legal profession until the late 1980s and which forms the basis for many critiques of change within the legal professions, was largely an illusion created by a relatively slow pace of technological change and a high level of workplace control by legal professionals. It would therefore be wrong to assume that there has been a rupture of continuity with the past as many (especially postmodern) theorists suggest. Rather, the utilisation of advanced technology and scientific management techniques have caused, and are still causing, the rate of occupational change to accelerate. It would be a mistake to say that we are experiencing the decline of the legal professions, instead we are experiencing

---

[57] Staudt, R.W., 'Practical Applications of Document Assembly Systems', in Nagel, S., *Law Decision Making and Microcomputers – Cross National Perspectives* (Quorum, New York, 1991).

[58] One firm mentioned that they were aspiring towards one secretary to four fee earners.

[59] *The Robson Rhodes Legal IT Survey* (RSM International, London, 1995) at p.47.

an example of reflexive legal professionalism. The legal professions are doing what they have always done, and that is adapt to market forces.

Summing up, there are some significant differences between 're-negotiated'[60] or reflexive professionalism, and the traditional concepts of legal professionalism.[61] During the past decade or so, four main types of change can be identified which have led to the redefining of traditional legal relationships and the diversification of the legal professions. Firstly, is the changing nature of the relationship between lawyer and client. The traditional 'trustee' relationship between the lawyer and client[62] has been superseded by a relationship in which lawyers are no longer seen to provide a legal *service* in the traditional sense but are now perceived as conducting legal *business* with the client. Secondly, there has been a change in the nature of the relationships between lawyers themselves. The development of a specialised division of labour within areas of law has brought about a marked decline in the general practitioner model of legal practice. Lawyers are now expected to specialise in an area of law. Thirdly, the relationship between lawyers and their employers has changed. The growth of the 'mega-law' firm has resulted in the decline of the self-employed legal professional which has led to changes in the employment structure of the legal professions. Fourthly, there is an increasing polarisation between legal practices which have engaged in the use of information technology and those which have not.

To conclude, legal cyberspace is a growing area of human social activity that has been created by the Internet and provides the potential for cheaper and more effective legal services and also independent personal access to legal information.[63] It is quite conceivable in the near future that consumers with legal needs will be able to seek advice, if not fulfilment of those needs, without ever consulting a lawyer. And, if they do consult lawyers, they may never meet them during the course of their dealings. The implications are quite profound as even our currently changing notions of legal professionalism will soon be outdated as more of the professions' mythical legal knowledge becomes publicly available and software is developed to undertake

---

[60] Paterson, A., 'Professionalism and the legal services market' (1996) 3(1) *International Journal of the Legal Profession* 137.

[61] Characterised by a) a governing body (or bodies) [that] represents a profession and has powers of control and discipline over its members; b) [mastery of] a specialised field of knowledge. This requires not only the period of education and training but also practical experience and continuing study of developments in theory and practice; c) admission is dependent upon a period of theoretical and practical training in the course of which it is necessary to pass examinations and tests of competence; d) [a] measure of self regulation so that it may require its members to observe higher standards than could successfully be imposed from without; e) a professional person's first and particular responsibility is to his client. . . . The client's case should receive the same level of care and attention as the client would himself exert if he had the knowledge and the means, *Final Report of the Royal Commission on Legal Services: Volume 1* (HMSO, London, 1979) at pp.28, 30.

[62] Johnson, T.J., *Professions and Power* (Macmillan, London, 1972).

[63] Wall, D.S. and Johnstone, J., 'The industrialisation of legal practice and the rise of the new electric lawyer: the impact of information technology upon legal practice' (1997) 25 *International Journal of the Sociology of Law* 95.

simple legal procedures; then legal practice will tend to relocate in areas of law which require greater specialist knowledge. At present it is by no means certain that lawyers will remain the 'gatekeepers of the law'. Lockley[64] identifies a growing view among some practice managers that if they 'cannot harness the power of the computer package to ensure we remain the source of legal advice, then we will not deserve to survive'.

As 'virtual' law rapidly develops on the Internet it is quite clear that our story is only half told.[65] We are entering the age of the new electric lawyer.

---

[64] Lockley, A., 'A new law: the client is king; Solicitors must learn to live with the empowered consumer' (1996) *The Independent*, 25 September, p.17.

[65] Wall, D.S. and Johnstone, J. loc. cit.

CHAPTER 6

Cyber-constitutionalism and digital democracy

*Clive Walker**

Introduction

> Information is the key to the modern age. The new age of information offers possibilities for the future limited only by the boundaries of our imaginations. The potential of the new electronic networks is breathtaking – the prospect of change as widespread and fundamental as the agricultural and industrial revolutions of earlier eras . . .[1]

Information technology has profoundly affected the ways in which late modern society operates and is configured, whether in the public and work spheres or in private and social spheres. Indeed, its influence and impact are themselves taken to be prime indicators of a transition from modernism to late modernism and the establishment of the 'informational society'.[2] Among the important features of the technology is its capacity for communication, as exemplified by facilities such as e-mail and the world wide web (often grouped under the heading of 'CMCs' – Computer Mediated Communication Systems).[3] The content of the communications carried by the new medium may often be tediously banal and uninformative. In this respect, the Internet discussion group can outdo the mindlessness of even the most inane tabloid newspaper or radio phone-in by providing an outlet for 'cheap speech'.[4] But at the same time, CMCs have some remarkable properties not shared by newspapers, broadcasting or other established mass media. They

---

* This chapter was developed from a presentation at the JETAI Conference, University of Glasgow, November 1997 and from the paper published as Walker, C. and Akdeniz, Y., 'Virtual democracy' [1998] *Public Law* 489. The author thanks Yaman Akdeniz and Huseyin Demir for valuable insights and source materials.

[1] Prime Minister Tony Blair in Department of Trade and Industry, *Our Information Age* (http://www.number-10.gov.uk/public/info/releases/publications/infoagefeat.html, 1998).

[2] See Castells, M., *The Information Age*, Vol. I: *The Rise of Network Society* (Blackwell, Oxford, 1996) p.21. See also Loader, B.D. (ed.), *The Governance of Cyberspace* (Routledge, London, 1997) chap. 1.

[3] The emphasis in this chapter on 'systems' is deliberate and is meant to emphasise forms of human interaction and involvement. The term will be preferred to Information and Communication Technologies (ICTs).

[4] Volokh, E., 'Cheap speech and what it will do' (1995) 104 *Yale Law Journal* 1805.

can thereby provide opportunities for communication which have attracted the title of a virtual marketplace of ideas – 'a constellation of printing presses and bookstores'.[5] The Millian[6] concept of a marketplace of ideas is of course very much bound up with the goal of the promotion of an informed and active political community in which individuals can achieve self-expression. In this chapter, the promise of the technology to be a vehicle for such an ideal will be gauged within the United Kingdom. The chapter will focus on the positive promotion of CMCs for constitutionalism while recognising also the less palatable political uses which have emanated as well as the limitations and shortcomings inherent in this choice of medium.

Meanings of constitutionalism and democracy

There are at least three aspects within constitutionalism, though these certainly overlap. One is the notion of democracy – that governments depend for their very existence and continuing legitimacy on the will of the people. Second is the doctrine of responsible government – that a government is under a constant obligation to explain its policies and actions – the word accountability is often used – and to provide remedies (including even resignation) in the event of faults and errors. Third is the notion of the rule of law. This is a term which has been assigned so many meanings over the centuries that it is almost as wide as constitutionalism and can be a synonym for it. However, for present purposes, I want the rule of law to mean negatively that the state must act according to preordained and clear laws but also positively that those laws must respect and develop the enjoyment of individual human rights. This chapter shall concentrate on democracy, and, through that, issues of accountability.

There is no single blueprint for the construction of a democracy.[7] As with all concepts of political philosophy, there is room for manoeuvre in how the ideal is to be understood and applied. However, the importance and desirability of democracy are now universal orthodoxies. Democracy is part of the political landscape which confers legitimacy on the distribution, and especially the exercise, of power through the concepts of popular control and political equality.[8] It is a further emanation of the conferment of liberal

---

[5] Wallace, J. and Mangan, M., *Sex, Laws and Cyberspace* (Henry Holt, New York, 1996) p.228.

[6] Mill, J.S., *On Liberty* (J.W. Parker, London, 1859).

[7] For general discussions, see: Macpherson, C.B., *The Real World of Democracy* (Clarendon Press, Oxford, 1966); Lively, J., *Democracy* (Blackwell, Oxford, 1975); Dunn, J. (ed.) *Democracy: the Unfinished Journey 508 BC to AD 1993* (Oxford University Press, Oxford, 1992); Arblaster, A. (ed.), *Democracy* (2nd ed., Open University Press, Milton Keynes, 1994).

[8] See Schumpeter, J., *Capitalism, Socialism, and Democracy* (George Allen and Unwin, London, 1943); Macpherson, C.B., *The Real World of Democracy* (Clarendon Press, Oxford, 1966); Beetham, D., *The Legitimation of Power* (Macmillan, Basingstoke, 1991); Beetham, D., 'Key principles and indices for a democratic audit' in Beetham, D. (ed.), *Defining and Measuring Democracy* (Sage, London, 1994); Beetham, D. and Boyle, K., *Introducing Democracy: 80 Questions and Answers* (Polity Press, Cambridge, 1995).

individual rights, which are thus extended (in a process which occurred in the nineteenth and early twentieth centuries in the West) into the sphere of public governance from the spheres of self-governance and inter-personal governance. The extent of democracy in Britain may be problematic; unlike the United States Constitution, the uncodified and traditional British constitution does not expressly recognise the will of 'We, the People' but tends to emphasise the State as personified in the Crown and as exercised through the sovereignty of Parliament.[9] Nevertheless, the practice of democracy is pragmatically established through laws of universal suffrage and regular elections which regularly command (at national level) an encouraging turnout of voters.[10]

In order to determine how CMCs might be said to relate to, and impact upon, democracy, it is first necessary to explore the meanings of democracy,[11] and this inquiry will be conducted by isolating the various characteristics essential of any democracy.[12]

Representative democracy involves most fundamentally accountability to an electorate. The ultimate test of that accountability comes at election time, but, in between elections, it is vital that public opinion can be expressed and can continue to exert an influence.[13] This feature of accountability is vitally important in large and complex democratic collectives, such as modern nation states, where democracy is more usually representative rather than direct and where responsiveness to the electorate provides the key to legitimacy.

In pursuit of the goals of accountability and the registering of choices, a number of other features come into play. Clearly, information and comprehension of public affairs are vital if autonomous and free choices are to be made by individual electors. Next, the informed citizen may also wish to play an active role in shaping opinion or adding to knowledge and understanding. In this way, the openness and accessibility of channels of communication and the possibility of participation, either through individual action or, more likely, through involvement in a pressure group or party, are important attributes on which the health of a democracy in part depends. A further feature is equality, which implies universal rights to partake in political discourse, universal suffrage and due regard to the interests and preferences of every citizen.

---

[9] See Ridley, F.F., 'There is no British Constitution: a dangerous case of the Emperor's clothes' (1988) 41 *Parliamentary Affairs* 340.
[10] See Blackburn, R., *The Electoral System in Britain* (Macmillan, London, 1995).
[11] The terminology used in the categorisation of democracy in this paper follows Pickles, D., *Democracy* (B.T. Batsford Ltd London, 1970). In other words, direct and representative democracies relate to the processes, while Liberal democracy relates to political and civic ends or outcomes. Economic and social democracy will not be considered in this paper, but see Seyers, S. and McLellan, D., *Socialism and Democracy* (Macmillan, London, 1991); Archer, R., *Economic Democracy* (Clarendon Press, Oxford, 1995); Bobbio, N., *Which socialism?: Marxism, Socialism, and Democracy* (Polity Press, Cambridge, 1986).
[12] See, for example, Jones, T., Newburn, T. and Smith, D.J., *Democracy and Policing* (PSI, London, 1994) chap. 11.
[13] Finer, S.E., *Comparative Government* (Penguin Press, London, 1970) p.63.

Democracies are expected to deliver. Though the process is a talking-shop, there should be practical outcomes. The desired outcomes will of course be expressed in election manifestos and may relate to home affairs, such as law and order, education or foreign affairs such as relations with the European Union. Promises relating to political processes rather than ends – better democracy or better government administration – may be part of the agenda on offer, but political parties which promise no more or even give pride of place to such an agenda tend not to rate highly in the affections of the United Kingdom electorate. Nevertheless, the Conservative government under Prime Minister John Major (1992–7) did place great faith in the improvement of the delivery of governmental services as not only a vote-winner but also an important facet of democracy. This policy was expressed most clearly through the Citizen's Charter.[14] Some question whether this initiative impacts at all upon citizenship (including its wider overtones of democratisation), since it 'neglects the role of the citizen as an active participant in the process of government'.[15] Accountability is to users not to citizens, and so there is a 'democratic deficit'.[16] The Public Service Select Committee of the House of Commons responded to such doubts (just before the General Election of 1997 and so with the benefit of a majority of Conservative members) that it would be wrong to rename it 'the Consumer's Charter' but on the lame grounds that Charter documents can state the balance between delivery and resources, though how this form of edict increases democracy is far from clear. The Labour government has affirmed that the Charter (relaunched as 'Service First') will continue but has also embarked on a programme of the 'modernisation' of the constitution which certainly does have substantial implications for the operation of democracy at local, regional and national levels.[17]

Finally, the proponents of direct democracy[18] would additionally contend that citizens should be able to decide political issues for themselves rather than always (or perhaps even ever) have decisions taken second-hand by elected representatives.[19] This degree of involvement might especially apply to key

---

[14] Cm. 1599, HMSO, London, 1991. See Barron, A. and Scott, C., 'The Citizen's Charter programme' (1992) 55 *Modern Law Review* 526; Barendt, E., 'The Citizen's Charter programme' (1993) 46 *Current Legal Problems* 116; Ridley, F.F., 'Reinventing British government' (1995) 48(3) *Parliamentary Affairs* 387; Prior, D., Stewart, J. and Walsh, K., *Citizenship: Rights, Community and Participation* (Pitman, London, 1995).

[15] Public Service Committee, *Citizen's Charter* (1996–7 HC 78) para. 26.

[16] Bogdanor, V., 'When the buck doesn't stop here anymore' (1993) *Guardian* 14 June p.18.

[17] See Cabinet Office, *Modernising Government* (Cm. 4310, Stationery Office, London, 1999); Blackburn, R. and Plant, R., *Constitutional Reform: the Labour government's constitutional reform agenda* (Longman, London, 1999); Hazell, R., *Constitutional Futures: A History of the Next Ten Years* (Oxford University Press, Oxford, 1999).

[18] See Pateman, C., *Participation and Democratic Theory* (Cambridge University Press, 1970); Barber, B., *Strong Democracy: Participatory Politics for a New Age* (University of California Press, Berkeley, 1984).

[19] For commentaries on representative democracy, see Schattschneider, E.E., *Party Government* (Farrar & Reinehart, New York, 1942); Schumpeter, J., *Capitalism, Socialism, and Democracy* (George Allen and Unwin, London, 1943) p.269; Lively, J., *Democracy* (Blackwell, Oxford, 1975); Holden, B. *Understanding Liberal Democracy* (Philip Allan, Oxford and

decisions about constitutional affairs, where the importance of the verdict demands a direct voice for the citizen.[20] Further, this mode of democracy is sometimes seen as desirable for very localised decisions, where the issues are not complex or where the outcome either way has limited impact on everyday life.[21]

The democratic potential of CMCs

How then can the CMCs relate to these different forms or characteristics of democracy?[22] An initial observation is that interconnectivity with the technological media may be an important protector of democratisation, since the new outlets present severe difficulties of control for authoritarian regimes.[23]

> Telecommunications played as much of a role as pickaxes and shovels in bringing down the Berlin Wall and the barbed wire of the Iron Curtain.[24]

There is clear evidence of major political change consequent upon global television coverage of events in the former Soviet Union and the Eastern Bloc. The scandal of Chernobyl, the tragic events leading to the overthrow of Ceausescu in Romania and the massive political upheavals following the attempted overthrow of Yeltsin's fledgling democracy, these could all be directly linked to the free flow of information and the power of modern communications media.[25] Along with television, other communications technologies such as satellites, fax machines and mobile phones, computers and modems played an important role in the globalisation of information systems, 'rendering national boundaries invisible'.[26]

New Jersey, 1988); Hirst, P., *Representative Democracy and Its Limits* (Polity Press, Cambridge, 1990); Schmitter, P.C. and Karl, T.L., 'What Democracy is . . . and is not' (1991) 2(3) *Journal of Democracy* 76; Dunn, J. (ed.) *Democracy: the Unfinished Journey 508 BC to AD 1993* (Oxford University Press, Oxford, 1992).

[20] Examples in the United Kingdom have primarily related to the European Communities and to devolution schemes: Alderson, S., *Yea or Nay? Referenda in the United Kingdom* (Cassell, London, 1975) chaps 4, 6; Norton, P., *The Constitution in Flux* (Basil Blackwell, 1984) chap. 11; Referendums (Scotland and Wales) Act 1997; Greater London Authority (Referendum) Act 1998.

[21] For examples, see Alderson, S., *Yea or Nay? Referenda in the United Kingdom* (Cassell, London, 1975) chap. 3.

[22] For overviews, see Fiorilli, L., 'Democracy and the Internet' (http://www.albany.net/%7efioril/democr.htm); Scolve, R.E., *Democracy and Technology* (Guildford Press, New York, 1995). There is of course a much wider agenda covering the use of technology for government purposes other than democratic engagement; see Parliamentary Office of Science and Technology, *Electronic Government – information technologies and the citizen* (London, 1998) chap. 3.

[23] Kedzie, C.R., 'Democracy and network interconnectivity' (http://www.isoc.org:80/HMP/PAPER/134/html/paper.html, 1995). See for example the Free Burma Coalition's website at the University of Wisconsin (http://freeburma.org) and the B92 Internet radio station in Belgrade during the Balkans conflicts (http://www.b92.net/).

[24] McGowan, W., 'The part as prologue: the impact of international telecommunications', in Chaloner, H. (ed.), *Telecom 91 Global Review* (Kline Publishing, London, 1991) p.56.

[25] Martin, W.J., *The Global Information Society* (Aslib Gower, Guildford, 1995) pp.9–10.

[26] See Hudson, H.E., *Global Connections: International Telecommunications Infrastructure and Policy* (Van Nostrand Reinhold, New York, 1997) chap. 1.

As for established democracies, there are several design features of CMCs which may not only mark them out as distinct from other media but also as having the potential to make a distinct contribution to democratic progress. At the same time, it seems inherently unavoidable that the cultural character of the technology will impact on the forms of democracy with which it interacts or attempts to interact – 'technology is cultural'.[27] This observation will also come into play later in this chapter in considering the limitations and drawbacks of the medium.

Among the positive features of CMCs is their ability to link on a mass scale, thereby overcoming problems of transmission. They have the capacity to store and disseminate vast amounts of information; the problem of limited spectrum space does not arise. Mainly because of this capacity, the CMCs comprise a relatively open mass medium as regards content production, content distribution and content oversight by bodies of governance, and this feature overcomes problems of entry into the political arena as well as freedom to operate within it. There is the advantage of instantaneity – the ability to publish and to receive messages without any delay and so to be able to respond to events and perhaps to influence them before it is too late. Potential problems of time lapse can thereby be overridden. Space is equally vanquished by the global nature of the CMCs which have roots now in virtually all countries and territories[28] (but many African states form an important exception) and can easily transcend national boundaries.

The foregoing features can easily be related to the attributes of democracy listed earlier. The capacity of CMCs means that the largest collectors and storers of information in most societies – governments[29] – should be able to make effective use of this medium. Accountability can be enhanced by interlinking, whether through e-mail or web pages, between elected representatives or bureaucrats and the citizen. These facilities allow for an increase in knowledge on the part of the citizen and the search for the truth or at least better understanding which in turn allows for critical debate and discussion, rational choice between proponents of policies or the assessment and refinement of policies. In this way, information technology can take us some way towards an ideal speech situation[30] which may result in improved decision-making[31] and can obviously assist with the rational choice between candidates at election time.[32]

[27] Street, J., 'Remote control?' (1997) 12(1) *European Journal of Communication* 27 at p.30.
[28] See Negroponte, N., *Being Digital* (Alfred A. Knopf, New York, 1995) p.165; Jones, S.G. (ed.), *Cybersociety* (Sage, Thousand Oaks, 1995); Johnson, D.R. and Post, D., 'Law and borders – the rise of law in cyberspace' (1996) 48 *Stanford Law Review* 1367.
[29] See *Report of the Committee on Data Protection* (Cmnd. 7341, HMSO, London, 1978).
[30] Habermas, J., *Communication and the Evolution of Society* (Heinemann Educational, London, 1979), *The Theory of Communicative Action* (Heineman, London, 1984), *The Structural Transformation of the Public Sphere* (Polity Press, Cambridge, 1992).
[31] Select Committee on the Parliamentary Commissioner for Administration, *Open Government* (1995–6 HC 84) para. 20.
[32] But the main political parties failed to make any distinct use of CMCs during the 1997 General Election: Yates, S.J. and Perrone, J.L., 'Politics on the web' (IRISS '98 Conference: The social impact of the information revolution, http://www.sosig.ac.uk/iriss/papers/paper46.htm).

As a result, the dissemination of information to the public becomes a key factor in avoiding political decisions being taken on uninformed, sectarian or simply technical/managerial grounds.[33] The provision of information is a democratic goal in itself, and the formats available through computers may be rather televisual and therefore attractive to many citizens, thereby aiding comprehension. This feature also tends towards accessibility. Recognising that most citizens are at most times more or less apathetic, participation via CMCs is far more convenient than attendance at public meetings in cold school halls or even the quinquennial trip to the polling booth. Democracy is available at the touch of the keyboard in the warmth of one's own home. So, here is the way to conduct 'a democracy for the moderately lazy'[34] and to overcome the problems of passivity and apathy. Many of the foregoing features of CMCs also contribute to the delivery of governmental services, especially the provision of information about services, points of contact and advice.

Another important characteristic of the new medium is interactivity. The capacity for citizens to act not only as the passive recipients of government but also as active communicators and directors is clearly very attractive. In this way, it can form the basis for deeper participation in the political process through online discussion as well as simple, one way information provision by government or representation or protest by citizen. For example, the 'Blue Ribbon' campaign was organised as a global protest against the censorship of the Internet by the United States government.[35] At the national level, for example, the availability of a previously suppressed United Kingdom local government Joint Enquiry Team ('JET') Report (about child abuse in Nottinghamshire) on more than 30 websites is a good example of direct citizen involvement.[36] It can even pave the way for direct democracy where CMCs are used to facilitate direct decision-making by active 'netizens'.[37] Thus, as well as the enhancement of representative democracy – the choice of the electorate entrusted to elected candidates – CMCs may provide pathways for the growth of direct democracy, and so some visionaries have talked of electronic town hall meetings which empower the netizen to make real policy choices without intercession.[38] In addition, and going back

---

[33] Habermas, J., *The Structural Transformation of the Public Sphere* (Polity Press, Cambridge, 1992); Benhabib, S., 'Models of public space' in Calhoun, C. (ed.), *Habermas and the Public Sphere* (MIT Press, Cambridge, MA, 1992); Hirst, P., *Associative Democracy* (Polity Press, Cambridge, 1994) p.20.

[34] Hirst, P., 'Democracy and accountability in a post-Liberal society' (Haldane Society, London, 1996).

[35] See: Communications Decency Act 1996 (47 USC s.223); *ACLU v Reno* 521 US 844 (1997); Akdeniz, Y., 'Censorship on the internet' (1997) 147 *New Law Journal* 1003.

[36] See Akdeniz, Y., 'Copyright and the Internet' (1997) 147 *New Law Journal* 965 at p.966.

[37] See Barber, B., *Strong Democracy: Participatory Politics for a New Age* (University of California Press, Berkley, 1984) p.307.

[38] See Adonis, A. and Mulgen, G., 'Back to Greece: the scope for direct democracy' (1994) 3 *Demos Quarterly* 2. This potential is often considered as a feature of emergent media: Street, J., 'Remote control?' (1997) 12(1) *European Journal of Communication* 27.

to previous features, interactivity can again assist with accountability, comprehension and accessibility. For example, it is reckoned that United States President Clinton receives more e-mail than any other person on earth.[39]

Finally, many of the features now rehearsed can tend in the direction of equality. These include the ability to provide mass links and to do so at low cost per paragraph or picture.[40]

Overall, the potential of CMCs for democratic advancement is immense, and politicians have laid out visions of CMCs 'reinvigorating local government and renewing informed public interest in national and international affairs'.[41] The arrival of the new media may also be timely. Several of their features seem distinct from the established media, even the broadcast media, which are said to be failing the democratic process by trivialising, sensationalising and even distorting political discourse,[42] egged on by eager politicians willing to play the same game.[43] But has the promise of democratic renewal in fact been realised? Was it ever realisable in the first place? This chapter will next examine the promotion and uses of CMCs with respect to the democratic accountability of different tiers of government in the United Kingdom. Attention will then be turned to the inherent obstacles to greater impact.

Promotion and uses of CMCs in practice

The central state

In terms of information and comprehension at least, one would suppose that the capabilities of information technologies to store, process and disseminate the vast amounts of data created by central government should have revolutionised the democratic accountability of the departments of state. In this way, the Public Records Acts 1958–67 and the Code on Open Government[44] could have been made much more effective, with far fewer records having to be culled than the current mortality rate,[45] and far more information

---

[39] See http://www.whitehouse.gov/WH/Welcome.html. US President Clinton's e-mail address is president@whitehouse.gov.

[40] Bonchek, M.S., 'Grassroots in Cyberspace: Using Computer Networks to Facilitate Political Participation', (The Political Participation Project, MIT Artificial Intelligence Laboratory, http://www.ai.mit.edu/people/msb/pubs/grassroots.html, 1995).

[41] Battle, J., 'Deepening democracy – the challenge of the new technology' (1995) 13(2) *Information Technology and Public Policy* 196. See also Bollier, D., 'Reinventing Democratic Culture in an Age of Electronic Networks' (http://www.netaction.org/bollier/index.html).

[42] Blumler, J. and Gurevitch, M., *The Crisis of Public Communication* (Routledge, London, 1995).

[43] Franklin, B., *Packaging Politics* (Edward Arnold, London, 1994).

[44] Cm. 2290, HMSO, London, 1993. The Code itself is also available at http://www.open.gov.uk/m-of-g/codete.htm. See Birkinshaw, P., 'I only ask for information' [1993] *Public Law* 557; Select Committee on the Parliamentary Commissioner for Administration, *Open Government* (1994–5 HC 84, 1995–6 HC 84); *Government Responses* (1995–6 HC 556, 1996–7 HC 75). The plans for the Code's replacement, the Freedom of Information Act 2000, are set out in the White Paper, Your Right to Know (Cm. 3818, Stationery Office, London 1997) and the Draft Bill (Cm. 4355, Stationery Office London, 1999).

[45] See Wilson Committee, *Modern Public Records* (Cmnd. 8204, HMSO, London, 1981) and *Government Response* (Cmnd. 8531, HMSO, London, 1982).

routinely being made available on the initiative of government departments. The Conservative government seemed to envisage such a trend in its White Paper, *Open Government*, in 1993.[46] But there are no signs that the grudging rules as to storage[47] and disclosure[48] have been at all transformed. Under pressure from the Select Committee on the Parliamentary Commissioner for Administration,[49] the government accepted that it would be good practice to consider the early release of information on the department's own initiative without waiting for any request.[50] But this undertaking is confined largely to factual information rather than internal discussion, and the flow of information has not increased dramatically since this promise was made. A far greater volume of materials has appeared through the Internet (as described below), and this accessibility is undoubtedly valuable on the ground that '[t]he well informed citizen needs the possibility to participate in constant public debate'.[51] An increased volume of materials has certainly emerged through the Internet, and this accessibility is very much to be welcomed – the government is probably the largest collector and user of data in our society. However, it should be emphasised that these publications are not by and large unique to that medium but largely duplicate the physical publication of papers – 'brochureware,'[52] so the overall volume of public information has not really increased, just its ease of accessibility.[53] The White Paper, *Your Right to Know*,[54] promises a proactive duty to publish certain information and an even more ambitious plan to change the civil service culture of secrecy, but the small print suggests that little more is on offer in this aspect of freedom of information than was available under the Code of Practice. It is disappointing that the 30-year rule is to be retained, and there is no commitment to retain electronically a wider range of records than was possible on paper.[55] Nor is there any sign that the release of information is going to be significantly increased after the passage of the Freedom of Information Act 2000, even though the Internet could provide an important vehicle for openness.

The main agency for transfer of central government information is the Central Computer and Telecommunications Agency ('CCTA'),[56] which

---

[46] Cm. 2290, HMSO, London, 1993.
[47] See *Government Response* (1996–7 HC 75) p.vi.
[48] See Birkinshaw, P., *Freedom of Information* (2nd ed., Butterworths, London, 1996) chap. 5.
[49] *Open Government* (1994–5 HC 84, 1995–6 HC 84).
[50] *Government Response* (1996–7 HC 75) p.v.
[51] See G7 Secretariat, 'Online support for democracy', at http://www.open.gov.uk/govoline/10101.pdf.
[52] National Audit Office, *Government on the Web* (1999–2000 HC 87) para. 1.5.
[53] But it should be noted that some of the Department of Trade and Industry papers are only published on the Internet. See Consultation Paper, *Licensing of Trusted Third Parties for the Provision of Encryption Services* (http://www.dti.gov.uk/pubs, 1997) and also *Regulatory Intent Concerning Use Of Encryption On Public Networks* (http://dtiinfo1.dti.gov.uk/cii/encrypt/, 1996).
[54] (Cm. 3818, HMSO, London, 1997) paras 2.17, 2.18, chap. 6.
[55] Compare Ryan, S.M., *Downloading Democracy* (Hampton Press, New Jersey, 1996).
[56] See http://www.open.gov.uk/ccta/thisccta.htm. See also the G7 Government On-Line Project at http://www.open.gov.uk/govoline/golintro.htm.

operates within the Cabinet Office. The CCTA has indeed taken up the new technology with some enthusiasm in conjunction with the technical agency, the Central Information Technology Unit.[57] The CCTA reckons that the United Kingdom government's site, http://www.open.gov.uk, is the largest public sector web gateway in Europe. It is undoubtedly both large and growing, but one is struck by the complexity, the detail and its prosaic nature. As noted above, its main impact (mainly post-1995)[58] has been to publish, through the World Wide Web, command papers and departmental papers which also appear in printed form. The resultant instantaneity and accessibility of publication on the web is certainly a boon to academic researchers and political lobbyists, but it surely does not have the same attraction to mass audiences. There is little by way of guidance for the non-expert. There is scant invitation to interact with what is read beyond the formulaic contact point by way of e-mail.

A far broader programme for engagement was suggested by the House of Lords Select Committee on Science and Technology in its paper, *Information Society*.[59] However, the government's *Response*[60] was rather disappointing. For example, the government adhered to the view that it was up to Departments to decide what information is provided free of charge.[61] There was no commitment to the web publication of all circulars and other 'hidden law' such as manuals, commissioned research, policy papers or maps of personnel and structures. Rather, the emphasis was upon the instrumental usage of information technology in commerce, such as through the Information Society Initiative aimed at small and medium-sized businesses and the Cabinet Office e-Envoy concerned primarily with e-commerce.[62]

An equally narrow approach to the democratic agenda, again emphasising information provision, accessibility and delivery of outcomes, but ignoring to a large extent accountability and participation, was also reflected in a paper issued by the Cabinet Office in 1996, *government.direct: A prospectus for the Electronic Delivery of Government Services*.[63] This stressed the value of information technology public service reform and the delivery

---

[57] See http://www.open.gov.uk/citu/pfi/citurole.htm. The CITU provides advice on IT strategy to ministers and departments, with a notable emphasis on the relevance of the Private Finance Initiative.

[58] The service opened on 17 July 1994 when there were 15 accesses (http://www.open.gov.uk/usage/); on Tuesday 17 March 1998, there were 189,089 accesses (http://www.open.gov.uk/analog/stats.html).

[59] House of Lords, Select Committee on Science and Technology, *Information Society: Agenda for Action in the UK* (1995–6 HL 77).

[60] Cm. 3450, HMSO, London, 1996.

[61] (Cm. 3450, HMSO, London, 1996) para. 6.14. A decentred strategy is also espoused by the current Minister for Science Energy and Industry, John Battle: 'HMG strategy for the internet', 18 March 1998 (http://www.dti.gov/Minspeech/btlspch3.htm).

[62] See http://www.isi.gov.uk/ and http://www.e-envoy.gov.uk.

[63] (Cm. 3438, HMSO, London, 1996). For the responses to the Green Paper, see: http://www.open.gov.uk/citu/gdirect/greenpaper/response/index.htm; Parliamentary Office of Science and Technology, *Electronic Government – information technologies and the citizen* (London, 1998) para. 2.3.

of high standards of administrative performance; the target is for 25 per cent of services to be accessible via the Internet by 2002[64] (later revised to 100 per cent by 2008[65]). In this way, there was a very firm link to the repressed vision of the Citizen's Charter programme, with its concern for New Public Management service delivery, rather than public participation in policy formation or review or accountability to the citizen rather than to the Treasury. This stance was reflected in three out of the four objectives set by the Cabinet Office paper, viz better and more efficient services; cost savings; the improvement of efficiency; the improvement of openness.[66] Only the last element has relevance to participative democracy, but it seemed not to be the driving principle as no specific proposals are built upon this observation, though the paper recognised that the flow of information 'will help citizens to involve themselves more in the democratic process'.[67] Similarly, the possibility of funding new links to the web which will be sited in public access places was raised not to allow accountability and participation in the political process but for the Citizen's Charter-like purposes of better service delivery and take-up in connection with job-seekers, vehicle licensing, income tax returns and benefits claims.[68]

This critical picture of central government blindness to a fuller democratic agenda could have been expected to change after the coming to office of the Labour Party in May 1997. Reform of the Constitution is a key part of the 1997 election manifesto and is evidenced by policies such as the incorporation of the European Convention, the reform of the House of Lords, freedom of information, devolution and a referendum on the voting system.[69] In terms of policy towards CMCs, there has been the emergence of an agenda much wider than the erstwhile preoccupation with industry and commerce and which especially emphasises access, an issue which will be taken up later. However, the organising principle of these changes has begun as modernisation rather than democratisation.[70] For example, even in relation to what is arguably the most politically radical step in the series of reforms, *Rights Brought Home: the Human Rights Bill*,[71] Prime Minister Tony Blair states in the Preface:

> The Government is pledged to modernise British politics. We are committed to a comprehensive programme of constitutional reform. We believe it is right to

[64] See Department of Trade and Industry, *Our Information Age* (http://www.number-10.gov.uk/public/info/releases/publications/infoagefeat.html, 1998).
[65] Cabinet Office, *Modernising Government* (Cm. 4310, Stationery Office, London, 1999) chap. 5 para. 16.
[66] (Cm. 3438, HMSO, London, 1996) para. 4.1.
[67] Ibid. para. 9.4.
[68] Ibid. para. 7. See further Bellamy, C. and Taylor, J.A., *Governing in the Information Age* (Open University Press, Buckingham, 1998) p.37.
[69] See the Labour Party Manifesto at http://www.labour.org.uk/views/index.html.
[70] Beetham, D., 'New Labour, democracy and constitutional reform' (Centre for Democratisation Studies Democracy Seminar, University of Leeds, 1997).
[71] Cm. 3782, HMSO, London, 1997.

increase individual rights, to decentralise power, to open up government and to reform Parliament.

It will be noted that the word 'democracy' does not appear, while modernisation is a term perhaps more closely associated with effectiveness and efficiency along the lines of the Citizen's Charter.

The restraint on Labour government thinking is evidenced by a consultation paper, *Crown Copyright in the Information Age*.[72] It depicts access to information as a key component of democracy and therefore considers whether the relaxation of copyright protection would help. But in terms of gains, the Paper thinks in terms of encouraging markets to exploit information rather than how this can spark democratic participation.[73] Likewise the later paper, *The Future Management of Crown Copyright*,[74] talks about 'evolution, not revolution' and offers few concessions in relation to official documents like statutes or court judgments. It seems that Crown papers are still at base depicted in property terms rather than as public goods which could be distributed via the Internet without enticing a private publisher.[75] More generally, the Cabinet Office paper, *Modernising Government*,[76] is based on 'a mission to modernise', and though there is mention of 'people as citizens',[77] it is their treatment as consumers which is really addressed. Thus, the paper emphasises 'Information Age Government' but again as a mode of better service delivery, especially through the 'joined-up working' of official agencies.[78] The National Audit Office paper, *Government on the Web*, once again depicts the public expectations in terms of service standards akin to private sector concerns.[79] Only the revamped website of the Prime Minister contains policy discussions and a 'Speaker's Corner', but the subjects tackled are often unrelated to specific government policy and there is a governmental response but not participation in the debate.[80]

As well as the executive, there has been much interest in the exploitation of CMCs on the part of Parliament. The Select Committee on Information in its paper in 1995, *Electronic Publication of House of Commons Documents*,[81] welcomed proposals to make parliamentary documents available free of charge via the Internet 'since it would . . . encourage wider public

---

[72] Cm. 3819, Stationery Office, London, 1998.
[73] Ibid., para. 4.12.
[74] *Future Management of Crown Copyright* (Cm. 4300, Stationery Office, 1999).
[75] Boyle, J., *Shamans, Software and Spleens* (Harvard University Press, 1996) chap. 4.
[76] (Cm. 4310, Stationery Office, London, 1999), foreword by Tony Blair. See also Lord Chancellor's Department, *Modernising Justice* (Cm. 4155, Stationery Office, London, 1998) paras 1.13, 2.13, 2.18.
[77] Ibid., Introduction by Jack Cunningham and see also chap. 2. Even the national responses as consumers are through a closed focus group (the People's Panel) rather than an open invitation through CMCs: chap. 3.
[78] (Cm. 4310, Stationery Office, London, 1999) para. 5.
[79] National Audit Office, *Government on the Web* (1999–2000 HC 87) para. 1.4.
[80] See http://www.number-10.gov.uk/YourSay/.
[81] (1995–6 HC 328).

interest in, and knowledge of, the business of the House'.[82] This was suggested even though it could present drawbacks in terms of intellectual property rights for the privatisation of HMSO. Since that time, an important website has been established,[83] but one might make the same criticism that it is primarily a vehicle for information transfer. This is very important and very useful (especially once again for researchers and academics). The Parliamentary site also contains some splendid guides to the workings of Parliament which are far more interesting and informative than anything offered by most government departments.[84] But the existing pages are not constructed to engender debate or to excite citizens to speak and vote. Apathy and ignorance cannot be entirely blamed on the electorate – it is the duty of the legislators to engage with it. A suitable medium, which will soon reach into schools and libraries, is at their disposal, but it has been found in a recent report by the Parliamentary Office of Science and Technology that the attitude of many is shaped by negative fears of 'a deluge of mail from constituents, lobbyists, advertisers and people from other countries [such as] US students with politics homework!'[85] Perhaps in response to such traffic, an educational site for schoolchildren related to the workings of Parliament opened in 1999.[86]

In summary, a picture emerges of the increasing provision of information transfer from both the executive and legislature. A unique opportunity exists for a new mode of interaction between government and citizen.[87] One hopes that this might aid comprehension, and it could be said to amount to a delivery of a service in itself. The information is offered at no charge by the producer and so complies with the principle of equality. But there is as yet little interactivity – attempts to foster discussion, participation and response, whether by citizens or by those in power, are sadly lacking. That task has seemingly been entrusted, as is often the British way, to 'amateur'[88] outsiders. Most prominent amongst them is an organisation called UK Citizen's On-line Democracy ('UKCOD').[89] This began in late 1995 to 'develop opportunities for wider public participation in the democratic process using online electronic communication'. It has provided information on

---

[82] Ibid., para. 5.

[83] See http://www.parliament.uk/.

[84] See for example, *The Judicial Work of the House of Lords* at http://www.parliament.the stationery-office.co.uk/pa/ld199697/ldinfo/ld08judg/ld08judg.htm.

[85] *Electronic Government – information technologies and the citizen* (London, 1998) para. 3.4.2.

[86] http://www.explore.parliament.uk/.

[87] Schorr, H. and Stolfo, S.J., 'Towards the Digital Government of the 21st Century: A Report from the Workshop on Research and Development Opportunities in Federal Information Services', (http://www.isi.edu/nsf/prop.html, 1997).

[88] This is certainly not intended in any pejorative sense – the point is that they are not professional politicians or public officials.

[89] See http://www.democracy.org.uk. Compare in Belgium, Cybercrate, which provides information, links and an electronic meeting space (http://www.axismundi.org/cybercrate) and in Germany Mehr Democratie (http://www.mehr-demokratie.de/). See Macpherson, M., 'Citizen politics and the renewal of democracy' (Bulletin of the European Institute for the Media (Duesseldorf, http://www.snafu.de/~mjm/CP/cp2.html, 1997).

matters of political interest, as well as structured online discussion forums for members of the public, interest groups and politicians. The organisation won financial support from companies and charities, and it has been utilised by the European Parliament for a discussion on monetary union. However, UKCOD remains relatively obscure even to web aficionados,[90] and it is also modest in terms of its coverage (with just a handful of topics for national online discussion). It also originates as a private rather than public initiative, though this line has become blurred through the support by the Cabinet Office of the site as a forum for the discussion of the White paper, *Your Right to Know*. Another example is the conference to discuss 'Public Information, Interactive Politics and the New Media', organised in October 1997 by the Hansard Society. This was the first conference in the United Kingdom exclusively devoted to an examination of the effects of new technologies, from the Internet to digital TV, on the democratic process. The conference concluded that the political process must open up to a more interactive dialogue between Parliament and citizens, and that the new technologies could be applied to the democratic process. These are stirring objectives, but it is remarkable that they come from a small and academic research group rather than Parliament itself.

While the use of CMCs by United Kingdom officialdom outstrips most of its European counterparts,[91] one might briefly compare the position in regard to the United States, where it is arguable that much more has been achieved.[92] At Federal level, there is wide dissemination of information by government webservers[93] and by Congress.[94] Individual legislators have also taken up CMCs; for example, there is an Internet Caucus within Congress which, through its website seeks interaction with the public about its policies and directions.[95] By 1998, 422 of the 535 members of Congress had established their own web pages, providing information about themselves and their

---

[90] Its discussion on *government.direct* garnered just 46 responses: Coleman, S., 'UK Citizens online democracy' (http://www.open.gov.uk/govline/chap17.htm).

[91] In France, see *Preparing France's Entry Into the Information Society* (http://www.premier-ministre.gouv.fr/DOSACTU/dpresang.htm). Ironically, the President of the Republic's site encourages contact by written letter (http://www.elysee.fr/mel/mel_.htm), citing the insecurity of Internet messages as a problem though it is one which is hardly assisted by French policies on encryption (see Global Internet Liberty Campaign, *Cryptography and Liberty* (Washington DC, 1998) pp.18–19). For an attempt to utilise the transnational nature of CMCs by linking all parliamentarians in European Union states, see Virtual Interparle (http://www.interparle.org/main.asp).

[92] See *Access America; Electronic Government – Serving The Public On Its Terms* (http://www.gits.fed.gov/htm/access.htm). In the report, Vice President Al Gore envisions 'a Government where all Americans have the opportunity to get services electronically and where, aided by technology, the productivity of Government operations will be soaring'. See for other electronic democracy initiatives from other countries 'Government On-Line and Democracy: Lessons, Issues, and Future Prospects: A White Paper of Contributed Chapters from Around the World', at http://www.state.mn.us/gol/democracy.

[93] See especially http://www.fedworld.gov/.

[94] See http://thomas.loc.gov/. See Casey, C., *The Hill on the Net* (AP Professional, Boston, 1996).

[95] See http://www.house.gov/white/internet_caucus/hello.html.

activities. Although all these sites have e-mail addresses, it is reported that it is very difficult to get a reply from the members of Congress, suggesting an initial interest in form rather than substance.[96] There also exists a number of initiatives involving collaborative ventures with private groups, such as democracy.net,[97] a joint project of the Center for Democracy and Technology and Voters Telecommunications Watch, which hosts live and interactive cybercasts of Congressional hearings and more local discussions with Senators and Representatives to illustrate the potential of the Internet to impact the democratic process in a constructive way. A wide variety of other independent groups also seeks to encourage debate about public affairs. One illustration is Votelink,[98] which organises referenda on national issues. Voters can record their votes and opinions, and they may be assisted by summaries of the issues to be decided and by the posted comments of other voters. This is an experimental organisation which does operate commercially by selling advertising, but it provides free listing space for any non-profit or governmental agency which is relevant to a topic under discussion. Though based in Boulder, Colorado, it is probably the only web-based organisation to have attempted an online debate on 'Should Britain leave the European Union'.

The local state

A similar pattern emerges at a local level in the United Kingdom. Information technologies are often seen as promotional – offering 'little more than electronic versions of brochures',[99] especially in connection with economic regeneration and urban development, and with an emphasis therefore on issues such as the availability of grants, transport and employment infrastructure, planning structures and industrial land information. The messages designed for citizens tend again towards the passive, typically with information about contact addresses for councillors and officials, and with little articulation of the links to democracy.[100] Nevertheless, there are some isolated attempts to create 'electronic town halls' and civic networking.[101]

---

[96] See Schmitt, E., 'Congress Stays in Touch on the Web', *The New York Times*, CyberTimes section, 24 November 1997.

[97] See http://www.democracy.net.

[98] See http://www.votelink.com. See also the Democracy and Internet Workgroup (http://www.sas.upenn.edu/~eumansky/net.dem.html) and Politics1 (http://www.politics1.com/).

[99] Parliamentary Office of Science and Technology, *Electronic Government – information technologies and the citizen* (London, 1998) Annex D para. 4.2.

[100] See Bellamy, C., Horrocks, I. and Webb, J., 'Exchanging information with the public' (1995) 21.1 *Local Government Studies* 11; Horrocks, I. and Zouridis, S., 'Electronic public information systems' in Bekkers, V., Koops, B.-J. and Nouwt, S. (eds), *Emerging Electronic Highways* (Kluwer, Hague, 1996).

[101] See Carter, D., '"Digital democracy" or "information aristocracy"' in Loader, B.D. (ed.), *The Governance of Cyberspace* (Routledge, London, 1997); Tsagarousianou, R., Tambini, D. and Bryan, C. (eds) *Cyberdemocracy* (Routledge, London, 1998) chap. 8; G7, 'Democracy and government on-line services' (http://www.open.gov.uk/govline/front.htm, 1998).

One prominent example used to be the People's Web run by the London Borough of Lewisham.[102] Although including the usual passive information provision and even a point of contact for council services, the service also comprised a more interactive area for citizens to post their opinions, so as to 'increase the participation of local people . . . in the decision-making process and enhance accountability'. This aspect was established in part through the influence of the DALI ('Delivery of and Access to Local Information and Service') Project. DALI is a project partly funded by DG XIII of the European Commission (telematics applications for urban and rural areas). Other cities throughout Europe (including in the United Kingdom, Bradford, Edinburgh, and Manchester[103]) have responded to the Global Bangemann Challenge[104] (in honour of the *Report on the Information Society*, by European Commissioner Bangemann[105]). The Challenge was launched by the City of Stockholm and invites all major cities in the world to participate in a competition for the 'best' information technology project. However, the Lewisham site is no longer supported, though ongoing local initiatives include Cambridge Online City, which aims to increase access to public information through the use of technology.[106]

The democratic agenda does now seem to be capturing the attention of government. The Department of the Environment's paper, *Modernising Local Government* issued in 1998, floated the idea of electronic voting and the use of communications technologies[107] to reverse the 'culture of apathy'[108] in what is seen as a flagging tier of democracy. Nevertheless, there again appears to be far more interest in active participatory democracy in localities within the United States, alongside the regular dissemination of information.[109] The notion of the town or village hall meeting has always had a revered symbolic importance in United States democratic history, and its revitalisation by electronic means has been the project of

---

[102] See http://www.lewisham.gov.uk/dali.htm.

[103] See http://www.tsl.fi/isc/.

[104] See http://www.challenge.stockholm.se/. See also Dr Martin Bangemann's speech, 'Access to information will remove curtains', at
http://www.challenge.stockholm.se/Bulletins/Articles/article_970528_1.htm.

[105] See The Bangemann Report, 'Recommendations to the European Council: Europe and the Global Information Society', (http://www.ispo.cec.be/infosoc/backg/bangeman.html, 1994).

[106] See http://www.worldserver.pipex.com/cambridge/. Free Public Internet access terminals are located at various points around Cambridge City giving members of the public the opportunity to use the information available within the Cambridge Online City pages, and to partake in discussions (see http://www.cambridge.gov.uk/forums/forums.htm). See also the Partnerships Online, (http://www.partnerships.org.uk/) which aims to put every community in Britain online and to bring back the sense of community and public discussion which this could engender.

[107] *Modernising Local Government* (Department of the Environment, 1998) para. 4.26.

[108] Ibid., para. 1.3.

[109] An important trend-setter for the Internet publication of state information was California State Law ab1624 (of 11 October 1993) which required the California state government to provide online access to state statutes and legislation in process (see now California Government Code s.10248 (1996)). See also The Progress & Freedom Foundation, *The Digital State* (http://www.pff.org/pff/tds.html, 1997).

many,[110] though the electronic version (which often uses a variety of media such as local or cable television as well as the Internet) is almost always confined to deliberation and does not include the effective mass vote of yesteryear. The wide varieties of community and civic networks are documented and encouraged by a number of private organisations including the Teledemocracy Action News and Network (TAN+N), which is the web site of the Global Democracy Movement.[111] In addition, some directly involve governmental organisations, whether municipalities (such as the City of Palo Alto[112]), states (such as the California online voter guide[113] and the Minnesota E-Democracy Project[114]), or departments within states (such as the Texas State Comptroller's On-Line Forum[115]).

Other levels of democratic engagement

The CMCs may be able to offer especially valuable assistance to democratic engagement by interest groups. The ability to link at low cost should encourage information flows and participation on a scale not hitherto within the reach of political groups used to life on a shoestring. Moreover, there will be an added bonus for those groups with aspirations and concerns which transcend national boundaries and who are seeking to counteract the anti-democratic tendencies of globalisation:[116]

> Globalization amounts to a *coup d'état* by the global economic élite. *Temporary* political ascendancy in the West is being systematically leveraged into *permanent* global political ascendancy, institutionalized in the network of élite-dominated commissions and agencies. The see-saw game has been abandoned by the élite, and the citizenry find themselves down on their backs.

Relevant groups include Amnesty International[117] and Greenpeace.[118] An interesting vehicle for them is GreenNet,[119] which handles over 20,000

---

[110] For example, it is part of the communitarian agenda: Etzioni, A., *The Spirit of Community* (Fontana, London, 1995).

[111] See http://www.auburn.edu/tann/. For other listings or uses, see Community Networks (http://ralph.gmu.edu/~pbaker/index.html; Democracy Network, http://www.democracynet.org.

[112] See http://www.city.palo-alto.ca.us/.

[113] See http://calvoter.org/. The guide comprises information about candidates for political or public office (including judges), election and referendum issues and other public controversies.

[114] http://www.e-democracy.org/. This is a non-profit group which works with the Minnesota state legislature and has established 'MN-Politics' – online sites for citizen interaction on public issues. Civic and political groups as well as candidates are invited to host online conferences. See also Clift, S., 'Democracies Online: Building Civic Life on the New Frontier', (http://www.e-democracy.org/do/library/build/, 1997).

[115] See http://www.window.state.tx.us/. This forum was established concerning taxation laws in Texas, so that the sponsoring governmental agency could gather public opinion and suggest reforms either by itself or through the legislature.

[116] Moore, R.K., 'Democracy and Cyberspace' in Hague, B.N. and Loader, B.D., *Digital Democracy* (Routledge, London, 1999) p.45.

[117] See http://www.io.org/amnesty/.

[118] See http://www.greenpeace.org/. Note also Green Party, http://www.gn.apc.org/greenparty/index.html.

[119] See http://www.gn.apc.org/gn.about/index.html.

groups (Greenpeace among them). Similar network servers are the HandsNet, the Institute for Global Communications (IGC) and the Association of Progressive Communications (APC) which offers Econet, Peacenet and Conflictnet. Other sites, such as Partnerships Online, seek to build and sustain localised communities.[120]

It is even claimed that the technology can be constitutive of such groups:[121]

> Whereas it took years for information and ideas to circulate by hand and to arrange the face-to-face meetings that drafted the Declaration of Independence and the Constitution, computer networks can greatly speed up the process of people-to-people exchanges of information, ideas, and plans of actions.

However, there is as yet little evidence of the political rather than social development of communities which would not otherwise have developed, save that there is now a burgeoning political movement concerned with the freedom of CMCs and their users. Its chief proponents include WIRED,[122] the Electronic Frontier Foundation[123] and the Computer Professionals for Social Responsibility.[124] But it is notable that the attack on the United States' Communications Decency Act 1996, which was criticised for imposing censorship on net content, was led by the long-established American Civil Liberties Union.[125]

Threats and limitations

Threats

Features which assist democracy – open access and the absence of state control – can also be exploited by those who would seek to undermine the freedoms or equality of others.[126] It is not intended to consider this issue in detail, as it has been fully documented elsewhere[127] and in any event, the

---

[120] http://www.partnerships.org.uk/.
[121] Hiltz, S.R. and Turoff, M., *The Network Nation* (MIT Press, Cambridge, MA, 1993) at p.480. Compare Rheingold, R., *The Virtual Community: Homesteading on the Electronic Frontier* (Secker and Warburg, London, 1993) (also at http://www.well.com/user/hlr/vcbook/index.html); Schuler, D., *New Community Networks: Wired for Change* (Addison-Wesley, Reading, MA, 1996); Jones, S.G. (ed.), *Virtual Culture* (Sage, London, 1997), *Cybersociety 2.0* (Sage, London, 1998); Smith, M.A. and Kollock, P., *Communities in Cyberspace* (Routledge, London, 1999).
[122] See http://www.wired.com/.
[123] See http://www.eff.org.
[124] See http://www.cpsr.org.
[125] See http://www.aclu.org. The case was *ACLU v Reno* 521 US 844 (1997). See Akdeniz, Y., 'The battle for the Communications Decency Act 1996 is over' (1997) 147 *New Law Journal* 1003.
[126] See, e.g., McAllester, M., 'Democracy of Internet threatens some nations: In Burma, Net access can be a path to prison', *The Inquirer, Philadelphia Online*, 20 November 1997, http://www.phillynews.com/inquirer/97/Nov/20/tech.life/FREE20.htm.
[127] Wallace, J. and Mangan, M., *Sex, Laws and Cyberspace* (Henry Holt, New York, 1996); US Anti-Defamation League Report, *High-Tech Hate: Extremist Use of the Internet* (New York, 1997); Craven, J., 'Extremism and the internet' (1998) 1 *Journal of Information Law and Technology*.

purpose of this chapter is to concentrate on the uses of CMCs positively for democracy and not against it.

The unscrupulous or unpalatable usages have fallen into various categories. They include the attempts to spread hate speech by right-wing, neo-Nazi groups.[128] The fear is that these sparsely spread and very marginal groups can utilise the lower communications costs of the Internet to make links with and increase solidarity amongst widely dispersed individuals. As with other media in which Nazis and racists have sought to disseminate their views,[129] there is considerable debate as to whether they should be banned from the Internet[130] or whether their new-found outlet will allow them to be exposed, controverted and educated.[131]

Similar debates surround groups which prominently appear on the world wide web to promote causes linked to political violence.[132] For example, the Sinn Féin site, originally at the University of Texas, moved after protests in May 1996.[133] The site associated with the Basque nationalist party, Herri Batasuna, has also been criticised.[134] There are even more direct concerns

---

[128] German authorities blocked access to 1,500 sites located at Web Communications in California because Ernst Zundel's (a German-born neo-Nazi resident in Toronto) WWW site in Toronto, which refers to the Holocaust as the 'lie of the century' and as 'an Allied propaganda tool concocted during World War II', is located on the server. See 'German Service Cuts Net Access' *San Jose Mercury News* (California), 27 January 1996. See also Vesely, R., 'Germany Restricts Internet Content' *Wired News*, 11 December 1996, at http://www.wired.com/news/news/politics/story/937.html.

[129] Compare Arkes, 'Civility and the restriction of speech' (1974) *Supreme Court Review* 281; Campisano, M.S., 'Group vilification reconsidered' (1979) 89 *Yale Law Journal* 308; Downes, 'Skokie revisited' (1985) 60 *Notre Dame Law Review* 629; Note, 'A communitarian defence of group libel laws' (1988) 101 *Harvard Law Review* 682; Greenawalt, K., *Speech, Crime and the Uses of Language* (Oxford University Press, Oxford, 1989) pp.294–5; Abrams, C., 'Hate speech' (1992) 37 *Villanova Law Review* 743; Mahoney, K., 'The constitutional approach to freedom of expression in hate propaganda and pornography' (1992) 55 *Law & Contemporary Problems* 77; Walker, S., *Hate Speech* (University of Nebraska Press, Lincoln, 1994); Jones, T.D., 'Human rights: freedom of expression and group defamation under British, Canadian, Indian, Nigerian and United States law' (1995) 18 *Suffolk Transnational Law Review* 427 at pp.501, 512; Greenawalt, K., *Fighting Words* (Princeton University Press, New Haven, 1995) chap. 4.

[130] Whine, M., 'The far Right on the internet' in Loader, B.D. (ed.), *The Governance of Cyberspace* (Routledge, London, 1997).

[131] Dworkin, R., 'A new map of censorship' (1994) 23 *Index on Censorship* May/June p.9.

[132] See for example Gori, Kevin, 'Like Smut, Terrorism Prompts Calls for Limiting Expression on the Net', *New York Times*, 23 June 1996 (CyberTimes section).

[133] The site (http://uts.cc.utexas.edu/~sponge/aprn/SFhome.html) moved to a commercial Internet service provider located in Philadelphia (http://www.serve.com/rm/sinnfein/index.html); the site is now on an Irish Internet service provider at http://sinnfein.ie/index.html. See Tendler, S., 'Ulster security details posted on the Internet' (1996) *The Times* 25 March, p.5.

[134] In July 1997, the Internet service provider, Institute for Global Communications, cut off access to the NewYork-based Euskal Herria Journal; see http://www.igc.apc.org/ehj/. The journal was the focus of a denial of service attack and e-mail 'bombings' by those who said the site's producers were sympathetic to the Euzkadi ta Azkatasuna (ETA). IGC staff members were reluctant to act in this way, but they said they had to remove the site because the attack had been crippling the entire service for its estimated 13,000 other subscribers. See the Global Internet Liberty Campaign press release supporting the IGC at http://www.gilc.org/speech/spain/igc-statement-en.html.

that Nazis or anarchist groups will use the Internet to spread information about bomb-making and other forms of attack.[135] Examples have indeed occurred, including the trial of the 'Gandalf' group of animal rights activists and anarchists who were charged with incitement and conspiracy to commit criminal damage arising out of the publication of the *Green Anarchist* magazine and materials placed on the Internet for the Animal Liberation Front Justice Department.[136] The circulation of such information among right-wing militias in the USA has also caused anxiety and has prompted attempts at legislation.[137] However, as with the political messages of extremists, one should hesitate before closing off channels of communications because they can be misused in these exceptional ways. Long before the advent of the Internet, Fascists were far more prominent in the 1930s and the amateurish Angry Brigade had the ability to make bombs in the 1970s which they learnt from freely available printed materials.[138]

There has been much discussion about how these irresponsible or undesirable netizens might be controlled or punished both nationally and internationally.[139] However, it is submitted that the Internet does not significantly increase our vulnerability but simply spreads risk. Normal constitutional protections should apply, and a democratic state must trust in the responsibility and self-control of the vast majority of its citizens.[140]

Limitations

It follows that the limitations inherent in the medium of CMCs and relevant to democratic success may be of greater importance than the foregoing forms of misbehaviour which have always occurred in one medium or another. The relevant limitations can be described in terms of non-use, barriers to use, terms of private use and terms of public use.

---

[135] See the US Anti-Defamation League Report, 'High-Tech Hate: Extremist Use of the Internet' (http://www.adl.org/ADLRept/HighTechHate/HTH_ExSum.html, 1997).

[136] Jenkins, L., 'Activists sent out guides on DIY anarchy' (1997) *The Times* 30 August p.6. Three of the four defendants were sentenced to three years' imprisonment, a fourth was acquitted. See Animal Liberation Frontline Information Service, 'Gandalf Trial Ends – Three Imprisoned For 3 Years', 15 November 1997 at http://www.envirolink.org/ALF/news/971115u.html. See also the Green Anarchist pages offered by Index on Censorship at http://www.indexoncensorship.org/greenanarchist.html.

[137] See Senate Bill S735 (1995); Wallace, J. and Mangan, M., *Sex, Laws and Cyberspace* (Henry Holt, New York, 1996) chap. 7; Caden, M.L. and Lucas, S.E., 'Comment, Accidents On the Information Superhighway: On-Line Liability And Regulation' (1996) 2 *Rich. J.L. & Tech.* 3. Consider also the school shootings in Colorado in April 1999, which were immediately placed at the door of the Internet: BBC Online Network, 'Americas school bombers' Internet link probed' http://news.bbc.co.uk/hi/english/world/americas/newsid_325000/325139.stm.

[138] See Walker, C., *The Prevention of Terrorism in British Law* (2nd ed., Manchester University Press, Manchester, 1992) p.4.

[139] See, for example, European Commission, Illegal and Harmful Content on the Internet (COM (96) 487 Final).

[140] Berman, J. and Weitzner, D.J., 'Abundance and user control' (1995) 104 *Yale Law Journal 1619*; Reidenberg, J.R., 'Governing networks and rule-making in cyberspace' (1996) 45 *Emory Law Journal* 911.

As for non-use, the problem is that, even if the CMCs are freely available to all and even if the different tiers of government offer the most attractive formats imaginable for democratic engagement, CMC users will choose to ignore the opportunities on offer and will self-insulate themselves and descend into (or remain within) worlds of fantasy, play and consumerism. This may be a depressing scenario, but it must surely be accepted since the Liberal tradition allows the feckless and the damned so to choose and remain. It would be wrong to configure the whole Internet on the grounds that it must be used primarily for lofty purposes.[141] It would also be wrong for governments to demand the dedication of private Internet service provider space for public purposes.[142] The demand here is that the government makes available facilities, including above all information about itself and avenues for participation in its processes, not that it somehow forces people to respond.

So, the real problem of non-use concerns barriers to use rather than the choice of non-use. One obvious problem under this heading is the inability to access the CMCs through poverty:[143] '... far too many ... believe that elite access to cyberspace means democratic enlightenment ... a middle class income is the basic password to Internet access'. The problem is at its most acute in Africa, where many countries scarcely have access to the Internet, with limited telephone lines and technology. In February 1995, South Africa's Deputy President Thabo Mbeki pointed out at a G7 conference that 'there were more telephone lines in Manhattan, New York than in the whole of sub-Saharan Africa' and that 'half of humanity has never made a telephone call'.[144]

There are also cultural problems in reaching out to apparently disinterested sectors of society. The CMCs are less heavily used by women and the elderly, partly because competence in their usage tends to be most linked to occupational familiarity which excludes many.[145] This basic fact of non-usage means that the Internet is not presently consistent with the aim of direct democracy. The Internet is not the 'public sphere' articulated by Habermas; in fact it is a very private sphere dependent on knowledge and

---

[141] Compare: Sunstein, C.L., 'The First Amendment in cyberspace' (1995) 104 *Yale Law Journal* 1757 at p.1788. Likewise freedom of information in the USA has been predominantly used by commercial users: Birkinshaw, P., *Freedom of Information* (2nd ed., Butterworths, London, 1996) p.57.

[142] Compare *Turner Broadcasting System Inc v FCC* 520 U.S. 180 (1997); *ACLU v Reno*, loc. cit.

[143] Lockard, J., 'Progressive politics, electronic individualism and the myth of virtual communities' in Porter, D. (ed.), *Internet Culture* (Routledge, London, 1997) at pp.219–20. See also Surman, S., 'Wired Words: Utopia, Revolution and the History of Electronic Highways' (http://www.web.apc.org/~msurman/wiredwords.html).

[144] Human Rights Watch, 'Silencing The Net: The Threat to Freedom of Expression On-line' (1996) 8(2) *Monitors: A Journal of Human Rights and Technology* (http://www.cwrl.utexas.edu/~monitors/1.1/hrw/index.html). See also Wresch, W., *Haves and Have-Nots in the Information Age* (Rutgers University Press, New Brunswick, NJ, 1996).

[145] Barnett, S., 'New media, old problems' (1997) 12(2) *European Journal of Communication* 193 at p.210.

power and so it allows a partial commodification of political debate by the relatively rich and powerful. However, the convergence of television and computer sets into a unique set with digital access capabilities and the growth of information technology teaching in schools (considered next) may eventually enhance both accessibility and interest.

Unlike the limitation of non-use through voluntary choice, these systemic or cultural aspects of non-use are troubling if the CMCs are to provide equal democratic access and opportunities. The issue was prominently raised by the House of Lords Select Committee on Science and Technology in its paper, *Information Society*.[146] The Conservative government's *Response*[147] accepted the desirability of wider access, but its projected methods of achievement left much to be desired. The programme, *IT for All*,[148] emerged, perhaps the most important part of which concerns how information technology is to be taught in schools. The applied programme was described by the Department of Education in its paper, *Superhighways for Education: Consultation Paper* and *Superhighways for Education: The Way Forward* in 1995. One would suppose that the inculcation of IT skills within children would be critical to the future health of a democracy within an information society and that its achievement should be central to educational infrastructure. By contrast, the Department of Education tamely asked for bids or pilot projects and offered only specific grants and not universal provision.[149] The result was that while there were many computers in schools – Britain leads the world in the ratio of computers to pupils – they were often the obsolete or inappropriate cast-offs from local businesses or ill-advised purchases, and another problem was lack of teacher training and expertise.[150] Access to a wider public was also not on offer, and there was no promise of funding for Citizen's Advice Bureaux to facilitate free access.[151] Perhaps private initiatives will do more to establish inclusion in the information age, and computer-related companies are prominent in these efforts.[152]

Following the Labour Party victory in the 1997 General Election, there came into play the pledges in the manifesto to supply Internet connections

---

[146] House of Lords, Select Committee on Science and Technology, *Information Society: Agenda for Action in the UK* (1995–6 HL 77).
[147] Cm. 3450, HMSO, London, 1996.
[148] *IT for All* is a four-year initiative designed to help people in all walks of life understand and exploit the benefits of new Information and Communication Technologies in their everyday lives. Further information is available at http://www.itforall.gov.uk/.
[149] (1995) p.40.
[150] See the Stevenson Report (*Information and Communication Technology in UK Schools*, McKinsey & Co., http://rubble.ultralab.anglia.ac.uk/stevenson/ICTUKIndex.html, 1997), as noted in Department for Education and Employment, *Excellence in Schools* (Cm. 3681, HMSO, London, 1997) chap. 4 paras 17, 18.
[151] (Cm. 3450, HMSO, London, 1996) para. 6.19.
[152] INSINC, the national working party on social inclusion in the information society, was set up by IBM in collaboration with Community Development Foundation in 1995, to examine the impact of new information technology on local communities, and the potential for greater social inclusion of people in communities within the information society. See Social Inclusion in the Information Society project, http://www.communities.org.uk/articles/insinc.html.

to all 32,000 state-run schools by agreement with BT – what is now called a 'National Grid for Learning'.[153] The link is expected to reduce costs by 80 per cent, and the plans have been approved by Director General of Fair Trading.[154] In total,[155] the modernisation strategy which is to be achieved by 2002 includes the training of teachers (with a £235m programme announced in January 1998), the connection of schools, the provision of software (some by donations from the Microsoft Corporation[156]) and ensuring access. There are also new commitments to link all 4759 public libraries to the Internet so as to provide a point of contact for all citizens and to establish 'IT for All' access sites and learning centres.[157] One must applaud such initiatives, but, as indicated earlier, one should remain sceptical as to the ultimate aims of these reforms. In other words, it remains to be seen whether the enthusiasm for pupil computing-power is based on securing the modernising goal of an efficient workforce for the future rather than a vibrant democracy.

Moving on to the terms of use rather than the issue of non-use, one might consider both the private and public aspects of limitation. As for the private sphere, advocates of democracy need to look with suspicion at the role of corporate powers in regard to CMCs. To take the Internet as an example, what started as cottage industries run by cyber-enthusiasts is now a vast business which is being increasingly consolidated within larger corporate entities.[158] The danger is that corporate interests in playing safe, avoiding offence and minimising conflict both with official regulators and with moral majority customers will eventually stifle some of the élan of the Internet in the interests of a growing commercial onslaught.[159] This stance has already begun to emerge after government arm-twisting over pornographic messages on the Internet.[160] More insidious, there is the fear that multinational

---

[153] Department for Education and Employment, *Excellence in Schools* (Cm. 3681, HMSO, London, 1997) chap. 4 para. 16. The National Grid for Learning operates a Virtual Teacher Centre at http://www.ngfl.gov.uk.

[154] (1997) *The Times* 12 July p.5.

[155] Department for Education and Employment, *Excellence in Schools* (Cm. 3681, HMSO, London, 1997) chap. 4 para. 19.

[156] (1997) *The Times* 7 October p.1.

[157] See Department of Trade and Industry, *Our Information Age* (http://www.number-10.gov.uk/public/info/releases/publications/infoagefeat.html, 1998); Department for Culture, Media and Sport, *New Library: the People's Network* (Cm. 3887, Stationery Office, London, 1998).

[158] Consider, for example, the takeover by Compuserve of America Online: C/Net News.Com Special Report, 'AOL buys rival service' 10 September 1997, at http://www.news.com/News/Item/0,4,14026,00.html. See Hague, B.N. and Loader, B.D., *Digital Democracy* (Routledge, London, 1999) p.15.

[159] Moore, R.K., 'Democracy and Cyberspace' in Hague, B.N. and Loader, B.D., *Digital Democracy* (Routledge, London, 1999).

[160] See DTI Press Release, 'Internet Safety-Net to Tackle Child Porn', 23 September 1996, at http://dtiinfo1.dti.gov.uk/safety-net/index.html. See American Civil Liberties Union, 'Fahrenheit 451.2: Is Cyberspace Burning? How Rating and Blocking Proposals May Torch Free Speech on the Internet', (http://www.aclu.org/issues/cyber/burning.html, 1997); Cyber-Rights & Cyber-Liberties (UK) Report, 'Who Watches the Watchmen: Internet Content Rating Systems, and Privatised Censorship', (http://www.cyber-rights.org/watchmen.htm, 1997).

communications companies will homogenise cultures and will instil compliance, as a function of gatekeeping, to given modes of expression or even policies.[161] It has been suggested that the pre-CMCs media will continue to dominate not only because of doubts about the take-up of the new CMCs but also because the old media will actually colonise and reshape the new.[162] In this way, an integrated transglobal media industry will emerge, in which CMCs are part of the industry that includes also broadcasting and the press. That industry will be driven by commercial, not political, considerations, though the customers may be introduced to the allure of virtual play through public forums including schools and libraries with donated software which carry an appropriate corporate logo designed to steer nascent consumer urges.

Limitations on the terms of public use – the use of the CMCs to engage with other members of the public or with public officials or representatives – next trigger questions about the modes of democratic participation. One issue is the possible commodification of access, through selling the addresses of logged users to commercial organisations. A second issue is whether contributions to debate can be made securely or anonymously through the use of encryption.[163] The issue was first explored by the Cabinet Office paper, *government.direct: A prospectus for the Electronic Delivery of Government Services*.[164] But the more detailed proposals on the regulation of the use of encryption technology came from a consultation paper entitled *Licensing of Trusted Third Parties for the Provision of Encryption Services*, from the Department of Trade and Industry ('DTI') in March 1997.[165] As described more fully later in this book,[166] the true goals of the DTI seemed to be to control and restrict encryption, not to promote it as an aid to political organisation and debate.[167] However, commercial pressures and practical realities prompted a reassessment, which was reflected in the *Secure Electronic Commerce Statement* of 1998[168] and the paper *Building Confidence*

The Government has supported the Internet Watch Foundation (http://www.internetwatch.org.uk/) as its favoured regulatory agent. But see Cyber-Rights & Cyber-Liberties (UK) Report, 'Who Watches the Watchmen', November 1997, at http://www.leeds.ac.uk/law/pgs/yaman/watchmen.htm.

[161] Sadar, Z, 'alt.civilizations.faq' in Sadar, Z. and Ravetz, J.R., *Cyberfutures* (Pluto Press, London, 1996).

[162] See Barnett, S., 'New media, old problems' (1997) 12(2) *European Journal of Communication* 193.

[163] See Raab, C., 'Privacy, democracy and information' in Loader, B.D. (ed.), *The Governance of Cyberspace* (Routledge, London, 1997).

[164] (Cm. 3438, HMSO, London, 1996) para. 8.3.

[165] DTI Consultation Paper, *Licensing of Trusted Third Parties for the Provision of Encryption Services*, (http://www.dti.gov.uk/pubs, 1997). See Akdeniz, Y. *et al.*, 'Cryptography and Liberty: Can the Trusted Third Parties be Trusted? A Critique of the Recent UK Proposals', 1997 (2) *The Journal of Information, Law and Technology*.

[166] See chap. 14.

[167] See Bowden, C. and Akdeniz, Y., 'Cryptography and Democracy – Dilemmas of Freedom,' in Liberty (ed.), *Liberating Cyberspace: Civil Liberties, Human Rights, and the Internet* (Pluto Press, London, 1998).

[168] http://www.dti.gov.uk/CII/ana27p.html. See Akdeniz, Y. and Walker, C., 'UK Government policy on encryption: trust is the key?' (1998) 3 *Journal of Civil Liberties* 110.

in Electronic Commerce in 1999.[169] The Electronic Communications Act 2000, Part I, proffers a more voluntary system, but the political debate remains fixated on the value of encryption solely for commercial ends and ignores its political aspects.

In conclusion, the United Kingdom government's desire for limits on the truly private uses of encryption has been described as a way of preserving the existing relations of force within society rather than as a mechanism for encouraging debate about them.[170] The computer provides vast new capabilities for officialdom to store information, conduct surveillance and to collect and generate evidence about the lives of citizens. The government does not seem as yet prepared to offer reassurance to the citizen that their suspicion of the state is well-understood and indeed well-founded and is to be encouraged rather than outlawed.

Conclusions

Putting the matter in a global context, it must be recognised that CMCs can be used as important channels of communication and that they can be of relevance to the flourishing of democracy. At the same time, there is no inherent linkage between the CMCs and nation-state democracy. Indeed, the two might be viewed as almost antithetical – one is a creature of late modernity, the other a creature of modernity.[171] So, one of the initial difficulties may be that while the Internet has power as a tool of democracy, this tool may not be most effectively sited within nation-state democracy. Its inherent tendencies to fragment and globalise mean that its greatest uses are at very localised[172] or very internationalised[173] levels of discourse. To take the case of international usage, if one accepts the late modern analysis of globalisation, then it becomes vital to subject to democratic accountability the new power-holders who flourish within and without the domains of nation states. These include bodies of public governance such as the European Union and the United Nations and also private bodies such as multinational corporations (including those dealing with the vitality of the Internet, such as the Microsoft Corporation). All have the potential to augment or undermine political freedoms, and rather than expect nation-state governments to represent the very diverse interests of their citizens, the Internet provides a direct channel of communication not only to make representations to the global bodies in question but also to organise globally into interest or monitoring groups. In this way, the perception of

---

[169] http://www.dti.gov.uk/CII/elec/elec_com_1.html.

[170] Poster, M., 'Cyberdemocracy' in Porter, D. (ed.), *Internet Culture* (Routledge, London, 1997) at p.202.

[171] Giddens, A., *The Consequences of Modernity* (Polity Press, Cambridge, 1990).

[172] See Bellamy, C. and Raab, C.D., 'Wiring up the deck' (1999) 52 *Parliamentary Affairs* 518.

[173] See Ithiel de Sola Pool, *Technologies without Boundaries* (Harvard University Press, Cambridge, MA, 1990).

the growing powerlessness of the nation state in the face of globalisation[174] might be balanced to some extent by the empowering of the citizen as an articulate player on the world stage through the mechanisms of the CMCs, where the boundaries of time and space become virtual rather than real. In this way, the world wide web, for example, 'interlaces with the emergence of a more reflexive citizenry'.[175] Some indications as to the groups working on this expansive stage have already been given.

Turning more specifically to the United Kingdom, utilisations of 'virtual democracy' have tended to be relatively conservative rather than trans-formative. The aim is often to enhance or modernise democracy rather than to change its nature or practice. So, most are about improving certain facets of representative democracy, such as the flow of information, compre-hension, accessibility and the delivery of state services. Rather fewer have attempted to augment accountability or participation or even to establish more direct democracy. More radical visions which seek to utilise CMCs to shift from dependence on representatives to self-assertion in a 'semi-direct democracy'[176] have not really come to fruition. The failure may not be entirely lamentable. For reasons given earlier, it must be feared that radical virtual democracy would not work satisfactorily and would give unequal power to organised interest and corporate groups.[177] Direct participative exercises do not necessarily debase democracy and may per-form a useful function of reinvigorating representative democracies which call for mass participation relatively infrequently.[178] For example, there was great interest and involvement in the Independent Television programme, 'The Monarchy – The Nation Decides'.[179] But this is no way to run a democracy as a general practice. In a society as diverse and complex as the United Kingdom, democracy should be on the model of deliberative demo-cracy,[180] which needs time for the development of reasoned public argument, reflection and discussion and so needs shielding to some extent from those foisting passionate opinions, often wildly popular but oppressive to minor-ities. In this way, direct virtual democracy – the aggregation of personal and

---

[174] McGrew, A. (ed.), *The Transformation of Democracy?* (Polity Press, Cambridge, 1997).

[175] Slevin, J., *The Internet and Society* (Polity Press, Cambridge, 2000) p.148.

[176] See Toffler, A. and Toffler, H., *Creating a New Civilization* (Progress and Freedom Founda-tion, Washington DC, 1994).

[177] Magleby, D.B., *Direct Legislation Voting on Ballot Propositions in the United States* (Johns Hopkins University Press, Baltimore, 1984); Wright, R., 'Hyperdemocracy' (1995) *Time* 23 January p.51; London, S., 'Teledemocracy vs. deliberative democracy' (1995) 3.2 *Jour-nal of Interpersonal Computing and Technology* 33; Papadopoulus, Y., 'Analysis of func-tions and dysfunctions of direct democracy: top-down and bottom-up perspectives' (1995) 23(4) *Politics and Society* 422. Compare Borinet, I. and Frey, B.S., 'Direct-Democratic Rules: The role of discussion' (1994) 47 *Kyklos* 341.

[178] Hirst, P., *Representative Democracy and Its Limits* (Polity Press, Cambridge, 1990).

[179] Barnett, S., 'New media, old problems' (1997) 12(2) *European Journal of Communication* 193 at p.213.

[180] See Miller, D., 'Deliberative democracy and social choice' (1992) XL *Political Studies* 54; Fishkin, J.S. *The Voice of the People* (Yale University Press, New Haven, 1997) chap. 5.

private preferences as the basis for choice in public policies – may become a threat to Liberal democracy.[181] Liberal democracy does of course recognise limits on the popular expression of will so as to preserve the liberty and equality which are essential to the ultimate health of society – it is not simply the aggregation of the largest number of individual preferences.[182] So, the ultimate facility of registering instant gratification by way of a vote on every issue may not be desirable (nor indeed desired[183]).

A more appropriate objective is that virtual democracy should involve access to governmental information on a far grander scale than ever before allowed or indeed conceivable. Further, it should provide a platform for engagement, so that discussions of the political issues of the day are at least available to, and encourage, mass public participation[184] and the 'civic orientation' of society.[185] There should be space for deliberation rather than just the recording of representations. In this way, the Internet may primarily be a vehicle for pluralism rather than democracy.[186] Thus, the relationship of CMCs to democracy should not be as a direct carrier of votes but as a means of political information, organisation, debate and feedback on behalf of active and competitive blocs of interest.[187] In short, it should trigger broad-based popular political activism[188] in a way which marries the late modern nature both of the medium and of society itself.[189] Nevertheless, one would hope that the observance of equal respect for the diversity of all citizens and their interest groups would also energise democratic involvement, though this does not necessarily involve a commitment to a radical pluralist 'associative democracy' based around group identity and self-governance[190] rather than a more centrally organised form of polity.

There are some pressing threats to this vision. The first is that it may fail on the grounds of political party discipline. This is far less pronounced in the United States of America, which may account in part for the more

---

[181] Mill himself talked about government by discussion: Mill, J.S., *Considerations on Representative Government* (Parker, Son, and Bourn, London, 1861) chap. 5.

[182] See Wintrop, N., *Liberal Democratic Theory and Its Critics* (Croom Helm, London, 1983); Sartori, G., *The Theory of Democracy Revisited* (Chatham House, New Jersey, 1987); Holden, B., *Understanding Liberal Democracy* (Philip Allan, Oxford and New Jersey, 1988).

[183] See 'Democracy and technology' (1995) *The Economist* 17 June p.21 at p.23: the average electoral turnout is generally higher in candidate elections than referendums.

[184] See Carr, E.H., *The New Society* (Macmillan, London, 1951).

[185] Ware, A., *Citizens, Parties and the State* (Princeton University Press, 1987) p.7. See also Tocqueville, A. de, *De la Democratie en Amerique* (Saunders & Otley, London, 1835).

[186] See Dahl, R.A., *Polyarchy: Participation and Opposition* (Yale University Press, New Haven, 1971), *Dilemmas of Pluralist Democracy* (Yale University Press, New Haven, 1982), *Democracy and Its Critics* (Yale University Press, New Haven, 1989); McLennan, G., *Pluralism* (Open University Press, Milton Keynes, 1995).

[187] See Miliband, R., *The State in Capitalist Society* (Basic Books, New York, 1969) pp.3, 4.

[188] Moore, R.K., 'Democracy and Cyberspace' in Hague, B.N. and Loader, B.D., *Digital Democracy* (Routledge, London, 1999).

[189] See McLennan, G., *Pluralism* (Open University Press, Milton Keynes, 1995) p.99.

[190] Hirst, P., *Associative Democracy* (Polity Press, Cambridge, 1994). See also Laclau, E. and Mouffe, C., *Towards a Radical Democratic Politics* (Verso, London, 1985).

participatory style of American virtual democracy. However, British citizens may find that more political influence can be secured through participation within parties rather than within governments which can be tightly controlled by party machines and are set on courses of action already predetermined in manifesto pledges. Though the present Labour government has begun a process of reform of political parties,[191] democracy within parties seems to be a receding prospect with no proposals to deal with increasing party manipulation over the selection of candidates and the control of national conferences, aided and abetted by the prospect of party lists at proportional elections for Scotland and Wales[192] and in European Parliament elections.[193] Nowhere are democratising devices such as primary elections[194] touted as possible democratic antidotes to the party machines, nor are the single-issue referenda, allowed in relation to devolution and the electoral system, likely to become sufficiently pervasive to weaken party clout.[195]

The proposed future may also falter on the allure of the medium and the risk that the audience may become forgetful of the message. Rather like television, the Internet could come to mean entertainment not information for most people, and any message which is not perceived as entertainment will be dismissed as unpalatable or amateurish. A kind of Gramscian hegemony will descend in which controversy is seen as wrong. As suggested by Rheingold,[196]

> Virtual communities could help citizens revitalise democracy, or they could be luring us into an attractively packaged substitute for democratic discourse. . . . Why should this new medium be any less corruptible than previous media? Why should contemporary claims for CMC as a democratising technology be taken any more seriously than the similar-sounding claims that were made for steam, electricity, and television?

---

[191] See Home Office Consultative Document, *The Prevention of Corruption. Consolidation and Amendment of the Prevention of Corruption Acts 1889–1916* (Home Office, London, 1997); Law Commission, *Legislating the Criminal Code: Corruption* (Consultation Paper No. 145, London, 1997); (Neill Committee), *Standards in Public Life: The Funding of Political Parties in the United Kingdom* (Cm. 4057, Stationery Office, London, 1998); Registration of Political Parties Act 1998; Political Parties, Elections and Referendums Act 2000.

[192] Scottish Office, *Scotland's Parliament* (Cm. 3658, HMSO, London, 1997) Annex C and Scotland Act 1998 s.5; Welsh Office, *A Voice for Wales* (Cm. 3718, HMSO, London, 1997) Annex C and Government of Wales Act 1998 s.4. But compare Northern Ireland Act 1998 s.34.

[193] European Parliamentary Elections Act 1999 s.3.

[194] See Lijpart, A., *Democracies* (Yale University Press, New Haven, 1984) pp.199–201.

[195] See Butler, D. and Ranney, A., *Referendums Around the World* (Macmillan, London, 1994).

[196] Rheingold, R., *The Virtual Community: Homesteading on the Electronic Frontier* (Secker and Warburg, 1993) chap. 10 (also at http://www.well.com/user/hlr/vcbook/index.html). See further UCLA Center for the Study of Online Community, http://netscan.sscnet.ucla.edu/csoc/; London, S., 'Civic Networks: Building Community on the Net', (http://www.west.net/~insight/london/networks.htm, 1997).

So, the danger is that the Internet will generate at best hyper-politics[197] – unreal images, jargon and movements which look and sound wonderful on screen but actually do little to improve the actual lives of real citizens. Whether the message is solely the medium takes us back to the debate rehearsed earlier over whether the Labour government's ultimate constitutional aims are modernisation or democratisation. It is as yet too early to say, but official development of the use of the CMCs should be scrutinised closely as a prime indicator either way.

---

[197] See Baudrillard, J., *Selected Writings* (Stanford University Press, Stanford, 1988).

CHAPTER 7

Policing the Internet: maintaining order and law on the cyberbeat

David Wall

Introduction[1]

A recurring theme that runs through many of the contemporary debates over the governance of the Internet is their reliance upon the rule of law compliance model. Central to this model is that revising existing laws, or introducing new ones, will change undesirable or harmful behaviour. So, understandably, these debates tend to take as their main focus, liabilities, obligations and prosecution strategies. While the 'law in the books' focus of such debates is important for the formation and development of law, it nevertheless tends to underplay the importance of the 'law in action'. Furthermore, it tends to assume that there exists a seamless link between statutory law, regulation, rules and policing. The problem with this emphasis, from the point of view of understanding the governance of the Internet, is that comparatively few complaints ever get to law, and even fewer are prosecuted. Rather, complaints tend to be dealt with not by law, but its 'shadow'[2], by a panoply of other, mediated, forms of resolution that exist to service the Internet and which seek to achieve a state of order maintenance. If the 'shadow of law' is the space that exists between social action and statute, where the law shapes action but does not determine it absolutely,

---

[1] This chapter is based upon the author's ongoing research into the cybercrimes and the regulation and policing of the Internet. See Wall, D.S., 'Cybercrimes: New wine, no bottles?' in Davies, P. Francis, P. and Jupp, V. (eds), *Invisible Crimes: Their Victims and their Regulation* (Macmillan, London, 1999) p.105; Wall, D.S., 'Policing and the Regulation of Cyberspace', in Walker, C. (ed.), *Crime, Criminal Justice and the Internet* (special edition, *Criminal Law Review*, Sweet & Maxwell, London, 1998), p.79; Wall, D.S., 'Catching Cybercriminals: Policing the internet' (1998) 12(2) *International Review of Law Computers and Technology* 201; Wall, D.S., 'Policing the Virtual Community: The internet, cyber-crimes and the policing of cyberspace', in Francis, P., Davies, P. and Jupp, V. (eds), *Policing Futures* (Macmillan, London, 1997) p.208.

[2] The term 'shadow of law' has hitherto tended to be used within the framework of alternative dispute resolution. See, for example, Mnookin, R.H. and Kornhauser, L., 'Bargaining in the Shadow of the Law: The Case of Divorce' (1979) 88 *Yale Law Journal* 954 at p.950; Norton, P.M., 'Between the Ideology and the Reality: The Shadow of the Law' (1976) 17 *Harvard Law Journal* 249; Kritzer, H.M. and Zemans, F.K., 'The Shadow of Punitives: An unsuccessful effort to bring it into view' [1998] *Wisconsin Law Review* 157.

then action within it is characterised by discretionary actions which are shaped by social norms. Thus the term 'policing', rather than 'law enforcement', is used here more in the traditional and colloquial sense of 'policing by consent' to describe the process by which order maintenance is achieved.[3] It is, however, important at this point to disaggregate the term 'policing' from the 'police', this forms part of the later discussion.

This chapter will explore the policing of the Internet, not by looking at the laws that could in an ideal situation be applied – these are dealt with elsewhere in this book – but by looking at how order and law on the Internet is kept. The terms 'order' and 'law' have been deliberately reversed here in order to break the conceptual link that has increasingly bound the two concepts since the late 1970s.[4] The first part of this chapter will look at what it is about the Internet that needs policing; it will seek to explore the deviant behaviour that has become known as 'cybercrime', by mapping out the contours of the behaviours (cybercrimes) which are generating so much concern. The second part will explore how order and law in cyberspace is currently being policed; it will look at the multi-tiered structure of order maintenance that already exists on the Internet.[5] The final part will discuss some of the key issues relating to the role of the public police in policing the Internet.

What needs to be policed?

At the dawn of the twenty-first century, the Internet is rapidly becoming an important part of everyday life. Not only will it continue to shape our future for many years to come, but it is already reformulating the ways in which we understand societal change, particularly the debates over modernity.[6] Although mass public use of the Internet has taken place for less than a decade, its social, educational, organisational and commercial benefits are already being felt. But if that is the good news, then the bad news is that along with the benefits come the social and personal costs, and it is these costs, in the form of harmful behaviours, upon which this chapter will concentrate.

---

[3] See further Reiner, R., *The Politics of the Police* (2nd ed., Harvester Wheatsheaf, London, 1992); Critchley, T.A., *A History of the Police in England and Wales 1900–1966* (Constable, London, 1967); Wall, D.S., *The Chief Constables of England and Wales: The socio-legal history of a criminal justice elite* (Dartmouth, Aldershot, 1998), chaps 2 and 3.

[4] See further, Fowles, A.J. 'Order and the Law' in Jones, K., Brown, J. and Bradshaw, J., *Issues in Social Policy* (Routledge and Kegan Paul, London, 1993) p.116.

[5] For a specific study of law enforcement in relation to child pornography, see chap. 10.

[6] See the discussion in the following: Escobar, A., 'Welcome to Cyberia: Notes on the anthropology of cyberculture' in Saradar, Z. and Ravetz, J R (eds), *Cyberfutures: Culture and Politics on the Information Superhighway* (Pluto Press, London, 1996), p.113; Loader, B. (ed.), *The Governance of Cyberspace* (Routledge, London, 1996); Rheingold, H., *The Virtual Community: Homesteading the Electronic Frontier* (Harper Perennial, New York, 1994); Barlow, J.P., 'Selling Wine Without Bottles: The Economy of Mind on the Global Net' http://www.eff.org/pub/Publications/John_Perry_Barlow/HTML/idea_economy_article.html; Wall, D.S., 'Policing the Virtual Community: The internet, cyber-crimes and the policing of cyberspace', in Francis, P., Davies, P. and Jupp, V. (eds), *Policing Futures* (Macmillan, London, 1997) p.208.

The Internet has engendered harmful behaviours in three broad ways. Firstly, it has provided a vehicle for the further facilitation of existing harmful activities.[7] Most typically, it has become a communications vehicle which facilitates the commission of 'traditional' criminal activities; for example, drugs dealers are known to be using e-mail to arrange their deals. Similarly, it has enabled paedophiles to communicate regarding their undesirable practices.[8]

Secondly, the Internet has generated new opportunities for harmful activities that are currently recognised by existing criminal or civil law; examples here would include the creation of new forms of obscenity through computer-generated images (pseudo-photographs),[9] various types of computer fraud (see later), deceptions and scams.

Thirdly, the unique characteristics of the Internet such as the acceleration and accentuation of what Giddens has described as the distanciation of time and space,[10] have led to it engendering entirely new forms of (unbounded) harmful activity. It has created an entirely new environment which has generated new opportunities for the development of novel forms of misbehaviour. These activities include the unauthorised appropriation of intellectual property such as visual imagery, software tools and music products.[11] Such activities will also include the waging of information warfare via the illegal invasion of computer space and the destruction of materials within it. In each case, the activity is largely free of traditional and terrestrial constraint. As such, the behaviours tend to lie outside our existing experiences, and they demand both new forms of understanding and also responses. Across these differential impacts lie four types of harmful activity which are currently raising concern. They are obscenity, trespass, theft and violence, and each group illustrates a range of activities rather than actual offences.[12] But each type of behaviour not only reflects areas of law but also specific sets of public debate.

(Cyber)obscenity refers to the trading of obscene materials within cyberspace. The cyberobscenity debate is very complex. Its newsworthiness not

---

[7] E-mail, for example, while being revolutionary because of its speed and interactive nature, is simply a communication method that is one step beyond the development of the fax.

[8] As recent police investigations, such as Operation Cathedral, have revealed, mostly through BBS and newsgroups. See 'Police swoop on computer porn suspects' (1999) *BBC Online*, 9 December.

[9] See, further, chap. 10.

[10] Giddens, A., *The Consequences of Modernity* (Polity Press, London, 1990) p.6. The debates over the development of cyberspace are causing a reformulation of the debates over modernity; see Escobar, A. 'Welcome to Cyberia: Notes on the anthropology of cyberculture' in Saradar, Z. and Ravetz, J.R., *Cyberfutures: Culture and Politics on the Information Superhighway* (Pluto Press, London, 1996) p.113.

[11] An example of such activity is the creation of software or design of imagery which never actually achieves physical expression.

[12] They are discussed in greater detail in Wall, D.S., 'Cybercrimes: New wine, no bottles?' in Davies, P., Francis, P. and Jupp, V. (eds), *Invisible Crimes: Their Victims and their Regulation* (Macmillan, London, 1999) p.105.

only drove the early debate over the regulation of cyberspace,[13] but its resolution is also marred by normative perceptions and definitional variations across legal jurisdictions. In Britain, for example, individuals daily consume images through the various facets of the mass media that might be classed as obscene in some Middle Eastern countries, and yet are acceptable in more permissive countries.[14]

(Cyber)trespass is the unauthorised access to computer systems, into spaces where rights of ownership or title have already been established. In its mildest form, cybertrespass is little more than an irritating intellectual challenge that results in a harmless trespass, but, at its worst, it is full-blown information warfare between social groups or even nation states. Somewhere between these positions lies the cybervandal, spy and terrorist.

(Cyber)theft relates to a range of different types of acquisitive harm that can take place within cyberspace. At one level are the more traditional patterns of theft, such as the fraudulent use of credit cards and (cyber)cash. Of particular concern is the increasing potential for the raiding of online bank accounts, and there have already been incidents of this activity.[15] At another level are behaviours, such as cyberpiracy (the appropriation of intellectual properties) which are causing us to reconsider our understanding of property and also the very act of theft itself. This is because the characteristics of the property, which exists as a digital code to create a product through a computer system, defies the 'permanently deprive' test under sections 1 and 6 of the Theft Act 1968.

(Cyber)violence describes the violent impact of the cyberactivities of another upon an individual or social or political grouping. While such activities do not have to have a direct physical manifestation, the victim nevertheless feels the violence of the act and can bear long-term psychological scars as a consequence. The activities referred to here range from cyberstalking[16] to hate speech and even bomb-talk.

While these four categories provide a coherent typology by which to demonstrate the range of behaviours that are generating demands for increased regulation, it is clear that their resolution is not simply a matter

---

[13] It could also be argued that the pornography trade also encouraged the development of reliable commercial software and it also demonstrated to the commercial world the viability of the WWW for e-commerce.

[14] For a fuller discussion of obscenity and the Internet see chaps 9 and 10.

[15] In one incident, some German students invited people to register to win an $50k prize. The students then used a program they had developed to search for online banking programs. If one was found, the student's program, or 'cookie', would automatically mail an invoice for $20. The students collected a total of $640k. See Lorek, L.A. 'Outwitting Cybercrime' *Sun-Sentinel of South Florida* (1997).
http://www.sunsentinel.com/money/09130018.htm. See also *Re Levin* [1997] 3 WLR 117.

[16] Ellison, L. and Akdeniz, Y. 'Cyber-stalking: the Regulation of Harassment on the Internet', in Walker, C. (ed.), *Crime, Criminal Justice and the Internet* (special edition, *Criminal Law Review*, Sweet & Maxwell, London, 1998) p.29. See also US Attorney General, Cyberstalking: A New Challenge for Law Enforcement and Industry
(http://www.usdoj.gov/criminal/cybercrime/cyberstalking.htm, 1999).

of engaging with specific bodies of criminal law. As stated in the introduction, the issue of creating order and law is rather more complex than the compliance model of law suggests as the harms are defined by a combination of normative, political and legal values. While the law tends to define the broader parameters, normative behaviour and political debate tend to shape the 'policing' response. So this policing response takes place in the shadow of law, a point that was made earlier. Consequently, each type of behaviour demonstrates quite different 'modalities of constraint'[17] which affect their regulatability and which render inadequate attempts to aggregate cybercrimes for the purpose of policy formation. In other words each type of cyber-behaviour requires a different strategic response towards it. This observation is based upon the following four observations.

Firstly, the increase in the scope of Internet use and the number of users has meant that the *architecture* of each type of harm varies in terms of opportunities to offend, potential victimisation and scale of impact. For example, opportunities for committing cyberfrauds have recently increased substantially with the development of e-commerce activities and also plug 'n' play technologies.[18] Secondly, each type of cybercrime is subject to distinct *bodies of law* and legal definitions can vary across jurisdiction, as is the case with definitions of obscenity, thus causing problems for enforcement both within and across borders. Thirdly, and similarly, *'social' norms* with regard to the harmful behaviour vary from one type of behaviour to another. Some forms of behaviour are viewed as minor harms while others are deemed more dangerous. Such norms also vary with regard to similar types of cybercrime across jurisdictions. Finally, the *markets* which influence and shape each type of behaviour vary not only in terms of the chronological development of Internet technologies, but also across jurisdictions, for example as has been the case with e-commerce.

The cybercrime issue is further complicated by the following seven tensions which themselves influence our understanding of the four groups of cyberbehaviours that were mentioned earlier and further complicate the role of law by shaping both legal and normative responses.

The ongoing power struggle for control and the definition of cybercrimes

Many definitions of offence and offender are being forged by the fight, or 'intellectual land grab'[19], that is taking place for control over cyberspace. Of particular importance here is the observation that the increasing political

---

[17] Lessig, L., 'The Laws of Cyberspace', paper presented at the Taiwan Net '98 conference, Taipei, March, 1998.
[18] Where computers automatically configure hardware and software thus not requiring the need for specialist knowledge about IT systems.
[19] Boyle, J., *Shamans, Software and Spleens: Law and the Construction of the Information Society* (Harvard University Press, Cambridge, MA, 1996) p.125.

and commercial potential of the Internet is giving rise to a new political economy of information capital.[20] As a consequence, a new set of power relationships is being established within which an increasing level of intolerance is being demonstrated by the new powerful towards various risk groups that the former perceive as a potential threat to their interests. Such intolerance tends to mould broader definitions of deviance. But the definitions of deviance are not so simply one-sided. Melossi has argued that definitions of crime and deviance arise, not only from the social activity of élite or power groups, but also from 'common members' of society and offenders themselves: 'the struggle around the definition of crime and deviance is located within the field of action that is constituted by plural and even conflicting efforts at producing control'.[21]

Civil or criminal wrongs?

There often exists some confusion as to whether or not some of the harms fall under civil or criminal laws, and to complicate matters further, some harms will be classed as criminal in some jurisdictions and civil in others. A further complication is the fact that within federated jurisdictions such as the USA, civil wrongs can subsequently become criminal once the state boundaries are crossed in the committing of an act. Indeed, this provides victims with alternative strategies to the public criminal justice model.

Jurisdiction

The trans-jurisdictional nature of cybercrimes creates a problem for the enforcement of law. Typically, policing often boils down to decisions that are made at a very local level over the most efficient expenditure of finite resources. Such decisions become complicated where different jurisdictions cover the location of the offence committed, the offender, victim and impact of the offence.

Yet, there are also examples where such trans-jurisdictionality has provided policing bodies with a flexible tool by which to maximise the potential for gaining a conviction, particularly with regard to 'forum shopping'[22] so that the prospect of achieving the most effective investigation and/or prosecution is achieved. A number of cases from both sides of the Atlantic demonstrate the enabling aspect of the trans-jurisdictionality of the Internet. In *United States of America v. Robert A. Thomas and Carleen Thomas*[23] the prosecutors 'forum shopped' to seek a site where they felt a conviction would best be secured. Consequently Tennessee, rather than California

---

[20] Ibid.

[21] Melossi, D., 'Normal Crimes, elites and social control', in Nelken, D. (ed.), *The Futures of Criminology* (Sage, London, 1994) p.205.

[22] See further Akdeniz, Y., 'Computer pornography: a comparative study of US and UK obscenity laws and child pornography laws in relation to the internet' (1996) 10(2) *International Review of Law, Computers and Technology* 235.

[23] 74 F.3d 701 (1996).

was chosen because of the greater likelihood of conviction. In *R v Arnold and R v Fellows*[24] the investigation was passed on from the US to the UK police because the former believed that the latter were more likely to gain a conviction.

Visibility of the harmful behaviour

Since the growth of the popular use of the Internet, there have been many reports which purport to estimate the extent of cybercrime, particularly with regard to hacking and commercial activities. Most of these reports have been produced by commercial organisations which constitute the emerging cybercrime security industry. Some are based upon systematic methodologies,[25] others tend to confuse risk assessment with reality. The impact of the latter has been an increase in public and commercial anxieties about the Internet. Yet there are a number of further factors which prevent the collection of the reliable data which many risk assessments talk so confidently about.

Identifying the victims

There is frequently some confusion over who the victims of cybercrime are and how they are being victimised. Not only can victims vary from being individuals, towards social or corporate groupings, but the (cyber)harms done to them can also range from the actual, to the perceived, to the implied. In cases such as cyberstalking or the theft of cybercash, the victimisation is very much directed towards the individual. However, in other cases the victimisation is more indirect, such as with cases of cyberpiracy or cyberspying/terrorism. Furthermore, as has been found to be the case with the reporting of white-collar crimes,[26] it is likely that many victims of cybercrimes, be they primary or secondary victims, may be unwilling to acknowledge that they have been a victim, or it may take them some time to realise it. Alternatively, where the victimisation has been imputed by a third party upon the basis of an ideological, political, moral or commercial assessment of risk, the victim or victim group may simply be unaware that they have been victimised or may even believe that they have not, such is the case with some forms of pornography.[27]

---

[24] [1997] 1 Cr.App.R. 244. The preliminary investigation in this case was carried out in the US before it was handed over to the police in the UK.

[25] See, for example, *Information Security Breaches Survey 2000* (http://www.dti.gov.uk/cii/dtiblue/dti_site_site/), which was conducted by Taylor Nelson Sofres as part of a DTI consortium. It was based upon a representative sample of 1000 organisations.

[26] See further Croall, H., *White Collar Crime, Criminal Justice and Criminology* (Open University Press, Buckingham, 1992); Levi, M., *Regulating fraud: White-collar crime and the criminal process* (Tavistock, London, 1987).

[27] For a general overview of the debates over invisibility see Davies, P., Francis, P. and Jupp, V. (eds), *Invisible Crimes: Their Victims and their Regulation* (Macmillan, London, 1999).

Under- and partial reporting of offences

Victims, both individuals and organisations, tend for a variety of reasons to be reluctant to admit that they have been the victim of an attack. At a personal level, this could arise because of individual embarrassment, ignorance of what to do or just simply 'putting it down to experience'. At a corporate level it might be the fear of the negative commercial impact of adverse publicity in terms of lost market share. Alternatively, the corporate victim may simply favour civil, rather than criminal, remedies, or they might find it easier to claim for losses through insurance, or pass on the costs directly to their customers.[28] Of importance here is the observation that the model of justice which public law enforcement organisations offer to corporate victims is not generally conducive to their business interests. Because of these reporting difficulties, cybercrimes are fairly invisible and some types will be more invisible than others.

Understanding the offender

The little evidence that does exist about cyberoffenders suggests that they are fairly atypical in terms of traditional criminological expectations. Although itself a contestable viewpoint, the debates over the criminology and policing of traditional crimes have tended to be located mainly within the analysis of working-class sub-cultures or the underclass. Cyberoffenders on the other hand, are more likely to share a broader range of social characteristics and the cases of hacking and other Internet-related offences that have been reported in the media would suggest they are more likely to be middle class, often without criminal records, often possessing expert knowledge and motivated by a variety of financial and non-financial goals. Consequently the study of the cyberoffender is more likely to be informed by, although not exclusively, the literature discussing white-collar crime.[29]

This section has demonstrated the complexity of the issue of cybercrimes, and it has also illustrated some of the ways in which those complexities impact upon the enforcement of law. These observations, combined with the many scare stories and woeful predictions about cybercrime waves forecast by the media, paint a fairly bleak picture for order and law on the Internet. Yet, this is not the picture that reflects the reality of the Internet. Given the exponential rate of growth in terms of its breadth and the sheer numbers of users, the Internet appears to be comparatively well ordered and the gloomy risk assessments have not yet become realities, if they ever will. The next section will suggest that the reasons for this lie in a multi-tiered structure of order maintenance that has emerged.

---

[28] Hamin, Z. and Wall, D.S., 'Ghosts in the Machine: Computer misuse within the organisation' (1999) 36 *Criminal Justice Matter*, 19.

[29] See further, Croall, H., op. cit., (1992); Levi, M., op. cit., (1987); Sutherland, E., *White collar crime: the uncut version* (Yale University Press, New Haven, 1983); Jordan, T. and Taylor, P., 'A Sociology of Hackers', (1998) 46(4) *The Sociological Review* 757; Taylor, P.A., *Hackers* (Routledge, London, 1999).

Order and law on the Internet

When exploring the ways by which the Internet is currently being policed to achieve and maintain order, it is important to distinguish between interest groups that seek to promote values or viewpoints, bodies which seek to create rules and laws, and bodies which seek to enforce them.

The interest groups draw their mandate from their support of a range of specific moral or political issues. Such interest groups range from organisations like Cyber-Rights and Cyber-Liberties,[30] to groupings of Internet service providers, such as the Internet Service Providers Association, which actively seeks to 'promote the interests of Internet Service Providers in the UK . . .'.[31] This category also includes the various pressure groups which represent specific concerns and who lobby in order to further their cause or protect the interests of their members.

The bodies which seek to create rules and law include policy-making groups and legislators[32] at both a national level and at an international level in the case of the OECD and the European Union.[33] The mandate of both is derived, directly or indirectly, from the formal democratic process.

Finally, there are the various organisations which are actively involved in the policing of cyberspace and which exist to enforce the norms of the former groups through various management strategies that effect a policing function.

In practice it is often hard to disaggregate one function from another because each impacts upon the activities of the others. Broadly speaking the groups tend to fall into one of two main viewpoints, the 'regulators' and the 'cyberlibertarians'. For the most part, these viewpoints oppose each other in terms of their interpretations of, and their respective solutions to, the perceived problems. In truth, the proponents of each viewpoint tend to respect the positions of the other,[34] however for the purposes of explanation it is useful to explore them in their extreme form.

The 'regulators' tend to depict the problem of cybercrimes as being an overall lack of effective regulation, so they demand changes in the law to empower or strengthen the existing powers of police and other regulatory organisations. The problem here is that this type of 'formalist' thinking tends to focus upon resolving disputes once the behaviour has taken place

---

[30] Cyber-Rights and Cyber-Liberties (http://www.cyber-rights.org), along with many others, have found an international expression under the umbrella of the Global Internet Liberty Campaign http://www.gilc.org.

[31] See http://www.ispa.org.uk/frame.htm.

[32] In the UK these organisations would include the DTI, the Home Office and the Houses of Parliament.

[33] Walker, C.P. and Akdeniz, Y. 'The governance of the Internet in Europe with special reference to illegal and harmful content' in Walker, C. (ed.), *Crime, Criminal Justice and the Internet* (special edition, *Criminal Law Review*, Sweet & Maxwell, London, 1998) p.5.

[34] See Strossen, N., 'Cybercrimes vs. Cyberliberties' in Wall, D.S. (ed.), 'Cybercrimes, Cyberspeech and Cyberliberties' (2000) 14(1) *International Review of Law, Computers and Technology* 11.

and seeks to resolve the symptoms, but not the causes. It therefore has little overall impact upon future behaviour.

Opposing the 'regulators' are the 'cyberlibertarians' who favour a more holistic solution which addresses the causes. So the 'cyberlibertarian' answer to most forms of cybercrime lies not so much in the rule of law, but in providing information and education on issues that will enable individuals to make informed choices, thus influencing normative behaviours. The problem with the pure cyberlibertarian position is that it emphasises the causes of behaviour at the expense of the symptoms. Thus, both positions are extremely problematic while also containing strengths, so a balance is required whereby legal rules have to reflect normative behaviours. In practice, both the 'regulators' and 'cyberlibertarians' openly acknowledge this point, and the focus of public debate mainly concentrates upon the nature of this balance.

These tensions have not only tended to shape the formation of norms, policy and law with regard to the Internet, but they have also shaped dynamically the maintenance of a semblance of order over the Internet. An analysis of the policing of the Internet shows that there are four main levels at which policing activity takes place within cyberspace: the Internet users and user groups; the Internet service providers; state-funded non-public police organisations; and state-funded public police organisations.[35]

Internet users and Internet user groups

The Internet users and Internet user groups are the largest group of individuals to be involved in the policing of the Internet. Within the larger group of netizens are a number of user groups which have formed around specific issues to police websites and individual behaviours that offend them. Often transnational in terms of their membership and operation, these groups tend to be self-appointed and possess neither a broad public mandate nor a statutory basis. Consequently, they lack any formal accountability for their actions, which themselves may be intrusive or in some cases even border on illegality. They would, however, appear to constitute a fairly potent regulatory force, and a number of visible examples of this virtual community policing have already occurred. Such examples and the organisations involved are discussed in greater detail elsewhere[36] but, in brief, they form a spectrum of actions which range from the creation of complaint

---

[35] These categories are more fully exhausted in Wall, D.S., 'Policing and the Regulation of Cyberspace', in Walker, C. (ed.), *Crime, Criminal Justice and the Internet* (special edition, *Criminal Law Review*, Sweet & Maxwell, London, 1998), p.79; Wall, D.S., 'Catching Cybercriminals: Policing the internet' (1998) 12(2) *International Review of Law Computers and Technology* 201.

[36] Wall, D.S., 'Policing the Virtual Community: The internet, cyber-crimes and the policing of cyberspace,' in Francis, P., Davies, P. and Jupp, V. (eds), *Policing Futures* (Macmillan, London, 1997) p.208; Wall, D.S., 'Policing and the Regulation of Cyberspace', in Walker, C. (ed.), *Crime, Criminal Justice and the Internet* (special edition, *Criminal Law Review*, Sweet & Maxwell, London, 1998) p.79.

'hotlines' to the formation of bodies of individuals who, on a voluntary basis, actively police the Internet to varying degrees. The Internet Rapid Response Team, for example, seeks to remove offensive (mainly spamming) materials, while the CyberAngels,[37] who are based on the Guardian Angel (exemplary citizen) model, have a broader purpose to actively promote, preserve and protect netiquette, which 'is the collection of common rules of polite conduct that govern our use of the internet'.[38] Importantly, they claim their citizen's right to question what they encounter on the Internet, arguing that they have a civil, legal and human right to bring it to the attention of the proper authorities if it offends them.[39]

Other groups align along a vigilante, rather than exemplary, model citizen, The Cyber-Vigilantes, for instance, seek to fight, via a fairly aggressive WWW site, on behalf of the 'little people' against what they see are inequities among insurance companies.[40] Farther towards the end of the spectrum of vigilantism are found more interventionist groups, such as Phreakers & Hackers (UK) Against Child Porn (PH(UK)ACP),[41] and Ethical Hackers Against Porn (EHAP).[42] Both 'want to stop child exploitation' and claim to work in loose cooperation with government and local officials, even though they admit to 'using unconventional means to take down the worst, most unscrupulous criminals known'. Of course it is impossible to know whether or not these claims are actually fulfilled.

A most interesting variant of the effective policing of one group of users by another is the policing of pornography on the Internet by the adult sites themselves. Since the mid-1990s first or one-click pornography (where pornography is immediately accessible with only one or two clicks of the mouse) has virtually been eliminated on the Internet and, while some of the credit for this achievement must be given to the user groups described earlier, the actions of adult sites themselves cannot be ignored. This is especially the case in the fight against child pornography on the Internet which has long been the concern of many user groups. Coalitions of adult sites, such as Adult Sites Against Child Pornography (ASACP),[43] have specifically been formed to combat child pornography on the Internet. The motivations of the adult sites and their coalitions, aside from their 'public spirit' in preserving public confidence in the Internet, is no doubt to distance themselves from child pornography and thereby seek to legitimise their own activities while also preserving their own markets.

---

[37] http://www.cyberangels.org/ and also at http://www.jex.com/cyberangels/.

[38] http://www.jex.com/cyberangels/mission.htm.

[39] http://www.jex.com/cyberangels/.

[40] http://www.insurancejustice.com/ but also see 'The Cyber Vigilantes are Alive and Well, And It's Time . . .' at http://www.refresher.com/!vigilante3.

[41] http://freespace.virgin.net/pure.kaos/PH(UK)ACP/index.htm.

[42] http://www.hackers.com/ehap/mission.htm.

[43] See the website of ASACP (Adult Sites Against Child Pornography) (http://www.asacp.org/) who claim to have over 700 members and represent over 300 adult websites.

The Internet service providers (ISPs)

The ISPs have a rather fluid status which arises from the fact that although they are physically located in a particular jurisdiction, they have to function transnationally. The moral panic[44] surrounding the Internet during the mid-1990s over the perceived threat of widespread pornography[45] and the subsequent threats of legal action[46] forced Internet service providers to consider the possibility of controlling some of the activities that are taking place on their servers: especially the news discussion groups – most declined to take such action. The general rule of thumb adopted across many jurisdictions is that (civil) liability tends to arise when an ISP fails to remove offensive material, whether it be obscene or defamatory, provided it has been brought to their attention following a complaint.[47]

Since the mid-1990s the legal status of ISPs as publishers has yet to be fully established in most jurisdictions; however, examples of case law are increasing annually. As a consequence, ISPs tend to tread fairly carefully and be responsive to police requests for cooperation. Not only are they very wary of their potential legal liabilities, but also it is probably fair to say that they are fearful of any negative publicity which might arise from their not being seen to act responsibly. Interestingly, the police themselves have also appeared to be fairly uncertain about their general position with regard to the prosecution of ISPs. While, since 1996, they have continued to warn the ISPs about possible prosecutions, few, if any, of the promised prosecutions have been brought against Internet service providers.[48]

In March 2000, the final settlement in the case of *Laurence Godfrey v Demon Internet Ltd*[49] caused ISPs to consider further their potential liability. The outcome of the case not only places ISPs in the uneasy situation of

---

[44] Cohen, S., *Folk Devils and Moral Panics* (Paladin, London, 1972); also see Chandler, A., 'The changing definition and image of hackers in popular discourse' (1996) 24 *International Journal of the Sociology of Law* 229.

[45] Wall, D.S., 'Policing the Virtual Community: The internet, cyber-crimes and the policing of cyberspace', in Francis, P., Davies, P. and Jupp, V. (eds), *Policing Futures* (Macmillan, London, 1997) p.208.

[46] Uhlig, R., ' "Safety Net" on Internet will catch child porn' (1996) 488 *Electronic Telegraph*, 23 September.

[47] See on the criminal side the case of Felix Somm in Germany, as discussed in Leong, G., 'Computer Child Pornography – the liability of distributors?' in Walker, C. (ed.), *Crime, Criminal Justice and the Internet* (special edition, *Criminal Law Review*, Sweet & Maxwell, London, 1998) p.25. See also for civil liability, *Godfrey v Demon Internet* [1999] 4 All ER 342, discussed at Akdeniz, Y., 'Case Analysis of Laurence Godfrey v Demon Internet Ltd.' (1999) 4(2) *Journal of Civil Liberties* 260 and at http://www.cyber-rights.org/reports/demon/htm; Nuttall, C., 'Demon drops libel appeal,' (1999) *BBC News Online*, 9 June; *Demon Internet statement on the Godfrey case and recent problems*, Press Release, 26 March 1999 at http://www.demon.net/info/helpdesk/announce/da1999-07-05a.shtml; Vick, W., Macpherson, L., Cooper, S., 'Universities, Defamation and the Internet' (1999) 62 *Modern Law Review* 58, at p.62.

[48] The main exception is the Felix Somm case in Germany, involving Compuserve. See Leong, G., loc. cit.

[49] (2000) *The Times* 31 March p.7.

being both 'judge and jury' when dealing with complaints, but it also causes them to run the risk of being sued if materials are not removed, and counter-sued if the removal of materials leads to an economic loss.[50]

In the UK the ISPs have, with strong Government encouragement, formed the Internet Watch Foundation which receives and processes complaints from netizens, mostly relating to pornography. Interestingly, the Internet Watch Foundation[51] has become the quasi-public face of Internet regulation in the UK. However, one of the criticisms levelled against the IWF is that it retains the status of being a private organisation that has a very public function and as such lacks the structures of accountability that are normally associated with organisations that have a public function. The relaunch of IWF in January 2000 following a Government review has broadened its remit and has more clearly defined both its role and function. The review has also redefined the IWF's relationship to government in terms of fostering the principle of 'co-regulation' among ISPs.[52]

State-funded non-public police organisations

The next level of policing involves state agencies, but these are bodies not normally perceived as 'police' nor are they given the title 'police'.[53] It is also arguable that their function often exists in parallel, although often with some overlap, to that of the state-funded police organisations.

Some governments, such as those of Singapore, China, Korea and Vietnam,[54] have, with varying degrees of effectiveness, actively sought to control their citizens' use of the Internet, either by directly controlling Internet traffic coming into their countries by only allowing government-controlled Internet service providers,[55] or by requiring users to register with a governmental monitoring organisation. Other governments have set up formal regulatory agencies, such as the Internet Content Task Forces in Germany and France. Aside from these regulatory agencies, a great number of state-funded non-public police organisations who draw upon the authority of the mandate of government also tend to be involved in policing the Internet.

Using the United States as an example, the trans-jurisdictional nature of Internet traffic involves federal rather than provincial state agencies, which accords with the US National Infrastructure Protection strategy towards the

---

[50] See further 'Piggy in the middle fear for ISPs' (2000) BBC News Online, Friday, 31 March.
[51] See chaps 9 and 10 for further details.
[52] See 'Relaunch of IWF' at http://www.internetwatch.org.uk/news/news.html.
[53] This implies that the public 'police' necessarily have a mandate to preserve the peace and enforce the criminal law.
[54] Surveys of censorship by country can be found at http://www.gilc.org/speech/.
[55] Center for Democracy and Technology, 'Regardless of Frontiers: Protecting the Human Right to Freedom of Expression on The Global Internet' (1998) Global Internet Liberty Campaign, 3, f/n 1; Caden, M. and Lucas, S.E., 'Accidents on the Information Superhighway: on-line liability and regulation' (1996) 2(1) Richmond Journal of Law and Technology 3; Standage, T. 'Web access in a tangle as censors have their say' (1996) 475 Electronic Telegraph, 10 September.

Internet.[56] Such federal organisations range from the United States Postal Service to the Inland Revenue Service, to Customs and Excise to the US Securities and Exchange Commission and the various security services and intelligence organisations. In most sovereignties a similar range of non-police organisations will be involved in policing the Internet.

In addition to the state-funded non-public police organisations are a strata of interesting hybrid organisations which are privately funded or organised but have a public function. One such example is the Computer Emergency Response Team (CERT), which exists to combat unauthorised access to the Internet and is based at Carnegie Mellon University in Pittsburgh, USA.[57] CERT is based within a publicly funded institution; however it appears to be funded mainly by private sources. Another example of this hybrid is the relaunched Internet Watch Foundation in the UK, which links the ISPs with government. Yet, it is a private organisation that has a public function.

State-funded public police organisations[58]

The final group of organisations to be involved in policing the Internet are the state-funded public police organisations whose status also allows them to draw upon the authority of the government's mandate. It is the state-funded police who, if the victimisation is serious enough, will engage the criminal justice process. In contrast, the non-police organisations, which vary considerably in function, tend to seek compliance by using alternative non-criminal forms of resolution and only seek to invoke the criminal law when all other avenues have failed.

Police forces tend to be organised either locally or nationally, depending upon the breadth of their jurisdiction. However, while they are mostly located within the boundaries of nation states, they are nevertheless joined by a tier of transnational policing organisations,[59] such as Interpol (worldwide) or Europol (EU specific), membership of which requires formal approved status.[60]

The public policing model and the investigation of cybercrimes

The previous section clearly demonstrates that there exists a pluralistic, multi-tiered structure which currently polices the Internet and achieves/maintains order under the shadow of law, but enforces rules and laws where required. This structure combines elements of both public and private

[56] See National Infrastructure Protection Center http://www.nipc.gov.
[57] http://www.cert.org/.
[58] The roles of the various security services are not included here.
[59] See further, Sheptycki, J., 'Policing, Postmodernism and Transnationalism' (1998) 38 *British Journal of Criminology* 485 and 'Reflections on the Transnationalisation of Policing: the case of the RCMP and Serial Killers' (1998) 26 *International Journal of the Sociology of Law* 17.
[60] Europol brings together national police forces from within the EU. See Convention based on Article K.3 of the Treaty on European Union, on the Establishment of a European Police Office (Europol Convention) with Declarations (Cm. 3050, HMSO, London, 1995).

models of policing. It also reflects the increasing plurality of policing in high modernity at both a national and transnational level,[61] as well as the 'organisational bifurcation'[62] or 'spatial polarisation'[63] that is also taking place within the sphere of terrestrial policing.

Importantly, this pluralistic policing structure bridges the tensions that currently exist on the Internet between behaviours, norms, the law and its enforcement. However, a number of questions arise regarding its future because it is likely that as the Internet becomes even further integrated into occupational and private life, the incidence of cybercrimes will continue to increase greatly each year in proportion to the numbers of Internet users. For example, during the two years between 1996 and 1998[64] the National Computing Centre found that the reporting of computer-related thefts rose by 60 per cent. Although this increase arose from a comparatively small base point, it is nevertheless likely that the annual increase will continue with the expansion of the many new innovative retail practices that fall under the banner of e-commerce. This expansion suggests that the demands placed upon the state-funded police organisations will also increase where the other tiers of policing fail or are found to be inappropriate to deal with the behaviours. So, the big question is whether or not this structure will endure, or whether the public policing function will eventually be expanded to include the Internet. While the history of the integration of technology by the police would point to the latter course of action, there are, however, a number of factors that have emerged during recent years to counteract the inevitability of this outcome, and these shall be explored here.

The purpose of the public police

Since its inception in the late 1820s, one of the dominant characteristics of the public police organisation has been its continued ability to adapt to the demands of modernity.[65] Indeed, the very birth of the full-time police was motivated by the need to deal with the knock-on effects of rapid industrialisation caused by the technological advancement of the industrial revolution.[66]

---

[61] Sheptycki, J., 'Policing, Postmodernism and Transnationalism' (1998) 38 *British Journal of Criminology* 485.

[62] Reiner, R., 'Policing a Postmodern Society' (1992) 55 *Modern Law Review* 761.

[63] Johnston, L., 'Privatisation and protection: spatial and sectoral ideologies in British policing and crime prevention' (1993) 56 *Modern Law Review* 771; Jones, T. and Newburn, T., *Private Security and Public Policing* (Clarendon Press, Oxford, 1998), p.260.

[64] Questionnaires were sent to 9,500 UK organisations and in-depth interviews were conducted with 25 organisations; 89 per cent of respondents reported at least one security breach. National Computing Centre, *The Information Security Breaches Survey 1996* (The National Computing Centre Limited, 1996).

[65] Wall, D.S., 'Cybercrimes: New wine, no bottles?' in Davies, P., Francis, P. and Jupp, V. (eds), *Invisible Crimes: Their Victims and their Regulation* (Macmillan, London, 1999) p.105.

[66] For useful accounts of the development and function of police, see Reiner, R., *The Politics of the Police* (2nd ed., Harvester Wheatsheaf, London, 1992); Johnston, L., *Policing Britain* (Longman, London, 1999); Critchley, T.A., *A History of the Police in England and Wales 1900–1966* (Constable, London, 1967); Manning, P.K., *Police Work* (MIT Press,

However, what marks out the Internet from previous technological eras is the rate of acceleration of the disembedding of time, space and place[67] and its impact upon harmful behaviours. Even the development of the automobile, telephone, radio and more recently the fax relied upon physical rather than purely electronic technologies. The Internet, by contrast is unique in that it creates a virtual environment which not only links different technologies but does so in ways that are virtually instantaneous. Consequently, the demands of the physical form do not tend to temper harmful behaviours in the way that it has done previously.

Furthermore, the range of harms that the Internet is generating, as described earlier, largely falls outside the ambit of traditional policing. Indeed, as discussed earlier, the public police do not always provide a model of justice that is always desired by the victims. This raises the pertinent question as to the extent to which the public police as a whole should seek to integrate the policing of the Internet within their normal daily routine.[68] Thus, an important task of public police organisations during this century will be to reconcile the traditional role and function of police with the new demands placed upon them and to define their involvement, or lack of involvement, more clearly.

Finite resources and shrinking government

Three conflicting factors will weigh heavily upon the minds of police policy-makers when deciding upon the level of public police involvement. The first is the fact that the police are now operating in a managerial environment in which the public's expectations made of the police are increasing. The second is that the resources made available to the police are finite and will remain so for the foreseeable future. Thirdly, the role of the state is also shrinking as more functions are shifted from central to local government.[69] The consequence of these three pressures for the public police is likely to be an increased gatekeeping function, but less responsibility for all but the most serious cases.

Organisational cultures and change

During the mid-1990s, Thackray and others argued that the UK police response to cybercrimes was under-resourced and suffered from a general lack of support from police forces because of an overall lack of general interest in computer-related crimes.[70] Thackray's observations supported those of others; the Metropolitan Police Computer Crime Unit at that time,

Cambridge, MA, 1977); Wall, D.S., *The Chief Constables of England and Wales: The socio-legal history of a criminal justice elite* (Dartmouth, Aldershot, 1998), chaps. 2, 3.

[67] Giddens, A., *The Consequences of Modernity* (Polity Press, London, 1990).

[68] Wall, D.S., 'Policing the Virtual Community: The internet, cyber-crimes and the policing of cyberspace,' in Francis, P., Davies, P. and Jupp, V. (eds), *Policing Futures* (Macmillan, London, 1997) p.208.

[69] See further, Crawford, A., *The Local Governance of Crime* (Clarendon Press, Oxford, 1997).

[70] McCormack, N., 'Criminals slip through the net' (1996) *Daily Telegraph*, 5 November p.3.

for example, reputedly suffered because of the limited number of cases that were reported to it. Case reports were felt to under-represent the total incidence of cybercrimes[71] and prevented the police from developing relative skills.[72] These concerns found a resonance in the DTI report on computer misuse[73] which questioned whether or not the public police have the appropriate skills to investigate cases of computer crime. Since the mid-1990s the UK police, in particular, have made considerable advancements in their understanding of the nature of the challenge of the Internet and how to establish organisational responses. Although they have yet to be fully integrated into policing, these advancements have largely been made through the initiatives of police officers, mainly those associated with the ACPO computer crime group and its subcommittees, but assisted by foresight research from the Home Office and National Crime Intelligence Service (NCIS).[74] Two outcomes of these deliberations have been the formation in many local UK police forces of computer crime units and also the prospective formation of a national computer crime capability.[75] This latter development brings the UK into line with a number of EU countries, such as Germany and France, which have also developed such national units, and also USA and Canada which have also developed federal capabilities.

The creation of specialist units to deal with new crime scenarios is quite a common police organisational response as they provide fora for assembling available expertise within a police organisation. However, there exists a number of organisational impediments to their efficient operation. One such impediment is the existence of conviction-led performance targets.[76] The combination of the requirement for the efficient expenditure of police resources and the Crown Prosecution Service's public-interest test, tend to favour those cases which have the stronger likelihood of investigation and conviction.

Another such impediment is the police policy of restricted tenure of office and the practice of rotating personnel and key staff, which is quite common to police forces in a number of jurisdictions, but perhaps more so in the UK. Designed to lead to the circulation of ideas and the occupational stimulation of individuals, while also preventing the development of corruptive contacts, rotation policy has the counter-productive side-effect of reducing the residual knowledge base and reducing the effectiveness of (some) specialist

---

[71] National Computing Centre, *The Information Security Breaches Survey 1996* (The National Computing Centre Limited, 1996).

[72] Akdeniz, Y., 'Section 3 of the Computer Misuse Act 1990: An antidote for Computer Viruses!' (1996) 3 *Web Journal of Contemporary Legal Issues*; Battcock, R., 'Computer Misuse Act 5 years on' (1995)
http://www.strath.ac.uk/Departments/Law/student/PERSONAL/R_BATTCOCK/.

[73] DTI (Department of Trade and Industry) *Dealing with Computer Misuse* (HMSO, London, 1992), p.29.

[74] National Criminal Intelligence Service (NCIS), *Project Trawler: Crime on the information highways* (Central Office of Information, London, 1999).

[75] For the Government Technical Assistance Centre, see chap. 14.

[76] Conviction rates are published in the reports of Her Majesty's Inspector of Constabulary and also by the Audit Commission.

units. It generates the dual problem of training new members in the use of relevant new technologies and also removing experienced personnel. This point was flagged by Thackray (see earlier) who, after spending time conducting research into the area of the police and the Internet, was moved back into the uniform branch.[77]

Occupational cultures

Although the police organisations, as stated earlier, have the capacity to respond quickly to new policing challenges by setting up specialist units, public policing practices have largely been moulded by the time-honoured traditions of policing and cannot themselves respond to such rapid change. In fact, the basic principles of policing, to keep the 'dangerous classes' off the streets through a dual mandate to keep the peace and bring felons to justice remain much the same almost one hundred and seventy years later, despite considerable social change. It is therefore arguable that the police occupational culture will prove much more resistance to change than that of the police organisations.

There are clear signs that the cultural discord between the public police model and the investigation of cybercrimes, identified in the mid-1990s, is still very present within police forces.[78] This discordance does not appear to be limited to the UK. Steele, for example, writing about the USA, argued that '[n]ot only are the police ill-equipped to deal with the growing and ever-changing criminal activity on the Internet, but most of the world either has no criminal laws for these crimes, or retains outdated ones that are in need of updating'.[79] While Steele perhaps overstated the role of the state-funded police in the overall policing of the Internet, he did identify the cultural discord that exists within the police. A graphic and interesting example of this discord was described by Barlow a few years earlier in the USA. Barlow found that, upon being interviewed by an FBI special agent about an alleged cybertheft, he spent much of the interview trying to educate the agent on the nature of the thing which had been stolen.[80]

Poor Agent Baxter didn't know a ROM chip from a Visc-grip when he arrived, so much of that time was spent trying to educate him on the nature of the thing

---

[77] McCormack, N., 'Criminals slip through the net' (1996) *Daily Telegraph*, 5 November p.3.

[78] See further Wall, D.S., 'Policing the Virtual Community: The internet, cyber-crimes and the policing of cyberspace,' in Francis, P., Davies, P. and Jupp, V. (eds), *Policing Futures* (Macmillan, London, 1997) p.208; Wall, D.S., 'Catching Cybercriminals: Policing the internet' (1998) 12(2) *International Review of Law Computers and Technology* 201.

[79] Steele, H.L., 'The Web That Binds Us All: The Future Legal Environment of The Internet' (1997) 19 *Houston Journal of International Law* 500.

[80] Barlow, J.P., 'Crime and puzzlement: in advance of the law on the electronic frontier' (1990) 14 *Whole Earth Review*. Although Barlow wrote this piece a decade or so ago, the example does, nevertheless, highlight the main processes involved in the paradigm shift. Today the FBI's training programme now annually trains many thousands of US police officers in procedures for dealing with cybercrimes. It is therefore likely that Agent Baxter would enter the same type of situation today with a greater knowledge of the computer medium.

which had been stolen. Or whether 'stolen' was the right term for what had happened to it . . . You know things have rather jumped the groove when potential suspects must explain to law enforcers the nature of their alleged perpetrations.

Barlow also felt that the special agent's problem was not just his low level of information technology literacy. Rather, he indicated the presence of the cultural discord, described earlier, between the immateriality of the Internet and police operational culture. One particular problem for the special agent was the fact that the biographies of the attendees of a hacker's conference, to which the cybertheft was linked, did not 'fit his model of outlaws'. Finally, Barlow was perplexed as to why the special agent 'had come all the way to Pinedale to investigate a crime he didn't understand, which had taken place (sort of) in 5 different places, none of which was within 500 miles?'[81]

Occupational culture is an important part of the way that policing takes place, often more so than the letter of the law[82] as it enables officers to make sense of the world which they have to police and without this cognitive map officers would have no understanding of their environment. But the broader debates over police culture suggest that it can also have a disabling function,[83] so when police officers come across cybercrimes, it is argued that they are very likely to interpret them in terms of their received public police culture. Sterling commented, in his influential work upon the policing of hackers, that he felt that the 'police want to believe that all hackers are thieves',[84] a view that has not changed in the years since his book was published. Sterling was describing a phenomenon commonly found in studies of police culture whereby the hard experience of policing causes the police to redefine the meaning and common understanding of life in the areas in which they become involved. Sacks puts it this way:[85]

> . . . objects and places having routine uses are conceived of in terms of favourite misuses. Garbage cans are places in which dead babies are thrown, schoolyards are places where mobsters hang out, stores are places where shop lifters go, etc.

By applying Sacks's observations to policing the Internet, it is therefore possible to understand some of the police statements of the late 1990s which demonstrate that they do not see it in terms of an exciting potential for the democratisation of knowledge or a growth in active

---

[81] Ibid.

[82] McBarnett, D., *Conviction: The Law, the State and the Construction of Justice* (Macmillan, London, 1981); Shearing, C. and Ericson, R., 'Culture as figurative action' (1991) 42(4) *British Journal of Sociology* 481.

[83] See further, Chan, J., *Changing Police Culture: Policing in a Multicultural Society* (Cambridge University Press, Cambridge, 1997); also the early chapters of Dixon, D., *Law in Policing* (Clarendon Press, Oxford, 1997); Shearing, C. and Ericson, R., 'Culture as figurative action' (1991) 42(4) *British Journal of Sociology* 481.

[84] Sterling, B., *The Hacker Crackdown: Law and Disorder on the Electronic Frontier* (Penguin Books, London, 1994), at p.63.

[85] Sacks, H., 'Notes on police assessment of moral character', in Sudnow, D. (ed.), *Studies in Social Interaction* (Free Press, New York, 1972) p.292; Shearing, C. and Ericson, R. (1991) loc. cit., p.490.

citizenship[86] through the levelling of social boundaries. Rather, they see it as a place where pornographers and other wrongdoers can ply their trade. It is no surprise, then, to see statements made by the police which likened the Internet newsgroups to 'libraries of pornography'[87] and which set the agenda for debates in which the police played a central role. It is also not surprising that, in articulating what they saw as the problem, the police drew from their experiences of the terrestrial world, conceiving of cyberspace as being 'like a neighbourhood without a police department'.[88] Moreover, the investigation of obscene materials, especially child pornography, is recognised as a fairly traditional police activity which carries a broad public mandate and is therefore fairly unproblematic from a police point of view. However, cybertheft and cybertrespass, by way of comparison, are more problematic for the police as they are not regarded as a mainstream police activity.

A further illustration of the cultural discord between traditional occupational police culture and the demands created by the Internet can be found in the shortcomings of laws that were introduced in the United Kingdom to deal with cybercrimes. The Computer Misuse Act 1990 created three new criminal offences, unauthorised hacking, unauthorised access with intent and unauthorised modification of the contents of any computer. However, the authors of this Act would appear to have given little thought to the difficulties of tracing and identifying hackers, and of being able to obtain enough evidence to put forward a convincing case for the prosecution.[89] Many of these outstanding issues are now being covered by legislation covering the interceptions of communications.[90] However, the Matthew Bevan case, for example, demonstrated that not only were there forensic problems in the gathering of evidence,[91] but the sheer cost of prosecution in this type of case was also fairly prohibitive.[92] The police are not the only criminal justice agency who are experiencing problems with computer-related crime. The courts have also encountered some difficulty in ascertaining the relative seriousness of computer thefts, as in the case of R v. Byrne,[93] which suggests that they would have serious problems where the victim has not so much

---

[86] See chap. 6.

[87] Uhlig, R., ' "Safety Net" on Internet will catch child porn' (1996) 488 *Electronic Telegraph*, 23 September.

[88] Sussman, V., 'Policing Cyberspace' (1995) 38 *U.S. News*, 23 January, p.54, citing the Director of the Federal Law Enforcement Training Center.

[89] Charlesworth, A., 'Between flesh and sand: rethinking the Computer Misuse Act 1990' (1995) 9, *International Year-book of Law, Computers and Technology*, 33. See also chap. 12.

[90] See chap. 14 and Council of Europe Committee on Crime Problems (CDPC), Committee of Experts of Crime in Cyberspace (PC-CY), 'Crime in Cyberspace; Draft Convention on Cyber-Crime' (Draft No. 19), April 2000 at http://conventions.coe.int/treaty/en/projets/cybercrime.htm.

[91] Campbell, D., 'More Naked Gun than Top Gun' [1997] *Guardian OnLine*, 27 November, p.2.

[92] Gunner, E., 'Rogue hacker turned legit code-cracker' [1998] *Computer Weekly*, 7 May, p.5.

[93] (1993) 15 Cr App R(S) 34. NB this case was primarily about the theft of computers. Wall, D.S., 'Technology and crime: increased capital investment in information technology and changes in victimisation patterns' (1995) 9 *International Year-book of Law, Computers and Technology* 97.

experienced a loss but a dilution of the value of the original property because it has been duplicated.

Conclusion

What this chapter has sought to demonstrate is that the governance of the Internet is not simply about law and engendering compliance; a study of the law in action suggests that the law merely shapes actions. So, while it is inevitable that there will always be a tension between the law itself and the order that it seeks to create, the Internet has also opened up a gap between what are perceived as undesirable behaviours and shortfalls in the law. This gap has been exacerbated by the anxiety of the new and the unknown, but it has been bridged by a pluralistic and multi-tiered structure of policing that involves individual users, user groups, the private sector and also the public sector. Collectively, it has effected a degree of order over harmful behaviours on the Internet. While care should be taken not to overstate the impact of this structure, it is nevertheless the case that it is an observable model that can provide the basis for an effective future policing system, particularly since there are various impediments to the increased role of the public police to incorporate the policing of the Internet.

It is, therefore, likely that any future policing structure will emerge from the existing mixed and multi-tiered structure of public, private and self-regulation. Since policing, in the guise of order maintenance, largely takes place in the shadow of law rather then under it, then one conceivable development is a mixed model in which the public police co-ordinate infra-structure protection according to national guidelines by facilitating a multi-agency approach which brings together and co-ordinates the users and user groups, ISPs and non-government organisations. However, the formalisa-tion of such a model would have to incorporate structures of accountability in order to maintain public confidence. This is particularly important in the case of self-policing which is not only inherently limited in scope but has a fairly low ceiling of efficacy.[94]

In the future, it is increasingly likely that the ISPs will become the hub of the Internet policing system, but this is a move that will be driven more by the ISPs' corporate culture, which encourages them to play safe in order to maintain profit margins, than by the need to maintain independence from external control or the desire to preserve freedoms of expression. On the other hand, the legal framework under which ISPs operate is becoming more clearly defined and as a consequence their legal accountability increases. So in this sense the future of policing the Internet might be less in the shadow of law and more under its direct rule with all its associated problems.

---

[94] See Walker, C.P., 'Cyber-contempt: Fair trials and the Internet', *Year Book of Media and Entertainment Law* (Oxford, Clarendon Press, 1997) p.28; Wall, D.S., 'Policing the Virtual Community: The internet, cyber-crimes and the policing of cyberspace,' in Francis, P., Davies, P. and Jupp, V. (eds), *Policing Futures* (Macmillan, London, 1997) at p.222.

CHAPTER 8

Criminal justice processes and the Internet

Clive Walker

The setting

The criminal justice process[1] essentially involves information networks applying their expertise in response to inputs from agencies within the system and from the public at large. Although one traditional product of the system might be the prison mail bag, the assembly line of justice is more about the manufacture of intangibles such as guilt or innocence rather than consumables:[2]

> Information enters the system in the form of pleadings and evidence; is processed through various pre-trial, trial, post-trial, and appellate operations; and exits the system in the form of orders and judgments, data, and opinions.

This emphasis upon information generation, processing, transmission and networking makes the process particularly appropriate for the application of information and communications technologies (ICTs).

In reality, the application of ICTs to courts processes within England and Wales[3] has made relatively slow progress, not only because of the usual cultural, political and financial obstacles,[4] but also because of deeper concerns about the negative impacts of ICTs. Some of these have been considered elsewhere, especially the advent of 'cybercontempts of court'.[5] They relate

---

[1] The 'process' involves plural networks (for example, courts, police, prisons, probation). For the relevance of ICTs to networks, see Castells, M., *The Information Age* Vol. I: *The Rise of Network Society* (Blackwell, Oxford, 1996) p.21.

[2] Anderson, R., *et al.*, 'The impact of information technology on judicial administration: a research agenda for the future' (1993) 66 *Southern California Law Review* 1762 at p.1769.

[3] The positions in Northern Ireland (see Lord Chancellor's and Officers' Departments, *Departmental Report* (Cm. 3909, HMSO, London, 1998) B para. 31 and Criminal Justice Review Group, *Review of the Criminal Justice System in Northern Ireland*, http://www.nio.gov.uk/review.pdf, 1998) Annex B p.34) and Scotland (see Scottish Office, *Serving Scotland's Needs* (Cm. 3914, HMSO, London, 1998) para. 10.13) are not covered in this paper. In terms of Internet development, those jurisdictions are well behind England and Wales.

[4] See Anderson, R. *et al.*, 'The impact of information technology on judicial administration: a research agenda for the future' (1993) 66 *Southern California Law Review* 1762 at p.1789.

[5] See Walker, C., 'Fundamental rights, fair trials and the new audio-visual sector' (1996) 57 *Modern Law Review* 517; 'Cybercontempt: fair trials and the internet' (1997–8) 3 *Oxford Yearbook of Media and Entertainment Law* 1. Contempt in this context even includes scandalising the court; see the case of James Hulbert whose website which was critical of

to the fact that the new channels of communication provided by the Internet easily transcend national boundaries (though are not universal),[6] and this transnationality is one feature which marks out the Internet as different at least in degree if not in kind from pre-existing mass media.[7] Another important feature is instantaneity, which both increases the likelihood of unreflected speech and at the same time decreases the opportunity for regulatory intervention. Perhaps the other accentuated characteristics are multiple linkages, ease of access, low establishment costs and interactivity, all of which tend to blur the distinction between publisher and audience so that users can easily switch between either mode. The effect is the encouragement of amateur legal commentators who are not versed in media law whether contempt, defamation[8] or otherwise and who can represent dangers[9] to the traditional weighing of values in the reporting of court cases. The values involve both free speech and fair trials. On the one hand, there are individual and collective interests in freedom of expression. That there is a free speech interest, especially based on the argument from democracy as articulated by Meiklejohn,[10] in what happens in the courts cannot readily be denied since it arises in at least three ways. First, courts are a fundamental state responsibility as they dispense state laws and justice. Consequently, no matter who is appearing in them, there is state interest and therefore a legitimate demand for democratic accountability and discussion. Next, there may be

---

named judges was closed by Kingston Internet under pressure from the Lord Chancellor's Department (*The Independent*, 7 November 1999).

[6] The vast bulk of the traffic is in North America, Western Europe and the Far East: http://www.nw.com/. For the UK's standing in the use of information and communications technologies, see: Department of Trade and Industry, *Moving into the Information Age: An International Benchmarking Study* (http://www.isi.gov.uk/isi/bench/mitia, 1998).

[7] See Johnson, D.R. and Post, D., 'Law and borders – the rise of law in cyberspace' (1996) 48 *Stanford Law Review* 1367.

[8] See: Lord Chancellor's Department, *Reforming Defamation Law and Procedure* (HMSO, London, 1995); Milmo, P., 'The Defamation Bill' (1995) 145 *New Law Journal* 1340; Braithwaite, N., 'The internet and information bulletin boards' (1995) 145 *New Law Journal* 1216; Defamation Act 1996 s.1. For the US case law, see: *Cubby Inc. v CompuServe Inc* 776 F. Supp. 135 (1991, SDNY); *Stratton Oakmont Inc and Porush v Prodigy Service Co* 23 Media L.Rep. (BNA) 1794 (NYSC, 1995); Branscomb, A.W., 'Anonymity, autonomy and accountability' (1995) 104 *Yale Law Journal* 1639. In regard to contempt, see: Contempt of Court Act 1981 s.3(2).

[9] The source of the dangers is primarily the (private) media outlets, but it is assumed there is at least state responsibility to react to their actions which threaten the rights of others, and it is arguable that fundamental rights are in any event directly applicable to relations between individuals: Clapham, A., *Human Rights in the Private Sphere* (Clarendon Press, Oxford, 1993); House of Lords Debates, vol. 583 col. 783 24 November 1997; Wade, W., 'Opinion: human rights and the judiciary' [1998] *European Human Rights Law Review* 520; Coppel, J., *The Human Rights Act 1998* (John Wiley, Chichester, 1999) p.26.

[10] See: Schauer, F., *Free Speech* (Cambridge University Press, Cambridge, 1982) chap. 3. The value of openness is recognised in English law in *Scott v Scott* [1913] AC 417 and in European Convention law in *Sunday Times v United Kingdom*, Appl. no.6538/74, Ser. A vol. 30 (1979–80) 2 EHRR 245; *Observer, Guardian etc. and Sunday Times (No. 2) v United Kingdom* Appl nos. 13166/87, 13585/88, Ser. A vols. 216, 217, (1992) 14 EHRR 153, 229; and *Goodwin v UK*, Appl. no. 17488/90, (1996) 22 EHRR 123 para. 39.

added public interest in discussion where the state is one of the litigants, as usually it is in regard to criminal prosecutions. Thirdly, even litigation brought between private litigants may air matters of public concern. On the other side to these pressures towards publication and discussion lie the individual and collective interests in upholding the fairness of trials and respect for the judicial system in general, both of which may be damaged by unregulated speech. Nevertheless, the clash of values may be more apparent than real. The individual can usually expect to benefit from the 'sunshine'[11] of public proceedings and the public scrutiny of legal proceedings in which the state is inevitably a stakeholder if not a direct party. Equally, the public has a collective interest in fair trials for suspected individual citizens – as was discovered with cases like the *Birmingham 6*,[12] miscarriages of justice are ultimately very damaging to the criminal justice process as a collective enterprise as well as representing personal tragedies for the defendants involved.

The accentuation of these negative impacts may now be on the decline, and a more positive attitude to ICTs was much in evidence in the Lord Chancellor's Department's *Consultation Paper: Resolving and Avoiding Disputes in the Information Age* issued in 1998. The governmental view in England and Wales, is that:[13]

> There can be no doubt that we are moving rapidly into the information age, into an era where a rich body of technologies will transform our lives, bringing changes as fundamental as the Industrial Revolution brought to society in the 18th century. No one will be exempt from these changes.

These sentiments are expressed not in connection with government administration, industry or education, favourite targets for governmental ICT strategies,[14] but in connection with the sedate and conservative courts system. On closer inspection, this technological pull is not entirely new but began as long ago as the *Roskill Report on Fraud Trials* in 1986.[15] Much of the recent attention has been focused on the civil process, notably by the *Woolf Report*, which expresses the belief that ICTs will not only streamline existing systems and processes but will also become 'a catalyst for radical change as well.'[16]

---

[11] 'Sunshine is said to be the best of disinfectants' (Brandeis, L., *Other People's Money* (FA Stokes, New York, 1932) p.92).

[12] *R v McIlkenny and others* [1992] 2 All ER 417. See: Walker C. and Starmer, K., *Miscarriages of Justice* (Blackstone Press, London, 1999) chap. 2.

[13] Lord Chancellor's Department, *Consultation Paper: Resolving and Avoiding Disputes in the Information Age* (London, 1998) chap. 1. For international comparisons, see Parliament of Victoria Law Reform Committee, *Technology and the Law* (1998–9 no, 52).

[14] See Walker, C. and Akdeniz, Y., 'Virtual democracy' [1998] *Public Law* 489.

[15] Roskill, L.J., *Fraud Trials Committee Report* (HMSO, London, 1986) paras 6.66, 9.25. This was followed up by the Report by Judge James Rant, *Fraud Trials, Report of a Working Party* (London, 1989) which considered the necessary equipment, finance and coordination. See Purnell, N., 'Technology and the courtroom' (1990) 140 *New Law Journal* 1064.

[16] *Access to Justice: Final Report* (London, 1996) chap. 21 para. 1. See Widdison, R., 'Beyond Woolf: the virtual court house' [1997] 2 *Web Journal of Current Legal Issues*, 'Electronic law practice' (1997) 60 *Modern Law Review* 143.

The reasons for singling out for special attention fraud trials and civil process are not hard to discern. Civil process is traditionally more paper and pre-trial based than criminal justice, so there is greater room for the intervention of ICTs. Fraud trials involve complexity both of evidence gathering and presentation, as well as contexts which might be very unfamiliar to the person in the jury box.[17] Yet, there are still pressures to apply ICTs in more run of the mill criminal cases. The criminal courts must process a historically large number of cases per year – recorded crime has risen 6 per cent per year in the 40 years up to 1993, though has since fallen.[18] There is concern for the treatment of defendants and increasingly victims – delay and confusing or aggressive treatment at trial are considered to be unacceptable.[19] Complexity has arguably increased in litigation, not only associated with a minority of serious fraud cases[20] but also, more generally, with an increase in legal representation. Above all, perhaps, there are concerns about costs. The courts are subjected to the New Public Management precepts[21] just as other 'services' of government. Accordingly, the Court Service[22] in its Framework Document of 1995 specifies, for example, the waiting time of defendants and unit costs of a courtroom as key performance indicators.

Having marked out the territory of this chapter as comprising positive rather than negative Internet impacts, and criminal rather than civil courts, the third aspect of the delineation is to distinguish the use of ICTs generally from the relevance of the Internet. ICTs aside from the Internet have certainly made a major impact on criminal justice, though there is still room for further improvement. The Lord Chancellor's Department's *Consultation Paper* sees ICT support for court processes as assisting with multi-media electronic filing and presentation, case management unified between agencies, and

---

[17] See Home Office, *Juries in Serious Fraud Trials* (Home Office, London, 1998). Compare Greenleaf, G. and Mowbray, A., 'Information Technology in Complex Criminal Trials' (http://www.austlii.edu.au/au/other/aija/aija.html, Australian Institute of Judicial Administration, 1993). Of course, ICTs may strengthen the jury by allowing ready and systematic access to transcripts and exhibits: Breheny, B.V. and Kelly, E.M., 'Note: Maintaining impartiality: does media coverage of trials need to be curtailed?' (1995) 10 *St. John's Journal of Legal Commentary* 371 at p.398.

[18] Home Office, *Protecting the Public* (Cm. 3190, HMSO, London, 1996) para. 1.6.

[19] See Report of the Interdepartmental Working Group on the treatment of Vulnerable or Intimidated Witnesses in the Criminal Justice System, *Speaking Up for Justice* (Home Office, London, 1998).

[20] See n. 17 above. Another area of growing complexity is the use of forensic science in criminal prosecutions: Walker, C., and Starmer, K., *Miscarriages of Justice* (Blackstone Press, London, 1999) chap. 6.

[21] See Le Vay, *Magistrates' Courts: Report of a Scrutiny* (Home Office, London, 1989); Home Affairs Committee, Home Office Expenditure (1988–9 HC 314); Home Office Working Group on Pre-Trial Issues (Home Office, 1991); Raine, J. and Wilson, M., *Managing Criminal Justice* (Harvester, Hemel Hempstead, 1993), 'Beyond managerialism in criminal justice' (1997) 36 *Howard Journal* 80.

[22] This is a Next Steps agency which administers the higher criminal and civil courts: http://www.courtservice.gov.uk/cs_home.htm.

litigation support systems.[23] All of these developments have been encouraged not only because they represent official objectives but also because of the ability of later commercially available software to capture the complexity of court processes.[24] Lord Woolf's *Report* discusses actual progress in the civil justice system.[25] As for the criminal courts,[26] the picture is more patchy.

The Lord Chancellor's Department has stated its ICT policy towards magistrates' courts as follows:[27]

> The Department is committed to the provision of standard computer services for use in all magistrates' courts. These services will be provided through partnership with the private sector under PFI. The main contract is due to be signed in June 1998. The ICT services will support the efficient operation and performance of magistrates' courts and enable a more effective means of delivering information across the criminal justice system.

To date, the Magistrates' Courts Standards Systems (MASS) has achieved limited interconnectivity. As a result, the influential *Narey Report* continues to express concern about delay at this level and recommends electronic data transfer between Crown Prosecution Service (CPS) and police as an important reform.[28] A more extensive LIBRA system has been devised at the end of 1998, including preparation of cases, listing, notifications and fine accounting. The system is designed so that information can be exchanged between courts and other criminal justice agencies.

In the Crown Court and Court of Appeal (Criminal Division), the Court Service has a more developed ICT strategy maintained by its Information Services Division which is under the control of the IT Sub-Group of the Court Service Management Board (CSMB).[29] The content of the strategy is

---

[23] Lord Chancellor's Department, *Consultation Paper: Resolving and Avoiding Disputes in the Information Age* (London, 1998), chap. 4. For later developments, see Court Service Information Services Division, *Information Technology (IT) Strategy* (http://www.courtservice.gov.uk/itstrat.htm, 1998) para. 1.1.3, Annex D.

[24] See Raine, J. and Wilson, M., *Managing Criminal Justice* (Harvester, Hemel Hampstead, 1993) chap. 7; McMillan, J.E., 'Case management systems in the USA, 1998' (http://www.netjustice.com.au/content/ausconf1.html).

[25] *Access to Justice: Final Report* (1996) chap. 21 paras 3, 13–20. The Local County Court System (LOCCS) Agreement, now called the Courts Computer Systems (CCS) Agreement has been the subject of a procurement contract with Electronic Data Systems Ltd (EDS) (see (1996) *The Times* 18 September p.2; Court Service Information Services Division, *Information Technology (IT) Strategy* (http://www.courtservice.gov.uk/itstrat.htm, 1998) para. 1.1.3, Annex D). This provides intranet operational IT support to the Court Service. A second PFI contract – the ARAMIS (A Resource And Management Information Service) Agreement – provides corporate management information, accounting and financial systems throughout the Court Service and was signed in December 1997: Annex E.

[26] For the Crown Prosecution Service, see (Glidewell) Review of the Crown Prosecution Service, *Report* (Cm. 3960, Stationery Office, London, 1998) chap. 12. See further n. 45, below.

[27] Lord Chancellor's and Officers' Departments, *Departmental Report* (Cm. 3909, Stationery Office, London, 1998) A para. 50.

[28] *Review of delay in the criminal justice system: A Report* (Home Office, 1997) chaps 2, 3.

[29] Court Service Information Services Division, *Information Technology (IT) Strategy* (http://www.courtservice.gov.uk/itstrat.htm, 1998) para. 1.5.1.

informed by meetings with the judiciary, through the Judicial Technology Group (JTG) and with other interested parties through the Information Technology and the Courts Committee (ITAC).[30] Future development is to include '. . . electronic communication with the professions and the public, with more information being provided both through the Internet and through suitably managed and secure access to Court Service systems'.[31] Applying these ideas to specific courts, most attention has been paid to the Crown Court, where the CREST system (an office program for backroom staff) dates from 1991 and has been upgraded as part of the CCS contract.[32] Future enhancements are being addressed following a Scoping Study conducted by Electronic Data Systems Ltd (the PFI supplier to the Court Service). They include: CDMIS (Central Determinations and Management Information System), which allows for automatic calculations for example in relation to legal aid and costs taxation; programs in relation to jury summoning and management service which will generate jurors' names from the Electoral Roll, produce summonses and records, record attendance and excusals, calculate expenses and maintain management information; and a case management project (CREDO), including the use of terminals in court, improvements to CREST, management information systems and links to external criminal justice agencies. As for the Court of Appeal (Criminal Division), the existing system (CACTUS – Criminal Appeals Case Tracking User System) apparently 'meets all the current requirements for case tracking and office support'.[33]

The effective interfacing of ICTs within different legal process agencies represents a major challenge,[34] both in civil[35] and criminal justice sectors.

---

[30] Formed in 1988, ITAC consists of court managers and user professions; see Purnell, N., 'Technology and the courtroom' (1990) 140 *New Law Journal* 1064.

[31] Court Service Information Services Division, *Information Technology (IT) Strategy* (http://www.courtservice.gov.uk/itstrat.htm, 1998) para. 1.1.3.

[32] See Waugh, P., 'The use of computers in the administration of justice in the United Kingdom' (1991) 5 *Yearbook of Law, Computers and Technology* 26; Court Service Information Services Division, *Information Technology (IT) Strategy* (http://www.courtservice.gov.uk/itstrat.htm, 1998) paras 1.1.2, 5.4.1.

[33] Court Service Information Services Division, *Information Technology (IT) Strategy* (http://www.courtservice.gov.uk/itstrat.htm, 1998) para. 5.2.1. The Crown Office is being treated in the same fashion: para. 5.3.1.

[34] The various systems to be linked include not only CREST and MASS but also the Prison Service Local Inmate Database System (LIDS), the Probation Service Case Record and Administration System (CRAMS), the CPS Standard Case Operations (SCOPE) and the police's Police/Home Office Enhanced Names Index (PHOENIX). The links are of course subject to the Data Protection Act 1998 – compare: Data Protection Registrar, *Annual Report 1992* (1992–3 HC 64, HMSO, London) p.5; *The Electronic Delivery of Government Services* (Cm. 3438, HMSO, London, 1996) para. 6.11., though concerns about the creation of a 'surveillance society' are certainly not allayed by the limited intervention to date of the Data Protection Registrar: see Hebenton, B. and Thomas, T., *Criminal Records: state, citizen and the politics of protection* (Avebury, Aldershot, 1993); Lyon, D., *The Electronic Eye* (Polity Press, Cambridge, 1994).

[35] See Lord Woolf, *Access to Justice: Final Report* (1996) chap. 21 para. 28. The Civil Justice Council (which was created by the Civil Procedure Act 1997 s.6) has not been prominent in ICT matters.

The task in regard to the latter has been entrusted to the Committee for the Co-ordination of the Computerisation of the Criminal Justice System (CCCJS).[36] Progress has been disappointing, with imperfect links between agencies and even within agencies.[37] Furthermore, its operation is far from comprehensive. For example, the development of police data handling systems, by far the most important in the criminal justice system, has never been within its clear purview and is the province of the distinct Police Information Technology Organisation (PITO).[38] There is no equivalent Criminal Justice Information Technology Organisation (CJITO),[39] far less one actually subsuming PITO.

Turning from ICTs mainly in court administration to ICTs in trial process, the Lord Chancellor's Department's consultation paper, *Resolving and Avoiding Disputes in the Information Age*, sees technology for judges as including:[40]

> ... document creation, electronic communications, document management, retrieval of external information, internal information resources, case management, courtroom technologies, and promulgation (putting their decisions on the Internet and on a judicial Intranet).

Thus, after years of neglect and underinvestment, the 'front-office' full-time judicial staff[41] have been issued with personal laptop computers by the Court Service from 1996 onwards under the JUDITH ('Judicial IT Help') project,[42] though there seems to be no plan to assist the 30,000 lay magistrates. Access to ICTs is meant to confer a number of benefits for the judiciary. It allows the efficient accessing or inputting of data in the courtroom, including the taking of benchnotes from which directions to a jury, a

---

[36] It was formed as a joint initiative between Home Office, Lord Chancellor's Department and Crown Prosecution Service. The first meeting was in 1989, and it comprises Magistrates' and Crown Courts, police, probation, Customs and Excise and DVLC representatives. See Bellamy, C.A. and Taylor, J., 'New ICTs and institutional change: the case of the UK criminal justice system' (1996) 9 *International Journal of Public Management* 51; Barrett, N., *Digital Crime* (Kogan Page, London, 1997) chap. 5.

[37] See Review of the Crown Prosecution Service, *Report* (Cm. 3960, Stationery Office, London, 1998) para. 8.

[38] Police Act 1997 Pt. IV.

[39] This is recommended by the Review of the Crown Prosecution Service, *Report*, loc. cit. para. 14, which also argues for PITO to manage the CPS's IT development: para. 26.

[40] Lord Chancellor's Department, *Consultation Paper: Resolving and Avoiding Disputes in the Information Age* (London, 1998), chap. 4.

[41] Lord Justice Brooke, 'IT and the Courts of England and Wales: the Next Ten Years', (13th BILETA Conference: 'The Changing Jurisdiction', Dublin, http://www.bileta.ac.uk/, 1998).

[42] Mander, M., The JUDITH Report (1993) 1 *International Journal of Law and Information Technology* 249; Lord Woolf, *Access to Justice: Final Report* (1996) chap. 21 para. 5; Gibb, F., 'Judges surf into court' (1996) *The Times* 13 August p.37; Court Service Information Services Division, *Information Technology (IT) Strategy* (http://www.courtservice.gov.uk/itstrat.htm, 1998) para. 3.2. For the background, see Lord Justice Brooke, 'IT and the Courts of England and Wales: the next Ten Years', (13th BILETA Conference: 'The Changing Jurisdiction', Dublin, http://www.bileta.ac.uk/, 1998). Compare Harvey, D., 'The New Zealand computers for judges project' (http://www.law.auckland.ac.nz/court/dc/judcomp.htm, 1998).

judgment or a sentence[43] can be compiled, dramatised by Judge Ito in the O.J. Simpson case.[44] A further important task identified for judges is the proactive formulation of case plans and their execution.[45] Even the humble personal laptop computer can facilitate easy access to court documents from home or while on circuit. Litigation support technologies include document indexing, review, search and full text retrieval and document image processing to assist with discovery and trial.[46] The expectation of the Court Service is that 'In the immediate future . . . all staff and all judges will need to have access to a computer to do their work.'[47]

Yet, the results so far are mixed. Some insiders relate that the uptake of ICTs has been 'an immense success', though it is driven by the personal initiative and enthusiasm of individuals from the cohort of higher judiciary and has not received the funding and training necessary to make the same outcome universal.[48] Others paint a less rosy picture. The Lord Chancellor's Department's *Consultation Paper* recognises two problems:[49]

> The first is that not all judges who want technology have yet been equipped, although plans are in hand to overcome this shortcoming. The second is that many judges will not want to use ICT even if it is available. There is scope here for firmer targets. It could be stipulated that, within five years, every judge in the land is expected to use IT in his or her daily work.

Whether this big stick materialises remains to be seen. It is in any event disappointing to hear that the judiciary may be forced to take up ICT strategies on the government's terms. The channel of communication provided by the Internet could be an important safeguard for independence – allowing the judges to explain themselves to the public without the spin of government or even the self-serving interests of the media interfering with the message.

Even if not all judges are self-motivated to take up ICTs, there may be pressures from other court users which force them to keep pace. For example, there is an increasing use of ICTs by solicitors and barristers,[50] with the

---

[43] See Strand, R.G., 'The computer integrated courtroom harnessing technology to enhance the justice system' (1991) 5 *Yearbook of Law, Computers and Technology* 1.

[44] Lord Woolf, *Access to Justice: Final Report* (1996) chap. 21 para. 23.

[45] Lord Woolf, *Access to Justice: Final Report* (1996) chap. 21 para. 16. The counterpart Criminal Courts Review (under Lord Justice Auld) is expected to report on practices and procedures (including the use of technology) by the end of 2000. See http:www.Criminal-courts-review.org.uk.

[46] Lord Woolf, *Access to Justice: Final Report* (1996) chap. 21 para. 6.

[47] Court Service Information Services Division, *Information Technology (IT) Strategy* (http://www.courtservice.gov.uk/itstrat.htm, 1998) para. 1.1.4. see also para. 3.1.

[48] Lord Justice Brooke, 'IT and the Courts of England and Wales: the next Ten Years', (13th BILETA Conference: 'The Changing Jurisdiction', Dublin, http://www.bileta.ac.uk/, 1998).

[49] Lord Chancellor's Department, *Consultation Paper: Resolving and Avoiding Disputes in the Information Age* (London, 1998), chap. 4.

[50] See Susskind, R., *The Future of Law: Facing the Challenges of Information Technology* (Clarendon Press, Oxford, 1996); Kelly, M., 'Getting support from litigation support' (13th BILETA Conference: 'The Changing Jurisdiction', Dublin, http://www.bileta.ac.uk/, 1998);

consequent need for protocols about systems and formats and the possible linkage of courts to professions already envisaged by the Court Service.[51] In practical terms, the links will involve electronic communications with courts, the electronic publication of information, and support for lawyers' ICT equipment in court and in court buildings.[52] The application of ICTs to the litigants in court could include the presentation and computer-aided transcription (CAT) in real time[53] of evidence.[54] This allows not only a clear and accurate record which avoids the need for any read-backs or note-taking, but also searching, indexing, linking, annotating and analytical procedures not possible with the printed word. The production of a transcript in this way could, of course, assist with publication via the Internet, a point considered later.[55] Technologies could also be used to facilitate the evidence-giving of litigants, for examples to screen juries or witnesses through video-conferencing or other linkages. This form of testimony is allowed in some circumstances under section 32 of the Criminal Justice Act 1988 (and in future under the Youth Justice and Criminal Evidence Act 1999, Part II), and the use of ICTs can bring enhanced scrutiny to the process,[56] though it does reduce the courtroom's atmosphere of solemnity and threat which are part of the pressure on the witness at least to take the proceedings very seriously, if not to tell the truth. The requisite technology has been installed in a number of Crown Court centres.

The Court Service has expressed great interest in all of this technology which it sees as having an important role in the 'courtroom of the future'.[57] The model often cited, drawing together many of these initiatives, is the Courtroom 21 Project, which is a joint project of the William & Mary School of Law (Virginia) and the National Center for State Courts,[58] and is

---

Wall, D.S. and Johnstone, J., 'The industrialisation of legal practice and the rise of the new electric lawyer' (1997) 25 *International Journal of the Sociology of Law* 95. Uses include more graphical presentations (though mainly confined to fraud cases to date): Tantum, M., 'The lawyer and the war' (1991) 5 *Yearbook of Law, Computers and Technology* 65.

[51] Court Service Information Services Division, *Information Technology (IT) Strategy* (http://www.courtservice.gov.uk/itstrat.htm, 1998) paras 1.1.6.

[52] Ibid. para. 8.1.

[53] The systems involve a computer-assisted stenograph machine which matches the court reporter's stenograph keystokes to full words in the computer's software (such as LiveNote or Lotus Notes).

[54] See Plotnikoff, J. and Woolfson, R., 'Replacing the judge's pen? Evaluation of a real-time transcription system' (1993) 1 *International Journal of Law and Information Technology* 90; O'Flaherty, D., 'Computer-generated displays in the courtroom: for better or worse? (1996) 4 *Web Journal of Current Legal Issues*; Harris, V., 'Overview of computerised transcript' (http://www.netjustice.com.au/content/VHARRIS.html, 1998).

[55] The Internet was used to distribute the judgment in the case of Louise Woodward: see http://www.courttv.com/trials/woodward/.

[56] Widdison, R., 'Beyond Woolf: the virtual court house' [1997] 2 *Web Journal of Current Legal Issues*.

[57] Court Service Information Services Division, *Information Technology (IT) Strategy* (http://www.courtservice.gov.uk/itstrat.htm, 1998) paras 5.4.6, 6.1.

[58] http://www.courtroom21.net/.

billed as 'The World's Most Technologically Advanced Courtroom' and used for both demonstration purposes and occasionally actual trials.

Having now set out the technological architectures and cultures which apply to the criminal justice system and especially its courts structure, attention will now be turned to the impact of the Internet. The examination in this chapter is split into two parts: actual and potential usage by the criminal courts themselves; and actual and potential usage by 'outsiders' in relation to criminal court processes.

Actual and potential Internet usage by courts

From the viewpoint of court administrators, judges and other legal professionals, the online court can perform a number of very valuable functions. These will revolve mainly around providing a better working system for the servants and the 'customers' of public justice through improvements in the quality of the process. There are also possible benefits to the outcomes of justice, including boosting the denunciatory function of justice. Other possible uses are directed more at the public, such as allowing active public participation in the justice system and educating the more passive wider community.[59] Finally, the Internet may provide an alternative forum for dispute resolution.

Improvements in the quality of the process

This objective is not just confined to the eradication of undue delay but also seeks to bolster the knowledge base of lawyers and the ways in which experiences can be shared. Of relevance here is the JUDITH project, mentioned earlier, which is to allow access to the judicial communications network known as FELIX, which comprises open and closed conference facilities, a messaging system including the ability to transfer files.[60] The provision of word processing, e-mail and conferencing facilities has been agreed between the Court Service and the Judicial Technology Group (JTG);[61] it is also planned that a pilot project to evaluate the benefits to the judiciary of using the Internet will be taken forward. This work will form part of the Government Secure Intranet (GSI), which will eventually replace the role of FELIX in providing e-mail and conferencing facilities for all judges.[62] So, all judges are to receive computers, and training is to be offered in consultation

---

[59] See Carlson, T.C., 'Information highway implementation guidelines' (Fifth National Court Technology Conference (CTC5), http://www.ncsc.dni.us/ctc5/ctc5arts.htm, 1997).

[60] Lord Woolf, *Access to Justice: Final Report* (1996) chap. 21 para. 5. There are around 490 judges with access to FELIX: Court Service Information Services Division, *Information Technology (IT) Strategy* (http://www.courtservice.gov.uk/itstrat.htm, 1998) para. 3.2.

[61] This is a liaison forum consisting of judges and Court Service (and sometimes representatives of EDS) which follows on from the Judges' Standing Committee on IT (JSCIT) founded in 1990.

[62] Court Service Information Services Division, *Information Technology (IT) Strategy* (http://www.courtservice.gov.uk/itstrat.htm, 1998) para.10.1.

with the Judicial Studies Board.[63] ICTs in the hands of judges could also allow access to new knowledge as well as the sharing of it. One example might be a greater reliance upon legal research through LEXIS.[64] This could eventually lead to an adjustment to the style of judgments, which become more dependent on reasoning and less on the inherent wisdom, pragmatism and authority of the judge, an approach which ties in with the expectation of the Lord Chancellor Irvine in human rights cases, where teleological reasoning is expected to play a greater role.[65] It is possible that what counts as precedent could also change. Internet technology allied to other forms of ICTs could ensure that most cases from Crown Court upwards could be recorded and reported. But should all cases be available for later citation?[66] In fact, the courts have tried to delimit unreported cases by placing strict restraints on them.[67] This may be less justifiable once issues of accessibility and cost cease to be important, and the effect will be to re-empower the parties rather than the judges to decide relevance and authority, with perhaps a greater emphasis on the standing of the authoring judge rather than the venue of judgment.

Another form of knowledge-based development could involve the use of local area networks to create localised guidelines and practices, for example in regard to sentencing. These might be especially relevant to magistrates, courts, though new managerialism has often been an excuse for the stifling rather than encouragement of local initiative.[68]

The ultimate achievement of ICTs would be the replacement of the judge with some kind of expert-system software which reaches smart decisions in response to the input of sets of data facts. It has indeed been suggested that the development of information technology will have profound impacts upon how legal professions deliver their services to clients and potential clients.[69] As legal information becomes readily accessible, it is arguable that the role of the lawyer will become less the demonstrator of legal texts or dispute resolver and more legal risk assessor and knowledge engineer. There may be at least two flaws to this thesis. One is that the inherent complexity and open texture of many laws mean that mere accessibility and knowledge do not, without the training of a lawyer, allow sound interpretation according to legal science. Law in the real world is not about 'rule-based, deterministic

[63] Lord Justice Brooke, 'IT and the Courts of England and Wales: the Next Ten Years', (13th BILETA Conference: 'The Changing Jurisdiction', Dublin, http://www.bileta.ac.uk/, 1998).
[64] See Bosworth, K., 'Taking up computer expectations' (1991) 5 Yearbook of Law, Computers and Technology 58 at p.59.
[65] See Walker, C. and Akdeniz, Y., 'Virtual democracy' [1998] Public Law 489.
[66] Lord Chancellor's Department, Consultation Paper: Resolving and Avoiding Disputes in the Information Age (London, 1998), chap. 2.
[67] See Roberts Petroleum Ltd v Bernard Kenny Ltd [1983] AC 192; Practice Statement [1998] 1 WLR 825 para. 8.
[68] Raine, J.W., Local Justice (T. & T. Clark, Edinburgh, 1989) p.176.
[69] Susskind, R., The Future of Law: Facing the Challenges of Information Technology (Clarendon Press, Oxford, 1996).

decisions' but is an interpretative life science which requires weighting and judgment between values based on moral precepts.[70] Given this normative setting, it seems most unlikely that any Internet-based program could either achieve the subtlety required or avoid undue legal conservatism by always rresorting to conventional terms.[71] The other doubt is whether the law is, or will ever be, electronically available to the citizen in the street. Such an objective is very difficult to achieve, given the rapidly and constant changing composition of law, especially in a common law, uncodified system.

Lord Woolf certainly saw this potential of ICTs:[72]

> . . . technology could provide the basis for information systems, available in court buildings and other public places, to guide the public and court and legal matters. . . . Given the projected level of usage of the World Wide Web, this should be one of the preferred means of delivery of information for the public. Additionally, I am impressed by the idea of using more general community information systems for the delivery of legal guidance.

The Court Service already has Internet pages[73] with organisational and policy information and a scattering of court judgments. Listing information for the Commercial Court is available on the Internet from other sources.[74] Another current source of information on the Internet is Smith Bernal, the official shorthand-writers, who are making available a wide range of court transcripts since May 1996, though now mainly on a subscription basis.[75] It is proposed that all Court Service related material will eventually be available on the Court Service site.[76] As far as the Lord Chancellor's Department is concerned:[77]

> Future plans include providing Daily Lists from other divisions of the High Court, and increasing the number and variety of judgments available on the site. It is also intended to put onto the site a large number of the most commonly used court forms and information leaflets, which would help small businesses, the professions and organisations such as Citizens Advice Bureaux.

---

[70] Anderson, R., *et al.*, 'The impact of information technology on judicial administration: a research agenda for the future' (1993) 66 *Southern California Law Review* 1762 at pp.1771, 1800.

[71] Compare Lord Chancellor's Department, *Consultation Paper: Resolving and Avoiding Disputes in the Information Age* (London, 1998), chaps 3, 4.

[72] Lord Woolf, *Access to Justice: Final Report* (1996) chap. 21 para. 9.

[73] http://www.courtservice.gov.uk/.

[74] See http://www.smlawpub.co.uk. The Court Alerting Service is accessible free of charge at this site.

[75] The former free access system (Casebase, http://www.smithbernal.com/casebase_frame.htm) has ceased, leaving the subscription based Casetrack (http://www.casetrack.com/casetrack_frame.htm). House of Lords' judgments are at http://www.parliament.the-stationery-office.co.uk/pa/ld199697/ldjudgmt/ldjudgmt.htm; Acts of Parliament at http://www.hmso.gov.uk/acts.htm.

[76] Court Service Information Services Division, *Information Technology (IT) Strategy* (http://www.courtservice.gov.uk/itstrat.htm, 1998) para. 11.2.1.

[77] Lord Chancellor's and Officers' Departments, *Departmental Report* (Cm. 3909, HMSO, London, 1998) A para. 105.

However, these grand plans also cause concern, as the Court Service has admitted that 'there has been no clear policy for co-ordinating publication of information . . . and this could lead to more fragmentation and an undue drain on Court Service resources'.[78] Furthermore, much of this initiative is consumerist in nature – the consumers here being the legal professions.

The Court Service does envisage the eventual use of intelligent kiosks to provide members of the public with a simple interface for requesting and providing information.[79] In this way, 'Kiosks are expected to support business strategy by improving the quality of service offered to the public and by reducing the level of routine and repetitive work being carried out [by court staff].' Members of the public and lawyers should be able to obtain or file court documents through the Internet which could be utilised for electronic data exchange. All these possibilities are strongly endorsed by the Lord Chancellor's Department's *Consultation Paper: Resolving and Avoiding Disputes in the Information Age*.[80] A practical step has been taken by the Community Legal Service, set up under section 4 of the Access to Justice Act 1999 and with one of its objects as 'the provision of general information about the law and legal system and the availability of legal services'. Pursuant to this aim, it has established the Just Ask! website,[81] though this as more a listing of other sites than a new source of information.

In these ways, the law could become more available to the 'latent legal market'.[82] This will leave private lawyers to cater for the wealthier sector of the legal needs market, though the implications of opening up in this way may be both palatable and unpalatable:[83]

> . . . the prospect that formal law might become broadly accessible, a part of everyday existence for most people, is quite revolutionary and not without controversy. But that revolution is what information technologies will make possible . . . Some observers note the increasing encroachment of law on daily life – the 'juridification' of the social sphere – with trepidation. Others, however . . . either assume or applaud it. The debate turns on many things, including fundamentally conflicting visions of what 'law' is: Is it a weapon of destruction that threatens to tear the social fabric as its influence spreads, or it is an essential system of support for valued and valuable social relationships?

---

[78] Court Service Information Services Division, *Information Technology (IT) Strategy* (http://www.courtservice.gov.uk/itstrat.htm, 1998) para. 8.3.

[79] Ibid., para. 11.3.1. The same strategy is to apply to other governmental services: *government.direct* (Cm. 3438, HMSO, London, 1996).

[80] Lord Chancellor's Department, *Consultation Paper: Resolving and Avoiding Disputes in the Information Age* (London, 1998) chaps 3, 5

[81] http://www.justask.org.uk/.

[82] See Susskind, R., *The Future of Law: Facing the Challenges of Information Technology* (Clarendon Press, Oxford, 1996); Lord Chancellor's Department, *Consultation Paper: Resolving and Avoiding Disputes in the Information Age* (London, 1998), chap. 3.

[83] Anderson, R., *et al.*, 'The impact of information technology on judicial administration: a research agenda for the future' (1993) 66 *Southern California Law Review* 1762 at p.1799. A similar concern is expressed in Lord Chancellor's Department, *Consultation Paper: Resolving and Avoiding Disputes in the Information Age* (London, 1998), chap. 6.

Certainly, such an approach would eventually have a radical impact on what constitutes 'the court', since in the future:[84]

> The marketplace for virtually all goods and services, including justice, [will be] the network itself, cyberspace. The courts' physical forums [will be] steadily, inexorably disappearing.

In this way, technology can be used to shift radically the nature of the court's persona; it becomes not just a paper-free and networked environment but takes on a virtual existence.[85] Other jurisdictions have already started along this path.[86]

They include in Arizona[87] 'Quick Court', which is an interactive multimedia computer system found in court and public library buildings that offers information and instructions to litigants and produces legal documents for use in court cases. Types of cases covered include family matters, probate; small civil claims, and landlord and tenant, as well as general court information and instructions on how and when to use alternative dispute resolution (ADR) services.[88] At US federal level, there is a significant availability of automated information (giving information about a case or files deposited in respect of it).[89] In Singapore, there is an Automated Traffic Offence Management System which comprises a network of self-operated kiosks at which accused persons may plead guilty to minor traffic offence; there is apparently still the involvement of a humanoid magistrate to accept the plea.[90]

The denunciatory function of justice – naming and shaming

The advent of a policy of naming and shaming, whether with felons, failing schools or feckless hospital surgeons, can offer yet another facet for Internet use. In the case of the criminal justice system, changes of policy have so far been related to the readier identification of juvenile and young defendants.[91] In addition, police forces in a number of US localities have also sought to

---

[84] Johnson, P.J., 'Introduction: planning for the next century in the California courts' (1993) 66 *Southern California Law Review* 1751 at p.1751.

[85] Hoch, F.C., 'Judicial philosophy in information technology' (http://www.netjustice.com.au/content/TCHJUS.html, 1998).

[86] For US court sites, see http://www.ncsc.dni.us/court/sites/courts.htm.

[87] http://www.supreme.state.az.us/courthelp/quick.htm. See Predavec, I., 'The automatic justice machine' (1995) 5(5) *Computers and Law* 18. There are also 'seven-foot tall, royal blue, bulletproof' interactive kiosks in Long Beach: Anderson, R., *et al.*, 'The impact of information technology on judicial administration: a research agenda for the future' (1993) 66 *Southern California Law Review* 1762 at p.1774. Colorado has also taken up similar ideas: http://www.courts.state.co.us/ct-index.htm.

[88] For ADR in the UK, see for example http://www.adrnet.co.uk/.

[89] See http://www.uscourts.gov/ttb/oct99ttb/newcases.html.

[90] Hoch, F.C., 'Judicial philosophy in information technology' (http://www.netjustice.com.au/content/TCHJUS.html, 1998). For computerisation in the Singapore Supreme Court (to include an electronic filing system), see http://www.gov.sg/judiciary/supremect/compute/computeindex.htm.

[91] See Report of the Interdepartmental Working Group on the treatment of Vulnerable or Intimidated Witnesses in the Criminal Justice System, *Speaking Up for Justice* (Home Office, London, 1998).

encourage publicity for certain categories of adult offender, such as those involved with prostitution. These are often relatively low-level offences, which might otherwise escape the attention of newspapers. But the posting of names and photos on the Internet, a record which certainly lasts longer than a newspaper and reaches a much wider audience may be a further disincentive to transgression. An example of this policy in action is the public notification pages of the police in St Paul, Minnesota, which even includes arrestees, and is billed as a 'direct response to the fears, anger and demands expressed by law-abiding men and women'.[92] Other conceivable offence types which might be treated in this way include shoplifters and child sex offenders, whose photographs are already circulated among police forces and by police forces to vulnerable localities.[93] Stolen vehicles registers might also benefit from the wider publicity of the Internet, though police education is necessary before many of the opportunities are realised.[94]

Naming and shaming can work for defendants as well as plaintiffs or prosecutors.[95] The low cost and accessibility of the Internet allow individuals and groups to obtain a hearing for their legal points to an extent which they could not afford in other media outlets and in circumstances where court appearances might not be available. The defendants in the so-called 'McLibel' case have made very effective use of the Internet as part of their campaign, which includes the pressurising of McDonalds to give up their legal action (and business practices).[96]

The Internet might also be used to produce dialogue about sentencing and the degree of naming and shaming. Rather than leaving it to a judge or magistrate to express the limits of tolerance of the community, sentencing levels and priorities might be shaped in this way, just as policing plans are supposed to embody the results of public soundings.

Active public participation in the justice system

The conflict between community involvement in, and professionalisation of, the criminal justice system provides the organising theme for this sub-issue. This conflict has become particularly acute in England and Wales, where trends of specialisation, technological sophistication and managerialism have tended to marginalise the role for lay persons within the environment of criminal justice. These trends can be evidenced by diminished lay involvement in the judiciary, for example, through an increase in professional ('stipendiary') magistrates.[97] Lay involvement in the trial process, focused on

[92] http://www.stpaul.gov/police/prostitution.htm
[93] See *Hellewell v Chief Constable of Derbyshire* [1995] 1 WLR 804; *R v Chief Constable of N Wales, ex p. AB* (1997) *The Times* 14 July.
[94] Hyde, S., 'A few coppers change' (1999) 2 *Journal of Information, Law and Technology*.
[95] See the links at http://www.leeds.ac.uk/law/hamlyn/1miscarr.htm. See also the materials about Mumia Abu Jamal at http://www.mumia911.org/home.htm.
[96] See: http://www.mcspotlight.org/home.html.
[97] See Seago, P., Walker, C. and Wall, D., The development of the professional magistracy in England and Wales [2000] *Criminal Law Review* 631.

the role of the jury, also seems to face official hostility in the UK. For example, there are also concerns about the efficiency of juries in either-way cases[98] and the viability of juries in dealing with complex frauds[99] which arises from a tension between efficiency and technical accuracy versus community involvement and the mediation of law through social standards. At the same time, it would be no advantage if professional oligarchies were to be replaced by the 'self perpetuation' of particular social strata, especially the middle class who 'provide the backbone of the Bench and form its dominant culture'.[100] So, the Internet could be used to reach out to a wider clientele and in that way improve the provision of justice within the system.

Problems such as these could be eased by informational campaigns which could include the medium of the Internet. Thus, it would help if the public were more familiar with the local courts and their processes. Becoming a juror or a magistrate might seem less extraordinary or difficult. In regard to the magistracy, a broader knowledge in this way might also avoid the 'self perpetuation' of particular social strata, especially the middle class who 'provide the backbone of the Bench and form its dominant culture'.[101] Of course, Internet users are at present predominantly middle class, though there are several government initiatives afoot to ameliorate this social exclusivity.[102] So, the immediate impact of Internet recruitment might be to encourage a younger, rather than a more socially diverse, cohort.

There is a more general audience to reach. Part of the characteristic of local justice at magistrates' court level is meant to be the accessibility of the local court house. This accessibility is diminishing as courthouses are closed. But even if the physical entity becomes more remote, its virtual presence can become more readily accessible and to a potentially greater audience than the relatively few members of the public who have ever bothered to sit in a public gallery. The two can be linked – the Internet could be used to advertise open days in the physical court buildings. Several magistrates' courts do operate open days.[103] But very few have websites, and fewer have sought to advertise their activities in general, or the roles of lay persons in particular. A praiseworthy exception was the advertising of the open day in 1996 at Bow Street Magistrates' Court.[104] It may be noted that the message was

---

[98] *Interdepartmental Committee on the Distribution of Criminal Business between the Crown Court and the Magistrates' Court* (Cmnd. 6323, HMSO, London, 1975); Home Office, *Mode of Trial* (Cm. 2908, HMSO, 1995); Home Office, *Determining mode of trial in either-way cases* (http://www.homeoffice.gov.uk/cpd/pvu/contrial.htm, 1999).

[99] Home Office, *Juries in Serious Fraud Trials* (Home Office, London, 1998).

[100] Raine, J.W., *Local Justice* (T. & T. Clark, Edinburgh, 1989) p.66.

[101] Ibid., p.66.

[102] See Walker, C. and Akdeniz, Y., 'Virtual democracy' [1998] *Public Law* 489.

[103] For example, the Leeds District Magistrates' Court held an open day on 26 September 1998. According to the Clerk to the Justices, Richard Holland, 'Today we wish to demonstrate to the people of Leeds the important role within our community, and the invaluable support given by other agencies, which make it possible for the highest quality of local justice to be administered.'

[104] http://www.cerbernet.co.uk/coventgarden/article2.htm.

carried by a non-court server and in the context of tourism and that Bow Street does have an exceptionally long and colourful history, being founded in 1740 and being the starting point for cases such as Oscar Wilde, Dr Crippen and the Kray Twins. However, most Crown Courts and magistrates' courts do have a rich history, even if the court building is modern.

In summary, the Internet could become the virtual welcome mat for the public. It could provide citizens a history of the court, details of its location, pictures of judges and personnel, audio clips of welcome and explanation and, above all, an invitation to participate.[105]

Educating the passive wider community

The courts may be the third and least dangerous estate,[106] but they are nevertheless part of the state and it behoves all democrats to take note of what is being transacted in their name. So, how far can ordinary citizens inform themselves as to the role of the courts and their business and personnel via the Internet? Potentially, the answer is a great deal, but the reality falls far short of that target.

Consider, for example, the availability of the basic building blocks of the law – the statutes and cases. Lord Woolf complained of the 'allegedly excessive costs' levied for permission to reproduce primary legal source materials such as statutes.[107] Since 1996, the position has significantly improved. Some statutes are now available from 1996 onwards – in the website of the Stationery Office.[108] But pre-1996 statutes are not available, and the presentation of contemporary individual statutes in this segmented way is of limited value. It makes no link to important factors such as commencement dates, secondary legislation, later amendments or case interpretation. As for case reports, House of Lords judgments have become officially available,[109] plus a scattering of selected cases from other tiers of the court structure.[110] Smith Bernal allows paid access to others,[111] though this is a private site and not well advertised to the general public. Official concerns about copyright seem to be diminishing,[112] but there is still no completion in sight for an official comprehensive and consolidated statute book, despite the plans for its birth around 1992.[113] Much more ambitious systems exist elsewhere.

---

[105] See Hambleton, J., 'Take a Walk on the Web Side' (1995) *Court Technology Bulletin* May/June 1995 vol. 7, no. 3.

[106] Alexander Hamilton, *The Judiciary Department* (Federalist Paper no. 78, New York).

[107] Lord Woolf, *Access to Justice: Final Report* (1996) chap. 21 para. 10.

[108] http://www.hmso.gov.uk/acts.htm. The Statutory Publication Office, an office within the Lord Chancellor's Department, is producing a database of United Kingdom legislation which is due to be completed in 2000: http://www.open.gov.uk/lcd/lawdatfr.htm, 2000.

[109] http://www.parliament.the-stationery-office.co.uk/pa/ld/ldjudinf.htm.

[110] http://www.courtservice.gov.uk/cs_home.htm. see also, the British and Irish Legal Information Institute, established in 2000: http://www.bailii.org/.

[111] http://www.casetrack.com/casetrack_frame.htm.

[112] *Crown Copyright in the Information Age* (Cm. 3819, HMSO, London, 1998).

[113] Waugh, P., 'The use of computers in the administration of justice in the United Kingdom' (1991) 5 *Yearbook of Law, Computers and Technology* 26.

The Australasian Legal Information Institute (AustLII),[114] a jointly operated 'research infrastructure facility' of the Faculties of Law at the University of New South Wales and the University of Technology, Sydney was established using a mixture of mainly public funding. The Law Foundation of New South Wales[115] also assists AustLII in obtaining access to primary legal materials to be included on AustLII. AustLII has a broad public policy role which is to put on the world wide web legal information of importance to the general public, which includes primary legal materials (legislation and decisions of courts); and secondary materials. In this way, it is building up a public law library on the Internet. In addition, the user-friendly site of the High Court of Australia[116] does not content itself with a list of judgments (though this does impressively comprise several thousand court decisions from 1947 onwards), but includes also a virtual tour and in future the submission of documents.

Similarly in Canada, LexUM, the law and computer team of the CRDP (Centre for Research in Public Law) of the University of Montreal is well on the way to producing a Virtual Canadian Law Library.[117] The website aims at making Quebec and Canadian law more accessible. Among the legal documents at this site are the Civil Code of Quebec and the Quebec Charter of Personal Rights and Freedoms as well as judgments of the Supreme Court of Canada and of the Human Rights Tribunal of Quebec.

Several American states have also provided Internet-based legal educational sites. For instance, the web pages, 'Colorado Courts At a Glance',[118] are expressly designed to give citizens:

> . . . a better understanding of your courts and the justice system. In a free society, it is important that citizens have an independent judiciary to protect their constitutional rights. To maintain an independent judiciary, it is important that all citizens understand the constitutional role and function of their courts.

Information available includes a description of rights in relation to criminal justice, types of courts, the appointment of judges, judicial discipline and performance.

In Arizona, court sites[119] includes information for the public, educators and students (such as general guides, encouragement, especially for high school students, to attend and observe, voter information in regard to judicial elections). A number of other US states carry information about judicial elections.[120]

In California,[121] a wide range of information is available about state courts at all levels, including documents about alternative dispute resolution, the

---

[114] http://www.austlii.edu.au/. A counterpart British and Irish Legal Information Institute is now being established: http://www.bailii.org.
[115] See Law Foundation Act 1979; http://www.fl.asn.au/.
[116] http://www.hcourt.gov.au/.
[117] http://www.droit.umontreal.ca/doc/biblio/en/index.html.
[118] http://www.courts.state.co.us/cctspam.htm.
[119] http://www.supreme.state.az.us/welcome.htm.
[120] See, for example http://ca94.election.digital.com/e/returns/judicial/page.html.
[121] http://www.courtinfo.ca.gov/.

Code of Judicial Ethics, interpreters, the impact of Three Strikes Law (apparently due to 'reader demand'), photographing, recording, and broadcasting in the courtroom. Specific municipal trial court sites include descriptions of criminal proceedings.[122]

The Peoples Law Library of Maryland[123] is an electronic library which provides clear explanations of legal subjects, explains procedures, and makes available legal forms and other legal information resources. In some sections of the Library, legal forms can be completed online and come with detailed instructions on how to use them. Other facilities include Legal Forum Participation – access to legal discussion groups; Periodic On-line Courses in law for non-lawyers on such subjects as consumer law, landlord–tenant law, and family law; Dispute Settlement Services using the On-Line Mediation Service; and Legal Updates. There is also a linked Legal Advice Line. For a fixed fee of $30.00 per telephone call, citizens can speak directly to a Maryland attorney about any legal matter.

The website of the New York State unified court system includes court forms, and the particular site of the Criminal Court of the City of New York contains a wide range of information about court processes and terms.[124]

Through the Texas Judiciary Online,[125] it is possible to obtain current information on the Internet about court schedules, locations, contact administrators and high profile cases. Documents can be sent and received by e-mail and stored electronically.

Responding to 'an ever-rising tide of "lawyerless litigation", developing information technology, and an economic landscape that increasingly makes qualified legal help too expensive for many people',[126] the Supreme Court of Florida pioneered in 1994 the 'Access Initiative'.[127] The technology was very much centred around the Internet and includes the distribution of detailed information, such as 'streaming audio' of oral arguments, court forms and Supreme Court judgments, quickly and inexpensively into every community served by a court. More detailed information has been developed, such as the 'Judge's Page', which informs court personnel about new developments in the law, and a 'Press Information Page' which quickly distributes information to the news media (including 'downloadable' briefs in pending cases, a 'Kids' Court', aimed at helping school-age children and their teachers (who may apply for fellowships from the Florida Justice

---

[122] See Los Angeles Municipal Court, http://www.lamuni.org/.

[123] http://www.peoples-law.com/

[124] http://www.courts.state.ny.us/crim0498.htm.

[125] See http://www.courts.state.tx.us/; Gibler, E., 'What to Expect When Courts Go On-Line' (Fifth National Court Technology Conference (CTC5), http://www.ncsc.dni.us/NCSC/TIS/CTC5/204.HTM, 1997).

[126] Waters, R.C., 'Tiptoeing through technology's graveyard on the way to the 21st Century: The Internet as the Backbone of Court Access Programs' (Fifth National Court Technology Conference (CTC5), http://www.ncsc.dni.us/NCSC/TIS/CTC5/205.HTM, 1997).

[127] See http://www.firn.edu/supct or http://www.flcourts.org/.

Teaching Institute to attend a series of workshops and seminars on law-related education) learn more about the legal system and an Internet 'Self Help Center', offering a large number of books, brochures and forms explaining Florida law to laypersons. Taking the last aspect further, it is a further aim that local court centres should develop community-based mediation programs, all linked together through the Internet with the Florida Supreme Court acting as the central repository of information and support material.

With these precedents in mind, it is obvious that, in England and Wales too, the Internet could 'change the distance between the Court and the public'.[128] An altered stance may in any event become necessary with the passage of the Human Rights Act and the further juridification of political and social life which means that 'the judicial system will serve as a forum for civic discourse about the norms and values that underlie those disputes and will play a significant role in building or reshaping the social, economic, and political institutions involved in them'.[129] In this way, technology and modes of communication can be (re)constitutive of the nature of the institution,[130] including by encouraging a wider range of evidence and advocacy becoming relevant at trial.[131] Admittedly, the Internet might not be the only way of achieving the goal of reaching out to a passive and ignorant public. An alternative is shown by the American-based cable channel, Court TV which commenced operations in 1991.[132] This tends to give greatest prominence to current reporting of well-publicised cases, especially those being reported on the cable TV side of the operation and so does not present an entirely balanced picture of life in the courts.[133] Yet, the prospect of a United Kingdom equivalent seems remote. Successive senior judiciary have turned their face against televising of the court proceedings.[134] Nevertheless, the judges have recognised the value of having some channel of communication

---

[128] Katsh, M.E., *Law in a Digital World* (Oxford University Press, Oxford, 1995) p.163.

[129] Anderson, R., *et al.*, 'The impact of information technology on judicial administration: a research agenda for the future' (1993) 66 *Southern California Law Review* 1762 at p.1762. See also Teubner, G., *Juridification of Social Spheres* (Walter De Gruyter, Berlin, 1987).

[130] The same applies to the legal professions as to the courts: see Susskind, R., *The Future of Law: Facing the Challenges of Information Technology* (Clarendon Press, Oxford, 1996) p.286; Wall, D.S. and Johnstone, J., 'The industrialization of legal practice and the rise of the new electric lawyer' (1997) 25 *International Journal of the Sociology of Law* 95.

[131] Chesterman, M., 'OJ and the Dingo: how media publicity relating to criminal cases tried by jury is dealt with in Australia and America' (1997) 45 *American Journal of Comparative Law* 109 at p.143.

[132] See: http://www.courttv.com/.

[133] See Harris, B.A., 'The Appearance of Justice: Court TV; Conventional Television, and Public Understanding of the Criminal Justice System' (1993) 35 *Arizona Law Review* 785.

[134] For the views of Lord Chief Justice Bingham, see (1997) *The Times* 9 October 1997 p.7. But the rejection of televising by Lord Chancellor Irvine does emphasise the dangers of a 'live media event' and 'live coverage' (LCD Press Release 244/97). The only exception is that very limited, non-contemporaneous filming by consent of all parties has been allowed in Scotland under a Practice Note of 6 August 1992: Gale, B., 'Televising and the courts' (1995–6) 22 *Criminal Justice Matters* 18; Metz, S.A., 'Justice through the eye of a camera: cameras in the courtrooms in the United States, Canada, England and Scotland' (1996) 14 *Dickinson Journal of International Law* 673.

within their own grasp and, following cases in which they felt they were misquoted or misrepresented (especially when dealing with sex offenders),[135] they have been advised by the Lord Chancellor's Department to ensure that journalists are provided with a written summary of sentencing remarks in cases likely to attract media interest.[136] The Internet could afford access directly by the public to such information. Indeed, the Internet could provide a third way to the debate about televising or not televising. The technology offers the possibility of real-time transcription which can then be published to a wide audience at low cost: for example, live 'webcasts' of proceedings are now available at courts in Florida, Indiana and Ohio.[137] This strategy has several advantages over live broadcasting (assuming livecasting is not utilised). It avoids the perceived intrusiveness and distraction of television. The emphasis is on what is said in court rather than, say, the colour of the defendant's eyes or the shortness of the advocate's skirt. The text (or at least the site) could also be linked to wider legal information which could provide explanations of terms and processes in more general terms. The second advantage is cost. Specialist television channels such as Court TV would probably not be viable in the UK since there is not sufficient volume of cases of interest to the public. It is notable that the Parliamentary Channel[138] likewise failed to survive as an independent operation.

If the courts and judiciary do not manage the public interface with the legal system, then it seems increasingly likely that the litigants and their lawyers will take that step. In fact, a recent study by the Lord Chancellor's Advisory Committee on Legal Education and Conduct, *Lawyers' Comments to the Media*,[139] found that the police were the principal utilisers of media outlets, outstripping the instances of defence lawyer intervention by a long way.[140] The media can be conceived as part of the criminal justice system which is meant to be both in public and publicly accountable; the media thus assist with account giving and the ability of the courts to give an account.[141] But the relationship is at present restricted by the bureaucratic nature of much court work and by the distance of key figures within it, such as the judge and jury. The Internet cannot alter these basic circumstances, but it could provide a way both for journalists and the public as a whole to be afforded greater insights into court work.

---

[135] See the case of Judge Griffith who was reported as saying that the defendant 'would not be in the dock [for rape] if he had sent his victim a bunch of flowers': Pearson, R., 'Limits to the privilege defence' (1996) *The Lawyer* 9 July p.8.

[136] 'Judges advised to brief media' (1997) 94/13 *Law Society's Gazette* 5.

[137] See Samborn, H.V., 'Plenty of seats in virtual courtroom' (2000) February *ABA Journal* 68.

[138] The BBC acquired the former Parliament Channel (http://www.parlchan.co.uk/), now BBC Parliament, and runs it as part of its BBC ONLINE digital service.

[139] Lord Chancellor's Department, London, 1997 paras 28, 50, 62. See further Schlesinger, P. and Tumber, H., *Reporting Crime* (Clarendon Press, Oxford, 1994).

[140] Compare *Gentile v State Bar* (1991) 501 US 1030; *Schopfer v Switzerland*, Appl. no. 25404/94, 1998-III.

[141] See Ericson, R.V., 'The news media and account ability in criminal justice' in Stenning, P.C. (ed.), *Accountability for Criminal Justice* (University of Toronto Press, Toronto, 1995).

An alternative forum for dispute resolution

There is great interest in alternative dispute resolution on the civil side. Almost as strongly in the criminal process, the victim support movement has prompted the questioning of traditional adversarial justice which is often seen as exclusionary from the point of view of the victim. In any event, boundaries between civil and criminal are breaking down.[142] Here again, the Internet may provide a possible model which can transcend the simple replication of traditional paper-based processes in a computerised environment.[143] In this way, 'the courtroom [becomes] only one component of a much greater dispute resolution system', all served by the same technology.[144]

Perhaps the best known example is the Virtual Magistrate.[145] This was a pilot project based in Villanova University for resolving disputes that arise on computer networks about online messages, postings and files. The Virtual Magistrate Project offered arbitration for rapid, interim resolution of disputes involving, for example, copyright or trademark infringement, misappropriation of trade secrets, defamation, fraud, deceptive trade practices, offensive materials, invasion of privacy and other wrongful content. The Virtual Magistrate made a judgment as to whether it would be reasonable for a system operator to delete, mask or otherwise restrict access to a challenged message, file or posting, or even to deny access to the speaker. The filing of complaints and communications between the parties and the Virtual Magistrate Project normally took place by e-mail. The linked Online Ombuds Office, from Massachussets University, was likewise founded in 1996 but is a *pro bono* operation and is not confined to online disputes.[146] A third such organisation, also starting in 1996 but terminating in December 1999 was CyberTribunal, based in the Centre de recherche en droit public at the University of Montreal.[147] Its fields of expertise, all related to the Internet, were electronic commerce, competition, copyright, trademark, freedom of expression, privacy and many others, but it did expressly exclude issues falling under criminal law. It emphasised the use of mediation as well as adjudicative resolutions. Another entrant into this field is iCourthouse, which provides a more commercially orientated virtual arbitration system (with juries making the decisions which are binding under contracts signed by the litigants).[148]

---

[142] Protection from Harassment Act 1997; Crime and Disorder Act 1998.

[143] See Anderson, R., *et al.*, 'The impact of information technology on judicial administration: a research agenda for the future' (1993) 66 *Southern California Law Review* 1762 at p.1767.

[144] Lederer, F.I. and Soloman, S.H., 'Courtroom Technology – An Introduction To The Onrushing Future' (Fifth National Court Technology Conference (CTC5), http://www.ncsc.dni.us/NCSC/TIS/CTC5/103.HTM, 1997).

[145] http://vmag.vcilp.org/. The system is described in Post, D.G., 'Dispute resolution in cyberspace' (Cyberspace Law Institute Working Paper #2, http://www.law.vill.edu/ncair/disres/dgp2.htm, 1996).

[146] http://www-legal.sbs.umass.edu/center/ombuds.

[147] http://www.cybertribunal.org/.

[148] http://www.i-courthouse.com/.

These initiatives, which admittedly more often substitute for a Sysop's decision than for formal litigation, have had limited impact. The Virtual Magistrate scheme was unable to find ISPs who would include resort to binding arbitration in their customer contracts, and parties would not agree to be bound in this way after a dispute had arisen.[149] Similarly, CyberTribunal found it difficult to bring respondents into an ADR procedure, but there is some hope that the concept will be taken up by 'CyberMerchants', as commerce on the Internet and disputes arising from it becomes more common.[150] One must assume that, until then, complainants can more often than not obtain satisfaction in terms of their private interests from either commercial Sysops (in terms of disputes about libel and other forms of offence) or can act through normal consumer channels in regard to purchases.

Breaking down the public–private divide along similar but more authoritative lines, the Court Service or the police could offer standard forms and advice for private mediation. In this way, the Court Service becomes multi-layered with different doors for different purposes (and, possibly as importantly, at different prices). The Lord Chancellor's Department is sympathetic to these ideas on the civil side.[151] But the avoidance of formal courts brings dangers. If courts, especially local courts, are to appreciate and reflect local concerns and outlooks, this almost certainly requires some public expression of the perceived culture of the locality.[152] And there is value in the solemnity of the court setting in terms of truth giving and truth finding.

Overall analysis

In common with its application in other 'political' settings,[153] the Internet has been both under-utilised overall and mainly confined to one-way information transfer rather than two-way communication. There is, of course, some benefit in information transfer in this way. Internet technology allows the disembedding of time and space,[154] so that, for example, knowledge which was once the preserve of an exclusive gatekeeping profession such as lawyers can be made more widely available even to those who do not attend courts or law libraries and can be made available instantaneously. The virtual legal community is far less bounded that its physical counterpart and could provide a forum for taking soundings on judicial policies and performance as well as providing more committed and informed lay

---

[149] The author thanks Professor David Johnson for this information (e-mail, 30 August 1988)
[150] The author thanks Aubert Landry for this information (e-mail, 10 September 1998).
[151] Lord Chancellor's Department, *Consultation Paper: Resolving and Avoiding Disputes in the Information Age* (London, 1998) chap. 4.
[152] See McInnes, R., 'Bordertown and the Globalisation of Justice: Using Computers in an Australian Magistrates Court' [1998] (2) *The Journal of Information, Law and Technology* (JILT).
[153] See Walker, C. and Akdeniz, Y., 'Virtual democracy' [1998] *Public Law* 489.
[154] See Giddens, A., *The Consequences of Modernity* (Polity Press, London, 1990).

participants within the process. As was said by the European Court of Human Rights in *Worm v Austria*:[155]

> There is general recognition of the fact that the courts cannot operate in a vacuum. Whilst the courts are the forum for the determination of a person's guilt or innocence on a criminal charge . . . this does not mean that there can be no prior or contemporaneous discussion of the subject matter of criminal trials elsewhere, be it in specialised journals, in the general press or amongst the public at large. . . .

But this wider perspective tends to be lost in the New Public Management approach largely taken to date. Though the criminal courts have not yet been audited in respect of the application of the Internet, this task has been undertaken in regard to the civil courts. The aims of the Lord Chancellor's Department Consultation Paper, *Resolving and Avoiding Disputes in the Information Age* appear wide and balanced:[156]

> So far, the most important benefits we have discussed have been:
> - increasing efficiency and so cutting costs
> - improved justice and access to justice
> - better productivity and so reduction in delays
> - greater public confidence in the justice system

Thus, alongside the usual concerns for economy, efficiency and effectiveness, there is an apparent concern with justice and access to justice, placing the emphasis on substance rather than process and even reorientating the nature of justice: 'We ask is the court a service or a place?'[157] But there is ultimately an overwhelming customer-service orientation, which means that: 'In the future, however, there is the possibility that IT will eventually enable legal service to change from being a form of advisory service to a type of information product.'[158] This runs the danger that the customer is king and will lead to even less being known to the public about court transactions and even less public involvement in the court process. The more the courts are conceived in terms of being a service at the behest of the private litigant, the more the consumer litigant will question the public aspects of the service. It also leads to the concern that the quality of justice must suffer, as is admitted in the following comment:[159]

> Even if a virtual hearing is less satisfactory than the conventional method, is it not preferable that many more cases could be disposed of, even if at a lesser standard (a Rolls Royce for a few or a Mondeo for many)?

---

[155] Appl. no. 22714/93, 1997-V, [1998] 25 EHRR 454 para. 50.
[156] Lord Chancellor's Department, *Consultation Paper: Resolving and Avoiding Disputes in the Information Age* (London, 1998), Preface. This paper arises out of the Civil Justice IT Strategy Development Group – charged with the tasks of exploring longer term possibilities and making recommendations for the role of IT in civil justice over the next five to fifteen years (ibid., Annex).
[157] Lord Chancellor's Department, *Consultation Paper: Resolving and Avoiding Disputes in the Information Age* (London, 1998), Preface.
[158] Ibid., chap. 2.
[159] Ibid., chap. 4.

Conversely, the *Consultation Paper* expresses very little concern for the non-consuming but onlooking public. They are hardly recognised in the Paper and are problematic when they do fleetingly make an appearance:[160]

> Future use of digital audio recording in courts opens up the prospect of the live, digitised sound from a hearing being transmitted back to a solicitor's office for study and research. In high-profile cases an audio feed might eventually be made available over the Internet, or via a private service running over the Internet. This may also prove possible with video in the longer term, but this would raise even more issues than audio transmissions.

Too often these wider matters are seen as merely 'ancillary effects'[161] or issues.

Actual and potential Internet usage by 'outsiders'

The production of a more informed citizenry is as much the responsibility of that citizenry as it is of the state. So, how have non-state institutions taken up this challenge as a form of education rather than commerce?[162]

In the US, the populist 'Lectric Law Library[163] has the goal of allowing easy access to law-related information and products all free of charge. It includes a substantial 'reference Room' and extensive sections on business law, data for legal professionals and a 'Lay Person's Lounge', which includes descriptions of the legal system in general, legal aid and assistance, wills and estate planning, consumer rights and protection, employment matters, information for investors, and some other family and contractual matters. Overall the pages are often informative, lively and engaging, though, at the same time, the humour can be distracting and the coverage patchy, as the site often relies on web materials obtained from other sources rather than generated internally and systematically.

As for the UK, the British Council have produced a very short overview of the British legal system,[164] but other substantial attempts to use the Internet to engage with the public in regard exclusively to legal matters are beginning to emerge. One is a site entitled, UK Law Online, operated through the CyberLaw Research Unit of the Department of Law at the University of Leeds.[165] This project, which commenced in 1997, took up as its main object the raising of public awareness, appreciation and understanding of the English, Scots and Northern Ireland Legal Systems by use of the medium

---

[160] Ibid., chap. 5.

[161] Anderson, R., *et al.*, 'The impact of information technology on judicial administration: a research agenda for the future' (1993) 66 *Southern California Law Review* 1762 at p.1765.

[162] Rosenor, J., *Cyberlaw* (Springer, New York, 1997) p.263. What is claimed to be the world's first Internet-only law firm, FirstLAW is regulated by the Law Society (http://www.firstlaw.co.uk/main.html). See also http://www.desktoplawyer.net/.

[163] http://www.lectlaw.com/.

[164] http://www.britcoun.org/governance/jusrig/uklaw/system/index.htm.

[165] http://www.leeds.ac.uk/law/hamlyn/. See further Walker, C. and Akdeniz, Y., 'UK Law Online' (1998) 11 *Amicus Curiae* 6. Other UK sites now include: http://www.bailii.org; http://www.lawontheweb.co.uk; http://www.startlawmachine.com/.

of the Internet. The project has involved the creation of a world wide website in order to educate the public as to the nature and impact of their legal system by providing complex legal information – including explanations and not just primary materials – in a comprehensible way.

The Internet is the chosen medium since it is a new interactive medium which involves a direct and continuous access to a mass audience. The users have direct access to our team by electronic mail, but the project is not intended for individual legal advice. Rather it is intended to offer generalised education and the improvement of comprehension of important legal issues. The main target audience comprises non-lawyers, especially school students, but the web pages also include some detailed information which would be of value to more professional users such as lawyers, law students, academics, researchers and journalists. The main subject headings to be made available comprise the legal system (domestic and European), criminal justice and civil process, civil liberties, contract and tort law, plus a section on current legal events in the news. The site also includes, by agreement with with the Incorporated Council of Law Reporting, around 25 case reports, mainly of seminal cases which are unreported elsewhere on the web.

Some of the limitations of this private enterprise path to public legal education must be admitted. One pressing concern is lack of finance. The initial year was sponsored by the Hamlyn Trust, but that income has now ceased, consequently the rate of progress must slow down. Yet, despite the modest nature of the site to date, it does indeed serve a 'latent legal market' of a kind predicted by Professor Susskind. However, it is important to note that it acts in the service of democratic empowerment rather than commercial niche-marketing.

One would expect that major sponsors of legal education would be the legal professions.[166] One would suppose that to inform the public of its rights and entitlements would be good for business if not the civic soul. However, the performance records of the professions are very disappointing in the United Kingdom. Contrary to popular image, it is not the case that lawyers are wholly averse to new technology.[167] Therefore, the problem relates more to the perceptions of their professional bodies in regard to their missions in life – that they exist to advance the interests, and to regulate the activities, of their members, rather to pursue any wider public policy agendas. The General Council of the Bar makes no mention of any interface with the public,[168] while the Law Society of England and Wales confines its

---

[166] Another possible candidate is the Law Commission (see http://www.open.gov.uk/lawcomm/homepage.htm). But its work is highly technical – it is certainly not a legal education body for the public.

[167] See Wall, D.S. and Johnstone, J., 'The industrialization of legal practice and the rise of the new electric lawyer' (1997) 25 *International Journal of the Sociology of Law* 95; Wall, D.S. and Johnstone, J., 'Lawyers, Information Technology and Legal Practice: The use of information technology by provincial lawyers' (1997) 11.1 *International Review of Law Computers and Technology* 117.

[168] http://www.barcouncil.org.uk/.

education to a 500-word description of the English legal system, though it does perform a more civic role of law reform (though whether on behalf of its members or the public may be debated).[169] The American Bar Association, perhaps reflecting the more political role which law plays in the USA, makes a much more impressive attempt, though not really via the Internet.[170] Its website has a section of ABA materials for consumers, educators and schools. These arise through the work of its Division for Public Education which has the objective of increasing public understanding of law and its role in society. However, most of the site simply advertises the extensive range of printed and video materials on sale from the ABA, and there is relatively little web-based instruction yet available. The one exception is 'Freedom of Expression at the National Endowment for the Arts', an interdisciplinary curriculum project funded by the American Bar Association, Commission on College and University Legal Studies through the ABA Fund for Justice and Education.[171]

Conclusions

Before complaining about the lack of progress by the courts in taking to the new modes of communication, it is worth entering some caveats. One is to challenge the assumption that ICTs are bound to deliver the expected benefits. Their use in organisational change is unpredictable, as the social contexts into which they are inserted can profoundly impact on the directions of exploitation.[172]

Conversely, their potential to achieve a powerful impact, bringing about the 'dematerialisation'[173] of court process, may not be as desirable as the advocates of change may pretend. The saving of the rainforest by the advent of the paperless court file is one thing, but the abolition of 'old style, face-to-face hearings', even on appeal or rehearing,[174] is quite another. The point is not simply about how well testimony and real evidence can be effectively tested in a virtual setting, a point raised earlier. Rather, participation and observance are important rights which signify the autonomy of the defendant and the legitimacy of public oversight, as has been recognised under Article 6[175] and 10[176] of the European Convention. Equally, the idea that

---

[169] http://www.lawsoc.org.uk/home.asp.
[170] http://www.abanet.org/.
[171] http://www.csulb.edu/~jvancamp/intro.html.
[172] Davenport, T.H., *Process Innovation: Re-engineering Work through Information Techno-logy* (Harvard Business School Press, 1993); Bellamy, C. and Taylor, J.A., *Governing in the Information Age* (Open UP, Buckingham, 1998).
[173] Katsh, M.E., *Law in a Digital World* (Oxford University Press, Oxford, 1995).
[174] This is suggested by Widdison, R., 'Beyond Woolf: the virtual court house' [1997] 2 *Web Journal of Current Legal Issues*.
[175] But see *Monnell and Morris v UK*, Appl. nos. 9562/81, 9818/82, Ser. A 115 (1987), (1988) 10 EHRR 205.
[176] *Crook and NUJ v UK*, Appl. no. 11552/85, *Atkinson, Crook, The Independent v United Kingdom*, Appl. no. 13366/87, *G. Hodgson, D. Woolf Productions Ltd and NUJ v United Kingdom*, *Channel Four Television Co. Ltd v United Kingdom*, Appl. no. 11553/85.

witnesses and the jury could operate more efficiently if dispersed (presumably to the costless site of their own abodes),[177] not only raises vulnerabilities in terms of contamination by attention to extraneous evidence,[178] intimidation and the insecurity of communications, but ignores the way in which personal interaction may assist in the verdict-making process. This is reflected by concerns which arise when jurors are separated when considering the verdict. An example is *R v Goodson*,[179] in which a juror, in the presence of a court bailiff, made a telephone call from a payphone within the court hallway. Not only was the juror discharged, but the defendant's appeal against conviction was allowed as the jury was incomplete 'in the jury room'.[180] Similarly, in *R v Tharakan*,[181] jury deliberation in the hotel to which they retired overnight resulted in the overturning of the conviction:[182]

> One of the strengths of the jury system is that they do act as a body, and if there is disagreement then individual jurors can look to others of the same view for support. If they continue their discussions outside the jury room, then those of a weaker disposition may be open to persuasion without having the support of others of the same mind.

The issue also arose in *The People of Colorado v Kriho*, in which there were complaints that a juror sought information from the Internet about possible sentences.[183] So, orality remains not just a 'ritual'[184] but a central feature of the adversarial process,[185] both in court and in the jury room, and the distanciation or dissolution of the courthouse can be seen to result in the diminution of justice as well as a silencing of civic expression. In addition, the complexities and costs of the new technologies may threaten the equality of arms between prosecution and defence with the result that the latter may be unable to explore and expose the defects in the former's construction of events.[186] Furthermore, the unco-ordinated use of technology may

---

[177] They can be allowed home overnight (Criminal Justice and Public Order Act 1994 s.43) but will be warned not to engage in any exchanges with others about the case until they return.

[178] See, for example, *R v Stewart and Sappleton* (1989) 89 Cr App R 273; *R v Maggs* (1990) 91 Cr App R 243; *R v Young* [1995] 2 Cr App R 379.

[179] (1975) 60 Cr App R 266.

[180] Ibid. at p.268 per James LJ.

[181] [1995] 2 Cr App R 368.

[182] Ibid. at p.374 per Swinton Thomas LJ.

[183] 2000 Colo. LEXIS 383 (see http://www.fija.org/).

[184] Anderson, R., *et al.*, 'The impact of information technology on judicial administration: a research agenda for the future' (1993) 66 *Southern California Law Review* 1762 at p.1777.

[185] It is arguable that, with Crime and Disorder Act 1998, we are moving into a 'third way' – the family or perhaps communitarian model; see Griffiths, J., 'Ideology in criminal procedure or a third "model" of criminal process' (1970) 79 *Yale Law Journal* 359.

[186] An example might be the analysis of 'heli-tele' pictures in the Casement Park cases: Committee on the Administration of Justice, *Pamphlet no. 19, The Casement Trials* (Belfast, 1992). The European Commission on Human Rights concluded that the screening of media witnesses from the defendants did not violate Article 6(1): *X v UK*, App. no. 20657/92, 15 EHRR CD 113.

confuse the jury and increase costs and delay.[187] Conversely, linkages be-tween different databases held by criminal justice agencies, as propounded by the inter-agency Committee for the Coordination of Computerisation in the Criminal Justice System, may threaten rights to privacy.

Yet we are far from the point when, through the intercession of the Internet, the court has become a conceptual rather than a concrete symbol. One of the reasons for the hesitation is that there is no body with overall charge of ICT policy. The Information Technology and the Courts (ITAC) Committee, formed in 1988 from seven constituent bodies – the Bar Coun-cil, the Law Society, the Society for Computers and the Law, the Crown Prosecution Service, the Lord Chancellor's Department, the Metropolitan Police and the Serious Fraud Office,[188] recommended in 1990 that a single policy body be established to direct and co-ordinate the introduc-tion of court technology. However, the policy and its implementation remains split even within the courts system, with no court-based equivalent to the Police Information Technology Organisation. One might compare the more directed approach in the US Federal Courts, where the Judicial Conference of the United States represents all Federal judges and controls the Administrative Office of the United States Courts and the Federal Judi-cial Centre (the principal function of which is judicial training).[189] It is responsible for the Long Range Plan for Automation in the US Courts of 1992 and for administration of the Judiciary Automation Fund which was created by Act in 1990,[190] approving the expenditure of $71.4 million on computerisation of the Federal Courts, to be spent in accordance with the annual revisions to the Long Range Plan through the Office of Automation and Technology (OAT) of the Administrative Office of the United States Courts. The Judicial Conference has a Committee on Auto-mation and Technology consisting of 14 judges. Likewise, the Technical Information Service of the National Center for State Courts (NCSC) is the principal co-ordinating body for the use of information technology in State Courts. The National Center for State Courts[191] was founded in 1971 on the advice of Chief Justice Warren E. Burger in order to provide leader-ship and service to the state courts. Its Court Technology Programs include a Technology Information Service (such as about available software and equipment suppliers).

---

[187] Trammell, G.W., 'Cirque du O.J.', (1995) 7(4) *Court Technology Bulletin* (available at http://www.ncsc.dni.us/).

[188] The membership has since grown to twelve, by inclusion of the Home Office (apparently replacing the Lord Chancellor's Department), the Central Computer and Telecommunica-tions Agency (CCTA), the Council of Circuit Judges, the Association of District Judges, the Legal Aid Board, and the Justices Clerks Society Information Technology Policy Committee.

[189] See Greenleaf, G. and Mowbray, A., 'Information Technology in Complex Criminal Trials' (http://www.austlii.edu.au/au/other/aija/aija.html, Australian Institute of Judicial Adminis-tration, 1993).

[190] 28 USC 612.

[191] See http://www.ncsc.dni.us/.

In terms of substantive goals to be achieved in England and Wales, what at first sight appears to be radically empowering policy developments turn out, like many other parts of the New Labour reform agenda, to be more about modernisation than democratisation. This may be true of development of ICT policy in general, and it certainly seems to be true of ICT strategy in the courts, as is reflected by the following, narrowly conceived principles on which the Court Service's overall strategy is based:[192]

> The Court Service IT strategy is based on the following principles:
> - the IT strategy will be determined by the business strategy, which will take full advantage of IT opportunities;
> - all new information systems (IS) services should be provided under a Private Finance Initiative (PFI) contract;
> - where possible existing PFI contracts will be used for the provision of such IS services;
> - no IS development or technical support work will be undertaken by Court Service staff.

The more specific objectives with respect to the criminal justice system are:[193]

> ... to modernise administrative procedures in the Crown Court and to improve links with all the other agencies involved in the criminal justice system. Improving procedures will result in much-enhanced efficiency and higher quality of service.

Without a single reference to accessibility, democracy, participation or even justice, this is the language of Arthur Anderson, not Thomas Paine. At a time when pressures are often for greater seclusion of the criminal process and certainly for greater technocratisation and managerialism, the Internet could counterbalance some of the exclusivity of the process.[194] It could provide concrete foundations for public debate and perhaps change that is even more radical and participatory than Lord Woolf and other commentators[195] have predicted.

---

[192] Court Service Information Services Division, *Information Technology (IT) Strategy* (http://www.courtservice.gov.uk/itstrat.htm, 1998) para. 2.1.

[193] Ibid. para. 5.1.

[194] Raine, J. and Wilson, M., *Managing Criminal Justice* (Harvester, Hemel Hampstead, 1993) p.52.

[195] See Katsh, M.E., *Law in a Digital World* (Oxford University Press, Oxford, 1995) p.196.

PART IV

LEGAL CONTROVERSIES
IN CYBERSPACE

CHAPTER 9

Sexually orientated expression

Yaman Akdeniz and Nadine Strossen[1]

Introduction to sexually explicit content on the Internet

Throughout history, one of the earliest and most widespread uses of each newly developed communications medium has been to purvey sexual words and images. Indeed, some experts see the persistent human desire for sexually orientated material as a major motivating factor that actually spurs the development of new communications media.[2] And that is precisely one of the major reasons why each new communications medium promptly triggers cries for censorship.

The Internet has been no exception to these general patterns. In the US, the Internet first hit the public and political headlines in 1995 as a result of sensationalistic media stories about the supposed prevalence of cyberporn. While some of these accounts were exaggerated at best and fabricated at worst,[3] it is indisputable that sexual expression – along with every other kind of expression – is more readily available online than through traditional media. This fact, in turn, fueled the enactment of the first US cybercensorship law, the Communications Decency Act ('CDA'),[4] in 1996. Moreover, despite the successful lawsuits that the American Civil Liberties Union ('ACLU') and other cyber-libertarians have brought against the CDA, as well as other laws that also have attempted to stifle online sexual expression, government officials all over the US are still busily pursuing various strategies for suppressing such expression.[5]

---

[1] Nadine Strossen authored only the portions of this chapter concerning the US; the credit and responsibility for the remainder of the chapter belong to Yaman Akdeniz, including the writing of all footnotes (Professor Strossen provided the substantive information reflected in the footnotes corresponding to the passages she authored). For research assistance with this chapter, the authors would like to thank Professor Strossen's Chief Aide, Amy L. Tenney. The authors also would like to thank Professor Clive Walker for his help on this chapter.

[2] See Tierney, J., 'Porn, the Low-Slung Engine of Progress' (1994) *New York Times*, 9 January

[3] See especially Rimm, M., 'Marketing Pornography on the Information Superhighway' (1995) 83 *Georgetown Law Journal*, 1839, the subject of a hyperbolic *Time Magazine* cover story, Elmer-Dewitt, P., 'On a screen near you: Cyberporn', *Time*, 3 July 1995, p.34. For a critique of the Rimm study see Wallace, J. and Mangan, M., *Sex, Laws, and Cyberspace: Freedom and Censorship on the Frontiers of the Online Revolution* (Henry Holt & Company, New York, 1996).

[4] 47 USC s.223 et seq.

[5] See, generally, American Civil Liberties Union, http://www.aclu.org/issues/cyber/hmcl.html, 2000.

While the US has a notoriously Puritanical attitude toward sex and sexual expression, in contrast to some Western European countries, the UK also shares with its former American colony both a long history of repressing sexual expression in all media, and current efforts to carry that tradition into cyberspace. But, rather than importing the US censorship initiatives into the English legal system, the UK government has adopted a self-regulatory approach towards Internet regulation. This approach is also consistent with the European Union's policy on Internet content that is deemed to be illegal and harmful. But, despite the popular perception, sexually explicit content is not necessarily illegal. Some argue that at least this kind of legal content may be harmful to some, especially to children. Therefore, the protection of children from such 'harmful content' has been the priority of regulators and quasi-regulators within the UK ever since the 'moral panic' about cyberporn started within the US in the summer of 1995.

The legal situation

The Internet is a global medium 'regardless of frontiers' in which national laws and regulations have limited or no effect. Still, it would be wrong to see this new hybrid communications medium as a 'lawless place'. It is therefore important to examine both the UK and US approaches to the regulation of online sexual expression in an analytical and critical way. It is not the purpose of this chapter to show which approach is better or worse but rather to consider the broader implications for suppression of cyberspeech. The message emerging from this commentary is that the impact of the US courts is libertarian in its nature in contrast to the English situation which is less principled and less judge-driven. Moreover, the current UK position is unlikely to change, despite the enactment of the Human Rights Act 1998.

The situation in England and Wales

UK obscenity legislation has been amended by the Criminal Justice and Public Order Act 1994 to take into account sexually explicit content in computer data format.[6] Still, the applicability of UK obscenity standards to a borderless medium like the Internet has its difficulties and limitations. It is also questionable whether such national standards should be enforced on a global medium as these may affect the rights of individuals in other countries.

Hitherto, there has been no explicit, documentary constitutional protection of free speech in the UK, so its regulation has depended upon vague common law principle and narrow parliamentary legislation.[7] But, following the enactment of the Human Rights Act 1998, the legal approach to civil liberties will change. The 1998 Act incorporates the European Convention on Human

---

[6] See House of Commons, Home Affairs Committee: *Computer Pornography* (1993–4 HC 126); Manchester, C., 'Computer Pornography' [1995] *Criminal Law Review* 546.
[7] Barendt, E., *Freedom of Speech* (Clarendon Press, Oxford, 1989) p.29.

Rights ('ECHR') into the English legal system. Therefore, such rights as freedom of expression will have express statutory recognition, although the rights cited in the ECHR are themselves subject to significant limitations.

So far, the European Convention, acting as an external bill of rights, has had an influence upon UK law in relation to freedom of expression issues. The European Court of Human Rights in the *Handyside* case[8] stated that the steps necessary in a democratic society for the protection of morals will depend to some extent on the standards to which a country is committed. The Court held that the prosecution of the *Little Red School Book* was within the margin of appreciation of Article 10(2) so that there was no breach. The intended audience was children, and the book was produced and marketed in a way to appeal to children.[9] The Court held that the forfeiture of copies of the book could be justified, and there was a 'pressing social need' for the interference in question.[10] But the *Otto Preminger*[11] case aside, there is a general reluctance on the part of the European Court to uphold interferences with the communication of ideas and information between willing producers and adult consumers,[12] and even more so if political ideas and information are involved.[13]

The Obscene Publications Acts 1959 and 1964 ('OPA') constitute the major legislation to regulate sexually explicit material of any kind in England and Wales. Section 1(1) of the OPA provides that 'an article shall be deemed to be obscene if its effect or the effect of any one of its items is, if taken as a whole, such as to tend to deprave and corrupt persons who are likely, having regard to all relevant circumstances, to read, see or hear the matter contained or embodied in it.'[14] Under Section 2(1) of OPA, it is an offence to publish an obscene article or to have an obscene article for publication for gain.[15] Section 1(2) of OPA 1964 makes it an offence to have an obscene article in ownership, possession or control with a view to publishing it for gain.[16]

---

[8] *Handyside v UK*, App. no. 5493/72, Ser A vol. 24 (1976) 1 EHRR 737.
[9] See Harris, D.J., O'Boyle, M., Warbrick, C., *Law of the European Convention on Human Rights* (Butterworth, London, 1995) at p.407.
[10] Jones, T.H., 'The Devaluation of Human Rights Under the European Convention' [1995] *Public Law* 430 at pp.435–6.
[11] *Otto Preminger Institut v Austria*, App. no. 13470/87, Ser. A vol. 295-A (1994).
[12] See Harris, D.J., O'Boyle, M., Warbrick, C., op. cit., at p.407.
[13] *Lingens v Austria*, App. no. 9815/82, Ser. A vol. 103 (1986) 8 EHRR 407; *Castells v Spain*, App. no. 11798/85, Ser. A vol. 236 (1992) 14 EHRR 445.
[14] This legal definition of obscene is narrower than the ordinary meaning of obscene which is filthy, lewd or disgusting. See *R v Anderson and others* [1971] 3 All ER 1152.
[15] See further Akdeniz, Y., 'Computer Pornography. A Comparative Study of the US and UK Obscenity Laws and Child Pornography Laws in Relation to the Internet' [1996] 10 *International Review of Law, Computers & Technology* 235.
[16] See *R v Arnold; R v Fellows* [1997] 1 Cr.App.R. 244. See also section 43 of the Telecommunications Act 1984 which makes it an offence to send 'by means of a public telecommunications system, a message or other matter that is grossly offensive or of an indecent, obscene or menacing character' and is an imprisonable offence with a maximum term of six months. In addition to dealing with indecent, obscene or offensive telephone calls, the Act also covers the transmission of obscene materials through the telephone systems by electronic means.

Until the abolition of the *Hicklin*[17] test on obscenity, one 'purple passage' could be enough to ban the material in question.[18] With the introduction of the Obscene Publications Act 1959 a very large measure of freedom for 'written materials' was secured even though these did not pass unchallenged. Cases involving D.H. Lawrence's *Lady Chatterley's Lover*,[19] *Last Exit to Brooklyn*,[20] and *Inside Linda Lovelace*[21] illustrated the freedom given by the 1959 Act.[22]

Internet-related cases under the OPA are relatively rare. They include that of Jason Manger, author of the *Internet Bible*, who was sentenced to one year's imprisonment (suspended) and was ordered to pay £1,000 costs, in March 1996 in Kingston Crown Court. Manger was selling hardcore pornographic material to customers all around the world. He pleaded guilty to four charges of having an obscene article for publication for gain. Thomas J. likened the case to 'a blue movies mail order business using new technology'.[23] In another case, a 21-year-old Lancashire University student pleaded guilty to four charges of publishing obscene articles on the Internet, contrary to the Obscene Publications Act, and another six of making indecent photographs of children, contrary to the Protection of Children Act 1978. He had linked his UK-based web pages to a US-based website which carried the obscene publications. Whether such a link amounts to 'publication' under the OPA is not clear,[24] though the police additionally discovered that the US-based pages were also owned by the defendant. A more recent example involves *R v Graham Waddon*.[25] Waddon was charged with publishing obscene articles contrary to section 2(1) Obscene Publications Act

---

[17] See *R v Hicklin* (1868) LR 3 QB 360 at p.371. The test in *R v Hicklin* was based on the harm principle, and Lord Chief Justice Cockburn defined the test of obscenity as 'whether the tendency of the matter charged as obscenity is to deprave and corrupt those whose minds are open to such immoral influences, and into whose hands a publication of this sort may fall'.

[18] Following the *Hicklin* test, D.H. Lawrence's, *The Rainbow* was destroyed in 1915 as well as *The Well of Loneliness* in 1928. See for a brief history of the UK obscenity laws Robertson, G. and Nicol, A., *Media Law* (3rd ed., Penguin Books, London, 1992) at pp.106–10.

[19] *R v Penguin Books* [1961] *Criminal Law Review* 176.

[20] *R v Calder & Boyars Ltd* [1968] 3 All ER 644.

[21] See Williams Committee, *Report of the Committee on Obscenity and Film Censorship* (Cmnd. 7772, HMSO, London, 1979) chap. 4.

[22] See for an extreme example of freedom for written materials applied to the Internet *in U.S. v Baker*, 890 F. Supp. 1375 (E.D. Mich. 1995) where Jake Baker posted e-mails to the Usenet group alt.sex.stories in which he seemed to be planning to abduct and torture someone.

[23] See 'Suspended Sentence for Computer Porn Man Caught in TV Trap' *PA News*, 16 March 1996. Note also *R v Jack (Colin Mason)*, CC; Norwich Crown Court, 4 July 1994. D pleaded guilty to having nine obscene articles, compact discs imported from the USA, for publication for gain. The discs contained obscene content, to which adult home computer-users gained access via an 0891 premium-rate telephone line. See further http://www.cyber-rights.org/reports/child.htm.

[24] See Akdeniz, Y., 'To Link or Not to Link: Problems with World Wide Web Links on the Internet' (1997) 11(2) *International Review of Law, Computers and Technology* 281; 'Porn Links lead straight to jail', *.Net magazine* May 1998, 'To link or not to link?', *.Net magazine* June 1998, p.89.

[25] *R v Graham Waddon* (1999), Southwark Crown Court (Judge Hardy) 30 June 1999, appeal dismissed 6 April 2000.

1959, the evidence being that he had maintained a commercial website featuring sexually explicit images in the USA. As publishing an article under section 1(3)(b) of the 1959 Act included data stored electronically and transmitted, Waddon was successfully prosecuted. He was given an 18-month prison sentence suspended for two years in September 1999 after pleading guilty to 11 sample counts.[26]

The OPA is often criticized; according to Pannick, it 'is poorly drafted, is inconsistently applied and it lacks any coherent principle'.[27] In practice the enforcement of the OPA is directed towards hard-core and child pornography. Robertson and Nicol argue that 'nudity is now acceptable and even artistic, but to erect a penis is to provoke a prosecution'.[28] Although in practice the OPA is not enforced within many police areas of Britain,[29] the Customs and Excise[30] on the other hand is enforcing and controlling the physical entry of obscene and indecent materials into the jurisdiction, though subject to some restraint by the operation of European Community law.[31] Apart from the Customs enforcement of physical content, the UK government has taken action against four satellite channels with adult-orientated content, namely Eurotica Rendez-Vous, Red Hot Television, TV Erotica, and Satisfaction Club TV.[32] Recently, Tim Brain, spokesman on pornography for the Association of Chief Police Officers, said:

> Since the introduction of the Obscene Publications Act, the law and technology have developed to a stage at which the legal position on pornography is unclear and which makes effective enforcement difficult.[33]

With the arbitrary application of national laws, the development of global communications systems, and recent calls for relaxation of obscenity standards, Britain presents a contrasting picture as far as obscenity is concerned. James Ferman, the outgoing president of the British Board of Film

---

[26] Wilson, J., 'Net porn baron escapes jail,' *Guardian*, 7 September 1999.
[27] See Pannick, D., 'Question: When is disgusting not obscene?', *The Times*, 8 September 1998.
[28] Robertson, G. and Nicol, A., *Media Law* (3rd ed., Penguin Books, London, 1992) at p.125.
[29] The current available statistics suggest that most of the prosecutions between the years 1980 and 1995 were brought within the Metropolitan Police area. See House of Commons Debs. vol. 290 col. 359wa, 17 February 1997.
[30] Section 42 of the Customs and Consolidation Act 1876 prohibits the importation into the UK of indecent or obscene prints, paintings, photographs, books, lithographic cards or other engravings, or any other indecent or obscene articles.
[31] Article 36 of the Treaty of Rome 1957 states that 'The provisions of Articles 30 to 34 shall not preclude prohibitions or restrictions on imports, exports or goods in transit justified on grounds of public morality, public policy or public security . . . Such prohibitions or restrictions shall not, however, constitute a means of arbitrary discrimination or a disguised restriction on trade between Member States.' See, for example *Henn & Darby v DPP* [1981] AC 850; *Conegate v HM Customs and Excise* [1987] 2 WLR 39; *R. v Bow St. Mag. Ct. ex p. Noncyp* [1989] 3 WLR 467; *R. v Uxbridge Justices, ex parte Webb* (1998) 162 J.P. 198; *Wright v Customs and Excise Commissioners* [1999] 1 Cr App R 69.
[32] See BBC News, European porn channel banned in UK, 10 September 1998; 'Smith bans Euro porn TV channel', *Daily Telegraph*, 11 September 1998.
[33] BBC News, Legalise hard-core porn, says chief censor, 8 August 1998.

Classification ('BBFC'), said if explicit material were legalised it would be easier to regulate.[34] According to Freeman 'the law has been applied by police and magistrates in too strict a manner to allow the material the customers want. Thus we are left with a flourishing black market which mixes pornography with obscenity, which is not conducive to a healthy society'.[35]

Currently there are no attempts to relax the obscenity standards within the UK, and there are also no initiatives to introduce any regulatory measures for the availability of sexually explicit content through the Internet. Therefore, while the state of sexually explicit content in Britain remains in flux, the government prefers the self-regulatory approach as also advocated by the European Union through the European Commission, as shall be described later in this chapter.

The US legal situation

Background – pre-Internet

Under current US law, the government's power to regulate sexually orientated expression turns on several factors: the nature of the expression; the type of regulation; and the communications medium.

The Supreme Court consistently has recognised that much sexual expression is valuable,[36] and it consistently has refused to uphold regulations that target such expression because of societal disapproval of the ideas it conveys. For example, the Court struck down a state statute that outlawed films condoning adultery.[37] Likewise, it affirmed lower court rulings invalidating a type of law advocated by some feminists, which targets sexually explicit materials that are 'degrading' to women.[38] Moreover, also resisting pressure from some feminists, the Court has refused to presume that sexually orientated expression necessarily gives rise to a claim of sexual harassment – no matter how offensive it may be to someone who hears or sees it.[39]

The Court has deemed only one, relatively narrow category of sexual expression – 'obscenity' – beyond the scope of the First Amendment's free speech guarantee,[40] and hence subject to banning in any medium because of

---

[34] See BBC News, Legalise porn – censor, 13 August 1998. See also 'Porn film industry is out of control', *Daily Telegraph*, 8 August 1998.

[35] Ibid. See further Akdeniz, Y., *Sex on the Net? The Dilemma of Policing Cyberspace*. South Street Press, Reading, 1999).

[36] See, for example, *Roth v US* 354 US 476, at p.487 (1957) (noting that sex is 'one of the vital problems of human interest and public concern').

[37] *Kingsley Int'l Pictures Corp. v Regents* 360 US 684 (1959).

[38] *American Booksellers Association v Hudnut* 771 F. 2d 323 (1985, affd. mem. 475 US 1001, 1986). See Hoffman, E., 'Feminism, Pornography and the Law' (1985) 133 *University of Pennsylvania Law Review* 497; Brest, P. and Vandenberg, A., 'Politics, feminism and the constitution' (1987) 39 *Stanford Law Review* 607; Mackinnon, C., *Only Words* (Harvard University Press, 1993); Strossen, N., *Defending Pornography* (Abacus, London, 1996).

[39] *Harris v Forklift Sys.* 510 US 17 (1993).

[40] 'Congress shall make no law respecting an establishment of religion, or prohibiting the free exercise thereof; or abridging the freedom of speech, or of the press; or the right of the people peaceably to assemble, and to petition the Government for a redress of grievances.'

its presumed communicative impact. The Court has held another category of sexual expression – child pornography – to be beyond the First Amendment pale, not because of any harm it inflicts upon those to whom it is communicated, but rather, because of the harm that is caused in producing it. Specifically, the Court has upheld laws defining illegal child pornography as material that is produced by exploiting actual children.[41]

To be constitutionally unprotected obscenity, the material, considered as a whole, must appeal to a 'prurient' or 'shameful'[42] interest in sex, and it must be 'patently offensive', according to local community standards. Moreover, it must lack any serious literary, artistic, political or scientific value, according to national standards.[43] Thanks largely to the last requirement, it is quite difficult for prosecutors to obtain an obscenity conviction, or to sustain it on appeal. For example, the notorious 1990 obscenity prosecution against an art museum, for displaying homoerotic photographs by the critically acclaimed Robert Mapplethorpe, failed on this ground.[44]

When the government's asserted regulatory rationale is not the sexual expression's communicative impact – its 'primary effect' – but, rather, its 'secondary effects,' such as causing increases in crime or decreases in property value, the US courts have upheld local zoning regulations that restrict 'adult' businesses to certain geographical areas.[45] Recognizing that similar zoning laws could not constitutionally ghettoise other types of expression, no matter how offensive they might be to members of the surrounding community, the Supreme Court has castigated the sexual expression in 'adult' theaters and strip clubs as of 'lesser value' than other constitutionally protected speech[46] – not outside the First Amendment scope, but relegated to its 'outer perimeters'.[47] Thus far, however, both the Supreme Court and other courts have refused repeated invitations to extend the 'secondary effects' rationale to other contexts, beyond the physical zoning of adult businesses.[48]

On the rationale that the broadcast media are 'uniquely pervasive' and 'uniquely accessible to children', the Supreme Court has upheld government regulations that are designed to shield children from sexually orientated expression in these media.[49] For example, broadcasts may not contain 'patently offensive' expression during times of the day when the audience is likely to include large numbers of children, even if the expression has serious value.

---

[41] See NY v Ferber 458 US 747 (1982); Osborne v Ohio 495 US 103 (1990).
[42] See Pope v Illinois Municipal Court 481 US 297 (1987).
[43] Paris Adult Theater v Slaton 413 US 49 (1973). See also Jenkins v Georgia 418 US 153 (1974).
[44] See City of Cincinnati v Contemporary Arts Center 566 N.E.2d 214 (1990).
[45] See Young v American Mini Theatres 427 US 50 (1976); Schad v Borough of Mt. Ephraim 452 US 61 (1981); City of Renton v Playtime Theatre 475 US 41 (1986).
[46] Young v American Mini Theatres 427 US 50, 70 (1976).
[47] Barnes v Glen Theatre, 501 US 560, 566 (1991). See also Arcara v Cloud Books 478 US 697 (1986); FW/PBS v Dallas 493 US 215 (1990).
[48] Reno v ACLU 521 US 844 (1997) at p.867. But see Erie v Pap's A.M. 120 S.Ct. 1382 (2000).
[49] FCC v Pacifica 438 US 726, 748–9 (1978).

All of these legal doctrines, which demote sexual expression to – at best – second-class status under the First Amendment, are highly contested, including by dissenting Supreme Court Justices. For example, the Court adopted the current obscenity exception to the First Amendment by a narrow 5–4 vote in 1973, and Justices who have subsequently joined the Court have also criticised that ruling.[50] Moreover, many Justices have urged a re-examination of the Court's diluted First Amendment protection of broadcast expression, contending that broadcast sexual (and other) expression should be subject to no more regulation than in print publications.[51] Similarly, dissenting Justices have assailed the majority's 'secondary effects' doctrine as a legal fiction that permits municipalities to stifle expression due to its disfavoured content.

All of these legal doctrines permitting restrictions on sexual expression squarely violate what the Court has called a 'bedrock principle' of America's proud free speech tradition: the notion of 'content' or 'viewpoint neutrality', which bars government from restricting expression merely because the majority of the community considers its content or viewpoint objectionable.[52] Enforcing this neutrality principle, for example, the Court recently has struck down efforts to punish such unpopular, offensive expression as burning the American flag[53] or burning a cross near the home of a black family.[54] Those rulings were joined by Justices across the Court's ideological spectrum. Indeed, the current Court is generally speech-protective. Thus, it might well ease some of the restrictions on sexual expression that are currently permissible in traditional – in other words, pre-cyberspace – media.

In any event, the Court resoundingly refused to permit additional new restrictions on sexual expression in cyberspace – beyond the prohibitions on obscenity and child pornography that have been upheld in traditional media[55] – in its 1997 decision *Reno v ACLU*[56] striking down the Communications Decency Act 1996 ('CDA'). Moreover, as explained further below, lower court judges have also struck down the second federal law that imposes special restrictions on sexually explicit expression in cyberspace, as well as similar state and local laws.[57] Indeed, one judge has opined that,

---

[50] See, for example, *Pope v Illinois Municipal Court* 481 US 497, at p.507 (Stevens J, dissenting).
[51] See, generally, Richards, D.A.J., 'Free speech and obscenity laws' (1994) 123 *University of Pennsylvania Law Review* 45.
[52] See *Texas v Johnson* 491 US 397 (1989); *US v Eichman* 496 US 310 (1990).
[53] Ibid.
[54] *RAV v City of St Paul* 505 US 377 (1992).
[55] The ACLU and others who have challenged the CDA and other cybercensorship laws have not challenged the provisions of these laws that simply extend to cyberspace the restrictions on obscenity and child pornography that have been upheld for traditional media; the new laws have been challenged only to the extent that they seek to outlaw additional categories of sexual expression online, beyond those that have been outlawed in other media.
[56] 521 US 844 (1997).
[57] See, for example, *ACLU v Johnson* 4 F. Supp. 2d 1029 (D.N.M. 1998); and *ALA v Pataki*, 969 F. Supp. 160 (S.D.N.Y. 1997).

because of their unique accessibility and interactivity, cybercommunications should receive more First Amendment protection than any other medium.[58]

The fall of the CDA

The ACLU and its allies challenged, and the Supreme Court struck down, the CDA's provisions outlawing 'patently offensive' or 'indecent' expression. Under the Court's medium-specific approach to the First Amendment, the government could not regulate such material at all in print or telephone communications[59] and could not wholly bar it even in broadcast media. Thus, the CDA's proponents sought to make cyberspace the least protected medium, subject to even more restrictions than the broadcast media, which now receive the least First Amendment protection. Seizing upon the Court's rationale for permitting regulation of 'patently offensive' broadcast communications, the CDA's advocates contended that cybercommunications are at least as 'pervasive' and 'accessible to children'.

The Supreme Court rejected this asserted broadcast analogy in an essentially unanimous[60] opinion that, significantly, was authored by Justice John Paul Stevens, who had written the 1978 opinion that did allow regulation of 'patently offensive' broadcast expression.[61] Justice Stevens distinguished that earlier ruling,[62] as well as every other precedent on which the government sought to rely, stressing the special nature of cyberspace and reading the earlier decisions narrowly. His opinion concluded that cyberspace is entitled to the same full First Amendment protection as print[63] – a holding that should serve as a speech-protective lodestar for evaluating any government measures that suppress cyberspeech. Accordingly, the Court analysed the CDA pursuant to the exacting 'strict scrutiny' standard that it applies to any restriction on print communications; the restriction is presumed unconstitutional and the government bears a heavy burden of demonstrating that it is (1) designed to advance a societal goal of 'compelling' importance, and (2) 'the least restrictive means' for advancing that goal – in other words that it restricts speech as little as possible.

While *ACLU v Reno* stated that shielding children from certain sexually orientated expression is a sufficiently important goal to satisfy the first element of this strict scrutiny standard,[64] it concluded that the CDA was

---

[58] *ACLU v Reno*, 929 F. Supp. 824 (E.D. Pa., 1996) at p.881 per Dalzell, J.
[59] See *Sable Communications v F.C.C.* 492 US 115 (1989).
[60] Justice O'Connor wrote a partial dissent, joined by Chief Justice Rehnquist, which concluded that the CDA should be constitutional only concerning a tiny percentage of online communications: those involving (1) only one adult and (2) one or more minors. As the majority noted, however, many communications of this type would likely be between family members – for example, e-mails between parents and their own children – thus raising constitutional problems even concerning this relatively narrow portion of the CDA's scope.
[61] *FCC v Pacifica*, 438 US 726 (1978).
[62] 521 US 844 (1997) at p.868.
[63] Ibid. at p.870.
[64] Ibid. at p.848.

unnecessarily overbroad. Following a line of precedents concerning other media, the Court stressed that government may not pursue its goal of denying children access to certain material through measures that also deny access to adults.[65]

The ACLU had urged additional, independently sufficient grounds for concluding that the CDA violates the First Amendment. For example, the ACLU argued, and one of the lower court judges ruled, that the Act's core terms – 'patently offensive' and 'indecent' – are unduly vague, thus chilling much valuable expression.[66] Furthermore, the ACLU argued, consistent with past Supreme Court decisions, that minors have their own First Amendment rights,[67] which the CDA also violates. Consistent with its general approach of reaching only those issues necessary to resolve a case, the Court did not rule on these additional arguments. Thus, it remains to be seen whether they might supply grounds for invalidating future cybercensorship laws.

Child Online Protection Act 1998

In the fall of 1998, Congress responded to the Supreme Court's ruling in *ACLU v Reno* by passing a second cybercensorship law, the Child Online Protection Act ('COPA'),[68] which is somewhat less sweeping than the CDA. COPA prohibits any online communication 'for commercial purposes' that 'includes any material that is harmful to minors'. A communication is 'for commercial purposes' if it is made 'as a regular course of . . . trade or business, with the objective of earning a profit', even if no profit is actually made. Material is 'harmful to minors' if it is obscene as to minors – in other words, if it appeals to the prurient interest, is patently offensive and lacks serious value, from a minor's perspective.

The ACLU and other cyberlibertarians promptly challenged COPA in *ACLU v Reno II*, and in February 1999 a federal judge granted plaintiffs' motion for a preliminary injunction, enjoining the government from enforcing COPA pending the trial on the merits.[69] The District Court held that the plaintiffs had shown the necessary 'likelihood of success' on the merits of their claim that COPA violates the First Amendment for many of the same reasons that the CDA did. Since COPA regulates expression that is protected at least 'as to adults',[70] the District Court ruled, it is subject to strict scrutiny. While the Court concluded that the government does have a compelling interest in shielding minors even from materials that are not obscene by adult standards, it also concluded that the government was unlikely to

---

[65] Ibid. at p.873.
[66] 929 F. Supp. 824 (E.D. Pa., 1996) at p.856.
[67] See *Tinker v Des Moines School District* 393 US 502 (1969); *Erznozvik v Jacksonville* 422 US 205 (1975).
[68] 47 USC s.231 et seq.
[69] *American Civil Liberties Union. v Reno* 31 F. Supp. 2d 473 (E.D. Pa., 1999) upheld by the Court of Appeals (3rd Circuit) 217 F.3d 162.
[70] Ibid. at p.497.

be able to show that COPA was the least restrictive means of achieving this goal. For example, the Court noted that the evidence before it 'reveals that blocking or filtering technology may be at least as successful as COPA would be in restricting minors' access to harmful material online without imposing the burden on constitutionally protected speech that COPA imposes on adult users or Web site operators'.[71] Since the Supreme Court has not addressed the 'harmful to minors' doctrine for many years,[72] it is difficult to predict COPA's ultimate constitutional fate.

Extending current doctrines permitting restriction of sexual expression in other media to cyberspace

Given the Supreme Court's reasoning in *Reno v ACLU*, it seems unlikely that laws directly suppressing online sexual expression would survive First Amendment challenges. However, in earlier cases involving other media, the Court has allowed the government to restrict sexual expression through less direct measures, which are now being advocated for cyberspace. Two examples are (1) the harmful-to-minors approach embodied in COPA and challenged in *ACLU v Reno II* which was discussed in the previous section, and (2) the government-as-employer approach, embodied in a Virginia law that is also being litigated.[73]

A third possible indirect route toward stifling online sexual expression is through the government's spending power. Although its rulings in this area are mixed, in some cases the Court has held that government may condition grants of public funds on the requirement that the grantee limit its expression.[74] In other words, the government may use the 'carrot' of its funding power to impose speech restrictions that it could not impose through the 'stick' of its regulatory power. Accordingly, some members of Congress have proposed measures that would cut off federal funds to public libraries and schools unless they block certain sexually orientated online material.[75]

Application of obscenity laws to cyberspace

Even without enacting new measures that specifically restrict sexual expression in cyberspace, government prosecutors are targeting much online sexual expression under existing laws that criminalise obscenity and child pornography in any media. Indeed, the second highest official in the US

---

[71] Ibid. at p.497.

[72] The Supreme Court's only direct ruling concerning such a law is *Ginsberg v New York* 390 US 629 (1968). For a discussion of other pertinent precedents, see Hefner, M., 'Note: "Roast Pigs" and Miller-Light: Variable Obscenity in the Nineties' [1996] *University of Illinois Law Review* 843.

[73] See *Urofsky v Allen* 995 F. Supp. 634, 636 (E.D. Va. 1998).

[74] See, for example, *Rosenberger v Rector and Visitors of Univ. of Va.* 515 US 819 (1995); *Rust v Sullivan* 500 US 173 (1991). See also *National Endowment for the Arts v Finley* 524 US 569 (1998).

[75] See, for example, S. 1619, 105th Cong. (1998) (the 'Internet School Filtering Act', sponsored by Senator John McCain).

Department of Justice has urged federal prosecutors to make it a priority to enforce anti-obscenity laws specifically in the cyberspace context.[76]

While cyberlibertarians do not oppose laws that punish individuals who actually exploit other human beings – as child pornography laws have traditionally done[77] – we do object to laws that suppress expression merely because the expression itself is disfavoured, as the obscenity laws do. As previously noted, many judges – including Supreme Court Justices – have criticised the obscenity exception to the First Amendment, and therefore it might ultimately be repudiated in its entirety.

Even if the concept of constitutionally unprotected obscenity should persist in other media, it does not make sense in cyberspace for two reasons. (Thus, the Court could well invalidate the extension of current obscenity doctrine to cyberspace even while continuing to approve it in other media.)

The first reason is that the Court's rationale for exiling obscenity from the First Amendment was to protect the local geographical community from the adverse impact allegedly caused by the physical presence of such establishments as adult bookstores and theaters.[78] This rationale is questionable – and, indeed, was rejected by the Justices who dissented from the decisions that embraced it.[79] But even if one accepted this rationale in traditional public spaces, it still makes no sense in cyberspace, where the only community in which the sexual expression is present is the voluntarily self-constituted, virtual community of individuals who choose to partake of this expression.

Second, even in traditional space, the Court has said that what would otherwise be constitutionally unprotected obscenity is nevertheless protected when viewed in the privacy of one's own home: 'If the First Amendment means anything, it means that [the government] has no business telling a man, sitting alone in his house, what books he may read or what films he may watch.'[80] Yet that is exactly what the government does when it prosecutes someone for accessing sexually orientated expression via computer, in his/her own living room or other private space.

For these reasons, the ACLU and other cyberliberties groups argued that the first obscenity prosecution against an online adult bulletin board service, in 1994, violated the First Amendment. Although both the lower court

---

[76] See McCullagh, D., 'Justice Department Memo Calls for Net Obscenity Crackdown', *Netly News*, 29 June 1998.

[77] In contrast, the federal Child Pornography Prevention Act 1996 (18 USC s.2256) criminalises sexually explicit depictions – including online images – of a minor, or that are advertised in such a way as to 'convey the impression that the material is or contains a visual depiction of a minor engaging in sexually explicit conduct . . .'. This law has been challenged as violating the First Amendment by, in effect, creating a 'thought crime', outlawing sexual fantasies about minors. The lower court held that the law was constitutional, but the appellate court disagreed: *Free Speech Coalition v Reno* (25 Media L. Rep. 2305, USDC N.D. Cal., 1997) and (198 F.3d 1083, 1999).

[78] See *Roth v US* 354 US 476 (1957) at p.487; *Paris Adult Theater v Slaton* 413 US 49 (1973).

[79] Ibid.

[80] *Stanley v Georgia* 394 US 557 (1969) at p.565 per Marshall, J.

and appellate court rejected these arguments,[81] the Supreme Court did not review the case, so the questions remain open.

Rating and filtering systems for Internet content

Following the fall of the CDA at the US Supreme Court, and the difficulties created by the enforceability of national laws, technology was seen as an answer to tackle the availability of sexually explicit Internet content that is legal but deemed harmful to minors. Rating systems and filtering software are therefore being developed with broad support from governments,[82] the Internet industry[83] and the European Union.[84] These new technologies are introduced as a means to avoid heavy-handed public regulation of Internet content by governments and with a vague rationale of the protection of children. But rating and filtering systems raise serious problems with regard to free expression.

Their possible drawbacks include the potential use of rating and filtering tools for censorship of Internet content, the development of such tools by unaccountable regulatory or quasi-regulatory bodies and limited protection offered to the users of such technological tools. In other words, most of these systems are currently defective; and they can be used for the exclusion of socially useful information on the Internet. At the same time, these defective systems give only a false sense of security for the concerned Internet users. In December 1997, the Electronic Privacy Information Center ('EPIC') released a report, *Faulty Filters: How Content Filters Block Access to Kid-Friendly Information on the Internet*.[85] The EPIC study showed that the

---

[81] See *US v Thomas* 74 F.3d 701 (6th Cir., 1996) cert. den. 519 US 820 (1996).

[82] See Uhlig, R., 'Minister's warning over Internet porn', *Daily Telegraph*, 18 August 1996. The *DTI Press Release* P/96/636 – 'Ian Taylor Challenges Internet Service Providers: Develop New Software to Come Clean' 14 August 1996, at http://www.coi.gov.uk/coi/depts/GTI/coi1319c.ok, the *DTI Press Release*, 'Internet Safety-Net to Tackle Child Porn' 23 September, 1996 at http://dtiinfo1.dti.gov.uk/safety-net/index.html. See Safety-Net proposal, 'Rating, Reporting, Responsibility, For Child Pornography & Illegal Material on the Internet' adopted and recommended by the Executive Committee of ISPA – Internet Services Providers Association, LINX – London Internet Exchange and the Internet Watch Foundation at http://dtiinfo1.dti.gov.uk/safety-net/r3.htm.

[83] Internet Watch Foundation consultation 'Rating and Filtering Internet Content – A United Kingdom Perspective', March 1998, is available at http://www.internetwatch.org.uk/rating.html.

[84] See Communication from the Commission to the European Parliament, the Council, the Economic and Social Committee and the Committee of the Regions, *Action Plan on promoting safe use of the Internet*, (Brussels, November 1997). See also, for a critique of the EU initiatives, Akdeniz, Y., 'The European Union and illegal and harmful content on the Internet' (1998) 3(1) *Journal of Civil Liberties* 31.

[85] See Electronic Privacy Information Center, 'Faulty Filters: How Content Filters Block Access to Kid-Friendly Information on the Internet,' (Washington, December 1997, http://www2.epic.org/reports/filter-report.html). See further Electronic Privacy Information Center (ed.), *Filters and Freedom – Free Speech Perspectives on Internet Content Controls* (Washington DC, 1999).

would-be family-friendly technologies result in the censorship of socially acceptable and legal content. It is also well known that these filtering tools are also used to exclude speech related to sexual minority groups.[86] Therefore, filtering software and rating systems will be used to exclude minority views and gripe sites more than protecting children. The Internet remains as a wonderful resource for online users including children, and it should be their parents' responsibility to supervise access, and therefore the parents should be educated on the benefits of the Internet rather than being affected by 'moral panics' about Internet content.[87] Moreover, any regulatory action intended to protect a certain group of people, such as children, should not take the form of an unconditional prohibition of using the Internet to distribute content that is freely available to adults in other media. In any event, if children want to access sexually explicit content, such technologies will not stop them because of the constantly changing profile of the Internet. Educating children is more important rather than placing trust in technology or in an industry that produces 'blunter instruments'[88] and believes it can do a better job of protecting children than parents. Although there may be a governmental duty to protect children when real harm to children is an issue (such as the use of children in the creation of child pornography), it remains at least questionable whether such a duty extends to the issue of protection of children from 'harmful Internet content' and whether this duty should be switched to a quasi-regulatory unaccountable bodies or industries.

Rating systems

The Platform for Internet Content Selections ('PICS') is a rating system for the Internet. PICS works by embedding electronic labels in the text or image documents to vet their content before the computer displays them.[89] The vetting system could include political, religious, advertising or commercial topics. These can be added by the publisher of the material, by an ISP, or by an independent vetting body. But rating systems are designed for the World Wide Web sites while leaving out other Internet-related communication systems such as the chat environments,[90] file transfer protocol servers ('ftp'),[91] Usenet discussion groups, real-audio and real-video systems which can

---

[86] See Gay & Lesbian Alliance Against Defamation report, 'Access Denied: The Impact of Internet Filtering Software on the Lesbian and Gay Community', (New York, December 1997), at http://www.glaad.org/glaad/access_denied/index.html.

[87] BBC News, 'Teachers' fears over Internet porn', 9 April 1998.

[88] Opinion of the Economic and Social Committee of the European Commission on the 'Proposal for a Council Decision adopting a Multiannual Community Action Plan on promoting safe use of the Internet' (Official Journal of the European Communities, 98/C 214/08, 10 July 1998), pp.29–32.

[89] See Computer Professionals for Social Responsibility, 'Filtering FAQ' http://quark.cpsr.org/~harryh/faq.html.

[90] Interactive environments like chat channels cannot be rated as the exchange and transmission of information takes place live and spontaneously.

[91] Estimated amount of ftp servers on the Internet is about a million. Some of these online libraries may have offensive content or legal content that may be considered harmful for children.

include live sound and image transmissions, and finally the ubiquitous e-mail communications. These systems cannot be rated with the above rating systems and therefore the assumption that rating systems would make the Internet a 'safer environment' for children is wrong as the WWW content represents only a fraction of the whole of the Internet content.

According to the UK Internet Watch Foundation, there is 'a whole category of dangerous subjects' that require ratings and these are information related to drugs, sex, violence, information about dangerous sports like bungee-jumping, and hate speech material.[92] This kind of content would include such publications as the *Anarchist's Cookbook*[93] which not only can be downloaded from WWW sites but also can be obtained through ftp servers or through the use of automatic e-mail services, apart from its availability through well-known bookshops such as Waterstones and Dillons within the UK.[94]

Filtering software

Most filtering software available is designed for the home market. This is intended to respond to the preferences of parents making decisions for their own children. There are currently around 15 filtering products, mainly US based[95] and therefore not reflecting the cultural differences in a global environment such as the Internet. It has been reported many times that, this kind of software is over inclusive and limits access to or censors inconvenient websites, or filters potentially educational materials regarding AIDS and drug abuse prevention. Therefore, 'censorware' enters homes under the guise of 'parental control' and as a purported alternative to government censorship but in fact imposes the standards of the program makers rather than the users. The companies creating this kind of software provide no appeal system to content providers who are 'banned', thereby 'subverting the self-regulating exchange of information that has been a hallmark of the Internet community'.[96]

UK and European rating and filtering

While the debate about the use of rating and filtering systems or policies that govern such usage is not settled in the US due to the First Amendment constraints (as shall be described later), the UK government favours self-regulatory schemes for Internet regulation and therefore supports the development of rating and filtering systems for Internet content. The UK

[92] Wired News, 'Europe Readies Net Content Ratings', 7 July 1997.
[93] See, for example, http://members.tripod.com/~bombland/.
[94] See Cyber-Rights & Cyber-Liberties (UK), *Who Watches the Watchmen: Internet Content Rating Systems, and privatised censorship* http://www.cyber-rights.org/watchmen.htm, 1997.
[95] See http://www.netparents.org/software/.
[96] See CPSR letter dated 18 December 1996 sent to Solid Oak, the makers of CyberSitter at http://www.cpsr.org/cpsr/nii/cyber-rights/.

policy is seen not only as suiting the environment of the Internet, but also fits with wider European policy and answers police (and allegedly public) concerns.

As for European policy, the European Union seeks the development of internationally compatible and interoperable rating and filtering schemes to protect users (especially children at risk from harmful content), and measures to increase awareness of the possibilities available among parents, teachers, children and other consumers to help these groups to use the networks while choosing the appropriate content and exercising a reasonable amount of parental control.[97] Accordingly, in November 1997, the European Commission adopted a proposal for an action plan,[98] promoting the safe use of the Internet, which would cover a three-year period between 1998 to 2001.[99] The Action Plan proposed by the European Commission concentrates on the regulation of illegal and harmful content on the Internet. The proposals followed the European Commission's Communication Paper on Illegal and Harmful Content on the Internet[100] and its Green Paper on the Protection of Minors and Human Dignity in Audiovisual and Information Services on 16 October 1996.[101] The European Commission Communication Paper suggested that: [102]

> . . . the answer to the challenge will be a combination of self-control of the service providers, new technical solutions such as rating systems and filtering software, awareness actions for parents and teachers, information on risks and possibilities to limit these risks and of international co-operation.

The UK Government welcomed the European Union initiatives with its emphasis on self-regulation by industry, as entirely consistent with the UK's approach: [103]

> The UK strongly agrees with the [European] Commission that since a legal framework for regulation of the Internet already exists in Member States, new laws or regulations are unnecessary.

---

[97] See Communication from the Commission to the European Parliament, the Council, the Economic and Social Committee and the Committee of the Regions, *Action Plan on promoting safe use of the Internet*, November 1997. For details of the programme, see http://158.169.50.95:10080/iap/.

[98] See EU Commission, *Communication on the follow-up to the Green paper on the protection of minors and human dignity in audiovisual and information services including a Proposal for a Recommendation* (COM (97) 570, Brussels, 1997).

[99] See Communication from the Commission to the European Parliament, the Council, the Economic and Social Committee and the Committee of the Regions, *Action Plan on promoting safe use of the Internet*, loc. cit.

[100] See European Commission Communication, Illegal and Harmful Content on the Internet (COM (96) 487, Brussels, 1996).

[101] See European Commission, *Green Paper on the Protection of Minors and Human Dignity in Audiovisual and Information Services* (COM (96) 483 final, Brussels, 1996).

[102] See European Commission Communication, *Illegal and Harmful Content on the Internet* (COM (96) 487, Brussels, 1996).

[103] Select Committee on European Legislation, *Fourth Report* (1996–7 HC 36-iv) para. 14.8.

However, apart from various civil liberties organisations, at least one Committee within the European Commission was not convinced that these technological systems would be the answer for the protection of children. In its opinion on the EU Action Plan, the Economic and Social Committee of the European Commission report[104] noted that the use of filtering tools may create a false sense of security for parents and teachers while children will quickly find any loopholes.[105] The Committee further questioned the claim that PICS will turn the Internet into an environment free of harmful content.[106] More importantly, the Committee was worried that the possibility of Internet service providers using filtering and rating systems at the level of entry would render these systems, dubbed as 'user empowering', an instrument of control, 'actually taking choice out of citizens' hands'.[107] The Committee considered it highly unlikely that the proposed measures will in the long term result in a safe Internet[108] with the rating and classification of all information on the Internet being 'impracticable'.[109] The Committee, therefore, 'sees little future in the active promotion of filtering systems based on rating'.[110]

In terms of police concerns, a defining moment occurred in mid-August 1996, when the Clubs & Vice Unit of the Metropolitan Police sent a letter to the UK ISPs supplying them with a list of Usenet discussion groups that they believe to contain pornographic material.[111] The list mainly covered newsgroups which carried child pornography such as 'alt.binaries.pictures.lolita.fucking, alt.binaries.pictures.boys', but it also included such newsgroups as 'alt.sex.fetish.tickling, alt.sex.fetish.wrestling, alt.homosexual', which might or might not include sexually explicit content. The action taken by the UK police appeared to have been ill-considered and did not do much to reduce the availability of obscene content on the Internet. Furthermore, the list of newsgroups provided by the UK police included much material that is not illegal, such as legitimate discussion groups for homosexuals and discussion groups which do not contain any pictures, but contain text, sexual fantasies and stories. These would almost certainly not infringe the Obscene Publications Act. The action of the police also amounted

---

[104] Economic and Social Committee of the European Commission, 'Opinion on the Proposal for a Council Decision adopting a Multiannual Community Action Plan on promoting safe use of the Internet' (OJEC, 98/C 214/08, 1998), pp.29–32.

[105] Ibid., para. 3.2.1.

[106] Ibid., para. 3.3.1.

[107] Ibid., para. 3.4.

[108] Ibid., para. 4.1.

[109] Ibid.

[110] Ibid., para. 4.1.1. for further criticism see also Akdeniz, Y., 'The European Union and illegal and harmful content on the Internet' (1998) 3(1) *Journal of Civil Liberties* 31 and Walker, C. and Akdeniz, Y., 'The governance of the Internet in Europe with special reference to illegal and harmful content', in Walker, C. (ed.), *Crime, Criminal Justice and the Internet* (Sweet & Maxwell, London, 1998).

[111] See Letter from the Metropolitan Police to the UK ISPs, August 1996, at http://www.cyber-rights.org/themet.htm.

to censorship of material without public debate in Parliament or elsewhere. Political action by the UK government would be preferable to random censorship by law enforcement authorities or by self-regulatory bodies. The Internet Watch Foundation ('IWF'), a private quasi-regulatory body strongly supported by the UK government, was set up as the primary vehicle for this purpose in September 1996.

The IWF operates first and foremost as a clearing house for complaints from the public about Internet content and liaises with both the ISPs and the police to respond to these complaints where well-founded. The IWF has also formulated more systematic plans for content controls. Thus, it announced a consultation paper for the development of rating systems at a national level in February 1998.[112] According to an IWF press release, rating systems would 'meet parents' concerns about Internet content that is unsuitable for children'. The consultation document by the IWF did not discuss whether these systems are suitable for the UK or whether they are needed at all. Nevertheless, the decision taken by the IWF consultation document is expressly supported by the UK government.[113]

The Department of Trade and Industry and the Home Office played key roles in the establishment of the self-regulatory body, the Internet Watch Foundation ('IWF') and continues to give it wide support.[114] Therefore, the IWF should be classified as a public regulatory body[115] and, as such, its activities should be more open and accountable and the public should be able to challenge its decisions and even participate in them. As for the latter, according to Barbara Roche, Minister of State in the Department of Trade and Industry, 'as part of its remit to help ensure that the Internet can be a safe place to work, learn and play, the Internet Watch Foundation has convened an advisory board comprising representatives of

---

[112] IWF, 'Rating and Filtering Internet Content – A United Kingdom Perspective' (March 1998, at http://www.internetwatch.org.uk/rating.html). For a critique of the IWF proposals see Cyber-Rights & Cyber-Liberties (UK), 'Who Watches the Watchmen: Internet Content Rating Systems, and privatised censorship' (1997) and 'Who Watches the Watchmen: Part II – Accountability & Effective Self-Regulation in the Information Age' (1998) both at http://www.cyber-rights.org/reports.

[113] See, for example, the statement by Alun Michael, Minister of State in the Home Department, HC Debs. vol. 307 col. 466 wa 2 March 1998: 'We also encourage other non-statutory schemes which are designed to protect young people from unsuitable material such as the working group of representatives from the Internet Watch Foundation and Internet Service Providers which is devising a common ratings system for United Kingdom Internet Users ...'

[114] Memorandum by the Hon John Battle MP, Minister for Science, Energy and Industry, House of Commons Adjournment Debate 'HMG Strategy for the Internet', 18 March 1998, at http://www.dti.gov.uk/Minspeech/btlspch3.htm. See also Department of Trade and Industry, *Secure Electronic Commerce Statement* (London, 1998, at http://www.dti.gov.uk/CII/ana27p.html) para. (iv).

[115] Compare the treatment of the Press Complaints Commission: *R v Press Complaints Commission, ex parte Stewart-Brady* [1997] EMLR 185, *The Times*, 22 November 1996. For the Irish approach see Irish Department of Justice, Equality and Law Reform, *Illegal and Harmful Use of the Internet* (Pn.5231, Dublin, 1998).

content providers, children's charities, regulators from other media, ISPs and civil liberties groups, to propose a UK-focused system for rating Internet content'.[116] It was later discovered that no civil liberties organisations were actually involved with the IWF's advisory board nor with its activities.[117]

Recently, Chris Smith, the Secretary of State for National Heritage has stated that:[118]

> It is vital . . . in considering how best to address [the problem of illegal and harmful content on the Internet], that we bear in mind that only a small fraction of the material available to the public poses a threat to the protection of minors or human dignity. It will be important, therefore, not to impose hasty regulation upon these new services and thereby constrain their development and the educational, commercial and social opportunities and other benefits they can engender.

However, the preference of self-regulatory solutions means that these solutions aim to restrict access by certain groups (e.g. by children) to otherwise legally available sexually explicit content rather than enforcing the current UK obscenity standards over the Internet.

US rating and filtering

Does the First Amendment apply?

Ever since it became clear that the CDA and other direct censorial measures were facing constitutional difficulties, advocates of suppressing online sexual expression stepped up their promotion of rating and filtering systems, which would also block access to the same expression.

It is impossible to generalise about whether such systems are (un)constitutional or have an adverse impact on free expression, since the analysis turns on the specific nature of the particular system.

In terms of the constitutional issues, the threshold question is whether the system is either directly imposed by the government or sufficiently connected to the government to be deemed 'state action' that triggers constitutional scrutiny.[119] At one end of the spectrum, when government officials require the installation of screening software – as increasing numbers of

---

[116] See HC Debs. vol. 296 col. 615 wa 26 June, 1997: 'My Department maintains frequent contact with the Internet Services Providers Association. The Department played a key role in the development and launch of a self-regulatory system for Internet content based on existing law, known as the Internet Watch Foundation (IWF) and continues to maintain contact with this organisation.'

[117] See Cyber-Rights & Cyber-Liberties (UK) report, 'Who Watches the Watchmen: Internet Content Rating Systems, and privatised censorship' (November 1997).

[118] See House of Commons, Select Committee on European Legislation, Second Report (1997–8 HC 155-ii). See particularly 'The Information Society and Protection of Human Dignity', at para. 60. See further Walker, C.P. and Akdeniz, Y., 'The Governance of the Internet in Europe with Special Reference to Illegal and Harmful Content', in Walker, C. (ed.), *Crime, Criminal Justice and the Internet* (special edition, *Criminal Law Review*, Sweet & Maxwell, London, 1998).

[119] See generally *Lee v International Society for Krishna Consciousness* 505 US 830 (1992).

public library and school officials are doing – such direct governmental action is clearly subject to the First Amendment. At the other end of the spectrum, when parents choose to install screening software on their home computers, to prevent their own children from viewing certain online material, there is no 'state action' that triggers First Amendment protection.

In between these two extreme situations, the government could provide various incentives to both the computer industry and parents to encourage the production, distribution and use of filtering software, which could raise close questions about whether the First Amendment should govern. If the computer industry attempts to deflect the numerous censorial threats from Congress and the Clinton Administration by 'voluntarily' adopting and promoting rating and blocking schemes, one could plausibly argue that such schemes resulted from government coercion, and therefore should be held to First Amendment standards.

While each rating and filtering scheme must be judged in light of its specific features and circumstances, analysis should always be guided by the simple lodestar principle that the Supreme Court enunciated in *Reno v ACLU*: online communications are entitled to the same high level of First Amendment protection as print communications. Therefore, just as it would violate the First Amendment, for example, to require that all authors rate their books, it should likewise violate the First Amendment to require everyone who posts something online to rate it.

Free speech values

Free speech values come into play in any use of rating and filtering schemes, even if the government is not sufficiently involved to invoke the Constitution formally. For example, if all Internet access were controlled by one or two private companies, due solely to economic and/or technological factors, and if those companies denied access to certain speakers or ideas, free speech values would be threatened, even if the First Amendment would not afford a legal basis for defending those values. Accordingly, cyberlibertarians have critiqued various rating and filtering schemes from the perspective of whether they advance or undermine free speech values, even if they involve only private, non-governmental, action.[120] From this perspective, too, no generalisation is possible, but each scheme must be judged individually.

At one end of the spectrum, one can imagine a rating and filtering scheme that would promote free speech values. The ideal system would maximise information about online sites, enabling all Internet users to make the most informed choices possible, consistent with their own tastes and values, about the material they would (or would not) access or permit their children to access. Users would be able to select from a wide variety of reviews and ratings sources, to choose those most likely to reflect their own preferences.

---

[120] See, generally, Electronic Privacy Information Center (ed.), *Filters and Freedom – Free Speech Perspectives on Internet Content Controls* (Washington DC, 1999).

No such system has yet been devised, and it is likely that economic, techno-logical and other pragmatic constraints will prevent such a hypothetical ideal from ever becoming a reality. The practical obstacles include: the overwhelming, and constantly proliferating and mutating, contents of cyber-space, thus impeding a review of all online material; and the inevitably subjective judgements required for determining the value of any particular material for any particular potential audience member. In the end, indi-vidual judgments by each Internet user – or, in the case of young children, individual judgments by each child's parents – may be the only approach that works in practice, as well as the only one that comports with free speech principles. In terms of receiving constructive assistance from others, the most feasible approach would seem to be – as with more traditional forms of expression – reviews that single out particular sites that are recommended, rather than filtering systems that completely deny access to certain sites.

At the other extreme end of the spectrum from the foregoing ideal scheme, which would facilitate and enhance informed individual decision-making, are rating and blocking systems that limit the range of information and choices available for each Internet user. As the ACLU wrote in one of its reports elaborating upon the free speech dangers of such systems: [121]

> In . . . the physical world, people censor the printed word by burning books. But in the virtual world, one can just as easily censor controversial speech by banish-ing it to the farthest corners of cyberspace using rating and blocking programs.

Unfortunately, rating systems that are currently in use – and that are being touted by government officials, industry leaders and pro-censorship advo-cacy groups – do have this constraining effect. For example, some filtering software is advertised as blocking only 'hard-core pornographic' materials, when it in fact blocks other, valuable sexually orientated material, and even material that has no sexual content whatsoever. Thus, individuals who install such software on their computers are, unknowingly, involuntarily deprived of access to expression that they would choose to see and to allow their children to see.

At best, practical constraints inevitably make filtering software both under-inclusive and over-inclusive in terms of blocking all the material it purports to, and only that material. At worst, ideological or value judg-ments that are not revealed to customers lead software manufacturers to screen out material whose perspectives they reject. While individual Internet users certainly have the right to install software that blocks out material they consider contrary to their values, almost all manufacturers of blocking software refuse to disclose either the sites they block or the criteria they use to determine which sites they will block. Therefore, the manufacturers are imposing their value choices on their customers, and not facilitating the customers' exercise of their own freedom of choice.

---

[121] *Fahrenheit 451.2: Is Cyberspace Burning?* (http://www.aclu.org/issues/cyber/burning.html, 1997).

These problems are compounded when filtering software is installed not as a matter of choice on the part of the individual user, but, rather, by someone else who controls the computer – for example, in the case of a public library or educational institution, government officials. Across the US, officials are installing or advocating blocking software on computers in libraries, schools and universities. Accordingly, individual choice is stripped from the many members of the public whose only access to the Internet is through such computers. For them, the installation of filtering software on library computers has the same censorial impact as the removal of books from library shelves.

Loudoun County litigation

Book banning is precisely the analogy that was invoked by the only court that to date has ruled on the (un)constitutionality of government-mandated filtering software in a public institution. In November 1998, Judge Leonie Brinkema upheld a First Amendment challenge to mandatory filtering software that had been installed in the Loudoun County, Virginia public libraries pursuant to a 'Policy on Internet Sexual Harassment', which requires software to block 'child pornography and obscene material', as well as material deemed 'harmful to juveniles' under state law.[122] To implement this policy, the library installed 'X-Stop', a commercial software product.

Judge Brinkema held that – along with such a direct censorial measure as the CDA – the filtering requirement had to withstand strict judicial scrutiny under the First Amendment.[123] She assumed that the government's asserted interests – in minimising access to obscenity and child pornography, and in avoiding the creation of a sexually hostile environment – were compelling.[124] However, she concluded that the blocking policy was unconstitutional on several, independently sufficient, grounds: (1) it is not necessary to further the government's asserted interests; (2) it is not narrowly tailored; (3) it limits adult patrons to accessing only material that is fit for minors; (4) it provides inadequate standards for restricting access; and (5) it provides inadequate procedural safeguards to ensure prompt judicial review.[125] Because of the fourth and fifth factors, Judge Brinkema ruled that the blocking policy constitutes an unconstitutional prior restraint.[126] According to Judge Brinkema:[127]

> Such a Policy offends the guarantee of free speech in the First Amendment and is, therefore, unconstitutional.

---

[122] *Mainstream Loudoun v Board of Trustees* 2 F. Supp. 2d 783 (E.D. Va. 1998) 24 F. Supp. 2d 552 (1998).

[123] 24 F. Supp. 2d 552 (1998) at p.561.

[124] Ibid. at p.565.

[125] Ibid. at pp.565–70.

[126] Ibid. at p.570. Government-mandated filtering schemes violate the First Amendment rights of not only the individuals who seek access to online materials, but also online speakers, who seek access to an audience. See ibid. (denying government's motion to dismiss claims of online publishers whose material was blocked).

[127] Ibid.

One particularly interesting feature of Judge Brinkema's analysis is her catalogue of 'less restrictive means' that Loudoun County could have used to pursue its asserted interests: installing privacy screens; charging library staff with casual monitoring of Internet use; installing filtering software only on some Internet terminals, and limiting minors to those terminals; and installing filtering software that could be turned off when an adult is using the terminal. Significantly, Judge Brinkema cautioned that, while all of the foregoing alternatives are less restrictive than the challenged policy, she did not 'find that any of them would necessarily be constitutional', since that question was not before her.[128]

Conclusion

The chapter has tried to explain two different policy and legal approaches to the availability of sexually explicit content over the Internet. When the US government tried to introduce new laws trying to restrict such content over the Internet, these attempts were unsuccessful. The UK government supports a self-regulatory approach in addition to its current restrictive obscenity laws. However, both governments choose to support technological solutions such as the rating and filtering systems as the way forward for dealing with Internet content deemed to be harmful to minors even though the intended Internet content often can be categorised as legal. The chapter has shown that both governments encourage the development of these systems and the implications for cyberspeech and censorship are the same in both jurisdictions. There remains a serious danger in excluding sexually explicit content and other controversial cyberspeech out of the screens of Internet users 'casting a far darker shadow over free speech, threatening to torch a large segment of the Internet community'.[129] The Supreme Court in *Reno v ACLU* stated that: [130]

> As a matter of constitutional tradition, in the absence of evidence to the contrary, we presume that governmental regulation of the content of speech is more likely to interfere with the free exchange of ideas than to encourage it. The interest in encouraging freedom of expression in a democratic society outweighs any theoretical but unproven benefit of censorship.

Considering that the Internet is a global medium and that a huge proportion of Internet content is generated from the US, it would be possible to argue that nothing less than the US Constitutional standards of the First Amendment should be acceptable over the Internet. But so far the most direct dangers and threats for cyberspeech came from the land of free speech – the United States. Legislation such as the CDA and COPA set a dangerous precedent for similar legislation in modern and developing societies including the UK.

---

[128] Ibid. at p.567.
[129] *Reno v ACLU* 521 US 844 (1997) at p.881.
[130] Ibid. at p.885.

In response, the House of Commons Select Committee on Culture, Media and Sport has commented that international initiatives will have an important impact on national Internet regulation but at the same time 'the question is whether such attempts at regulation can be anything more than optimistically indicative rather than genuinely effective'.[131] This statement is true and promising, but many governments are ready to follow such bad examples as the CDA or to use the currently available technology for cybercensorship.

The chapter has also noted that the development of rating and filtering systems may not be a sound response to content problems. However, the European Union and the Internet industry continues to promote the development of such systems,[132] and more governments are supporting the use of such systems.[133]

The battle for free cyberspeech is therefore far from over. But one difficulty faced by cyberlibertarians is that the regulatory initiatives are switching from public hands into private hands where there is no accountability. This is already the case within the UK with the IWF acting as a private body with important public duties, and a similar approach will be followed within the European Union following the European Commission's Action Plan. The regulation of sexually explicit content will move into the hands of private organisations and ISPs and, due to the commercial pressures, the private sector will be more proactively involved with Internet content regulation.[134] However, government inspired and enforced pre-censorship is no better than government-imposed censorship.[135] Such restrictions and complex regulations will make the UK (and the US if it follows suit) a very hostile place for network development and an ideal environment for cybercensorship.

---

[131] *The Multimedia Revolution* (1997–8 HC 520) Vol. I, para. 108.
[132] See the Bertelsmann Foundation's Memorandum on Internet Self-Regulation (September 1999, at
http://www.stiftung.bertelsmann.de/internetcontent/english/download Memorandum.pdf).
For a critique of the Bertelsmann proposals see the Cyber Rights & Cyber-Liberties (UK) Memorandum for the Internet Content Summit 1999 (September, 1999, at
http://www.cyber-rights.org/reports/summit99.htm).
[133] The Australian Government introduced the Broadcasting Services Amendment (Online Services) Act 1999 which mandates blocking of Internet content based upon existing national film and video classification guidelines. For details see
http://www.efa.org.au/Issues/Censor/cens1.html.
[134] See the Bertelsmann Foundation's Memorandum on Internet Self-Regulation, loc. cit.
[135] Akdeniz, Y., Cyber-Rights & Cyber-Liberties (UK) Report: 'Who Watches the Watchmen: Part II – Accountability & Effective Self-Regulation in the Information Age', loc. cit.

CHAPTER 10

Child pornography

Yaman Akdeniz

Introduction

There have been more concerns raised about the availability of child pornography over the Internet and the usage of the Internet by paedophiles than any other online criminal activity. As a response, and ever since Operation Starburst,[1] undertaken within the UK by the West Midlands Police, solutions for the suppression of child pornography have been sought in different fora including at both national and international levels involving both public and private bodies. The *Marc Dutroux Affair* in Belgium[2] was one of the main reasons why the European Union decided to take action with respect to the availability of illegal and harmful content on the Internet in late 1996.[3] The main purpose and concern of the EU regulators was the protection of children. The chapter will therefore analyse the specific problem of child pornography in relation to the Internet.

While the problem of child pornography is global and not medium-specific, this chapter will address this problem both within the UK and in relation to the Internet. Still, it would be wrong to exclude from the overall picture supranational and international developments in relation to the governance of child pornography especially in the field of law enforcement. Therefore, there will be references to such developments outside the UK as far as they are relevant to the problem of child pornography over the Internet.

---

[1] Darbyshire, N., 'Nine arrested in raid on Internet child porn ring', *Daily Telegraph*, 27 July 1995; Davis, D., *The Internet Detective – An Investigator's Guide* (Police Research Group, Home Office, 1998), Appendix D; Davis, D., 'Criminal Law and the Internet: The Investigator's Perspective', in Walker, C. (ed.), *Crime, Criminal Justice and the Internet* (special edition, *Criminal Law Review*, Sweet & Maxwell, London, 1998).

[2] See Walsh, J., 'The Terror and Pity', *Time International*, vol. 148, no. 11, 2 September 1996 and Millward, D., 'Belgian plea for help to crush child porn rings', *Daily Telegraph*, 20 August 1996.

[3] European Commission, *Communication to the European Parliament, The Council, The Economic and Social Committee and the Committee of the Regions: Illegal and Harmful Content on the Internet* (COM (96) 487, Brussels, 16 October 1996).

Child pornography on the Internet

Although the usage of the Internet by paedophiles to circulate child pornography causes enormous public concern, this is not a new problem specifically related to the Internet or use of the Internet by paedophiles. Paedophilia networks have been using computer networks for similar purposes since as early as 1986,[4] and references to child pornography were made within local computer bulletin board systems within Britain as early as in 1985.[5] Therefore, we are witnessing the continuation of existing crimes with the use of a global medium, the Internet, rather than the development of new crimes.

There is no doubt that, in most cases, child pornography is a permanent record of the sexual abuse of an actual child (except in the case of pseudo-photographs or within the context of written materials). Child pornography, therefore, in most cases, is a form of sexual abuse and exploitation in which depiction of children engaging in sexually explicit conduct, poses a serious threat to the physical and mental health, safety and well-being of children. For these reasons, in most countries, its creation or distribution is considered a serious crime. Possession of child pornography is normally a lesser offence, and in some countries it may not be an offence to possess child pornography at all.[6] Therefore, there are differences in relation to how the problem of child pornography is dealt with in different jurisdictions. The UK's laws (as will be explained later) do criminalise the creation, possession and distribution of child pornography (including pseudo-photographs) under the Protection of Children Act 1978, as amended by the Criminal Justice Act 1988 and by the Criminal Justice and Public Order Act 1994.

With the advancement of new technologies and the Internet, child pornography has become more visible in the 1990s even though it mainly remains as a cottage industry created and distributed by paedophilia networks. Mostly, the activities of paedophilia networks do remain underground and

---

[4] The Meese Commission Report, in 1986, provides evidence that paedophile offenders and child pornographers had begun to use personal computers and computer networks for communication and distribution of materials. See Attorney General's Commission on Pornography, *Final Report* (US Government Printing Office, Washington DC, 1986) p.629.

[5] PBBS was an adult-orientated Bulletin Board with at least 500 users in 1985. The Surrey-based PBBS was closed down in June 1987 following allegations involving discussions of paedophilia and child pornography within the system. PBBS was reported to the Metropolitan Police Obscene Publications Squad and this resulted in its closure. However, no charges were ever brought, and the System Administer traced the allegations to a single message involving one user's interest with 'young girl' material. For further information see Tate, T., *Child Pornography: An Investigation* (Methuen, London, 1990), p.209.

[6] Sweden is one country in which the possession of child pornography is not a specific offence. The United Nations was concerned in October 1997 that many governments in Eastern Europe have not adopted special legislation to prohibit child prostitution and child pornography. Note also the decision of the Court of Appeal for British Columbia in *R v Sharpe* [1999] BCD Crim. J. 265: 'Making it an offence to possess expressive material, when that material may have been created without abusing children and may never be published, distributed or sold, constitutes an extreme invasion of the values of liberty, autonomy and privacy', *per* Madam Justice Anne Rowles.

hidden, and it is not possible to assess the real extent of this problem and availability of such materials over the Internet. Child pornography mainly and visibly exists within some newsgroups, while it is difficult to claim the same for the World Wide Web. However, a University College, Cork study claims that the amount of child pornography accessible through the Internet is considerable, with the situation being fluid and dynamic due to sites frequently changing addresses.[7] The Cork Study (in research carried out in January 1998) further suggests that 0.07 per cent of the 40,000 newsgroups carry 'child erotica' or 'pornography', plus there existed at that time 238 'girl-related child pornography or erotica' web pages[8] (albeit out of around 50 million web pages).

While web search engines on child pornography would normally direct inquirers towards sites campaigning against the availability of child pornography on the Internet,[9] one of the major problems for the future may be the availability of channels devoted to child pornography within the Internet Relay Chat or ICQ environment. The Cork Study on this front concluded that 'due to the organised dynamic nature of paedophile activity, it is not possible to estimate with accuracy the amount of traffic generated on IRC channels'.[10] However, the definitions used within the Cork study are far from tight,[11] and claims that this source of child pornography is either 'major' or 'increasing' are unsubstantiated in the absence of earlier measures or measures of other forms of trafficking. However, such studies are useful for assessing the problem of child pornography over the Internet, and regular studies are needed for assessing the issue.

In any event, the problem of child pornography is global:[12]

> Child pornography is a pressing problem on local, national, and international levels and . . . all nations have an important part to play in the solution.

The Internet is a global communication medium regardless of frontiers and therefore solutions for specific problems created by the misuse of the Internet would undoubtedly involve global responses. There may be a role to play for different players at different levels within a multi-layered governance mechanism in which the role of the governments as rule-makers and the police as

---

[7] See a summary of the Cork Study in the Irish Department of Justice, Equality and Law Reform, *Illegal and Harmful Use of the Internet* (Pn.5231, Dublin, 1998) pp.33–5.

[8] An unspecified larger number were boy-related according to the Cork Study.

[9] Reports submitted by the Special Rapporteur of the Commission on Human Rights on the sale of children, child prostitution and child pornography to the General Assembly, Sale of children, child prostitution and child pornography, Note by the Secretary-General, A/52/482, issued on 16 October 1997, http://www.unhchr.ch/html/menu4/garep/52ga482.htm, para. 101.

[10] Irish Department of Justice, Equality and Law Reform, *Illegal and Harmful Use of the Internet* (Pn.5231, Dublin, 1998), p.34.

[11] See ibid., p.30.

[12] Healy, M.A., 'Child Pornography: an international perspective', paper presented at the World Congress against Commercial Sexual Exploitation of Children, Sweden, 1996, at http://www.usis.usemb.se/children/csec/215e.htm.

law enforcers are not exclusive.[13] Still, their role remains pivotal, but current initiatives show that private sector and the Internet industry has been under pressure to do the undoable – 'policing the information superhighway'.

This chapter will now proceed into the examination and analysis of these issues from a UK perspective.

Governance of child pornography in the UK

At a national level, the availability of laws dealing with child pornography is the most important weapon to fight the creation, possession and distribution of child pornography whether on the Internet or elsewhere. This part of the chapter will show the crucial role that laws and the law enforcement bodies play in the fight against child pornography. However, in some instances, even a solid system may malfunction since law enforcement often remains limited to the borders of the individual nation states.

Following a report by the House of Commons Home Affairs Committee, the UK obscenity laws were amended by the Criminal Justice and Public Order Act 1994 to include publications in data format. Although computer-based child pornography was the main issue in the House of Commons Home Affairs Committee Report, the Internet was not directly mentioned.[14] The definition of child pornography within the Protection of Children Act 1978 was also amended to include computer-generated images of children ('pseudo photographs') by the 1994 legislation.[15]

Illegality is a specific national issue to be dealt with by the law enforcement and courts of law and the Internet is of course not a 'lawless place'.[16] The following sections will briefly examine the current state of UK laws following these amendments, together with law enforcement issues.

Protection of Children Act 1978

The 1978 Act was passed in response to the problem of child pornography. Its main purpose was to close some potential gaps in the measures available to police and prosecutors.[17] The definition of 'photograph' given in section

---

[13] See, generally, Akdeniz, Y., 'Governance of Pornography and Child Pornography on the Global Internet: A Multi-Layered Approach', in Edwards, L. and Waelde, C. (eds), *Law and the Internet: Regulating Cyberspace* (Hart Publishing, Oxford, 1997).

[14] By the time the House of Commons, Home Affairs Committee's report (*Computer Pornography*, 1993–4 HC 126) came out in 1994, the existence of computer pornography was not known.

[15] The US Child Pornography Prevention Act 1996 (18 USC s.2256) follows from the UK legislation to criminalise computer-generated images. This law has been successfully challenged as violating the First Amendment by, in effect, creating a 'thought crime', outlawing sexual fantasies about minors: *Free Speech Coalition v Reno* (1999) 198 F. 3d 1083. See further chap. 9.

[16] Reidenberg, J.R., 'Governing Networks and Cyberspace Rule-Making' (1996) 45 *Emory Law Journal* 911.

[17] Gibbons, T., 'Computer Generated Pornography' 9 *International Yearbook of Law Computers and Technology* 83, at p.87.

7(4) of the 1978 Act was extended to include photographs in electronic data format following the amendments made by section 84(4) of the Criminal Justice and Public Order Act 1994 ('CJPOA 1994'). As mentioned previously, the CJPOA 1994 also introduced the concept of 'pseudo-photographs' of children.

Therefore, it is now an offence under section 1 of the 1978 Act 'for a person to take, or permit to be taken or to make, any indecent photographs or pseudo-photographs of a child; [or] to distribute or show such indecent photographs or pseudo-photographs'. Under section 6(1) of the 1978 Act, a person may be punishable either on conviction on indictment or on summary conviction with a term of not more than three years, or to a fine or to both on indictment and for a term not exceeding six months or to a fine or to both for a summary conviction.

Further, under section 160 of the Criminal Justice Act 1988, as amended by section 84(4) of the CJPOA 1994, it is an offence for a person to have an indecent photograph or pseudo-photograph of a child in his possession. This offence is now a serious arrestable offence with a maximum imprisonment term not exceeding six months. To have a defence,[18] the defendant will have to prove under section 160(2):

(a) that he had a legitimate reason for having the photograph or pseudo-photograph in his possession; or
(b) that he had not himself seen the photograph or pseudo-photograph and did not know, nor had any cause to suspect, it to be indecent; or
(c) that the photograph or pseudo-photograph was sent to him without prior request made by him or on his behalf and that he did not keep it for an unreasonable time.

The foregoing legislation has been successfully used in many cases involving the possession and distribution of child pornography ever since they were amended to take into account the technological developments. According to official figures, a total of 238 prosecutions were commenced between 1994 and 1996 for possession of child pornography (including pseudo-photographs) in England and Wales plus a total of 173 prosecutions for taking, making, distributing, showing, possessing with intent to distribute or show, or publishing any advertisement conveying the distribution of indecent photographs or pseudo-photographs of children in the same period.[19] The figures went up to 265 for possession related offences within the period between 1996 and 1998, and 254 for the more serious

---

[18] See the decision of the Court of Appeals in the cases of *Atkins v Director of Public Prosecutions* and *Goodland v Director of Public Prosecutions* [2000] 1 WLR 1427 in relation to this issue.
[19] The above figures are taken from an announcement by the Home Office under House of Commos Written Answers on Child Pornography, 15 July 1998, column 191. Later figures are not available. See, further, Akdeniz, Y., *Sex on the Net? The Dilemma of Policing Cyberspace* (Reading: South Street Press, 1999).

offences of taking and making for the same period.[20] However, it is not possible to say how many of these prosecutions involved child pornography obtained through the Internet or child pornography possessed or distributed in data format. But still the figures show a considerable rate of prosecutions. Therefore, the following cases will offer examples of how such cases are dealt with and interpreted under the UK laws.

Possession offences

As a result of Operation Starburst, many cases of simple possession offences were brought to courts in England and Wales. *Christopher Sharp* was the first person to be prosecuted in a case involving the Internet and he was fined £9,000.[21] Sharp admitted two charges of possessing indecent photographs of children under the age of 16 contrary to section 160 of the Criminal Justice Act 1988. In early 1996, *Martin Crumpton*, was sentenced to three months' imprisonment in a Birmingham magistrates' court.[22] He also admitted possession of indecent pictures of children and was the first person to be jailed in the UK for an offence concerning child pornography and the Internet.

John Payne, 48, a GP in Warminster, Wiltshire, admitted four counts of possessing images of children in indecent poses stored on his home computer in November 1996[23] at West Wiltshire Magistrates' Court, Trowbridge. Dr Payne was sentenced to 120 hours' community service in December 1996. Charles Goodbody, defending, stated that, 'Payne wasn't the photographer. He was not inciting the actions. He was an innocent witness of material he should not have seen.'[24]

Graham Warren, 34, a statistician, at Newcastle University admitted 10 specimen charges of possessing indecent photographs of children in November 1996. Mark Saunders, defending, said 'Warren was certainly not involved in distributing this material and did not pass it on to anyone else.' Warren was fined £1,000 and also ordered to pay £300 costs in November 1996 by the Newcastle upon Tyne magistrates.[25]

The most publicised case of all was that of *Paul Gadd* (better known as Gary Glitter), who was sentenced to four months' imprisonment following conviction for a possession offence in November 1999.[26] The crime was reportedly detected when the defendant's personal computer was taken for repair to a retailer who alerted the police.

---

[20] House of Commons, Hansard, Written Answers (8 December 1999, pt. 1) Home Department, Child Pornography Prosecutions.
[21] Bunyan, N., 'Man fined £9,000 for Internet porn', *Daily Telegraph*, 27 October 1995.
[22] 'Man jailed over child pornography on Internet', *Daily Telegraph*, 5 January 1996.
[23] Reid, T., 'Doctor got child porn on Internet', *Daily Telegraph*, 11 November 1996.
[24] O'Neill, S., 'GP stored child porn on home computer', *Daily Telegraph*, 7 December 1996.
[25] Stokes, P., 'Man is fined £1,000 over child porn from Internet', *Daily Telegraph*, 27 November 1996.
[26] (1999) *The Times*, 13 November p.1.

So, the above examples show that the application of the 1978 Act in relation to possession offences is straightforward, and in most cases the defendants plead guilty.

Distribution offences

Distribution offences are more serious offences, and the above-mentioned statistics prove that the issue has been taken seriously by the law enforcement agencies.[27]

Arnold and Fellows,[28] the Birmingham University case, is the most famous case and first of its kind. It also pre-dates the amendments made by the CJPOA 1994. Arnold and Fellows were charged with a total of 18 charges, under the Protection of Children Act 1978, and the Obscene Publications Act 1959 following a referral from Jefferson County Police, in Kentucky USA via US Customs[29] who had identified a server of child pornography at Birmingham University. Fellows had built up an extensive library of explicit pornography called 'The Archive', featuring children as young as three, on a computer at Birmingham University where he worked. The material could be accessed through the Internet across the world. After the ruling of the trial judge that computerised images could be legally regarded as photographs, Fellows admitted four charges of possessing indecent photographs of children with a view to distributing them, and one of possessing obscene photographs of adults for publication. Arnold also admitted distributing indecent photographs of children. Fellows was jailed for three years, and Arnold for six months for providing Fellows with up to 30 pornographic pictures of children. Owen J. stated:

> The pictures could fuel the fantasies of those with perverted attitudes towards the young and they might incite sexual abuse on innocent children.

On appeal, Evans LJ upheld the ruling of the trial judge that images stored on computer disc constitute photographs.[30] His Lordship reviewed the terms of the 1978 Act and decided that although the computer disk was not a photograph, it was 'a copy of an indecent photograph'.

Simon Jackson, a computer consultant of Andover was jailed for four months at Swindon Crown Court for sending indecent photographs of young children on the Internet in September 1996. Jackson admitted two counts of distributing indecent photographs or pseudo-photographs of children under the age of 16. He also admitted to one count of possession with intent to distribute indecent photographs of young children and one

---

[27] In addition to the 1978 Act, prosecutions have been brought under the Customs Consolidation Act 1876 s.42: *R v Forbes* (2000) *The Times*, 4 April.

[28] *R v Fellows; R v Arnold* [1997] 1 Cr.App.R. 244. See Manchester, C., 'More About Computer Pornography' [1995] *Criminal Law Review* 645.

[29] See Davis, D., *The Internet Detective – An Investigator's Guide* (Police Research Group, Home Office, 1998), Appendix D.

[30] See *R v Fellows; R v Arnold* [1997] 1 Cr.App.R. 244.

count of indecent assault on a child. The evidence obtained from Jackson's computer revealed that the age of the children in the photographs ranged from eight to 12, with some possibly younger. Assistant Recorder Simon Privett told Jackson:

> Every picture of a child of that age is an abuse of that child. The possession and exchange of these photographs fuels the appetite so offences of this nature are practised. It is a pernicious exchange and by distributing the photographs you spread the evil around the world.

Father Adrian McLeish, a Roman Catholic priest, at St Joseph's church in Gilesgate, Durham was sentenced for six years by Newcastle upon Tyne Crown Court in November 1996. Durham Police mounted 'Operation Modem' after they received information from their counterparts in Germany.[31] McLeish had two hard disks which he referred to as his 'nice disk' and his 'naughty disk'. McLeish admitted 12 specimen charges of indecent assaults against two boys of 10, one aged 12 and another aged 18. He also admitted distributing indecent photographs, possessing them with intent to distribute them and being involved in the importation of pornographic videos of children. Mr Justice Moses told McLeish:

> You corrupted those children and damaged them emotionally. You, and other paedophiles like you, dangerously delude yourselves if you think there is one iota of care, affection or even thought for those children. There is none.[32]

The police discovered that McLeish was linked to the Internet through at least four different companies and used encryption software.[33] However, McLeish's use of encryption was not a problem for the Durham police as McLeish handed over his encryption keys together with his private passphrase – 'Overhead the moon is beaming'.

Graham Fitchie, of Merstham, Surrey had 10,751 pictures, 81 films and more than 500 pages of stories about child sex stored on computer hard disks and CD drives. Fitchie pleaded guilty to sending obscene images and films via the Internet, and to indecently assaulting the 11-year-old boy in the original film. He was jailed for three years in July 1997.[34]

Making offences

Perhaps the most problematic application of the Protection of Children Act 1978 has been in relation to 'making' offences. It was recently held by the Court of Appeal in the *R v Bowden*[35] case that the downloading and/or printing out of computer data of indecent images of children from the

---

[31] Stokes, P., 'Six years for priest who broadcast abuse of boys to Internet paedophiles', *Daily Telegraph*, 13 November 1996.

[32] Wilkinson, P. and Gledhill, R., 'Paedophile priest circulated porn on the Internet', *The Times*, 13 November 1996.

[33] See further chap. 14.

[34] Fleet, M., 'Pornographer is trapped by paedophile', *Daily Telegraph*, 26 July 1997.

[35] *R v Bowden* [2000] 2 All ER 418.

Internet was capable of amounting to a 'making' offence within the meaning of section 1(1)(a) Protection of Children Act 1978.

Jonathan Bowden, a school teacher, had downloaded photographs containing indecent images of young boys from the Internet and either printed them out or stored them on computer discs, for his own personal use. During the police investigation of his computer, Bowden did not contest that all the photographs were indecent and involved children under the age of 16. He admitted that he had printed out some of the photographs that he had downloaded from the World Wide Web pages on the Internet. Bowden was charged with 12 counts of having 'made an indecent photograph' contrary to section 1(1)(a) Protection of Children Act 1978, and nine other offences of possession in the Cambridge Crown Court. Initially, Bowden pleaded not guilty to the making offences under the 1978 Act but changed his plea after a ruling from the judge that his behaviour had amounted to taking or making an indecent photograph and he was not merely in possession of them. Bowden was sentenced to four months' imprisonment for the offences involving 'making an indecent photograph' and three months' concurrent for the possession of indecent photograph offences. Bowden appealed on the ground that he possessed the images but did not make them under the 1978 Act.

The Court of Appeal on 10 November 1999 held that section 1 of the 1978 Act remains clear and unambiguous in its true construction. Lord Justice Otton stated that the 1978 Act rendered unlawful the making of a photograph or a pseudo-photograph. The words 'to make' had to be given their natural and ordinary meaning. In this context it is: 'to cause to exist; to produce by action, to bring about' (*Oxford English Dictionary*). According to the Court of Appeal, such a meaning applies as a matter of construction, not only to original photographs but also to negatives, copies of photographs and data stored on computer disk by virtue of section 7 of the 1978. The Court of Appeal preferred a submission made on behalf of the Crown that:[36]

> ... a person who either downloaded images on to disc or who printed them is making them. The Act is not only concerned with the original creation of images, but also their proliferation. . . . To download or print the images within the jurisdiction was to create new material.

The Court of Appeal concluded that:[37]

> ... despite the fact that he made the photographs and the pseudo-photographs for his 'own use', his conduct is clearly caught by the Act. The judge's ruling was correct ... the convictions must stand and we dismiss the appeal.

---

[36] Ibid. at p.423.

[37] Ibid. at p.424. However, a conditional discharge of 12 months for all counts was substituted because the appellant was of good character and there was no breach of trust nor any evidence of risk to the public.

But the case illustrates the fact that the 'making approach' adopted by the Court of Appeal remains problematic. This is due to the fact that Bowden did not 'create' the images himself, and his actions resulted in 'copying' existing images from the Internet. Therefore, it is very questionable whether Bowden should be regarded as the original creator of the images or even a child abuser. According to the Court of Appeal, he was certainly of good character and he did not cause any 'risk to the public'.

It is also very doubtful whether it was the intention of the Parliament to regard 'downloading' or 'copying' from the Internet as a 'making' offence rather than a simple possession (or, where appropriate, distribution) offence. However, these arguments were rejected by the Court of Appeal in the *Bowden* case. It was certainly the intention of the Parliament to create a new offence of 'making' in relation to pseudo-photographs during the passage of the Criminal Justice and Public Order Act 1994 through Parliament:[38]

> It simply provides that a pseudo-photograph is an image, whether *made* [emphasis added] by computer graphics or by any other means of technology that *make it* [emphasis added] appear to be a photograph.[39]

The original version of the 1978 Act only included the verb 'take' and only with the amendments provided by section 84 of the Criminal Justice and Public Order Act 1994 was the verb 'to make' added to the section 1 offence. However, the Court of Appeal in the *Bowden* case thought that there was no 'necessity to refer to Parliamentary material for assistance in interpretation' of the legislation in question.

The same approach was adopted in the cases of *Atkins v Director of Public Prosecutions* and *Goodland v Director of Public Prosecutions*,[40] in which the Court of Appeals stated that *R v Bowden* was rightly decided and that 'making' photographs included copying, provided it was done with knowledge. So, for example, there was no 'making' involved in images stored in computer caches according to the Court. A further interesting point was in relation to the issue of whether two photographs sellotaped together constituted a pseudo-photograph. The Court concluded that, 'were this item to have been photocopied it could have constituted a pseudo-photograph'.

The whole issue of 'making' child pornography remains obscure in the light of these recent cases and judgments.

Law enforcement and child pornography

The previous section showed that the legal system is capable of dealing with the problem of child pornography on the Internet at a national level as far as those who perpetrate child pornography-related offences are within the

---

[38] See generally House of Commons, Standing Committee B, Criminal Justice and Public Order Bill (1993–4, vol. II, Sixteenth Sitting, 15 February 1994, at cols 741–2).
[39] Ibid. at col. 733, *per* Mr David Maclean.
[40] [2000] 1 WLR 1427.

jurisdiction. However, the global nature of the Internet and the technical development of the computer networks have presented law enforcement bodies with new challenges.[41] How are the police to deal effectively with the distribution of child pornography in these new conditions?

The main problem for law enforcement agencies is the transnational nature of these crimes. Policing activity normally takes place within the borders of a nation state. Even at a national level, traditional policing activity is localised. Within the UK, the National Criminal Intelligence Service ('NCIS') was established in April 1992 to produce intelligence on serious and organised crime and criminals nationally. NCIS has a Paedophile Intelligence Section whose main function is to maintain a database of intelligence relating to known or suspected paedophiles, and to develop intelligence and pass it to operational teams for action.[42] By the end of 1996, NCIS held over 25,000 names of those suspected or convicted of paedophile-related offences in its databases.[43] Therefore, NCIS has been active in gathering information on paedophile rings and has also been successful in bringing into light such crimes, as have some other police forces in local jurisdictions. However, the Paedophile Intelligence Section of NCIS has noted a dramatic increase in the use of the Internet as a medium for transmitting child pornography, according to its 1996–7 Annual Report.[44]

Secondly, the understanding of the computer technology and global communications networks remains a problem for the law enforcement bodies. The police forces within the UK (and elsewhere in Europe) are in a learning process, and the sources and manpower to deal with such crimes remain limited. For example, the UK police were said to know 'nothing about the Internet or the strange world they were about to encounter'[45] during *Operation First-Out* in April 1994, which involved the above-mentioned *Arnold and Fellows* prosecutions. At the time there was no competent police officer to examine the UNIX computer machine confiscated by the police, and the enquiry was possible thanks to help provided by the US Customs officers. This 'enormous step into the unknown'[46] still remains unknown territory to many police officers with a few having computer crime specialists or cybercops. According to Davis:[47]

> Failure to fully embrace the technology will result in the Police being left behind and missing out on the most effective and dynamic communications system since the invention of the telephone.

---

[41] See further chap. 7.
[42] See http://www.ncis.co.uk/pa.html, 2000.
[43] NCIS, *Annual Report for 1996–7* (London, 1997).
[44] Ibid.
[45] See Davis, D., *The Internet Detective – An Investigator's Guide* (Police Research Group, Home Office, 1998), Appendix D.
[46] Ibid. at p.117.
[47] Ibid. at p.15.

Apart from the NCIS Paedophile Intelligence Section, three police forces have units dedicated to the investigation of obscene publications within the UK: the Metropolitan Police Service, Greater Manchester police and West Midlands police.[48] These do deal with Internet crime in collaboration with NCIS.

Trans-border law enforcement operations into child pornography

It is suggested that the following UK police operations will show that co-operation between local, national and foreign police forces is by far the most important element for dealing with child pornography transmitted via the Internet.

In July 1995, the British police were involved in *Operation Starburst*, an international investigation of a paedophile ring who used the Internet to distribute graphic pictures of child pornography. The paedophile section of NCIS assisted the West Midlands Police in ensuring the successful conclusion of *Operation Starburst* between May and July 1995.[49] Nine British men were arrested as a result of the operation which involved other arrests in Europe, America, South Africa and the Far East. The operation identified 37 men worldwide.

In September 1998, about 100 people in 12 countries were arrested in what the UK police claims to be the biggest-ever world wide swoop on paedophiles operating over the Internet.[50] British police co-ordinated the raids, code-named *Operation Cathedral*, in Europe, Australia and the United States. The police recovered more than 100,000 indecent images of children as young as two from one US-based paedophile club known as 'Wonderland'.[51] US Customs officials tipped off police in Sussex, England, who raided the house of one of the members. Analysis of his computer system revealed the existence of the far larger and more sophisticated Wonderland club.[52] According to the police, 11 people were arrested in Britain across the country. Seven men in Britain were charged in November 1998 with conspiracy to distribute indecent images of children in Hastings, East Sussex.[53]

More recently, *Operation Queensland*, was conducted by the Greater Manchester Police's Obscene Publications Unit and involved 20 forces across

[48] See HC Debs, vol. 318 col. 388wa, 2 November 1998, Paul Boateng.
[49] NCIS, *Annual Report for 1995–6* (London, 1996), p.16. See, further, Akdeniz, Yaman, 'The Regulation of Pornography and Child Pornography on the Internet' 1997 (1) *The Journal of Information, Law and Technology*.
[50] Lusher, A., 'Child sex victims' faces to be revealed', *Daily Telegraph*, 2 November 1998.
[51] Wonderland's name stemmed from *Alice in Wonderland* author Lewis Carroll's reputed penchant for photographing young girls. See Reuters, 'Police crack down on Net child porn', 2 September 1998; Livraghi, G., 'Alice nel paese delle ipocrisie', (Alice in the country of hypocrisies), *Gandalf*, 5 September 1998.
[52] See Allbritton, C. and McShane, L., 'Suicide only option for some charged in online kiddie porn roundup', Associated Press, 8 November 1998, at http://www.nandotimes.com.
[53] *Guardian*, Home News section, 19 November 1998, p.4. Four of the WOnderland suspects killed themselves within the USA: Allbritton, C. and McShane, L., 'Suicide only option for some charged in online kiddie porn roundup', Associated Press, 8 November 1998.

the UK following a six-month investigation.[54] Warrants were executed at 27 addresses by the combined task force and the vast majority of suspects targeted in the operation were said to be previously unknown to police or the social services.[55]

Improvement in law enforcement techniques

The involvement of the UK law enforcement bodies and police forces in dealing with such operations has helped them to develop their investigative techniques. Although it is so far claimed that the Internet involves high-tech crimes and therefore the competency of the police is often questioned, the examination of the above-mentioned UK cases and policing operations suggests otherwise.

The police have been active in combating these so called high-tech crimes, and even though there are no specific police units focused on Internet-related criminal matters,[56] traditional forms of policing methods have been successful in dealing with child pornography offences. For example, in the *Graham Fitchie* case, it was an informant, namely a paedophile serving a six-year jail sentence who led police to another offender who appeared to be the respectable employee of a school publishing company. The police who searched Fitchie's home and discovered one of the largest digital child pornography collections found in England and Wales.[57] Fitchie's computer records were also used to trace other paedophiles around the world. In the Belfast case of *Morris*,[58] the police raided Morris's home, after a disk he left behind at a Belfast Internet café was found to contain child pornography. The police found images of child pornography on computer disks and also on Morris's computer's hard disk. Next, it was a burglary that prompted the police investigation into *Father McLeish* after the thieves tipped off the police about McLeish's illegal activities.

Therefore, law enforcement has secured significant achievements within the UK and elsewhere by a mixture of traditional policing activities, traditional policing activities applied to the Internet-related crimes and also

---

[54] BBC News, 'Police swoop on computer porn suspects', 9 December 1999, at http://news2.thls.bbc.co.uk/hi/english/uk/newsid%5F556000/556626.stm. The forces which took part in the operation were Cleveland, Devon and Cornwall, Durham, Essex, Gloucestershire, Greater Manchester, Gwent, Hertfordshire, Kent, Lothian and Borders, Merseyside, Metropolitan Police, Norfolk, Northamptonshire, Northern, Northumbria, South Wales, Surrey, West Midlands and West Yorkshire.

[55] Ibid.

[56] NCIS called for a dedicated national taskforce to be set up to target cybercrimes: *Project Trawler: Crime on the Information Highways* (http://www.ncis.co.uk/, 1999). Funding of £25m was committed for a Government Technical Assistance Centre in March 2000; see chap. 14 for details.

[57] Fleet, M., 'Pornographer is trapped by paedophile', *Daily Telegraph*, 26 July 1997.

[58] *Peter James Morris*, 28, was fined £4,000 for possession of child pornography in July 1997 in Belfast, Northern Ireland. Resident Magistrate Chris Milner at the Antrim Magistrates Court said that the 'spread of pornography on the Internet is a matter of public concern' and anyone found with illegal photos of children will be hit with severe penalties. 'Cyber-Porn Rap: Internet man fined £4,000 for indecent photos', *Belfast Telegraph*, 26 July 1997.

new techniques. Within the UK, a book, *Internet Detective: An Investigator's Guide*,[59] that explains the Internet to police officers has been compiled by Detective Inspector David Davis of the West Midlands police. The Home Office, which commissioned Inspector Davis's research, has produced 2,000 copies for distribution among police forces in the UK.[60]

Cooperation with the Internet industry

Concerns about the availability of child pornography over the Internet and pressures on the Internet service providers ('ISPs') was first marked in public in the UK in the summer of 1996. The initial warning to ISPs providing services within the UK came from the then Science and Technology Minister, Ian Taylor, in August 1996, following the Metropolitan Police's attempt to ban around 130 Usenet discussion groups allegedly carrying child pornography.[61] At that time both Mr Taylor and the Metropolitan Police made it clear that the police would prosecute ISPs who provided their users with illegal content.

Following the Metropolitan Police warning, self-regulation of the Internet industry rather than government regulation was seen as the best way forward. The result was the establishment of the Internet Watch Foundation ('IWF') in September 1996 (initially known as the Safety-Net),[62] while the Internet industry produced the 'Rating, Reporting, Responsibility, For Child Pornography & Illegal Material on the Internet'[63] proposals. The Safety-Net scheme stated that the UK ISPs should be responsible for their services and should implement reasonable, practicable and proportionate measures to hinder the use of the Internet for illegal purposes, and to provide a response mechanism in cases where illegal material or activity is identified.[64]

The IWF follows a similar initiative in Holland although there are differences between the two hotline systems.[65] The IWF is a predominantly industry-based organisation, albeit one which is supported by the UK Government, the Home Office, the DTI and the UK police. The IWF launched its

---

[59] See Davis, D., *The Internet Detective – An Investigator's Guide* (Police Research Group, Home Office, 1998), Appendix D.

[60] There are no plans to make the book more widely available (Campbell, D., 'On the bit beat: PCs are getting to know their PCs', *Guardian*, Online Section, 9 July 1998).

[61] See Uhlig, R., 'Minister's warning over Internet porn', *Daily Telegraph*, 18 August. See also the *DTI Press Release* P/96/636 – 'Ian Taylor Challenges Internet Service Providers: Develop New Software to Come Clean' 14 August 1996. See, further, Akdeniz, Y., 'The Regulation of Pornography and Child Pornography on the Internet' (1997) *The Journal of Information, Law and Technology* (1) at http://elj.warwick.ac.uk/jilt/internet/97_1akdz/default.htm.

[62] See http://www.internetwatch.org.uk.

[63] See DTI, 'Rating, Reporting, Responsibility, For Child Pornography & Illegal Material on the Internet', September 1996, at http://dtiinfo1.dti.gov.uk/safety-net/r3.htm.

[64] See Safety-Net proposal, 'Rating, Reporting, Responsibility, For Child Pornography & Illegal Material on the Internet' adopted and recommended by the Executive Committee of ISPA – Internet Services Providers Association, LINX – London Internet Exchange and The Safety-Net Foundation at http://dtiinfo1.dti.gov.uk/safety-net/r3.htm.

[65] The Dutch hotline was established by the Dutch Foundation for Internet Providers ('NLIP'), Dutch Internet users, the National Criminal Intelligence Service ('CRI'), National Bureau

hotline for reporting illegal material on the Internet in December 1996. The IWF has an e-mail, telephone and fax hotline so that users can report materials related to child pornography and other obscene materials.[66] The IWF undertakes to inform all British ISPs once they locate illegal content such as child pornography. The ISPs concerned then have no excuse in law that they are unaware of the offending material, and the UK police will be entitled to take action against any ISP which does not remove the relevant content requested from the IWF.[67]

The activities of the IWF have mainly concentrated on Usenet discussion groups so far, even though Internet content does not only generate through this system. It is certainly tempting to identify and try to block particular newsgroups, websites or other Internet forums that seem devoted to illegal material, but such measures set dangerous precedents. It is wrong to make ISPs solely responsible for content provided by third parties on the Internet. It establishes an act of privatised censorship that could come to be applied too broadly over time, and could change the role of Internet service providers. The law enforcers should instead concentrate their efforts on the posters to the Usenet discussion groups and not on the carriers (the ISPs). Prosecuting the ISPs would have a chilling effect on the development of the Internet within the UK, and prosecuting an ISP will not reduce the real-life problem of child abuse.[68]

However, *Net Benefit: the electronic commerce agenda for the UK*,[69] a document launched by the Department of Trade and Industry in October 1998, implies otherwise:[70]

---

against Racial Discrimination and a psychologist. See
http://www.xs4all.nl/~meldpunt/meldpunt-eng.htm.

[66] See http://www.internetwatch.org.uk/hotline/.

[67] See Safety-Net proposal, 'Rating, Reporting, Responsibility, For Child Pornography & Illegal Material on the Internet' adopted and recommended by the Executive Committee of ISPA Internet Services Providers Association, LINX London Internet Exchange and The Safety-Net Foundation at http://dtiinfo1.dti.gov.uk/safety-net/r3.htm.

[68] Felix Somm, the general manager for CompuServe in Germany was found guilty of having assisted in the dissemination of pornographic writings in thirteen legally coinciding cases (mainly child pornography and other Internet content deemed as illegal within Germany), committed jointly, factually coinciding with a negligent violation of the German Dissemination of Publications Morally Harmful to Youth Act in three legally coinciding cases. Somm received a two-year suspended sentence and a fine of DM100,000 from the Munich district court in May 1998. See the Criminal case of Somm, Felix Bruno, File No: 8340 Ds 465 Js 173158/95, Local Court (Amtsgericht) Munich. An English version of the case is available at http://www.cyber-rights.org/isps/somm-dec.htm. The conviction was reversed on appeal in November 1999. (*CompuServe Ex-Official's Porn Case Conviction Reversed*, *Associated Press*, 17 November 1999.) Compare the CompuServe case with the US case of *Doe v America Online, Inc.*, 25 Media L. Rep. (BNA) 2112, 1997 WL 374223 (Fla. Cir. Ct. June 26, 1997); Case No. 97-2587 (Fourth District Court of Appeal, Fla, October 14, 1998). See also *Zeran v AOL*, 129 F. 2d 327 (4th Cir., 1997) cert. denied, 524 US 937 (1998).

[69] DTI, *Net Benefit: The Electronic Commerce Agenda for the UK* (DTI/Pub 3619, London, October 1998). See also Speech by Mrs Barbara Roche MP at the OECD Electronic Commerce Ministerial Meeting, Ottawa: 9 October 1998, at http://www.dti.gov.uk/Minspeech/roche.htm.

[70] Ibid. p.20.

Primary responsibility for illegal material on the Internet would clearly lie with the individual or entity posting it. Under UK law, however, an Internet service provider (ISP) which has been made aware of the illegal material (or activity) and has failed to take reasonable steps to remove the material could also be liable to prosecution as an accessory to a crime.

A similar point was made by the Parliamentary Under-Secretary of State for the Home Department, Kate Hoey:[71]

> In general, Internet service providers in the UK are not required to vet the material which their customers store and transmit. They do however acquire responsibilities once they become aware of material which is illegal. Should they not remove child pornography from their servers once they are made aware of it, they could be prosecuted under the Protection of Children Act 1978 for the dissemination of such material. In general, UK Internet service providers are diligent in removing illegal material once they are made aware of it and in cooperating with law enforcement when investigations into crime are under way.

Furthermore, *Net Benefit* claims that 'clarification of the liability of ISPs has been addressed by collaboration among UK industry, Government and the police' and that:[72]

> Compliance with this code of practice (essentially the removal of material from their UK servers following IWF notification) would likely be taken in court as evidence of the ISP having made reasonable efforts to comply with the law.

These are strong words, but in reality the industry regulators that are mentioned (the IWF and also the Internet Service Providers Association) do not represent the whole of the ISP industry within the UK. While the Internet Magazine suggests that there are more than 300 UK-based ISPs,[73] the ISPA has 85 members. There is no unique body representing the interests of the Internet industry at a national level within the UK and reliance on its code of practice and the IWF scheme do not necessarily clarify ISP liability at a national level.

The issue of ISP liability will be resolved at the European Union level with an EU Directive on certain legal aspects of electronic commerce in the internal market which was adopted in May 2000.[74] The Directive on Certain Legal Aspects of Electronic Commerce in the Internal Market[75] which

---

[71] See House of Commons European Scrutiny Committee, *Child Pornography on the Internet* (1998–9 HC 34-ii), para. 12.3. See, further, Leong, G., 'Computer Child Pornography – The Liability of Distributors?' in Walker, C. (ed.), *Crime, Criminal Justice and the Internet* (special edition, *Criminal Law Review*, Sweet & Maxwell, London, 1998).

[72] Ibid.

[73] *Internet Magazine*, December 1998.

[74] See European Commission, *Proposal for a European Parliament and Council Directive on certain legal aspects of electronic commerce in the internal market* (COM(1998) 586 final, Brussels, 18 November 1998, as amended by COM(1999) 427 final, Brussels, 1999); Press Release, 'Electronic Commerce: Commission welcomes final adoption of legal framework Directive', (IP/00/442, Brussels, 4 May 2000).

[75] See European Commission, *Proposal for a European Parliament and Council Directive on certain legal aspects of electronic commerce in the internal market* (COM(1998) 586 final,

was drafted by the European Commission (through DGXV) in November 1998 would ensure that information society services benefit from the Single Market principles of free movement of services and freedom of establishment provided they comply with the law in their country of origin. The proposed Directive covers a wide range of issues including the establishment of the definition of where operators are established, electronic contracts, liability of intermediaries, dispute settlement and role of national authorities.[76] However, the EU Directive (by article 14) favours an 'actual knowledge' test for removal of third-party content from ISP servers. So, the EU Directive would limit liability, though 'notice and takedown' provisions may lead into complex legislation and procedures. The 'notice and takedown' procedures have already proved to be problematic as far as the defamatory content on the Internet is concerned.[77]

Conclusion

Criminal law is traditionally associated with nation states, and policing is a core activity of nation states. This chapter has shown that the problem of child pornography has been so far dealt with adequately by the law enforcement bodies within the UK, though the agencies are troubled by the borderless nature of the Internet. Therefore, as far as the global dimension of the problem is concerned, cooperation at an international level is essential to deal with Internet-related criminal activity. According to the Austrian Presidency of the European Union in December 1998, 'child pornography on the Internet [is] recognised as a global problem requiring a coordinated approach also at international level, especially at the United Nations'[78] and so even beyond the scope of the European Union. A Draft Joint Action to combat Child Pornography on the Internet, under the initiative of the Austrian government,[79] is also under development by the European Union and is supported by the UK government.[80] The Parliamentary Under-Secretary of State for the Home Department, Kate Hoey, commented that:[81]

98/0325 (COD), Brussels, 18 November 1998, as amended by COM(1999) 427 final, Brussels, 1999).
[76] See generally
http://www.ispo.cec.be/ecommerce/legal/documents/com1999-42//com427en.pdf.
[77] See further chap. 13 and the Defamation Act 1996 s.1.
[78] See Presidency Conclusions, Vienna European Council, 11 and 12 December 1998, para. 92 at http://europa.eu.int/council/off/conclu/dec98.htm
[79] Initiative of the Republic of Austria with a view to adopting a Council Decision to combat child pornography on the Internet (1999/C 362/06, C 362/8 Official Journal of the European Communities, Brussels, 16 December 1999).
[80] See House of Commons European Scrutiny Committee, *Child Pornography on the Internet* (1998–9 HC 34-ii). This is a contribution to the implementation of Recommendation 5 of the EU Action Plan to combat organised crime which was endorsed by the Amsterdam European Council in June 1997.
[81] See ibid., para. 12.3.

The Government endorses the need for effective action by Member States to deal with child pornography and broadly supports the provisions of the draft joint Action. The UK has been a leader within the EU in developing measures of the kind . . .

Ms Hoey's comments also directly refer to the setting up of the Internet Watch Foundation and reinforces the fact that 'in respect of child pornography, the law has adequately accommodated technical developments and should enable law enforcement authorities to take necessary measures to combat this activity on computer networks'. Therefore, no change to UK legislation would be needed to meet the provisions of the Joint Action as currently drafted.[82]

The main concern of enforcement authorities and regulators should remain as the prevention of child abuse – the involvement of children in the making of pornography.[83] Conversely, the utility of industry-based hotlines to report illegal activity with the aimed result of removing such content through the servers of local ISPs remains doubtful. Privatised policing organisations do not have the legitimacy to judge the suitability or illegality of Internet content, and there is a serious risk in allowing hotline operators to act as 'self-appointed judges' with an 'encouragement for vigilantism.'[84] According to Nadine Strossen, 'these hotlines violate due process concepts that are also enshrined in international, regional, and national guarantees around the world'.[85]

Therefore, it should not be forgotten that child pornography is not an Internet-specific problem and it remains rather as a problem within society. It should be dealt with accordingly and not specifically in relation to the Internet. The Internet is just another convenient tool for paedophiles who wish to traffic in these kind of materials. But in most cases, child pornography is used as an excuse for further general regulation of the Internet or as an excuse to provide law-enforcement bodies with new general powers for dealing with the Internet.[86] This overreaction must be strongly resisted.

---

[82] See ibid., para. 12.4. See further European Council decision of 29 May 2000 to combat child pornography on the Internet (2000/375/JNA, Official Journal L138/1–4).

[83] See further Akdeniz, Y., 'Governance of Pornography and Child Pornography on the Global Internet: A Multi-Layered Approach', in Edwards, L. and Waelde, C. (eds), *Law and the Internet: Regulating Cyberspace* (Hart Publishing, Oxford, 1997).

[84] 'ACLU Joins International Protest Against Global Internet Censorship Plans', 9 September 1999, at http://www.aclu.org/news/1999/n090999a.html.

[85] Ibid.

[86] See the Regulation of Investigatory Powers Act 2000 and chap. 14.

CHAPTER 11

Hate speech

Barry Steinhardt

Introduction

Speech on the Internet is entitled to the same First Amendment protection available to speech in other mediums

The massive growth of the Internet over the last few years is empowering millions of people to speak their minds freely. Nothing could be more damaging to this communications revolution than the fear of censorship. Although 'hate speech' and other vile utterances can be found in cyberspace, censoring speech in this medium would go against the free, open, anarchic and global nature of the Internet, and severely impede its growth. While the law on cyberspace is still in its infancy, the well-established principles of free speech should apply with even greater force to speech on the Internet. Public networks provide free and easy access to public discourse, and allow everyone to disseminate their views. This is the life blood of a true democracy.

Presently, there is little direct guidance from the United States Supreme Court about the constitutional protection or lack of protection of 'hate speech' on the Internet. Two cases, *Reno v ACLU* ('*Reno*')[1] and *ApolloMedia Corp v Reno* ('*AppolloMedia*'),[2] both challenges to the Communications Decency Act ('CDA'), signed by President Clinton on 8 February 1996 to protect minors from harmful material on the Internet, reflect the Court's generally strong inclination towards unrestricted speech on the Internet.

In the first case, the Supreme Court found that the terms 'indecent' and 'patently offensive' in sections 223(a)(1)(B) and 223(d) of the CDA to be unconstitutionally overbroad, thereby extending First Amendment protection to 'patently offensive' and 'indecent' speech on this medium. In a similar case, *ApolloMedia Corp. v Reno*, the Supreme Court affirmed a lower court ruling which upheld section 223(a)(1)(A) of the CDA that makes it a felony to transmit communications over the Internet that are 'indecent' and made with the intent to 'annoy'. Although this ruling seems

---

[1] *Reno v ACLU* 521 US 844, 138 L. Ed. 2d 874 (1997), *aff'g* 929 F. Supp. 824 (ED Pa. 1996).
[2] *ApolloMedia Corp. v Reno* 19 F. Supp. 2d 1081 (ND Cal. 1998), *affirmed*, 526 US 1061 (1999).

to conflict with that of the earlier case, it was apparent from the opinion that the two-judge majority read the provision carefully so as to avoid complete discord with the ruling in *Reno v ACLU*.

Reno v ACLU and ApolloMedia

Reno v ACLU is a solid indication by the Supreme Court that for the purposes of constitutional protection, it is irrelevant whether speech appears in a printed pamphlet or travels through cyberspace. The same protections should apply with at least equal force to electronic communications including e-mail, list services, mail exploders, newsgroups, chatrooms and the World Wide Web.[3] In fact, the Court's rulings seem to suggest that speech on the Internet is worthy of a high level of protection, since this is a dynamic medium that has experienced phenomenal growth recently, is highly participatory and accessible to people, and is not invasive like certain broadcast mediums. The courts, cognizant also of the current unavailability of technology that would effectively restrict speech on the Internet to protect minors without chilling the free speech of adults, are reluctant to regulate and penalise speech in this medium.

Justice Stevens, who wrote the majority opinion, acknowledged the vast, evolving and diverse nature of the Internet and concluded:[4]

> As a matter of constitutional tradition, in the absence of evidence to the contrary, we presume that governmental regulation of the content of speech is more likely to interfere with the free exchange of ideas than to encourage it. The interest in encouraging freedom of expression in a democratic society outweighs any theoretical but unproven benefit of censorship.

Judge Sloviter of the US District Court wrote that tagging material and allowing readers to screen out unwanted transmissions through verification schemes was not 'technologically or economically feasible'.[5] The Supreme Court too rejected the government's 'tagging' defence, which would have restricted speech, yet through supposed verification schemes would have allowed adults access to certain online discourse. Noting that it is not economically feasible for most non-commercial speakers to employ such verification schemes, the burden on adult free speech remains. The Supreme Court compared the speech restriction to 'burn[ing] the house to roast the pig' and stated '[t]he CDA, casting a far darker shadow over free speech, threatens to torch a large segment of the Internet community'.[6]

US District Court's Judge Dalzell reviewed 'the special attributes of the Internet' and concluded that the Internet, 'the most participatory form of mass speech yet developed', is entitled to 'the highest protection from

---

[3] *Reno* 138 L. Ed. 2d at pp.896–7.
[4] Ibid. at p.906.
[5] *Reno* 929 F. Supp. at p.856.
[6] *Reno* 138 L. Ed. 2d at p.904 (quoting *Sable Communications of Cal., Inc. v FCC* 492 US 115, 127 (1989)).

governmental intrusion'.[7] The District Court compared the Internet to the broadcast medium, noting that the former not 'as invasive', is not a 'scarce' expressive commodity and is 'as diverse as human thought'.[8] The lower federal court concluded and the Supreme Court affirmed that 'our cases provide no basis for qualifying the level of First Amendment scrutiny that should be applied to this medium'.[9]

The Supreme Court rejected several of the government's arguments that the CDA was not overbroad because other channels of communication still existed for free speech. For example, the government suggested that even if the CDA censors speech on chat groups, news groups and mail exploders, the statute was not overbroad because the World Wide Web was still available. The Court analogised this argument to allowing a statute that banned distributing leaflets on certain subjects as long as individuals are free to publish books.[10] Similarly, the government contention that the 'unregulated availability of "indecent" and "patently offensive" material on the Internet is driving countless citizens away from the medium because of the risk of exposing themselves or their children to harmful material' was found to be wholly unpersuasive.[11] To the contrary, the Court concluded that 'the growth of the Internet has been and continues to be phenomenal'.[12] Hence in finding the disputed provisions of the CDA to be overbroad and not narrowly tailored, thereby imposing a great burden on speech, the Supreme Court makes an important indication of its desire to extend constitutional protections of free speech to the Internet with equal or more force.

In *ApolloMedia*, the Supreme Court upheld Section 223(a)(1)(A) of the CDA, which makes it a felony to transmit communications over the Internet that are 'obscene, lewd, lascivious, filthy, or indecent' with intent to 'annoy, abuse, threaten, or harass another person . . .'.[13] The case involved a request from the plaintiff, ApolloMedia, a multimedia technology company, seeking preliminary and permanent injunctive relief, as well as declaratory judgment that the challenged provision violated the First Amendment. ApolloMedia created and maintained an Internet site at 'annoy.com.'[14] The website was used by the company and visitors to express strong views, freely criticize public officials, annoy people and use whatever expression they wish.[15] There were four sections on the website; one called the 'heckle'

---

[7] *Reno* 929 F. Supp. at p.856. Judge Dalzell discusses four factors: 'First the Internet presents very low barriers to entry. Second, these barriers to entry are identical for both speakers and listeners. Third, as a result of these low barriers, astoundingly diverse content is available on the Internet. Fourth, the Internet provides significant access to all who wish to speak in the medium, and even creates a relative parity among speakers.' Ibid. at p.877.

[8] Ibid. at pp.842–4.

[9] *Reno* 138 L. Ed. 2d at p.897.

[10] Ibid. at p.903.

[11] Ibid. at p.906.

[12] Ibid.

[13] *ApolloMedia Corp.* 19 F. Supp. 2d at p.1081.

[14] Ibid. at p.1085.

[15] Ibid.

section contained articles with strong and provocative positions on issues, a second section called 'gibe' was a threaded message board that allowed visitors to read previous messages and add their own. These were not censored by ApolloMedia. A third section called 'censure' allowed people to mail postcards to people to their e-mail addresses. Finally, the CDA (Created and Designed to Annoy) section contained pages of commentary and visuals. ApolloMedia claimed that some of its material of social and political value was sexually explicit, employed vulgar language and might be found by many to be indecent.[16]

ApolloMedia claimed that the challenged CDA provision to the extent it prohibits 'indecent' communications made with an intent to annoy was impermissibly overbroad and vague and thus violated the First Amendment. The plaintiff did not challenge the provision's regulation of 'obscene' speech which is not protected by the First Amendment.[17] But ApolloMedia noted that Congress used the terms 'indecent' to bear a meaning quite distinct from 'obscene' throughout the CDA; since 'indecent' could not imply one thing in other parts of the CDA and quite another in the challenged provision, Congress intended the word to mean something distinct.[18] The majority disagreed with this proposition in light of their interpretation of the legislative history. In their assessment of the legislative history, the majority compared the challenged provision to 18 USC section 1462 and 18 USC section 1465, enacted to add 'interactive computer services' and to criminalise obscene Internet communications. The same 'string of words' in the challenged provision were used here as well. The Court stated that Congress's conference report reflect that the amendments were meant to 'clarify current obscenity statutes'. Since these amendments employed the exact same 'string of words', stated the Court, Congress intended the challenged provision of the CDA to cover obscenity as well. The Court overlooked the plaintiff's argument that the two statutes could not be compared since sections 1462 and 1465 covered 'interactive computer service' and the provision of the CDA covered 'telecommunication devices'.[19]

The dissenting United States District Judge, Susan Illston wrote: '*Reno v ACLU* represents the Supreme Court's direction that in this statute, separate words used in the disjunctive are to be separately considered.' She concluded:[20]

> The present debate over the language of the CDA seems academic until one considers the application of this criminal statute to the Internet, a communication medium being used daily by tens of millions of people in dozens of countries around the world. It is unrealistic to expect these users to know that the words of

---

[16] Ibid. at pp.1085–6.
[17] Ibid. at p.1084. See *Roth v US* 354 US 476 (1957); *Memoirs of a Woman of Pleasure v AG for Massachusetts* 383 US 413 (1966); *Miller v California* 413 US 15 (1973).
[18] Ibid. at p.1093.
[19] Ibid.
[20] Ibid. at p.1099.

this statute do not mean what they say, and that the government has promised not to enforce the statute in accordance with its terms.

The dissent pointed out that, in the lower court's opinion, the majority avoided reading the statute in a way that would render it unconstitutional. It read the string of words 'lewd', 'lascivious', 'filthy' and 'indecent' as synonyms to the word 'obscene'. Hence, by reading this 'string of words' to simply imply obscenity the court found the statute to be constitutionally valid.[21] Had the court read the statute as the plaintiff suggested (i.e. that it prohibits speech that is 'indecent' and with the intent to 'annoy'), it would have been unconstitutional pursuant to *Reno*; merely 'indecent' speech is protected by the Constitution, while 'obscene' speech is not.

Political 'hate speech' and 'fighting words'

Introduction to the fighting words doctrine

Only those words that are directed to inciting or producing imminent lawless action and are likely to incite or produce such action are outside the purview of First Amendment protection. Such utterances, coined as 'fighting words', include words, expressive conduct and symbolic speech like wearing a jacket with the words 'fuck the draft' in a US courthouse, or burning the American flag. Fighting words were first discussed in a 1942 case, *Chaplinsky v New Hampshire*, and are defined as words that inflict injury or tend to incite an immediate breach of the peace.[22] Since then 'fighting words' have been narrowed and redefined, and now apply only in situations where there is a clear and present danger of a violent physical reaction in the audience to such words. Mere advocacy and rhetorical speech is not proscribed. Generally, speech that is directed at racial, ethnic, national or other groups or that may be applied in racial confrontations is still protected under the Constitution. The utterance of derogatory or hateful language uttered against racial groups may be penalised if such verbiage falls within the 'fighting words' exception; otherwise those words would constitute protected speech. There is no group defamation law in the United States.

In contrast the United Kingdom does not have a 'fighting words' doctrine but has enacted specific legislation to cover group defamation and to regulate speech that incites racial hatred. Sections 17 to 28 of the Public Order Act of 1986 (the 'POA') is preceded by several other statutes proscribing group defamation and incitement to racial hatred. Section 17 defines racial hatred as 'hatred against a group of persons defined by reference to colour, race, nationality (including citizenship) or ethnic or national origins'. Section 18 of the 1986 Act provides that it constitutes a criminal offence to use 'threatening, abusive or insulting words or behaviour' of a racially derogatory character. Words, behaviour and display of written material must be

---

[21] Ibid. at p.1097.
[22] *Chaplinsky v New Hampshire* 315 US 568 (1942), at p.572.

likely to stir up racial hatred, and used with the intent to do the same. Section 19 applies this law to publishing and section 23 to possession of racially inflammatory material. Although these laws are enacted to protect racial minorities, as a caveat, the consent of the Attorney General is always needed to bring legal action.[23]

United States fighting words doctrine: Chaplinsky

In 1942, the Supreme Court in *Chaplinsky v New Hampshire* held that fighting words are not protected by the First Amendment. Chaplinsky, a Jehovah's witness, spoke as he stood on a street corner outside the City Hall of Rochester, a town in New Hampshire. Among other statements addressed to plaintiffs, he pronounced: 'You are a damned racketeer' and 'a damned Fascist and the whole government of Rochester are Fascists or agents of Fascists'. He was prosecuted for these statements under a New Hampshire public peace statute.

In upholding the conviction, the Court defined fighting words as 'those which by their very utterance inflict injury or tend to incite an immediate breach of the peace'.[24] The Court stated that such words '[a]re of such slight social value as a step to truth that any benefit that maybe derived from them is clearly outweighed by the social interest in order and morality'.[25]

Since *Chaplinsky*, the Supreme Court has essentially narrowed the category of fighting words to those expressions that constitute a face-to-face incitement to immediate violence as reflected in cases like *Brandenberg v Ohio*,[26] *Cohen v California*[27] and progeny. The *Brandenberg* test is generally considered the most protective standard for free speech ever developed by the Supreme Court.[28] It protects speech unless the fighting words are directed to inciting immediate lawless action and are likely to incite that action. Some commentators call it the modern version of the 'clear and present danger' test.

The 'clear and present danger test' first came about in *Schenck v United States*[29] in an opinion delivered by Justice Holmes. In August 1917 Schenck distributed about 15,000 leaflets proclaiming a capitalist conspiracy, and protesting war proscriptions. Schenck was convicted of violating the Espionage Act. Holmes admitted that his speech may be protected at other times but not at this time. 'The most stringent protection of free speech would not protect a man in falsely shouting fire in a theater and causing a

---

[23] See Wolffe, W.J., 'Values in Conflict' [1987] *Public Law* 85; Jones, T.D., 'Human Rights: Freedom of Expression and Group Defamation Under British, Canadian, Indian, Nigerian, and United States Law – A Comparative Analysis' (1995) 18 *Suffolk Transnational Law Review* 427. For the future impact of the Human Rights Act 1998, see *Jersild v Denmark* App. No. 15890/89, 19 EHRR 1.

[24] Ibid. at p.572.

[25] Ibid.

[26] *Brandenberg v Ohio* 395 US 444 (1969).

[27] *Cohen v California* 403 US 15 (1971).

[28] See Lessig, L., 'The Regulation of Social Meaning' (1995) 62 *University of Chicago Law Review* 944, at pp.1035–6.

[29] *Schenck v United States* 249 US 47 (1919).

panic.'[30] He then coined the 'clear and present danger test' which in turn was based on proximity and degree. He stated: 'The question in every case is whether the words used are used in such circumstances and are of such a nature as to create a clear and present danger that they will bring about the substantive evils that Congress has a right to prevent.'[31] The clear and present danger test has developed since its inception in *Schenck*. A long and confusing line of cases from the 1950s used this test as the Supreme Court's decisions in this decade echoed the communist phobia of the McCarthy era.

In *Brandenberg*, a leader of the white supremacist group, the Ku Klux Klan (KKK), made racially derogatory comments about Blacks and Jews at a rally in Cincinnati and was prosecuted under Ohio's criminal syndicalism statute.[32] The rally, captured on a reporter's film, was filled with racist and incendiary bile. The Klan leader pronounced 'We're not a revengent organization, but if our President, our Congress, our Supreme Court, continues to suppress the White Caucasian race, it's possible that there might have to be some revengence taken.'[33] Ohio's criminal syndicalism statute punished people who '[a]dvocate or teach the duty, necessity, or propriety' of violence as a means of accomplishing industrial or political reform. The Supreme Court overturning this statute held that it 'falls within the condemnation of the First and Fourteenth Amendments'.[34] The Court distinguished between mere advocacy and expression as incitement to imminent lawless action.[35] No one was present at the Klan rally besides Klan members themselves. In these circumstances, the Court said, the Klan was guilty only of the 'abstract teaching' of the 'moral propriety' of racist violence. The Court noted that the guarantees of free speech 'do not permit a State to forbid or proscribe advocacy of the use of force or of law violation except where such advocacy is directed to inciting or producing imminent lawless action and is likely to incite or produce such action'.[36]

The *Brandenberg* test was applied quite literally in *Hess v Indiana*.[37] Anti-Vietnam war demonstrators had blocked the street and were consequently moved to the kerb by police officers. As a police office passed by, Hess, a demonstrator remarked, 'We'll take the fucking street later.'[38] Applying the *Brandenberg* standard, the court held that Hess was not guilty of incitement to immediate lawless action. His words reflected 'present moderation' or advocacy of unlawful action 'at some indefinite future time,' and neither were enough to constitute a direct incitement likely to lead to disorder.[39]

[30] Ibid. at 52.
[31] Ibid.
[32] *Brandenberg* 395 US at pp.444–5.
[33] Ibid. at p.446.
[34] Ibid. at p.449.
[35] Ibid. at p.448.
[36] Ibid. at p.447.
[37] *Hess v Indiana* 414 US 105 (1973).
[38] Ibid. at p.106.
[39] Ibid. at pp.107–8.

Claiborne Hardware further elucidates the Brandenberg standard

Speech does not lose constitutional protection just because it is coercive and effectuates political and social change. In *NAACP v Claiborne Hardware Co.*, a 1982 case, a local NAACP voted to boycott white merchants in the area to protest racial discrimination against blacks.[40] Charles Evers, one of the NAACP leaders, was quoted as warning boycott violators during 1 April 1966, '[i]f we catch any of you going in any of them racist stores, we're gonna break your damn neck'. Evers at this time addressed a group of 8,000 assembled individuals. These statements along with several others were made at a time when blacks in the county were engaged in various political activities aimed at ending racial discrimination; most of these were uniformly peaceful and orderly and involved organised picketing.[41] Some activities involved a process of disciplining where certain black groups like the 'Black Hats' stood outside individual stores and identified those who traded with white merchants.[42] The names of these people were later published in a black newspaper and they were branded as traitors. Various reported incidents or acts of violence targeted against these alleged traitors are reported, varying from throwing bricks at home windows, damaging flowers to firing gunshot at homes.

The Supreme Court held that the speech of the NAACP was entitled to constitutional protection, despite the fact that individuals perpetrated a scattering of non-peaceful activities. The Court emphasised that those non-peaceful activities could be circumscribed and punished for 'conspiracy against the public peace and order' and for other violations of valid law, without impinging important constitutional First Amendment protections.[43] The Court recognised 'the strong governmental interest in certain forms of economic regulation, even though such regulation may have an incidental effect on rights of speech and association'.[44] The impact on the white merchants was one entailing economic loss that requires such regulation. The Court nevertheless held that the boycott was a constitutionally protected activity:[45]

> Through exercise of the First Amendment Rights, petitioners sought to bring about political, social, and economic change. Through speech, assembly and petition – rather than through riot or revolution – petitioners sought to change a social order that had consistently treated them as second class citizens.

The Court also held that Charles Evers's speech did not fall under the 'fighting words' and 'threats' exceptions to constitutional protection of speech. The Court specified that the *Chaplinsky/Brandenberg* standard on

---

[40] *NAACP v Claiborne Hardware Co.* 458 US 886 (1982) at p.889.
[41] Ibid. at p.903.
[42] Ibid.
[43] Ibid. at p.909.
[44] Ibid. at p.912.
[45] Ibid. at pp.912–13.

speech is 'directed to inciting or producing imminent lawless action and is likely to incite or produce such action'.[46] The Court found that Evers's speech was mere advocacy and did not meet the *Brandenberg* standard; '[t]he emotionally charged rhetoric of Charles Evers' speeches did not transcend the bounds of protected speech set forth in *Brandenberg*'.[47] The Court noted that '[s]trong and effective extemporaneous rhetoric can not be nicely channeled in purely dulcet phrases'.[48] The Court's reasoning was also grounded in the fact that violent or non-peaceful incidents did not occur immediately after Evers' rhetorical speech and that there was no evidence that he 'authorized, ratified, or directly threatened' acts of violence.[49]

'Captive audience'

As noted before, cases such as *Cohen v California* and its progeny altered the *Chaplinsky* doctrine of fighting words and its principle of social interest in order and morality. These cases limited the circumstances under which speech could be designated fighting words to 'captive' situations in which the target of the speech has no reasonable means of escape.

For example, in *Cohen*, the defendant wore a jacket in a California courthouse with words 'Fuck the Draft' written on its back.[50] He was convicted under a state 'public peace' statute for his 'offensive conduct'. The Supreme Court did not find this conduct to fall within the *Chaplinsky* 'fighting words' exception to the First Amendment. Quoting *Chaplinsky*, Justice Harlan described 'fighting words' as those which 'when addressed to the ordinary citizen, are . . . likely to provoke violent reaction'.[51] He noted further that the *Chaplinsky* exception did not apply in the present case, 'since no one could reasonably have regarded the words on [Cohen's] jacket as a direct personal insult . . . [nor were the words] thrust upon unwilling or unsuspecting viewers . . .'[52] '[W]hile the particular four-letter word being litigated here is perhaps more distasteful than most others of its genre, it is nevertheless often true that one man's vulgarity is another's lyric.'[53]

In *Gooding v Wilson*,[54] the Supreme Court overturned a conviction in which a defendant said to the policeman, 'You son of a bitch, I'll choke you to death.' In *Lewis v City of New Orleans*,[55] the Supreme Court overturned a similar conviction. Here, the defendant had said to a policeman, 'you goddamn motherfucking police'. In both cases, the court held that the laws used to prosecute the defendants were overbroad. For example, in *Lewis*,

---

[46] Ibid. at p.927.
[47] Ibid. at p.928.
[48] Ibid.
[49] Ibid. at p.929.
[50] *Cohen* 403 US at p.16.
[51] Ibid. at p.20.
[52] Ibid.
[53] Ibid. at p.25.
[54] *Gooding v Wilson* 405 US 518 (1972).
[55] *Lewis v City of New Orleans* 415 US 130 (1974).

the ordinance made it unlawful '[w]antonly to curse or revile or to use obscene or opprobrious language toward or with reference to any member of the city police while in the actual performance of his duty'. The court found that this ordinance plainly has a broader sweep than the constitutional definition of 'fighting words' announced in *Chaplinsky*.[56]

Before *Cohen* restricted the application of the 'fighting words' doctrine, in at least one case a defendant was arrested and convicted for his speech. In *Feiner v New York*,[57] the defendant made a speech to about 75 onlookers. In his speech he referred to President Truman as a 'bum'. He further proclaimed that 'The negroes don't have equal rights; they should rise up in arms and fight for their rights.'[58] In upholding his conviction and the policeman's right to arrest Feiner, Justice Vinson wrote for the Supreme Court that '[h]ere the speaker passes the bounds of argument or persuasion and undertakes incitement to riot. . . .'[59] Such a conviction would not stand today.

Expressive conduct constitutes speech and is protected

In *Texas v Johnson*,[60] a 1984 case, Johnson was one of about 100 participants in a political demonstration to protest the policies of the Reagan government. Johnson doused an American flag and burned it at the end of the demonstration, and was consequently charged under a Texas criminal statute. The court found that Johnson's expressive conduct did not constitute 'fighting words' and quoting *Chaplinsky*, stated that it was not 'likely to provoke the average person to retaliation, and thereby [causing] a breach of peace'.[61] In dicta, the Court noted that restriction on Johnson's expression was 'content-based'. Hence, Texas's asserted interest in prosecuting Johnson, claiming that the flag's special symbolic character must be preserved, is subjected to the 'the most exacting scrutiny'.[62]

Group libel is not a viable doctrine

Introduction: there are no group defamation statutes in the United States

Statutes in the United Kingdom like the Race Relations Act of 1965 and the Public Order Act of 1986, which regulate group defamation and speech that incites racial hatred, would not pass constitutional muster in the United States. There is no equivalent group libel statute or common law doctrine in the United States. Group libel doctrine was discussed in an earlier Supreme

---

[56] Ibid. at p.132.
[57] *Feiner v New York* 340 US 315 (1951).
[58] Ibid. at p.330.
[59] Ibid. at p.321.
[60] *Texas v Johnson* 491 US 397 (1989).
[61] Ibid. at p.409 (quoting *Chaplinsky*, 315 US at p.574).
[62] Ibid. at p.412 (quoting *Boos v Barry* 485 US 312 (1988) at p.321).

Court case, but was implicitly overruled in *R.A.V. v City of St Paul*.[63] In *R.A.V.*, the Court held a city ordinance that rendered it a misdemeanor to make certain expressions reasonably likely to arouse anger, alarm or resentment in others on the basis of race, colour, creed, religion or gender as unconstitutional.

Hence, there is no 'hate speech' or racist speech exception to the First Amendment. Racist speech is often used synonymously with the phrase 'hate speech', but is really a generic term that has come to embody the use of speech attacks based on race, ethnicity, religion and sexual orientation or preference.[64] Racial and other slurs directed at specific groups are not held to a different standard. These slurs are subjected to *Brandenberg* scrutiny: whether they were directed at producing imminent, lawless action and were likely to produce that action. Furthermore, even though *Brandenberg* was a racist speech case, and even though the case involved racially derogatory statements by the Ku Klux Klan against blacks, the test that was put forth by that decision did not carve out a particular racist speech exception. It is rather a general 'clear and present danger' exception to constitutional protection of speech.

The death knell of group libel

The Supreme Court of the United States has discussed group libel or defamation only once – in *Beauharnais v Illinois*.[65] Since that decision, the Supreme Court has not revisited the issue. Smolla and Nimmer write that the *Beauharnais* decision, if it was still good law, would have created a 'hate speech' exception. They continue, '[f]or a variety of reasons of doctrine and policy that reach to the heart of contemporary First Amendment jurisprudence, *Beauharnais* must be understood as discredited and overruled'.[66] They consider *R.A.V.* to be the death knell of the group libel doctrine.

In *R.A.V.*, the Supreme Court held 5-4 (with Justice Scalia writing the majority opinion) that a city ordinance which banned hate speech was unconstitutional.[67] Under this ordinance it was a misdemeanor 'to place on public or private property a symbol, object, appellation, characterization, or graffiti, including a burning cross, which one knows or has reasonable grounds to know arouses anger, alarm, or resentment in others on the basis of race, color, creed, religion, or gender'. While the majority held it to be unconstitutional, the four concurring judges found the ordinance impermissibly overbroad and unconstitutional on narrower grounds.

---

[63] *R.A.V. v City of St Paul* 505 US 377 (1992).
[64] See Delgado, R., 'Words that Wound: A Tort Action for Racial Insults and Epithets, and Name-Calling' (1982) 17 *Harvard Civil Rights-Civil Liberties Law Review* 133.
[65] *Beauharnais v Illinois* 343 US 250 (1952).
[66] Smolla, R.A., *Smolla and Nimmer on Freedom of Speech* (3rd ed., Clark Boardman Callaghan, New York, 1996) § 12:7 at 12-8.
[67] *R.A.V.* 505 US at p.377.

A white teenager who allegedly placed a burning cross inside the fenced yard of a house belonging to a black family was charged under this statute. The city of St Paul, Minnesota, defended the ordinance specifying its goals as protection of a group, rather than impingement of free speech, stating 'the ordinance is intended not to impact on the right of free expression of the accused, but rather to protect against the victimization of . . . persons who are particularly vulnerable because of their membership in a group that has historically been discriminated against'.[68] The Court rejected this argument, in light of the 'danger of censorship presented by a facially content-based statute'.[69]

Justice Scalia wrote against such content-based regulation in the majority opinion: 'Displays containing abusive invective, no matter how vicious or severe, are permissible unless they are addressed to one of the specified disfavored topics. Those who wish to use "fighting words" in connection with other ideas – to express hostility, on the basis of political affiliation, union membership or homosexuality – are not covered'.[70] Scalia noted that '[t]he dispositive question in this case, therefore, is whether content discrimination is reasonably necessary to achieve St Paul's compelling interests; it plainly is not'.[71] An ordinance not limited to the favoured topics would have exactly the same beneficial effect.[72]

The Court disapproved of a statute that further narrowed the 'fighting words' exception for the special prohibition of words spoken on disfavoured topics of race, color, creed, gender or religion. Under *R.A.V.* a 'fighting words' statute not singling out any particular subclass of fighting words, but aimed at 'fighting words' in general would be constitutional *vis-à-vis* the First Amendment. Hence, *R.A.V.* truly sounded the 'death knell' of the group libel doctrine of *Beauharnais*. A fighting words statute may be applied to racial or other group confrontations, but simply may not be limited to such confrontations.

The decisions of other courts even before *R.A.V.* significantly undermined the group libel doctrine. In *Collin v Smith*,[73] for example, a federal appeals court expressly rejected the argument that group libel could be regulated solely on the basis of its offensiveness without regard to its likelihood to lead to violence.[74]

By contrast, statutes that limit 'fighting words' to racial confrontations exist in the United Kingdom; the Race Relations Act of 1965 created the offence of incitement to racial hatred. This statute punished libellous and slanderous communications that were likely to stir up racial hatred against

---

[68] Ibid. at p.394.
[69] Ibid. at p.395.
[70] Ibid. at p.391.
[71] Ibid. at pp.395–6.
[72] Ibid. at p.396.
[73] *Collin v Smith* 578 F. 2d 1197 (7th Cir. 1978). See further *Phelps and Engel v Hamilton* 59 F. 3d 1058 (10th Cir, 1995).
[74] Ibid. at pp.1207–10.

a particular segment of British community on the basis of race, colour, ethnic or national origins.[75] Among other cases, the Race Relations Act of 1965 was used in cases such as *R. v Malik* to prosecute the defendant, a Black Muslim leader of the Racial Adjustment Action Society, who spoke against Whites.

The current version of the Race Relations Act (of 1976) is amended by the Public Order Act of 1986. It defines racial hatred 'as hatred against a group of persons in Great Britain defined by reference to colour, race, nationality (including citizenship) or ethnic or national origins. Very generally, threatening, abusive or insulting words of a racially derogatory character, whether spoken or written, are proscribed, if these are intended to stir up racial hatred and are likely to stir up racial hatred.'[76] This can be compared to the United States, *Chaplinsky/Brandenberg* 'fighting words' doctrine in a specifically racial context. It can also be analogised to the United States group libel/*Beauharnais* doctrine. But nothing like this exists in the United States.

Despite the presence of the doctrine of group libel, commentators note that for one reason or another prosecutions under the Race Relations Act in the UK have been few in number. For one thing, the Attorney General's consent is required for criminal prosecutions under the sections mentioned above. Secondly, anxieties regarding the invasion of the right to the freedom of speech run high.[77] Some prosecutions under the 1986 Act include the 1988 conviction of a 'soapbox operator' who made racist speech and distributed racist literature; the 1990 charging of Major Galbraith of the Conservative party who described a Black parliamentary candidate as a 'Bloody Nigger'; the 1991 conviction of Lady Birdwood for distributing anti-Semitic publications, and the 1991 conviction of three Ku Klux Klan members for possessing racially inflammatory material. Such convictions would not survive under the race-neutral constitutional 'fighting words' doctrine in the United States.

The court upholds a group libel statute in Beauharnais

The only case where group libel is discussed is *Beauharnais* which in light of subsequent cases must be seen as overruled by implication.[78] Here the Court adopted the view that offensive public speech that contained epithets and words of personal abuse 'which by their very utterance inflict injury' could be prohibited. Writing for the Court, Justice Frankfurter sustained the conviction of a white supremacist, president of a racist Chicago organisation, the White Circle League, for distributing racist leaflets calling upon the

---

[75] Jones, loc. cit. at p.438.
[76] Ibid. at pp.448–9.
[77] Ibid. at pp.451–2.
[78] *Beauharnais* 343 US at pp.258–67. The leaflets also stated that '[i]f persuasion and the need to prevent the white race from becoming mongrelized by the Negro will not unite us, then the aggressions, [rapes], robberies, knives, guns, and marijuana of the Negro surely will.' Ibid. at p.252.

mayor and the City Council of Chicago to take action to halt the 'encroachment, harassment and invasion of white people, their property, neighborhoods and persons by the Negro'.[79] The Court upheld the power of Illinois to punish distribution of the leaflets under a group libel statute prohibiting dissemination of any publication that 'portrays depravity, criminality, unchastity, or lack of virtue of a class of citizens, of any race, color, creed or religion which exposes the citizens of any race, color, creed or religion to contempt, derision, or obloquy or which is productive of breach of the peace or riots'.[80]

The Court's reasoning combined the doctrines of common law libel with the *Chaplinsky* fighting words doctrine. It identified the issue in the case as 'whether the protection of "liberty" in the Due Process Clause of the Fourteenth Amendment prevents a State from punishing such libels – as criminal libel has been defined, limited and constitutionally recognized time out of mind – directed at designated collectivities and flagrantly disseminated'.[81] It then sustained Beauharnais's conviction for group libel because his leaflet communicated 'extreme racial and religious propaganda . . . in public places and by means calculated to have a powerful emotional impact on those to whom it is presented'. The Court quoted the *Chaplinsky* rationale in its entirety and observed, '[if] an utterance directed at an individual may be the object of criminal sanctions, we cannot deny to a State power to punish the same utterance directed at a defined group, unless we can say that this is a willful and purposeless restriction unrelated to the peace and well-being of the State'.

What remains of the fighting words doctrine?

The fighting words doctrine has clearly evolved since its inception in *Chaplinsky*. In *Cohen* and *Brandenberg*, 'fighting words' were redefined within the 'clear and present danger' requirement. Words must be an incitement to imminent lawless action and likely to produce such action to constitute an exception to the First Amendment. Furthermore, a statute condemning speech must be neutral in order to meet the *R.A.V.* standard and not a general one that condemns hate speech only, since there is no concept of group libel in the United States.

True threats are not protected by the First Amendment

Watts v United States: the Supreme Court first discusses true threats

True threats, as separate from mere political hyperbole or rhetoric, are outside the purview of First Amendment protected speech. A speaker is not

---

[79] Ibid. at p.251.
[80] Ibid.
[81] Ibid. at p.258.

protected by the First Amendment when he or she threatens another with death or serious bodily injury. In *R.A.V.*, the Supreme Court articulated three reasons why threats should not be protected: to protect individuals from threats of violence, to protect people from disruption that threats engender, and to protect them from the possibility that the threatened violence will occur.[82]

Most often, courts cite *Watts v United States* as support for the proposition that threats stand outside the coverage of the First Amendment. The 'true threats' doctrine was first discussed in this leading 1969 case, which was issued in the same term as the *Brandenberg* decision.[83] Since *Watts*, the Supreme Court has not offered any extensive analysis of the 'true threats' doctrine, and various strands of conflict have since arisen regarding the doctrine.

In *Watts*, at a 1966 anti-war rally near the Washington Monument, Robert Watts told a crowd of demonstrators that '[if] they ever make me carry a rifle the first man I want to get in my sights is L.B.J. [President Lyndon B. Johnson]. They are not going to make me kill my black brothers'.[84] He was arrested and convicted under 18 USC section 871(a), a criminal statute, of 'knowingly and willfully . . . [making] any threat to take the life of or to inflict bodily harm upon the President of the United States'.[85] The *Watts* court upheld the constitutionality of the statute forbidding threats against the life of the President, but reversed a conviction under that statute on First Amendment grounds. It held that Watts's statements were not intended as literal incitements to violence, but were rather angry statements amounting to 'political hyperbole'.[86] Generally, in analysing whether a 'true threat' exists under Watts, courts will defer to a jury's factual determination, rather than treat the question as a mixed question of fact and law appropriately left to independent judicial review.

United States v Kelner – true threats must be unequivocal and unconditional

The next major step after *Watts* towards discussing the constitutional dimension of 'true threats' came in *United States v Kelner*.[87] Russell Kelner, a leader of the Jewish Defense League (JDL), a radical organisation, threatened to kill Yassir Arafat, leader of the PLO on his controversial trip to New York in 1974. He was charged under 18 USC section 875(c), a 'threat' statute similar to the one in the *Watts* case. That section provides:[88]

Whoever transmits in interstate or foreign commerce any communication containing any threat to kidnap any person or any threat to injure the person of

---

[82] R.A.V. 505 US at p.388.
[83] *Watts v United States* 394 US 705 (1969).
[84] Ibid. at p.706.
[85] Ibid. at p.705, citing 18 USC s.871(a) (1969).
[86] Ibid. at p.708.
[87] *United States v Kelner* 534 F. 2d 1020 (2d Cir. 1976).
[88] Ibid. at p.1020, n.1 (citing 18 USC s.875(c) (1969)).

another, shall be fined under this title or imprisoned not more than five years, or both.

Summarising its approach to section 875(c), the *Kelner* court ruled that '[s]o long as the threat on its face and in the circumstances in which it is made is so unequivocal, unconditional, immediate and specific as to the person threatened, as to convey a gravity of purpose and imminent prospect of execution, the statute may properly be applied'.[89] The court continued that its clarification of section 875(c)'s scope was consistent with a rational approach to First Amendment construction which provides for governmental authority in instances of inchoate conduct, where a communication has become 'so interlocked with violent conduct as to constitute for all practical purposes part of the [proscribed] action itself'.[90]

The factual context of threats

To assess whether speech is a threat, courts will usually look at the factual context of the statements. In deciding whether Robert Watts's words were a true threat the court evaluated various factors including whether the statement had a political dimension, whether it was conditional and the reaction of the listeners.[91] While statements that are true threats need not identify a specific individual as their target, these must be sufficiently specific as to their potential target or targets to render the statement more than hypothetical.[92]

In *Claiborne Hardware*, NAACP leader Charles Evers's speech was coercive, yet the Court did not engage in a 'true threats' analysis and instead went the incitement route under the *Brandenberg* standard. Threats must be directed at specific victims to be true threats. In *Claiborne Hardware* the Supreme Court briefly discusses the question of why Evers's speech did not constitute a threat. One reasonable conclusion is that Evers did not direct his words at anyone in particular, but spoke to a vague and general class of people who failed to abide by the boycott.

In a slightly different setting in *United States v Khorrami*,[93] the US Court of Appeals for the Seventh Circuit upheld the conviction of a defendant accused of mailing threatening communications and making threatening telephone calls to New York headquarters of the Jewish National Fund. Mailings here were specifically addressed to the organisation and phone calls were made to the organisation's number.

Usually the paradigmatic subjects are 'coercive and extortionate' threats for a section 875(c) prosecution for threats.[94] 'At their core, threats are

---

[89] Ibid. at p.1027.
[90] Ibid., quoting Emerson, T.I., *The System of Freedom of Expression* (Random House, New York, 1970) at p.329.
[91] See *United States v Baker* 890 F. Supp. 1375 (E.D. Mich. 1995) at p.1380, *aff'd sub nom. United States v Alkhabaz*, 104 F. 3d 1492 (6th Cir. 1997).
[92] See ibid. at p.1386.
[93] *United States v Khorrami* 895 F. 2d 1186 (7th Cir. 1990).
[94] See *Baker*, 890 F. Supp. at p.1384.

tools that are employed when one wishes to have some effect, or achieve some goal, through intimidation. This is true regardless of whether the goal is highly reprehensible or seemingly innocuous'.[95] The threat can be coercive and extortionate and has to be taken seriously by its recipient such that it implicates a real possibility that 'threatened' violence would occur.[96] Sometimes, however, the alleged threat is proscribable even if it is not extortionate and or coercive. This was the situation in *Kelner*, where the defendant sought to further his political objectives by intimidating the PLO with warnings of violence. Even if the speech's goal is innocuous, it may still be proscribable; a frivolous bomb scare would be an example.

Conflicts have arisen among the federal circuit courts of appeals, both in applying the 'true threat' doctrine and on 'specific intent'

The *Kelner* court did not resolve the statutory issue of whether 'specific intent' or 'general intent' is required in determining whether speech constitutes a true threat. General intent requires an objective, low-threshold inquiry of whether a reasonable person would consider the speech at issue a threat, while the second is a more involved inquiry of the defendant's subjective state of mind. The question of intent (general or specific) and the question of whether something is a true threat are two distinct inquiries and part of the confusion among circuits arises because the term 'true threats' has been used to describe both the statutory intent requirement and the constitutional 'unconditional, unequivocal, immediate and specific' requirement.[97]

Most circuits require only a showing of 'general intent' for true threats. For example, the Sixth Circuit, like most others, has held that section 875(c) requires only general intent, stating '[b]ecause Section 875(c) is a general intent crime, intent must be proved by "objectively looking at the defendant's behavior in the totality of circumstances", rather than "probing the defendant's subjective state of mind"'.[98] Stated in another way, section 875(c) requires proof that a reasonable person would have taken the defendant's statement as a serious expression of an intention to inflict bodily harm. Nevertheless, not all circuits agree with this holding; in *United States v Twine*, the Ninth Circuit found a specific intent requirement in section 875(c).[99]

The Baker and Nuremberg legacies

Cyberspace communications are not devoid of threatening speech; surfers on the World Wide Web and recipients of listservs may occasionally encounter such offensive language. The same question of whether something constitutes an unlawful threat or protected speech arises in the context of the

---

[95] *Alkhabaz*, 104 F. 3d. at p.1495.
[96] *Baker* 890 F. Supp. at p.1384.
[97] Ibid. at p.1383.
[98] Ibid. at p.1384 (quoting *United States v DeAndino* 958 F. 2d 146 (6th Cir. 1992) at p.148).
[99] *United States v Twine* 853 F. 2d 676 (9th Cir. 1988).

Internet. Some aspects of the Internet though are unique and communications via this medium are distinct from all other communications. Threatening words may appear on a website. These websites then can be linked to other existing websites with ease, thus creating a multitude of interlinked sites with the same message. Similarly mirror sites may appear. Websites are dynamic and are continually updated, and often evolve through online interactions of Internet users. Distinct in its dynamic nature from oral and printed speech, speech on the Internet poses new complexities for the doctrine of true threats.

At least two cases, *United States v Baker* and *Planned Parenthood v American Coalition of Life Activists* (the 'Nuremberg' case) are about cyberspace speech that could be perceived as threatening. The threat inquiry in the *Baker* case involved e-mail interactions of two individuals who expressed their desires to inflict violence on women and girls. The alleged threats in the Nuremberg case included a website with the personal information of certain abortion providers whom the creators of the site promised to bring to trial for war crimes against humanity. While the subjects of the *Baker* case threats were 13–14 year old girls in the sender's neighborhood and women in his college dorm, they were not the recipients of his e-mail; his e-mail interactions were private. In the Nuremberg trial case, the threats were largely directed at abortion providers and others whom the anti-abortion movement regarded as 'accomplices' in the provision of abortion. Posters, bumper stickers and Internet sites containing the alleged threats were visible to people who saw these, or clicked a mouse button, to access the Nuremberg Files site.

The Baker case

In this case, Abraham Jacob Alkhabaz, a University of Michigan student also known as Jake Baker, posted a story to a newsgroup in which he described the rape, torture and murder of a woman.[100] He used a classmate's name to describe these incidents. In response Baker received several e-mails and began to correspond with someone called Gonda in Ontario, Canada. Between 29 November 1994 and 25 January 1995, the two exchanged at least 41 e-mails regarding their desires to inflict violence on women and girls, and it was these 'shared fantasies' that led to the case.[101]

Baker was prosecuted under the federal statute, 18 USC section 875(c), prohibiting interstate communications to threat or injure another person.[102] Upholding the subjective intent requirement and the true threat standard conveyed in *Kelner*, the district court stated, '[a] *Kelner* transmission, or series of transmissions, in order to constitute a true threat must on its face be so unequivocal, unconditional, immediate, and specific as to the person

---

[100] *Alkhabaz* 104 F. 3d at pp.1492–3.
[101] Ibid. at p.1493.
[102] *Baker* 890 F. Supp. at p.1380.

threatened, as to convey a gravity of purpose and imminent prospect of execution'.[103] The court held that the statements made in the e-mails did not meet the *Kelner* standard and reversed Baker's earlier conviction. The court stated, '[s]tatements expressing musings, considerations of what it would be like to kidnap or injure someone, or desires to kidnap or injure someone, however unsavory, are not constitutionally actionable under § 875(c) absent some expression of an intent to commit the injury or kidnapping'.[104]

The Sixth Circuit affirmed this judgment after a heated dissent. It upheld the general intent standard, stating that for a communication to constitute a threat under section 875(c) it must be such that a reasonable person, (1) would take the statement as a serious expression of an intention to inflict bodily harm (the *mens rea*), and (2) would perceive such expression as being communicated to effect some change or achieve some goal through intimidation.[105] In conclusion the Sixth Circuit stated, '[e]ven if a reasonable person would take the communications between Baker and Gonda as serious expressions of an intention to inflict bodily harm, no reasonable person would perceive such communications as being conveyed to effect some change or achieve some goal through intimidation. Quite the opposite, Baker and Gonda apparently sent e-mail messages to each other in an attempt to foster a friendship based on shared sexual fantasies.'[106]

The District Court opinion in the *Baker* case reflected on the Internet in the context of hate speech and true threats, and expressed its strong preference to hold speech on the Internet to the same constitutional standard of protection as if it appeared anywhere else:[107]

> Baker is being prosecuted under [section 875(c)] for his use of words, implicating fundamental First Amendment concerns. Baker's words were transmitted by means of the Internet, a relatively new communications medium that is itself currently the subject of much media attention. The Internet makes it possible with unprecedented ease to achieve worldwide distribution of material, like Baker's story, posted to its public areas. When used in such a fashion, the Internet may be likened to a newspaper with unlimited distribution and no locatable printing press – and with no supervising editorial control. But Baker's e-mail messages, on which the superseding indictment is based, were not publicly published but privately sent to Gonda. While new technology such as the Internet may complicate analysis and may sometimes require new or modified laws, it does not in this instance qualitatively change the analysis under the statute or under the First Amendment.

The Nuremberg files case

The factual context of the Nuremberg case includes a wave of violence directed against abortion providers in 1993 and 1994; this resulted in three

---

103 Ibid.
104 Ibid. at p.1386.
105 Ibid. at p.1495.
106 Ibid. at p.1496.
107 *Baker* 890 F. Supp. at p.1391.

murders of abortion providers. A distribution of wanted-style posters identifying the doctors preceded these murders. Following this wave of violence,
the anti-abortion movement splintered on doctrinal lines and the American
Coalition of Life Activists (ACLA), a group that believes in 'justifiable
homicide' for abortion providers, was formed. In ACLA meetings held in
1995, the group issued more wanted-style posters, including one entitled
the 'deadly dozen list'.[108]

During a January 1996 ACLA meeting, the Nuremberg files containing
information on abortion providers was revealed. A website appeared in
January 1997 when the Nuremberg files were posted online, and these
among other threats were subject of *Planned Parenthood v American
Coalition of Life Activists*. The first page of these files began with the following words:[109]

> The American Coalition of Life Activists (ACLA) is cooperating in collecting
> dossiers on abortionists in anticipation that one day we may be able to hold them
> on trial for crimes against humanity. *Click the Hot Link at the bottom of this
> page to vote to make this site a 'Starting Point hot Site.'* Your vote can bring tens
> of thousands of people face to face with the fact that everybody faces a payday
> someday, a day when what is sown is reaped. [The site further listed more rhetoric
> under the heading] Why this must be undone.

The site further contained names of 200 alleged 'abortionists' along with
200 other names. No further personal information was listed online, except that on Plaintiff Warren Hern under the heading 'Third Trimester
Butchers'. In addition to the Nuremberg files, both off-and online, the other
threats in the case were the deadly dozen poster, and other wanted-style
posters, a bumper sticker with 'Execute' in large black letters written on it.
In a summary judgment decision, the US district court of Oregon assessed
whether these were true threats, and held that all but the bumper sticker
were actionable.[110]

In March 1999, the District Court granted a permanent injunction that
would restrain the defendants in the case from engaging in certain speech in
the future. Before this decision, the ACLU submitted a memorandum of
amicus curiae questioning the granting of such an injunction in light of the
unique and dynamic nature of the Internet. Before the injunction's issuance,
a proposed injunction enjoined defendants from publishing, republishing,
reproducing and/or distributing anywhere or in any way the Nuremberg
Files. Since the nature of the Internet is dynamic and content at a site such
as the Nuremberg files can potentially change each second, the notion of
republishing raises a more complex issue compared to print mediums that
are static.

---

[108] *Planned Parenthood v American Coalition of Life Activists* 23 F. Supp. 2d 1182 (D. Or.
1998) at pp.1185–7, *later opinion*, 41 F. Supp. 2d 1130, 1131 (D. Or. 1999). For the
background constitutional law relating to abortion, see *Roe v Wade* 410 US 113 (1973).
[109] *Planned Parenthood* 23 F. Supp. 2d at p.1187.
[110] Ibid. at p.1194.

The permanent injunction then issued followed much of the language suggested by the ACLU in their *amicus curiae*. The ACLU suggested that the nature of the Internet medium, being quite distinct from the printed word, counselled against applying the same language that might be appropriate to enjoin repeated publications of the Deadly Dozen Posters of the poster of Dr Crist. The content of a website such as the Nuremberg files may change from moment to moment, quite unlike the poster, books, periodicals. In the future, there may be less or more threatening material on this website.

In addition, wrote the ACLU, a 'website typically contains links or references to discrete pages to which the user can seamlessly move with a single click of the mouse'. Some of these pages might be found on the same website, while others might be on different websites and controlled by third parties. The publisher of the referring page might not even be familiar with the full content of that third-party website as it existed at the time the link was established. In most cases the publisher of the referring page would not even be familiar with the changes that were made to the content of the other website.

ACLU raised the issue of republication as well, which was more complicated on the web due to the existence of links. The ACLU proposed that the plaintiffs could be enjoined from downloading and distributing in paper form, with the specific intent to threaten, the Nuremberg Files concerning the plaintiffs that the court would find in its order to be threatening. ACLU proposed that defendants could be enjoined from electronically reproducing that information with a specific intent to threaten by, for example, creating their own mirror site.

A more complicated issue involving republication regarded publicising the address of the Nuremberg Files or providing a link to it or any of the mirror site. The ACLU stated in the *amicus curiae* that even assuming a specific intent requirement, in light of the evolving nature of the Internet, republication was a complex question. The ACLU then suggested amended language which the court took verbatim to issue the following injunction, restraining defendants from:[111]

(d) Providing additional material concerning Robert Crist . . . [other names of Plaintiffs] . . . with a specific intent to threaten, to the Nuremberg Files or any mirror website that may be created. In addition, defendants are enjoined from publishing, republishing, reproducing and/or distributing in print or electronic form the personally identifying information about plaintiffs contained in . . . [the Nuremberg Files] with specific intent to threaten.

Tort and other remedies for victims of harmful speech

Speech that causes emotional harm and interferes with some relational interest can be penalised or remedied in other ways besides group libel.

---

[111] *Planned Parenthood* 41 F. Supp. 2d at p.1156.

Remedies include tort actions such as libel, slander, invasion of privacy, holding someone in false light, intentional infliction of emotional distress. These are alternatives to criminal prosecutions for fighting words and true threats and could be available in some situations to provide damages to victims of hate speech. Such remedies might avoid, at least in part, possible severe impingement and narrowing of First Amendment protections.

Claiborne Hardware suggests other remedies may be available to victims of harmful speech. In this case, certain boycott violators were subjected to non-peaceful coercion. Although none of these actually decided to join the boycott, they did suffer some minor property and other damage. The Court emphasised that those non-peaceful activities could be circumscribed and punished for 'conspiracy against the public peace and order' and for other violations of valid law, in a way that would not conflict as drastically with important constitutional First Amendment protections.[112] Remedies were also available for the white merchants whose businesses were targeted. Reiterating that law provides other remedies for economic and business losses and constitutional freedoms need not be inhibited, Justice Stevens continued: 'The First Amendment does not protect violence. . . . No federal rule of law restricts a State from imposing tort liability for business losses that are caused by violence and by threats of violence. When such conduct occurs in the context of constitutionally protected activity, however, "precision of regulation" is demanded.'[113]

The defendants in *Baker* too could be penalised through tort actions. The District Court in that case expressed its scepticism that the Attorney General was pushing the issue (of whether the true threats statute had been violated) a bit too far:[114]

> Whatever Baker's faults, and he is to be faulted, he did not violate [section 875(c)] The case would have been better handled as a disciplinary matter, as the University of Victoria proceeded in a similar situation, despite whatever difficulties inhere in such a course.

In some situations, there are various courses of action available to the victims of harmful speech. Aside from disciplining Baker, the alleged victims of Baker's speech could, as an example, pursue a tort path and sue him for 'invasion of privacy'.

Conclusion

In 1995 and 1996, several states enacted statutes to regulate Internet content. Despite the Supreme Court's ruling in *Reno v ACLU*, these statutes aim to control speech on the Internet and there are several pending bills related to material harmful to minors. For example, Michigan has recently

---

[112] *Claiborne Hardware* 458 US at p.909.
[113] Ibid. at p.916, citing *NAACP v Button* 371 US 415 (1963) at p.438.
[114] *Baker* 890 F. Supp. at pp.1391–2.

amended its laws, which already forbid the dissemination or displaying of sexually explicit matter to minors. The new amendments extend the ban to include furnishing such material over the Internet. The laws, as amended, prohibit both visual and verbal material.[115]

While the subject of such proposed bills usually targets speech harmful to minors, and the repercussions from the passage of such bills are not yet clear, some conclusions can be made about protecting speech on the Internet.

All speech on the Internet should be protected before any rash restrictions impede the growth of this powerful medium of communication. Fighting words in a very narrow and limited context can be proscribed. However, the speech that is proscribed must be inciteful to imminent lawless action and likely to cause that action. Because one must access the Internet wilfully and click buttons to read fighting words and hate speech, any potential incitement is diluted. There is no captive audience issue here since people are free to leave the vicinity of a computer screen. In fact, net surfers who want to avoid hateful speech and/or fighting words should not go to websites where they are likely to be offended. One doesn't have to go to a KKK or an Aryan Brotherhood website, any more than one feels compelled to attend their rallies.

In the words of Supreme Court Justice Brandeis, '[the] remedy to be applied is more speech, not enforced silence'.[116] Since the Internet facilitates easy, free and instantaneous public discourse in various forums, the best revenge against what one perceives as hateful is more speech and not less.

At the same time, true threats are not protected by the First Amendment. While this standard applies to speech on the Internet, one must keep sight of the doctrine's limitations. Inadvertent misstatements that amount to nothing more than jest, or mere political commentary and hyperbole are not true threats. True threats are those that on the face and in the circumstances are so unequivocal, unconditional, immediate and specific that a gravity of purpose and imminent prospect of execution is conveyed to the threatened person and are intended to achieve a certain end-goal of intimidation.

Again, the nature of the Internet is such that a threatening message on the Internet is never static. The Internet has unique attributes that may require a more complex analysis under the constitutional standards that have emerged so far. Courts are cognizant of the unique nature of the Internet. Nevertheless, as at least one judge has noted, courts are reluctant to apply a new standard for constitutional protection or lack thereof for speech on the Internet.[117]

---

[115] Mich. Comp. Laws ss.722.673, 722.675, 722.676, and 722.677 (1999).
[116] *Whitney v California* 274 US 357 (1927), at p.377 (Brandeis J, concurring).
[117] *Baker* 890 F. Supp. at p.1390.

CHAPTER 12

Hacking, viruses and fraud

Martin Wasik

Introduction

The aim of the present chapter is to give an account of the current law relating to three of the main forms of IT misuse – hacking, viruses and fraud, and to consider to what extent the Internet creates new problems for the criminal law in these areas.[1] Barrett, in a useful survey,[2] observes that 'The Internet . . . brings the facilities and the threats of the information age closer to home – literally so: home shoppers using the Internet are as likely to be targeted by computer hackers, viruses and fraudsters as are the banks and building societies.' The three areas forming the title of this chapter were the subject of review by the Law Commission for England and Wales, and the equivalent body for Scotland, in the late 1980s. The English Law Commission produced a Report on *Computer Misuse*[3] – which, in turn, prompted legislative reform in the Computer Misuse Act 1990. Hacking and viruses, but not fraud, are dealt with in the Act. This legislative story has been related in detail elsewhere,[4] and it is not proposed to tread that ground again. Suffice it to say that the 1990 Act has provided some useful deterrent, educational and opinion-forming functions in relation to the wrongfulness of IT misuse. By and large, the Act also appears to have worked reasonably well in practice when called upon, although this is to judge it on the basis of relatively few prosecutions and even fewer reported cases.

It is also clear, however, that while industry and commerce lobbied very hard for the Act at the time, individual victims of computer misuse do not see the criminal law as a useful resource when things go wrong.[5] Many victims choose not to report incidents of computer misuse, either through embarrassment, through the belief that the investigative authorities lack the time, experience and technical skill to deal with such offences, or through the knowledge that a criminal investigation will generate bad publicity.

---

[1] See National Criminal Intelligence Service, *Project Trawler*, 1999: http://www.ncis.co.uk. For complaints relating to computer misuse see http://www.web-police.org.
[2] Barrett, N., *Digital Crime* (Kogan Page, London, 1997) p.22.
[3] Report No. 186, *Computer Misuse* (Cm. 819, HMSO, London, 1989). See also Scottish Law Commission, *Report on Computer Crime* (Cm. 174, HMSO, London, 1987).
[4] See Wasik, M., *Crime and the Computer* (Clarendon Press, Oxford, 1990).
[5] Department of Trade and Industry, *Dealing With Computer Misuse* (London, 1992).

There is no requirement in English law to report incidents of computer misuse to the police. The Law Commission considered whether there should be, and decided not, on the basis that since there is no general duty to report crime in the UK, the creation of a duty in a narrow class of case would be anomalous.[6] There is also a common preference for dealing with computer security breaches quietly and informally. From the point of view of the victim, prevention by way of adequate IT security is a far better option than prosecution after the harm has been caused. Perpetrators of computer misuse, when identified, are usually disciplined by the firm or required to leave, rather than being reported to the police. According to the Audit Commission, only twenty per cent of those detected are prosecuted.[7]

While there have been no serious calls for a review of the hacking and virus provisions of the 1990 Act, one or two prosecutions have failed unexpectedly, and these are considered further, below. Offences of fraud, however, are to be found mainly in the Theft Acts 1968 and 1978 and, apart from some recent difficulties over fraud involving electronic funds transfer,[8] these offences have been little affected by the IT revolution. The Law Commission has recently issued a Consultation Paper on Fraud and Deception,[9] which acknowledges the importance of the IT revolution but recommends only minor adjustment to the Theft Acts offences to take account of it. Apart from the substantive law, other developments need to be borne in mind. Special jurisdictional and procedural rules in relation to offences of dishonesty have been on the statute book since 1993, but these only came into force on 1 June 1999. The jurisdictional rules for computer misuse offences are to be found in the Computer Misuse Act. Where computer misuse takes the form of fraud, both sets of provisions may be in play.

Hacking: Computer Misuse Act, sections 1 and 2

This issue first came to general attention in the UK during the 1980s, through reports of computer hacking cases in the US, and the gathering of various 'computer crime casebooks' comprising newspaper and other accounts of such incidents. Legal opinion in the UK was at first divided over whether such misconduct could simply be prosecuted under pre-existing laws of theft and fraud, or whether tailor-made new crimes were required.[10]

---

[6] There are such duties elsewhere; e.g. Colorado: Col.Rev.Stat. 18-15.5 – 101, 102; 18-8 – 115. Those who work in the financial sector must report their knowledge or suspicion that money laundering is taking place: Drug Trafficking Act 1994 s.52.
[7] Audit Commission, *Opportunity Makes a Thief: An Analysis of Computer Abuse* (London, 1994).
[8] *Preddy* [1996] AC 815.
[9] Law Commission, *Consultation Paper No. 155: Legislating the Criminal Code: Fraud and Deception* (London, 1999, at http://www.open.gov.uk/lawcomm/).
[10] See, for example, Tapper, C., 'Computer Crime: Scotch Mist?' [1987] *Criminal Law Review* 4.

The decision of the House of Lords in *Gold and Schifreen*[11] established that computer hacking, as such, was not an offence under the existing criminal law. The House held that a prosecution for forgery under the Forgery and Counterfeiting Act 1981 was in reality a desperate attempt by the prosecution to force the facts to fit a law inappropriate to them. The quashing of the convictions in that case made it clear that a 'purpose-built' hacking law was essential. This important case provided the spur for change. Acting on the recommendations of the Law Commission, Parliament implemented the Computer Misuse Act of 1990. This statute remains the principal substantive criminal law provision in the area.

The Act deals both with hacking and the deliberate introduction of computer viruses into computer systems. Sections 1 and 2 of the Act are designed to outlaw the gaining of unauthorised access to computer-held programs or data, whether by an outsider acting remotely, or by an insider such as a company employee gaining access to computer-held information which he has no authority to see. The Act incorporates the Commission's view that the best legislative arrangement was to have the two offences arranged hierarchically, the first being a 'basic' hacking offence, the second a more serious 'ulterior' offence to be used by the prosecution where it could be proved that the hacker intended by unauthorised access thereby to commit a further crime, such as theft. Section 1 of the Act provides:

1 (1) A person is guilty of an offence if –
  (a) he causes a computer to perform any function with intent to secure access to any program or data held in any computer;
  (b) the access he intends to secure is unauthorised; and
  (c) he knows at the time when he causes the computer to perform the function that that is the case.
 (2) The intent that a person has to have to commit an offence under this section need not be directed at –
  (a) any particular program or data;
  (b) a program or data of any particular kind; or
  (c) a program or data held in any particular computer.
 (3) A person guilty of an offence under this section shall be liable on summary conviction to imprisonment for a term not exceeding six months or to a fine not exceeding level 5 on the standard scale or to both.

It should be noted that there is no definition of 'computer', 'data' or 'program' in the Computer Misuse Act, although a range of other terms is defined. It was felt by the Law Commission that the pace of technological change would soon render any such definition outdated. This was perhaps the best approach. It may create some future problems, however, where there is a doubt over whether a particular device should count as a 'computer', or not. A court could make a ruling on the matter at that stage, but it is arguable that judge-made law could turn out to be less satisfactory than

---

[11] [1988] AC 1063.

a statutory definition.[12] An alternative would be for the judge simply to leave the matter to the jury to decide, on the basis that 'computer' is now an ordinary word of the English language, and so its meaning is a question of fact, not law.[13] So far there have been no cases to test the boundaries of the meaning of 'computer' in the 1990 Act.

Section 1 creates a summary offence, triable only in magistrates' courts. The *actus reus* of the offence requires the defendant to 'cause a computer to perform any function'. This is meant to exclude mere physical contact with the computer and the scrutiny of data without any interaction with the computer. The computer must be made to 'respond' in some way by performing a function. Thus, if a person simply reads confidential computer output, or reads data displayed on the computer screen, these activities are not covered by the Act.[14] The reason is that they do not amount to unauthorised 'access'. They are simply an invasion of privacy or a form of 'snooping', which is not generally regulated by the criminal law. It follows that 'computer eavesdropping'[15] is not covered either, subject to one possible counter-argument. This is that if the device used by the eavesdropper can itself be termed 'a computer' then the wording of section 1 may be fulfilled: the defendant has caused a 'computer' (the eavesdropping device) to perform a function with intent to secure access to data held in the (target) computer. Such an argument has not been tested in the courts and, indeed, no prosecution for computer eavesdropping has yet come to light.

It should be noted that there is no requirement that the defendant must *succeed* in obtaining access to the program or data, or be successful in subverting computer security devices in place. A remote hacker would, thus, 'cause a computer to perform any function' if he accessed it remotely and the computer responded, such as by activating a computer security device, or by offering a log-on menu. The substantive offence is thus drafted in such a way as to include conduct which might usually be thought to fall within the scope of attempted crime: 'knocking on the door of the computer', as the Law Commission put it. Such conduct (provided the other elements of the crime were made out) would amount to the full offence, rather than an attempt.[16] It can also be seen that the offence can be committed without there having been any computer security measures in place for the hacker to overcome. Any material held on a computer is covered by the Act, whether

---

[12] There is also no definition of 'computer' in the Police and Criminal Evidence Act 1984. Section 69 of that Act deals with admissibility of documentary evidence which has been generated by a computer. In *Blackburn*, 1992, *The Times*, 1 December, the Court of Appeal held that a PC when being used as a word processor was *not* a 'computer', and hence that word-processed documents were not subject to section 69.

[13] *Brutus v Cozens* [1973] AC 854.

[14] Although the Data Protection Acts 1998 may apply. See below.

[15] See Steele, D., 'Eavesdropping on Electromagnetic Radiation Emanating from Video Display Units' (1989–90) 32 *Criminal Law Quarterly* 253.

[16] There is general provision in English criminal law that liability for attempted crime does not extend to summary offences: Criminal Attempts Act 1981, s.1(4).

or not it is protected. This is a difference between English law and some similar provisions in other jurisdictions, where the view is taken that no offence should be committed where access to the material was unrestricted.[17] The Law Commission felt that to confine the offence of hacking to protected data was equivalent to saying that no burglary is committed where a householder leaves the doors and windows unlocked.

The prosecution must also establish that the access was an 'unauthorised' access. By section 17(5), access is defined as 'unauthorised' if the defendant is not himself entitled to control access to the relevant program or data, and he does not have the necessary consent to access from the person who is entitled to give that consent. While this lack of authorisation will usually be easy to show, especially where remote hacking is involved, it may be more difficult to prove where an insider, operating from their own terminal, gains access to material on the computer which they are not authorised to see. It may then be a matter of some dispute whether the access was in fact authorised, or whether the appropriate person has in fact given their consent. In the context of a commercial organisation, a prosecution is thus more likely to be effective where lines of responsibility for IT matters are clear. A warning about the restricted nature of access to categories of computer-held information should appear on the screen as soon as the machine is switched on by an employee and again as soon as an attempt is made to access sensitive or restricted material.

The question whether access was 'unauthorised' caused problems in *DPP v Bignell*,[18] where the Divisional Court held that an offence under section 1 was not committed where two police officers (husband and wife) instructed a computer operator to extract details of cars from the Police National Computer. It was shown that the two officers required that information for private, rather than official, purposes, the cars being owned by a male acquaintance of Mr Bignell's ex-wife. The Divisional Court stated that what mattered here was the fact that the officers *were* authorised to access information of that kind from the PNC, albeit only for legitimate police purposes. In the case Astill J commented that the Computer Misuse Act was designed to criminalise 'breaking into computer systems', and noted that the misuse of data once it had been obtained was not covered by the Act. Such misuse might nonetheless constitute an offence under the Data Protection Act 1984 (which was then in force), and this fact clearly influenced the Divisional Court in reaching its view that the conduct lay outside the scope of the Computer Misuse Act.[19] The decision in *Bignell* is open to criticism on the ground that, on an ordinary construction of language, authorising a

---

[17] For example, the Summary Offences Act 1953 (South Australia) as amended in 1989, where hacking is committed only where unauthorised access is gained to 'information stored in a restricted-access system'. See also German Penal Code s.202a (Data Espionage), which extends only to 'specially protected' computers.

[18] [1998] 1 Cr App R 1.

[19] See below.

person's access for one (legitimate) purpose ought not to be regarded as authorising his access for another (non-legitimate) purpose.[20] In the analogous area of burglary, it has been held that where D has been given a general permission by V to enter V's house as a guest, he is in law regarded as a trespasser (and hence a burglar) if he enters V's house with a secret dishonest intention to steal V's property.[21]

The authority of *Bignell* was undermined to some extent by the decision of the House of Lords in *Bow Street Metropolitan Stipendiary Magistrate, ex parte Government of the United States*.[22] In that case an exployee of American Express had authorisation to access client accounts referred to her by her employers to check matters relating to credit. She in fact obtained access to 189 other accounts as well, and passed on confidential details of those to one Allison, the defendant in the case. That information was used by Allison to encode credit cards and supply PIN numbers, enabling fraudsters to obtain cash from automated teller machines. Money in the order of $1 million was obtained. The issue in the case was whether Allison could be extradited from England to the United States to face charges and the House of Lords, reversing the decision of the Divisional Court, held that he could be extradited. Lord Hobhouse had no difficulty in finding that the conduct of the American Express employee fell 'fairly and squarely' within the provisions of section 1. His Lordship then considered the decision in *Bignell*, and pointed out that the Divisional Court had erred in asking itself whether the police officers had 'authority to access the *kind* of data in question', a mistake also made by the same court in the instant case. The correct issue was whether the officers had authority to access the *actual data* involved. Even so, his Lordship thought that, on the facts, the acquittal in *Bignell* was 'probably right'. It was distinguishable from the instant case because the police officers in *Bignell* had instructed the (innocent) computer operator to access the computer on their behalf. The only access to the computer had therefore been made by the computer operator, and he had not exceeded his authority in doing so. In the circumstances, there had been no 'unauthorised access', and hence an essential element of the *actus reus* of the offence was missing.[23] The *Bow Street* case confirms the correctness of a number of earlier unreported convictions, such as *Bonnett*.[24] There, a special constable was convicted under section 1 of the Act, where he himself accessed the Police National Computer to find out who owned the car with the registration number BON1T, because he wanted to buy it. It puts in

---

[20] Commentary on the case at [1998] *Criminal Law Review* 53 by Professor J.C. Smith.

[21] *Jones and Smith* [1976] 3 All ER 54; *Barker* (1983) 7 AJLR 426.

[22] [2000] 1 Cr App R 61; see O'Doherty, S., 'Computer Misuse' (2000) 164 *Justice of the Peace* 179, and for the decision of the Divisional Court see [1999] QB 847.

[23] It might be suggested that the Bignells made an authorised access to the computer through the *innocent agency* of the computer operator. This argument would fail, since 'authorised access' is clearly part of the *actus reus* of the offence, and cases of innocent agency relate to the *mens rea* of the principal offender and not *actus reus*.

[24] Unreported, Newcastle under Lyme Magistrates' Court, 3 November 1995.

doubt some other earlier cases, such as *Farquharson*,[25] where the defendant asked another person to access the data, but was convicted under section 1 and sentenced to six months' imprisonment.

There are two limbs to the *mens rea* of the offence under section 1. The first limb is the 'intent to secure access to any program or data held in any computer'. The 1990 Act provides that the defendant intends to 'secure access' to a program or data where he intends, by causing the computer to perform any function, to alter or erase the data or program, to copy it, or move it, or use it, or display it. The words 'any computer' seem, on the face of it, to make it clear that the intent may, but need not, relate to the computer which the defendant is at that time operating. In the case of *Cropp*,[26] however, the trial judge ruled that the offence under section 1 was only available where *two* computers were involved, the defendant having used one computer to access the other. The defendant in that case was acquitted, but the Attorney-General referred the point of law to the Court of Appeal[27] in *Attorney General's Reference (No 1 of 1991)*,[28] where the Court held that the judge's interpretation had been wrong, that the meaning of the provision was in fact clear, and that 'direct' access to the target computer was covered by section 1 as well as 'remote' access. This point was re-emphasised by the House of Lords in the *Bow Street* case, discussed above, where the Divisional Court had appeared to stray into error. Lord Hobhouse stated that the term 'hacking', was 'used conveniently to refer to all forms of unauthorised access whether by insiders or outsiders . . .'[29]. In another case, *Bedworth*, reported only in the newspapers which covered his trial and not in the law reports, the defendant was acquitted of a charge under section 1, apparently on the basis that he was 'addicted' to computer hacking[30] and did not form the necessary intent to commit the offence. This view was reached by the jury in the face of a clear direction by the judge that such 'addiction' could be no defence to the charge, and so the acquittal in this case must be regarded as perverse and wrong.[31] Subsection (2) explains that the defendant's intent need not be directed at any *particular* program or data, so as to include the hacker who accesses a computer without any clear idea of what he will find there. Intention must, however, be proved – recklessness is not enough.[32]

---

25 Unreported, Croydon magistrates' court, 9 December 1993.
26 Unreported, Snaresbrook Crown Court, 4 July 1991. See Wasik, M., 'A Simple Case of Computer Hacking' (1992) 156 *Justice of the Peace* 694.
27 Under powers in the Criminal Justice Act 1972, s.36.
28 [1993] QB 94.
29 [2000] 1 Cr App R 61, at p.72.
30 For a book-length treatment of the subject of 'internet addiction', see Young, K.S., *Caught in the Net* (Wiley, Chichester, 1998).
31 'Addiction' to taking goods from shops without paying for them is no defence to theft! Two other defendants who had been involved with Bedworth pleaded guilty to the charges and both received custodial sentences of six months.
32 Recklessness would have been enough for liability under an earlier Bill on Computer Misuse, sponsored by Emma Nicholson MP, which never became law: see Wasik, M., op. cit., App 2.

Still less would careless or inattentive accessing of unauthorised material suffice for liability.

The second limb to the *mens rea* for this offence is that the defendant must know, at the time when he causes the computer to perform the function, that the access which he intends to secure is unauthorised. 'Knowledge' is a clear *mens rea* term. Mere suspicion on the part of the defendant would not be enough to meet this requirement, but knowledge can be established by proof that the defendant realised that the access might be unauthorised, and then deliberately closed his mind to that possibility.[33] It is, of course, clear from the decisions in *Bignell* and *Bow Street* that the defendant's belief that the access was unauthorised cannot make the act criminal if it turns out that, in fact, the access was authorised. Ignorance of the law, however, provides no defence. In *Bonnett* the defendant policeman claimed that he did not realise that accessing the PNC for private purposes was against the law but such a mistake, even if it is believed, does not excuse.

Secondary (accomplice) liability may arise in respect of anyone who supplies information which is useful to a hacker, such as a computer system password, intending that it should be so used by him.[34] This is behaviour equivalent to providing a safebreaker with the combination to the safe, and as such amounts to counselling and procuring the relevant offence.[35] Under English law liability depends upon proof that the person supplying the information intended so to assist and was aware of the kind of offence which would be committed.[36] A person supplying information by posting it on their website, or possibly an Internet service provider having knowledge that the information was being displayed, might therefore come within the reach of this offence, although personal responsibility for posting the information and the requisite intent might be very difficult to establish. No such prosecution has been reported in England.[37] The provision of information in this way could also amount to an incitement to commit the relevant offence, but it would have to be proved that the person who placed the information knew of all the relevant circumstances and intended that the material should be used for the particular purpose.[38]

The maximum sentence for the section 1 offence is six months' imprisonment and/or a fine up to £5,000. The criminal courts have a range of other sentencing powers which might also come into play in such a case. In particular, the magistrates' court may require the convicted offender to pay compensation of up to £5,000 for any 'injury, loss or damage' occasioned

---

[33] *Westminster City Council v Croyalgrange* [1986] 2 All ER 353.
[34] Magistrates' Courts Act 1980 s.44(1).
[35] Accessories and Abettors Act 1861 s.8 (a provision applicable to indictable offences).
[36] *DPP v Maxwell* [1978] 3 All ER 1140.
[37] See Leong, G., 'Computer Child Pornography – The Liability of Distributors?' in Walker, C. (ed.), *Crime, Criminal Justice and the Internet* (special edition, *Criminal Law Review*, Sweet & Maxwell, London, 1998) at p.19.
[38] See *Invicta Plastics v Clare* [1976] RTR 251, concerning the advertising and sale of radar detection equipment.

to the victim by the offence,[39] and to confiscate any property of the offender which was used or was intended for use in the commission of the offence.[40] Clearly this would include, where appropriate, confiscation of the offender's computer, modem and other equipment forming part of the hacker's stock-in-trade.

Time limits are specified in the Act within which a prosecution for the section 1 offence must be brought. Normally prosecutions for summary offences must be brought within six months of the date of commission of the offence.[41] Exceptionally for the section 1 offence, however, a prosecution may be brought within six months of the date on which evidence sufficient in the opinion of the prosecutor to warrant the proceedings came to his knowledge but, in any event, there can be no prosecution later than three years after the offence was allegedly committed. This exception was considered, and strictly construed against the prosecution, by the Divisional Court in *Morgans v DPP*.[42] It was held that the relevant date is when the prosecutor (or other officer in charge of the case) acquires the evidence, not when he decides that proceedings are warranted.

Section 2 of the Computer Misuse Act 1990 provides:

(1) A person is guilty of an offence under this section if he commits an offence under section 1 above ('the unauthorised access offence') with intent –
    (a) to commit an offence to which this section applies; or
    (b) to facilitate the commission of such an offence (whether by himself or by any other person);
(2) This section applies to offences –
    (a) for which the sentence is fixed by law; or
    (b) for which a person of twenty-one years of age or over (not previously convicted) may be sentenced to imprisonment for a term of five years (or, in England and Wales, might be so sentenced but for the restrictions imposed by section 33 of the Magistrates' Courts Act 1980).
(3) It is immaterial for the purposes of this section whether the further offence is to be committed on the same occasion as the unauthorised access offence or on any future occasion.
(4) A person may be guilty of an offence under this section even though the facts are such that the commission of the further offence is impossible.
(5) A person guilty of an offence under this section shall be liable –
    (a) on summary conviction, to imprisonment for a term not exceeding six months or to a fine not exceeding the statutory maximum, or both; and
    (b) on conviction on indictment, to imprisonment for a term not exceeding five years or to a fine or both.

Section 2 creates an offence which is triable either in the Crown Court or in a magistrates' court, depending upon the seriousness of the case. The offence is made out where the defendant commits the unauthorised access

---

[39] Powers of Criminal Courts Act 1973 s.35(1).
[40] Powers of Criminal Courts Act 1973 s.43.
[41] Magistrates' Courts Act 1980, s.127.
[42] [1999] 2 Cr App R 99.

offence under section 1 with intent to commit, or facilitate the commission of, a more serious 'further' offence. All of the above case law and discussion on the section 1 offence is, therefore, just as relevant to section 2. If any element of the section 1 offence has not been proved, the section 2 offence has not been proved either. It is not necessary for the prosecution to show that the further offence has actually been committed. Indeed, in many cases the further offence will not have been committed, the gravamen of the charge under section 2 being the seriousness of the ulterior intent. If the further offence has been committed, it is likely that the prosecution would charge that offence instead, or in addition. The offences in sections 1 and 2 are hierarchical, so that where a charge is brought under section 2 a conviction may be returned for the section 1 offence if the further ulterior intention cannot be proved.[43] It should be noted, however, that since the section 2 offence is an indictable offence, there may be a prosecution for an attempt to commit that offence but, as we have seen, no conviction may be returned for an attempt to commit the summary offence under section 1.

A defendant may be found guilty of the section 2 offence in a wide range of different factual situations. Obtaining the unauthorised access may, for example, be done with the intention of committing theft, such as by diverting funds which are in the course of electronic transfer, to the defendant's own account or to the account of an accomplice. In the *Bow Street* case the defendant was ultimately extradited for two offences under section 2; namely, securing unauthorised access to the American Express computer system (i) with intent to commit theft, and (ii) with intent to commit forgery. The section 2 offence would also apply where a defendant gains unauthorised access to sensitive information held on computer with a view to later blackmailing a person to whom the information relates. The section also refers to a case where the sentence for the further offence is 'fixed by law', which is the mandatory life sentence for murder. Such a case might arise where the defendant hacked into a hospital computer to alter drug dosages with the intention to kill or cause really serious injury.[44]

Section 2(2) explains what qualifies as a further offence for these purposes. Most offences of fraud and dishonesty (which will be the offences typically concerned here) are punishable with at least five years' imprisonment on indictment. These offences also qualify as 'arrestable offences' under the Police and Criminal Evidence Act 1984. Subsection (3) makes it clear that the defendant may intend to commit the further offence on the same occasion (as in the example of diverting funds to the defendant's bank account, above) or on a future occasion (as in the blackmail example). Subsection (4) makes it possible to convict a person who intended to commit the further offence even though, as it turns out, its commission would be factually impossible. An example would be where the intended blackmail

---

[43] Computer Misuse Act 1990, s.12.
[44] A variation on the facts of *Rymer*; considered below.

victim was, unknown to the defendant, dead. This so-called 'impossibility' rule is analogous to that contained in the law on inchoate offences,[45] as applied in *Shivpuri*.[46]

The maximum penalties for this offence are set out in section 2(5). The fine can be up to a maximum of £5,000 in the magistrates' court, but is unlimited in the Crown Court. The additional sentencing options referred to in relation to section 1, also apply here. In Crown Court there is no limit to the amount of compensation which may be ordered. The offence under section 2 is an arrestable offence.

Viruses: Computer Misuse Act 1990, section 3

Section 3 of the Computer Misuse Act provides:

(1) A person is guilty of an offence if –
  (a) he does any act which causes an unauthorised modification of the contents of any computer; and
  (b) at the time when he does the act he has the requisite intent and the requisite knowledge.
(2) For the purposes of subsection (1)(b) above the requisite intent is an intent to cause a modification of the contents of any computer and by so doing –
  (a) to impair the operation of any computer;
  (b) to prevent or hinder access to any program or data held in any computer; or
  (c) to impair the operation of any such program or the reliability of any such data.
(3) The intent need not be directed at –
  (a) any particular computer;
  (b) any particular program or data of any particular kind; or
  (c) any particular modification or a modification of any particular kind.
(4) For the purposes of subsection (1)(b) above the requisite knowledge is knowledge that any modification he intends to cause is unauthorised.
(5) It is immaterial for the purposes of this section whether an unauthorised modification or any intended effect of it of a kind mentioned in subsection (2) above is, or is intended to be, permanent or merely temporary.
(6) For the purposes of the Criminal Damage Act 1971 a modification of the contents of a computer shall not be regarded as damaging any computer or computer storage medium unless its effect on that computer or computer storage medium impairs its physical condition.
(7) A person guilty of an offence under this section shall be liable –
  (a) on summary conviction, to imprisonment for a term not exceeding six months or to a fine not exceeding the statutory maximum or to both; and
  (b) on conviction on indictment, to imprisonment for a term not exceeding five years or to a fine or to both.

Section 3 creates an offence of 'unauthorised modification of computer material' which is an offence triable either in the Crown Court or in a

[45] Criminal Attempts Act 1981, s.1(2).
[46] [1987] AC 1.

magistrates' court, depending upon the seriousness of the facts. When read in the context of section 17 of the Act (the 'interpretation section'), it is clear that a wide range of different forms of conduct is included. It certainly covers all forms of intentional alteration or erasure of programs or data (s.17(1)(a)) where the defendant intends thereby to impair a computer's operation, hinder access to computer material by a legitimate user or impair the operation or reliability of computer-held material, and where he knows that the intended modification is unauthorised. As with the unauthorised access offence(s), recklessness is *not* sufficient *mens rea* for this offence. Intention must be proved but, again, wilful blindness can be taken to be equivalent to knowledge. It does not have to be proved that the defendant had any specific target computer, program or data in mind.

The central case covered by the section is one where the defendant intentionally introduces a computer virus into a computer system, by way of a floppy disk or an e-mail attachment. Where, for example, D deliberately introduces into circulation a floppy disk contaminated with a virus and A, an innocent party, uses the disk in a computer, impairing its operation, D is guilty of the offence as soon as he introduces the disk into circulation, since section 17(7) states that any act which contributes towards causing such a modification shall be regarded as causing it. The liability of D would be unaffected by A passing the disk to B, who then uses the disk and impairs the operation of any computer, since the intent of A need not be directed at any particular computer, program or data. The first such case prosecuted under the 1990 Act was *Pile*,[47] where a programmer who called himself 'The Black Baron' admitted planting viruses called Pathogen and Queeg that costs hundreds of thousands of pounds to eradicate. He also designed and spread a program called Smeg, which made the viruses particularly difficult to detect. The defendant pleaded guilty to five offences under section 3 as well as to five offences under section 1. In mitigation the defence claimed that Pile was 'a sad recluse' who had worked alone on the offences. The judge imposed a sentence of eighteen months' imprisonment.

In many cases the defendant will have committed an offence under section 1 of the 1990 Act before proceeding to make the unauthorised modification. It is clear, for example, that were the facts of *Gold and Schifreen* to recur the defendants could be convicted of the section 3 offence. In the *Bow Sreeet* case the defendant was extradited for two offences under section 2 of the Act as well as one offence of causing unauthorised modification to the contents of the American Express computer system. In *Rymer*[48] a nurse gained unauthorised access to a hospital's computer system using a doctor's personal identification number which the nurse had memorised some time earlier. Patient drug doses and treatment records were altered. There was a

---

[47] Unreported; see 'Programmer jailed for planting computer virus', *The Times*, 16 November 1995.
[48] This case is referred to by the Audit Commission, loc. cit. p.17, and appears to be the same case which appears in *The Times*, 21 December 1993.

successful prosecution under section 3. The offence is also designed to apply in a case where the defendant intentionally introduces a computer 'worm', the program rapidly using up spare capacity on the computer by replicating itself or by adding additional data to file contents. The defendant may be motivated by mischief, but a likely effect of the introduction of such a program is to prevent or hinder access to a legitimate user (section 3(2)(b)). Where such hindrance is the defendant's clear intention the offence also applies. An example is the Canadian case of *Turner*,[49] where a hacker placed a 'locking device' on data, rendering it inaccessible to others. By section 3(5) it is irrelevant whether such hindrance is, or is intended to be, temporary rather than permanent.

It is unclear whether the offence in section 3 properly extends to the situation which arose in *Whittaker*.[50] There, a private writer of software was supplying copies of his software on approval and asking for payment to be sent if the recipient wished to keep the software. He inserted into the software a program which was automatically activated after 30 days and wiped the program. If the recipient ordered the softwares he would be supplied with a further copy, without the self-destruct program. When the programs supplied did indeed self-destruct, the software supplier was prosecuted and convicted before the magistrates of an offence under section 3. It is true that he had, literally, caused 'an unauthorised modification of the contents of any computer'. The result may be questionable, however, since much turns on the meaning of 'unauthorised modification', and on the precise terms of the licence. The software remains the property of the writer unless purchased (it is not intended as a gift). The owner of property is ordinarily entitled to destroy it if he wishes. That is one of the badges of ownership. If the information supplied with the software made it clear that the program would self-destruct if used after 30 days, by using it after that time the recipient may be taken to have authorised the 'modification' which then took place. Matters might be different again if, say, the program was in the form of a database which invited the recipient to enter data to try out its operation. Self-destruction of the program would then also destroy the recipient's data, and it would seem that this 'modification' is not authorised.[51]

Subsection (6) deals with the relationship between the section 3 offence and the offence of criminal damage under the Criminal Damage Act 1971. Liability for damage under the 1971 Act does not extend to intangible property.[52] In *Cox v Riley*[53], a pre-1990 Act case, the defendant deliberately erased programs from a printed plastic circuit card. His conviction for

---

[49] (1984) 13 CCC(3d) 430.

[50] Unreported, Goole magistrates' court, April 1993. This is thought to be the same case which is referred to at (1994) 10 *Computer Law and Security Report* 39.

[51] If there was a threat to destroy the recipient's data unless payment was received, a charge of blackmail would lie, but there is a possible defence under Theft Act 1968, s.21(1).

[52] Criminal Damage Act 1971, s.10(1).

[53] (1986) 83 Cr App R 54. The decision in *Whiteley* (1991) 93 Cr App R 25 (also a pre-Act case) is to the same effect.

criminal damage was upheld by the Divisional Court, on the basis that the *card* (rather than the intangible programs) had been damaged by the erasure. Section 3(6) declares that the scope of the 1971 Act in computer cases is confined to circumstances in which the physical condition of the computer, or computer storage medium, has been impaired. The intended effect of this is that, were the facts of this case to recur, the defendant would be guilty of unauthorised modification of computer material under section 3, rather than criminal damage. It will be seen that this will be effective so long as the card, or disk, was at the relevant time *in* the computer, since it would then form part of the 'contents of any computer' (sections 3(1)(a) and 17(6)), but it would not apply where the defendant removed the disk from the computer and wiped it with a magnet. In such a case it would still seem to be necessary to rely on the Criminal Damage Act 1971. The relationship between these two statutory provisions does not seem to have given rise to any practical difficulties.

The penalties for this offence are the same as for the offence under section 2 of the 1990 Act. The additional sentencing options referred to in relation to the section 1 offence are also applicable here. The section 3 offence is an arrestable offence.

Offences Under the Data Protection Acts 1984 and 1998

The United Kingdom Data Protection Acts, in contrast with equivalent provisions elsewhere in Europe, are essentially educative and regulatory in character, placing little emphasis upon criminal sanctions. Nevertheless, section 5 of the 1984 Act (as amended by the Criminal Justice and Public Order Act 1994) created a number of offences, relating principally to breach of the registration requirements under the Act and related matters. The offences are all non-imprisonable regulatory offences, punishable by way of a fine. The 1984 Act is currently in the process of being repealed and replaced by the 1998 Act over various dates up to 2007, but with the relevant criminal provisions of the 1998 Act coming into force during 2000. There are some situations where an incident of computer misuse may fall within the criminal provisions, and for convenience reference is made here to both sets of provisions.

Section 5 of the 1984 Act provides that:

(1) A person shall not hold personal data unless an entry in respect of that person as a data user, or as a data user who also carries on a computer bureau, is for the time being contained in the register.
(2) A person in respect of whom such an entry is contained in the register shall not –
  (a) hold personal data of any description other than that contained in the entry;
  (b) hold any data, or use any data held by him, for any purpose other than the purpose or purposes described in the entry;
  (c) obtain such data, or information to be contained in such data, to be held by him from any source which is not described in the entry;

(d) disclose such data held by him on any person who is not described in the entry; or

(e) directly or indirectly transfer such data held by him to any country or territory outside the UK other than one named or described in the entry.

By subsection (3) a servant or agent of a person to whom subsection (2) applies is made subject to the same restrictions. Subsection (4) requires that a person carrying on a computer bureau must register accordingly. Subsection (5) provides that a person contravening subsection (1) (which is an offence of strict liability) or knowingly or recklessly contravening any other provision of section 5 shall be guilty of an offence. For the purposes of section 5 it has been held that the term 'recklessly' bears the 'objective' meaning ascribed to it by the House of Lords decision in *Lawrence*.[54] Proceedings for any criminal offence under the 1984 Act may be brought only by the Data Protection Registrar, or by or with the consent of the Director of Public Prosecutions.[55] Annual Reports of the Data Protection Registrar reveal that most prosecutions brought under section 5 are for the offence of non-registration under section 5(1), with a small number being brought under section 5(2)(b) and section 5(2)(d).

In the important case of *Brown*[56] the defendant was a serving police officer entitled to make use of the Police National Computer for official purposes, but who accessed the computer to obtain information about vehicles owned by debtors of clients of a debt collection agency which was run by a friend of his. The House of Lords quashed his conviction for an offence under section 5(2)(b) of the 1984 Act, deciding that he could not be said to have 'used' personal data for a purpose other than that described in the entry where he had done no more than simply look at the personal data displayed on a computer screen, and where there was no evidence that he had taken further steps to make use of it. The facts of this case took place before the Computer Misuse Act came into force, so there was no possibility of prosecution under that Act. A prosecution under section 1 of that Act would succeed provided that, in the light of the *Bignell* and *Bow Street* cases, discussed above, the prosecution could show that the defendant's access to the relevant material was unauthorised, and that he knew it to be unauthorised. The decision in *Brown* contrasts with a Scottish case,[57] where a police officer acting for a friend ran a check on the police computer relating to the boyfriend of the man's daughter. The police officer found that the man was a hepatitis risk, and he telephoned the daughter, telling her that the man was 'riddled with AIDS'. Here the police officer had clearly taken steps to 'use' the information obtained, and he was properly convicted

---

[54] [1982] AC 510.

[55] 1984 Act, s.19(1).

[56] [1996] 2 Cr App R 72. For comment see Gaskill, S., 'Lords' Ruling on Computer Privacy' *The Times*, 14 February 1996.

[57] Unreported, *Glasgow Herald*, 20 February 1993 (case referred to by Lloyd, I., *Information Technology Law* (Butterworths, London, 1993), p.164.

under section 5 of the 1984 Act and fined. In another case, a nurse working at an outpatients' department accessed a patient's file and passed on information about the patient's illness to her colleagues, one of whom reported the matter. This seems a clear breach of section 5(2)(d), assuming of course that the hospital was properly registered under the Act. The nurse in this case was disciplined rather than being prosecuted.[58]

Under the Data Protection Act 1998, section 17(1) requires that personal data within the (newly extended) meaning of the Act must not be processed unless an entry in respect of the data controller (formerly 'data user') is included in the register maintained by the Data Protection Commissioner (formerly 'Registrar') under section 19. Contravention of section 17(1) by a data controller is an offence under section 21(1). Section 20 imposes a duty on every data controller included in the register to notify the Commissioner, as and when required by regulations, of details of the registrable particulars and of measures taken by the data controller to ensure compliance with the seventh data protection principle (which is: that appropriate technical and organisational measures shall be taken against unauthorised or unlawful processing of personal data and against accidental loss or destruction of, or damage to, personal data). Failure to comply with this duty is an offence under section 21(2). This is an offence of strict liability, but a due diligence defence is available in section 21(3). It is an offence for a person to fail to comply with an enforcement notice issued under section 40 of the 1998 Act where the Commissioner is satisfied that a data controller has contravened or is contravening any of the data protection principles. Again, this is a strict liability offence, but with a due diligence defence available.

The Criminal Justice and Public Order Act 1994 created new offences relating to procuring the disclosure of, or selling or offering to sell, computer-held personal information. The relevant provisions were inserted into the 1984 Act as subsections (6) to (11) of section 5.[59] The changes to the law were prompted by an Audit Commission Report[60] published in 1994 in which sixteen cases involving 'browsing through computer systems' were reported. Her Majesty's Treasury's Central Computer and Telecommunications Agency had also identified browsing of personal data and associated information misuse as a key area of concern.[61] In addition, a number of commercial agencies had been set up, offering quite openly to obtain and to sell confidential information about the affairs of others. One such agency offered to obtain information on a person's bank account balance, credit

---
[58] Case reported by the Audit Commission, loc. cit., p.16.
[59] 1994 Act, s.161 (in force from 3 February 1995). For the background to these offences see Wasik, M., 'Dealing in the Information Market: Procuring, Selling and Offering to Sell Personal Data' (1995) 9 *International Yearbook of Law, Computers and Technology* 193.
[60] Audit Commission, *Opportunity Makes a Thief: An Analysis of Computer Abuse* (London, 1994).
[61] Discussed by the Audit Commission, loc. cit., p.16.

card details, salary or pension details for a fee of about £250.[62] The relevant provisions make it clear that the personal data concerned must be within the scope of the Data Protection Act. Thus, for example, data relating to companies, or to persons now deceased, are not covered. The relevant information must be held on computer (although this is to be extended to some manual records by the 1998 Act) and the data user must be registered under the Act. The procurer must be a person who does not come within the description in the entry in the register. 'Procure' means 'to produce by endeavour',[63] so there must clearly be a causal link between the efforts of the defendant and the obtaining of the information. Thus, an unsolicited leak to a journalist of personal data damaging to a person in the public eye would not be covered. Procurement normally suggests a deception of some kind (such as pretending to be a person entitled to receive the data[64]) but it could also extend to obtaining the information by other means, including bribery, threat or blackmail. The procurer must know, or have reason to believe, that disclosure of the information constitutes a contravention of section 5. Liability under section 5(7) for selling personal data cannot arise if the personal data has been lawfully acquired in the first place, and is restricted to 'selling' – revealing the information to another person for non-financial motives is not within its scope. Further, and somewhat surprisingly, the seller of such information is only liable if *he* is the person who procured the information in the first place – the wording is not apt to cover the case where one person procures the information and then passes it to another person to sell. Offering to sell is covered by section 5(8). It can be seen that liability will only arise if and when the defendant actually procures the information. The publishing of a 'prospectus' advertising such services may constitute an offer to sell the data (section 5(9)).

The Data Protection Act 1998 restructures these more recent offences, with section 55 of the 1998 Act making it an offence for a person 'knowingly or recklessly, without the consent of the data controller [to] obtain or disclose personal data ... or procure the disclosure to another person of the information' (section 55(1)). Section 55(2) offers a range of possible defences to cover cases where, *inter alia*, the obtaining, disclosing or procuring was necessary for the purpose of preventing or detecting crime, or was required or authorised by law. The wording indicates that the burden of proof here rests on the defendant, and that the defence is available only where the obtaining, etc. *was* necessary or required. A mistaken belief that it was so necessary or required would not be enough. Of particular interest is the defence now made available where the obtaining, disclosing

[62] House of Lords Debates vol. 556 col. 1668, 12 July 1994. See also *Sunday Times*, 'Private Lives for Sale in Illicit Info-Market' 18 July 1993.

[63] *AG's Reference (No 1 of 1975)* [1975] 2 All ER 684, at p.684.

[64] Such as in the prosecution referred to in the *Thirteenth Annual Report* of the Data Protection Registrar, where a private investigator used a deception to obtain details of the owner of a motor vehicle from the DVLA (1997–8 HC 122, p.21).

or procuring 'was justified as being in the public interest'. Again it seems that justification can be measured by the court with the benefit of hindsight, and this wording will surely be the subject of appellate consideration in due course. The activities of investigative journalists not infrequently involve the obtaining of personal information by deception. Such activities may conflict with Article 8(1) of the European Convention on Human Rights (that 'everyone has the right to respect for his private and family life, his home and his correspondence'), argument in respect of which can be used before English courts from October 2000 when the Human Rights Act 1998 comes into force. It remains to be seen how readily, in that context, a criminal court will construe the journalist's 'public interest' defence in section 55(2) of the Data Protection Act 1998. The provisions in the former section 5(7), (8) and (9) are substantially replicated in the new section 55(4), (5) and (6).

Fraud

Despite the existence of the more specialist offences referred to so far in this chapter, it has always been clear that the majority of cases involving misuse of information technology will continue to be prosecuted under more traditional theft and related offences in the Theft Acts 1968 and 1978. This continues to be the case, as the Audit Commission Reports have demonstrated. Most computer-related fraud which has come to light in the UK has taken the form of input rather than program fraud and, as such, requires a relatively unsophisticated *modus operandi*. The indications thus far are that frauds committed via the Internet will again be little different in criminal law terms from what has gone before.[65] As the Law Commission has observed recently, 'the Internet is really acting as no more than a sophisticated communications system, and any fraudulent use is likely to involve the commission of existing offences'.[66] Various UK regulators and the police have been expressing concern over the potential for fraud on the Internet, now that people are becoming more used to purchasing goods and services online.[67] As Barrett[68] explains, 'home shoppers are vulnerable in the provision of credit card or other electronic payment mechanisms over the Internet connections'. Goods ordered over the Net may have been misdescribed, they may turn out to be counterfeit, or they may just never be delivered. The Securities and Investment Board has identified several cases of unauthorised investment business being carried out, but it is understood that no prosecutions have yet been brought. Long-established forms of fraud can, of course, be committed just as well over the Net, and here it is the problems of

---

[65] 'Compared with the totality of fraud, Internet fraud should not be overstated': NCIS, *Project Trawler*, loc. cit.
[66] Law Commission, *Legislating the Criminal Code: Fraud and Deception*, loc. cit., para. 8.42.
[67] See 'Cyber Surfers of Internet Must Beware the Sharks', *The Times*, 20 May 1995.
[68] Barrett, N., op. cit., p.22.

evidence and identification of the fraudster, rather than problems over the law itself, which may be quite considerable. The SIB points out that, while it can be difficult to discover who is behind a particular e-mail or website, fraudsters still need to make direct contact with their potential victims.[69] Thus far, no particular substantive legal problems, as opposed to problems of proof, have come to light.

There have been some examples of more novel methods of commission of fraud in recent years. In each case, however, convictions for long-established fraud offences were successfully obtained. In the first unreported trial[70] two defendants were convicted of conspiracy to defraud. They had built and installed their own bogus cashpoint machine which purported to be one belonging to the Halifax. The machine contained a magnetic card reader which took information from customers' cards and downloaded it to a computer. Numerous customers tried to use the machine, which paid out no money but recorded the account details and PINs of those who tried to use it. These details were passed via a modem to the defendants' head-quarters. Counterfeit cards were then manufactured and used to withdraw more than £120,000. The defendants pleaded not guilty but were convicted.[71] In a second unreported trial seven defendants were convicted of conspiracy to steal.[72] The defendants, acting with the help of corrupt British Telecom employees, were planning to intercept telephone communications linking the national networks of 21,000 automated cashpoint machines with main-frame computers at banks. The gang intended to decrypt the information and download account details on to plastic cards which had already been prepared for that purpose. These cards would then have been used to with-draw cash, although it was argued in court that the fraud would not have succeeded because of the security chips now included in plastic cards and because the decrypting equipment used by the conspirators would not have been adequate for the purpose. In a third unreported case several defend-ants pleaded guilty to conspiracy to steal where they had been caught filming cashpoint customers keying in PINs when withdrawing cash. Two of the defendants received custodial sentences of four years and two years.[73] An interesting variation on the theme of fraud occurred in *Munden*.[74] The defendant police officer was convicted of an attempt to obtain property by deception after claiming that 'phantom' cash machine withdrawals had been made from his building society account. He was given a conditional discharge by magistrates, and ordered to pay prosecution costs.

---

[69] See 'Surf Boards on the Lookout for Shysters in Space', *The Times*, 25 January 1996.
[70] *Moore and Hedges*, *The Times*, 15 September 1996.
[71] This case is thought to be the first example of a home-made cash machine being used. Earlier cases have involved stolen cash machines, and of course there has been a batch of cases in which thieves have used JCB diggers in 'ram raid' thefts of cash dispenser machines. See 'Bank Offers £20,000 after JCB Raiders Rip Out Cashpoints', *The Times*, 21 April 1992.
[72] See 'How Gang Planned to Tap into 30 Million Accounts', *The Times*, 5 December 1996.
[73] See 'Card Fraudsters Jailed', *The Times*, 5 December 1996.
[74] Unreported, *The Times*, 8 April 1994.

The Law Commission has recently undertaken a review of offences of fraud and dishonesty, and issued a Consultation Paper[75] in March 1999. While recognising the 'phenomenal growth and increased sophistication of the Internet', the Commission has not seen the need for substantial change to take account of technological development. One possible loophole which has been known about for years, but which has never received legislative attention is the English case law which establishes that a computer cannot be 'deceived', thus rendering the various deception-based Theft Act offences impotent where the fraudster has caused a machine to pay out.[76] In fact this 'loophole' has caused virtually no problems in practice. This is for two reasons. First, virtually every case of criminal deception can now, since the decision of the House of Lords in *Gomez*[77] be prosecuted equally effectively as one of theft. This possibility is only available, however, in relation to the obtaining of *property* by deception under the Theft Act 1968, section 15. Where the relevant charge is obtaining *services* by deception under the Theft Act 1978, section 1, theft is not available as an alternative charge. The second point is that even in a case where a deception charge has been brought in relation to a computer fraud, or a fraud committed over the Internet, a human mind will usually have been deceived at some point, thus fulfilling the deception offence requirement. It is nonetheless possible to imagine some cases in which this loophole could frustrate an otherwise meritorious prosecution.[78] The Law Commission's provisional view is that it should be criminal to obtain a service without the permission of the person providing it, albeit without the deception of a human mind. They propose that this should be done by extending the offence of theft, or by creating a new theft-like offence, rather than by artificially extending the definition of 'deception' to include 'deception of machines'.[79]

A significant problem emerged in 1996 in relation to the prosecution of frauds involving electronic funds transfer. In *Preddy*[80] the House of Lords held that where a defendant dishonestly and by deception procured a debiting of the victim's bank account by a certain sum and the crediting of his own or an accomplice's account by the same sum the defendant

---

[75] Law Commission, *Legislating the Criminal Code: Fraud and Deception*, loc. cit.

[76] The issue was discussed in Wasik, M., op. cit., pp.104–8. 'To deceive is . . . to induce a man to believe a thing which is false, and which the person practising the deceit knows or believes to be false', per Buckley, J. in Re *London and Globe Finance Corpn* [1903] 1 Ch 728 at p.732.

[77] [1993] AC 442. The case decided that the consent of the owner of the property was irrelevant when deciding whether there had been an appropriation for the purposes of theft, thereby approving the earlier decision of *Lawrence v MPC* [1972] AC 626.

[78] As in *Moritz*, unreported, 17–19 June 1981, a case relating to tax fraud, which was soon reversed by statute.

[79] Law Commission, loc. cit., para. 8.58.

[80] [1996] 3 All ER 481. See further [1996] *Criminal Law Review* 726 and commentary on the case. For consideration of the Court of Appeal decision see [1995] *Criminal Law Review* 564.

was not guilty of obtaining property by deception. Although the Court of Appeal had been prepared to uphold the defendant's original conviction, the House of Lords found that this conduct did not come within the wording of the offence charged. The problem was that, in law, the defendant had not obtained anything which had actually belonged to the victim. The property which belonged to the victim was in the form of an intangible bank credit. The activities of the defendant had diminished that property and had enlarged or created a different intangible bank credit belonging to the defendant. Although it is true that the effect of what the defendant did was to obtain dishonestly and by deception a certain sum of money belonging to the victim, this was not in law what had actually happened. It is clear that the effect of the decision was to deprive the prosecution of the use of the offence of obtaining property by deception, under the Theft Act 1968, section 15, in all cases involving electronic funds transfer (and, by implication, transfer by way of cheque, where the analysis of the House of Lords seemed to be equally applicable). Shortly after the decision in *Preddy* the Court of Appeal in *Graham* held that, generally, the reasoning in the former case would also be fatal to a conviction for theft on the same facts.[81] The Law Commission acted speedily to remedy this serious defect in the law,[82] bypassing its normal procedure of issuing a Consultation Paper. It consulted informally, and then moved straight to a Report and Draft Bill. The resulting legislation was the Theft (Amendment) Act 1996, which creates a new offence of obtaining a money transfer by deception, contrary to the Theft Act 1968, section 15A. This is now the offence on which the prosecution should rely. It may be that other charges might succeed in this context, but the law is less than clear.[83]

Finally, a whole range of substantive offences might on occasion be appropriate to deal with particular cases of computer misuse or fraud. Perhaps the most likely is criminal copyright under the Copyright, Designs and Patents Act 1988, section 107. The criminal provisions in this Act are confined to copyright infringement committed 'in the course of a business', unless the infringement is to such an extent as to 'affect prejudicially the owner of the copyright'. The commercial copying of computer software, or of other goods via the Internet thus falls within the scope of the offence, while persons who copy material for their own personal use may incur civil liability but rarely infringe the criminal law. On the other hand the *mens rea* requirements under section 107 extend to a defendant who 'has reason to

---

[81] For discussion see Sir John Smith's comments at (1996) 9 *Archbold News* 3.

[82] For details see Sir John Smith, 'Money Transfers: What Preddy Did to be an Offence' (1996) 9 *Archbold News* 4.

[83] Where the defendant secures a mortgage advance by deception, it is now clear that the relevant offence is obtaining services by deception, under the Theft Act 1978, s.1(3), as inserted by the 1996 Act. The decision in *Halai* [1983] *Criminal Law Review* 624 is now widely accepted to be wrong.

believe' that a relevant article is an infringing copy of a copyright work. This may be contrasted with the Computer Misuse Act offences, where full intent and knowledge must be established by the prosecution. Other possible offences are conspiracy to defraud, of which some mention was made earlier, and a range of specific Theft Act and Companies Act offences, as well as telecoms offences,[84] which may be infringed on the facts of a particular case.

---

[84] Corbitt, T., 'Telecommunications Fraud' (1999) 163 *Justice of the Peace* 668.

CHAPTER 13

Defamation on the Internet

Yaman Akdeniz and Horton Rogers

Introduction

Applying the present libel laws to cyberspace or computer networks entails rewriting statutes that were written to manage physical, printed objects, not computer networks or services. Consequently, it is for the legislature to address the increasingly common phenomenon of libel and defamation on the information superhighway.[1]

There are few specific laws and regulations with respect to defamation on the Internet (though the UK Defamation Act 1996 is a notable exception). At the same time, there is no reason why existing laws including common law decisions on defamation should not apply to Internet-related cases. The greatest difficulties for the common law centre around the liability of Internet service providers for defamatory statements published by third parties who use their systems.

Other chapters in this book have shown that freedom of speech is not absolute, and speech that contains 'obscenity' or 'child pornography' is not protected. Likewise, the law of defamation can be seen as a limitation on freedom of speech and so can have implications for censorship of the Internet. Inevitably, it is difficult to find a balance between the protection of reputation and the right of others to express themselves freely. Where do we draw the line, and how do we draw the line and is there a balance? The law of defamation may have a chilling effect on freedom of speech, and decisions such as *New York Times v Sullivan*[2] in the US and recently the UK decisions in *Derbyshire County Council v Times Newspapers*[3] and *Reynolds v Times Newspapers*[4] have moved from concerns for the private reputations of individuals towards interests of democracy and truth, which is consistent with free speech theories. Such an approach is fostered by the European Convention on Human Rights, though the Convention also recognises the necessity to balance this with the protection of reputation. These matters of course go far beyond the context of the Internet, and the core issues are

---

[1] *It's in The Cards, Inc. v Fuschetto* 535 NW2d 11 (Wis 1995).
[2] 376 US 254 (1964).
[3] [1993] AC 534.
[4] [1999] 4 All ER 609.

likely to be fought out in cases involving pre-existing media. Hence this chapter is mainly concerned with more technical problems presented by the Internet for the traditional law of defamation.

Internet defamation

Defamation can occur on the Internet in a number of different forms. E-mails can contain defamatory statements, as can e-mails posted to Usenet discussion groups, electronic journals and WWW pages. The multi-purpose hybrid Internet provides the possibility to any user to publish web pages; to enter into any discussion group; or to communicate via e-mail. Online users with basic computing skills can easily use Internet browsers, e-mail programs, Usenet news reader programs, and Internet Relay Chat ('IRC') channels. This results in a massive daily turnover of publications on the Internet. Now every single Internet user is a potential publisher, and the Internet allows every single publisher a ready opportunity to reach a global audience.

The World Wide Web

The World Wide Web ('WWW') may be regarded as closely comparable to paper publications or to the kind of newspapers or magazines available in the printed form in newsagents. What is new with the Internet is the opportunity to communicate cheaply, effectively and directly with a massive audience. The Internet potentially provides the opportunity for almost anyone to reach an audience comparable with those of media broadcasting giants such as CNN, BBC and national newspapers such as *The Times* and the *Guardian*. They may be small-scale traditional publishers such as *Shetland News*,[5] *The Thamesmead Gazette*,[6] web-based organisations such as Cyber-Rights & Cyber-Liberties (UK)[7] or purely private individuals. You can read and may comment through these WWW pages, but you cannot change the context of the web pages[8] and, as in the normal daily papers, there is no guarantee that your comments will be published. Therefore, these WWW sites provide a 'one-way' communications system, though there is always the opportunity for individuals to establish their own web pages.

Electronic mail and Usenet discussion groups

The basis of the Internet and the tool most employed by those who use it is the e-mail program. Electronic mail is a two-way communication different from WWW pages. It may be used between two persons in the same manner as sending personal and private letters but e-mails are also used for posting messages to Usenet discussion groups or any other mailing list.

---

[5] See http://www.shetland-news.co.uk/.
[6] See http://www.idiscover.co.uk/superscript/thamesmead/index1.html.
[7] See http://www.cyber-rights.org.
[8] Unless you are a hacker.

An early decision involving defamation and Usenet discussion groups, is the Australian case of *Rindos v Hardwick*.[9] Mr Rindos, an anthropologist, claimed that he had been libelled in a discussion group called 'sci.anthropology' by Mr Hardwick. The initial defamatory statement was transmitted from a computer in Derby, Western Australia. Ipp J found that Rindos was 'well known internationally in academic, anthropological and archaeological circles and that he was a person of high standing in those circles' and that his reputation would suffer from the defamatory statements. Rindos was awarded $40,000 in damages.[10] There are over 30,000 Usenet discussion groups available over the Internet. A Usenet discussion group like 'sci.anthropology' will be available through many Internet news servers though not many people will have an interest in anthropology.[11]

UK defamation laws[12]

Defamation is the publication of a statement which reflects on a person's reputation and tends to lower him in the estimation of right-thinking members of society generally or tends to make them shun or avoid him.[13]

In order to succeed in an action for defamation the plaintiff must prove: that the statement was defamatory; that it referred to him; and that the defendant published it to a third person. The purpose of the law is the protection of reputation, and the wrong is remedied almost exclusively by an award of damages. Although there may be no actual financial loss in a defamation case, the damages may be very high, and it is very expensive to bring a defamation claim to the courts.

Libel and slander

Defamation can occur in two forms. Libel (the more important in practice) is the publication in permanent form of a defamatory statement, and slander is the transitory form. Libel is actionable *per se*, i.e. without proof of damage; slander generally requires proof of 'special' damage. While any writing, picture or an effigy are examples of libel, spoken words

---

[9] No. 1994 of 1993, judgment delivered by the Western Australian Supreme Court, 31 March 1994.

[10] Auburn, F., 'Usenet News and the Law' [1995] 1 *Web JCLI* at http://www.ncl.ac.uk/~nlawwww/.

[11] Defamatory material may of course be conveyed in other forms on the Internet. See *Charleston v News Group Newspapers Ltd* [1995] 2 AC 65, at p.313 where the libel action arose from a news report of indecent computer game material (noted by Prescott, P., 'Libel and Pornography' (1995) 58 *Modern Law Review* 752).

[12] There are no significant differences between the law of Northern Ireland and that of England. Differences in Scots law are pointed out where relevant.

[13] Rogers, W.V.H., *Winfield and Jolowicz on Tort* (15th. edition, Sweet & Maxwell, London, 1998) p.391.

and gestures would be slander.[14] Broadcasting both by radio and television are treated as libel by section 166 of the Broadcasting Act 1990. There appears to be no decisive case on whether defamatory statements over the Internet should be classed as libel or slander. The nature of the Internet and the diversity of the services available over it create some difficulties. The difference between libel and slander was not in issue in the American cases such as *Cubby, Inc. v CompuServe Inc.*[15] and *Stratton Oakmont, Inc. v Prodigy Servs. Co.*[16] Equally, Ipp J in *Rindos v Hardwick* did not specifically address the question whether the defamatory statement was libel or slander, but he did allow damages for mental distress seemingly assuming the news postings to be libel not slander.[17] Ipp J stated that:

> The messages that appear on the bulletin board can remain on the computer of a subscriber or participant for a number of days, or weeks, depending on the storage capacity of the computer in question. . . . Items of interest on the bulletin board can be printed on hard copy.

This suggests that he had in mind a permanent form,[18] but it may also be argued that Ipp J did not give much importance to this matter because even if it were slander it was actionable *per se*, the defamatory statement involving an imputation of unfitness or incompetence of the plaintiff.[19]

If, as seems likely, newsgroup postings are to be regarded as libel, the same should be true for WWW pages and material transferred via file-transfer protocols, though the situation is less clear for e-mails. Arnold Moore argues that with e-mails a permanent form will exist at the time of publication to the receiver but a permanent form will not always be retained.[20] However, a conventional letter (undoubtedly libel) may have a very transitory existence. Internet Relay Chat, Internet phone and video teleconferencing[21] on the other hand are likely to be slander rather than libel where the data is not stored permanently.

For the foregoing reasons, it would be difficult to argue that WWW publications are slander rather than libel on the ground that WWW addresses are not permanent and many pages appear and disappear everyday. The legal classification can hardly depend on the circumstances of the particular website. While these issues have not been tackled by the UK courts yet, the

---

[14] It has been accepted since *Youssoupoff v Metro-Goldwyn-Mayer Pictures Ltd* (1934) 50 T.L.R. 581, that a film constitutes libel.

[15] 776 F. Supp. 135 (S.D.N.Y. 1991).

[16] 23 Media L. Rep. (BNA) 1794 (NY Sup. Ct. No. 31063/94, 25 May 1995).

[17] See Arnold-Moore, T., 'Legal pitfalls in cyberspace' [1994] 5 *Journal of Law and Information Science* 165 at p.176 (also available at http.//www.kbs.citri.edu.au/law/defame.html).

[18] Loc cit. "Permanence" should not be taken too literally.

[19] The statement related to the plaintiff's academic standing.

[20] Arnold-Moore, T., 'Legal pitfalls in cyberspace' [1994] 5 *Journal of Law and Information Science* 165 at p.177.

[21] Video teleconferencing or the transmission of Internet Radio may be considered libel under the provisions of the Broadcasting Act 1990 s.166.

likelihood is that libel, rather than slander, is the dominant tort in the context of the Internet.[22]

Publication

The material part of the cause of action in libel is not the writing, but the publication of the libel.[23]

This statement means that there has to be a publication of the defamatory statement and publication must be communicated to a third party.[24] It is not enough that A sends a statement defamatory of B by electronic mail only to B but it has to be communicated to at least one other party, C. This requirement is not part of Scots Law[25] nor of criminal libel.[26]

Where a claim is brought against the publisher of a newspaper or a book, it is presumed that the matter came to the attention of at least some of those who bought it. Many WWW sites incorporate mechanisms for counting the number of accesses and in some cases a user is required to register and log in on each access.[27] More difficulty may arise if such mechanisms are absent, but accesses may still leave a trace within the log files. However, there may be difficulty in obtaining information about these matters from an ISP who is not liable for the publication.[28] The situation may be even more complicated for newsgroups because it is never clear who accesses them. While the number of posters can be discovered, it is impossible to find out the number of the readers worldwide. Ipp J in *Rindos v Hardwick*[29] held that damages

---

[22] Some jurisdictions avoid the problem by never having had the distinction between libel and slander, as in Scotland, or by abolishing it, as in New South Wales. The Faulks Committee (*Report of the Committee on Defamation* (Cmnd.5909, HMSO, London, 1975) chap. 2) recommended that the distinction be abolished.

[23] Per Lord Esher MR in *Hebditch v MacIlwaine* [1894] 2 QB 58, at p.61, per Davey, L.J. at p.64.

[24] See *Pullman v W. Hill & Co. Ltd* [1891] 1 QB 524 where Lord Esher MR stated that publication is 'The making known of the defamatory matter after it has been written to some person other than the person of whom it is written.'

[25] In Scotland, publication to a third party is not essential because the defamation is regarded by the system as an injury to a person's feelings as well as to his reputation, see e.g. *Mackay v M'Cankie* (1883) 10 Rettie 537.

[26] In criminal libel publication to the prosecutor alone suffices, see e.g. *R v Adams* (1888) 22 QBD 66 where reference is made to the tendency to provoke a breach of the peace, but the law was reviewed in *Gleaves v Deakin* [1980] AC 477 where the House of Lords held that there is no requirement that the libel should tend to a breach of the peace but it should be of a sufficiently serious nature to justify the use of criminal process.

[27] For example the Electronic Telegraph requires users to complete a registration form before accessing the site and the number of possible users of the service is known to the company.

[28] See Mackie, I. and Poulton, A., 'Untangling the web of deceit' *The Times*, 19 January 1999, p.41. For a very liberal approach to discovery see *A v B Ltd* [1997] IRLR (not an Internet case). Milmo, P. and Rogers, W.V.H., *Gatley on Libel and Slander* (9th ed, Sweet & Maxwell, London, 1998) Appendix 1.16, has a precedent statement of claim for an Internet libel which pleads that 'at all material times the said Web site has been open to general access by any user of the World Wide Web'.

[29] Loc. cit.

should be assessed on the basis of publication to approximately 23,000 persons worldwide whose computers had access to 'science anthropology'. It was not stated in the judgment how this figure was arrived at, but being a special-interest discussion group, the potential number of users may be much less than those who have access to a general newsgroup.[30] Where a defamatory statement is sent to a moderated newsgroup, it is thought that it will at least be presumed that the moderator himself read the post before forwarding it to his moderated group.

E-mail communications may create more problems than WWW pages and newsgroups. A letter posted by A to C containing a statement defamatory of B would be a publication if proven[31] and that will also be the case for e-mails. There may be problems when A sends a statement defamatory of B only to B and B claims that the e-mail has been read by others. E-mails are unsecure except for encrypted e-mails, which can only be read by the holder of the private key in a public key encryption system.[32] An e-mail sent from A to B may pass through different computers, and it may be read by others. It is possible to set up routines which scan e-mails for key words and intercept them without being detected. It is also possible for a system operator to read the e-mails of a user in its system, and curious sysops probably do this from time to time. It is possible to argue that there is an analogy with postcards.

> . . . a postcard being an unclosed document, the writing is necessarily visible to every person through whose hands it passes.[33]

In the case of a postcard it will be presumed in the absence of evidence to the contrary, that it has been read by persons other than the one to whom it was sent.[34] But there is also authority supporting the view that a libellous letter sent by post in an unfastened envelope insufficiently stamped is no evidence of a publication to the post officials. *Huth v Huth*[35] supports the view that there is no presumption that the post officials will read the letter and that the plaintiff will need evidence in support of his claim that it has been read by a third party. Lord Reading CJ with respect to postcards stated that:

> if the defendant could establish that the postcard was never read by a single person – although it would be very difficult to conceive that the proof could be given – he would, notwithstanding the presumption, succeed in the action, because he would have proved that there was no publication.[36]

---

[30] See Auburn, F., 'Usenet News and the Law' [1995] 1 *Web JCLI* at www/ncl.ac.uk/~nlawwww/.
[31] *Warren v Warren* (1834) I C.M. & R. 250.
[32] See chap. 14.
[33] Per Palles C.B. in *Robinson v Jones* (1879) 4 L.R. Ir. 391, at p.395.
[34] See Lord Reading CJ in *Huth v Huth* [1915] 3 KB 32 at p.39.
[35] [1915] 3 KB 32.
[36] Per Lord Reading CJ ibid. at p.41.

On balance it seems likely that the courts would reject the analogy with a postcard.[37]

A person who by negligence allows a defamatory statement to go into circulation is treated as publishing it,[38] and a person who sends a communication to a business address should expect that in the normal course of things it may be opened by an employee rather than the person to whom it is addressed.[39] There seems no reason why these principles should not be applicable, with suitable modifications, to the sending or accessing of an electronic communication.

Publishers and distributors: the common law

Where a libel is published in a newspaper or book, everyone who has taken part in publishing it is *prima facie* responsible at common law.[40] The meaning of 'publisher' is very wide including not only the writer of the defamatory statement but also the editor, the printer, the publisher and the owner of the newspaper or the publishing company. There is, however, a distinction between a mere distributor such as newsagents, libraries and booksellers, and a person who takes an active part in the production of the defamatory statement such as the editor or the author. While such a person is liable even if he is not negligent in publishing the defamatory statement, the same does not hold true for distributors.

In *Thomson v Lambert*,[41] Duff CJ stated that:

> The analogy between the delivery of a consignment of newspapers to distributors for distribution among newsvendors, or a parcel of newspapers to a vendor, and the delivery of an article by an author to an editor is a wholly false one. The editor exercises an independent judgment determined by the character of the article. . . . A consignment of newspapers is dealt with as a commercial commodity and not otherwise.

The distributor of defamatory material will not be liable at common law if he succeeds in showing: (i) that he was innocent of any knowledge of the libel contained in the work disseminated by him, (ii) that there was nothing in the work or the circumstances under which it came to him or was disseminated by him which ought to have led him to suppose that it contained a libel, and (iii) that, when the work was disseminated by him, it was not by any negligence on his part that he did not know that it contained a libel.[42] But the onus of proving such facts lies on him, and the question of

---

[37] In any case, the range of publication is clearly very relevant on damages.
[38] See Milmo, P. and Rogers, W.V.H., *Gatley on Libel and Slander* (9th ed., Sweet & Maxwell, London, 1998) para. 6.12.
[39] Ibid., para. 6.11.
[40] Ibid., para. 6.2. For the position under the Defamation Act 1996 see below.
[41] [1938] S.C.R. 253 at p.267.
[42] See *Vizetelly v Mudie's Select Library Ltd* [1900] 2 QB 170, at p.180, applied in *Bottomley v Woolworth* (1932) 48 T.L.R. 521.

publication or non-publication is, in such a case, one for the jury. In *Sun Life Assurance Co. of Canada v W.H. Smith & Sons Ltd*[43] Scrutton LJ said that it might be better if the jury were asked only one question, whether the defendants were negligent in carrying on their business.

The responsibility for defamation of Internet service providers

There is a persistent debate in jurisdictions where the matter is governed by the common law over whether electronic publishers such as system operators ('sysops') of computer bulletin boards ('BBS') and Internet service providers ('ISPs'), are primary publishers or only distributors. ISPs and the sysops of the BBS may be the target of defamation claims as secondary parties for publishing or republishing defamatory statements. This may be the case considering that many of the defamatory statements over the Internet come from 'anonymous sources', as in the US cases of *Prodigy*[44] and *Zeran*.[45] It may be very difficult to find the original author of the defamatory statement and in any case the defendants will try to sue the ISPs with 'deep pockets'. There have been recent cases in this area in the United States, and they are helpful to understand the position at common law before considering the UK Defamation Act 1996.

The American case law from *Cubby, Inc. v. CompuServe Inc.*[46]

In 1991, CompuServe, which develops and provides computer-related products and services, including CompuServe Information Service ('CIS'),[47] was sued by the plaintiffs Cubby, Inc.[48] and Robert Blanchard. One publication in its journalism forum was Rumorville USA ('Rumorville'), a daily newsletter that provided reports about broadcast journalism and journalists. Rumorville carried false and defamatory statements about the plaintiffs, Cubby, Inc. CompuServe did not dispute that the statements were defamatory of the plaintiffs. Instead CompuServe's argument was that 'it acted as a distributor, and not a publisher, of the statements and cannot be held liable for the statements because it did not know and had no reason to know of the statements'.

CompuServe's argument was based on the fact that Cameron Communications, Inc. ('CCI'), an independent company, had contracted to control

---

[43] (1934) 150 L.T. 211 at 212.
[44] 23 Media L. Rep. (BNA) 1794 (NY Sup. Ct 1995).
[45] 129 F 3d 327 (1997), cert. den. 48 S Ct 2341 (1998).
[46] 776 F. Supp. 135 (S.D.N.Y. 1991).
[47] An online general information service or 'electronic library' that subscribers might access from a personal computer or terminal. Subscribers to CIS paid a membership fee and online time usage fees, in return for which they had access to the thousands of information sources available on CIS. Subscribers might also obtain access to over 150 special interest 'forums', which comprised electronic bulletin boards, interactive online conferences and topical databases.
[48] Cubby and Blanchard developed Skuttlebut, a computer database designed to publish and distribute electronically news and gossip in the television news and radio industries.

the contents of the Journalism Forum in accordance with editorial and technical standards established by CompuServe. CompuServe argued that it had no contractual or other direct relationship with Don Fitzpatrick Associates of San Francisco ('DFA') who published Rumorville. DFA provided Rumorville to the Journalism Forum under a contract with CCI and DFA accepted total responsibility for the contents of Rumorville.[49] CompuServe had no opportunity to review the contents of publications before they were uploaded into its servers. The plaintiffs, on the other hand, argued that CompuServe was a 'publisher' of the false statements and should be held to the higher standard of liability accompanying such designation.

Leisure, District Judge, giving the judgment in *Cubby v CompuServe* stated that:[50]

> CompuServe's CIS product is in essence an electronic, for-profit library that carries a vast number of publications and collects usage and membership fees from its subscribers in return for access to the publications. CompuServe and companies like it are at the forefront of the information industry revolution. While CompuServe may decline to carry a given publication altogether, in reality, once it does decide to carry a publication, it will have little or no editorial control over that publication's contents. This is especially so when CompuServe carries the publication as part of a forum that is managed by a company unrelated to CompuServe.

The judge then, taking into account the relevant First Amendment considerations,[51] found Compuserve to be a distributor and stated that the appropriate standard of liability to be applied to CompuServe was whether it knew or had reason to know of the allegedly defamatory Rumorville statements.

If CompuServe was found to have 'published' the defamatory statement, it would have been liable as a culpable party because a publisher who republishes or repeats a defamatory statement is subject to the same liability as if it had originally published the statement.[52] Whether or not a party will be characterised as a publisher will depend upon how much editorial control is exercised over a publication. For example, newspapers have a high degree of editorial control of their publication. In *Miami Herald Publishing*

---

[49] Affidavit of Jim Cameron.

[50] *Cubby, Inc. v CompuServe Inc.* 776 F. Supp. 135, 140 (S.D.N.Y. 1991).

[51] 'First Amendment guarantees have long been recognised as protecting distributors of publications. . . . Obviously, the national distributor of hundreds of periodicals has no duty to monitor each issue of every periodical it distributes. Such a rule would be an impermissible burden on the First Amendment': *Lerman v Flynt Distributing Co.* 745 F.2d 123, at p.139 (2d Cir.1984), cert. denied, 471 US 1054 (1985). See also *Daniel v Dow Jones & Co.* 137 Misc.2d 94, 102, 520 N.Y.S.2d 334, 340 (NYCiv.Ct.1987) (computerised database service 'is one of the modern, technologically interesting, alternative ways the public may obtain up-to-the-minute news' and 'is entitled to the same protection as more established means of news distribution').

[52] See Restatement (Second) of Torts para. 578 (1976) which states that 'one who repeats or otherwise republishes defamatory matter is subject to liability as if he had originally published it'.

Co. v Tornillo,[53] the Supreme Court held that the 'choice of material to go into a newspaper, and the decisions made as to limitations on the size and content of the paper and treatment of public officials . . . constitute the exercise of editorial control and judgment'.[54] A newspaper proprietor is considered a publisher of the entire contents of the newspaper, but the same is not necessarily true of Internet service providers.

A different outcome was reached in *Stratton Oakmont Inc v Prodigy Services Co.*[55] Prodigy, another US Internet service provider, as a part of its services contracted with Bulletin Board Leaders, who among other things, participated in board discussions and undertook promotional efforts to encourage usage and increase users. 'Money Talk' was one of Prodigy's bulletin boards where members could post statements regarding stocks, investments and other financial matters.[56] In October 1994, an unidentified person posted on Money Talk allegedly defamatory statements about the plaintiffs, Stratton Oakmont, Inc., a securities investment banking firm. The statements accused Stratton and its president of committing criminal and fraudulent acts in connection with a public stock. This was described as a 'major criminal fraud', and the posting also alleged that the president of Stratton was 'soon to be a proven criminal' and his firm Stratton Oakmont was characterised as a 'cult of brokers who either lie for a living or get fired'. The plaintiffs asked the court to determine whether Prodigy was a 'publisher' of the alleged defamatory statements.

The plaintiffs' claim that Prodigy was a publisher was based on Prodigy's family orientated online service policy. In an effort to provide a family environment, Prodigy edited the content of messages posted on its bulletin boards:[57]

> We make no apology for pursuing a value system that reflects the culture of the millions of American families we aspire to serve. Certainly no responsible newspaper does less when it chooses the type of advertising it publishes, the letters it prints, the degree of nudity and unsupported gossip its editors tolerate.

The plaintiffs contended that this was tantamount to an admission that Prodigy was akin to a newspaper and, as such, should incur liability for defamatory statements posted on its bulletin boards as a publisher. The question for the court was whether or not Prodigy had exercised enough editorial control to be considered as a publisher with the same liabilities as a newspaper publisher. The plaintiffs' argument was also supported by the content guidelines and the software screening program with an emergency delete function used by Prodigy's Bulletin Board Leaders.

The Court in *Stratton Oakmont v Prodigy* distinguished the *Cubby* decision on two counts. First, Prodigy held itself out to the public and its

---

[53] 418 U.S. 241 (1974).
[54] Ibid. at p.258.
[55] 23 Media L. Rep. (BNA) 1794 (NY Sup. Ct 1995).
[56] Money Talk was one of the most widely read financial computer bulletin boards in the US.
[57] NY Sup. Ct. No. 31063/94, 25 May 1995, Exhibit J.

members as controlling the content of its computer bulletin boards. Secondly, Prodigy implemented this control through its automatic software screening program and the Guidelines which Board Leaders were required to enforce. By actively utilising technology and the human agency to delete notes from its computer bulletin boards on the basis of, for instance, offensiveness and 'bad taste', Prodigy was clearly making decisions as to content, and such decisions constituted editorial control. The Court concluded that for the purposes of plaintiffs' claims in this action, Prodigy was a publisher rather than a distributor. The Court in *Stratton Oakmont* agreed that ISPs 'should generally be regarded in the same context as bookstores, libraries, and network affiliates' as decided in *Cubby*. However, according to the Court, it was Prodigy's own policy to apply an editorial control over its bulletin boards which altered its liability and resulted in it being labelled as a publisher.

The *Stratton Oakmont* case was distinguished and doubted by higher New York courts in *Lunney v Prodigy Services Co.*[58] Here Prodigy were sued for libel in respect of an abusive e-mail message which an unidentified person had sent in the plaintiff's name to his Boy Scout leader, and in respect of similar false messages posted on a bulletin board. Granting Prodigy summary judgment, the Appellate Division reasoned that in carrying e-mail messages the defendants were acting in a manner closely analogous to a telephone company, and it had been held in New York that such a 'carrier' was not to be treated as publishing defamatory messages transmitted via its lines, even if it was aware of their content.[59] In other words, it did not even bear the restricted liability of a 'distributor'. The fact that the defendants might have instituted some automatic system to screen out offensive words in messages did not make them 'editors' of the material: 'application of any unintelligent automated word-exclusion program of this type cannot be equated with editorial control . . . Intelligent editorial control involves the use of judgment, and no computer program has such a capacity.' An alternative (but in the Court's view less accurate) analogy would equate the defendants with a telegraph company[60] and it was established law that, while a telegraph company was a publisher, since it participated in a more active way in the transmission, nevertheless it was protected under New York law unless it was aware that the message was defamatory. All this was sufficient to distinguish *Stratton Oakmont*. But the court went further, remarking that in that case 'Prodigy was punished for allegedly performing in an inadequate way the very conduct (exercise of editorial control) which, initially, it had no legal duty to perform at all. The rule of law announced in *Stratton Oakmont* discourages the very conduct which the plaintiff in *Stratton Oakmont* argued should be encouraged.'[61]

[58] 683 NYS 2d 557 (1998) (AD); 701 NYS 2d 684 (1999) (Ct of Appeals).
[59] *Anderson v New York Telephone Co* 320 NE 2d 647 (NYCA 1974).
[60] The court described e-mail as 'in substance, nothing but an updated version of the telegraph'.
[61] Loc. cit.

On a further appeal,[62] the Court of Appeals agreed that in respect of e-mail the ISP was directly analogous to a telephone company – 'merely a conduit'. With regard to the bulletin board messages the Court declined to hold that because Prodigy had reserved the power to screen these it was therefore to be regarded as a publisher of each and every message on them.

US Communications Decency Act 1996

The discouragement of desirable conduct point made in *Lunney* also underlies a legislative initiative which was not applicable in *Lunney* because the complaint was launched before it was passed. The Communications Decency Act passed in 1996[63] was an attempt to regulate Internet indecency.[64] By section 223(f)(1) a person who makes a good faith effort to restrict the access of minors to offensive material is not to be subject to civil or other liability (for example at the suit of the person who originates the material) on account of that effort; and in order to protect such a person from the collateral risk that by making such an effort he will be classed as a 'publisher' for defamation purposes, section 230(c)(1) provides that 'No provider or user of an interactive computer service shall be treated as the publisher or speaker of any information provided by another information content provider.'[65]

This provision was considered by the Fourth Circuit Court of Appeals in *Zeran v America Online Inc*,[66] which held that 'by its plain language, section 230 created a federal immunity to any cause of action that would make service providers liable for information originating with a third-party user of the service'.[67] Nor did the fact that the provider had notice of the transmission of wrongful material prevent the operation of the immunity or allow reliance on the alternative argument that it was liable as a 'distributor'. *Zeran*, like *Lunney*, arose from an anonymous posting, in the inception of which the defendants were no more than a conduit. A case closer on its facts

---

[62] 701 NYS 2d 684 (1999).

[63] 47 USC s.223 et seq.

[64] Only partially successful because part of the Act was found incompatible with the First Amendment in *ACLU v Reno* 521 US 844 (1997); Akdeniz, Y., 'Censorship on the Internet' (1997) 147 *New Law Journal* 1003; Vick, D.W., 'The Internet and the First Amendment' (1998) 61 *Modern Law Review* 414. See further chap. 9.

[65] S.230 defines 'interactive computer service' as 'any information service, system, or access software provider that provides or enables computer access by multiple users to a computer server, including specifically a service or system that provides access to the Internet and such systems operated or services offered by libraries or educational institutions' 47 USC s.230(e)(2). The term 'information content provider' is defined as 'any person or entity that is responsible, in whole or in part, for the creation or development of information provided through the Internet or any other interactive computer service' (s.230(e)(3)).

[66] 129 F 3d 327 (1997), *cert. den.* 524 US 937 (1998); *Doe v America Online Inc* 718 So 2d 385 (Fla 1998). The plaintiff's claim, which arose out of a false bulletin board posting that the plaintiff was selling t-shirts with offensive messages about the Oklahoma City bombing, was framed as one for negligence in failing to remove the posting, but the court said that the allegations were in substance indistinguishable from a 'garden variety defamation action': 129 F 3d at p.332.

[67] Ibid. at p.330.

to *Stratton Oakmont* is *Blumenthal v Drudge and America Online Inc*,[68] a defamation claim brought in respect of allegations in the first defendant's 'Drudge Report', an electronic scandal sheet. The second defendants, AOL, made the Drudge Report site available to its subscribers, advertised it as a means of promoting its service, paid Drudge a licence fee and by its contract with him had extensive editorial rights in respect of content, though no control had been exercised on the occasion in question. With some reluctance,[69] the Court found that AOL were protected by the clear words of the statute, though it warned that section 230 did not preclude joint liability where a service provider had taken some active role in the creation of material.[70] There is, therefore, a stark contrast between the position of a service provider and a newspaper or magazine publisher or even a television station, which are prima facie responsible for anything appearing in their product. The service provider may 'tout someone as a gossip columnist or rumour monger who will make such rumours and gossip "instantly accessible" to [its] subscribers, and then claim immunity when that person, as might be anticipated, defames another'.[71]

UK Law: the Defamation Act 1996 and *Godfrey v Demon Internet*

The Defamation Act 1996 reforms the law of defamation in many respects: here we are concerned with the provisions on responsibility for publication in section 1(1) of the Act. Section 1 came into force on 4 August 1996 and applies to the whole United Kingdom.[72] Section 1 was preceded by a consultation paper[73] on 'The Defence of Innocent Dissemination' issued by the Lord Chancellor in July 1990. The common law on this defence has been outlined above.

While the principle underlying the common law defence was a desirable one, it had failed to keep pace with changing technology and practices. For example, printers were not entitled to rely on the defence, but in modern conditions they often do not see a word of the material, which may be input by electronic means and in a language which they cannot understand. The Lord Chancellor explained section 1 in the House of Lords as:[74]

---

[68] 992 F Supp. p.44 (US District Ct, DC 1998).

[69] The court remarked (at p.52) 'that AOL in this case has taken advantage of all the benefits conferred by Congress in the Communications Decency Act, and then some, without accepting any of the burdens that Congress intended'. The NYCA in *Lunney* (above) declined to enter into the debate on the effect of s.230(c)(1).

[70] 992 F Supp. at p.50.

[71] Ibid. at p.51.

[72] S.18(1), (2), (3).

[73] A later consultation paper, *Reforming Defamation law and Procedure: Consultation on Draft Bill* (Lord Chancellor's Department, London, 1995) covered the whole Bill.

[74] House of Lords Debates vol. 571, col. 214, 2 April 1996. It is not wholly clear that the section *replaces* the common law: see Milmo, P. and Rogers, W.V.H., *Gatley on Libel and Slander* (9th ed., Sweet & Maxwell, London, 1998) para. 6.25.

... intended to provide a defence for those who have unwittingly provided a conduit which has enabled another person to publish defamatory material. It is intended to provide a modern equivalent of the common law defence of innocent dissemination, recognising that there may be circumstances in which the unwitting contributor to the process of publication may have had no idea of the defamatory nature of the material he has handled or processed.

Section 1(1) of the 1996 Act provides:

In defamation proceedings a person has a defence if he shows[75] that –
(a) he was not the author, editor or publisher of the statement complained of,
(b) he took reasonable care in relation to its publication, and
(c) he did not know, and had no reason to believe, that what he did caused or contributed to the publication of a defamatory statement.

By section 1(5),

in determining ... whether a person took reasonable care, or had reason to believe that what he did caused or contributed to the publication of a defamatory statement, regard shall be had to –
(a) the extent of his responsibility for the content of the statement or the decision to publish it;
(b) the nature or circumstances of the publication, and
(c) the previous conduct or character of the author, editor or publisher.

Section 1(2) defines the author, the editor and the publisher respectively. An author is 'the originator of the statement'; an editor is 'a person having editorial or equivalent responsibility for the content of the statement or the decision to publish it'; and 'publisher' means 'a commercial publisher, that is, a person whose business is issuing material to the public, or a section of the public, who issues material containing the statement in the course of that business'. However, section 1(3) then specifically excludes certain persons from the category of author, editor or publisher, such as printers and (in certain circumstances) broadcasters of live programmes. The provisions primarily relevant to ISPs are as follows:

A person shall not be considered the author, editor or publisher of a statement if he is only involved ...
(c) in processing, making copies of, distributing or selling any electronic medium in or on which the statement is recorded, or in operating or providing any equipment, system or service by means of which the statement is retrieved, copied, distributed or made available in electronic form;
(e) as the operator of or provider of access to a communications system by means of which the statement is transmitted, or made available, by a person over whom he has no effective control.[76]

---

[75] The burden of proof of establishing these matters is clearly upon the defendant.
[76] One must distinguish the case where A, an employee of B, in the course of his employment, uses B's network or Internet access to distribute a defamatory statement. In such a case B would be vicariously liable for A's act and it would be quite irrelevant whether B had taken reasonable care. An insurance company recovered £450,000 in an out of court settlement

Section 1(3)(c) may be applied[77] to the ISP whose servers are indirectly used by the subscribers to the system to download files through File Transfer Protocols ('FTP'), access WWW pages, and send e-mails. Section 1(3)(e) exempts from liability the operator of a communication system by means of which a defamatory statement is transmitted. Lord Inglewood, Parliamentary Under-Secretary of State, Department of National Heritage stated that:[78]

> In the notes accompanying the draft Bill . . . we invited views as to whether it would be helpful to introduce legislation clarifying any doubts as to when and where publication has taken place when computer networks are used. Those who responded were strongly in favour of legislation and several offered detailed models. However, it would not be right to attempt legislation without full consideration and consultation on all policy issues arising in the context of both defamation law and diverse other areas of law relevant to the use of those networks. Service providers would fall within the example under Clause 1(3)(e) of those who will not be considered publishers.

Since section 1 is built on the common law, there are two issues. First, is the ISP a publisher in the common law sense? Secondly, if it is, can it avail itself of the section 1 defence?

On the first issue, *Godfrey v Demon Internet Ltd*[79] is authority that (in contrast to what may be the position under American common law) the ISP does publish material held on his newsgroup server and accessed by others. As Morland J put it, 'The situation is analogous to that of the bookseller who sells a book . . . to that of the circulating library who provided books to subscribers. . . . and to that of distributors [of magazines]. . . . I do not accept [the] argument that the defendant was merely the owner of an electronic device through which postings were transmitted.'[80] On the second issue, *Godfrey* holds that an ISP can in principle avail itself of the protection of section 1 of the 1996 Act because it is not a 'publisher' in the special, narrow sense used there.[81] However, it will have been noticed that the

---

against another insurer in respect of e-mails circulated by employees of the first casting doubt on the solvency of the second: see 'Insurance firm wins £450,000 for e-mail libel', *Daily Telegraph*, 18 July 1997.

[77] It is of course much broader. For example it covers retailers of CD-ROMS.

[78] House of Lords Debates vol. 570, col. 605, 8 March 1996.

[79] [1999] 4 All ER 342. See Akdeniz, Y., 'Case analysis' (1999) 4 *Journal of Civil Liberties* 260. The case was settled out of court (on payment of £15000 damages plus costs) on 30 March 2000.

[80] At p.348. The implication here and at p.349 seems to be that the telephone service is in the same position as in the USA. It is submitted that here, as in the USA, ISPs do not publish private e-mails which they carry.

[81] The position is perhaps less clear in the case of a moderated newsgroup since this would seem to amount to an editorial function under s.1(2) and the defendant is not then 'only involved' as the operator of a communication system under s.1(3)(e). That said, of course, it may be exceedingly difficult to identify any but the most egregious defamatory messages. However, it has been pointed out that there is an element of contradiction in s.1, for the more rigorous the steps taken by way of reasonable care, the more likely it is that the defendant will be exercising an editorial function: Edwards, L., 'Defamation and the Internet: Name Calling in Cyberspace' in Waelde, C. and Edwards, L. (eds), *Law and the Internet: Regulating Cyberspace* (Hart Publishing, Oxford, 1997).

complaints in some of the American cases have arisen not in respect of the original publication but because the ISP has failed to remove them on complaint – liability 'on notice'. Although section 1 is not explicit on this point, yet bearing in mind that the material may be continually accessed,[82] it seems that the intention was that once notice is given the ISP may lose the section 1 defence,[83] and *Godfrey* so holds:[84]

> After 17 January 1997 after the receipt of the plaintiff's fax the defendant knew of the defamatory posting but chose not to remove it from its Usenet news servers. In my judgment this places the defendant in an insuperable difficulty so that it cannot avail itself of the defence under section 1.

The ISP would seem in fact to be in a somewhat invidious position, for the provider of the information may contend that it is true or privileged or fair comment on a matter of public interest, matters which it may be difficult or impossible for the ISP to judge.[85] It would not seem to be possible for the ISP to contend that, for example, it had received legal advice that, say, the matter was fair comment, for it is required to show not that it had no reason to believe that it was contributing to an *actionable* publication but to one that was *defamatory*. The likelihood is, therefore, that an ISP will err on the side of caution and more or less automatically remove the material on complaint.[86] This is certainly not the position in the United States, for reasons clearly explained by the court in the *Zeran* case:[87]

> Notice-based liability would deter service providers from regulating the dissemination of offensive material over their own services. Any efforts by a service provider to investigate and screen material posted on its service would only lead to notice of potentially defamatory material more frequently and thereby create a stronger basis for liability. Instead of subjecting themselves to further possible lawsuits, service providers would likely eschew any attempts at self-regulation. More generally, notice-based liability for interactive computer service providers would provide third parties with a no-cost means to create the basis for future lawsuits. Whenever one was displeased with the speech of another party conducted over an interactive computer service, the offended party could simply 'notify' the relevant service provider, claiming the information to be legally defamatory. In light of the vast amount of speech communicated through interactive computer services, these notices could produce an impossible burden for service providers, who would be faced with ceaseless choices of suppressing controversial speech or sustaining prohibitive liability. Because the probable effects of distributor liability

---

[82] Compare a newspaper or television publication where there is no further publication except by the publisher's deliberate choice.

[83] It would in effect be in the same position as the golf club committee in *Byrne v Deane* [1937] 1 KB 818, whose liability arose from failing to remove the defamatory material from its notice board.

[84] [1999] 4 All ER at p.346.

[85] The point is made generally about s.1 by Lord Lester of Herne Hill in the House of Lords Debates vol. 570, cols 584–5, 8 March 1996.

[86] See Akdeniz, Y., 'Can He Not Stay Free' *The Guardian*, Online, 27 April 2000 p.6. See further the case of Hulbert at http://www.cyber-rights.org/documents/hulbert.htm.

[87] Loc. cit. at p.334.

on the vigour of Internet speech and on service provider self-regulation are directly contrary to [the Communications Decency Act] section 230's statutory purposes, we will not assume that Congress intended to leave liability upon notice intact.

The contrast between the two systems may be illustrated by a case which was brought in this country by a British lecturer in respect of defamatory postings about him to newsgroups by students at Cornell University. It is understood that the matter was settled without any payment.[88] In fact the University was not hosting the newsgroups and its network was merely the conduit through which access was gained to the Internet, but in either event it would have fallen under section 1 of the 1996 Act. The form of section 1 would seem to preclude regarding it as an 'author, editor or publisher'. Nevertheless, section 1 clearly contemplates that a person who does not fall within these categories may incur liability by 'contributing' to the publication of a defamatory statement and upon receipt of a reasonably substantiated complaint, failure to block further access[89] (and, if the University were the host, to remove the material) would seem to be prima facie a failure to exercise reasonable care under section 1. But under United States law, as *Zeran* shows, neither action would be required. Whether or not that is a desirable state of affairs is of course a matter for debate. The present state of the law in the United States would seem to leave the victim of Internet attack, even in extreme cases involving threats to individuals and going far beyond the bounds of legitimate free speech, in the position where he may be dependent for an effective remedy upon the grace of the ISP.

Place of publication; republication

Quite apart from the question of *who* publishes, the Internet presents more challenges to libel rules framed around paper publications. The basic principles of English law in this area are as follows. First, a statement is published in the place where it is seen or heard.[90] Secondly, leave may be obtained to serve process on a defendant outside the jurisdiction (i.e. England) where the damage is sustained, or resulted from an act committed, within the jurisdiction and again damage is sustained and the relevant act is committed where the publication takes place. Thirdly, where the Brussels Convention of 1968 applies (as it does in the case of most European countries) a person abroad may be sued here if the 'harmful event' occurred here, and this again means publication.[91] Fourthly, each separate publication gives rise to a

---

[88] Legal Watch, University Business, July/August 1998: http://universitybusiness.com/9807/legal.html. The plaintiff was the Dr Godfrey of *Godfrey v Demon Internet*.

[89] In itself of course that may present problems. A defamatory statement may be found in a newsgroup or WWW site over which the University has no control and which contains academically useful information. See generally for the risks to universities and their response, Vick, D., Macpherson, L. and Cooper, S., 'Universities, Defamation and the Internet' (1999) 62 *Modern Law Review* 58.

[90] *Bata v Bata* [1948] WN 386.

[91] *Shevill v Presse Alliance* [1995] 2 AC 18 (European Court of Justice). See further chap. 4.

separate cause of action, and there is a separate publication for this purpose not only where material previously issued is reissued, but to each person who receives a statement issued on a single occasion. The practice is, however, that if a book or newspaper is published in this country one action is brought in respect of the entire publication,[92] and it is unlikely that the courts would tolerate multiple actions; it is thought that a similar attitude would be taken to an Internet publication here. Fifthly, where the libel is published abroad,[93] it must be actionable both by English law and by the law of the place where the defendant acted[94] but where the tort is committed in England only English law is relevant. There have been a number of actions in respect of foreign newspapers with small circulations in England, but the Internet clearly has enormous possibilities for 'cross-border' litigation if it can be shown, for example, that a WWW site was accessed outside the country where the material was input. The 'double actionability' rule will not help the defendant where the plaintiff can show that the site was accessed in England because the tort will then have been committed here. English libel law is perceived to be rather more 'plaintiff-friendly' than that of some other countries,[95] particularly the United States. For example, an American ISP sued here in respect of a libel on a politician would be unable to take advantage of either section 230 of the Communications Decency Act or of the rule in *New York Times v Sullivan*.[96] The defendant may apply to stay the action on the ground of *forum non conveniens*, but it is most unlikely to succeed where the plaintiff resides here and sues in respect of a publication here. In a foreign newspaper case the Court of Appeal said: 'Where the tort of libel is allegedly committed in England against a person resident and carrying on business in England by foreigners who are aware that their publication would be sent to subscribers in England, that English resident is entitled to bring proceedings here . . . and to limit his claim to publication in England, even though the circulation of the article . . . was extremely limited in England and there was a much larger publication elsewhere.'[97] Of course where the defendant does not have substantial assets here, the plaintiff may find it very difficult to enforce

---

[92] Some American states have a 'single publication rule' – see the Uniform Single Publication Act adopted by the Commissioners on Uniform State Laws in 1952. However, this is largely directed at the prevention of multiple actions in different US states in respect of one issue. This problem is of course much less serious within the UK.

[93] The defendant may be sued because he is present here.

[94] This has been modified in other tort cases but is retained for defamation by s.13 of the Law Reform (Miscellaneous Provisions) Act 1995. There is, however, some doubt whether it still applies to cases where the Brussels Convention is applicable: see Tugendhat, M., 'Media law and the Brussels Convention' (1997) 113 *Law Quarterly Review* 360 and Briggs, A., 'Two undesirable side-effects of the Brussels Convention?' (1997) 113 *Law Quarterly Review* 364.

[95] See further Braithwaite, N., *The International Libel Handbook* (Butterworth-Heinemann, London, 1995).

[96] 376 US 254 (1964).

[97] *Schapira v Ahronson* [1999] EMLR 735. See also *Berezosky v Michaels* [2000] 2 All ER 986.

his judgment abroad if there is a divergence between English law and the foreign system, since the foreign court may consider enforcement as against its local public policy.[98]

Even if we leave aside the international dimension, the nature of the Internet presents more problems. Although we have concentrated upon ISPs, it is self-evident that individual contributors are personally liable for what they write. A very large proportion of Newsgroup content consists of material 'quoted' from previous postings and, though it is probably not very widely known, there is no doubt that a person who repeats a libel originated by someone else is as liable as the source. If I say 'A told me that B murdered his wife', it is not sufficient for me to prove that A did tell me that: I have to prove that B did the act charged.[99] It is difficult to see how someone who posts a message quoting a previous defamatory posting can escape this rule. On the other hand, a complete failure to include the previous message in a response, apart from being impracticable, runs the risk that the poster will be unable to rely on the defence of fair comment, because the defence is only available for comments upon matters which are 'indicated' in the statement and whether a statement is a comment or an assertion of fact (in which case it has to be shown to be true) has to be determined from the publication itself.[100] It may be reasonable to expect a newspaper editor to have some understanding of these subtleties, but they are not likely to be known to many newsgroup posters.

Slightly different from the above is the widespread practice of one website incorporating links to others. Is the creator of the link an 'author or editor' of the linked statement accessed through his site?[101] If the author of a book incorporates a defamatory passage from another work, it would seem plain that he cannot rely on the defence of innocent dissemination at common law. Even under the Defamation Act 1996, while he may not literally be the 'originator' of the statement, he surely has editorial responsibility for the decision to publish the statement. There is of course a substantial practical difference between this case and that of the creator of a link, and it is arguable that he is closer to, say, someone providing a library service. If, on this basis, the creator of the link may rely on section 1(3) of the Act, the question then arises, at least where the linked statement is defamatory on its face, whether he will be able to show that he took all reasonable care and did not know that he was contributing to the publication of the defamatory statement. This may depend very much upon the facts. At one extreme, take the case of the person who creates a link to general news

---

[98] See for example *Bachchan v India Abroad Publications* 585 NYS (2d) 661 (NYSC, 1992).
[99] See *Lewis v Daily Telegraph* [1964] AC 234 at p.260.
[100] *Telnikoff v Matusevitch* [1992] 2 AC 343.
[101] See also Akdeniz, Y., 'To Link or Not to Link: Problems with World Wide Web Links on the Internet' (1997) 11 *International Review of Law, Computers and Technology* 281. Drawing attention to an existing defamatory statement can amount to publishing it: *Hird v Wood* [1894] 38 SJ 235.

service (for example the BBC News website). It cannot conceivably be the law that he automatically becomes liable, via the link, for any future defamatory statement on the service. The answer would seem to be the same even in respect of existing libels where it would be unreasonable to expect him to peruse the entire content of the linked site – it would be theoretically possible for a bookseller to arrange to have his entire stock read for libel before it is put on sale, but no one has ever suggested that this is the price of reliance on the common law defence of innocent dissemination.[102] The position is not, however, necessarily the same in two cases: where the linked site has acquired a 'reputation for libel' or where the link is made to a specific article on the site, at least where the libel in it is obvious.[103]

It is also possible that where A publishes a defamatory statement, he may be liable for its repetition by B. In some cases this is obviously so because A intends and authorises the repetition of the statement, as where an author submits a manuscript to a publisher or a politician makes a statement at a press conference. As a general principle, however, it has been said that there may be liability for republication by another whenever that is the 'natural and probable consequence'.[104] Does a person who publishes a statement on his website bear responsibility for publications via links which others create to the site?[105] This point is of course of much more importance in relation to the print or broadcast media, because there it may lead to a person who has made only a limited initial publication being liable for a much more widespread one, whereas it tends to be in the nature of an Internet publication that it is generally available from the beginning. Nevertheless, as a practical matter links in popular sites may vastly increase the distribution of the statement.

Conclusion

So far as is known, no Internet libel case in England has yet been fought right through to judgment, though there have been settlements.[106]

---

[102] It is thought that an author in the conventional media who merely refers to another publication does not thereby publish it in any sense for the purposes of the law of defamation. While in a sense a link is a mere reference, nevertheless it must be relevant that in practice it is much easier to follow up than a reference in a book.

[103] It is thought that the court should set a low standard of care for this purpose.

[104] See *Slipper v BBC* [1991] 2 QB 283.

[105] Where the creation of a link is invited, the answer is surely 'Yes'.

[106] In March 1995 Dr Laurence Godfrey was involved in a case where he alleged libel by another physicist Mr Phillip Hallam-Baker. However the claim never came to final trial because Dr Godfrey accepted an out of court settlement in July. See McGourty, C., 'Internet libel laws creep up on cyberspace' *Daily Telegraph*, 29 March 1995; Marks, P., 'Internet's free flow faces libel law curbs' *Daily Telegraph*, 5 June 1995. See also Marks, K., 'Asda pays PC damages for E-mail slur', *Daily Telegraph*, 20 April 1995; McCormack, M., 'Tell it to the Judge', *.Net Magazine* [1995] 9; Graves, D., 'Insurance firm wins £450,000 for e-mail libel,' *Daily Telegraph*, 18 July 1997; *Godfrey v Demon Internet*, n.79 above.

Defamation actions are generally expensive, legal aid is not available, legal costs are high and jury awards are unpredictable. These financial aspects of defamation actions mean that no matter how strongly individual potential plaintiffs wish to utilise defamation claims to protect their reputation, in reality it tends to be well-off people who take action against the media. Recent case law on damages may have reduced further the attraction of defamation as a source of potential reward for the rich.[107] Furthermore, the House of Lords has moved towards extending the law of qualified privilege in discussions of matters of public interest in *Reynolds v Times Newspapers*.[108] England may now therefore become less of a happy hunting ground for libel plaintiffs, though the action may also become conversely more accessible because the Defamation Act 1996 includes a fast track summary procedure with damages up to £10,000 and a new offer of amends defence.[109] The Internet undoubtedly gives ordinary people a much greater capacity to 'broadcast' their views to a wide audience than has ever been the case before. Whether one takes the view that this requires contributors to have some special treatment from defamation law in the interests of free discussion is likely to turn on one's broader conception of the proper balance between free speech and reputation. A great deal of Internet 'discussion' is at the level of puerile abuse, and it can be argued that it would not be in society's interests to encourage this. On the other hand, the nature of the Internet makes it comparatively easy to reply to defamatory statements – it has a built-in 'right of reply' so to speak. Such a right exists as a matter of law in some systems[110] and may be broadly defined as the right of a person to require a media publisher to publish a counter-statement by that person in respect of anything said about him by the media publisher which is claimed to be inaccurate. This right is not necessarily confined to defamatory inaccuracy. Enforcement is by criminal sanctions, and there is generally no enquiry into the truth of the media statement or the response. The right of reply in this sense does not exist in any common law country, and in the USA it would seem to be unconstitutional to require the media to publish any statement.[111] In England it was considered by the Faulks Committee[112] and rejected for two principal reasons. First, the structural and historical background of systems using the right of reply were different from those in England, in particular because of less reliance on large awards of damages and more reliance on the criminal law. Secondly, the Committee found 'objectionable a principle which entitles a person, who may be without

---

[107] See *John v Mirror Group Newspapers* [1997] QB 586; *Rantzen v Mirror Group Newspapers (1986) Ltd* [1994] QB 670; *Tolstoy Miloslavsky v United Kingdom* App.no. 18139/91, Ser.A vol. 316, 323 (1995) 20 EHRR 442.

[108] [1999] 4 All ER 609.

[109] See Milmo, P., 'Fast track or gridlock?' [1996] 146 *New Law Journal* 222. These provisions came into force on 28 February 2000.

[110] See generally Braithwaite, N., n.25 above.

[111] See *Miami Herald Publishing Co. v Tornillo* 418 US 241 (1974).

[112] The Faulks Committee, loc. cit. paras 618–24.

merits, to compel a newspaper to publish a statement extolling his non-existent virtues'. It may also be added that defamed persons must feel some doubt about the effectiveness of such a system if used as a primary restraint upon or deterrent to false statements. And from the contradictory perspective of the media there is a fear that an enthusiastic exercise of rights of reply would very seriously hamper editorial discretion or even swamp the primary news dissemination function. There is something of a similar but not identical nature in English law in the shape of Part II of Schedule 1 to the Defamation Act 1996.[113] This gives the protection of qualified privilege[114] to a huge range of reports, and those in Part II are 'subject to explanation or contradiction'. In other words, the defendant can only plead qualified privilege in respect of a Part II report if he is willing to publish a reasonable counter-statement by the plaintiff. This is not identical with the 'right of reply' because it depends upon the defendant's decision to plead qualified privilege, rather than, say truth. Perhaps we might say that we do not have a right of reply but a right of reply is attached as a condition to the pleading of one defence. A defendant may, of course, allow the plaintiff to make a statement independently of these provisions, either as the price of a settlement or in order to be seen to be fair.

So, it may be argued, the Internet provides the defamed person with a remedy in his own hands, and this justifies the withdrawal (or at least the shackling) of libel law in this area. But it is doubtful if the argument is compelling on a practical level. Not only is there a retributory element in libel law, but those who feel defamed by others are likely to feel that replying to a charge will not vindicate their reputation in the same way as a court verdict and monetary award. Furthermore, the argument seems to rest on the dubious assumption of a populace with easy and universal access to the Internet (not to mention the time to peruse it). Next, while there may be a built-in right of reply in newsgroups, there are large parts of the Internet, such as the WWW, where one cannot respond in this way within the same arena because from the point of view of input, as opposed to access, they are as tightly sealed off as any newspaper or TV programme.

The problem of the position of ISPs is an intractable one. Although section 1 of the Defamation Act 1996 goes some way to alleviate their position, there is still a serious potential of liability 'on notice'[115] as well as some practical uncertainty about what must be done to ensure compliance, and there is an attraction in the simple, clear rule provided by the United States legislation. Yet as the *Blumenthal* case shows, that system allows a provider to increase market share with seeming impunity on the back of

---

[113] In force on 1 April 1999, replacing more restricted provisions in the Defamation Act 1952. The principle dates back to the Law of Libel Amendment Act 1888.

[114] Qualified privilege is a defence to an action for defamation. The defence of qualified privilege can be defeated by proof of malice by the defendant.

[115] See Akdeniz, Y., 'Can He Not Stay Free?' *The Guardian*, Online, 27 April 2000 p.6; 'Case analysis: *Laurence Godfrey v Demon Internet Limited*' (1999) 4 *Journal of Civil Liberties* 260.

material which it knows is defamatory; and the contribution of ISPs to news distribution or meaningful public discussion is, for all the accessibility of the Internet,[116] at present minimal in comparison with newspapers[117] and the broadcast media.

More intractable still are the jurisdictional issues. As in most of this area, the problems are not really new in analytical terms: just as it can be argued that e-mail is only a progression from the telegraph or fax, so here we have had cross-border newspaper publication for many years. But because the Internet is virtually instantaneous and literally worldwide the problems appear to move into another dimension. In theory the matter should be dealt with by an international convention, but the prospects of getting even all the advanced countries to sign up to a common system seem remote and it is not obvious upon what principle such a convention would be based.[118]

---

[116] See Rose, L., *Netlaw: Your Rights in the Online World* (Osborne McGraw-Hill, Berkeley, 1995) p.130.
[117] Of course newspapers now publish electronic versions via the Internet. However, with regard to their liability there is no reason to distinguish the electronic and paper versions of the product.
[118] To give jurisdiction to the place where the posting was made and to apply its laws would be just as arbitrary as the present English approach: an American resident could shelter behind his own libel law if sued by someone in England but could take advantage of English law in respect of statements about him emanating from England. One way forward might be to apply a 'double actionability' rule in all cases. But it is hard to see why this should not apply to the conventional media as well.

CHAPTER 14

Whisper who dares: encryption, privacy rights and the new world disorder

Yaman Akdeniz and Clive Walker

Introduction*

In common with the modes of communication it succeeds and to some extent supplants, the Internet entails both positive and negative consequences for personal privacy. At the outset it must be admitted that the very concept of privacy is highly contested. Its boundaries have been stated in international law by article 8(1) of the European Convention on Human Rights and Fundamental Freedoms (1950)[1] as comprising a right 'to respect for . . . private and family life . . . home and . . . correspondence', though subject, under article 8(2), to interferences such as might be necessary in a democratic society:

> . . . in the interests of national security, public safety or the economic well-being of the country, for the prevention of disorder or crime, for the protection of health or morals, or for the protection of the rights and freedoms of others

The relationship between the positive statement of right and limitations thereto under article 8 is far from straightforward.[2] Reflecting similar difficulties at a national level within Europe, the UK Government has on several occasions rejected attempts to devise a legislative formula for the specific protection of privacy.[3] Problems of definition and the concern that privacy protection would be at the cost of free speech have been the primary reasons cited. Instead, the UK government has opted under the Human Rights Act 1998 simply to make legally relevant in domestic law the European Convention's catalogue of rights – not only its privacy protections but also its concern under article 10 for free speech. This is a neat sidestep, but it

---

* An earlier version of this paper was presented at the Internet Society Conference, San Jose, June 1999.
[1] Council of Europe, 87 UNTS 103, ETS 5, Strasbourg, 1950.
[2] See Warbrick, C., 'The structure of Article 8' [1998] *European Human Rights Law Review* 32.
[3] See especially Government Response to the National Heritage Select Committee, *Privacy and Media Intrusion* (Cm. 2918, HMSO, London, 1995).

will have the effect of juridifying the future development of privacy laws in the UK. The US precedent of *Roe v Wade*[4] suggests this strategy will not offer a free home run for those wishing to smooth the path to the protection of privacy and that legislative solutions from the political system may eventually prove as necessary in the UK as elsewhere.[5]

So, the polycentric problems arising from privacy are difficult enough to manage, and no easier solutions are evident when we turn to the relationship between privacy and the Internet. It may seem paradoxical that there can arise any expectation of privacy on this most open and unregulated mode of electronic communication, but privacy remains a legitimate demand in the Information Age and involves a claim by an individual to control information and personality (or personalities)[6] created or transmitted via the Internet, including immunity from unwarranted usage or intrusions by others. The relationships between privacy and the Internet can be both positive and negative.

Amongst the negative impacts might be the ability to gather and transfer data concerning subjects in ways which at best commodify the personality of the individual and at worst facilitate unaccountable and even mistaken interferences with autonomy. The ability of technological devices to enable the collection, processing and distribution of personal data[7] is a major factor behind the public concern about losses of privacy, and so action against technology is at one level very popular.[8] These concerns are reflected in data protection laws which, more so in Europe than the USA, restrict the free market in data use for the sake of subject privacy. The European data protection legislation is, broadly speaking, based around article 8 of the European Convention, which in turn was the inspiration for the Council of Europe's Convention on Data Protection.[9] Arising from the patchy ratification and implementation of the Convention, the European Communities have now issued the Directive on Data Protection,[10] the compliance with which henceforth becomes a matter of enforceable Community law.[11] Already, implementing legislation has begun to appear within the Member States,

---

[4] *Roe v Wade* 410 US 113 (1973), further discussed at
http://www.cnn.com/specials/1998/roe.wade/.
[5] Global Internet Liberty Campaign, *Privacy and Human Rights: An International Survey of Privacy Laws and Practice* (Washington DC, 1998) at http://www.gilc.org/privacy/survey/.
[6] Carnow, C.E.A., *Future Codes* (Artech House, Boston, 1997) p.125.
[7] Wacks, R., 'Privacy in cyberspace' in Birks, P. (ed.), *Privacy and Loyalty* (Oxford, Clarendon Press, 1997).
[8] *Report of the Committee on Data Protection* (Cmnd. 7341, HMSO, London, 1978); *Report of the Committee on Privacy* (Cmnd. 5012, HMSO, London, 1972).
[9] Council of Europe, *Convention for the Protection of Individuals with regard to Automatic Processing of Personal Data* (ETS No. 108, Strasbourg, 1980).
[10] European Communities, Directive on Data Protection (95/46/EC, OJ L281, 23 November 1995 p.31, at http://www2.echo.lu/legal/en/dataprot/dataprot.html.
[11] Kosten, F. and Pounder, C. (1996), 'The EC Data Protection Directive' [1996] 2 *Web JCLI*, at http://www.ncl.ac.uk:80/~nlawwww/; Lloyd, I. (1996), 'An outline of the European Data Protection Directive' [1996] 1 *Journal of Information Law and Technology*, at http://jilt.law.strath.ac.uk/elj/jilt/.

such as the UK's Data Protection Act 1998.[12] Lurking behind this impetus towards ever more widespread regulation of data-sets is the fear that it is technology which threatens privacy.[13]

The Internet cannot absolve itself of all responsibility for mass technophobia. Though it has increasing allure for the individual sitting in the sanctity of the home, there are major concerns about the mechanisms it provides for personal snooping not only by commercial institutions[14] but also (and more seriously) by governmental organisations,[15] all keeping track of individual usage of the Internet for the purposes of marketing, policing or otherwise.

More positively from the point of view of privacy interests, the technological mode of delivery of Internet communications can be utilised to afford effective protection for communications, especially through the use of strong encryption tools.[16] It will be noted that article 8 expressly incorporates a right to privacy in regard to 'correspondence', and this has long been interpreted by the European Court of Human Rights as demanding privacy in relation to communications via telecommunications networks. Indeed, the United Kingdom has already been found to be in breach of article 8 on several occasions for failing to pay adequate attention to this value of privacy. It is therefore fortuitous that in many respects the technically aware Internet user can achieve a greater degree of privacy than available through the postal service or many other forms of telecommunications.[17] Facilities such as anonymous remailers and encryption can be so effective against oversight that law enforcement agencies have begun to voice concerns about the viability of future crime detection in cyberspace.[18] These

---

[12] Home Office, *Data Protection: The Government Proposals* (Cm. 3725, Stationery Office, London, 1997).

[13] See, for example, on the Intel Pentium III controversy, Cyber-Rights & Cyber-Liberties (UK), 'Report on the Intel PIII Processor Serial Number Feature', by Dr Brian Gladman, 1999, at http://www.cyber-rights.org/reports/intel-rep.htm.

[14] BBC News, 'E-mail: Our right to write?,' 4 May 2000, at http://news2.thls.bbc.co.uk/hi/english/uk/newsid%5F734000/734844.stm.

[15] Campbell, D., 'Echelon: Interception Capabilities 2000 Report', April PE 168.184/Part 4/41999 (STOA publication) at http://www.cyber-rights.org/interception/stoa/stoa_cover.htm.

[16] See Denning, D.E., *Information Warfare and Security* (ACM Press, New York, 1999) Pt. III.

[17] JUSTICE (1998), *Surveillance* (London, 1998).

[18] Freeh, L., 'The Impact of Encryption on Public Safety', Director of Federal Bureau of Investigation before the Permanent Select Committee on Intelligence United States House of Representatives Washington, DC, 9 September 1997 at http://www.fbi.gov/pressrm/congress/congress97/encrypt4.htm; Freeh, L., 'Threats to US National Security Statement', Director of Federal Bureau of Investigation before the Senate Select Committee on Intelligence Washington, DC 28 January 1998 at http://www.fbi.gov/pressrm/congress/congress98/threats.htm; National Criminal Intelligence Service, Press Release, 'NCIS calls upon Government to ensure law enforcement powers do not fall behind technology in fight against "crypto criminals"', no: 02/99, 26 January 1999 at http://www.ncis.co.uk/web/Press%20Releases/encryption.htm; Davies, D., 'Criminal Law and the Internet', in Walker, C. (ed.), *Crime, Criminal Justice and the Internet* (Sweet & Maxwell, London, 1998) pp.48–60. The famous remailer operated by Johan Helsingius, anon.penet.fi, closed in August 1996.

concerns remind us that all rights, including rights to anonymity, can be exercised in ways which become abusive of other rights (whether to property in the cases of fraud or theft, or to life and liberty in the cases of terrorism and racism):[19]

> ... cryptography surely is the best of technologies and the worst of technologies. It will stop crimes, and it will create new crimes. It will undermine dictatorships, and it will drive them to new excuses. It will make us all anonymous, and will track our every transaction.

Encryption and the benefits to privacy

Among the many advantages of computer-mediated communications systems are their offer of privacy and security for their users. Encryption[20] is one technique which can be used to achieve secrecy for the contents of a message, but there are other methods of hiding identities and information which will not be covered in this paper, including steganography, remailers, account cloning and spoofing. Although encryption and cryptography have a long and colourful tradition in the military defence field, encryption technologies are increasingly integrated into commercial computer applications and the 'exclusive' military character of encryption belongs to the past.

Encryption can provide confidentiality, integrity and authenticity of the information transferred from A to B, countering the open nature of electronic documents.[21] It can provide a protected transmission of content, ensuring that the message's integrity has not been tampered with. Furthermore, with the use of encryption technology, B can authenticate that the information was sent by A. All these points may be important for different reasons for the transmission of data over the Internet. While, for example, governmental and commercial correspondents will require a confidential and secret communication, others will only be interested with the accuracy and authenticity of the information transmitted or received. Digital signatures can be created by the use of encryption, and these can authenticate the sender of the information. The danger that someone will assume an identity can be avoided by some form of certification of the digital signature; the certification can be based on hierarchical authority (perhaps, but not necessarily, dependent on governmental or third-party[22] recognition) or on horizontal recognition based on vouched personal relationships.

So, encryption has the potential to protect the privacy of communications and, despite the mathematical sophistication of the techniques being used,[23]

---

[19] Baker, S.A. and Hurst, P.R., *The Limits of Trust* (Kluwer, Hague, 1998) p.xv.

[20] See Schneier, B., *Applied Cryptography* (2nd ed. John Wiley & Sons, London, 1995); Koops, B.-J., *The Crypto Controversy* (Kluwer, The Hague, 1999) chap. 3.

[21] Katsh, M.E., *Law in a Digital World* (Oxford University Press, New York, 1995) p.98.

[22] See for example Thawte (http://www.thawte.com/) and Verisign (http://www.verisign.com/).

[23] Bowden, C. and Akdeniz, Y., 'Cryptography and Democracy: Dilemmas of Freedom', in Liberty (eds), *Liberating Cyberspace: Civil Liberties, Human Rights, and the Internet* (London Pluto Press, 1999).

does so by programs which can be increasingly utilised by non-experts. This is due to the desktop computer revolution which has made it possible for cryptographic techniques to become widely used and accessible to non-experts (even though the science of cryptography is very old). Nowadays, it is possible to buy cheap but strong encryption software from local computer shops. Moreover, one of the most popular encryption softwares, the Pretty Good Privacy ('PGP') is freely available over the Internet for personal use.[24] Over time, it might be predicted that these will become a standard part of common software, and this future is already becoming a reality with programs such as Microsoft's Windows 2000, which incorporates 128-bit encryption specifically permitted by relaxed US regulations on encryption exports and announced in January 2000.[25]

The use of encryption seems to give rise to an element of suspicion – it is often assumed that the use of secret codes are associated with the world of spies and industrial espionage. Nevertheless, there are many legitimate purposes of secrecy in general[26] and encryption in particular. Many are connected with business transactions and the desires to keep financial information away from the prying eyes of third parties and to authenticate and prevent repudiation of the communication as between the intended parties to the transaction. In this way, encryption technology is a fundamental element for the development of a global electronic commercial system.

Other personal purposes include being able to obtain advice or counselling in private and perhaps even without identification. Thus, the technology has been used by the Samaritans organisation in the UK as part of its voluntary counselling service. Equally, the same encryption technology can be used for securing true private communications concerning public affairs. It has enabled the use of the Internet as a mode of information gathering and dissemination concerning, for example, human rights abuses. Organisations such as Amnesty International and Human Rights Watch communicate with dissidents all around the world with the use of encryption technology which ensures not only the secrecy of the content of messages but also the authenticity of their authors.[27] More specifically, Anonymizer.com's Kosovo Project, which relied on strong encryption, allowed individuals to report on conditions and human rights violations from within the war zone without fear of government retaliation.[28]

---

[24] A full list of sites (many with ftp download facilities) is available at http://www.ssh.fi/tech/crypto/sites.html. The existence of such sites makes the banning of encryption a futile policy: Koops, B.-J., *The Crypto Controversy* (Kluwer, The Hague, 1999) chap. 6½.

[25] http://www.microsoft.com/WINDOWS2000/news/bulletins/encryption.asp, 2000. The impact is better system security. For the revised US Encryption Export Control Regulations, 2000 (65 FR 2492), see www.epic.org/crypto/export_controls/regs_1_00.html.

[26] Bok, S., *Secrets: on the ethics of concealment and revelation* (Oxford University Press, Oxford, 1982).

[27] Network Week, 'From internal briefings to remote links, Amnesty International needs secure systems', 9 December 1998.

[28] http://info.anonymizer.com/kosovo.shtml, 2000. See Akdeniz, Y., 'Anonymous now' (2000) (3) *Index on Censorship*, Privacy Issue, June 57.

Encryption policy in Europe

In response to the needs for establishing trust and confidence through the use of encryption technology in the Information Age, a regulatory framework must be established at national, supranational and international level. However, there have been considerable differences between the various regulatory framework initiatives offered in the European Union and in the USA. Furthermore, there are even conflicting policy initiatives between the European Union Member States (for example the United Kingdom and France). The absence of consensus hampers not only the growth and development of e-commerce but also the possibility of providing a stable and trustworthy environment for netizens.

At European Union level, there is no doubt that there is a strong commitment, based on global economic competition but equally political populism, to embrace in principle 'the age of the Information Society'.[29] The desire to encourage the vigorous growth of electronic commerce in Europe is a significant part of the agenda.[30] Yet, because of cultural, historical and socio-political diversity, there will inevitably be divergent approaches to the growth and governance of the Internet in different European societies. Faced with the fragmentation of both the Internet and the all-purpose nation state, and having regard to the cardinal principles of respect for difference and subsidiarity, it is not surprising that the supranational European Union has sought to avoid domineering stances and the imposition of monopolistic forms of governmentality.

As early as 1994, the Bangemann Report to the European Commission, *Europe and the Global Information Society*,[31] dealt with the use of encryption tools and stated that a solution at a national (Member States) level will inevitably prove to be insufficient because communications reach beyond national frontiers and because the principles of the internal market prohibit measures such as import bans on decoding equipment. Therefore, according to the Bangemann Report, a solution at the European level was needed:[32]

> ... which provides a global answer to the problem of protection of encrypted signals and security. Based on the principles of the internal market it would create parity of conditions for the protection of encrypted services as well as the legal framework for the development of these new services.

In October 1997, the European Commission, published a communication paper, *Towards a European Framework for Digital Signatures and*

---

[29] House of Lords Select Committee on Science and Technology, *Information Society* (1995–6 HL 77, HMSO, London) paras 1.1, 1.6.

[30] European Commission, Communication to the European Parliament, the Council, the Economic and Social Committee and the Committee of the Regions, *A European Initiative in Electronic Commerce*, COM(97)157.

[31] *Europe and the Global Information Society* (Bull.6-1994, point 1.2.9 and Supplement 2/94 – Bull., at http://www.igd.fhg.de/wise/english/rd/prog/general/bangemann.html, 1994).

[32] *Europe and the Global Information Society*, ibid., chap. 3.

Encryption.[33] In contrast to many Member State initiatives (including those of the UK) and despite years of US attempts to propagate government access to keys,[34] the European Commission paper found key escrow and key recovery systems to be inefficient for business purposes and ineffective for crime control:[35]

> ... most of the (few) criminal cases involving encryption that are quoted as examples for the need of regulation concern 'professional' use of encryption. It seems unlikely that in such cases the use of encryption could be effectively controlled by regulation.

This view is echoed, albeit indistinctly, in the OECD Guidelines on Cryptography Policy.[36] These Guidelines are intended to promote electronic commerce, data security and privacy protection. Encryption plays a vital role, as is recognised by Principle 5 which states that 'the fundamental rights of individuals to privacy, including secrecy of communications and protection of personal data, should be respected in national cryptography policies and in the implementation and use of cryptographic methods'. Principle 6 provides that national policies may allow lawful access to plaintext or encryption keys but does not require such a regime and renders it subject to other principles. Likewise, the Council of Europe has concluded that Internet users should be able to use all available means to protect communications, including encryption.[37] Though these international statements may be categorised as 'soft' law, the European Commission's Communication on Encryption and Electronic Signatures reminds us that:[38]

---

[33] European Commission Communication, 'Towards a European Framework for Digital Signatures and Encryption', Communication from the Commission to the European Parliament, the Council, the Economic and Social Committee and the Committee of the Regions ensuring Security and Trust in Electronic Communication, COM (97) 503, October 1997, at http://www.ispo.cec.be/eif/policy/97503toc.html.

[34] This initiative was personified by the US Special Ambassador, David Aaron, who met with UK officials between 1996 and 1998: http://www.cyber-rights.org/foia/, 1999; HC Debs. vol. 336 col. 460wa Ms Patricia Hewitt, 19 October 1999.

[35] European Commission Communication, 'Towards A European Framework for Digital Signatures And Encryption,' Communication from the Commission to the European Parliament, the Council, the Economic and Social Committee and the Committee of the Regions ensuring Security and Trust in Electronic Communication, COM (97) 503, October 1997, at http://www.ispo.cec.be/eif/policy/97503toc.html at para. 2.2.

[36] *Cryptography Policy Guidelines: Recommendation of the Council Concerning Guidelines for Cryptography Policy*, 27 March 1997, at http://www.oecd.org/dsti/sti/it/secur/prod/e-crypto.htm. See Baker, S.A. and Hurst, P.R., *The Limits of Trust* (Kluwer, The Hague, 1998) p.41.

[37] Recommendation R(99)5, 'Protection of Privacy on the Internet' (Strasbourg, 1999). This is now in contrast with the Council of Europe's draft Convention on Cyber-crime (PC-CY (2000), Draft N° 19), at http://conventions.coe.int/treaty/en/projets/cybercrime.htm which contains provisions mandating that every Member State enact laws that require an individual to release encryption keys and unencrypted data when required by government officials.

[38] European Commission Communication (1997), 'Towards A European Framework for Digital Signatures And Encryption,' Communication from the Commission to the European Parliament, the Council, the Economic and Social Committee and the Committee of the

International treaties, constitutions and laws guarantee the fundamental right to privacy including secrecy of communications (Art. 12 Universal Declaration of Human Rights, Art. 17 International Covenant on Civil and Political Rights, Art. 8 European Convention on Human Rights, Art. F(2) Treaty on EU, EU Data Protection Directive) . . . Therefore, the debate about the prohibition or limitation of the use of encryption directly affects the right to privacy, its effective exercise and the harmonisation of data protection laws in the Internal Market.

As far as digital signatures are concerned, the Commission decided to separate the need for a regulatory framework for the use of digital signatures from that of the use of encryption. The Commission also dismissed any claims that the use of digital signatures would create problems for law enforcement. For the purpose of creating a legal framework for the use of digital signatures, the European Commission, in May 1998, published a proposed Directive on a Common Framework for Electronic Signatures.[39] The draft directive was finalised in October 1998 and highlighted the problem that '. . . divergent rules with respect to legal recognition of electronic signatures and the accreditation of certification service providers in the Member States may create a significant barrier to the use of electronic communications and electronic commerce and thus hinder the development of the internal market . . .'.[40] It warns against compulsory certification schemes, though there may be voluntary provision. The Directive for a Community framework for electronic signatures was finalised on 13 December 1999[41] and is intended to guarantee the recognition, and free circulation of digital signatures or related services within the European Union. Furthermore, an electronic signature cannot be legally discriminated against solely on the grounds that it is in electronic form, but it can be used as evidence in legal proceedings. The Directive also requires Member States to include mechanisms for cooperation with third countries on the basis of mutual recognition of certificates and on bilateral and multilateral agreements.

At the time of writing, the European Commission was yet to formulate a common policy on the use of encryption. This will be the more problematic task for the Commission as there are completely different policy views

---

Regions ensuring Security and Trust in Electronic Communication, COM (97) 503, October 1997, at http://www.ispo.cec.be/eif/policy/97503toc.html, para. III.1.

[39] 'Proposal for a European Parliament and Council Directive on a common framework for electronic signatures: European Commission Communication from the Commission to the European Parliament, the Council, the Economic and Social Committee and the Committee of the Regions' COM(1998) 297 final, Official Journal C 325, 23/10/98, at http://www.ispo.cec.be/ecommerce/docs/DigitalSignatures.pdf. See Angel, J., 'Why use Digital Signatures for Electronic Commerce?' 1999 (2) *Journal of Information, Law and Technology* at http://www.law.warwick.ac.uk/jilt/99-2/angel.html.

[40] Ibid., Preamble para. 4. Divergent state legislation has arisen in the USA: Baker, S.A. and Hurst, P.R., *The Limits of Trust* (Kluwer, The Hague, 1998) chap. 8.

[41] Directive 1999/93/EC of 13 December 1999 on a Community framework for electronic signatures. It remains the position that States cannot make the provision of services related to electronic signatures subject to mandatory licensing.

within the Member States of the European Union. We shall now explore one such Member State, namely the United Kingdom.

UK government encryption policy

Regulatory stances

The UK government has been trying to formulate a policy on encryption since 1994, but the many policy twists and turns have been caught up between two different governments (before and after the May 1997 General Election) and have also been strongly affected by supranational (the European Union) and international (the OECD) policy initiatives described above.[42]

At the outset in June 1996, the UK's Department of Trade and Industry ('DTI') published a discussion paper, *On Regulatory Intent Concerning Use of Encryption on Public Networks*,[43] to meet the growing demands to safeguard the integrity and confidentiality of information sent electronically over the Internet. The UK government proposed the introduction of the licensing of Trusted Third Parties ('TTPs') who would hold the copies of all private encryption keys to facilitate key recovery and verification. In this way, law enforcement access would become part of the public key infrastructure (and therefore much less visible). The discussion was continued by the Consultation Paper, *Licensing of Trusted Third Parties for the Provision of Encryption Services*, in March 1997.[44] This DTI document addressed many issues which would have an impact on the use of encryption tools on the Internet, but the threat to privacy of whether blanket escrow of encryption keys (the central policy being put forward both to encourage trust in the integrity of encryption and to allow for investigation of those criminals and terrorists who abuse its facilities) was not addressed.[45] In addition to its refusal to examine the core of the controversy, the DTI paper was provincial and ahistorical. There was no mention of the four years of continual proposals for key escrow systems by the US government,[46] even

---

[42] See generally Liberty (ed.), *Liberating Cyberspace* (Pluto Press, London, 1999) chaps 3, 4.

[43] Department of Trade and Industry, *On Regulatory Intent Concerning Use of Encryption on Public Networks* (DTI, London, http://dtiinfo1.dti.gov.uk/cii/encrypt/, 1996. See Akdeniz, Y., 'UK Government Encryption Policy', [1997] *Web Journal of Current Legal Issues* 1 at http://www.ncl.ac.uk/~nlawwww/1997/issue1/akdeniz1.html.

[44] Department of Trade and Industry, Consultation Paper, *Licensing of Trusted Third Parties for the Provision of Encryption Services* (http://elj.warwick.ac.uk/jilt/Consult/ukcryp/ukdtipap.htm, 1997). See Akdeniz, Y. and Walker, C., 'UK Government Policy on Encryption: Trust is the Key?' (1998) 3 *Journal of Civil Liberties* 110.

[45] Akdeniz, Y., 'No Chance for Key Recovery: Encryption and International Principles of Human and Political Rights', [1998] *Web Journal of Current Legal Issues* 1, at http://webjcli.ncl.ac.uk/1998/issue1/akdeniz1.html.

[46] Schneier, B. and Banisar, D., *The Electronic Privacy Papers: Documents on the Battle for Privacy in the Age of Surveillance* (New York, John Wiley & Sons, 1997), Ruiz, B.R., *Privacy in Telecommunications* (Kluwer, The Hague, 1997); Diffie, W. and Landau, S., *Privacy on the Line: The Politics of Wiretapping and Encryption* (London, MIT Press, 1998), ACLU, *Special Report, Big Brother in the Wires: Wiretapping in the Digital Age*, March 1998 at

though their proposals had much in common with the DTI proposal and clearly inspired the latter.[47] And the viability of key escrow, when many TTPs would not normally store private keys to carry out most of their services and when 'horizontal' certification can verify further unescrowed keys, was not established.

Since the Labour Party had objected to key escrow while in opposition,[48] it was expected that there would be a fresh look at encryption policy after the General Election in 1997. No doubt, the politicians did look again, but they seem to have been readily convinced by their civil servants to dust off and advance the existing policies. This continuum was first signalled in February 1998 with the announcement by the Home Secretary of a plan to allow government access to encrypted communications for the prevention of crime. The European Union ministers at a meeting in Birmingham warned that unbreakable encryption systems would mean organised crime could pursue its activities unhindered.[49]

A re-packaged version of the UK government policy was therefore announced in spring 1998 by the Department of Trade and Industry under the title of *Secure Electronic Commerce Statement.*[50] This policy statement reflected the previous government's Trusted Third Party initiative, but this time, and in line with the forthcoming European Directive, the Trusted Service Providers (TSPs) (who must combine TTP and Certification Authority functions) could be employed by Internet users on a 'voluntary basis', though those Internet users who did not employ them could not avail themselves of certain presumptions of authenticity. In addition, it remained a licensing condition for the TTPs to use key recovery systems favoured by the government and therefore the risks associated with the key recovery systems remained. Phill Zimmermann, the creator of Pretty Good Privacy ('PGP'), stated after reviewing the government statement that 'in principle it's voluntary; but, *de facto*, it's compulsory. This is exactly what so many of us in the US have worked very hard to stop'.[51] The Internet industry likewise did not favour the UK government's policy since the framework proposed did not provide the necessary confidence and trust for the development of e-commerce.

---

http://www.aclu.org/issues/cyber/wiretap_brother.html; Baker, S.A. and Hurst, P.R., *The Limits of Trust* (Kluwer, The Hague, 1998) chap. 2.

[47] Akdeniz, Y. *et al.*, 'Cryptography and Liberty: Can the Trusted Third Parties be Trusted? A Critique of the Recent UK Proposals,' [1997] (2) *Journal of Information, Law and Technology*, http://elj.warwick.ac.uk/jilt/cryptog/97_2akdz/. See further Cyber-Rights & Cyber-Liberties (UK), 'Freedom of Information Files,' at http://www.cyber-rights.org/foia/, 2000.

[48] Labour Party, *Policy on Information Superhighway: Communicating Britain's Future* (http://www.labour.org.uk/views/info%Dhighway/content.html, 1995).

[49] Akdeniz, Y., 'Global Internet Liberty Campaign Member Statement: New UK Encryption Policy criticised', February 1998, at
http://www.cyber-rights.org/crypto/gilc-dti-statement-298.html.

[50] Department of Trade and Industry, *Secure Electronic Commerce Statement* (DTI, London, 1998), at http://www.dti.gov.uk/CII/ana27p.html.

[51] Campbell, D., 'Coded Message,' *The Guardian* (Online Section), 30 April 1998.

The DTI's statement was the inspiration behind the announcement within the Queen's Speech in November 1998 of proposed legislation in the form of an Electronic Commerce Bill, the aim of which was to make the UK the most propitious place in the world to trade online. A consultation paper detailing the proposals was announced,[52] and more details were given in a document issued in October 1998 by the DTI called, *Net Benefit: The Electronic Commerce Agenda for the UK*.[53] The paper still contended that 'encryption, has a major drawback – the same technology used to protect sensitive business communications can be used by criminals and terrorists to circumvent the legal powers of interception by governments'.[54] Therefore the *Net Benefit* paper stated that:[55]

> In the UK, the Government is proposing to encourage the establishment of Trusted Third Parties (TTPs) where users of encryption keys could deposit their private encryption keys with licensed organisations which would provide legal access by law enforcement agencies. Introducing legislation to license such bodies will give both the public and business confidence that they are dealing with organisations providing professional key management and storage facilities.

It can be seen that key escrow remained central to the *raison d'être* of TSPs, and so the widespread criticism remained that this would significantly hamper e-commerce while being of marginal assistance to law enforcement.

A further DTI Consultation Paper, *Building Confidence in Electronic Commerce*, appeared in March 1999.[56] In continued pursuance of 'the ambitious goal of developing the UK as the world's best environment for electronic trading by 2002' and rendering the law 'technology neutral',[57] the means chosen remained stubbornly regulatory. So, on electronic signatures, the European Commission Draft Directive on Electronic Signatures[58] is turned on its head and is interpreted to mean that there should be legal regulation; registration with the Certification Authority cannot be compulsory (and TSPs are not to have access to private signature keys), but businesses were warned that (unlike the position in regard to plaintext

---

[52] Department of Trade and Industry, *Our competitive future: building the knowledge driven economy* (Cm. 4176, Stationery Office, London, 1998).

[53] Department of Trade and Industry, *Net Benefit: The Electronic Commerce Agenda for the UK*, DTI/Pub 3619, October 1998, at http://www.dti.gov.uk/CII/netbenefit.html.

[54] Ibid. at p.15.

[55] Ibid. at p.15.

[56] Department of Trade and Industry, *Building Confidence in Electronic Commerce* (http://www.dti.gov.uk/CII/elec/elec_com 1.html, 1999). See Angel, J., 'Why use Digital Signatures for Electronic Commerce?' 1999 (2) *Journal of Information, Law and Technology* at http://www.law.warwick.ac.uk/jilt/99–2/angel.html; Price, S., 'Towards privacy, security and trust on the information superhighway' (1999) 149 *New Law Journal* 886.

[57] Ibid., paras 1, 3.

[58] European Commission, 'Proposal for a European Parliament and Council Directive on a common framework for electronic signatures: European Commission Communication from the Commission to the European Parliament, the Council, the Economic and Social Committee and the Committee of the Regions' COM(1998) 297 final, Official Journal C 325, 23/10/98, at http://www.ispo.cec.be/ecommerce/docs/DigitalSignatures.pdf.

signatures) they could lose the presumption of validity if they did not act through officially licensed TSPs.[59] Furthermore, the core strategy of key escrow and third-party recovery and licensed Trust Service Providers, with OFTEL as the licensing authority, was again to the fore, though it remained in theory voluntary and more flexible licensing was envisaged in which key escrow would not be a condition to obtain a licence.[60] This agenda went well beyond the relatively minor and technical legislative adjustments necessary to put electronic writing and signatures on a par with physical versions,[61] and primarily evoked a plea from respondents for a 'light touch'.[62]

Encryption policy was to be finalised in April 1999 in intensive discussions with the information technology industry and in the light of the consultation paper. Three developments halted the achievement of this goal. First, the meetings with industry sectors resulted in powerful lobbying against many of the preferred solutions as very damaging to e-commerce. Secondly, the considerable delay on the part of the government to embark upon its legislative implementation allowed agencies and groups championing civil liberties interests to gather their forces. They were encouraged to do so by the House of Commons Select Committee on Trade and Industry, which decided in late 1998 to embark upon an inquiry into electronic commerce. Lobbying ensued from the officially appointed Data Protection Registrar and also from non-governmental organisations.[63] The latter again criticised the government approach as fixated on the value of encryption solely in connection with commerce and ignoring wider social and political purposes.[64] In regard to law enforcement, it was suggested that the government was naive in believing that criminals would adopt the very encryption procedures most likely to be vulnerable to penetration by law enforcement bodies.

The resultant House of Commons Select Committee Report on *Building Confidence in Electronic Commerce*,[65] became a third obstacle to government blueprints. It heavily criticised the government's attachment to key escrow, which was seen as satisfying law enforcement concerns at the expense of economic competitiveness. It doubted whether there was a need

---

[59] Department of Trade and Industry, *Building Confidence in Electronic Commerce* (http://www.dti.gov.uk/CII/elec/elec_com_1.html., 1999) para. 19.

[60] Ibid. para. 37.

[61] Compare the examples (California Government Code s.16.5 and Code of Regulations Title 2 s.22002; German Digital Signatures Act 1997 and the Utah Digital Signatures Act 1995, 46–3–101) discussed in New Zealand Law Commission, *Electronic Commerce* (Report no. 50, Wellington, 1998) chap. 7.

[62] Department of Trade and Industry, Responses to *Building Confidence in Electronic Commerce* (http://www.dti.gov.uk/cii/elec/conrep.html, 1999).

[63] See Akdeniz, Y., Bohm, N. and Walker, C., 'Internet privacy: Cyber-Crimes versus Cyber-Rights' (1999) 10 *Computers & Law* 34.

[64] See Cyber-Rights & Cyber-Liberties (UK), Memorandum to the House of Commons Trade and Industry Select Committee on Electronic Commerce Inquiry, February 1999, at http://www.cyber-rights.org/reports/crcl-hc.htm.

[65] House of Commons Select Committee on Trade and Industry, *Report on Building Confidence in Electronic Commerce* (1998–9 HC 187).

for more than minimal technical legislation and rejected outright the official reliance upon enforcement of key escrow:[66]

> We are disappointed . . . that the Government should still hold a candle for key escrow and key recovery. If these technologies are likely to be of benefit to firms and consumers, perhaps because of the need to store vital private keys or to facilitate law enforcement access to decrypted data, then the market will provide for them. We can foresee no benefits arising from the Government promotion of key escrow or key recovery technologies.

These attacks were followed up in July 1999 with another Trade and Industry Select Committee Report, *Electronic Commerce*.[67] This paper took a wider view of the Internet and commerce (including ideas such as proselytising functions for the Director General of Telecommunications and an e-Envoy in the DTI)[68] rather than focusing upon the issue of encryption.

The initial governmental response came from the Cabinet Office's Performance and Innovation Unit, which had conducted a review of *Encryption and Law Enforcement*[69] at much the same time as the Commons Select Committee. Rather than imposing closure upon three years of debate, it emphasised that the way forward was for a 'partnership' approach, with the partners being government and information technology industry. Civil liberties groups were not mentioned, though some did respond to the proposals.[70] The DTI paper, *Response to 'Building Confidence in Electronic Commerce'*,[71] likewise accepted as the most striking message to emerge in reaction to its last report was the plea for a 'light touch', including the decoupling of e-commerce issues from law enforcement concerns and the end to the pursuit of key escrow.

Intended as the closure to the debate was the DTI Command Paper, *Promoting Electronic Commerce*, which incorporated draft legislation which has now become the Electronic Communications Act 2000.[72] Significant shifts in regulatory policy included the shelving of plans for compulsory licensing of TSPs, to be replaced by a voluntary 'approvals regime' in which the industry itself was to adopt self-regulatory kite-marking, but the threat of an imposed (and virtually unspecified) registration scheme

---

[66] House of Commons Select Committee on Trade and Industry, *Building Confidence in Electronic Commerce* (1998–9 HC 187) at para. 90.

[67] House of Commons Select Committee on Trade and Industry, *Electronic Commerce* (1998–9 HC 648).

[68] See http://www.e-envoy.gov.uk/.

[69] Cabinet Office's Performance and Innovation Unit, *Encryption and Law Enforcement* (http://www.cabinet-office.gov.uk/innovation/1999/encryption/report.htm, 1999).

[70] Cyber-Rights & Cyber-Liberties (UK), (http://www.cyber-rights.org/reports/blair-letter.pdf, June 1999); *Guardian*, 'Call for fairer encryption code: Groups say rights are suffering in e-gold rush', 17 June 1999.

[71] Department of Trade and Industry, *Responses to 'Building Confidence in Electronic Commerce'* (http://www.dti.gov.uk/cii/elec/conrep.htm, 1999) para. 3.

[72] Department of Trade and Industry, *Promoting Electronic Commerce* (Cm. 4417, Stationery Office, London, 1999).

for cryptography support services loomed under Part I of the legislation if industry did not deliver.[73] The Alliance for Electronic Business (AEB) have drawn up an industry-led scheme (known as the 'T' Scheme).[74] The government has said that it will not commence Part I of the legislation if it continues to be satisfied that the T Scheme meets the government's objectives. Next, to achieve a greater degree of technology neutrality, it was also been accepted that all electronic signatures, certified or not, of British origin or not, will be legally admissible, leaving it to the courts case-by-case to work out authenticity and impact.[75] Less surprising features of Part II of the legislation included a sweeping power to alter existing legislation as to the form of 'signature' or 'writing'.[76] Aside from the legislative proposals, the White Paper also contained further encouragement to police/ISP forum meetings as fostering the partnership approach.[77]

Since it remains so prominent in shaping the debates concerning privacy and the Internet,[78] this chapter will now address in greater depth the issue of law enforcement and its balance with privacy rights.

Law enforcement concerns

It should be made clear from the outset that the European Convention on Human Rights does not forbid electronic surveillance. According to *Klass v Germany*:[79]

> The Court has therefore to accept that the existence of some Legislation granting powers of secret surveillance over the mail, post and telecommunications is, under exceptional conditions, necessary in a democratic society in the interests of national security and/or for the prevention of disorder or crime.

The need for surveillance in connection with organised crime in the UK was likewise accepted in *Malone v UK*.[80] But law enforcement concerns cannot be exclusive, and since the introduction of the discussion paper in June 1996, the government has consistently failed to recognise the importance of encryption to private communications over the Internet. This attitude is especially remarkable in the light of other governmental initiatives, such as the Human Rights Act 1998 and the strengthened Data Protection Act 1998.

This blindness is equally evident within the official stance in regard to investigative powers in response to the risk that criminals and terrorists will

---

[73] paras 4, 23, 24. The Electronic Communications Act 2000 s.1 imposes a duty on the Secretary of State to establish and maintain a register of approved providers of cryptography services.
[74] See http://www.fei.org.uk/fei/news/tscheme.html.
[75] paras 4, 20. See Electronic Communications Act 2000 s.7.
[76] para. 21. See Electronic Communications Act 2000 s.8.
[77] para. 51. But see note Akdeniz. Y., 'New Privacy Concerns: ISPs, Crime prevention, and Consumers' Rights', (2000) 14 *International Review of Law, Computers and Technology* 55.
[78] House of Commons Select Committee on Trade and Industry, *Report on Building Confidence in Electronic Commerce* (1998–9 HC 187) para. 20.
[79] *Klass v Germany* App.no. 5029/71, Ser. A 28 para. 48.
[80] *Malone v United Kingdom* App.no. 8691/79, Ser. A 82, (1984) 7 EHRR 14 para. 81.

exploit strong encryption techniques to protect their activities from detection by law enforcement agencies and that the law enforcement agencies such as the National Criminal Intelligence Service (NCIS) will not be able to access 'private encryption keys'.[81] The original plans for encryption involved key escrow on a wide scale, so that new powers to access encrypted data held by TTPs could bear fruit.[82] However, later plans afforded access to encrypted messages which had been seized independently on the basis of pre-existing powers only (under the Interception of Communications Act 1985 ('IOCA'), the Intelligence Services Act 1994 and the Police Act 1997 Part III)[83] and did not create new powers to intercept. The policy paper, *Secure Electronic Commerce Statement*, asserted that 'the new powers will apply to those holding such information (whether licensed or not) and to users of encryption products'.[84] Those plans were given shape by the command paper, *Promoting Electronic Commerce*, and have been pursued since that time. There are several objections to reliance upon pre-existing powers of surveillance.

First, there is no proven need for any extension built upon interception powers in order to obtain deciphered messages. Though warrants are regularly used for the interception of communications within Britain,[85] there is no claim that the interception of encrypted messages through the use of the Internet was decisive in any single case out of the 2,600 interception warrants issued during 1996 and 1997 by the Home Secretary. These statistics are called in aid by the Cabinet Office's Performance and Innovation Unit paper,[86] which also mentions that the 2,600 warrants resulted in 1,200 arrests. These are also claimed to be reliable and cost effective, but not one is linked to the Internet or to encryption, as the following sample case-studies (selected as the strongest and most frequently cited instances) attest.

- Possibly the largest survey of the impact of 'computer crime' (meaning that '[c]omputer interconnectivity is the essential characteristic') in the UK has been *Project Trawler*, a report from National Criminal Intelligence Service ('NCIS').[87] The report catalogued a considerable increase in complaints in computer crime but did not relate these to the even greater rate rise in computer usage and ownership. Nor did the report

---

[81] Department of Trade and Industry, *Building Confidence in Electronic Commerce* (http://www.dti.gov.uk/CII/elec/elec_com_1.html, 1999) para. 49. See further NCIS, *Project Trawler: Crime On The Information Highways*, 22 June 1999, at http://www.ncis.co.uk/.

[82] Department of Trade and Industry, *On Regulatory Intent Concerning Use of Encryption on Public Networks* (DTI, London, http://dtiinfo1.dti.gov.uk/cii/encrypt/, 1996) para. 2.

[83] See further EU Council Resolution of 17 January 1995 on the lawful interception of telecommunications (OJ C 329), requiring network operators and service providers to install appropriate facilities.

[84] Ibid., para. 14.

[85] Ibid., para. 13.

[86] Cabinet Office's Performance and Innovation Unit, *Encryption and Law Enforcement* (http://www.cabinet-office.gov.uk/innovation/1999/encryption/report.htm, 1999) at para. 4.2.

[87] NCIS, *Project Trawler: Crime on the Information Highways* (http://www.ncis.co.uk/, 1999).

necessarily distinguish possible breach of civil from criminal law (especially in the case of infringements of intellectual property, pornography and gambling, none of which is *per se* illegal in the UK). Nor did the report clearly isolate cases in which the Internet (as opposed to intranets) has played a part.[88] One of the largest computer crime incidents to date has been 'Operation Starburst' which entailed the arrest of 37 persons in the UK, USA, Germany, South Africa, Hong Kong and Singapore.[89] It is claimed that encryption was a hindrance, but detection was nevertheless effected through a mixture of physical surveillance of suspects, telephone and financial checks to establish their usage of their ISPs, and then the physical seizure of their computers. Though some of the material was encrypted (with PGP), there was plenty of unencrypted material available on which to base prosecutions and convictions. Another example, given by NCIS in early 1998, related to police enquiries into an attempted murder and sexual assault were said to be impeded by the discovery of encrypted material on a suspect's computer.[90] The investigator was able to proceed only after the private encryption key was discovered by the police among other material seized from the suspect. But the private encryption key was in fact recovered rather than not. According to NCIS, there are examples of terrorists in the UK using encryption as a means of concealing their activities. In late 1996, a police operation culminated in the arrests of several leading members of a terrorist group and the seizure of computer equipment containing encrypted files. The files held information on potential terrorist targets such as police officers and politicians. The data was eventually retrieved, but only after considerable effort.[91] But, again, we note that the data was retrieved.

- It is asserted in the DTI Consultation Paper, *Building Confidence in Electronic Commerce* that there are 'numerous' cases of paedophiles using encryption and some involving terrorists.[92] But there is no proof that this blocked detection and prosecution. The Paper admits that 'At present, the impact of encryption is significant but is not having a major operational impact on the fight against serious crime.'[93]

---

[88] It is admitted that most hacking offences are committed by insiders: para. 23.

[89] See Davies, D., 'Criminal Law and the Internet', in Walker, C. (ed.), *Crime, Criminal Justice and the Internet* (Sweet & Maxwell, London, 1998) pp.48–60; NCIS, *Project Trawler: Crime on the Information Highways* (http://www.ncis.co.uk/, 1999) para. 81.

[90] National Criminal Intelligence Service, Press Release, 'NCIS calls upon Government to ensure law enforcement powers do not fall behind technology in fight against "crypto criminals"', no: 02/99, 26 January 1999 at
http://www.ncis.co.uk/web/Press%20Releases/encryption.htm.

[91] National Criminal Intelligence Service, Press Release, 'NCIS calls upon Government to ensure law enforcement powers do not fall behind technology in fight against "crypto criminals"', no: 02/99, 26 January 1999 at
http://www.ncis.co.uk/web/Press%20Releases/encryption.htm.

[92] Department of Trade and Industry, *Building Confidence in Electronic Commerce* (http://www.dti.gov.uk/CII/elec/elec_com_1.html, 1999) para. 50.

[93] Ibid., para. 83.

- Another case sometimes discussed is Father Adrian McLeish, a Roman Catholic priest, who was sentenced to six years' imprisonment in November 1996 for child abuse and child pornography offences.[94] During Operation Modem by the Durham Police, it was discovered that McLeish used encryption software. But McLeish's use of encryption was not a problem for investigators, as McLeish handed over his encryption keys together with his private passphrase – 'Overhead the moon is beaming'. McLeish admitted 12 specimen charges of indecent assaults against two boys. He also admitted distributing indecent photographs, possessing them with intent to distribute them and being involved in the importation of pornographic videos of children.

Second, the interception powers themselves appear wildly out of constitutional control. The number of IOCA warrants has risen alarmingly in the last few years (2,031 warrants issued in 1998 compared to 473 in 1990).[95] This suggests that the current powers are more than adequate for law enforcement purposes. One problem concerns the broad criteria which can relate to concepts such as 'national security' and 'economic well-being'.[96] Another problem is whether existing surveillance powers are properly or strictly regulated.[97] The increase in the volume of warrants per annum must cast doubt on the value of having the Home Secretary in charge. Are we really to believe that the Home Secretary has time to scrutinise carefully and individually somewhere in the region of five warrants every day of the year in addition to dealing with the renewal of some of the interception warrants from time to time? A further point to note is that by building enforcement on the basis of existing powers, the government is not wholly committed to searches purely under the authority of a judge. In the *Statement*, a vague distinction is made between judicial involvement in 'criminal investigations' and other 'interceptions' which will be by order of the Secretary of State.[98] To some extent, it must be admitted that this follows the lax pattern of earlier legislation (such as the Interception of Communications Act 1985, the Intelligence Services Act 1994 and the Police Act 1997 Part III), but the replication of this absence of proper oversight should hardly be welcome. Following a secretive review,[99] the Home Office Consultation Paper,

---

[94] See http://www.cyber-rights.org/reports/ukcases.htm, 1999. See further chap. 10.
[95] Report of the Commissioner (Cm. 4364, Stationery Office, London, 1999) p.11.
[96] These concepts were accepted by the Commission in *Christie v United Kingdom*, App.no. 21482/93, 78A D&R; *Esbester v United Kingdom*, App.no. 18601/91; *Hewitt and Harman (no. 2)*, App.no. 20317/92; *Redgrave v United Kingdom*, App.no. 20271/92. But see the view of the Court in Amman v Switzerland, App.no. 27798/95, February 2000.
[97] Walker, C.P. and Taylor, N. (1996), 'Bugs in the System', (1996) 1 *Journal of Civil Liberties* 105.
[98] Department of Trade and Industry, *Secure Electronic Commerce Statement* (DTI, London, 1998), at http://www.dti.gov.uk/CII/ana27p.html, para. 14. Compare Electronic Communications Privacy Act 1986 (18 USC s.2516); *Steve Jackson Games v US Secret Service* 36 F 3d 457 (1994).
[99] The process is criticised by the House of Commons Select Committee on Trade and Industry, *Report on Building Confidence in Electronic Commerce* (1998–9 HC 187) para. 101.

Interception of Communications in the United Kingdom, rejected judicial authorisations for IOCA interceptions and most forms of surveillance have been treated likewise.[100] A further worry is that systems of oversight under the Police Act 1998 Part III are very lax,[101] for there is no outside authorisation save for especially sensitive cases (homes, offices, hotel bedrooms, legal and journalistic materials). The contrary argument is made in the Consultation Paper[102] that forms of executive authorisation subject to later judicial oversight have been upheld by the European Commission of Human Rights.[103] But later Court judgments cast some doubt on this interpretation,[104] and supervisory control by a judge was recommended in *Klass v Germany*.[105] The effectiveness of oversight is particularly doubtful in the case of warrants for bulk interception, where an underlying certificate is used to specify the intercepted material which may be examined. Effect is given to the certificate by computer-based word searching of intercepted material, and the choice of words for searching is of course crucial in determining what is examined. There appears to be no oversight that ensures that the selection corresponds properly to what is specified in the certificate.

The *Consultation Paper* failed to support two further possible safeguards (as reflected in the subsequent Regulation of Investigatory Powers Act 2000, which is described later). One is disclosure after the close of the investigation to the subject.[106] The other is the use of intercepted material as evidence in court (forbidden by section 9 of IOCA),[107] though this aversion is narrowly confined to telecommunications interceptions and not surreptitious surveillance in general. Strangely, the Cabinet Office Performance and Innovation Unit report, *Encryption and Law Enforcement*, more or less acknowledged this inconsistency, suggesting that more openness might be helpful in terms of justifying to the public the importance and necessity of interception.[108] Usage in court (and the prior stage of disclosure) would also be a further valuable check against breach of due process during the collection process.

---

[100] (Cm. 4368, Stationery Office, London, 1999) para. 7.2. The reason given is that the involvement of judges would be unthinkable for warrants in connection with national security and economic well-being, but such powers already exist under the Official Secrets Acts 1911 s.9 and 1989 s.11.

[101] At least it answers charges that practices are not in accordance with law: *Govell v United Kingdom* App.no. 27237/95 [1997] EHRLR 438; *Khan v UK*, App.no. 35394/97, (2000) *The Times* 20 May.

[102] *Consultation Paper*, para. 2.10.

[103] *Christie v United Kingdom* App.no. 21482/93, 78A D&R; *Matthews v UK*, App.no. 28576/95; *Preston v UK*, App.no. 24193/94; *Redgrave v United Kingdom* App.no. 20271/92.

[104] *Chahal v UK*, App.no. 22414/93, Reports 1996-V, (1996) 23 EHRR 413; *Tinnelly v UK*, App.nos. 20390/92, 21322/93, Reports 1998-IV, (1999) 27 EHRR 249.

[105] App.no. 5029/71, Ser A 28 para. 56.

[106] The failure to grant this safeguard is not *per se* a breach of Article 8: *Klass v Germany* App.no. 5029/71, Ser A 28 para. 58.

[107] See *Morgans v DPP* [2000] 2 WLR 386. See also *R v Aujla and others* [1998] 2 Cr App R 16 (admission of intercepted information obtained abroad).

[108] The repeal of section 9 of the Interception of Communications Act 1985 was supported by the Lloyd Report on Terrorism Legislation in 1996 (*Inquiry into Legislation against Terrorism* (Cm. 3420, HMSO, London, 1996).

Third, the deficient controls which prevailed before the Regulation of Investigatory Powers Act 2000 were easily evaded by a system of permissive disclosures on the request of a police inspector under the Data Protection Act 1998, section 29 (formerly section 28(3) of the 1998 Act),[109] which arguably fell short of the demand of the European Convention that interferences with communications be expressly provided for by law. Section 29 is used (in combination perhaps with section 45 of the Telecommunications Act 1984) to obtain disclosure of materials (mainly in the form of traffic data) from ISPs where the material has ceased to be on a public telecommunications network within IOCA. It afforded an immunity from what would otherwise be a breach of data protection legislation by exceeding the bounds of registered disclosures so long as necessary for the prevention or detection of crime or for the purpose of any criminal proceedings by the users (holders) of personal data. Whether or not this practice was in accordance with law, in truth section 29 was never meant to be transformed *de facto* into a systematic positive power. Accordingly, it lacked safeguards such as prior independent authorisation or review,[110] though the standard form which had been unofficially developed required the authorisation of a police inspector. Reasons did not have to be given if it would prejudice the investigation. The request did not have to be in connection with any identified offences; there was no limit on the relevant offences; there were no safeguards for legal privilege;[111] and it was not specified how long the material should be held or whether there should be destruction.[112]

There are further techniques of surveillance which were in legally uncharted territory. These included telephone metering,[113] interceptions on private communications networks[114] or by the 'consent' of a party,[115] interceptions of portable phone transmissions,[116] certain international traffic (especially if

---

[109] LINX, 'Data Protection Act s.28(3) form' (http://www.linx.net/misc/dpa28-3form.html, 1999).

[110] Compare *Lambert v France* App.no. 23618/94, 1998-V.

[111] Compare *Kopp v Switzerland* App.no. 23224/94, 1998-II.

[112] Compare *Kruslin v France* App.no. 11801/85, Ser A 176A; *Huvig v France* App.no. 11105/84, Ser A 176B.

[113] *Malone v United Kingdom* App.no. 8691/79, Ser A 82, (1984) 7 EHRR 14; *Valenzuela Contreras v Spain* App.no. 27671/95, 1998-V. But see the wide interpretation of 'communications' in *Morgans v DPP* [2000] 2 WLR 386).

[114] *R v Ahmed* [1995] *Criminal Law Review* 246; *Halford v UK*, App.no. 20605/92, 1997-III, (1997) 24 EHRR 523; *R v Owen and Stephen* [1999] 1 WLR 949 (overruled in respect of the admissibility of evidence by *Morgans v DPP* [2000] 2 WLR 386). See Uglow, S., 'Covert surveillance and the European Convention on Human Rights' [1999] *Criminal Law Review* 287; Home Office Circular 15/1999. *Interception of Non-Public Telecommunications Networks* (London); OFTEL, Recording telephone conversations on private networks (http://www.oftel.co.uk/releases/pr47-99.htm).

[115] *R v Rasool* [1997] 1 WLR 949; *R v Owen and Stephen* [1999] 1 WLR 949 (overruled in respect of the admissibility of evidence by *Morgans v DPP* [2000] 2 WLR 386).

[116] *R v Effik* [1995] 1 AC 309 (overruled in respect of the admissibility of evidence by *Morgans v DPP* [2000] 2 WLR 386).

by radio wave rather than wire),[117] the planting in private or public places of listening devices (bugs) which do not intercept but 'overhear'[118] and the use of undercover agents.[119] Infra-red cameras and long-range external microphones were also not covered by any of the legislation, and those cases had no statutory system of authorisation or independent scrutiny.

The Home Office Consultation Paper[120] dealt with the demand for assistance from ISPs. Though this might be viewed as an imposition which chills speech contrary to article 10 and discriminates in comparison to other media under article 14, this demand is broadly in line with the European Council Resolution on the lawful interception of telecommunications.[121] Nevertheless, two concerns might be voiced. One is that any change in UK law should accord with a pan-European timetable and that financial burdens placed upon UK ISPs (which could amount to 10 to 15 per cent of running costs)[122] should not become more onerous than elsewhere so as to conduce them to relocate within or without the European Union. A further point is that the imposition of significant burdens on ISPs is unlikely to be proportionate to the advantages obtained, because these are in any event bound to be quickly eroded by technical progress. A combination of steganography[123] and communications sessions encrypted by transient keys will over the next two to three years nullify the advantages of extending interception to ISPs. The advance of these technologies is effectively beyond legislative control, and

---

[117] *R v Taylor-Sabori* [1999] 1 All ER 160. Chapter 6 of the *Consultation Paper* deals with the international developments in relation to interception of communications but makes no attempt to engage with the interception capabilities of the Echelon system and the Enfopol proposals at a European Union level.

[118] See *Govell v UK*, App.no. 27237/95 [1997] EHRLR 438; *Khan v UK* App.No. 35394/97, (2000) *The Times* 20 May.

[119] See *Teixeira de Castro v Portugal*, App.no. 25829/94, Reports 1998-IV; Uglow, S., 'Covert surveillance and the European Convention on Human Rights' [1999] *Criminal Law Review* 287.

[120] Loc. cit. chap. 5. See further Cyber-Rights & Cyber-Liberties (UK), 'Response to the Home Office Consultation Paper on Interception of Communications in the UK', at http://www.cyber-rights.org/reports/ioca99-response.htm, 1999; and Home Office, 'Interception of Communications in the United Kingdom: An Analysis of Responses to the Government's Consultation Paper', at http://www.homeoffice.gov.uk/oicd/iocresp.htm, 1999.

[121] (OJ C 329, 17 January 1995). This Resolution is subject to proposed amendment (draft Council Resolution on the lawful interception of telecommunications in relation to new technologies (10951/2/98 – C4-0052/99 – 99/0906(CNS) and these changes have been criticised by the Committee on Civil Liberties and Internal Affairs in a report on 23 April 1999 (see http://www.cyber-rights.org/interception/schmid-0243.htm). See also Recommendation of the Council of Europe 'for the Protection of Privacy on the Internet' should also be taken into account while developing a policy for the ISPs (Council of Europe Recommendation (No R (99) 5 of the Committee of Ministers to Member States, at http://www.coe.fr/cm/ta/rec/1999/99r5.htm).

[122] See the views of Demon at http://www.dispatches.demon.net/pr/1999/pr1999-08-19a.html. The Home Office estimates costs of around £20m: HC Debs vol. 345 col. 828 6 March 2000, Charles Clark.

[123] It is also difficult to distinguish compressed from encrypted material at first glance. It is not lawful to seize in order to sift for relevant material: *R v Chesterfield Justices ex p. Bramley* [2000] 2 WLR 409.

law enforcement bodies should be devoting their efforts to adapting their practical strategies to the new technical environment rather than trying to delay the incoming technical tide by ineffectual legislative means.

The launch in 1999 by the Association of Chief Police Officers and others of five codes of practice (including one entitled, *Interception of Communications and Accessing Communications Data*) in 1999[124] was a heartening recognition of the lack of constitutionalism in the field but did not redeem the situation. Though some of the legal desert was mapped, the means chosen could not amount to 'law' for the purposes of the European Convention[125] and the safeguards were woefully weak.[126] The Home Office Consultation Paper, *Interception of Communications in the United Kingdom*, helpfully recognised the need for a single legal framework wide enough to regulate not only public telecommunications but also, for example, e-mail on ISP servers and on intranets and traffic data.[127] However, in substance, it was defective as it did not address all the forms of surveillance covered by the ACPO codes. There remained the concern that it was fixated on one form of interception (via telecommunications systems) and would thereby be open to evasion by the use of other forms of surveillance techniques. The subsequent Regulation of Investigatory Powers Act 2000 thankfully avoids this narrow focus, but the failure of the Consultation Paper meant that most of the Act's contents were not pre-announced or discussed. Even within the field of telecommunications interception, the Consultation Paper is curt. For example, it is not clear why it concedes that 'communication data' should be subject to surveillance for wider purposes and with lesser authorisation than under IOCA.[128] The fact and pattern of traffic is as much a matter of personal preference (including preference as to the level of privacy protection) as the content of a message.

In any event, the idea that officially certified TSPs could satisfy law enforcement concerns was always far-fetched and was largely laid to rest by the close of 1999.[129] Such a structure can easily be evaded by criminals who

---

[124] See NCIS, Convention of Human Rights Codes of Practice (http://www.ncis.co.uk/web/Publications/Publications.htm, 1999). The codes also covered: Surveillance; Use of Informants; Undercover Operations; Recording and Dissemination of Intelligence Material.

[125] ACPO codes of practice would inevitably be perceived, as far as the general public are concerned 'somewhat obscure and open to differing interpretations' (*Malone v United Kingdom* App.no. 8691/79, Ser A 82, (1984) 7 EHRR 14 para. 79).

[126] Under the Code of Practice on Accessing Communications Data, para. 6, access to data under the Telecommunications Act 1985 s.45 (such as subscriber information from a licensed telecommunications operator) or the Data Protection Act 1998 s.29 (such as the contents of messages stored by a service provider) could be authorised by senior police officers, in connection with any crime and without any subsequent notification. The interception of messages entirely within a private network (such as e-mails within a company) required the authorisation of a chief constable: para. 5.

[127] (Cm. 4368, Stationery Office, London, 1999) chap. 4.

[128] Consultation Paper, chap. 10.

[129] House of Commons Select Committee on Trade and Industry, *Report on Building Confidence in Electronic Commerce* (1998–9 HC 187) para. 90.

can take their business abroad or use uncertified systems of encryption.[130] Only the Cabinet Office's Performance and Innovation Unit managed to see merit in key escrow, believing that lazy criminals would use it by default or would be forced to do so by legitimate correspondents.[131] However, the Cabinet Office did conclude that the balance of arguments had turned against key escrow because of uncertainty, costs and lack of global support.[132] This failure to convince the world to dance to the Anglo-American tune is finally conceded in the consultation paper, *Promoting Electronic Commerce* which accepted there would be no mandatory key escrow.[133] The policy is enacted by section 14 of the Electronic Communications Act 2000.

The interception of messages is an important technique of modern law enforcement, but it should be remembered that terrorists and organised criminals are detected through a variety of techniques involving mainly informers and surveillance. It should also be remembered that encryption is a means to an end and that at some stage a decrypted message is quite likely to be produced and physically reproduced in a form which allows for traditional search methods.

A further alternative to the discovery of the codes of keys from trusted third parties is to demand directly the decrypted information from a key holder who is either an innocent recipient of a key code or is even the criminal suspect.[134] The position in regard to innocent recipients, depending on their identity, might give rise to issues of legal privilege or journalistic confidences. Even more difficult, the position of suspects is subject to the privilege against self-incrimination. It is true that already in English (but not Scottish) law, those suspects who choose to exercise their 'right to silence' by not disclosing information to unlock encrypted files will risk adverse inferences being drawn from their silence under sections 34 and 35 of the Criminal Justice and Public Order Act 1994. An even more draconian power to order an explanation of seized materials (such as a computer disk) exists in relation to terrorism investigations under Schedule 5 paragraph 13 of the Terrorism Act 2000. This form of erosion of due process rights is now to be applied more directly to users of encryption. The DTI Consultation Paper, *Building Confidence in Electronic Commerce*[135] argued that there should be a new power to allow the police to require the disclosure of

---

[130] Koops, B.-J., *The Crypto Controversy* (Kluwer, The Hague, 1999) p.160.
[131] Cabinet Office's Performance and Innovation Unit, *Encryption and Law Enforcement* (http://www.cabinet-office.gov.uk/innovation/1999/encryption/report.htm, 1999) para. 6.5.
[132] Ibid. para. 6.10.
[133] Department of Trade and Industry, *Promoting Electronic Commerce* (Cm. 4417, Stationery Office, London, 1999) para. 36.
[134] See Koops, B.-J., *The Crypto Controversy* (Kluwer, The Hague, 1999) chap. 8.
[135] Department of Trade and Industry, *Building Confidence in Electronic Commerce* (http://www.dti.gov.uk/CII/elec/elec_com_1.html, 1999) at para. 64. The idea is endorsed by the House of Commons Select Committee on Trade and Industry, *Report on Building Confidence in Electronic Commerce* (1998–9 HC 187) para. 98.

encryption keys on service of a written notice when encrypted data has been uncovered pursuant to existing search or intercept powers.

The bones of the same idea were followed in the Cabinet Office paper and were given greater flesh in mid-1999 by the consultation paper, *Promoting Electronic Commerce* and Part III of the draft Electronic Communications Bill.[136] Broadly speaking, under clause 10, the authority which authorised the search or seizure by which the encrypted material comes into the possession of the investigating authorities could also issue (either at the time of initial authorisation or later) the written notice to decrypt and could do so without any further proof as to degree of possession on the part of the holder or the importance to the investigation or whether an order for the production of plaintext would suffice.[137] It followed from the provenance of the original seizure of the material that the written notice to decrypt would not necessarily be issued on the foot of judicial authority (it would be in the cases of search and seizure under the Police and Criminal Evidence Act 1984, sections 8 and 9), but could be authorised by the Home Secretary as a follow-up to an authorisation under IOCA or by a senior police officer as a follow-up to a bug under the Police Act 1997.[138] Even worse, for lawful seizures not pursuant to warrant (say, under the Police and Criminal Evidence Act 1984, sections 17, 18, 19, 32 or the Telecommunications Act 1984, section 45), the police and Customs (and soldiers) could be self-authorising in regard to the appropriate permission to issue a notice to decrypt (though secret agents must have written permission from a circuit judge).[139] The relevant authorities could decide at their discretion whether it is sufficient to supply plaintext or whether a key must be disclosed,[140] even though the disclosure of a key potentially is much more intrusive than disclosure of plaintext. The forced disclosure of documentation may not be considered as serious as the demand for personal testimony, but it can be personally incriminating (especially if invoked against the suspect rather than a third-party professional) as implying the admission of the existence and possession of keys.[141] Accordingly, it was strongly possible that such a requirement could breach Article 6(1) to (3) of the European Convention by being considered unfair in the circumstances and by reversing the burden of proof, especially since: it was not made clear what suspicion or belief in relation to what levels of offence should be established by the prosecution or what other evidence should be possessed by the law enforcement authorities, or what other avenues of investigation should be exhausted prior to the issuance of a notice; the difficulty for the suspect to prove ignorance is

---

[136] Department of Trade and Industry, *Promoting Electronic Commerce* (Cm. 4417, Stationery Office, London, 1999) para. 32.

[137] See Bill cl.10 and Sched.1.

[138] Sched.1 para. 1.

[139] Sched.1 para. 2, 4.

[140] cl.11.

[141] See *Saunders v UK*, App.no. 19187/91, 1996-VI, (1997) 23 EHRR 313 *Funke v France*, App.no. 10828/84, Ser. A 256-A. Compare *US v Doe* (1984) 465 US 605.

substantial; and the need for the power in relation to the threat to society is highly variable given that the notice could apply to any offence.[142] It was also not certain that legal advice would be available;[143] but it was certain that a failure to comply would itself automatically be an offence (with the onus therefore on the recipient of the notice to prove no knowledge[144]) and not just a matter of evidence whose weight can be expressly evaluated in the trial as a whole.[145] The device could help in a few cases (though the availability of other avenues under the likes of the Terrorism Act 2000 should be recalled) but could only be legitimate if the foregoing conditions are met.

Part III proved to be the most contentious part of the draft Electronic Communications Bill and, to avoid undue delays, it was dropped from the proposals which have become the Electronic Communications Act 2000. At the same time, it was decided to combine the former Part III with other pending legislation which was to replace both IOCA and the ACPO Codes. The result is the Regulation of Investigatory Powers Act 2000 (the 'RIP Act').

Part I Chapter II of the RIP Act concerns the acquisition and disclosure of communications data. This replaces the procedures under the Data Protection Act 1998, sections 29, and should be welcomed as providing a surer footing for the disclosure by ISPs of traffic data. Section 21 expressly confines itself to traffic data not in the course of transmission (such interception falls within Chapter I) and to the routing information (including sender and recipient) but not including content. Section 22 imposes new requirements of necessity and proportionality (section 22(5)), but the purposes for which an authorisation may be issued are breathtakingly wider than for interception warrants[146] and are not subject to any external warrant process but can be authorised at a specified level of seniority by the policing or intelligence services themselves. Surely these limits (or lack of them) do not have sufficient regard to the value of privacy at the time of issuance, even if there is some later oversight by the Interception of Communications Commissioner under section 57? Though privacy is not given much priority, the potential expenditure to the communications industry and the concern that the legislation will render uncompetitive UK-based ISPs can be addressed under section 24 by which the government may contribute to the costs incurred

---

[142] These tests in relation to article 6(2) especially are rehearsed in *R v Home Secretary, ex p Kebilene* [1999] 3 WLR 972.

[143] Compare Youth and Criminal Evidence Act 1999 s.58.

[144] Cabinet Office's Performance and Innovation Unit, *Encryption and Law Enforcement* (http://www.cabinet-office.gov.uk/innovation/1999/encryption/report.htm, 1999) para. 7.7.

[145] cl.12 of Bill. See *Salabiaku v France*, App.no. 10519/83, Ser A vol. 141-A, (1988) 13 EHRR 379; *Murray (John) v UK*, App.no. 18731/91, (1996) 22 EHRR 29; *R v Home Secretary, ex p Kebilene* [1999] 3 WLR 175. The House of Lords reversed on other grounds and suggested that once the Human Rights Act 1998, s.3, comes into force, there will be an evidential burden on the defendant but not the ultimate burden: [1999] 3 WLR 972 at pp.984–7.

[146] The extra purposes include preventing any crime or disorder, as well as health, taxation or indeed any purpose which might be specified by a statutory order.

through the installation of equipment necessary to allow forms of interception and recording.[147]

Decryption powers are granted by Part III of the RIP Act. Under section 49, there must be some triggering power under which the material is first captured, and this potentially allows for safeguards to be introduced. Accordingly, the government often talks in terms of this power being based on a warrant. The seizure under judicial warrant (such as the Police and Criminal Evidence Act 1984, section 9) is the least controversial example, since in that situation there is independent judicial oversight.[148] The government claims that oversight by the Secretary of State under Part I powers (formerly IOCA) (or under section 5 of the Intelligence Services Act 1994) is no less searching (and it can produce the raw material under section 49(1)(b)). But one might question how far it is as searching or as clinical as a judge's oversight; there is also concern about 'case-hardening' on the part of a politician dealing with 2,000 or so applications per year. However, initial scrutiny is in any event less certain since there are alternative ways of capturing the material which do not require any independent oversight or formality. This criticism applies to some extent to Part I Chapter II (Acquisition and disclosure of communications data). Those powers (which can produce the raw material under section 49(1)(c)) will be authorised internally by the police or security services (section 25(2)), but there is the limitation that the powers in that connection do not include the surveillance of content (section 21(4)(b)). The more worrying case, where the police, Customs and Excise or security services can seek the key to content, will be where they have entered premises either pursuant to a non-warrant power such as to make an arrest or to 'rummage', followed by a search or seizure power under PACE sections 18, 19 or 32 or a power under the Customs and Excise Management Act 1979 (this is envisaged by section 49(1)(a)) or pursuant to the consent of the occupier of the premises who may or may not be the owner or subject of the encrypted data or simply by provenance such as when a disk is found lying in the street having been dropped in error (this is envisaged by section 49(1)(e)).

The next concern is how searching scrutiny will be once the police have seized the encrypted raw material and wish to force the erstwhile possessor to provide a key. Before the issuance of a notice requiring a key, there must be the 'appropriate permission' under section 49(2). The default position again gives some reassurance in that there must be written permission from an independent judicial officer under Schedule 2 paragraph 1. But this default

<hr/>

[147] See The Smith Group Limited Report for the Home Office on technical and cost issues associated with interception of communications at certain Communication Service Providers, CIR221D009-1.1 (19 April 2000), at http://www.homeoffice.gov.uk/oicd/techcost.pdf.

[148] This falls within section 49(1)(a). The same argument will apply to at least some disclosures under section 49(1)(d) – the receipt of material pursuant to a statutory duty (an example being a disclosure order under section 2 of the Criminal Law Act 1987 in connection with serious fraud).

position can be overridden under paragraphs 2 to 5 (though the default process would seem to be available in these cases if preferred: paragraph 1(2)). The following exceptions are listed in Schedule 2 and largely negate the default safeguard.

Under paragraph 2 it will be possible to ask for permission to issue a decryption notice at the time of asking for permission to search or conduct surveillance – to bundle both the search and decryption requests together (paragraph 2(2)(a)) – or to go back to the same issuing authority after seizure (paragraph 2(2)(b). This not only applies to judicial permission under PACE and to the Secretary of State's authorisation under Part I (formerly IOCA) or under section 5 of the Intelligence Services Act 1994, but also applies to authorisations under the Police Act 1997 Part III. So in these cases, there may never be any judicial scrutiny, aside from those cases falling under section 97 (dwellings, hotel bedrooms, offices and confidential journalistic, legally privileged and personal information). However, these exceptional permissions apply only to the material identified in the warrant or authorisation and not to material seized (such as under PACE section 19) at the same time as a search under warrant or authorisation (paragraph 2(9)).

Under paragraph 3, for material coming into the possession of the intelligence services under statutory power but without a warrant such as evidence seized under PACE sections 18, 19 or 32 or communications data under Part I Chapter II (the immediate provenance being another public authority such as the police, which has passed on the information to the intelligence services), the permission to issue a decryption notice under section 49 can be given by the Secretary of State.

Paragraph 4 deals with the incidental obtaining of information under statutory powers such as PACE sections 18, 19 and 32.[149] In these very common cases the police (and customs and excise and the armed forces) can secure the 'appropriate permission' without actually having to apply for it externally (subject to senior level internal approval under paragraph 6). Other agencies must apply to a judge.

Finally, paragraph 5 deals with the encrypted data obtained without legal formality either by consent or through provenance under section 49(1)e). For the intelligence services, judicial permission under paragraph 1 may be avoided by the granting of permission from the Secretary of State. If the information is not passed to the intelligence services in this way, then the default position applies to the police and customs and excise.

The RIP Act improves upon the position in the draft Electronic Communications Bill in several respects, though whether it is 'a significant step forward for the protection of human rights in this country'[150] may be more

---

[149] The incidental powers are excluded from paragraph 2 by para. 2(9) and the security services are not invested with these powers under PACE and so they cannot be relevant to para. 3.
[150] HC Debs vol. 345 col. 767 6 March 2000, Jack Straw.

debatable. There is express regard to necessity and proportionality in terms of the issuance of a notice under section 49 (section 55) which may counter the concern that notices can be issued in connection with any offence (section 49(3)(b). Next, the exercise of the powers will be kept under review by the Covert Investigations Commissioner (section 57). Furthermore, section 50 allows for the disclosure of plaintext as the normal response to a notice to decrypt 'in almost all cases'[151] – the handing over of the key must be specifically demanded and be a proportionate imposition (section 51(4)). In terms of the section 53 offence of failure to comply with a notice, there is now a burden of proof on the prosecution to show that the defendant 'has or has had possession of the key' and the original requirement to disclose under section 49(2) must be based on an objective not subjective belief of possession. However, the burden is not predicated upon proof of any conspiracy in the crime, any neglect or any wilful failure to comply. Equally, the statutory defences allow for failure to disclose or facilitate access only if not 'reasonably practicable', so possessors still have a burden of proof that the failure was reasonable or, indeed, that they never possessed a key in the first place or had ceased to do so at the time of the request, despite some objective evidence that they once did.[152] This shift in burden occurs even though possession of an encryption key may well be transitory if good security practices are maintained.

Overall, the Trade and Industry Select Committee Report on the Draft Electronic Communications Bill saw 'nothing that would substantiate some hysterical comment to the effect that the Government's proposed new power to require decryption represents a major assault on our rights'.[153] But there remain great concerns about the overall scheme and detailed provisions. In terms of the overall scheme, one should remain doubtful about the need for these powers which are not (as yet) replicated in other comparable jurisdictions. In the light of this lack of demonstrable need, one wonders whether the cost of security for seized materials will be money well-spent.[154] Furthermore, the concerns remain about potential breaches of articles 6 and 8 of the European Convention.

The world view

In contrast to the UK position, the law enforcement policy stances of states in the non-Anglo-American world, including the European Union and OECD

---

[151] HC Debs vol. 345 col. 834 6 March 2000, Charles Clark.
[152] A useful summary of the arguments, especially as contended by the Foundation for Information Policy Research, is set out in the House of Commons Library, Research Paper 00/25 (http://www.parliament.uk/commons/lib/research/rp2000/rp00-025.pdf, 2000).
[153] (1998–9 HC 852) para. 23. See further the government's observations at 1999–2000 HC 199.
[154] Funding of £25m was committed for a Government Technical Assistance Centre in March 2000. See (2000) *The Sunday Times* 30 April p.1; Gladman, B.R., 'The Regulation of Investigatory Powers Bill – The Provisions for Government Access to Keys', (Foundation of Information Policy Research, 23 February, 2000, at http://www.fipr.org/rip/RIPGAKBG.pdf).

policy statements as described already, look rather different, and the trend is towards greater liberalisation.[155] There was even a dramatic turn away from encryption controls by the French government, when Prime Minister Lionel Jospin announced on 19 January 1999 that France was dropping its long-held restrictions on the use of cryptography.[156] The Irish government had already rejected internal and export controls in June 1998.[157] Further afield, the Canadian government has confined its attention largely to the technical issue of the acceptance of digital signatures as evidence equivalent to physical writing.[158] According to EPIC's Report, *Cryptography and Liberty 2000*, only Malaysia and Singapore have existing laws mandating lawful access to encryption keys similar to the UK's RIP Act approach.[159] The stances elsewhere sometimes relate more to slower progress down the information superhighway than conscious and considered decisions about the appropriate role of encryption. However, in order to explain the remaining differences between those information societies like the US and UK which are favourably disposed towards regulation of encryption and those like the European Union (and France) which are less so inclined, we offer the following explanations.

In the first place, we suggest that the Anglo-American official position is reflective of underlying geo-policies and tensions, in other words the dominance of a state security agenda on the part of executives whose world authority is in large part based on military might.[160] Set in the context of the richest and most militarily powerful country in the world, the US concerns that the dissemination of encryption techniques will weaken this power seem strikingly implausible. There is no more convincing evidence that the use of encryption has created insuperable new problems for law enforcement or security interests in the US than in the UK.[161]

---

[155] Global Internet Liberty Campaign, *Cryptography and Liberty: An International Survey of Encryption Policy* (http://www.gilc.org/crypto/crypto-survey.html, Washington DC, 1998); Electronic Privacy Information Center, *Cryptography and Liberty 1999* (http://www.epic.org/reports/crypto1999.html, Washington, 1999) and *Cryptography and Liberty 2000*, (http://www.epic.org/reports/crypto2000.html, Washington, 2000).

[156] Jospin, L. (1999), at http://www.premier-ministre.gouv.fr/GB/INFO/FICHE1GB.HTM.

[157] Irish Government, *Framework for Ireland's Policy on Cryptography and Electronic Signatures* (http://www.irlgov.ie:80/tec/communications/signat.htm, 1998).

[158] Canadian Ministry of Justice, *Consultation Paper on facilitating electronic commerce: statutes, signatures and evidence* (http://www.canada.justice.gc.ca/consultations/facilt7_en.html, 1998).

[159] See Electronic Privacy Information Center, *Cryptography and Liberty 2000*, loc. cit.

[160] See also Campbell, D., 'Echelon: Interception Capabilities 2000 Report', April PE 168.184/ Part 4/41999 (STOA publication) at http://www.cyber-rights.org/interception/stoa/stoa_cover.htm; Barth, R.C. and Smith, C.N., 'International regulation of encryption' in Kahin, B. and Neeson, C., *Borders in Cyberspace* (MIT Press, Cambridge, 1997) at p.283.

[161] But see Denning, D.E. and Baugh, W.E. Jr, 'Cases involving encryption in crime and terrorism' (http://guru.cosc.georgetown.edu/~denning/crypto/cases.html, 1997); Grabosky, P.N. and Smith, R.G., *Crime in the Digital Age* (Transaction Publishers, Annandale, 1998) p.210; FBI, *Encryption: Impact on Law Enforcement* (http://www.fbi.gov/library/, 1999) p.9.

Our conclusion is that the perfect criminal could use encryption technology to make detection very difficult, just as the perfect criminal could use a fast car to make a speedy getaway or wear overalls and plastic gloves to avoid the deposit of DNA materials. In reality, criminals are rarely perfectly conscientious or error-free, and we value fast cars, overalls – and encryption – for purposes other than their possible applications in the commission of crime. None of these devices is the electronic equivalent of a sawn-off shotgun whose very design points invariably to nefarious purposes.

Despite the absence of convincing security concerns, the US government has pursued the curtailment of encryption based on what it perceived as national security interests.[162] The most overt illustration of this policy was the attempted control of exports of encryption codes, especially as applied against Phil Zimmerman, though these attempts have now effectively foundered after the investigation of his alleged contravention of the US International Traffic in Arms Regulations[163] was dropped in 1996. More recently, the commercial might of the information technology sector has also secured some relaxation, as in the case of Windows 2000 cited earlier. But national security concerns about encryption remain embodied in the multilateral mechanisms of the Wassenaar Arrangement of 1995 (On Export Controls for Conventional Arms and Dual Use Goods and Technologies),[164] even though it is arguable that they cannot be justifiable within that context in relation to encryption which is a defensive/passive technology and has an established role in clearly distinguishable civil transactions.

A second explanation for Anglo-American restrictive approaches to encryption is that the different approaches also reflect distinct cultural stances in regard to the value of privacy. The UK especially has had a tradition of being a privacy-free legal zone. The USA does recognise privacy at federal and state level but, even so, the protection is at best patchy and is heavily tempered by the dominant value of First Amendment free speech. Only where encryption is utilised in pursuance of political speech is there likely to be positive constitutional protection.[165] In contrast, the more regulated and corporatist polities of Western Europe have long developed respect for privacy, and their lead in data protection laws are a prime indicator of the difference from the Anglo-American position. Yet, these differences may now be diminishing. With the Maastricht

---

[162] See Barth, R.C. and Smith, C.N., 'International regulation of encryption' in Kahin, B. and Neeson, C., *Borders in Cyberspace* (MIT Press, Cambridge, MA, 1997); Baker, S.A. and Hurst, P.R., *The Limits of Trust* (Kluwer, The Hague, 1998) chap. 3.

[163] 22 C.F.R. ss 120–130 (made under the Arms Export Control Act, 22 USC s2778). See Carnow, C.E.A., *Future Codes* (Artech House, Boston, 1997) Pt VI chap. 13; Baker, S.A. and Hurst, P.R., *The Limits of Trust* (Kluwer, The Hague, 1998) chap. 3.

[164] See Cyber-Rights & Cyber-Liberties (UK), (http://www.cyber-rights.org/crypto wassenaar.htm, 1998); Baker, S.A. and Hurst, P.R., *The Limits of Trust* (Kluwer, The Hague, 1998) p.71.

[165] *McIntyre v Ohio Elections Commission* 514 US 334 (1995). See further Karnow, C., *Future Codes* (Artech House, Boston, 1997) chaps 10, 13.

Treaty[166] and the establishment of a Third Pillar competency including home affairs and justice, the European Union has been drawn into not only policing matters in relation to police cooperation on interception of communications, including encryption, but also is alleged to be considering controversial plans (under the project title, ENFOPOL) for wide-ranging and co-ordinated electronic surveillance[167] which seem at odds with its underlying respect for privacy. In the background, there are also allegations of a much bigger and better US-led electronic surveillance system, ECHELON, which may account for lukewarm UK support for ENFOPOL in the DTI's consultation paper of 1999.[168] At the same time, most Western European jurisdictions regulate surveillance far more strictly and with greater concern for individual privacy than the UK, as evidenced by judicial authorisation, disclosure to the suspect (after the end of surveillance) and the use of evidence in court.[169]

Our third explanation is that the Anglo-American distaste for private encryption is also motivated by forms of moral entrepreneurship on the part of the policing and security organisations within those jurisdictions. As some forms of policing business diminish, whether through the end of the Cold War or (in the US) through the endless incarceration of an ever-increasing proportion of the population, other forms of business will be sought. Set against recent falling crime rates, the invocation of the threat of boundless pornography, fraud, organised crime and vile racism has proven a useful bedrock on which the enterprising police or security officer can found a new empire and secure funding for it. The threat may turn out to be exaggerated,[170] but part of the exaggeration relates to encryption. An example might be the recommendation at the end of NCIS's *Project Trawler* report that NCIS itself should provide a single, dedicated, national unit to investigate the most serious computer crimes and to act as a centre of excellence.[171]

---

[166] Maastricht Treaty (1992) (Cm. 1934, HMSO, London, 1992). See further Colvin, M. and Noorlander, P., 'Human rights and accountability after the Treaty of Amsterdam' [1998] *European Human Rights Law Review* 191; Betten, L. and Grief, N., *European Union Law and Human Rights* (Longman, London, 1998).

[167] See C 13/32 EN 18.1.1999 Official Journal of the European Communities – (1999/C 13/043) written question, subject Enfopol, E-1402/98 by Gerhard Hager (NI) to the Commission (7 May 1998); ENFOPOL 98, Rev 1, Draft Council Resolution on New Technologies, Brussels, 4 November 1998 (10951/1/98), at http://www.telepolis.de/tp/english/special/enfo/6389/1.html. See further the ENFOPOL Timeline 1991–9, 10 March 1999, at http://www.telepolis.de/tp/english/special/enfo/6382/1.html.

[168] Department of Trade and Industry, *Promoting Electronic Commerce* (Cm. 4417, Stationery Office, London, 1999) para. 42. See Campbell, D., 'Somebody's listening', (1998) *New Statesman*, 12 August, p.10; Hager, N., 'Secret Power: New Zealand's Role in the International Spy Network', at http://www.fas.org/irp/eprint/sp/index.html, 1996.

[169] See Nash, S., 'Interception of communications in the European Union' 1996 *Juridical Review* 321.

[170] Wall, D., 'Policing and the regulation of the Internet' in Walker, C. (ed.), *Crime, Criminal Justice and the Internet* (Sweet & Maxwell, London, 1998) pp.79–91.

[171] NCIS, *Project Trawler: Crime on the Information Highways* (http://www.ncis.co.uk/, 1999) paras 110.111. But the command paper, Department of Trade and Industry, *Promoting*

In this way, the Internet provides a paradigm of a late modern sub-society,[172] in which the traditional structures of class or other socio-political commonality are replaced by new élites whose privilege is measured in terms of knowledge and technological access.[173] In this case, the self-selecting élite are the cybercops who seek to claim better insights into the threats of the Internet than are understood by its users themselves. To help them further, a national encryption resource unit has been established in the security services,[174] a location which should remind us of the political importance of this area of policing.

Conclusion

This chapter has suggested that national government access to encryption keys would undermine and hold back both the development of e-commerce and would be harmful to individual rights of privacy and free speech. The development of the Internet requires the instillation of trust in Internet users and affirmation that their expectation of privacy in correspondence is legitimate. But it seems to be the government which has no trust and instead seeks to assert 'Orwellian mischief'[175] over them:[176]

> Until recently, the Government intended to use legislation to control crypto-graphy rather than to encourage the development of electronic commerce . . . UK electronic commerce policy was for so long entrapped in the blind alley of key escrow that fears have been expressed that UK's reputation as a competitive environment for electronic commerce is now severely damaged. It is unfortunate that legislation to deal with the recognition of electronic signatures in law, and related measures, should have become entangled with the requirements of law enforcement agencies to tackle criminals' use of encryption

We also suggest, in the light of case studies of Internet 'misuse' which have been processed by the police in the United Kingdom, that there is no com-pelling state interest in such an invasion of privacy, as the perpetrators have been detected and evidence gathered without any new powers to survey or search. Part of the reason for that outcome, too often ignored in

---

Electronic Commerce (Cm. 4417, Stationery Office, London, 1999) para. 52, simply suggests notification of encryption in criminal activity.

[172] Giddens, A., *The Consequences of Modernity* (Polity Press, Cambridge, 1990).

[173] Castells, M., *The Information Age Vol. 1: The Rise of Network Society* (Blackwell, Oxford, 1996); O'Malley, P. and Palmer, D., 'Post-Keynsian policing' (1996) *Economy and Society* 25(2), 137.

[174] See House of Commons Select Committee on Trade and Industry, *Report on Building Confidence in Electronic Commerce* (1998–9 HC 187) para. 110; Cabinet Office's Performance and Innovation Unit, *Encryption and Law Enforcement* (http://www.cabinet-office.gov.uk/innovation/1999/encryption/report.htm, 1999) para. 7.6; House of Commons Debates, col. 195 wa 26 May 1999; Government Technical Assistance Centre (http://www.homeoffice.gov.uk/oicd/ecu/partind.htm).

[175] *Arizona v Evans* 514 US 1 at p. (1995) per Ginsburg, J. (dissenting).

[176] House of Commons Select Committee on Trade and Industry, *Report on Building Confidence in Electronic Commerce* (1998–9 HC 187) para. 116.

the equation, is that the Internet itself, aside from encryption, produces 'many technological windfalls for security'.[177] Criminals cannot be entirely prevented from having access to strong encryption and from bypassing escrowed encryption. The benefits of regulation for crime fighting are therefore not easy to assess and often expressed in a fairly general language. However, the chilling effect on Internet usage, especially for legitimate political purposes in opposition to states, is easier to discern. Equally, the RIP Act's demand that suspects provide information on pain of an offence is expressed in terms which are far too wide and unguarded and are incompatible with government policy to make Britain a favourable location for e-commerce and network development. So, like some other academic commentators,[178] we favour a 'zero option' in which alternative approaches to policing are adopted, including through the use of the Internet for intelligence-gathering.[179]

Fortunately, the underlying conditions of Internet governance are set firmly against eccentric national regulation, as this is a medium that demands global coherence so as to achieve an effective regulatory framework.[180] The steps taken by the European Union and the OECD seem to be in the right direction. Now that the benefits of encryption are increasingly widely recognised for the development of e-commerce and supported by regulators and the industry, it is time to recognise other beneficial and legitimate uses of such technology. So the debate about the balance between privacy versus law enforcement[181] will continue and the authors foresee that there will be differences within the policies of individual nation states in relation to the policing issues which are firmly connected to the cultural, political and historical backgrounds of individual nation states. However, we believe that encryption is more likely to help than to hinder the prevention and detection of cybercrimes. It should become a core utility in the correspondence of a netizen, who should attract no penalty or even suspicion for taking perfectly reasonable precautions for the sake of privacy.

---

[177] Zimmerman, P., 'The rise and reform of public law in the Internet' (INET99 Conference, San Jose, 1999).

[178] Koops, B.-J., *The Crypto Controversy* (Kluwer, The Hague, 1999) chap. 10. Compare Ruez, B.R., *Privacy in Telecommunications* (Kluwer, The Hague, 1997) p.255.

[179] See Hyde, S., 'A few coppers change' 1999 (2) *Journal of Information Law and Technology* (http://www.law.warwick.ac.uk/jilt/99-2/hyde.html).

[180] Walker, C. and Akdeniz, Y. (1998), 'The governance of the Internet in Europe with special reference to illegal and harmful content' in Walker, C. (ed.), *Crime, Criminal Justice and the Internet* (Sweet & Maxwell, London, 1998) p.5. See also New Zealand Law Commission, *Electronic Commerce* (Report no. 50, Wellington, 1998) para. 28.

[181] As in *R v Preston* [1994] 2 AC 130 at pp.145–6 per Lord Mustill.

CHAPTER 15

Electronic commerce – law and policy

*Paul Eden**

The invention of the steam engine two centuries ago and the harnessing of electricity ushered in an industrial revolution that fundamentally altered the way we work, brought the world's people closer together in space and time, and brought us greater prosperity. Today, the invention of the integrated circuit and computer and the harnessing of light for communications have made possible the creation of the global Internet and an electronic revolution that will once again transform our lives . . .

One of the most significant uses of the Internet is in the world of commerce. Already it is possible to buy books and clothing, to obtain business advice, to purchase everything from gardening tools to high-tech telecommunications equipment over the Internet. This is just the beginning. Trade and commerce on the Internet are doubling or tripling every year – and in just a few years will be generating hundreds of billions of dollars in sales of goods and services. If we establish an environment in which electronic commerce can grow and flourish, then every computer can be a window open to every business, large and small, everywhere in the world.

William J. Clinton, 'Message to Internet Users' 1 July 1997[1]

Introduction

The profound effect that Internet technology is having on the global trade in goods and services is impossible to deny.[2] World trade involving computer software, entertainment products (such as motion pictures, video games and sound recordings), information services (such as databases and online newspapers), technical information, product information, product licences, financial and professional services (including business and technical consulting, accounting, architectural design, legal advice and travel services)

---

* A working draft of this chapter was delivered to a Socrates Workshop on Information Law and Technology at the School of International Studies and Law, University of Coventry on 12 March 1999. Unless otherwise indicated all Internet source sites were visited 10–11 May 2000.
[1] The White House, Office of the Press Secretary, 'Text of the President's Message to Internet Users' 1 July 1997, http://www.whitehouse.gov/WH/New/Commerce/message.html.
[2] See 'The Net Imperative: A Survey of Business and the Internet' (1999) *The Economist*, 26 June p.5.

has grown rapidly over the last ten years.[3] An increasing amount of these transactions occurs online. What has been termed the Global Information Infrastructure (GII) is still in the early stages of its development, but it has the potential to revolutionise commerce by lowering transaction costs and facilitating new types of commercial transactions.

Many businesses and consumers are wary of conducting business over the Internet because of the lack of a predictable legal environment governing transactions. Therefore, this chapter seeks to introduce some of the legal policy issues surrounding electronic commerce. It will first examine the applicability of existing commercial law, including the classification of contracts for the purchase of computer software and the validity of shrinkwrap and clickwrap licences. It will then consider the legal policy issues underlying the establishment of a new legal framework for electronic commerce. Particular attention will be paid to the proposals of the British government to facilitate electronic commerce. Because of the large number of legal and regulatory issues that exist with regard to electronic commerce, this chapter can only offer an introduction to some of the main issues.

What is electronic commerce?

The Organisation for Economic Co-operation and Development (OECD) has stated:[4]

> Electronic Commerce generally refers to all forms of commercial transactions involving both organisations and individuals, that are based on the electronic processing and transmission of data, including text sound and visual images. It also refers to the effects that the electronic exchange of commercial information may have on the institutions and processes that support and govern commercial activities.

In the view of the World Trade Organisation (WTO), 'electronic commerce' includes both products which are bought and paid for over the Internet but are delivered physically, and products that are delivered as digitalised information over the Internet.[5] These broad definitions of electronic commerce include transactions involving telephones, faxes, televisions, electronic payment and money transfer systems that are well established. The most significant development is the mass-market potential of the simple-to-use browsers for surfing the World Wide Web that have transformed the Internet

---

[3] In 1997, the US Framework for Global Electronic Commerce estimated that this form of trade accounted for over US$40 billion of US exports alone:
http://www.whitehouse.gov/WH/New/Commerce/read.html.
[4] OECD, *Electronic Commerce: Opportunities and Challenges for Government* (OECD, Paris, 1997) 11. See Dickie, J., *Internet and Electronic Commerce in the European Union* (Hart Publishing, Oxford, 1999) chap. 1.
[5] See WTO Secretariat *Electronic Commerce and the Role of the WTO* (WTO, Geneva, 1998). See generally the Electronic Commerce section of the WTO website at http://www.wto.org/wto/ecom/ecom.html.

from being the medium of choice for geeks and paedophiles into an electronic marketplace for businesses and consumers alike. Since the 1980s, the software industry has evolved to become the United States' third largest manufacturing industry and information commodities such as books, films, videos, multi-media and software have grown to become 'either the largest sector of the modern economy or the second largest'.[6]

The classification of computer software contracts

The contract of sale is, by far, the most common type of commercial contract, and most of the essential elements of the law relating to the sale of goods governed by English law can be found in a single statutory code, the Sale of Goods Act. The title of the original Sale of Goods Act of 1893 stated that it was '[a]n Act for Codifying the Law Relating to the Sale of Goods'. The 1893 Act, as drafted by the noted statutory draftsman and commercial law author, Sir Mackenzie Chalmers, was envisaged as a merchants' code.[7] Its partial failure to provide satisfactory remedies for buyers in consumer contracts led to statutory amendments in 1973[8] and 1977.[9] In 1979, the 1893 Act was repealed and replaced by a new Sale of Goods Act 1979, which embodied all the amendments to the 1893 Act,[10] in particular the alterations made by the Unfair Contract Terms Act 1977. The Sale of Goods Act 1979 was further amended by the Sale and Supply of Goods Act 1994 which came into force on 3 January 1995. The Sale and Supply of Goods Act 1994 is the legislative expression of the Law Commission's recommendations contained in *Sale and Supply of Goods*,[11] and it seeks to reinforce the role of the Sale of Goods Act 1979 as an instrument of consumer protection.[12]

Sections 12–15 of the Sale of Goods Act 1979 lay down seven statutory terms in favour of the buyer of goods. Sections 13 and 14 are of particular interest. Section 13 states that '[w]here there is a contract for the sale of goods by description there is an implied term that the goods will correspond with the description'. Section 14(2) states that '[w]here the seller sells in the

---

[6] Nimmer, R.T., 'Information Age in Law: New Frontiers in Property and Contract' (1996) 68 *New York State Bar Journal* 28, as quoted by Rustad, M.L., 'Commercial Law Infrastructure for the Age of Information' (1997) 15 *Journal of Computer and Information Law* 258.

[7] See Chalmers, Sir M.D., *The Sale of Goods Act, 1893. including the Factors Acts, 1889 & 1890* (Butterworth, London, 1924).

[8] Supply of Goods (Implied Terms) Act 1973.

[9] Unfair Contract Terms Act 1977.

[10] For a brief account of the legislative history of the major changes to the 1893 Act see the judgment of Lord Justice Potter in *Stevenson v Rogers* [1994] 1 All ER 613 (CA) at pp.619–22. See further Guest, A. (ed.), *Benjamin's Sale of Goods* (5th ed., Sweet & Maxwell, London, 1997).

[11] *Report no. 160: Sale and supply of goods* (Cm. 137, HMSO, London, 1987).

[12] See Bridge, M., 'The Sale and Supply of Goods Act 1994' [1995] *Journal of Business Law* 398; Howells, G., 'The Modernization of Sales Law' [1995] *Lloyd's Maritime and Commercial Law Quarterly* 191.

course of a business, there is an implied term that the goods supplied under the contract are of satisfactory quality'. Prior to the coming into force of the Sale and Supply of Goods Act 1994, section 14(2) of the 1979 Act required goods sold in the course of a business to be of 'merchantable quality'. Section 14(3) states:

> Where the seller sells goods in the course of a business and the buyer, expressly or by implication, makes known . . . to the seller . . . any particular purpose for which the goods are being bought, there is an implied term that the goods supplied under the contract are reasonably fit for that purpose, whether or not that is a purpose for which such goods are commonly supplied, except where the circumstances show that the buyer does not rely, or that it is unreasonable for him to rely, on the skill or judgment of the seller.

Section 6(2) of the Unfair Contract Terms Act 1977 provides that the sellers' implied undertakings as to conformity of the goods with description, or as to their quality, or as to their fitness for any particular purpose cannot be excluded by reference to any contract term where the buyer deals as a consumer. Where a buyer does not deal as a consumer, section 6(3) of the Unfair Contract Terms Act states that the statutory implied terms in favour of the buyer contained in sections 13–15 of the Sale of Goods Act 1979 can be excluded by reference to a contract term in so far as the term satisfies the requirement of reasonableness. The concept of dealing as a consumer has been interpreted broadly and, in *R & B Customs Brokers Co Ltd v United Dominions Trust Ltd*,[13] the Court of Appeal held that a firm of customs brokers that bought a company car for its managing director was dealing as a consumer for the purposes of section 12 of the Unfair Contract Terms Act 1977.

Although the Sale of Goods Act 1979 offers, to both consumers and non-consumers alike, an unrivalled degree of legal certainty as regards the essential elements of the contract of sale, its application to 'cybershopping' is not without conceptual difficulties. Section 2(1) of the Sale of Goods Act 1979 states that:

> A contract for the sale of goods is a contract by which the seller transfers or agrees to transfer the property in the goods for a money consideration called the price.

Section 61(1) of the Sale of Goods Act 1979 defines 'goods' as including all personal chattels other than things in action (also known as intangible movables) and money. Thus, the Sale of Goods Act 1979 only applies to transactions where the property (broadly ownership) in a tangible movable (other than money) is transferred to a buyer for a money consideration. The sale of computer hardware is undoubtedly a sale of goods governed by the Sale of Goods Act 1979[14] and, in *Toby Constructions Products Pty Ltd v Computer Bar (Sales) Pty Ltd*,[15] the Supreme Court of

---

[13] [1988] 1 All ER 847 (CA).
[14] See *Amstrad plc v Seagate Technology* (1998) 86 BLR 34.
[15] [1983] 2 NSWLR 48.

New South Wales held that a contract for the sale of both computer hardware and software is a contract for the sale of goods. Rogers J who delivered the judgment in the *Toby* case specifically left open the question whether the sale of software by itself constituted a sale of goods and he suggested that consideration should be given to the need for legislative action.

Prior to the Court of Appeal's decision in *St Albans City and District Council v International Computers Limited*,[16] when English Courts were faced with claims arising out of computer software transactions[17] they generally declined to express a view as to whether the sale of computer software was a sale of goods governed by the Sale of Goods Act 1979, holding instead that the implied terms of mechantability and fitness for purpose would be assumed to exist. In *St Albans City and District Council v International Computers Limited* the majority of the Court of Appeal declined to consider whether the supply of computer software constituted a sale of goods governed by the Sale of Goods Act 1979 but held instead that the defendants were under an express contractual undertaking to provide a computer system that would enable the plaintiff local authority to administer accurately the collection of the community charge.

In a separate concurring judgment in the *St Albans* case, Sir Iain Glidewell considered the legal basis of the implied terms as to quality and fitness for purpose in computer software contracts. Sir Iain Glidewell stated that the decision in the *Toby* case was 'clearly correct',[18] and he went on to consider the question left open in the *Toby* case namely whether the sale of software by itself constitutes a sale of goods. Although the trial judge in the *St Albans* case, Scott Baker J, was of the view that software was 'probably' goods for the purposes of section 2(1) of the Sale of Goods Act 1979 since '[p]rograms are . . . of necessity contained in some physical medium otherwise they are useless',[19] Sir Iain Glidewell stated that if a computer disk was not sold or hired[20] by the computer manufacturer, as the program itself was not 'goods' within the statutory definition,[21] there would be no statutory implication of terms as to quality or fitness of purpose. In Sir Iain Glidewell's view any implied terms as to quality or fitness of purpose in such contracts would have to satisfy the strict test for the implication of terms into a contract at common law.[22]

---

[16] [1996] 4 All ER 481 (CA).

[17] See *Eurodynamics Ltd v General Automation Ltd* (6 September 1988, unreported, QBD) and *Saphena Computing Limited v Allied Collection Agencies Ltd* [1995] FSR 616 (CA).

[18] [1996] 4 All ER 481 (CA) at p.493.

[19] [1995] FSR 686 at 699. For support for this approach see Reed, C., *Computer Law* (3rd ed., Blackstone, London, 1996) p.57.

[20] The Supply of Goods and Services Act 1982 s.9 contains statutorily implied terms regarding quality and fitness (which are, for all practical purposes, identical to the Sale of Goods Act 1979 s.14) where goods are hired or bailed.

[21] [1996] 4 All ER 481 (CA) at p.493.

[22] [1996] 4 All ER 481 (CA) at p.494.

Sir Iain Glidewell's *obiter* statements in the *St Albans* case are controversial. If correct, they will enable suppliers of computer software to avoid the statutory implied terms in favour of the buyer contained in the Sale of Goods Act 1979 by the simple expedient of supplying the software over the Internet or, alternatively, expressly retaining the ownership of any computer disk on which software is supplied.

In *The Salvage Association v Cap Financial Services Limited*,[23] Thayne Forbes J accepted that the supply of a computer program in the circumstances similar to those described above (albeit for bespoke software) if not a sale of goods governed by the Sale of Goods Act 1979 would at least be the supply of a service governed by section 13 of the Supply of Goods and Services Act 1982. Section 13 of the Sale of Goods and Services Act 1982 provides that:

> In a contract for the supply of a service where the supplier is acting in the course of a business, there is an implied term that the supplier will carry out the service with reasonable skill and care.

Many suppliers of services attempt to exclude or limit their obligation to take due care contained in section 13 of the Supply of Goods and Services Act 1982. Section 2(2) of the Unfair Contract Terms Act 1977 permits suppliers of services to exclude their liability for loss or damage (other than death or personal injury) caused by negligence in so far as the term or notice excluding such liability satisfies the requirement of reasonableness. Unlike section 6 of the Unfair Contract Terms Act 1977, section 2 does not draw a distinction between persons dealing as consumers and persons dealing otherwise than as consumers. Suppliers of computer software services governed by the Supply of Goods and Services Act 1982 thus not only escape the 'strict' obligations of the sellers of goods contained in sections 12–15 of the Sale of Goods Act 1979, they also enjoy greater powers to exclude the due care obligation contained in section 13 of the Supply of Goods and Services Act 1982. Where consumers purchase 'off-the-shelf' software (whether via the Internet or not), there cannot be any sound reason for imposing on the suppliers of such software fewer legal duties than the sellers of tangible goods, if the goals of 'medium neutrality' and a predictable, consistent and simple legal environment for electronic commerce are to be achieved.

Given the fact that electronic commerce is essentially a global rather than a national issue, the classification of computer software contracts in other legal regimes is also relevant. The two most important legal regimes to consider are:

- The Uniform Commercial Code of the United States of America, and
- The United Nations Convention on Contracts for the International Sale of Goods 1980 also known as the Vienna Convention on International Sales.

---

[23] [1995] FSR 654 (QBD) at pp.664–71.

US law

In *Advent Systems Limited v Unisys Corporation*,[24] the Third Circuit of the United States Court of Appeal held that computer software was a 'good' within the meaning of the Pennsylvania version of Article 2 of the Uniform Commercial Code (UCC). Applying the Article 2 of the UCC to computer software contracts offers substantial benefits to litigants, since Article 2 contains a uniform body of law on a wide range of questions likely to arise in computer software disputes: implied warranties, consequential damages, disclaimers of liability and the statute of limitations to name but a few. It should, however, be noted that the Court in the *Advent Systems* case determined the applicability of the UCC by examining the predominance of goods or services.

Given the conceptual difficulties of applying the notion of 'goods' to sales of computer software and the fact that Article 2 of the UCC does not specifically address licensing issues, the American Bar Association, the American Law Institute and the National Conference of Commissioners on Uniform State Laws began drafting a comprehensive amendment to the Uniform Commercial Code that would create a uniform body of law which would apply to software transactions (including both sales and licences, and service contracts), including retail software transactions.[25]

The drafting of proposed Article 2B – Licences became entangled in a wide-ranging debate about intellectual property issues and whether the suppliers of computer software should offer the same level of consumer protection as Article 2 of the UCC.[26] In April 1999 the American Law Institute and the National Conference of Commissioners on Uniform State Laws announced that legal rules for computer information transactions would not be promulgated as Article 2B of the Uniform Commercial Code, but the Conference would instead promulgate the rules for adoption by states as the Uniform Computer Information Transactions Act.

On 29 July 1999, the National Conference of Commissioners on Uniform State Laws (NCCUSL), by a vote of 43 to 6, promulgated the Uniform Computer Information Transactions Act (UCITA) for consideration by the

---

[24] 925 F.2d 670 (3rd Cir. 1991).

[25] See The 2B Guide at http://www.2bguide.com/bkgd.html.

[26] For a survey of some of the issues involved see Hillebrand, G., 'The Uniform Code Drafting Process: Will Articles 2, 2B and 9 be fair to Consumers?' (1997) 75 *Washington University Law Quarterly* 69; Selman, J.C. and Chen, C.S., 'Steering the Titanic Clear of the Iceberg: Saving the Sale of Software from the Perils of Warranties' (1997) 31 *University of San Francisco Law Review* 531; Dodd, J.C., 'Time and assent in the formation of information contracts: the mischief of applying article 2 to information contracts' (1999) 36 *Houston Law Review* 195; Frisch, D., 'Commercial Common Law, the United Nations Convention on the International Sale of Goods, and the Inertia of Habit' (1999) 74 *Tulane Law Review* 495; Founds, G.L., 'Shrinkwrap and Clickwrap Agreements: 2B or Not 2B?' (1999) 52 *Federal Communications Law Journal* 99; Kobayashi, B.H. and Ribstein, L.E., 'Uniformity, choice of law and software sales' (1999) 8 *George Mason Law Review* 261; Towle, H.K., 'The politics of licensing law' (1999) 36 *Houston Law Review* 121.

various state legislatures for adoption.[27] To date no American state has adopted the Uniform Computer Information Transactions Act.

In 1999 the Uniform Law Commissioners also promulgated the Uniform Electronic Transactions Act (UETA).[28] The primary objective of UETA is to establish the legal equivalence of electronic records and signatures with paper writings and manually signed signatures, removing barriers to electronic commerce. To date, the Uniform Electronic Transactions Act has been adopted in eleven states and introduced in fifteen other states (and the District of Columbia).[29]

The Vienna Sales Convention

The UN Convention on the International Sale of Goods (CISG) was drafted by the United Nations Commission on International Trade (UNCITRAL) and was adopted by a United Nations Conference held at Vienna from 10 March to 11 April 1980. The CISG entered into force on 1 January 1988, twelve months after the tenth instrument of adoption. To date the CISG has been adopted by over 57 nations (but not the United Kingdom). The CISG is now the uniform international sales law of the North American Free Trade Association (NAFTA) and two thirds of the European Union. Substantially more than one half of world trade is conducted on the terms of the CISG. Article 1(1) of CISG states that '[t]his Convention applies to contracts of sale of goods between parties whose places of business are in different States'. At first glance, this would seem to limit the sphere of application of CISG to sales of movable tangible objects, but the intention of the parties to the CISG was that the notion of 'goods' should be understood to cover all objects that form the subject matter of commercial sales contracts. In the view of the authors of the most exhaustive commentary on CISG, 'Computer programs (software) will have to be recognised as goods falling under the CISG'.[30] This view is supported by the decision in a case before the Landgericht München I.[31] It is less certain whether the sale of 'know-how' that is not incorporated in a physical medium will fall under the CISG as it has no link whatsoever with the notion of goods. By virtue of

---

[27] See Shah, P.A., 'The Uniform Computer Information Transactions Act' (2000) 15 *Berkeley Technology Law Journal* 85.

[28] See Boss, A.H., 'Electronic Commerce and the Symbiotic Relationship Between International and Domestic Law Reform' (1998) 72 *Tulane Law Review* 1931; Boss, A.H., 'The Internet and the Law: Searching for Security in the Law of Electronic Commerce' (1999) 23 *Nova Law Review* 583; Overby, A.B., 'UNCITRAL model law on electronic commerce: Will Cyberlaw Be Uniform? An Introduction to the UNCITRAL Model Law on Electronic Commerce' (1999) 7 *Tulane Journal of International and Comparative Law* 219.

[29] For information on the Legislative Status and Information on Uniform Acts see the National Conference of Commissioners on Uniform State Laws (NCCUSL) at http://www.nccusl.org/.

[30] Schechtriem, P., *Commentary on the UN Convention on the International Sale of Goods* (2nd ed. (in translation), Clarendon Press, Oxford, 1998) p.23.

[31] Landgericht München I, 8. Kammer für Handelssachen, 08.02.1995, 8 HKO 24667/93. The full text of the decision is available at http://www.jura.uni-freiburg.de/ipr1/cisg/.

article 2(a) of the CISG, the Vienna Sales Convention does not apply to sales of goods bought for personal family or household use.

Shrinkwrap and clickwrap licences

Computer software programs that are sold as commodities also embody intellectual property rights, and the users of such programs require a licence from the copyright owner to ensure that running the program and storing it on a hard disk will not infringe the copyright owner's intellectual property rights. Copyright owners may also wish to limit the number of copies of the program that can be made and, although this is not strictly an intellectual property issue, to limit their liability for losses caused by faults in the program.

Because the software copyright owner rarely contracts directly with the end-user, the software industry has evolved the concept of the shrinkwrap licence (also known as an end-user licence) with regard to the selling of mass-market software. It became standard practice for software manufacturers to include a notice in or on software packaging indicating that the software was subject to strict end-user licence conditions. Where the packaging was 'shrinkwrapped', the notice would state that the opening of the package indicated the end-user's acceptance of the terms and conditions contained in the notice.

The enforceability of shrinkwrap licences has been the subject of considerable debate. The conceptual difficulties include issues such as privity of contract, consideration and incorporation of terms.[32] The validity of a shrinkwrap licence was upheld by the Outer House of the Court of Session in *Beta Computers (Europe) Limited v Adobe Systems (Europe) Limited*.[33] The Seventh Circuit of the United States Court of Appeals has also upheld the general validity of shrinkwrap licences in *ProCD Incorporated v Zeidenberg*.[34] As the *Beta Computers* case was resolved by reference to a doctrine of Scottish law (the doctrine of *ius quaesitum tertio*), it is unlikely to have much persuasive authority before an English court.[35] By contrast Circuit Judge Easterbrook's finding in *ProCD*, that shrinkwrap licences are enforceable unless their terms are objectionable on grounds applicable to contracts in general, is based on careful balancing of the interests of

---

[32] For a detailed treatment of the relevant issues see Gringas, C., 'The Validity of Shrink-Wrap Licences' (1996) 4 *International Journal of Law and Information Technology* 77; Bainbridge, D., *Introduction to Computer Law* (3rd ed., Pitman, London, 1996) Pt. 2; Rowland, D. and MacDonald, E., *Information Technology Law* (Cavendish, London, 1997) chaps 3, 4; Chissick, M. and Kelman, A., *Electronic Commerce* (Sweet & Maxwell, London, 1999) chap. 3; Saxby, S. (ed.), *Encyclopaedia of Information Technology Law* (Sweet & Maxwell, London, 1990–9) chap. 6.
[33] [1996] FSR 367.
[34] 86 F.3d 1447 (7th Cir. 1996).
[35] See Goodger, B., 'Beta Plus for Effort: Beta Minus for Clarity' (1996) 11 *European Intellectual Property Review* 636. But see also Gretton, G.L., 'Software: binding the end-user' [1996] *Journal of Business Law* 524.

consumers and the software industry. It is submitted that the *ProCD* case, by injecting commercial reality and flexibility into the area of shrinkwrap licensing, should prove to be highly influential both inside and outside the United States.[36]

In English law objectionable contract terms are regulated by the Unfair Contract Terms Act 1977 and the Unfair Terms in Consumer Contracts Regulations 1999.[37] The principles of reasonableness and fairness contained in these provisions are likely to be invoked in relation to both shrinkwrap and clickwrap licences. Clickwrap licences are the electronic commerce equivalent of shrinkwrap licences but without the same conceptual difficulties. When buying goods or services online, buyers are often required to click on an icon that indicates acceptance of the seller's standard terms and conditions of sale. Unlike shrinkwrap licences, the seller's terms and conditions in clickwrap licences are always inserted pre-contractually and the problems of privity and consideration do not occur in that scenario.

The development of a new framework for electronic commerce

As important as transactional issues such as the classification of computer software contracts and the validity of shrinkwrap and clickwrap licences are, the unique nature of the Internet and the economic potential of electronic commerce have prompted proposals to develop an appropriate legal framework for electronic commerce. The three most significant attempts to develop a framework for the growth of electronic commerce are –

- the UNCITRAL Model Law on Electronic Commerce;[38]
- the EU Initiative in Electronic Commerce;[39] and
- the US Framework for Global Electronic Commerce.[40]

Other important initiatives include –

---

[36] For a detailed commentary on *ProCD v Zeidenberg* see Baker, D.C., 'Commercial Reality, Flexibility in Contract Formation, and Notions of Manifested Assent in the Arena of Shrinkwrap Licences' (1997) 92 *Northwestern University Law Review* 379.

[37] 1999 SI No. 2083.

[38] The text of the Model Law is set forth in annex I to the report of UNCITRAL on the work of its twenty-ninth session. Official Records of the General Assembly, Fifty-first session, Supplement No. 17(A/51/17), Annex I and it is also available at http://www.uncitral.org/. See further chap. 2.

[39] See *A European Initiative in Electronic Commerce* COM(97) 157, and COM(98)586 and COM(99) 427 final,
http://www.ispo.cec.be/ecommerce/legal/documents/com1999-427/com427en.pdf. See generally *Electronic Commerce and the European Union* at http://www.ispo.cec.be/Ecommerce/. For an introduction to the relevant draft directives see John Dickie *Internet and Electronic Commerce Law in the European Union* (Hart, Oxford, 1999) chap. 3; Kelleher, D. and Murray, K., *IT Law in the European Union* (Sweet & Maxwell, London, 1999) chap. 8. There is further commentary in chap. 3.

[40] See *The Framework for Global Economic Commerce* at
http://www.whitehouse.gov/WH/New/Commerce/.

- the OECD Cryptography Policy Guidelines[41] and
- the ICC General Usage for International Digitally Ensured Commerce.[42]

The UNCITRAL Model Law on Electronic Commerce was adopted by the United Nations Commission on International Trade Law (UNCITRAL) in 1996 in furtherance of its mandate to promote the harmonisation and unification of international trade law. The UNCITRAL Model Law on Electronic Commerce was approved by the General Assembly of the United Nations on 16 December 1996. The decision by UNCITRAL to formulate model legislation on electronic commerce was taken in response to the fact that in a number of countries the existing legislation governing communication and storage of information was inadequate or outdated because it did not contemplate the use of electronic commerce. The objectives of the Model Law include enabling or facilitating the use of electronic commerce and providing equal treatment to users of paper-based documentation and to users of computer-based information. The Model Law relies on a 'functional equivalent approach', that is based on an analysis of the purposes and functions of the traditional paper-based requirements with a view to determining how those purposes or functions could be fulfilled through electronic-commerce techniques.

A *European Initiative in Electronic Commerce*[43] built on the European Commission's work on the 'Information Society' and sought to provide a coherent policy framework for future Commission action in the field of electronic commerce. The four principles that inform the Commission's creation of an appropriate regulatory framework for electronic commerce in the European Union are –

- no regulation for regulation's sake;
- any regulation must be based on Single Market Freedoms;
- any regulation must take account of market realities;
- any regulation must meet general interest objectives efficiently and effectively.

An amended proposal for a Directive to establish a coherent legal framework for electronic commerce within the Single Market was put forward on 1 September 1999 by the European Commission. The amended proposal takes into account the favourable opinion from the European Parliament, adopted on the 6 May 1999, on the original proposal that fully supported the Commission's Single Market approach.[44] A number of clarifications

---

[41] See generally the Organisation for Economic Co-operation and Development (OECD) *Electronic Commerce* at http://www.oecd.org/subject/e_commerce/.

[42] See GUIDEC *General Usage for International Digitally Ensured Commerce* at http://www.iccwbo.org/home/guidec/guidec.asp.

[43] COM (97) 157.

[44] Opinion of the Economic and Social Committee on the 'Proposal for a European Parliament and Council Directive on certain legal aspects of electronic commerce in the internal market', Official Journal C169, 16/06/99.

were introduced in the amended proposal to strengthen the link between the electronic commerce proposal and existing consumer protection and data protection Directives. Also considered in the amending proposal are the treatment of unsolicited commercial communications via electronic mail and determination of the moment when an online contract is concluded. The European Commission has maintained the proposed rules limiting the liability of online service providers who act as intermediaries.

In 1997 the United States government prepared a strategy, under the leadership of Vice President Al Gore, to help accelerate the growth of global commerce across the Internet. *A Framework for Global Electronic Commerce*,[45] published in July 1997, establishes a set of five principles to guide policy development. The principles are:

1. The private sector should lead.
2. Governments should avoid undue restrictions on electronic commerce.
3. Where governmental involvement is needed, its aim should be to support and enforce a predictable, minimalist, consistent and simple environment for commerce.
4. Governments should recognise the unique qualities of the Internet.
5. Electronic commerce over the Internet should be facilitated on a global basis.

The *Framework* document also covered nine areas where the US government considered that international agreements were needed to preserve the Internet as a non-regulatory medium. These included financial issues such as customs, taxation and electronic payments; legal issues such as a 'Uniform Commercial Code' for electronic commerce, intellectual property protection, privacy and security; and market access issues such as telecommunications infrastructure and technical standards.[46]

Building the framework – the legal issues

The major legal issues associated with the creation of a framework for electronic commerce include the legal recognition of electronic instruments, encryption, jurisdiction and taxation.

Legal recognition of electronic instruments

The development of an adequate legal framework for the legal recognition of electronic instruments is generally regarded as an essential element in the development of a legal framework for electronic commerce. Many legal systems require writing for the formal validity of certain transactions. Article 2–201 of the Uniform Commercial Code for example stipulates that

---

[45] See *The Framework for Global Economic Commerce* at
http://www.whitehouse.gov/WH/New/Commerce/.
[46] For a comparative analysis see Vittet-Philippe, Patrick, 'US and EU Policies for Global Electronic Commerce' (1998) 14 *Computer Law and Security Report* 87.

contracts for the sale of goods where the price is more than US$500 require 'some writing sufficient to indicate that a contract for sale has been made by the parties and signed by the party against whom enforcement is sought' in order to be enforceable. The UNCITRAL Model Law on Electronic Commerce was adopted to assist States modernising their legislation to ensure that the communication of legally significant information in the form of paperless messages would not be hindered by legal obstacles to the use of such messages, or by uncertainty as to their legal effect or validity. The UNCITRAL Model Law on Electronic Commerce together with additional article 5bis as adopted in 1998 has been very influential. The United Kingdom's Electronic Communications Act 2000 was drafted to ensure consistency with the UNCITRAL Model Law as well as with the draft EU Electronic Signatures Directive.[47]

Encryption

Encryption is the process of turning normal text into a series of letters and/or numbers which can only be deciphered by someone who has the correct password or key. Encryption is used to prevent others reading confidential, private or commercial data. The OECD, the International Chamber of Commerce and UNCITRAL all recognise that trustworthy cryptography service providers are essential to encourage the growth of electronic commerce. The fear that encryption may encourage criminal activity on the Internet has led to calls for cryptography service providers to deposit encryption keys with trusted third parties. Although the British government was initially attracted to the idea of 'key escrow' (i.e. the concept of depositing encryption keys with trusted third parties), opposition from the business community lead to the abandonment of key escrow in the Electronic Communications Act 2000 and a more flexible, facilitative approach.[48]

Jurisdiction

All national legal systems are based on the premise that a sovereign state enjoys exclusive jurisdiction within its own territory. The territoriality principle is difficult to apply to the Internet because the Internet is designed to transcend boundaries.[49] In *American Library Association v Pataki*[50] District Judge Preska noted that:

> The Internet is wholly insensitive to geographic distinctions. In almost every case, users of the Internet neither know nor care about the physical location of the

---

[47] As the Electronic Communications Bill was introduced in Parliament on 18 November 1999 and EU Electronic Signatures Directive was only adopted on 13 December 1999 (Directive 1999/93/EC, Official Journal 2000 L13/12), the Electronic Communications Bill was based on the draft Directive only.

[48] See chap. 14.

[49] See the remarks of District Judge Gertner in *Digital Equipment Corporation v Altavista Technology Inc* 960 F.Supp 456 (D. Mass, 1997) at p.462. Compare also chap. 4.

[50] 969 F.Supp 160 (SDNY, 1997) at p.170.

resources they access. Internet protocols were designed to ignore rather than document geographic locations; while computers on the network do have 'addresses,' they are logical addresses on the network rather than geographical addresses in real space.

The unique nature of cyberspace places considerable strain on the traditional approaches to jurisdiction. Jurisdiction over electronic contracts concluded by parties domiciled in the European Union is generally determined by reference to the Brussels Convention on Jurisdiction and the Enforcement of Judgments in Civil and Commercial Matters 1968. Section 2 of the Civil Jurisdiction and Judgments Act 1968 provides that the Brussels Convention shall have the force of law in the United Kingdom. As regards non-consumer contracts, the primary rule is contained in Article 2 of the Brussels Convention that provides that a party to a contract who is domiciled in a state party to the Brussels Convention can only be sued in his or her state.[51] In consumer contracts for goods or services, the consumer can only be sued in his or her domicile,[52] but the consumer can choose to sue in either his or her domicile or in the seller's domicile.[53]

The global nature of electronic commerce also raises the issue of choice of law in contracts.[54] The 1980 Rome Convention on the law applicable to contractual obligations is the principal choice of law instrument in the European Union. Section 2 of the Contracts (Applicable Law) Act 1990 provides that (subject to certain limited exceptions) the Rome Convention shall have the force of law in the United Kingdom. Article 3(1) of the Rome Convention sets out the basic principle that '[a] contract shall be governed by the law chosen by the parties.' Unfortunately, when buying goods or services online, consumers are frequently required to click on an icon that indicates acceptance of the seller's standard terms and conditions of sale. It is entirely conceivable that the seller's standard terms will also include a choice of law clause. In relation to consumer contracts, Article 5(2) of the Rome Convention provides that:

> Notwithstanding the provisions of Article 3, a choice of law shall not have the result of depriving a consumer of the protection afforded to him by the mandatory rules of the law of the country in which he has his habitual residence . . . if in that country the conclusion of the contract was preceded by a specific invitation addressed to him or by advertising, and he had taken in that country all the steps necessary on his part for the conclusion of the contract.

---

[51] One exception to the principle contained in Article 2 of the Brussels Convention is Article 5(1) that permits a defendant to be sued in the place of performance of the obligation in question.

[52] Article 13 of the Brussels Convention.

[53] Article 14 of the Brussels Convention.

[54] See generally Schu, R., 'The Applicable Law to Consumer Contracts Made Over the Internet: Consumer Protection Through Private International Law?' (1997) 5 *International Journal of Law and Information Technology* 192.

Both the European Council and the European Parliament believe that the proposed EU Directive on electronic commerce should not affect the law applicable to contractual obligations relating to consumer contracts and should not have the result of depriving the consumer of the protection afforded to him by the mandatory rules relating to contractual obligations of the law of the Member State in which he has his habitual residence.[55]

There is a growing conviction that both the Brussels and Rome Conventions will have to be amended to ensure effective protection of consumers in the world of e-commerce.[56] Article 9 of the Unfair Terms in Consumer Contracts Regulations 1999 provides that '[t]hese Regulations shall apply notwithstanding any contract term which applies or purports to apply the law of a non-Member State, if the contract has a close connection with the territory of the Member States'.

The EU's Distance Selling Directive[57] is also potentially relevant to the development of the legal framework for electronic commerce for consumers living in the European Union as electronic mail is included in the indicative list of the means of communication covered by Article 2(4) of the Distance Selling Directive.[58] The Directive seeks to introduce a minimum set of common rules in relation to distance selling within the Community. Article 4(1) of the Directive states that the consumer must be provided with certain fundamental information before the contract is concluded, namely:

(a) the identity of the supplier and, in the case of contracts requiring payment in advance, his address
(b) the main characteristics of the goods or services
(c) the price of the goods or services including all taxes
(d) delivery costs, where appropriate
(e) the arrangements for payment, delivery or performance
(f) the existence of a right of withdrawal . . .
(g) the cost of using the means of distance communication, where it is calculated other than at the basic rate
(h) the period for which the offer or the price remains valid
(i) where appropriate, the minimum duration of the contract in the case of contracts for the supply of products or services to be performed permanently or recurrently

---

[55] Para. 55 of the *Common position adopted by the Council with a view to the adoption of Directive of the European Parliament and of the Council on certain legal aspects of Information Society services, in particular electronic commerce, in the Internal Market* ('Directive on electronic commerce') adopted by the European Parliament on 4 May 2000 (2000/31/EC) available at http://www.ispo.cec.be/Ecommerce/.

[56] See Seaman, A., 'E Commerce, Jurisdiction and Choice of Law' (1999) 10 *Computers and Law* 28–31, Rowe, H. (ed.), *A Practitioner's Guide to the Regulation of the Internet* (City & Financial Publishing, Old Woking, 1999) chap. 5 and the remarks of the Minister for Small Business and E-Commerce, Ms Patricia Hewitt MP, during the Second Reading of Electronic Commerce Bill (HC Debs, vol. 340 col. 48 29 November 1999).

[57] Directive 97/7/EC of the European Parliament and of the Council of 20 May 1997 on the Protection of Consumers in respect of Distance Contracts, Official Journal No L 144, 4/6/97.

[58] See Annex 1 of the Directive.

Article 5(1) of the Distance Selling Directive provides that the consumer must receive confirmation in a durable medium of the Article 4(1) information, at the latest, at the time of delivery of the goods. Article 6 of the Directive provides for a cooling-off period of at least seven working days within which the consumer may withdraw from the contract without penalty and without giving any reason.

Taxation

Taxation is traditionally based on one of two concepts – source or residence. As both concepts are linked to territorial boundaries, the borderless nature of cyberspace poses problems for the application of the law of taxation.[59] Since users of the internet neither know nor care about the physical location of the resources they access, there is considerable temptation for suppliers of goods and services to domicile their electronic commercial activities within a low tax jurisdiction.[60]

In October 1998, following discussion with business, the British Government published a paper on its policy on the taxation of e-commerce.[61] A major policy principle is that taxation should aim to be neutral as between electronic commerce and more conventional forms of commerce so that no form of commerce is advantaged or disadvantaged. In addition to the customer service opportunities offered by electronic communication, a number of specific issues were addressed by the policy paper. These included royalties, permanent establishment, transfer pricing, customs duties and VAT.

With regard to indirect taxation, the relevant tax within the European Union is value added tax (VAT) which is the only permissible general sales tax within the European Union.[62] The primary legislative basis is the Sixth VAT Directive[63] which has been the subject of substantial amendment since its promulgation in 1977. At present, if goods are supplied to a person in the UK, from a non-EU supplier, VAT is payable. By contrast, an EU domiciled

---

[59] See generally Eden, S., 'The Taxation of Electronic Commerce' in Edwards, L., and Waelde, C., *Law and the Internet: Regulating Cyberspace* (Hart Publishing, Oxford, 1997); Gersheny, P., and Major, C., 'Tax implications of the Internet' in Rowe, H. (ed.), *A Practitioner's Guide to the Regulation of the Internet* (City & Financial Publishing, Old Woking, 1999); Singleton, S., *Business, the Internet and the Law* (Tolley's, Croydon, 1999) chap. 12; Chissick, M., and Kelman, A., *Electronic Commerce* (Sweet & Maxwell, London, 1999) chap. 9; Saxby, S., (ed.), *Encyclopaedia of Information Technology Law* (Sweet & Maxwell, London, 1990–99) chap. 12; Dickie, J., *Internet and Electronic Commerce in the European Union* (Hart Publishing, Oxford, 1999) chap. 2; Hickey, J.J.B., 'The Fiscal Challenge of E-Commerce' [2000] *British Tax Review* 91.

[60] Consider the competitive advantage of a British domiciled bookmaker who, by locating his/her on-line betting activities in Gibraltar, is able to avoid the general betting duty that is chargeable in respect of any off-course bet made with a bookmaker in the United Kingdom.

[61] Inland Revenue Press Release 128/98: *Electronic commerce UK policy on taxation* available at http://www.inlandrevenue.gov.uk/e-commerce/release128_98.html.

[62] VAT was introduced in the United Kingdom on 1 April 1973 by the Finance Act 1972. Successive Finance Acts made amendments to the law and VAT has now been consolidated in the Value Added Tax Act 1994 with effect from 1 September 1994.

[63] Directive 77/388/EEC, official Journal No. L. 145 13/6/77.

purchaser can acquire services from outside the EU without paying VAT. The European Commission is currently working to close the loophole that allows suppliers of services based outside the European Union to avoid paying VAT.[64]

On 26 November 1999 the Inland Revenue and HM Customs and Excise published *Electronic Commerce: The UK's Taxation Agenda*,[65] which details the work the two departments are undertaking to meet the British Government's objectives for e-commerce and e-government in the UK. In particular the paper acknowledged that '[t]he international nature of e-commerce brings with it the need to find global solutions to the taxation issues that it raises.'[66] The paper highlighted the major role that the British government is playing in the OECD's work on the tax issues raised by e-commerce.[67]

At present, under the terms of most of the UK's double taxation treaties, a British non-resident will only be taxed on profits arising from trading within the UK if the non-resident has a 'permanent establishment' in the United Kingdom. The use of the concept of permanent establishment[68] as a threshold for the taxation of non-residents may be traced back to the 1920s,[69] but there is some doubt about its application to electronic commerce. The OECD is currently in the process of clarifying the definition of permanent establishment in the context of electronic commerce.[70] On 11 April 2000, in order to encourage investors, the UK announced that it took the view that a web site of itself is not a permanent establishment and that a server is insufficient of itself to constitute a permanent establishment of a business that is conducting e-commerce through a web site on the server.[71]

As well as having impact on the raising of taxes, the Internet has other relationships with the taxation system. On 21 March 2000, The Chancellor of the Exchequer (Mr Gordon Brown) announced that in order to encourage one million small businesses to go on line, he would introduce a special tax reduction. Between 1 April 2000 and 31 March 2003, any small business buying computers, or investing in e-commerce and new information technologies, will be able immediately to write off against tax the full 100 per cent of the cost in the year of purchase.[72] At the same time, the Chancellor also

[64] *Indirect Taxes and E-commerce* – Commission Paper XXI/99/1201-EN. See also Nissé, J., 'EU's Net Traders may shed tax handicap' (1999) *The Times* 7 July p.30.
[65] Available at http://www.inlandrevenue.gov.uk/taxagenda/ecom.pdf.
[66] *Ibid*. para. 3.1.
[67] *Ibid*. paras 3.4–3.16.
[68] 'For the purposes of this Convention, the term "permanent establishment" means a fixed place of business through which the business of an enterprise is wholly or partly carried on.' Article 5(1) of the 1998 OECD and United Nations Model Double Taxation Conventions.
[69] See generally Picciotto, S., *International Business Taxation* (Woidenfeld and Nicolson, London, 1992).
[70] See *The application of permanent establishment definition in the context of electronic commerce: proposed clarification of the commentary on article 5 of the OECD Model Tax Convention* available at http://www.oecd.org/daf/fa/treaties/art5rev_3march.pdf.
[71] See Inland Revenue press release 84/2000 *Electronic Commerce: Tax Status of Web Sites and Servers* available at http://www.inlandrevenue.gov.uk/e-commerce/ecom15.html.
[72] HC Debs. Vol. 346 col. 862 21 March 2000.

announced that to promote the use of the Internet, the British government would legislate for a £100 tax cut for electronic filing of tax and VAT returns, and a further £50 tax cut for electronic filing for those paying the working families tax credit.

Other jurisdictions have also been uneasy about the (potential) loss of their tax revenues to cyberspace. In November 1996 the US Department of Treasury published a discussion paper on the tax policy implications of global electronic commerce.[73] The US Treasury's stated policy goals with respect to electronic commerce included neutrality (in other words, treating economically similar income equally) and avoiding double taxation so that the new technology may be permitted to reach its full potential.[74] In 1998 the US Congress passed the Internet Tax Freedom Act that placed a moratorium on the rights of American states to impose new taxes on interstate electronic commerce.[75] The Act is in conformity with the position taken in the *Framework* document that 'no new taxes should be imposed on Internet commerce.' At the second WTO Ministerial Conference held in Geneva on 18–20 May 1998, the Ministers declared that members would continue their current practice of not imposing customs duties on electronic transmissions.[76]

The ability of suppliers of goods and services over the Internet to route themselves around fundamental tax concepts (such as residence and source) has led to the suggestion that only way the Internet can be taxed is by reference to a 'bit tax'. A bit tax is a tax on data transmitted over the Internet (at around a rate of 0.0000001c) to be collected by telecommunications companies and passed onto the relevant treasury. As intriguing as the concept of a bit tax is, it is inherently unworkable. A bit tax would be unable to discriminate on the nature of the data transmitted or the status of the parties involved. As it would tax information transmitted over the Internet for educational purposes at the same rate as business information, it would be unfair.[77] Further, international agreement would have to be reached on the division between governments of the revenue raised from cross border

[73] International Tax Counsel, US Department of Treasury *Selected Tax Policy Implications of Global Electronic Commerce* November 1996.
[74] See generally Bloom, A.S., and Guisti, R.S., 'International Tax Implications of Electronic Commerce on Outbound Transactions' (1997) 23 *International Tax Journal* 45.
[75] Pub. L. No. 105–277, 112 Stat. 2681 (1998). See Sweet, J.E., 'Formulating international tax laws in the age of electronic commerce' (1998) 146 *University of Pennsylvania Law Review* 1949; Forst, D.L., 'Old and New Issues in the Taxation of Electronic Commerce' (1999) 14 *Berkeley Technology Law Journal Berkeley Technology Law Journal* 711; McLaughlin, M.G., 'The Internet Tax Freedom Act: Congress Takes a Byte Out of the Net' (1998) 48 *Catholic University Law Review* 209.
[76] 'Declaration on Global Electronic Commerce' adopted on 20 May 1998 WT/MIN(98)/DEC/2. See also Cockfield, A.J., 'Balancing national interests in the taxation of electronic business commerce' (1999) 74 *Tulane Law Review* 137.
[77] Swindells, C., and Henderson, K., 'Legal Regulation of Electronic Commerce' (1998) 3 *Journal of Information, Law and Technology* para. 6.3 available at http://www.law.warwick.ac.uk/jilt/98-3/swindells.html.

data flow. Although the EC High Level Expert Group indicated that they were interested in the possibility of an EU bit tax in 1997, this proposal has been abandoned in the desire to avoid a 'server flight' from the European Union.

Electronic commerce – the British response

In a White Paper, *Our Competitive Future: Building the Knowledge Driven Economy*,[78] the British Government set out the ambitious goal of developing the UK as the world's best environment for electronic trading by 2002. In her speech to both Houses of Parliament on 24 November 1998, the Queen announced that legislation would be introduced to promote electronic commerce, to modernise the law and to improve competitiveness by enabling the United Kingdom to compete in the new digital marketplace.[79]

The government's broader electronic agenda was set out in *Net Benefit: the electronic commerce agenda for the UK*[80] published in October 1998 and, on 5 March 1999, the Government issued the Consultation Document *Building Confidence in Electronic Commerce*[81] which was prepared jointly by the DTI and the Home Office. In July 1999, the Department of Trade and Industry published *Promoting Electronic Commerce* which consisted of a consultation document that invited comments on the government's proposals for an Electronic Communications Bill and which also set out the government's response to the Trade and Industry Committee's Report on the government's previous consultation document.[82]

The Electronic Communications Bill was introduced in the House of Commons on 18 November 1999. The main purposes of the Bill were again stated to be to help build confidence in electronic commerce and the technology underlying it. The Electronic Communications Act 2000 which emerged is divided into three parts. Part I concerns the arrangements for registering providers of cryptography support services, such as electronic signature services and confidentiality services.[83] Although section 1 of the Act requires the Secretary of State to establish and maintain a register of approved suppliers of cryptography support services, section 3 makes clear the government's goal of 'co regulation'. According to the Minister for Small Business and E-Commerce, Ms Patricia Hewitt MP, co-regulation means that the government should define the public policy objectives, but that industry should deliver the solutions through self-regulation.[84] If

[78] (Cm. 4176, HMSO, London, 1998).
[79] HC Debs, vol. 321 col. 4 24 November 1998.
[80] Department of Trade and Industry, *Net Benefit: The Electronic Commerce Agenda for the UK*, DTI/Pub 3619, October 1998, at http://www.dti.gov.uk/CII/netbenefit.html.
[81] Department of Trade and Industry, *Building Confidence in Electronic Commerce* (http://www.dti.gov.uk/CII/elec/elec_com_1.html, 1999).
[82] Department of Trade and Industry, *Promoting Electronic Commerce* (Cm. 4417, Stationery Office, London, 1999).
[83] See further chap. 14.
[84] HC Debs, vol. 340 col. 43 29 November 1999.

self-regulation fails, Part I of the Act provides for a statutory default option. Significantly, section 14 explicitly prohibits key escrow requirements being imposed in any order made under the Act. Part II makes provision for the legal recognition of electronic signatures. Section 7 of the Act confirms the legal validity of electronic signatures. Section 8 of the Act empowers the appropriate Minister, by order made by statutory instrument, to amend references to paper signatures, documents and records to include their electronic equivalents. It has been estimated that there are about 40,000 such references to paper signatures, documents and the like. Part III involves miscellaneous and supplemental matters – the removal of obstacles in other legislation to the use of electronic communication and storage in place of paper.

Concluding thoughts

Governments can have a profound effect on the growth of electronic commerce. By their actions, they can facilitate electronic trade or inhibit it. Government officials should respect the unique nature of the medium and recognise that widespread competition and increased consumer choice should be the defining features of the new digital marketplace. They should adopt a market-oriented approach to electronic commerce that facilitates the emergence of a global, transparent, and predictable legal environment to support business and commerce.

William J. Clinton, 'Message to Internet Users' 1 July 1997[85]

It is difficult to provide accurate assessments of the economic significance of 'cybershopping'. US analysts initially expected online business to double to US$ 2.3 billion during the 1998 festive season. Those estimates may have been too conservative. The Boston Consulting Group and shop.org, an organisation of online retailers, reported that revenues grew by 230 per cent.[86] It is estimated that £14.2 billion was spent in the United Kingdom during Christmas 1999. If the growth of Internet sales in the United Kingdom matched the growth in the United States, a sizeable proportion of that £14.2 billion will have been spent online.

In January 1999 Yahoo! announced a US$ 3.6 billion takeover of GeoCities. GeoCities, which helps Internet users to build their own web pages, was founded in 1994 and at the date of the takeover it had never made a profit or earned any significant revenues. 'GeoCities was a complete unknown on Wall Street until autumn 1998. Its floatation was delayed because of market turbulence and the offer price was dropped from $14 per share to $9. Yahoo! offered to pay $113.66 a share, a premium of 52 per cent over the last closing price.'[87] In January 1999, Alan Greenspan, the Chairman of the Federal Reserve Board, warned investors that the 'hype'

---

[85] The White House, Office of the Press Secretary, 'Text of the President's Message to Internet Users' 1 July 1997, http://www.whitehouse.gov/WH/New/Commerce/message.html.
[86] 'Americans push cyberspace stores to $13bn boom' *Guardian* 29 December 1998, p.18.
[87] 'Yahoo! set to challenge AOL's Net dominance' *The Times* 29 January 1999, p.30.

surrounding Internet companies had introduced a 'lottery premium' into their stock market valuations.[88] However, this warning did not daunt America Online and Time Warner Inc., who combined in January 2000 in the largest merger deal in history.[89] The worth was put at £220 billion because of the potential to dominate the market for Internet shopping in the future.

In the United Kingdom shares in the Internet service provider, Freeserve, soared to $205^1/_2$p on their first day of trading in July 1999, a 37 per cent premium on their initial offer price. Freeserve was launched in September 1998, and by its launch had not made a profit but was still valued at over £1bn.[90] Although shares in Freeserve continued to rise quickly to be valued at just over 240p per share at the beginning of August 1999, by the end of September 1999 the shares had fallen to below their 150p offer price set at floatation.[91] Investing in the 'dot.com' sector is not for the faint-hearted. In the twelve months from their first day of trading, Freeserve shares traded between lows of $123^1/_2$ per share and highs of 930p per share.

In the light of this short but turbulent history, it has been commented that, 'The Internet has been said to be both over-hyped and undervalued.'[92] The economic potential of the Internet is as difficult to predict at the beginning of the twenty-first century as the economic potential of the motor car was at the beginning of the twentieth century. Like the motor industry, the limits of the Internet's economic potential depend on both technological and legal factors. Most of the legal issues surrounding electronic commerce have been identified, but the creation of a global, transparent and predictable legal environment for electronic commerce, although in the process of rapid development, is far from complete.

---

[88] 'Greenspan attacks "hype" as Yahoo! pays $3.5bn' *The Times* 29 January 1999, p.29.
[89] *The Times* 11 January 2000, p.1.
[90] 'Freeserve shares soar 37% on first day' *Financial Times* 27 July 1999, p.1.
[91] 'Net investors log on to www.loss.com' *Guardian* 21 September 1999 p.3.
[92] 'The Net Imperative: A Survey of Business and the Internet', *The Economist* June 26 1999 p.5.

BIBLIOGRAPHY

This listing is confined to sources which are either fundamental to the study of the Internet in the context of the law and society or are not specific to one chapter. For further sources, see the footnotes of each chapter and additionally the following website:

http://www.booksites.net

Akdeniz, Y. *et al.*, 'Cryptography and Liberty: Can the Trusted Third Parties be Trusted? A Critique of the Recent UK Proposals', [1997] (2) *Journal of Information, Law and Technology*, http://elj.warwick.ac.uk/jilt/cryptog/97_2akdz/

Akdeniz, Y., 'UK Government Encryption Policy', [1997] *Web Journal of Current Legal Issues* 1 (February), at
http://www.ncl.ac.uk/~nlawwww/1997/issue1/akdeniz1.html.

Akdeniz, Y., 'Governance of Pornography and Child Pornography on the Global Internet: A Multi-Layered Approach', in Edwards, L. and Waelde, C. (eds), *Law and the Internet: Regulating Cyberspace* (Hart Publishing, Oxford, 1997) 223

Akdeniz, Y., 'No Chance for Key Recovery: Encryption and International Principles of Human and Political Rights', [1998] *Web Journal of Current Legal Issues* 1, at http://webjcli.ncl.ac.uk/1998/issue1/akdeniz1.html

Akdeniz, Y. and Walker, C., 'UK Government Policy on Encryption: Trust is the Key?' (1998) 3(2) *Journal of Civil Liberties* 110

Angel, J., 'Why use Digital Signatures for Electronic Commerce?' 1999 (2) *Journal of Information, Law and Technology* at
http://www.law.warwick.ac.uk/jilt/99-2/angel.html

Bainbridge, D., *Introduction to Computer Law* (3rd ed., Pitman, London, 1996)

Baker, S.A. and Hurst, P.R., *The Limits of Trust* (Kluwer, The Hague, 1998)

Bangemann Report, *Europe and the Global Information Society*
(http://www.ispo.cec.be/infosoc/backg/bangeman.html, 1994)

Barrett, N., *Digital Crime* (Kogan Page, London, 1997)

Bellamy, C. and Taylor, J.A., *Governing in the Information Age* (Open University Press, Buckingham, 1998)

Boyle, J., *Shamans, Software and Spleens* (Harvard University Press, Cambridge, MA, 1996)

Cabinet Office, *Crown Copyright in the Information Age* (Cm. 3819, HMSO, London, 1998)

Cabinet Office, *government.direct: A prospectus for the Electronic Delivery of Government Services* (Cm. 3438, HMSO, London, 1996)

Cabinet Office, *Modernising Government* (Cm. 4310, Stationery Office, London, 1999)

Cabinet Office's Performance and Innovation Unit, *Encryption and Law Enforcement* (http://www.cabinet-office.gov.uk/innovation/1999/encryption/index.htm, 1999)

Castells, M., *The Information Age*, Vol. I: *The Rise of Network Society* (Blackwell, Oxford, 1996); *The Information Age*, Vol. II: *The Power of Identity* (Blackwell, Oxford, 1997); *The Information Age*, Vol. III: *End of Millennium* (Blackwell, Oxford, 1998)

Chissick, M. and Kelman, A., *Electronic Commerce* (Sweet & Maxwell, London, 1999)

Coleman, S., Taylor, J.A. and Van de Dok, W., 'Parliament in the age of the Internet' (1998) 52 *Parliamentary Affairs* 365

Council of Europe, Recommendation R(99)5, *Protection of Privacy on the Internet* (Strasbourg, 1999)

Cyber-Rights & Cyber-Liberties (UK), *Report, Who Watches the Watchmen: Internet Content Rating Systems, and Privatised Censorship* (http://www.cyber-rights.org/watchmen.htm, 1997)

Cyber-Rights & Cyber-Liberties (UK), *Report: Who Watches the Watchmen: Part II – Accountability & Effective Self-Regulation in the Information Age* (http://www.cyber-rights.org/watchmen-ii.htm, 1998)

Delta, G.B. and Matsuura, J.H., *Law of the Internet* (Aspen Law & Business, New York, 1998)

Denning, D.E., *Information Warfare and Security* (ACM Press, New York, 1999)

Department for Culture, Media and Sport, *New Library: the People's Network* (Cm. 3887, HMSO, London, 1998)

Department for Education and Employment, *IT for All* (Cm. 3450, HMSO, London, 1996)

Department of Trade and Industry, *Secure Electronic Commerce Statement* (DTI, London, 1998), at http://www.dti.gov.uk/CII/ana27p.html

Department of Trade and Industry, *Net Benefit: The Electronic Commerce Agenda for the UK* (DTI/Pub 3619, London, 1998), at http://www.dti.gov.uk/CII/netbenefit.html

Department of Trade and Industry, *Building Confidence in Electronic Commerce* (DTI, London, 1999) at http://www.dti.gov.uk/CII/elec/elec_com_1.html

Department of Trade and Industry, *Our Information Age* (DTI, London, 1999) at http://www.number-10.gov.uk/public/info/index.html

Department of Trade and Industry, *Regulating Communications* (Cm. 4022, Stationery Office, London, 1998)

Dickie, J., *Internet and Electronic Commerce Law in the European Union* (Hart Publishing, Oxford, 1999)

Diffie, W. and Landau, S., *Privacy on the Line: The Politics of Wiretapping and Encryption* (MIT Press, London, 1998)

Edwards, L. and Waelde, C., *Law and the Internet* (Hart Publishing, Oxford, 1997)

Electronic Privacy Information Center, *Cryptography and Liberty 1999* (http://www.epic.org/reports/crypto1999.html, Washington DC, 1999)

European Commission, *Proposal for a European Parliament and Council Directive on a common framework for electronic signatures: European Commission Communication from the Commission to the European Parliament, the Council, the Economic and Social Committee and the Committee of the Regions* (COM(1998) 297 final, Official Journal C 325, Brussels, October 1998)

European Commission Communication, *Towards A European Framework for Digital Signatures and Encryption, Communication from the Commission to the European Parliament, the Council, the Economic and Social Committee and the Committee of the Regions ensuring Security and Trust in Electronic Communication* (COM(97) 503, Brussels, October 1997)

Global Internet Liberty Campaign, *Cryptography and Liberty: An International Survey of Encryption Policy* (Washington DC, 1998), at http://www.gilc.org/crypto/crypto-survey.html

Grabosky, P.N. and Smith, R.G., *Crime in the Digital Age* (Transaction Publishers, Annandale, MN, 1998)

Gringras, C. (ed.), *The Laws of the Internet* (Butterworth, London, 1997)

Hague, B.N. and Loader, B.D., *Digital Democracy* (Routledge, London, 1999)

House of Commons Select Committee on Culture, Media and Sport, *The Multimedia Revolution* (1997–8 HC 520, HMSO, London)

House of Commons European Scrutiny Committee, *Child Pornography on the Internet* (1998–9 HC 34-ii, HMSO, London)

House of Commons Select Committee on Home Affairs Committee: *Computer Pornography* (1993–4 HC 126, HMSO, London)

House of Commons Select Committee on Procedure, *Electronic Publication of House of Commons Documents* (1995–6 HC 328, HMSO, London)

House of Lords, Select Committee on Science and Technology, *Information Society: Agenda for Action in the UK* (1995–6 HL 77, HMSO, London), and *Government Response* (Cm. 3450, HMSO, London, 1996)

House of Commons Select Committee on Trade and Industry, *Building Confidence in Electronic Commerce* (1998–9 HC 187, HMSO, London)

House of Commons Select Committee on Trade and Industry, *Electronic Commerce* (1998–9 HC 648, HMSO, London)

Jordan, T., *Cyberpower: The Culture and Politics of Cyberspace* (Routledge, London, 1999)

Kahin, B. and Neeson, C., *Borders in Cyberspace* (MIT Press, Cambridge, MA, 1997)

Karnow, C., *Future Codes* (Artech House, Boston, MA, 1997)

Katsh, M.E., *Law in a Digital World* (Oxford University Press, New York, 1995)

Kelleher, D. and Murray, K., *IT Law in the European Union* (Sweet & Maxwell, London, 1999)

Koops, B.-J., *The Crypto Controversy* (Kluwer, The Hague, 1999)

Lessig, L., *Code and Other Laws of Cyberspace* (Basic Books, New York, 1999)

Liberty (ed.), *Liberating Cyberspace: Civil Liberties, Human Rights, and the Internet* (Pluto Press, London, 1998)

Loader, B.D. (ed.), *The Governance of Cyberspace* (Routledge, London, 1997)

Manchester, C., 'Computer Pornography', [1995] *Criminal Law Review* 546

Milmo, P. and Rogers, W.V.H., *Gatley on Libel and Slander* (9th ed, Sweet & Maxwell, London, 1998)

National Audit Office, *Government on the Web* (1999–2000 HC 87)

National Criminal Intelligence Service, *Project Trawler: Crime on the Information Highways* (London, 1999)

Negroponte, N., *Being Digital* (Alfred A. Knopf, New York, 1995)

Parliamentary Office of Science and Technology, *Electronic Government* (http://www.parliament.uk/post/egov.htm, 1998)

Rheingold, R., *The Virtual Community: Homesteading on the Electronic Frontier* (Secker and Warburg, London, 1993)

Rosenor, J., *Cyberlaw* (Springer, New York, 1997)

Rowe, H. (ed.), *A Practitioner's Guide to the Regulation of the Internet* (City & Financial Publishing, Old Woking, 1999)

Saradar, Z. and Ravetz, J.R. (eds), *Cyberfutures: Culture and Politics on the Information Superhighway* (Pluto Press, London, 1996)

Saxby, S. (ed.), *Encyclopaedia of Information Technology Law* (Sweet & Maxwell, London, 1990–9)

Schneier, B. and Banisar, D., *The Electronic Privacy Papers: Documents on the Battle for Privacy in the Age of Surveillance* (John Wiley & Sons, New York, 1997)

Singleton, S., *Business, the Internet and the Law* (Tolley's, Croydon, 1999)

Slevin, J., *The Internet and Society* (Polity Press, Cambridge, 2000)

Smith, G.J.H., *Internet Law and Regulation* (FT Law and Tax, London, 1996)

Smith, M.A. and Kollock, P., *Communities in Cyberspace* (Routledge, London, 1999)

Sommerlad, H. and Wall, D.S., *Legally Aided Clients and their Solicitors: Qualitative perspectives on quality and legal aid* (Research Study No. 34, Law Society, London, 1999)

Susskind, R., *The Future of Law* (2nd ed., Oxford University Press, Oxford, 1998)

Taylor, P.A., *Hackers* (Routledge, London, 1999)

Tsagarousianou, R., Tambini, D. and Bryan, C. (eds), *Cyberdemocracy* (Routledge, London, 1998)

Volokh, E., 'Cheap speech and what it will do' (1995) 104 *Yale Law Journal* 1805

Wacks, R., 'Privacy in cyberspace' in Birks, P. (ed.), *Privacy and Loyalty* (Clarendon Press, Oxford, 1997)

Walker, C. (ed.), *Crime, Criminal Justice and the Internet* (special edition, *Criminal Law Review*, Sweet & Maxwell, London, 1998)

Walker, C. and Akdeniz, Y., 'Virtual democracy' [1998] *Public Law* 489

Wall, D.S., 'Catching Cybercriminals: Policing the internet' (1998) 12(2) *International Review of Law Computers and Technology* 201

Wall, D.S., 'Cybercrimes: New wine, no bottles?' in Davies, P., Francis, P. and Jupp, V. (eds), *Invisible Crimes: Their Victims and their Regulation* (Macmillan, London, 1999) p.105

Wall, D.S. (ed.), 'Cybercrimes, Cyberspeech and Cyberliberties' (special issue of the *International Review of Law Computers and Technology*, 2000) vol. 14, no. 1

Wall, D.S. (ed.), 'E-commerce' (special issue of the *International Review of Law Computers and Technology*, 1999) vol. 13, no. 2

Wall, D.S. and Johnstone, J., 'The industrialisation of legal practice and the rise of the new electric lawyer: the impact of information technology upon legal practice' (1997) 25 *International Journal of the Sociology of Law* 95

Wallace, J. and Mangan, M., *Sex, Laws and Cyberspace* (Henry Holt, New York, 1996)

INDEX